FOURTH EDITION

UNDERSTANDING MOTIVATION AND EMOTION

JOHNMARSHALL REEVE
University of Iowa

WILEY

John Wiley & Sons, Inc.

EXECUTIVE EDITOR   Ryan Flahive
ASSOCIATE EDITOR   Lili DeGrasse
EDITORIAL ASSISTANT   Deepa Chungi
MEDIA EDITOR   Tom Kulesa
MARKETING MANAGER   Kate Stewart
SENIOR PRODUCTION EDITOR   Patricia McFadden
SENIOR DESIGNER   Karin Gerdes Kincheloe
SENIOR PHOTO EDITOR   Lisa Gee
PHOTO RESEARCHER   Lisa Passmore
PRODUCTION MANAGEMENT SERVICES   Pine Tree Composition
COVER IMAGE   © Images.com/CORBIS

This book was set in 10/12 Times Roman by Pine Tree Composition and printed and bound by Malloy Lithographing. The cover was printed by Phoenix Color, Inc.

This book is printed on acid free paper.   ∞

ISBN 0-471-45619-5
WIE ISBN 0-471-65770-0

Printed in the United States of America

10 9 8 7 6 5 4 3 2 1

Welcome to the golden age of motivation and emotion. Never in its 100 years of formal study has the field been more exciting than it is today. Every month, new and important findings appear in the scholarly journals, and many of these findings make their way into the popular press. Every year, new scholars join those already studying motivation and emotion. So more people are interested in understanding motivation and emotion, and what they are discovering is proving to be both interesting and relevant to people's lives.

Just 20 years ago, this was not the case. The field was stagnant. But something changed in the 1990s. Creative ideas appeared, new theories emerged, life-changing applications became obvious, and the sheer number of people interested in understanding and applying motivation and emotion exploded. All this activity produced an enormous amount of new knowledge, and these advances opened up new areas of application in the home, at work, during sports and exercise, and in caring for people's health and well being. As you read this text today, you are in the intellectual wake of what has been the explosion of new interest in motivation study. This means that now is the best possible time to take a course in motivation and emotion. Had you taken this same course 10 or 15 years ago, the field could not have offered you material that is as exciting and as meaningful as it is now. I hope this book will help you identify what we in the field are so terribly enthusiastic about.

In this book, you will find some of the most useful information in psychology and in life. Motivation is about human strivings, wants, desires, and aspirations—both your own, and the strivings and wants of those you care for, such as your future students, employees, and own children. Motivation study concerns all conditions that exist within the person and within the environment and culture that explain "why we want what we want" and "why we do what we do."

By the end of the book, I hope you will feel comfortable with motivation study at two levels. First, theoretically, an understanding of motivation and emotion provides answers to questions such as, "Why did she do that?," "How does that work?," and "From where does the sense of 'want to' come?" Second, practically, an understanding of motivation and emotion provides the means to develop the art of motivating both self and others. Each chapter seeks to provide concrete answers to questions such as, "How do I motivate myself?" and "How do I motivate others?"

I assumed some background knowledge on the part of the reader, such as an introductory course in psychology. The intended audience is upper-level undergraduates enrolled in courses in a department of psychology. I also write for students in other disciplines, largely because motivation research itself reaches into so many diverse areas of study and application. Among these are educational, health, counseling, clinical, sports, industrial/organizational, and business. The book concentrates on human, rather than on nonhuman, motivation. It includes some experiments in which rats, dogs, and monkeys served as research participants, but the information gleaned from these studies is always framed within an analysis of human motivation and emotion.

WHAT'S NEW IN THE FOURTH EDITION

What's new in the fourth edition is also what's new in the field of motivation itself. Since the third edition, motivation study has expanded, diversified, and picked up many new allies. This growth has introduced a number of new theoretical perspectives and areas of application. The third edition stood out in the sheer number of new ideas it introduced, including achievement goals, personal strivings, types of extrinsic motivation, implementation intentions, personal empowerment, the non-Freudian unconscious, and so forth. What is new in the fourth edition is a concerted effort to expand these theoretical ideas further into practical applications, especially in the areas of education, work, therapy, sports, and the home, including parenting.

Each chapter features a chapter box that addresses a specific concern. For instance, the box in Chapter 3 uses the information on the motivated and emotional brain to understand how anti-depression drugs work to alleviate depression. The box in Chapter 8 uses the information on goals to lay out a step-by-step goal-setting program that can be applied to many different objectives. At the end of each chapter, I list a number of recommended readings. These articles represent suggestions for further study. I selected these readings using four criteria: (1) its focus represents what is central to the chapter; (2) its topic appeals to a wide audience; (3) its length is short; and (4) its methodology and data analysis are reader-friendly.

INSTRUCTOR'S MANUAL/TEST BANK

For the fourth edition, I expanded the Instructor's Manual/Test Bank to include classroom discussion questions, recommended activities, brief demonstrations of motivational principles, and other tools to help instructors teach their students. Interested instructors should contact their Wiley representative for more information.

ACKNOWLEDGMENTS

Many voices speak within the pages of the book. Much of what I write emerged from conversations with colleagues and through my reading of their work. I have benefited from so many colleagues that I now find it impossible to acknowledge them all. Still, I want to try.

My first expression of gratitude goes to all those colleagues who, formally or casually, intentionally or inadvertently, knowingly or unknowingly, shared their ideas in conversation: Roy Baumesiter, Daniel Berlyne, Virginia Blankenship, Jerry Burger, Steven G. Cole, Mihaly Csikszentmihalyi, Richard deCharms, Ed Deci, Andrew Elliot, Wendy Grolnick, Alice Isen, Carroll Izard, Richard Koestner, Randy Larsen, Wayne Ludvigson, David McClelland, Henry Newell, Glen Nix, Brad Olson, Dawn Robinson, Tom Rocklin, Richard Ryan, Carl Rogers, Lynn Smith-Lovin, Richard Solomon, Silvan Tomkins, Robert Vallerand, and Dan Wegner. I consider each of these contributors to be my colleague and kindred spirit in the fun and struggle to understand human strivings.

My second expression of gratitude goes to those who explicitly donated their time and energy to reviewing the early drafts of the book, including Sandor B. Brent, Gustavo Carlo, Robert Emmons, Valeri Farmer-Dougan, Eddie Harmon-Jones, Wayne Harrison, Carol A. Hayes, John Hinson, Mark S. Hoyert, Wesley J. Kasprow, Norman E. Kinney,

John Kounios, Robert Madigan, Randall Martin, Michael McCall, Jim McMartin, James J. Ryan, Peter Senkowski, Michael Sylvester, Ronald R. Ulm, and A. Bond Woodruff.

My third expression of gratitude goes to those colleagues who provided valuable comments and suggestions for this edition: Debora R. Baldwin, University of Tennessee; Herbert L. Colston, University of Wisconsin-Parkside; Richard Dienstbier, University of Nebraska; Todd M. Freeberg, University of Tennessee; Teresa M. Heckert, Truman State University; August Hoffman, California State University Northridge; Kraig L. Schell, Angelo State University; Henry V. Soper, California State University Northridge; and Wesley White, Morehead State University.

I sincerely thank all the students I have had the pleasure to work with over the years. It was back at Ithaca College that I first became convinced that my students wanted and needed such a book. In a very real sense, I wrote the first edition for them. The students who occupy my thoughts today are those with me at the University of Iowa, here in Iowa City. For readers familiar with the earlier editions, this fourth edition presents a tone that is decidedly more practical and applied. This balance comes in part from my daily conversations with students. Every chapter now presents both what motivation researchers know and also what students see as most worth learning.

Ithaca is doubly important to me, because it was in this beautiful town in upstate New York that I met Deborah Van Patten of Wiley (then Harcourt College Publishers). Deborah was every bit as responsible for getting this book off the ground as I was. Though 15 years have now passed, I still want to express my heartfelt gratitude to you, Deborah. The professionals at Wiley have been wonderful. Everyone at Wiley has been both a valuable resource and a source of pleasure, especially Anne Smith, Ryan Flahive, Deepa Chungi, Christine Cordek, Kate Stewart, Lisa Gee, Karin Kincheloe, and Trish McFadden.

I am especially grateful for the advice, patience, assistance, and direction provided by my psychology editor Lili DeGrasse. Thanks.

—Johnmarshall Reeve

To Richard Troelstrup, who introduced me to psychology.

To Edwin Guthrie, who interested me in psychology.

To Steven Cole, who mentored me so I could participate in this wonderful profession.

BRIEF CONTENTS

Detailed Contents

Chapter 1

Introduction

What is motivation? What is emotion? One reason to read this book is, of course, to find answers to these questions. But as a way of beginning the journey, pause for a moment and generate your own answers to these two questions, however preliminary, however tentative. Perhaps scribble your definitions on a notepad or in the margins of this book.

To define motivation and emotion, notice that you first need to choose a noun to begin your definition (as in "motivation is a ___"). Is motivation a desire? a feeling? a way of thinking? a sense of striving? a need, or a collection of needs? a process, or a set of processes? On page 6, the text offers a definition with which almost everyone who studies motivation would agree (see Subject Matter section). On page 7, the text offers a definition of emotion (see Internal Motives section). As you progress throughout the pages of this book, your definitions will grow in sophistication to the point where you will be increasingly able to explain the full range of motivational phenomena and also successfully apply motivational principles in your own life.

But the journey to understand motivation and emotion can be a long one. So pause yet again and consider why take the journey in the first place. Why read these pages? Why ask questions in class? Why stay up until two in the morning pondering questions of human motivation? Consider two reasons that justify the journey.

First, learning about motivation is quite an interesting thing to do. Few topics spark and entertain the imagination so well. Anything that tells us about who we are, why we want what we want, and how we can improve our lives is going to be interesting. And anything that tells us about what other people want, why they want what they want, and how we can improve their lives is also going to be interesting. When trying to explain why people do what they do, we can turn to theories of motivation to learn about topics such as human nature, strivings for achievement and power, desires for biological sex and for psychological intimacy, emotions like fear and anger, cultivating talent and promoting creativity, developing interests and growing competencies, and making plans and setting goals.

Second, few topics are more useful to our lives. Motivation is important for its own sake, but it is further important because of its capacity to foreshadow those life outcomes that we care deeply about, including the quality of our performances and our well-being. So learning about motivation can be an extremely practical and worthwhile undertaking. It can be quite useful to know from where motivation comes, why it sometimes changes and why other times it does not, under what conditions motivation increases or decreases, what aspects of motivation can and cannot be changed, and which of these types of motivation produce engagement and well-being and which types do not. Knowing such things, we can apply our knowledge to situations such as trying to motivate employees, coach athletes, counsel clients, raise children, tutor students, or change our own ways of thinking, feeling, and behaving. To the extent that a study of motivation can tell us how we can improve our lives and also how we can improve the lives of those of others, the journey to learn about motivation will be time well spent.

Studying motivation brings both theoretical understanding of how motivation and emotion work, and it also brings the practical know-how we need to accomplish whatever it is we think is important. As a case in point, consider exercise.

Think about it for a moment: Why would anyone *want* to exercise? From where does the motivation to exercise come? Are people more willing to exercise under some conditions than under other conditions? Can anything be done to increase people's motivation to exercise? If someone hated to exercise, could another person encourage him or her to truly want to exercise? The following paragraph is about exercising, but it could be about the motivation underlying almost any activity—studying, developing a talent, learning to read, practicing the piano, graduating from school, eating less, improving a tennis serve, and so on.

Why run laps around a track, jump up and down during aerobics, climb stairs on a machine that does not really go anywhere, walk briskly in the park, or swim laps in a pool? Why run when you know your lungs will collapse for want of air? Why jump and stretch when you know your muscles will rip and tear? Why take an hour out of the day for a brisk walk when you just do not feel like it or when your schedule will not allow it? Why exercise when life offers so many other interesting things to do?

Thirteen different motivation-based reasons to exercise appear in Table 1.1. Who is to say which of these reasons are valid and which other reasons are erroneous? It is the goal of motivation research to investigate a phenomenon (like exercise) and construct theories and test hypotheses to explain how motivation works to affect the phenomenon. For in-

Table 1.1   Motivational Reasons to Exercise

Why Exercise?	Source of Motivation	Illustration
For fun	Intrinsic motivation	Children exercise spontaneously—they run and jump and chase, and they do so simply for the sheer fun of it.
Personal challenge	Flow	Athletes get "in the zone" when their sport optimally challenges their skills.
To live up to the expectations of others	Extrinsic motivation	Athletes begin an exercise program because their coach tells them to do so.
To accomplish a goal	Goal	Runners see if they can run a mile in 6 minutes or less.
Because it's a useful thing to do.	Value	People exercise to lose weight or to strengthen the heart.
Inspired to do so	Possible self	People watch others exercising and becomes inspired to do the same.
To meet a standard of excellence	Achievement strivings	Snow skiers race to the bottom of the mountain trying to beat their previous best time.
For the satisfaction of a job well done	Perceived competence	As exercisers make progress, they feel more competent, more effective.
An emotional kick	Opponent process	Vigorous jogging can produce a runner's high (a rebound to the pain).
Good mood	Positive affect	Beautiful weather can pick up exercisers' moods and invigorate exercise spontaneously, as they skip along without knowing why.
To alleviate guilt	Introjection	People exercise because they think that is what they should, ought to, or have to do to feel good about themselves.
To relieve stress, silence depression	Personal control	After a stressful day, people go to the gym, which they see as a structured, controllable environment.
To hang out with friends	Relatedness	Exercise is often a social event, a time simply to enjoy hanging out with friends.

stance, once a motivation researcher decided to focus his or her attention on understanding why people exercise, the researcher might ask any or all of the following questions: Will people really want to exercise more when they adopt a goal? Does exercise really relieve stress, reduce depression, provide a sense of accomplishment, or produce a "runner's high"? If exercise produces any of these effects, then under what conditions does it do so? Once a hypothesis can be validated through research findings, it allows for both a deeper understanding of the phenomenon (i.e., gain theoretical knowledge) and also insights to construct workable solutions to solve the problems we and others face in our lives (i.e., gain practical know-how).

TWO PERENNIAL QUESTIONS

The study of motivation revolves around providing the best possible answers for two fundamental questions:

1. What causes behavior?
2. Why does behavior vary in its intensity?

What Causes Behavior?

Motivation's first fundamental question is, "What causes behavior?" Or, stated in another way, "Why did she do that?" We see people behave, but we cannot see the underlying cause or causes that generated their behavior. We watch people show great effort and persistence (or none at all), but the reasons why they show great effort and persistence remain unobserved. Motivation exists as a scientific field to answer this question.

To really explain "What causes behavior?" we need to expand this one general question into a series of five specific questions:

- Why does behavior start?
- Once begun, why is behavior sustained over time?
- Why is behavior directed toward some goals yet away from others?
- Why does behavior change its direction?
- Why does behavior stop?

In the study of motivation, it is not enough to ask why a person practices a sport, why a child reads books, or why an adolescent refuses to sing in the choir. To gain a sophisticated understanding of why people do what they do, we must also ask why athletes begin to practice in the first place. What energizes their effort hour after hour, day after day, season after season? Why do these athletes practice one particular sport rather than another? Why are they practicing now rather than, say, hanging out with their friends? When they do practice, why do these athletes quit for the day, or quit during their lifetimes? These same questions can be asked of children as they read their books: Why begin? Why continue reading past the first page? Past the first chapter? Why pick that particular book rather than one of the other books sitting on the shelf? Why stop reading? Will their reading continue in the years to come? For a personal example, let me ask, Why did you begin to read this book today? Will you continue reading to the end of this chapter? Will you continue reading until the end of the book? If you do stop before the end, at what point will you stop? Why will you stop? After reading, what will you do next? Why?

Motivation's first perennial question—What causes behavior?—can, therefore, be elaborated into the study of how motivation affects behavior's initiation, persistence, change, goal directedness, and eventual termination. This question is either one grand question, or it is five interrelated questions. Either way, the first essential problem in a motivational analysis of behavior is to understand how motivation participates in, influences, and helps explain a person's ongoing stream of behavior.

Why Does Behavior Vary in Its Intensity?

Motivation's second fundamental question is, "Why does behavior vary in its intensity?" Another way of asking this same question would be, Why is desire sometimes strong and resilient but at other times it wanes and disappears altogether? Behavior varies in its intensity, and it varies both within the individual and between different individuals. The idea that motivation can vary within the individual means that at one time a person can be actively engaged, yet at another time that same person can be passive and listless. The idea that motivation can vary between individuals means that, even in the same situation, some people can be actively engaged while others are passive and listless.

Within the individual, motivation varies over time. When motivation varies, behavior also varies, as people show high or low effort and their persistence is strong or fragile. Some days an employee works rapidly and diligently; other days the work is lethargic. One day a student shows strong enthusiasm, strives for excellence, and shows determined goal-directed striving; yet the next day, the same student is listless, does only the minimal amount of work, and avoids being challenged academically. Why the same person shows strong and persistent motivation at one time yet weak and unenthusiastic motivation at another time needs to be explained. Why does the worker perform so well on Monday but not on Tuesday? Why do children say they are not hungry in the morning, yet the same children complain of urgent hunger in the afternoon? So the second essential problem in a motivational analysis of behavior is to understand why a person's behavior varies in its intensity from one moment to the next, from one day to the next, and from one year to the next.

Between different people, motivation varies. We all share many of the same basic motivations (e.g., hunger, need for affiliation, anger), but people do clearly differ in what motivates them. Some motives are relatively strong for one person yet relatively weak for another. Why is one person a sensation seeker, who continually seeks out strong sources of stimulation, such as riding a motorcycle, whereas another person is a sensation avoider, who finds such strong stimulation more of an irritant than a source of excitement? In a contest, why do some people strive diligently to win, whereas others care little about winning and strive more to make friends? Some people seem so easy to anger, whereas others rarely get upset. For those motives in which wide individual differences exist, motivation study investigates how such differences arise and what implications they hold. So another motivational problem to solve is to recognize that individuals differ in what motivates them and to explain why one person shows intense behavioral engagement in a given situation while another does not.

SUBJECT MATTER

To explain why people do what they do, we need a theory of motivation. The point of a motivation theory is to explain what gives behavior its energy and its direction. It is some motive that energizes the athlete, and it is some motive that directs the student's behavior toward one particular goal rather than another. *The study of motivation concerns those processes that give behavior its energy and direction.* Energy implies that behavior has strength—that it is relatively strong, intense, and persistent. Direction implies that behavior has purpose—that it is aimed or guided toward achieving some particular goal or outcome. It is the responsibility of a theory to explain what those motivational processes are and also how they work to energize and direct a person's behavior.

The processes that energize and direct behavior emanate from forces in the individual and in the environment, as shown in Figure 1.1. Motives are internal experiences—needs, cognitions, and emotions—that energize the individual's approach and avoidance tendencies. External events are environmental incentives that attract or repel the individual to engage or to not engage in a particular course of action.

Internal Motives

A motive is an internal process that energizes and directs behavior. It is therefore a general term to identify the common ground shared by needs, cognitions, and emotions. The difference between a motive and a need, cognition, or emotion is simply the level of analysis. Needs, cognitions, and emotions are just specific types of motives (see Figure 1.1).

Needs are conditions within the individual that are essential and necessary for the maintenance of life and for the nurturance of growth and well-being. Hunger and thirst exemplify two biological needs that arise from the body's requirement for food and water. Food and water are both essential and necessary for biological maintenance, well-being, and growth. Competence and belongingness exemplify two psychological needs that arise from the self's requirement for environmental mastery and warm interpersonal relationships. Competence and belongingness are both essential and necessary for psychological maintenance, well-being, and growth. Needs serve the organism, and they do so by generating wants, desires, and strivings that motivate whatever behaviors are necessary for the maintenance of life and the promotion of well-being and growth. Part I discusses specific

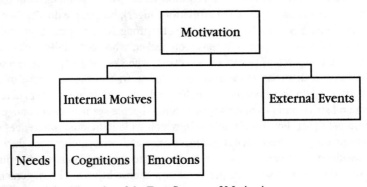

Figure 1.1   Hierarchy of the Four Sources of Motivation

types of needs: biological needs (Chapter 4), psychological needs (Chapter 5), and social needs (Chapter 7).

Cognitions refer to mental events, such as beliefs, expectations, and the self-concept. Cognitive sources of motivation revolve around the person's ways of thinking. For instance, as students, athletes, or salespersons engage in a task, they have in mind some plan or goal, they hold beliefs about their abilities, they harbor expectations for success and failure, they have ways of explaining their successes and failures, and they have an understanding of who they are and what their role in the larger society is. Part II discusses specific cognitive sources of motivation: plans and goals (Chapter 8), expectancies (Chapter 9), and the self (Chapter 10).

Emotions are short-lived subjective-physiological-functional-expressive phenomena that orchestrate how we react adaptively to the important events in our lives. That is, emotions organize and orchestrate four interrelated aspects of experience:

- Feelings—subjective, verbal descriptions of emotional experience.
- Physiological preparedness—how our body physically mobilizes itself to meet situational demands.
- Function—what specifically we want to accomplish at that moment.
- Expression—how we communicate our emotional experience publicly to others.

By orchestrating these four aspects of experience into a coherent pattern, emotions allow us to react adaptively to the important events in our lives. For instance, when we face a threat to our well-being, we feel afraid, our heart rate increases, we strive to escape, and the corners of our lips are drawn backward in such a way that others can recognize and respond to our experience. Other emotions, such as anger and joy, show similar coherent patterns that organize our feelings, physiological preparedness, function, and expression in ways that allow us to cope successfully with the circumstances we face. Part III discusses the nature of emotion (Chapter 11), as well as its different aspects (Chapter 12).

External Events

External events are environmental incentives that have the capacity to energize and direct behavior. Offering money as an incentive to take some action, for instance, often energizes approach behavior, just as an unattractive odor often energize defensive avoidance. The incentive (money, odor) gains the capacity to energize and direct behavior to the extent that it signals that a particular behavior will likely produce rewarding or punishing consequences. So incentives precede behavior and functionally pull the person closer to external events that promise pleasant experiences or functionally push the person away from external events that promise unpleasant experiences. From a broader perspective, external events include not only specific environmental stimuli but also more general situations, such as those that emerge in the classroom, family, and workplace. At an even broader level, external events include sociological forces such as culture. Chapter 6 discusses how incentives and larger social contexts add to a motivational analysis of behavior.

EXPRESSIONS OF MOTIVATION

In addition to identifying motivation's perennial problems and its subject matter, one more introductory task remains—namely, specifying how motivation expresses itself. In other words, How can you tell when someone is motivated? Or is not motivated? Or is only a little bit motivated? To some extent, all people are motivated, so we could reframe the question as, How can you tell the intensity of another person's motivation? We also need to ask, How can you tell the quality of another person's motivation? For instance, as you watch the behavior of two people—say two teenagers playing a tennis match—how do you know that one person is more motivated than is the other? How do you know whether one player harbors a higher quality of motivation than does the other player?

Two ways exist to infer motivation in another person. The first way is to observe motivation's behavioral manifestations. To infer hunger, for instance, we watch to see whether Joe eats more quickly than usual, chews vigorously, talks about eating during conversation, and forgoes social manners for the opportunity to eat. Behaving quickly, vigorously, and narrowly implies that some force must be energizing and directing Joe's consummatory behavior. The second way to infer motivation is to pay close attention to the antecedents known to give rise to motivational states. After 72 hours of food deprivation, a person will be hungry. After feeling threatened, a person will feel fear. After winning a competition, a person will feel competent. Food deprivation leads to hunger, a threat appraisal leads to fear, and objective messages of effectance lead to feeling competent. When we know the antecedents to a person's motivation, we do not have to infer motivation from behavior. That is, we can predict people's motivational states in advance, and we can do so rather confidently, at least to the extent that we take notice that the person has gone without food, been threatened, or just won the championship. But these antecedents are not always knowable. Sometimes, motivation must be inferred from its expressions—its behavior, physiology, and self-report.

Behavior

Seven aspects of behavior express the presence, intensity, and quality of motivation (Atkinson & Birch, 1970, 1978; Bolles, 1975; Ekman & Friesen, 1975): effort, latency, persistence, choice, probability of response, facial expressions, and bodily gestures. The seven aspects of behavior shown in Table 1.2 provide the observer with data to infer the presence and intensity of another person's motivation. When behavior shows intense effort, short latency, long persistence, high probability of occurrence, facial or gestural expressiveness, or when the individual pursues a specific goal-object in lieu of another, such is the evidence to infer the presence of a relatively intense motive. When behavior shows lackadaisical effort, long latency, short persistence, low probability of occurrence, minimal facial and gestural expressiveness, or the individual pursues an alternative goal-object, such is the evidence to infer an absence of a motive or at least a relatively weak motive. The term "engagement" nicely captures an overview sense of how intense a person's motivation is. Engagement refers to the intensity and emotional quality of a person's involvement with an activity (Connell & Wellborn, 1991; Skinner & Belmont, 1993). It features both behavioral and emotional aspects, such that an engaged student expresses

Table 1.2   Behavioral Expressions of Motivation

Effort	Extent of exertion put forth while trying to accomplish a task.
Latency	The time a person delays a response following an initial exposure to a stimulus event.
Persistence	The time between the initiation of a response until its cessation.
Choice	When presented with two or more courses of action, showing a preference for one course of action over the other course of action.
Probability of response	Given a number of different opportunities for the behavior to occur, the number (or percentage) of occasions that particular goal-directed response occurs.
Facial expressions	Facial movements, such as wrinkling the nose, raising the upper lip, and lowering the brow a bit (e.g., a disgusted facial expression).
Bodily gestures	Bodily gestures like posture, weight shifts, and the movements of the legs, arms, and hands (e.g., a clenched fist).

not only high effort, persistence, attention, and the like, but also a positive emotional tone (e.g., high interest, low anxiety) during that effort.

Physiology

As people and animals prepare to engage in various activities, the nervous and endocrine systems manufacture and release various chemical substances (e.g., neurotransmitters, hormones) that provide the biological underpinnings of motivational and emotional states (Andreassi, 1986; Coles, Ponchin, & Porges, 1986). In the course of a public speech, for example, speakers experience acute emotional stress to various degrees, and that emotionality manifests itself physiologically through a rise in plasma catecholamines (e.g., adrenaline; Bolm-Avdorff et al., 1989). To measure such neural and hormonal changes, researchers use blood tests, saliva tests, urine analyses, and a host of psychophysiological measures involving complex electrical equipment to observe neural activity in the brain (e.g., EEG, or electroencephalogram). Using these measures, motivation researchers monitor a person's heart rate, blood pressure, respiratory rate, pupil diameter, skin conductance, contents of blood plasma, and other indices of physiological functioning to infer the presence and intensity of underlying motivational and emotional states. The six bodily arousal systems that express motivation and emotion are cardiovascular, plasma, ocular (eye), electrodermal, skeletal muscle activity, and brain activity, as listed in Table 1.3.

Self-Report

A third way to collect data to infer the presence, intensity, and quality of motivation is simply to ask. People can typically self-report their motivation, as in an interview or on a questionnaire. An interviewer might assess anxiety, for instance, by asking how anxious the interviewee feels in particular settings or by asking the interviewee to report anxiety-related symptoms, such as an upset stomach or thoughts of failure. Questionnaires have several advantages. They are easy to administer, can be given to many people

Table 1.3   Psychophysiology Expressions of Motivation

Cardiovascular activity	Activity of heart and blood vessels increases with the pursuit of difficult/challenging tasks and attractive incentives.
Plasma activity	Contents of the bloodstream, particularly the catecholamines of epinephrine and norepinephrine, which regulate the fight-or-flight reaction.
Ocular activity	Eye behavior—pupil size, eye blinks, and eye movements. Pupil size correlates with the extent of mental activity; involuntary eye blinks express changing cognitive states and transition points in the information-processing flow; and lateral eye movements increase in frequency during reflective thought.
Electrodermal activity	Electrical changes on the surface of the skin, as during sweating. Novel, emotional, threatening, and attention-getting stimuli all evoke electrodermal activity to express threat, aversion, and stimulus significance.
Skeletal activity	Activity of the musculature, as with facial expressions and bodily gestures.
Brain activity	Activity of various brain sites, such as the cerebral cortex and limbic system.

simultaneously, and can target very specific information (Carlsmith, Ellsworth, & Aronson, 1976). But questionnaires also have pitfalls that raise a red flag of caution as to their usefulness. Many researchers lament the lack of correspondence between what people say they do and what they actually do (Quattrone, 1985; Wicker, 1969). Further, there is also a lack of correspondence between how people say they feel and what their psychophysiological activity indicates they probably feel (Hodgson & Rachman, 1974; Rachman & Hodgson, 1974). Hence, what people say their motives are sometimes are not what people's behavioral and physiological expressions suggest their motives are. What conclusion, for instance, can one draw when a person verbally reports low anger but shows a quick latency to aggress, a rapid acceleration in heart rate, and also eyebrows that are drawn tightly downward and together? Because of such discrepancies, motivation researchers typically trust and rely on behavioral and physiological measures but mistrust and rely only conservatively on self-report measures. Therefore, self-report measures are used mostly to confirm the validity of behavioral and physiological measures.

THEMES IN THE STUDY OF MOTIVATION

Motivation study includes a wide range of assumptions, hypotheses, theories, findings, and domains of application, as you will see in the chapters to come. But motivation study also has a number of unifying themes that integrate these assumptions, hypotheses, theories, findings, and applications into a coherent field of study, including the following:

- Motivation benefits adaptation.
- Motives direct attention.
- Motives vary over time and influence the stream of behavior.

- Types of motivation exist.
- Motivation includes both approach and avoidance tendencies.
- Motivation study reveals what people want.
- To flourish, motivation needs supportive conditions.
- There is nothing so practical as a good theory.

Motivation Benefits Adaptation

People are complex adaptive systems. This is important because the environments we live in always change. Job demands rise and fall, educational opportunities come and go, relationships improve and decline, the momentum in an athletic season quickens and reverses, personal health suffers crisis and recovers, and so on. Motivation benefits adaptation to ever-changing circumstances because motivational states allow people to be complex adaptive systems in the sense that whenever discrepancies occur between moment-to-moment demands and our well-being then people experience motivational states that ready them to take corrective action.

When people go for hours without food and when food supply is scarce, hunger arises. When deadlines become too numerous, stress arises. When a person gains control over a difficult problem, a sense of mastery arises. Therefore, one theme that runs throughout this book is that motivational states (e.g., hunger, stress, mastery) provide a key means for individuals to cope successfully with life's inevitable demands. Take away the motivational states, and people would quickly lose a vital resource they rely on to adapt and to maintain well-being. Anyone who tries to lose weight, write a creative poem, or learn a foreign language without first recruiting motivation will quickly realize that motivation benefits adaptation. The lesson we learn from such an undertaking is that motivation readies and allows us to lose weight, perform creatively, and learn complex skills.

When motivation sours, personal adaptation suffers. People who feel helpless in exerting control over their fates tend to give up quickly when challenged (Peterson, Maier, & Seligman, 1993). Helplessness sours the person's capacity to cope with life's challenges. People who are bossed around, coerced, and controlled by others tend to become emotionally flat and numb to the hopes and aspirations embedded within their inner psychological needs (Deci, 1995). Being controlled by others sours the person's capacity to generate motivation of his or her own. In contrast, when the quality of a person's motivational states is strong and purposive, personal adaptation thrives. When kids are excited about school, when workers are confident in their skills, and when athletes set higher goals for their performances, then their teachers, supervisors, and coaches can rest assured each of these persons will be able to adapt successfully to his or her unique environment. People with high-quality motivation adapt well and thrive; people with motivational deficits flounder.

Motives Direct Attention

Environments constantly demand our attention, and they do so in a multitude of ways. Just driving down the road, for instance, we have many things to do—find our destination, cooperate with other drivers, avoid hitting other cars, listen and respond to our passenger's conversation, avoid spilling our coffee, and so forth. Similarly, a college student must simultaneously make good grades, maintain old friendships, eat healthy, balance budgets of money and time, plan for the future, wash clothes, develop artistic talents, keep abreast of world news, and so on. Who is to say whether our attention is allocated in one direction or the other? Much of that "say" comes from our motivational states. Motives have a way of gaining, and sometimes demanding, our attention so that we attend to one aspect of the environment rather than to another.

Motives affect behavior by directing attention to select some behaviors and courses of action over others. An illustration of how motives grab our attention and channel our behavior appears in Table 1.4. The table's four columns list, from left to right, (a) various aspects of the environment, (b) a motive typically aroused by that environmental event, (c) a motive-appropriate course of action, and (d) a hypothetical priority or sense of urgency given to each course of action as determined by the intensity of the underlying motive. While six courses of action are possible, attention is not allocated equally to each because the motive strengths associated with them vary (as denoted by the number of asterisks in the far-right column). Because interest, thirst, and rest are not urgent at that particular time (one asterisk), their salience is low and they fail to grab attention. The motive to avoid a headache's pain is highly salient (five asterisks) and therefore a strong candidate to grab attention and direct behavior toward taking an aspirin. Pain, like many motives, has an intrinsic ability to grab, hold, and direct our attention (Bolles & Fanselow, 1980; Eccleston & Crombez, 1999). Motives, therefore, influence behavior by capturing attention, interrupting what we are doing, distracting us from doing other things, and imposing a priority onto our behaviors.

Motives Vary over Time and Influence the Stream of Behavior

Motivation is a dynamic process—always changing, always rising and falling—rather than a discrete event or static condition. Not only do motive strengths constantly rise and fall, but people always harbor a multitude of different motives at any one point in time. Harboring a multitude of motives is important to adaptation because circumstances and

Table 1.4 How Motives Influence Behavior for a Student Sitting at a Desk

Environmental Event	Aroused Motive	Motive-Relevant Course of Action	Motive's Urgency Attention-Getting Status
Book	Interest	Read chapter.	*
Cola	Thirst	Drink beverage.	*
Familiar voices	Affiliation	Talk with friends.	***
Headache	Pain avoidance	Take aspirin.	*****
Lack of sleep	Rest	Lie down, nap.	*
Upcoming competition	Achievement	Practice skill.	**

Note: The number of asterisks in column 4 represents the intensity of the aroused motive. One asterisk denotes the lowest intensity level, while five asterisks denote the highest intensity level.

situations are complex and people need to be motivationally complex to adapt. Typically, one motive is strongest and situationally-appropriate, while other motives are relatively subordinate (i.e., one motive dominates our attention, while others lie relatively dormant, as in Table 1.4). The strongest motive typically has the greatest influence on our behavior, but each subordinate motive can become dominant as circumstances change and can therefore influence the ongoing stream of behavior.

As an illustration, consider a typical study session in which a student sits at a desk with book in hand. Our scholar's goal is to read the book, a relatively strong motive on this occasion because of an upcoming examination. The student reads for an hour, but during this time, curiosity becomes satisfied, fatigue sets in, and various subordinate motives—such as hunger and affiliation—begin to increase in strength. Perhaps the smell of popcorn from a neighbor's room makes its way down the hallway, or perhaps the sight of a close friend passing in the hallway increases the relative strength of an affiliation motive. If the affiliation motive increases in strength to a dominant level, then our scholar's stream of behavior will shift direction from studying to affiliating.

An ongoing stream of behavior in which a person performs a set of three behaviors, X, Y, and Z (e.g., studying, eating, and affiliating; Atkinson, Bongort, & Price, 1977) appears in Figure 1.2. The figure plots the changes in the strength of each of these three motives that produce the observed stream of behavior. At time 1, motive X (studying) is the dominant motive, while motives Y and Z are relatively subordinate. At time 2, motive Y (eating) has increased in strength above motive X, while motive Z remains subordinate. At time 3, motive Z (affiliating) gains relative dominance and exerts its influence on the stream of behavior. Overall, Figure 1.2 illustrates that (a) motive strengths change over time, (b) people forever harbor a multitude of motives of various intensities, any one of which might grab attention and participate in the stream of behavior, given the appropriate circumstances, and (c) motives are not something a person either does or does not have, but instead, these motives rise and fall as circumstances change.

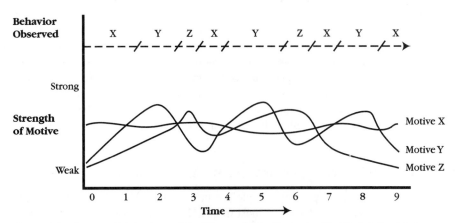

Figure 1.2   Stream of Behavior and the Changes in the Strength of Its Underlying Motives

Source: Adapted from *Cognitive Control of Action,* by D. Birch, J. W. Atkinson, and K. Bongort, in B. Weiner's (Ed.), *Cognitive View of Human Motivation* (pp. 71–84), 1974, New York: Academic Press.

Types of Motivation Exist

In many people's mind, motivation is a unitary concept. Motivation's key feature is its amount, or intensity level. From this popular point of view, the only concern about motivation is "how much?" As a unitary construct, motivation therefore varies from none, to a little, through a moderate amount, to high, and to a great deal. Practitioners (teachers, managers, coaches) accordingly focus their attention on the perennial question of, How do I foster more or higher motivation in my students, workers, or athletes?

In contrast, several motivation theorists suggest that important types of motivations exist (Ames, 1987; Ames & Archer, 1988; Atkinson, 1964; Condry & Stokker, 1992; Deci, 1992a). For instance, intrinsic motivation is different from extrinsic motivation (Ryan & Deci, 2000a). The motivation to learn is different from the motivation to perform (Ames & Archer, 1988). And the motivation to approach success is different from the motivation to avoid failure (Elliot, 1997). In other words, human beings are motivationally complex (Vallerand, 1997).

Watch as an athlete practices, a student studies, an employee works, and a doctor cares for a patient, and you will see variations in the intensity of their motivation. But an equally important observation to make is to ask the question of why the athlete practices, why the student studies, why the employee works, and why the doctor provides care. Attending to the person's type of motivation is important because some types yield a higher quality of experience, more favorable performances, and psychologically healthier outcomes than do other types. For instance, students who learn out of an intrinsic motivation (via interest, curiosity) show more creativity and positive emotion than do students who learn out of an extrinsic motivation (via stickers, deadlines; Deci & Ryan, 1987). In achievement situations, students whose goal is to approach success ("My goal is to make an A.") dramatically outperform equally able students whose goal is to avoid failure ("My goal is to not make an F."; Elliot, 1999). Often—in a school full of students, a hospital full of doctors, and a team of hard-working athletes—the people do not vary all that much in the level of their motivation but, instead, in the type—or in the quality—of their motivation.

Emotions also show that motives vary not only in intensity but also in type. For instance, a person who is intensely angry behaves quite differently from a person who is intensely afraid. Both are highly motivated and "how much?" matters, but "which type" (of emotion) is an equally important question to consider. So a complete motivational analysis of behavior answers both questions—How much? What type? Experience has probably already taught you that "how much?" matters; the 15 chapters to come further illustrate that "which type?" is an equally important consideration.

Motivation Includes Both Approach and Avoidance Tendencies

Generally speaking, people presuppose that to be motivated is better than to be unmotivated. Indeed, the two most frequently asked questions in motivation are, "How can I motivate myself to do better (or more)?" and "How can I motivate another person to do better (or more)?" In other words, how might one possess more motivation than one presently has, either for oneself or for others? Clearly, motivation is a state that people long to achieve for themselves and for others.

The problem is that you sometimes get what you wish for. In actuality, several motivational systems are aversive in nature—pain, hunger, distress, fear, dissonance, anxiety, pressure, helplessness, and so on. Motivational states do ready us to approach environmental opportunities and to improve upon our lives, and we have many such motives to ready us to do so (e.g., interest, hope, joy, achievement motivation, self-actualization). But some other motivational states ready us to avoid aversive, threatening, and anxiety-providing situations. Attention-getting motives like anxiety and tension essentially poke the proverbial needle in our side until we give the aversive motive its due and adjust our behavior accordingly. And, more often that not, "the greater the irritation, the greater the change" (Kimble, 1990, p. 36).

Human beings are curious, intrinsically motivated, sensation-seeking animals with goals and plans for striving to master challenges, for developing warm interpersonal relationships, and for moving towards attractive incentives, psychological development, and growth. It is also true, however, that people are stressed, frustrated, plagued by insecurities, pressured, afraid, in pain, depressed, and encounter aversive situations from which they wish to flee. Further, people often, and perhaps even typically, feel these positive and negative motivational and emotional states at the same time. To adapt optimally, human beings have a motivational repertoire that features just as many aversive, avoidance-based motives as positive, approach-based motives.

Motivation Study Reveals What People Want

The study of motivation reveals why people want what they want. It also reveals what people want—literally, the contents of human nature. The subject matter of motivation and emotion concerns what we all hope for, desire, want, need, and fear. It examines questions such as whether people are essentially good or evil, naturally active or passive, brotherly or aggressive, altruistic or egocentric, free to choose or determined by biological demands, and whether or not people harbor within themselves tendencies to grow and to self-actualize.

Theories of motivation reveal what is common within the strivings of all human beings by identifying the commonalities among people from different cultures, different life experiences, and different genetic endowments. All of us harbor physiological needs such as hunger, thirst, sex, and pain. All of us inherit biological dispositions such as temperament and neural circuits in the brain for pleasure and aversion. We all share a small number of basic emotions, and we all feel these emotions under the same conditions, such as feeling fear when threatened and distress after losing something or someone of value. We all interact with our surroundings with the same constellation of needs as we explore our surroundings, develop our competencies, refine our skills, and form close attachments to those we love. We are all hedonists (approach pleasure, avoid pain), but we seem to want enjoyment, well-being, and personal growth even more (Seligman & Csikszentmihalyi, 2000).

Theories of motivation also reveal those motivations that are learned through experience—motives that are clearly outside the realm of human nature. For example, through our personal and unique experiences, we learn ability beliefs, performance expectations, ways of explaining our successes and failures, values, personal aspirations, a sense of self, and so forth. These ways of energizing and directing our behavior arise from environmental, developmental, social, and cultural forces (e. g., incentives, reinforcers, role models, socially inspired possible selves, cultural roles). The study of motivation therefore informs us what part of want and desire stem from human nature but also what part of want and desire stem from personal, social, and cultural learning.

To Flourish, Motivation Needs Supportive Conditions

A person's motivation cannot be separated from the social context in which it is embedded. That is, a child's motivation is strongly affected by the social context provided by his or her parents, and a student's motivation is strongly affected by the social context provided by the school. The same could be said for the motivation of athletes affected by coaches, patients affected by physicians, and citizens affected by their culture. For the motivation of children, students, athletes, and the like, environments can be nurturing and supportive or environments can be neglectful and damaging. Those who are surrounded by social contexts that support and nurture their needs and strivings show greater vitality, experience personal growth, and thrive more than those who are surrounded by social neglect and frustration (Ryan & Deci, 2000a). Recognizing the role that social contexts play in people's motivation and well-being, motivation researchers seek to apply principles of motivation in ways that allow people's motivation to flourish.

Four areas of application are stressed in this book:

- Education
- Work
- Sports and Exercise
- Therapy

In education, an understanding of motivation can be applied to promote students' classroom engagement, to foster the motivation to develop talents like those in music, and to inform teachers how to provide a supportive classroom that will nurture students' needs and interests. In work, an understanding of motivation can be applied to improve worker productivity and satisfaction, to build confident and resilient beliefs, to keep stress at bay, and to structure jobs so that they offer workers optimal levels of challenge, variety, and relatedness with their coworkers. In sports, an understanding of motivation can be applied to identify the reasons youths participate in sports, to design exercise programs that promote long-term adherence, and to predict the effects on performance of factors such as interpersonal competition, performance feedback, and goal-setting. In therapy, an understanding of motivation can be applied to improve mental and emotional well-being, to cultivate a sense of optimism, to foster mature defense mechanisms, to explain the paradox of why mental control efforts so often backfire, and to appreciate the contribution the quality of one's interpersonal relationships play in motivation and mental health.

As you watch parents, teachers, workplace managers, coaches, and therapists attempt to motivate their children, students, workers, athletes, and clients, you will observe that not all attempts to motivate others are successful and that there really is an art to motivating others. The same can be said to attempts to motivate the self. For instance, take the time to actually monitor the emotions expressed by children, students, workers, athletes, and clients as they are being motivated by others. When people adapt successfully and

BOX 1	*Why We Do What We Do*

Question: Why is this information important?

Answer: To gain the capacity to really explain why people do what they do.

Explaining motivation—why people do what they do—is not easy. People have no shortage of possible motivation theories ("He did that because . . ."), but the problem is that many of the theories people come up with to explain behavior are not very helpful in the effort to explain why people do what they do.

When I talk to people in everyday life, ask students about their motivation theories during the first week of class, and when I read Dear Abbey's advice in the newspaper, the most popular theories people embrace are:

• Self-esteem
• Incentives
• Rewards
• Praise

At the top of the list of people's theories of motivation is "increase self-esteem." The view on self-esteem sounds something like, "Find a way to make people feel good about themselves, and then good things will start to happen." "Praise them, reward them, compliment them, give them stickers or trophies; give them some affirmation that they are worthy as a person and that brighter days are ahead." The problem with this strategy is that it is wrong. It is wrong because there is practically no empirical evidence to support it (Baumeister et al., 2003). Educational psychologists, for instance, routinely find that increases in students' self-esteem do not produce increases in their academic achievement (Marsh, 1990; Scheier & Kraut, 1979; Shaalvik & Hagtvet, 1990). A former President of the American Psychological Association (APA) went so far as to conclude that "there are almost no findings that self-esteem causes anything at all" (Seligman, quoted in Azar, 1994, p. 4).

There is value in self-esteem. It's ludicrous to wish low self-esteem on someone. The problem is that self-esteem is not a causal variable. Instead, it is an effect—a reflection of how our lives are going. It is a barometer of well-being. When life is going well, self-esteem rises; when life is going poorly, self-esteem drops. This is very different from saying that self-esteem *causes* life to go well, however. The logical flaw in thinking about self-esteem as a source of motivation is the act of putting the proverbial cart before the horse. Self-esteem is an expression, not a cause, of motivation. Self-esteem is a cart, not a horse.

If motivation does not flow outwardly from a reservoir of high self-esteem, then from where does motivation come? How do people succeed in their attempts to study more, start exercising, reverse bad habits, resist temptation, or overcome impulses and appetites like alcohol abuse, overeating, smoking, gambling, shopping, and aggression? To understand the sources of motivation that can influence behavior in a causal way, consider shifting some of your attention away from self-esteem as a motivation theory and toward the theories listed in Table 1.5. These are the theories that empirical evidence shows are the ways to change the way people think, feel, and behave. Some theories revolve around supporting people's needs, other theories revolve around cultivating optimistic and resilient ways of thinking (cognitions), other theories establish conditions that promote positive emotions, and still other theories address the judicious management of incentives and consequences. Hence, I recommend the reader put self-esteem somewhere on the proverbial back burner for the time being so to make room on the front burner of one's intellectual stove for some new theories of motivation (those that rely on needs, cognitions, emotions, and incentives to explain why people do what they do).

their motivational states flourish, people express positive emotions such as joy, hope, interest, and optimism. But when people are overwhelmed by their environment and their motivational states flounder, people express negative emotions such as sadness, hopelessness, frustration, and stress. In the chapters to come, much of the text will be devoted to practical applications and to the art of motivating the self and others.

There Is Nothing So Practical As a Good Theory

Consider how you might answer a motivational question such as, "What causes Joe to study so hard and for so long?" To generate an answer, you might begin with a common-sense analysis (e.g., "Joe studies so hard because he has such high self-esteem."). Additionally, you might recall a similar instance from your personal experience when you tried very hard, and you might then generalize that experience to this particular situation (e.g., "The last time I studied that hard, it was because I had a big test the next day."). A third strategy might be to find an expert on the topic and ask her (e.g., "My neighbor is a veteran teacher, I'll ask her why she thinks Joe might be studying so hard."). These are all fine and informative resources for helping answer motivational questions, but another resource to answer motivational questions is a good theory.

A theory is a set of variables (e.g., self-efficacy, goals, effort) and the relationships that are assumed to exist among those variables (e.g., strong self-efficacy beliefs encourage people to set goals, and once set, goals encourage high effort). Theories provide a conceptual framework for interpreting behavioral observations, and they function as intel-

Table 1.5   Twenty-Four Theories in the Study of Motivation and Emotion
(with a Supportive Reference Citation)

Motivation Theory	Supportive Reference Citation for Further Information
Achievement motivation	Elliot (1997)
Arousal	Berlyne (1967)
Attribution	Weiner (1986)
Cognitive dissonance	Harmon-Jones and Mills (1999)
Cognitive evaluation	Deci and Ryan (1985a)
Differential emotions	Izard (1991)
Drive	Bolles (1975)
Dynamics of action	Atkinson and Birch (1978)
Effectance motivation	Harter (1981)
Ego development	Loevinger (1976)
Expectancy x value	Vroom (1964)
Facial feedback hypothesis	Laird (1974)
Flow	Csikszentmihalyi (1997)
Goal setting	Locke and Latham (2002)
Learned helplessness	Peterson, Maier, and Seligman (1993)
Opponent process	Solomon (1980)
Positive affect	Isen (1987)
Psychodynamics	Westin (1998)
Reactance	Wortman and Brehm (1975)
Self-actualization	Rogers (1959)
Self-determination	Ryan and Deci (2000a)
Self-efficacy	Bandura (1997)
Sensation seeking	Zuckerman (1994)
Stress and coping	Lazarus (1991a)

lectual bridges that link motivational questions and problems with satisfying answers and solutions. With a motivation theory in mind, the researcher approaches a question or problem along the lines of, "Well, according to goal-setting theory, the reason Joe studies so hard and so long is because . . ." As you read through the pages of each chapter and become familiar with each motivation theory, consider its usefulness in answering the motivational questions you care about most.

Table 1.5 introduces 24 motivation theories that appear in the chapters to come. The theories are listed here for two reasons. First, the list introduces the idea that the heart and soul of a motivational analysis of behavior is its theories. Instead of existing as dry and abstract playthings of scientists, a good theory is the most practical, useable tool for solving the problems faced by students, teachers, workers, employers, managers, athletes, coaches, parents, therapists, and clients. To paraphrase Kurt Lewin, there is nothing so practical as a good theory. A theory can serve as a useful guide in how to solve a problem.

Second, the list of theories can serve as a means for monitoring your growing familiarity with contemporary motivation study. At the present time, you probably recognize very few of the theories listed in the table, but your familiarity will grow week by week. Months from now, you will feel more comfortable with the two dozen theories listed in Table 1.5. If so, then you can then be confident that you are developing a sophisticated and complete understanding of motivation and emotion. When you know motivation theories, you know motivation.

PUTTING IT ALL TOGETHER: A FRAMEWORK TO UNDERSTAND THE STUDY OF MOTIVATION

One way to integrate the perennial questions, subject matter, and expressions of motivation is summarized in Figure 1.3. Antecedent conditions affect the person's underlying motive status, and the rise and fall of the person's motive status creates a sense of "wanting to" that expresses itself through energetic and goal-directed behavior, physiology, and self-report.

Consider a few illustrative examples. Hours of food deprivation (antecedent condition) will cause a subsequent drop in plasma glucose (change in physiological need) which will be represented in consciousness as felt hunger and a sense of wanting to eat that energizes and directs one's forthcoming behavior, physiology, and self-report. Likewise, receiving positive feedback from a job well done (antecedent condition) nurtures a perception of competence that cultivates a sense of wanting to improve that enhances persistence behavior, calms upset physiology, and inspires self-reports like, "This is fun." Similarly, a personal threat (antecedent condition) can give rise to fear (emotion) and hence a sense of wanting to flee and protect the self, a sense that foreshadows the person's behavior (running away), physiology (heart rate), and self-report (worry, feeling nervous).

The summary model (Figure 1.3) illustrates how motivational psychologists answer their perennial questions. That is, the model identifies the conditions under which motives rise and fall (as influenced by antecedent conditions), illustrates the subject matter of motivation study (needs, cognitions, emotions), and illustrates how changes in motivation overtly express themselves (behavior, physiology, self-report). How all these processes work together to explain a specific motivational phenomenon is the job of a theory. The

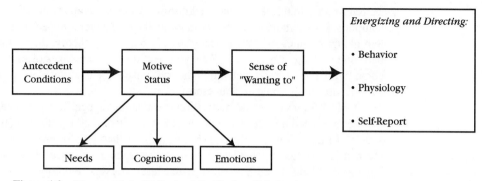

Figure 1.3 Framework to Understand the Study of Motivation

essential purpose of each of the theories listed in Table 1.5, for instance, is to explain how the model in Figure 1.3 works in relation to a particular motive (e.g., achievement, arousal, attribution).

SUMMARY

The journey to understand motivation and emotion begins by asking the perennial question, "What causes behavior?" This general question invites the more specific questions that constitute the core problems to be solved in motivation study: What starts behavior? How is behavior sustained over time? Why is behavior directed toward some ends but away from others? Why does behavior change its direction? Why does behavior stop? What are the forces that determine behavior's intensity? Why does a person behave one way in a particular situation at one time yet behave in a different way at another time? What are the motivational differences among individuals, and how do such differences arise?

The subject matter of motivation concerns those processes that give behavior its energy and direction. The four processes capable of giving behavior strength and purpose—its energy and direction—are needs, cognitions, emotions, and external events. Needs are conditions within the individual that are essential and necessary for the maintenance of life and for growth and well-being. Cognitions are mental events, such as beliefs, expectations, and self-concept, that represent rather enduring ways of thinking. Emotions are short-lived subjective-physiological-functional-expressive phenomena that organize feelings, physiology, purpose, and expression into a coherent response to an environmental condition, such as a threat. External events are environmental incentives that energize and direct behavior toward those events that signal positive consequences and away from those that signal aversive consequences.

Both in its presence and in its intensity, motivation can be expressed in three ways: behavior, physiology, and self-report. The seven aspects of motivated behavior include effort, latency, persistence, choice, probability of response, facial expressions, and bodily gestures. Psychophysiological states express the activity of the central nervous and hormonal systems, and they provide further data to infer the biological underpinnings of motivation and emotion. Self-report ratings measure motivational states as through interviews or questionnaires. All three of these expressions can be helpful in inferring motivation, but researchers rely heavily on behavioral and physiological measures and only lightly on self-report ratings.

Eight themes run through motivation study. These themes are as follows: (1) motivation benefits adaptation, (2) motives affect behavior by directing attention, (3) motive strengths vary over time and influence the stream of behavior, (4) types of motivation exist, (5) motivation includes both approach and avoidance tendencies, (6) motivation study reveals what people want, (7) to flourish, motivation needs supportive conditions, and (8) there is nothing so practical as a good theory. These principles are important because they provide an overall perspective for unifying motivation study's diverse assumptions, hypotheses, perspectives, theories, findings, and applications into a coherent, interesting, and practical field of study. A general framework for understanding the motivational phenomenon in the chapters to come appears in Figure 1.3.

Chapter 2

Motivation in Historical and Contemporary Perspectives

Have you seen the Michael J. Fox movie *Back to the Future?* In this movie, the hero drives a car that acts as a time machine capable of transporting its passengers back in time to the 1950s. While Michael J. Fox skateboards around town and makes his movie, we can drop by the local university to see what the college motivation course looks like.

Besides the students' bobby-socks and funny haircuts, one item to notice in this college course on motivation would be the lack of a textbook. The first textbook in motivation was not written until 1964 (Cofer & Appley, 1964). Another item would be the syllabus. Featured topics on the mimeographed handout would be drive theory, incentives and reinforcement, acquired drives, conflict, and emotion. You could search the syllabus all you wanted, but none of the really interesting stuff about how to apply motivation would be included—nothing about motivation in the schools, sports psychology, work motivation, obesity and dieting, personal control beliefs, and so on. The course would, however, likely include psychoanalytic and self-actualization concepts—a week on Freud, another week on Maslow. The course would feature a weekly laboratory assignment. Each student would receive a rat and would spend his or her time testing what effects manipulations such as 24 hours of food deprivation had on the rat's running speed toward a goal box filled with sunflower seeds. Once you returned to the De Lorean time machine and drove back to the present, you would probably agree that the study of motivation has changed and improved itself even more than the haircuts and fashions have.

PHILOSOPHICAL ORIGINS OF MOTIVATIONAL CONCEPTS

If our science-fiction technology sent you back 100 years, then you would not be able to find a motivation course at all. Courses in motivation (and the field of motivation itself) have not been around very long—less than 100 years.

The roots of motivation study owe their origin to the ancient Greeks—Socrates, Plato, and Aristotle. Plato (Socrates's student) proposed that motivation flowed from a tripartite, hierarchically arranged soul (or mind, psyche). At the most primitive level was the soul's appetitive aspect, which contributed bodily appetites and desires, such as hunger and sex. At a second level was the competitive aspect, which contributed socially referenced standards, such as feeling honored or shamed. At the highest level was the calculating aspect, which contributed the soul's decision-making capacities, such as reason and choosing. For Plato, these three different aspects of the soul motivated different realms of behavior. Also, each higher aspect could regulate the motives of the lower aspects (e.g., reason could keep bodily appetites in check). Interestingly, Plato's portrayal of motivation anticipated Sigmund Freud's psychodynamics rather well (e.g., see Plato's Book IX, pp. 280–281): Roughly speaking, Plato's appetitive aspect corresponds to Freud's id, the competitive aspect to the superego, and the calculating aspect to the ego (Erdelyi, 1985).

Aristotle endorsed Plato's hierarchically organized, tripartite soul (appetitive, competitive, and calculating), though he preferred different terminology (nutritive, sensitive, and rational). The nutritive aspect was the most impulsive, irrational, and animal-like. It contributed bodily urges necessary for the maintenance of life. The sensitive aspect was also bodily related, but it regulated pleasure and pain. The soul's rational component was unique to human beings, as it was idea-related, intellectual, and featured the will. The will operated as the soul's highest level as it utilized intention, choice, and that which is divine and immortal.

Hundreds of years later, the Greek's tripartite psyche was reduced to a dualism—the passions of the body and the reason of the mind. The two-part soul retained the Greek's hierarchical nature as it made its chief distinction between that which was physical, irrational, impulsive, and biological (the body) versus that which was nonmaterial, rational, intelligent, and spiritual (the mind). The impetus for this reinterpretation rested mostly in the era's intellectual commitment to motivational dichotomies, such as passion versus reason, good versus evil, and animal nature versus human soul. Thomas Aquinas, for example, suggested that the body provided irrational, pleasure-based motivational impulses, whereas the mind provided rational, will-based motivations.

In the post-Renaissance era, René Descartes, a French philosopher, added to this mind-body dualism by distinguishing between the passive and active aspects of motivation. The body was a mechanical, machine-like, and motivationally passive agent, whereas the will was an immaterial, spiritual, and motivationally active agent. As a physical entity, the body possessed nutritive needs and responded to the environment in mechanistic ways through its senses, reflexes, and physiology. The mind, however, was a spiritual, thinking entity that possessed a purposive will. The mind could control the body; the spirit could govern the body's desires. This distinction was a tremendously important one because it set the agenda for motivation study during the next 300 years: What was needed to understand the passive and reactive motives was a mechanistic analysis of the body (i.e., the study of physiology); what was needed to understand active and purposive motives was an intellectual analysis of the will (i.e., the study of philosophy).

WILL: THE FIRST GRAND THEORY

For Descartes, the ultimate motivational force was the will. Descartes reasoned that if he could understand the will, then he would understand motivation. The will initiated and directed action; it chose both whether to act and what to do when acting. Bodily needs, passions, pleasures, and pains created impulses to action, but these impulses only excited the will. The will was a faculty (a power) of the mind that controlled the bodily appetites and passions in the interests of virtue and salvation by exercising its power of choice. By assigning exclusive powers of motivation to the will, Descartes provided motivation with its first grand theory.

The phrase "grand theory" is used here and throughout the chapter to connote an all-encompassing theory, one general model that seeks to explain the full range of motivated action—why we eat, drink, work, play, compete, fear certain things, read, fall in love, and so on. The statement that "the will motivates all action" is a grand theory of motivation in the same way that "the love of money is the root of all evil" is a grand theory of evil. Both identify a single, all-encompassing cause that fully explains a phenomenon (all motivation, all evil).

Descartes's hope was that once he understood the will, then an understanding of motivation would inevitably unfold. Understanding motivation was reduced to, and became synonymous with, understanding the will. For this reason, a great deal of philosophical energy was invested in the effort. Some progress was made as the acts of willing were identified to be choosing (i.e., deciding whether to act or not; Rand, 1964), striving (i.e., creating impulses to act; Ruckmick, 1936), and resisting (i.e., self-denial or resisting temptation). In the end, however, two centuries of philosophical analysis yielded disappointing results. The will turned out to be an ill-understood faculty of the mind that arose, somehow, out of a congeries of innate capacities, environmental sensations, life experiences, and reflections upon itself and its ideas. Further, once the will emerged, it somehow became endowed with intentions and purposes. And it turned out that some people showed more willpower than did other people.

To make a long story short, philosophers found the will to be as mysterious and as difficult to explain as was the motivation it supposedly generated. Philosophers discovered neither the will's nature nor the laws by which it operated. Essentially, philosophers painted themselves into the proverbial corner by multiplying the problem they were trying to solve. In using the will, philosophers now had to explain not only motivation but also the motivator—the will. As you can see, the problem only doubled. For this reason, those involved with the new science of psychology, which emerged in the 1870s (Schultz, 1987), found themselves in search of a less mysterious motivational principle. They found one, not within philosophy, but within physiology—the instinct.

Before leaving the historical discussion of the will, consider that contemporary psychologists do recognize that the mind (the will) does think, plan, and form intentions that precede action. If it is not the will that is doing the thinking and planning, then from where is all this thinking and planning coming? In other words, how do people resist temptation (Mischel, 1996), sustain effort (Locke & Kristof, 1996), exercise self-control (Mischel & Mischel, 1983), control their thoughts (Wegner, 1994), form intentions to act (Gollwitzer, 1993), and concentrate their attention on the task at hand (Rand, 1964)? Consider two explanations. In the first, consider how children summon the willpower they need to delay gratification and resist temptation (Mischel, Shoda, & Rodriguez, 1989; Patterson & Mischel, 1976). In one experiment, a preschool child sits alone at a table with a tempting cookie. The experimenter gives the child a choice—one cookie now or two cookies if he or she could wait 20 minutes. Rather than calling on their willpower (i.e., self-denial, grim determination), the researchers found that the children successfully resisted the temptation and delayed their gratification by converting the frustrating wait into something more tolerable or enjoyable (i.e., playing a game, singing, or even taking a nap). Children who used such strategies resisted the temptation, whereas children who did not use such strategies acted on impulse (ate the available cookie immediately). In the second example, college students took an exam as researchers tried to predict how well or poorly they would do (Locke & Kristof, 1996). The researchers recorded each student's goal (desired grade) and study methods. Students with clear plans and effective study methods performed well, whereas students with no goals and superficial study methods performed poorly. Thus, goals and strategies, not personal willpower, produced effective performance. Therefore, in the contemporary study of motivation, researchers put aside general models of motivation like "willpower" and instead specify the psychological processes that they can more readily link to people's behavior. That is, researchers study measurable mental processes like plans, goals, and strategies, rather than the mysterious will (Gollwitzer & Bargh, 1996).

INSTINCT: THE SECOND GRAND THEORY

Charles Darwin's biological determinism had two major effects on scientific thinking. First, Darwin's biological determinism provided biology with its most important idea (evolution). In doing so, biological determinism turned the mood of scientists away from mentalistic motivational concepts (e.g., will) toward mechanistic and genetic ones. Second, Darwin's biological determinism ended the man-animal dualism that pervaded early motivation study. Instead, it introduced questions such as how animals use their resources (i.e., motivation) to adapt to the prevailing demands of an environment. For the earlier philosophers, the will was a uniquely human mental power, and breaking down the distinction between the motivation of humans and the motivation of animals was yet another reason to drop the will as a grand explanation of motivated behavior.

For Darwin, much of animal behavior seemed to be unlearned, automated, and mechanistic (Darwin, 1859, 1872). With or without experience, animals adapted to their prevailing environments: Birds built nests, hens brooded, dogs chased rabbits, and rabbits ran from dogs. To explain this apparently prewired adaptive behavior, Darwin proposed the instinct.

Darwin's achievement was that his motivational concept could explain what the philosopher's will could not—namely, where the motivational force came from in the first place. Instincts arose from a physical substance, from the genetic endowment. Instincts were physically real—they existed in the genes. The animal had a material substance within it that led the animal to act in a specific way. Motivation study left philosophy and entered the natural sciences.

Given the presence of the appropriate stimulus, instincts expressed themselves through inherited bodily reflexes—the bird built a nest, the hen brooded, and the dog hunted, all because each had a genetically endowed, biologically aroused impulse to do so. Essentially, motivation thinkers in the 19th century stripped away the inanimate part of the philosopher's dualism (i.e., the rational soul) and kept that which remained, namely the biological urges, impulses, and appetites.

The first psychologist to popularize an instinct theory of motivation was William James (1890). James borrowed heavily from the intellectual climate of Darwin and his contemporaries to endow human beings with a generous number of physical (e.g., sucking, locomotion) and mental (e.g., imitation, play, sociability) instincts. All that was needed to translate an instinct into goal-directed (i.e., motivated) behavior was the presence of an appropriate stimulus. Cats chase mice, run from dogs, avoid fires simply because they biologically must (i.e., because a mouse brings out the cat's instinct to chase, a dog brings out the instinct to flee, and the fire's flames bring out the instinct to protect). That is, the sight of a mouse (or dog or fire) activates in the cat a complex set of inherited reflexes that generated impulses to specific actions (e.g., chasing, running). Through the instinct, animals inherited a nature endowed with impulses to act and the reflexes needed to produce that purposive action.

Psychology's affection for, and commitment to, its second grand theory of motivation grew rapidly. A generation after James, William McDougall (1908, 1926) proposed an instinct theory that featured instincts to explore, to fight, to mother offspring, and so on. McDougall regarded instincts as irrational and impulsive motivational forces that oriented the person toward one particular goal. It was the instinct that "determines its possessor to perceive, and to pay attention to, objects of a certain class, to experience an emotional excitement of a particular quality upon perceiving such an object, and to act in regard to it in a particular manner, or, at least, to experience an impulse to such action" (McDougall, 1908, p. 30). Thus, instincts (and their associated emotions) explained the goal-directed quality so readily apparent in human behavior. In many respects, McDougall's instinct doctrine paralleled James's ideas. The greatest difference between the two was McDougall's rather extreme assertion that without instincts human beings would initiate no action. Without these "prime movers," human beings would be inert lumps, bodies without any impulses to action. In other words, all of human motivation owes its origin to a collection of genetically endowed instincts (i.e., a grand theory of motivation).

Once researchers embraced the instinct as a grand theory of motivation, the next task became identifying how many instincts human beings possessed. Things quickly went out of control. The instinct doctrine became hopelessly speculative as different lists of instincts grew to include over 6,000 different instincts (Bernard, 1924; Dunlap, 1919). In the practice of compiling lists of instincts, intellectual promiscuity reigned: "If he goes with his fellows, it is the 'herd instinct' which activates him; if he walks alone, it is the 'antisocial instinct'; if he twiddles his thumbs, it is the 'thumb-twiddling instinct'; if he does not twiddle his thumbs, it is the 'thumb-not-twiddling instinct'" (Holt, 1931, p. 428). The problem here is the tendency to confuse naming with explaining (e.g., the reason people are aggressive is because they have an instinct to be aggressive). Confusing naming and explaining adds nothing to the understanding of motivation and emotion.

In addition, the logic underlying instinct theory was exposed as circular (Kuo, 1921; Tolman, 1923). Consider the explanation of how the instinct to fight motivates acts of aggression. The only evidence that people possess an instinct to fight is that they sometimes behave aggressively. For the theorist, this is the worst kind of circularity: The cause explains the behavior (instinct → behavior), but the behavior is evidence for its cause (behavior → instinct). What is lacking here is some independent way to determine if the instinct really exists. One way to determine this is to raise two very similar animals (i.e., animals endowed with similar instincts) in a way that gives them different life experiences. Then wait until the animals mature into adulthood, and check if their behaviors are essentially the same. If instincts direct behavior, then two genetically matched animals should behave in essentially the same way, despite the differences in their life circumstances and experiences. When researchers performed such experiments on the mothering instinct in rats (Birch, 1956) and the handedness (right- or left-handed) instinct in humans (Watson, 1924), the rats and humans acted in ways that reflected their different experiences (rather than their similar instincts).

The instinct concept arose to fill a gap of what motivation is and from where it came (Beach, 1955). Psychology's affair with instinct theory began with wholehearted acceptance but ended with sweeping denial.[1] Just as psychology previously abandoned the will,

---

[1]Contemporary psychology no longer uses the instinct to explain complex human behavior. Nonetheless, the proposition that nonhuman animals show consistent, unlearned, stereotypical patterns of behavior is an undeniable observation. Bees build hexagonal cells, male stickleback fish attack red coloration, and birds build nests. Contemporary psychologists (but especially ethologists) concede that such stereotypical acts can be attributed to instincts in animals. As James wrote over a century ago, "that instincts . . . exist on an enormous scale in the animal kingdom needs no proof" (1890, p. 383). In using the term "instinct," ethologists (Eibl-Eibesfeldt, 1989; Lorenz, 1965; Moltz, 1965) now speak of inherited neuronal structures that are unmodified by the environment during development. These inherited neuronal structures give rise not to general patterns of behavior but to particular bits of situationally specific behavior, referred to as "fixed action patterns." Changing instinct's focus from the cause of complex behavior to the cause of bits of behavior (fixed action patterns) proved to be a comfortable theoretical compromise. While theoretically expedient, such a compromise clearly shows the decline of a grand theory. Explaining bits of behavior or bits of motivation is just not the same as explaining all of behavior and all of motivation.

it abandoned the instinct and found itself in search of a substitute motivational concept to explain behavior's purposive nature.

DRIVE: THE THIRD GRAND THEORY

The motivational concept that arose to replace instinct was drive (introduced by Woodworth, 1918). Drive arose from a functional biology, one that understood that the function of behavior was to service bodily needs. As biological imbalances occurred (e.g., lack of food and water), animals experienced these biological need deficits psychologically as "drive." Drive motivated whatever behavior was instrumental to servicing the body's needs (e.g., eating, drinking, approaching). The two most widely embraced drive theories came from Sigmund Freud (1915) and Clark Hull (1943).

Freud's Drive Theory

Freud, a physiologist by training, believed that all behavior was motivated and that the purpose of behavior was to serve the satisfaction of needs. His view of the nervous system was that biological urges (e.g., hunger) were constantly and inevitably recurring conditions that produced energy buildups within a nervous system that revolved around an inherited tendency to maintain a constant low level of energy (Freud, 1915). While it tried to maintain a constant and low-energy level, the nervous system was perpetually being displaced from this objective by the emergence and reemergence of biological urges. Each energy buildup upset nervous system stability and produced psychological discomfort (i.e., anxiety). If the energy buildup rose unchecked, it could threaten physical and psychological health. Drive therefore arose as a sort of emergency warning to take action. Behavior continued until the drive or urge that motivated it was satisfied. In other words, behavior served bodily needs, and anxiety (drive) acted as a sort of middleman for ensuring that behavior occurred as and when needed.

One way to understand Freud's view of nervous system energy (i.e., "libido") is through the analogy of a hydraulic system in which energy (like constantly flowing water) continues to rise and rise. As the bodily drives continue to build up energy, the anxious urge to discharge that energy becomes increasingly urgent and expedient (or else the water would overflow). The higher the psychic energy rose, the greater the impulse to act. Adaptive behavior quieted the drive, for a time, but the ever-constant buildup of nervous-system energy would return (i.e., the water's inflow never shuts off).

Freud (1915) summarized his drive theory with four components: source, impetus, aim, and object. The source of drive was a bodily deficit (e.g., lack of food). Drive had an impetus (force) that possessed the aim of satisfaction, which was the removal (via satisfaction) of the underlying bodily deficit. To accomplish this aim, the individual experienced anxiety on a psychological level, and it was this anxiety that motivated the behavioral search for an object capable of removing the bodily deficit. Satisfaction of the bodily deficit quieted drive/anxiety. Given this introduction, Freud's drive theory can be represented as follows:

Source of Drive →	Impetus of Drive →	Object of Drive →	Aim of Drive
Bodily Deficit	Intensity of the psychological discomfort (anxiety)	Environmental object capable of satisfying bodily deficit	Satisfaction by removing the bodily deficit

Despite its creativity, Freud's drive theory suffered at least three criticisms: (1) a relative overestimation of the contribution of biological forces to motivation (and hence, a relative underestimation of factors related to learning and experience); (2) an overreliance on data taken from case studies of disturbed individuals (and hence, an underreliance on data taken from experimental research with representative samples); and (3) ideas that were not scientifically (i.e., experimentally) testable (e.g., How can you create an empirical test of whether or not people possess a drive to be aggressive?). None of these three criticisms applied, however, to the second major drive theory, that by Clark Hull.

Hull's Drive Theory

For Hull (1943, 1952), drive was a pooled energy source composed of all current bodily deficits/disturbances. In other words, particular needs for food, water, sex, sleep, and so forth summed to constitute a total bodily need. For Hull, as for Freud, motivation (i.e., drive) had a purely physiological basis and bodily need was the ultimate source of motivation (i.e., a grand theory of motivation).

Hull's drive theory had one outstanding feature that no motivation theory before it had ever possessed—namely motivation could be predicted before it occurred. With both the instinct and the will, it was impossible to predict in an *a priori* fashion when and whether or not a person would be motivated. But if an animal was deprived of food, water, sex, or sleep, however, then drive would inevitably increase in proportion to the duration of that deprivation. Motivation was responsive to antecedent conditions in the environment. Drive was an increasing monotonic function of total bodily need, and total bodily need was an increasing monotonic function of hours of deprivation. The fact that drive could be known from antecedent environmental conditions marked the beginning of a *scientific* study of motivation. This was so because if one knew which environmental conditions created motivation, then one could manipulate (and predict) motivational states in the laboratory. One could also explore the effects of the manipulated motivational state on a host of outcomes (e.g., performance, effort, well-being).

Drive arose from a range of bodily disturbances, including hunger, thirst, sex, pain, air, temperature regulation, urination, sleep, activity, nest building, and care for one's young (Hull, 1943, pp. 59–60). Once it arose, drive energized behavior (Bolles, 1975). Although drive energized behavior, it did not direct it. Habit, not drive, directed behavior. As one contemporary phrased it, "Drive is an energizer, not a guide" (Hebb, 1955, p. 249). Behavior-guiding habits came from learning, and learning occurred as a consequence of reinforcement. Hull's research led him to argue that if a response was followed quickly by a reduction in drive, learning occurred and habit was reinforced. Any response that decreased drive (e.g., eating, drinking, mating) produced reinforcement, and the animal learned which response produced drive reduction in that particular situation. To show how habit and drive (i.e., learning and motivation) produced behavior, Hull (1943) developed the following formula:

$$_sE_r = {_sH_r} \times D$$

The variable $_sE_r$ is the strength of behavior (E stands for "excitatory potential") in the presence of a particular stimulus. $_sH_r$ is habit strength (i.e., probability of a particular drive-reducing response given a particular stimulus). D is drive.[2] The observable aspects of behavior—running, persisting, etc.—are denoted by $_sE_r$. The variables $_sH_r$ and D refer to behavior's underlying, unobservable causes. The multiplication sign is important in that behavior occurred only when habit and drive were at nonzero levels. In other words, without drive ($D = 0$) or without habit ($H = 0$), there is no excitatory potential ($E = 0$).

Later, Hull (1952) extended his behavior system beyond $H \times D$ to include a third cause of behavior: incentive motivation, abbreviated as K.[3] In addition to the motivational properties of D, the incentive value of a goal object (its quality, its quantity, or both) also energized the animal. After all, people generally work harder for $50 than they do for $1. Because he recognized that motivation could arise from either internal (D) or external (K) sources, Hull (1952) proposed the following formula:

$$_sE_r = {_sH_r} \times D \times K$$

Both D and K were motivational terms. The principal difference between the two was that D was rooted in internal stimulation via bodily disturbances, whereas K was rooted in external stimulation via the quality of the incentive.

Hull's behavior theory gained enormous popularity. In its zenith, his drive theory was as popular as any theory in the history of psychology. That is obviously a strong statement, but consider three historical occurrences that validate this claim. First, approximately half of all the articles published in the leading psychology journals in the early 1950s (e.g., *Psychological Review*, *Journal of Experimental Psychology*) included a reference to Hull's 1943 book. Second, books on motivation went from being practically nonexistent at mid-century to commonplace 10 years later (Atkinson, 1964; Bindra, 1959; Brown, 1961; Hall, 1961; Lindzey, 1958; Madsen, 1959; McClelland, 1955; Maslow, 1954; Olds, 1956; Peters, 1958; Stacey & DeMartino, 1958; Toman, 1960; Young, 1961). Third, in the 1950s the American Psychological Association (APA) invited its members to list the most important figures in the history of psychology (through mid-century). The survey rankings appear in Table 2.1. Notice the two names at the top of the list.[4]

---

[2]The subscripts *s* and *r* stand for "stimulus" and "response" to communicate that $_sH_r$ refers to a particular response in the presence of a particular stimulus. Similarly, the subscripts joined with $_sE_r$ refer to the potential "energy" of that response in the presence of that particular stimulus.

[3]Incidentally, if you happen to wonder why incentive motivation was abbreviated as K instead of as I, K stood for Kenneth Spence (Weiner, 1972). Spence convinced Hull of the necessity of incorporating incentive motivation into his behavior system. Besides, I was used for another variable, inhibition, which is not discussed here.

[4]By the dawn of the 21st century, the list of eminent psychologists had changed quite a bit (Haggbloom et al., 2002). In 2002, Sigmund Freud dropped to 3rd, while Clark Hull dropped to 21st. The current top 10, in order from 1st to 10th, still features a number of motivation researchers: B. F. Skinner, Jean Piaget, Sigmund Freud, Albert Bandura, Leon Festinger, Carl Rogers, Stanley Schachter, Neal Miller, Edward Thorndike, and Abraham Maslow.

Table 2.1   Mid-Century Rankings of the 10 Most Important Historical Figures in Psychology

1. Sigmund Freud
2. Clark Hull
3. Wilhelm Wundt
4. Ivan Pavlov
5. John Watson
6. Edward Thorndike
7. William James
8. Max Wertheimer
9. Edward Tolman
10. Kurt Lewin

Decline of Drive Theory

Drive theory—both the Freudian and Hullian versions—rested on three fundamental assumptions:

1. Drive emerged from bodily needs.
2. Drive reduction was reinforcing and produced learning.
3. Drive energized behavior.

Throughout the 1950s, empirical tests of these three assumptions revealed much support but also reason for concern. First, some motives existed with or without any corresponding biological need. For instance, anorexics do not eat (and do not want to eat) despite a strong biological need to do so (Klien, 1954). Thus, motivation could emerge from sources other than one's bodily disturbances. Second, learning often occurred without any corresponding experience of drive reduction. Hungry rats, for instance, learn even when reinforced only by a nonnutritive saccharin reward (Sheffield & Roby, 1950). Because saccharin has no nutritional benefit, it cannot reduce drive (i.e., cannot serve the needs of the body). Other research showed that learning occurred following drive induction (i.e., drive increase; Harlow, 1953). Eventually, it became clear that for learning to occur, drive reduction was neither necessary nor sufficient (Bolles, 1972). Third, research recognized the importance of external (nonphysiological) sources of motivation. For example, a person who is not necessarily thirsty can feel a rather strong motive to drink upon tasting (or seeing or smelling) a favorite beverage. Hull did add incentive motivation (K), but the important point is that motives arose from more than just bodily physiology. To explain motivational phenomena like eating, drinking, and having sex, it became clear that researchers needed to focus at least some of their attention on external (environmental) sources of motivation.

Post-Drive Theory Years

The 1950s and 1960s were transitional decades in the study of motivation. In the early 1950s, the prevalent motivation theories were the well-known, historically entrenched grand theories. Drive theory was the dominant perspective on motivation (Bolles, 1975;

Hull, 1952). Additional prominent mid-century motivational theories included optimal level of arousal (Hebb, 1955; Berlyne, 1967), pleasure centers in the brain (Olds, 1969), approach-avoidance conflicts (Miller, 1959), universal needs (Murray, 1938), conditioned motives (Miller, 1948), and self-actualization (Rogers, 1959). As motivation study progressed and as new findings emerged, it became clear that if progress was to be made, the field was going to have to step outside the boundaries of its grand theories. In the post-drive theory years, alternative theories of motivation did emerge and try to take their place as the new grand theory of the day. But motivation psychologists were simply gaining too much new information to be restricted to a grand theory. To investigate their new findings, the motivation psychologists of the 1970s began to embrace mini-theories of motivation (Dember, 1965). The next section discusses these mini-theories. But it will be helpful to pause here and consider the two motivational principles from the 1960s that were offered as possible post-drive theory replacements for a grand theory of motivation: incentive and arousal.

Consider incentive. An incentive is an external event (or stimulus) that energizes and directs approach or avoidance behavior. Drive reduction theory asserted that people were motivated by drives, which "pushed" them toward particular goal objects (e.g., hunger pushed the person out into the environment to find food). Incentive motivational theories asserted that people were motivated by the incentive value of various objects in their environment that "pulled" them toward these objects (e.g., the sight of strawberry cheesecake pulled the person toward the dessert table). Notice that the primary motivation is not to reduce drive but, rather, to increase and maintain contact with incentive stimuli. The incentive theories that emerged in the 1960s fundamentally sought to explain why people approached positive incentives and why they avoided negative ones. These theories essentially focused on Hull's K instead of his D, and they adopted the concept of hedonism, which essentially postulates that organisms approach signals of pleasure and avoid signals of pain. Through learning, people formed associations (or expectancies) of which environmental objects were gratifying and thus deserved approach responses, and which other objects were pain-inflicting and thus deserved avoidance responses. Incentive theories offered three new features: (1) new motivational concepts, such as incentives, (2) the idea that motivational states could be acquired through experience, and (3) a portrayal of motivation that highlighted moment-to-moment changes (because environmental incentives can change from one moment to the next).

Consider arousal. The rising disaffection with drive theory was countered by a rising affection for arousal theory. The discovery that lay the foundation for this transition came from the neurophysiological finding of an arousal system in the brain stem (Lindsley, 1957; Moruzzi & Magoun, 1949). The central ideas were that (1) aspects of the environment (how stimulating, novel, stressful) affected how aroused the brain was, and (2) variations in level of arousal had a curvilinear (the inverted-U shape) relationship to behavior. That is, unstimulating environments generated low arousal and emotions like boredom; somewhat stimulating environments generated optimal arousal and emotions like interest; and overly stimulating environments generated high arousal and emotions like fear. Eventually, level of arousal came to be understood as something "synonymous with a general drive state" (Hebb, 1955, p. 249): People prefer an optimal level of arousal and shun too little or too much arousal. So notice what happened to drive theory—it had been reinterpreted away from its biological roots and brought into the age of neurophysiology and cognition. By the late 1960s, the motivational psychologist of the day could focus on biological needs (drive), environmental incentives, or brain states of arousal.

With the growing disaffection with drive theory, it became increasingly evident that any one grand theory was simply unable to carry the whole burden of explaining motivation (Appley, 1991). In its attempt to cover the full range of motivational phenomena, the contemporary landscape of motivation study is now characterized by a wide-ranging diversity of theories ("mini-theories") rather than by any consensus to a single grand theory.

RISE OF THE MINI-THEORIES

Unlike grand theories to explain the full range of motivation, mini-theories limit their attention to specific motivational phenomenon. Mini-theories seek to understand or investigate one particular:

- Motivational phenomenon (e.g., the flow experience)
- Circumstance that affects motivation (e.g., failure feedback)
- Groups of people (e.g., extraverts, children, workers)
- Theoretical question (e.g., What is the relationship between cognition and emotion?)

A mini-theory explains some but not all of motivated behavior. Thus, achievement motivation theory (a mini-theory) arose to explain how people respond to standards of excellence, and hence why some people show enthusiasm and approach, whereas others show anxiety and avoidance when facing a standard of excellence. Achievement motivation theory leaves a great deal of motivated action unexplained, but it does a very good job of explaining an interesting slice of motivated action. The following list identifies some of the mini-theories (with a seminal reference) that emerged in the 1960s and 1970s to replace the fading grand theories of drive, incentive, and arousal:

- Achievement motivation theory (Atkinson, 1964)
- Attributional theory of achievement motivation (Weiner, 1972)
- Cognitive dissonance theory (Festinger, 1957)
- Effectance motivation (White, 1959; Harter, 1978a)
- Expectancy $\times$ Value theory (Vroom, 1964)
- Flow theory (Csikszentmihalyi, 1975)
- Intrinsic motivation (Deci, 1975)
- Goal-setting theory (Locke, 1968)
- Learned helplessness theory (Seligman, 1975)
- Reactance theory (Brehm, 1966)
- Self-efficacy theory (Bandura, 1977)
- Self-schemas (Markus, 1977)

Three historical trends explain why motivation study left behind its tradition of the grand theories in favor of mini-theories. First, motivation researchers reevaluated the wisdom of the idea that human beings are inherently passive. The next section discusses this trend. Second, motivation, like all of psychology, turned markedly cognitive. This trend became known as the cognitive revolution. And third, motivation researchers became increasingly interested in applied, socially relevant questions and problems. In addition to these historical trends, the first journal devoted exclusively to the topic of motivation emerged in 1977, *Motivation and Emotion*. This journal has focused almost all of its attention on the empirical exploration of mini-theories of motivation.

Active Nature of the Person

The purpose of drive theory was to explain how an animal went from inactive to active (Weiner, 1990). The mid-century assumption was that animals (including humans) were naturally inactive, and the role of motivation was to arouse the passive to become the active. Indeed, "motive" means "to move." So drive, like all early motivational constructs, explained the instigating motor of behavior. As a point of illustration, a common mid-century definition of motivation was, "the process of arousing action, sustaining the activity in progress, and regulating the pattern of activity" (Young, 1961, p. 24). Motivation was the study of energizing the passive.

The psychologists of the second half of the century saw things differently. They emphasized that the person was always getting to and doing something. People were inherently active, always motivated. According to one of the proponents of the active nature of people, "Sound motivational theory should . . . assume that motivation is constant, never ending, fluctuating, and complex, and that it is an almost universal characteristic of practically every organismic state of affairs" (Maslow, 1954, p. 69). Perhaps there is no place where this is more evident than in little children: "They pick things up, shake them, smell them, taste them, throw them across the room, and keep asking, 'What's this?' They are unendingly curious" (Deci & Ryan, 1985a, p. 11).

In their mid-1960s review of motivation theories, Charles Cofer and Mortimer Appley (1964) divided the motivation theories of the day into those that assumed a passive, energy-conserving organism and those that assumed an active, growth-seeking organism. The passive-oriented portrayals outnumbered the active-oriented portrayals by 10 to 1. But theories assuming an active organism were beginning to emerge. Today's ideas about motivation and emotion accept the premise of the active organism, and they deal little with deficit motivations (e.g., tension reduction, homeostasis, equilibrium) and much with growth motivations (e.g., creativity, competence, possible selves, self-actualization; Appley, 1991; Benjamin & Jones, 1978; Rapaport, 1960; White, 1960). Motivation study is now the study of directing purpose in inherently active people.

Cognitive Revolution

The early motivational concepts—drive, arousal, homeostasis—were grounded in biology and physiology. Much of the thinking about motivation was therefore molded by a biological heritage and perspective. Contemporary motivation study continues to maintain this alliance with biology, physiology, and sociobiology. In the early 1970s, however, psychology's *Zeitgeist* (its "intellectual climate") turned decidedly cognitive (Gardner, 1985; Segal & Lachman, 1972), and the cognitive revolution spilled into motivation just as it spilled into virtually all areas of psychology (D'Amato, 1974; Dember, 1974). Motivation researchers began to supplement their biological concepts with those that emphasized internal mental processes. Some of these mentalistic motivational constructs include plans (Miller, Galanter, & Pribram, 1960), goals (Locke & Latham, 1990), expectations (Seligman, 1975), beliefs (Bandura, 1977), attributions (Weiner, 1972), and the self-concept (Markus, 1977).

The cognitive revolution had two additional effects on thinking about motivation. First, intellectual discussions about motivation emphasized cognitive constructs (e.g., expectancies, goals) and de-emphasized biological and environmental constructs. These discussions changed psychology's image of human functioning to become "human rather than mechanical" (McKeachie, 1976, p. 831). This ideological shift from mechanical to dynamic (Carver & Scheier, 1981, 1990; Markus & Wurf, 1987) was captured nicely in the title of one of the popular motivation texts of the day, *Theories of Motivation: From Mechanism to Cognition* (Weiner, 1972). A review of motivation studies from the 1960s and 1970s shows a marked decline in experiments manipulating the deprivation states of rats and an equally marked increase in experiments manipulating success or failure feedback given to human performance (Weiner, 1990). The experimental design is not much different, but the focus on human, instead of nonhuman, animals is unmistakable.

Second, the cognitive revolution complemented the emerging movement of humanism. Humanistic psychologists critiqued the prevailing motivation theories of the 1960s as decidedly de-human. Humanists resist the machine metaphor that portrays motivation in a deterministic fashion in response to unyielding biological forces, developmental fates (e.g., traumatic childhood experiences), or controls in the environment or society (Bugental, 1967; Wertheimer, 1978). Ideas from Abraham Maslow and Carl Rogers (Chapter 15) expressed psychology's new understanding of human beings as inherently active, cognitively flexible, and growth motivated (Berlyne, 1975; Maslow, 1987; Rogers, 1961).

Applied, Socially Relevant Research

A third important change that helped usher in the mini-theories era: Researchers turned their attention to questions that were relevant to solving the motivational problems people faced in their lives (McClelland, 1978)—at work (Locke & Latham, 1984), in school (Weiner, 1979), in coping with stress (Lazarus, 1966), in solving health problems (Polivy, 1976), in reversing depression (Seligman, 1975), and so on. As researchers studied nonhuman animals less and humans more, they discovered a wealth of naturally occurring instances of motivation outside the laboratory. Hence, motivation researchers began focusing increasingly on socially relevant, applied questions and problems. Motivation psychologists began to initiate more frequent contact with psychologists in other areas, such as social psychology, industrial/organizational psychology, clinical and counseling psychology, and so on. Overall, the field became less interested in studying, for instance, hunger as a source of drive and more interested in studying the motivations underlying eating, dieting, obesity, and bulimia (Rodin, 1981; Taubes, 1998).

Emphasizing applied, socially relevant research placed contemporary motivation study in a sort of "Johnny Appleseed" role in which individual motivation researchers left their laboratories to take their questions ("What causes behavior?") into psychology's areas of specialization. Motivation's new alliances with other fields in psychology can be

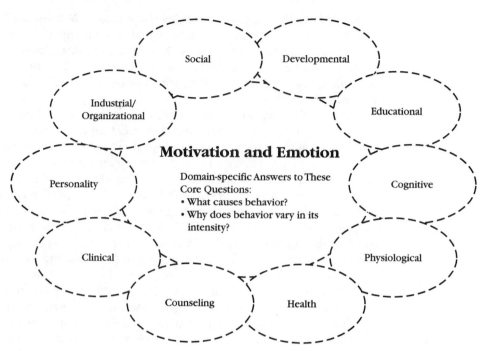

Figure 2.1   Relationship of Motivation Study to Psychology's Areas of Specialization

illustrated in Figure 2.1. The figure illustrates explicitly how motivation links itself with the reader's other courses in psychology. That is, courses in social psychology, personality, and educational psychology will have some content that is decidedly motivational. Because of this overlap, it is sometimes difficult to say where the study of cognition ends and where the study of motivation begins (Sorrentino & Higgins, 1986) or where the study of perception ends and where the study of motivation begins (Bindra, 1979). Weak boundaries between motivation and allied fields generally suggest an identity crisis within motivation study, but in practice, the absence of sharp boundaries facilitated the exchange of ideas and fostered an exposure to different perspectives and methodologies (Feshbach, 1984), including those outside of psychology (e.g., sociology; Turner, 1987). As a consequence, contemporary motivation study has gained a special richness, interest, and vitality (McNally, 1992).

CONTEMPORARY MINI-THEORIES ERA

Thomas Kuhn (1962, 1970) described the history of most sciences, emphasizing that a discipline makes both continuous and discontinuous progress. With continuous progress, participants make slow, incremental, and cumulative progress as new data add to and supplant old data and new ideas add to and supplant outworn ideas. With discontinuous progress, however, radical ideas appear and rival (rather than add to) old ideas. If the radical ideas gain acceptance, researchers' ways of thinking quickly and drastically change, as old models are torn down to make room for new models to take their place.

Kuhn's developmental view appears in Table 2.2. In its pre-paradigmatic stage, the primitive beginnings of a discipline take root as participants ask different questions, use different methods, pursue different problems, endorse different solutions, and basically disagree and argue a lot. In its paradigmatic stage, the discipline's participants succeed in reaching a consensus as to what constitutes their common theoretical and methodological framework. This shared framework (a "paradigm") allows each contributor to understand the discipline's methods and problems in the same way. Participants are then able to work collectively to gain an increasingly detailed and refined understanding of their subject matter. Over time, however, the limitations and inadequacies of the accepted paradigm become apparent as an anomaly surfaces that cannot be explained with the prevailing paradigm. A general discomfort soon runs throughout the field. As a result, fresh insights and new discoveries arise, and these insights and discoveries breed a new way of thinking (a "paradigm shift"). Armed with their new way of thinking, researchers eventually settle into a new and improved paradigm, a process that typically takes multiple generations of scientists. Two classic examples of paradigm shifts, for instance, occurred when the Copernican revolution replaced astronomers' ideas of earth centrality and when Einstein's general theory of relativity unseated Euclidean geometry. Astronomy and physics were forever changed.

As a discipline, motivation study has participated in the rise and fall of three major ways of thinking: will, instinct, and drive. Each of these motivational concepts gained wide acceptance, but as new data emerged, each concept proved to be too limiting for further progress. Eventually, each was replaced by the next new-and-improved radical idea. Motivation study is currently in the midst of its mini-theories era, and the three recent developments reviewed above help explain why the mini-theories era has proved more fruitful than the drive theory era (i.e., active nature of the person, cognitive revolution, and socially relevant research). Another current in contemporary motivation study is that the discipline has effectively moved a bit further away from the natural sciences and a bit closer to the social sciences. The current specializations, debates, and disagreements have left motivation in a "crisis stage."

Table 2.2 Outline of the Typical Development of a Scientific Discipline

1. Pre-paradigmatic	A budding science emerges. It consists of participants who do not share the same language or the same knowledge base. Debates are frequent about what should be the discipline's methods, problems, and solutions.
2. Paradigmatic	Pre-paradigmatic factionalism merges into a shared consensus about what constitutes the discipline's methods, problems, and solutions. This shared consensus is called a paradigm. Participants who share this paradigm accumulate knowledge and make incremental advances.
3. Crisis and revolution	An anomaly emerges that cannot be explained by the existing consensus/paradigm. A clash erupts between the old way of thinking (that cannot explain the anomaly) and the new way of thinking (that can explain the anomaly).
4. New paradigm	The new way brings discipline-changing progress. Embracing the new consensus, participants settle back into the new paradigm (a new Paradigmatic stage). Progress returns to making incremental advances.

The "crisis stage" transition from drive theory to the current mini-theories era has produced consequences that are both good and bad. On the bad side, motivation was dethroned as perhaps psychology's most important discipline to a sort of second-class field of study. The dethronement of motivation was so severe that, to some degree, the field collapsed for a decade and a half.

Motivation study did not, however, disappear. The questions that define motivation, discussed in Chapter 1, endured. Instead of disappearing, motivation specialists dispersed themselves into virtually all areas of psychology. Learning theorists, personality psychologists, social psychologists, clinicians, and others were unable to explain all the behavior they sought to explain without using motivational concepts. In other words, psychology's other fields needed answers to their motivational questions. What emerged were theories of social motivation (Pittman & Heller, 1988), physiological motivation (Stellar & Stellar, 1985), cognitive motivation (Sorrentino & Higgins, 1986), developmental motivation (Kagan, 1972), and so on. Further, motivation theories specific to particular domains of application emerged: theories to explain the motivation underlying dieting and bingeing (Polivy & Herman, 1985), work (Locke & Latham, 1984, 1990; Vroom, 1964), sports (Roberts, 1992; Straub & Williams, 1984), education (Weiner, 1979), and so on. By 1980, motivation psychologists were in literally every area of psychology, as they investigated the motivational underpinnings of cognition, social interaction, health, personality, education, and so on.

In the 1960s, the study of motivation basically collapsed. Motivational concepts were set aside as the dicipline was dominated by behaviorists who saw motivation as something that took place outside the person (in the form of incentives and reinforcers). When forces inside the person were acknowledged, they were either physiological, unconscious, or subconscious forces. Hence, studying the conscious aspects of motivation was somehow out-of-bounds, so to speak (Locke & Latham, 2002). Motivation study needed theories to explain how people intentionally regulated their own behavior. Fortunately, nonmotivational psychologists in other fields wanted the same thing. That is, the questions of motivation proved to be significant for and relevant to practically every aspect of psychology. Motivation researchers therefore branched out in alliances with other fields to form a loose network of researchers who shared a common concern and commitment to motivationally relevant questions and problems. It was in the specialty areas of psychology—social psychology, educational psychology, industrial/organizational psychology, etc.—that the theories of how people intentionally regulate their behavior were created.

Given the prevailing "crisis stage," there are two ways to conceptualize contemporary motivation study. The first way is to basically admit that the field of motivation is young, immature, and basically stuck in a 100-year-long pre-paradigmatic stage (see Table 2.2). Rather than existing as its own established discipline, contemporary motivation study depends on its alliances with other fields in psychology, as depicted in Figure 2.1. Figure 2.1 shows the intellectual overlap between the core of motivation study and these 10 allied fields. As one illustration, educational psychology studies how students learn and how teachers help them learn (Renninger, 1996). Because motivation affects how students learn and because teachers affect students' motivation to learn, the field of motivation is relevant to educational psychology. This mutual interest is shown by the overlapping circles in Figure 2.1, and it manifest itself in research studies carried out by educational psychologists who ask questions like, "What is the role of interest in learning?" (Ainley,

Hidi, & Berndorff, 2002) and "How does a teacher's praise affect students' motivation?" (Henderlong & Lepper, 2002).

A second way to conceptualize contemporary motivation study can be seen in Figure 1.1 (from Chapter 1). That figure identified the subject matter of motivation study as revolving around the four constructs of needs, cognitions, emotions, and external events. All motivation researchers emphasize the contribution of one or more of these constructs to explain behavior's energy and direction. In the study of needs, for instance, some theorists argue that "the study of human motivation is the study of human needs and the dynamic processes related to these needs" (Deci, 1980, p. 31). Emotion-minded motivational theorists argue that "emotions are the primary motivation system" (Tomkins, 1970, p. 101). A cognitive study of motivation assumes "people's . . . beliefs determine their level of motivation" (Bandura, 1989, p. 1,176). Other theorists focus on the motivational properties of external events and favor an analysis of how environmental events energize and direct behavior (Baldwin & Baldwin, 1986; Skinner, 1953).

The organization of the chapters in this book reflects this latter conceptualization of motivation study. That is, one chapter covers how needs motivate behavior, another chapter covers how cognitions motivate behavior, and so on. This is a critical point to make, because it reveals that those who study motivation and emotion recognize that motivational phenomena are inherently multileveled (Driver-Linn, 2003). That is, a motivational state can be understood at a neurological level, at a cognitive level, at a social level, and so on (see Box 2). Acknowledging that motivation and emotion are inherently multilevel phenomena means that the field will necessarily include contradictory assumptions, varying methods, and different ways of understanding.

A good way to conclude this analysis of motivation as a developing discipline is to review the current definitions of motivation and emotion. These definitions are repeated from Chapter 1:

> *Motivation:* Those processes that give behavior its energy and direction.
>
> The phrase *those processes* admits that motivation researchers cannot agree as to whether motives are essentially needs, cognitions, emotions, or reactions to environmental events. The phrase is therefore a dead-giveaway that contemporary motivation study is multi-paradigmatic and, hence, in a pre-paradigmatic stage of development.
>
> *Emotion:* Short-lived subjective-physiological-functional-expressive phenomena that orchestrate how we react adaptively to the important events in our lives.
>
> The phrase *subjective-physiological-functional-expressive* recognizes that motivation researchers understand emotions by looking at them from many different points of view. The phrase is therefore another dead-giveaway that contemporary emotion study is multilevel and, hence, in a pre-paradigmatic stage of development.

Admitting that motivation study is in a pre-paradigmatic stage of development might come across as pejorative. After all, any discipline would rather see itself as mature, advanced, paradigmatic, and cohesive (like physics) rather than as immature, slow, pre-paradigmatic, and splintered (like motivation; Driver-Linn, 2003). So, motivation study exists as an intellectual "work in progress."

BOX 2 *The Many Voices in Motivation Study*

Question: Why is this information important?

Answer: To become aware of the full range of voices participating in the effort to understand motivation.

Motivational phenomena are complex events that exist at multiple levels (e.g., neurological, cognitive, social, environmental). In practice, however, most attempts to explain a motivational experience rely on a single perspective. For instance, when a teenager loses interest in schooling, a parent (or researcher) typically goes in search of "the" explanation of why interest is low. People tend to choose the first reasonable and satisfying idea that comes to mind. Another way to think about motivation, however, is to become aware of a full range of possible ideas and then select those that best fit the particular experience.

Many voices participate in discussions of contemporary motivation study, though seven are particularly prominent:

Perspective:	Motives emerge from...
Behavioral	Environmental incentives and rewards (e.g., money)
Physiological/ neurological	Brain and hormonal activity (e.g., hunger)
Cognitive	Mental events and ways of thinking (e.g., goals)
Social-cognitive (cultural)	Ways of thinking after being exposed to other people such as a role model (e.g., possible selves)
Evolutionary	One's genetic endowment (e.g., extraversion)
Humanistic	Encouraging the human potential (e.g., self-actualization)
Psychoanalytical	Unconscious mental life (e.g., anxiety)

As a point of illustration, consider how to best understand and explain sexual motivation. Behaviorists point to that part of desire that stems from how attractive or reinforcing another person is, as in physical attractiveness. Physiological psychologists point to that part of desire that depends on dopamine released into the brain's limbic system. Cognitivists add that desire further comes from expectancies, goals, values, schemas, and beliefs about what is and is not possible. Social-cognitive researchers add that our beliefs and expectations arise from interactions with others, such as peers and cultural role models. Evolutionists add that men and women have different mating strategies, and they therefore desire different qualities in a mate. Humanists point to that part of desire that stems from the opportunity to participate in an intimate, growth-promoting relationship. And psychoanalysts add that we desire relationships with those who fit our early attachments and childhood-rooted mental model of what an ideal romantic partner should be.

Listening to the many voices that participate in the conversation about motivation brings both a strength and a weakness. As to a weakness, you might get the impression (justly) that motivation does not look like a single field of study—that it is divided into specialties, and no one seems to agree on how to understand and explain motivation and emotion. As to a strength, however, you gain an opportunity to put together more pieces of the puzzle. Researchers from different perspectives ask different questions about motivation, many of which you might never have thought of had they not first been raised by these unfamiliar perspectives. You might not find all these answers satisfactory, but a deep and sophisticated understanding of motivation and emotion begins by first putting all available knowledge on the table and then selecting those ideas that are most empirically defensible and personally useable.

The 1990s Return of Motivation Study

Starting in 1952, the University of Nebraska invited the most prominent motivation theorists of the day to gather annually for a symposium on motivation. In its inaugural year, contributors included Harry Harlow, Judson Brown, and Hobart Mowrer (famous names in motivation study). The next year, John Atkinson and Leon Festinger presented papers, and Abraham Maslow, David McClelland, James Olds, and Jullian Rotter presented papers in the third year (again, all famous names in motivation study). The symposium quickly became a success and served a leadership role in defining and reflecting the field. The symposium continued uninterrupted for 25 years, until a fundamental change occurred in 1978 (Benjamin & Jones, 1978). In 1979, the symposium discontinued its motivational theme and, instead, considered topics that changed from one year to the next, none of which had much if anything to do with motivation. The 1979 symposium focused on attitudes, and later symposiums focused on topics such as gender, addictive behaviors, and aging. Recall that these years correspond to motivation's dethronement as perhaps psychology's most important field to a second-class field. Basically, the Nebraska Symposium, like psychology in general, lost interest in the study of motivation (for reasons described earlier). With the decline of its grand theories, motivation study lost its focus and identity.

The story does not end with motivation in hopeless crisis, however. In recognition of motivation's revival and its contemporary accomplishments (i.e., the mini-theories era), the organizers of the 1990 Nebraska Symposium once again invited prominent motivation researchers to gather for a symposium devoted exclusively to the concept of motivation (Dienstbier, 1991). During that conference, the organizers asked the participants— Mortimer Appley, Albert Bandura, Edward L. Deci, Douglas Derryberry, Carol Dweck, Don Tucker, Richard Ryan, and Bernard Weiner (again, all famous names in motivation study)—if they thought motivation was once again strong enough and mature enough as a field to support an exclusive return to motivation topics. Unanimously and enthusiastically, the contributors agreed that motivation was once again a rich enough field of study to justify an annual gathering in Nebraska. The organizers agreed and, in doing so, gave motivation study a vote of confidence and a sense of public identity. Every year since, the symposium has continued its focus on motivation.

In the 1970s, motivation study was on the brink of extinction, "flat on its back," as one pair of researchers put it (Sorrentino & Higgins, 1986, p. 8). The mere fact that the conference organizers had to ask the symposium participants whether or not motivation was a field that could stand on its own says something about the field's identity crisis. Motivation study survived by allying itself with other fields of study, and the 1990 Nebraska Symposium symbolically heralded its return toward an integrated, coherent field of study. With a new millennium, motivation study once again has its critical mass of interested and prominent participants. To document such an optimistic conclusion, the reader can glance through psychology's major journals (e.g., *Psychological Review, Psychological Bulletin, Psychological Science*) and expect to find an article related to motivation in practically each issue. Motivational questions and problems are just too interesting and too important to ignore, it seems. And the same can be said for journals in a number of specialty areas as well (e.g., *Journal of Educational Psychology, Journal of Personality and Social Psychology*). In the new millennium, motivation study is clearly back at the frontier of psychology. In the 14 chapters to come, the reader can expect to encounter a growing field in its prime—a bit disorganized but interesting, relevant, and vital.

As one participant phrased it, "If what you have is a way to help people address the significant questions in their lives, then there are 'Help Wanted' signs all over the place."

CONCLUSION

Much can be gained by wading through 24 centuries of thinking about motivation. Consider the ancient questions: Why behave? Why do anything—why get out of the bed in the morning and do anything? Given these questions, the history of motivation began with the search for the instigators of behavior—that is, the search to identify that which energizes or initiates behavior. For two millennia (from Plato [ca. 428–348 B.C.] to Descartes [ca. 1596–1650]), the intellectual effort to understand motivation focused on the will, which resided within the immaterial soul. Studying an immaterial, spiritual substance proved to be too difficult an undertaking for the new science of psychology. Biology (physiology) proved to be a more suitable alternative because its subject matter was material and measurable. In answering the "Why behave?" question, the answer came to be that behavior serviced the needs of the organism. Instinct, drive, and arousal all gained appeal because each clearly energized behavior that served the needs of the organism (e.g., people get out of bed because they are hungry and need to eat something). Incentive added to these motivational constructs because hedonism (approach pleasure, avoid pain) explained why environmental events could also energize behavior (i.e., people get out of bed to approach pleasure and to avoid pain). Century by century, thinkers were improving their answers to the question of what instigates behavior: will, instinct, drive, incentive, arousal.

The whole process was going along rather nicely until a critical mass of motivation researchers realized that they were asking and pursuing the wrong question! The question of the instigation of behavior presumes a passive and biologically regulated organism; that is, one who is asleep and upon awaking, needs some motive to get into a behaving mode. At some point, motivation thinkers realized that sleeping was behaving and that the proverbial sleeper was actively engaged in his or her environment. The realization was that to be alive is to be active: Organisms are therefore always active, always behaving. There is no time in which a live organism is not behaving; there is no time in which a live organism is not showing both energy and direction. The fundamental questions of motivation therefore shifted: Why does behavior vary in its intensity? Why does the person do one thing rather than another?

These two questions expanded the charge of motivation study. Contemporary motivation study focuses not only on behavior's energy but also on its direction. This is why the three historical trends of the active organism, cognitive revolution, and concern for applied, socially relevant research, are so important—namely, because the field became less entrenched in the instigators of behavior, biology, and animal laboratory experiments and increasingly interested in the directors of behavior, cognition, and human motivational problems.

This change in perspective opened the intellectual floodgates for the arrival of the field's mini-theories. In place of the grand theories, the contemporary landscape now offers a collection of mini-theories like achievement motivation, goal-setting, and self-efficacy. These mini-theories answer specific questions and explain motivation in particular situations rather well, as we shall see in the pages to come.

SUMMARY

A historical view of motivation study allows the reader to consider how the concept of motivation came to prominence, how it changed and developed, how ideas were challenged and replaced, and finally, how the field reemerged and brought together various disciplines within psychology (Bolles,

1975). Motivational concepts have philosophical origins. From the ancient Greeks through the European Renaissance, motivation was understood within the two themes of that which is good, rational, immaterial, and active (i.e., the will) and that which is primitive, impulsive, biological, and reactive (i.e., bodily desires). The philosophical study of the will turned out to be a dead end that explained very little about motivation, as it actually raised more questions than it answered.

To explain motivation, the new field of psychology pursued a more physiological analysis of motivation by focusing on the mechanistic, genetically endowed concept of the instinct. The appeal of the instinct doctrine was its ability to explain unlearned behavior that had energy and purpose (i.e., goal-directed biological impulses). The physiological study of the instinct proved to be an intellectual dead end as well, at least in terms of its capacity to serve as a grand theory of motivation. Motivation's third grand theory was drive. In drive theory, behavior was motivated to the extent that it served the needs of the organism and restored a biological homeostasis. Like will and instinct, drive appeared to be full of promise, especially because it could do what no motivation theory had ever done before—namely, predict motivation before it occurred from antecedent conditions (e.g., hours of deprivation). Consequently, the theory enjoyed wide acceptance, especially as manifest in the theories of Freud and Hull. In the end, drive theory, too, proved itself to be overly limited in scope, and with its rejection came the field's disillusionment with grand theories in general, though several additional grand motivational principles emerged with some success, including incentive and arousal.

Eventually, it became clear that if progress was to be made in understanding motivation, the field had to be willing to step outside the boundaries of its grand theories and embrace the less ambitious, but more promising, mini-theories. Three historical trends explain this transition. First, motivation study rejected its commitment to a passive view of human nature and adopted a more active portrayal of human beings. Second, motivation turned decidedly cognitive and somewhat humanistic. Third, the field focused on applied, socially relevant problems. The field's changed focus toward mini-theories was part disaster and part good fortune. As to disaster, motivation lost its comfortable status as psychology's flagship discipline and descended rapidly into a second-class status. In reaction, motivation researchers dispersed into virtually all areas of psychology (e.g., social, developmental, clinical) and forged alliances with other fields to share ideas, constructs, methodologies, and perspectives. This turned out to be motivation's good fortune because the field's scattering into a wide range of other fields of study proved to be fertile ground to develop a host of enlightening mini-theories.

The theme throughout this chapter is that motivation study has undergone a constant developmental process, though it continues to remain in a pre-paradigmatic stage of development. In retrospect, motivation study progressed from relatively simplistic conceptualizations of motivation to an ever-increasing collection of sophisticated and empirically defensible insights about the forces that energize and direct behavior. With the turn of the new millennium, the grand theories have passed. What has arisen to replace a once unified field dominated by a consensus commitment to a series of grand theories is an eclectic group of researchers who embrace three commonalities: (1) core questions (e.g., What causes energetic and directed behavior?); (2) core constructs (i.e., needs, cognitions, emotions, and external events), and (3) a shared history.

READINGS FOR FURTHER STUDY

Grand Theories Era

Bolles, R. C. (1975). Historical origins of motivational concepts, In *A Theory of Motivation*, 2nd ed., (pp. 21–50). New York: Harper & Row.

Cofer, C. N., & Appley, M. H. (1964). Motivation in historical perspective, *Motivation: Theory and Research* (pp. 19–55). New York: Wiley.

Hull, C. L. (1943). Primary motivation and reaction potential, *Principles of Behavior* (pp. 238–253). New York: Appleton-Century-Crofts.

KOCH, S. (1951). The current status of motivational psychology. *Psychological Review, 58*, 147–154.

KUO, Z. Y. (1921). Giving up instincts in psychology. *Journal of Philosophy, 17*, 645–664.

Mini-Theories Era

APPLEY, M. H. (1991). Motivation, equilibration, and stress. In R. A. Dienstbier (Ed.), *Nebraska symposium on motivation* (Vol. 38, pp. 1–67). Lincoln: University of Nebraska Press.

BENJAMIN, L. T., JR., & JONES, M. R. (1978). From motivational theory to social cognitive development: Twenty-five years of the Nebraska Symposium. *Nebraska symposium on motivation* (Vol. 26, pp. ix–xix). Lincoln: University of Nebraska Press.

BOLLES, R. C. (1972). A motivational view of learning, performance, and behavior modification. *Psychological Review, 81*, 199–213.

DEMBER, W. N. (1974). Motivation and the cognitive revolution. *American Psychologist, 29*, 161–168.

WEINER, B. (1990). History of motivational research in education. *Journal of Educational Psychology, 82*, 616–622.

Chapter 3

The Motivated and Emotional Brain

The more you diet, the hungrier you get. As comedian Jerry Seinfeld used to say, "What's up with that?" The hunger-causing culprit is probably ghrelin, a hormone manufactured in the stomach, circulated in the blood, and detected by the brain. When a person goes for an extended period of time with little or no food (i.e., diets), the stomach and intestines detect the lack of nutrients and begin to release ghrelin into the bloodstream. A brain structure (the hypothalamus) constantly monitors how much ghrelin is in the blood, and when ghrelin levels rise, the hypothalamus detects the message received from the stomach and intestines—namely, nutrients are low, send supplies. This message stimulates the hypothalamus to create the psychological experience of hunger.

Consider how this works. It is lunchtime, and some friendly psychologists invite you to join a group of volunteers at an all-you-can-eat buffet (Wren et al., 2001). The lunch is free, and everyone may eat as much as they would like. But there is a catch. Thirty minutes before the feast, the researchers give some volunteers an intravenous injection of ghrelin while other volunteers receive only a placebo injection. Following the injections, the researchers take a chair, sit back, and watch what happens. What happens is that while the volunteers with the placebo eat a normal meal those with extra ghrelin in their bloodstreams pig out.

Consider a second illustration. Researchers monitored adults' naturally-occurring ghrelin over the course of several days (Cummings et al., 2002). After measuring the adults' natural day-to-day levels of ghrelin, the researchers asked some of the adults to start a 3-month diet. The diet was carefully designed and included a program of vigorous exercise. The diet worked. On average, the dieters lost about 20% of their body weight, and they maintained their weight loss for another 3 months. Over this time, the researchers continued to monitor the dieters' levels of ghrelin. Unbeknownst to the dieters, their ghrelin levels continued to rise. Even three months after the diet was over, many dieters still felt "hungry all the time." How much ghrelin was in the former dieters' bloodstreams over the course of a typical day appears in Figure 3.1. It shows the dieters' daily ghrelin levels both before they started the diet (dashed line) and three months after their successful weight loss (darker line).

Figure 3.1 communicates four points. First, it shows that ghrelin was chronically high for the dieters (the darker line is always higher than the dashed line). Second, ghrelin rises and falls throughout the normal day (peaking around breakfast, lunch, and dinner). Third, eating food led to a rapid fall in ghrelin. Fourth, the lowest level of ghrelin (and hence the least hunger) after the diet equaled the highest level of ghrelin (and hence the most hunger) before the diet, which means that the least hunger felt by dieters equaled the most hunger felt by nondieters.

The message is that diet-induced food deprivation leads the body to generate a potent counter-force against further dieting and food deprivation (i.e., the spike in ghrelin). As one woman who experienced the diet-induced ghrelin spike phrased it, "When I look at a frosted butter cookie, the bells in my head that go off are like standing on the top of a cathedral." From a motivational point of view, the role of ghrelin is to stimulate the brain: "Eat, eat, eat!"

On a more optimistic note, the body also has hunger-suppressing hormones. Just like the stomach and intestines secrete ghrelin into the bloodstream to stimulate appetite (feeling hungry), the stomach and intestines also secrete leptin into the blood to communicate satiety (feeling full). But during food deprivation, leptin levels drop (Cummings et al., 2001). So, during a diet, dieters get hit with a motivational double-whammy—increased ghrelin stimulates hunger, while decreased leptin suppresses satiety. While this is bad news for dieters, it does help explain hunger and satiety. By manufacturing, secreting, and

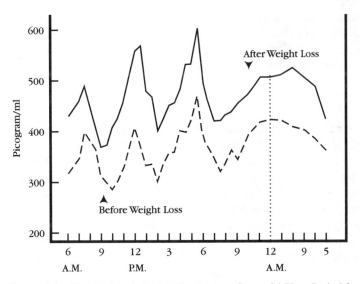

Figure 3.1 Ghrelin Levels in the Bloodstream Over a 24-Hour Period for Dieters and Nondieters

Note. The darker line represents the hour-to-hour ghrelin levels of dieters who lost 20% of their body weight three months before. The dashed line represent the hour-to-hour ghrelin levels of these same individuals before they began their diet and hence before they lost 20% of their body weight.

Source: From *Plasma Ghrelin Levels After Diet-induced Weight Loss or Gastric Bypass Surgery,* D.E. Cummings, D.S. Weigle, R.S. Frayo, P.A. Breen, M.K. Ma, E.P. Dellinger, and J.Q. Purnell, 2002, *New England Journal of Medicine, 346,* 1623–1630. Copyright © 2002 Massachusetts Medical Society. All rights reserved.

monitoring these two hormones, our bodies regulate motivational states in the face of both scarce food and weight loss (ghrelin increases, leptin decreases) and abundant food and weight gain (ghrelin decreases, leptin increases).

THE MOTIVATED AND EMOTIONAL BRAIN

Why is the brain important? Most people, maybe just about everyone, will say that the brain is important because it carries out cognitive and intellectual functions, including thinking, learning, remembering, decision making, and problem solving. These are very important brain processes indeed, but the brain does more. The brain is not only a thinking brain, it is also the center of motivation and emotion. It generates cravings, needs, desires, pleasure, and the full range of the emotions. In other words, as the brain performs its functions, it cares not only about what task it is doing (using its cognitive-intellectual functions), but it also very much cares about whether you want to do it (motivated brain) and what your mood is while doing it (emotional brain) (Gray, Braver, & Raichle, 2002).

All motivational and emotional states involve brain participation. To check such a claim, try an experiment on yourself by trying to experience anger, hunger, or curiosity without first recruiting the participation of the brain. Tough to do. As you work through such an exercise, you will learn that when it comes to understanding motivation and emotion the brain is the star of the show. The brain does, however, have a long list of supporting actors, including the major organs (e.g., liver, stomach) and all the biochemical activity throughout the body (e.g., hormones). To illustrate how the brain creates, maintains, and regulates motivational and emotional states, consider the following three principles that organize how motivational researchers study the brain.

Three Principles

As the pair of examples listed in Table 3.1 introduce, motivational researchers map out which brain structures are associated with which motivational states, how these brain structures become activated, and how day-to-day events create this activation process. In the case of hunger, for instance, dieting leads the intestines to produce ghrelin, ghrelin circulates in the blood and thus stimulates the lateral hypothalamus, and hypothalamic stimulation generates felt hunger. In the case of feeling good, an unexpectedly pleasant event occurs (you receive a letter in the mail from a friend) and activates the ventral tegmental area to release dopamine, dopamine release stimulates limbic structures, and stimulation of limbic structures like the medial forebrain bundle generate a warm glow of feeling good.

Table 3.1   Two Illustrations of the Motivated (Feeling Hungry) and Emotional (Feeling Good) Brain

Feeling Hungry: Food deprivation generates hunger via its affects on ghrelin, hypothalamus:

A. Environmental Event →	B. Biochemical Agent →	C. Activated Brain Structure →	D. Aroused Motivational State
Food deprivation (i.e., dieting)	Ghrelin (a hormone) produced and circulated in bloodstream	Ghrelin stimulates hypothalamus	Stimulated hypothalamus creates the experience of hunger

Principle 1:   The hypothalamus generates felt hunger (C → D).
Principle 2:   Increased ghrelin stimulates the hypothalamus (B → C).
Principle 3:   Food deprivation (dieting) increases ghrelin (A → B).

Feeling Good: Unexpectedly good event generates pleasurable feelings via its affects on dopamine, limbic structures:

A. Environmental Event →	B. Biochemical Agent →	C. Activated Brain Structure →	D. Aroused Emotional State
Unexpected pleasant event	Dopamine (a neurotransmitter) released into brain	Dopamine stimulates limbic structures, such as medial forebrain bundle (MFB)	Feeling good, pleasure

Principle 1:   Limbic structures (e.g., MFB) generate pleasure, feeling good (C → D).
Principle 2:   Increased dopamine stimulates limbic structures (B → C).
Principle 3:   Unexpectedly pleasant events stimulate dopamine release (A → B).

1. Specific brain structures generate specific motivational states.

Stimulating a specific brain site generates the subjective experience of a specific motivational state. In the example above, hypothalamic stimulation gave rise to feeling hungry. Another way of saying this would be that if something happened to damage a particular brain structure (as through an accident or surgery), the person's capacity to experience that specific motivational state would be compromised. In some cases, it is not the stimulation of one particular brain structure that gives rise to a motivational experience, but is instead the stimulation of a neural circuit—a number of interconnected brain structures—that generates the motivational state. As we shall see, many brain structures in the limbic system are interconnected and stimulation of the circuit generates a specific motivational state. In still other cases, the stimulation of a neurotransmitter pathway generates a specific motivational state. Throughout the chapter, we will explore how the stimulation of specific brain structures, neural circuits, and chemical pathways in the brain give rise to specific motivational states.

2. Biochemical agents stimulate these brain structures.

If specific brain structures give rise to specific motivational states, then the next question to ask is, How do these brain structures get stimulated in the first place? Brain structures have receptor sites on them that endow them with the potential to be stimulated. The biochemical agents that stimulate these receptor sites are neurotransmitters and hormones. Neurotransmitters are the communication messengers of the nervous system (allowing one neuron to communicate with another), while hormones are the communication messengers of the endocrine system (allowing glands to communicate with bodily organs like the heart or lungs). Thus, to understand the rise and fall of motivational states, we need to look at how neurotransmitters and hormones stimulate and suppress specific brain sites.

3. Day-to-day events stir biochemical agents into action.

To carry out their research studies, surgeons and motivation researchers artificially stimulate brain structures (see Figure 3.2). In doing so, they can isolate the function of specific brain structures. But outside the laboratory in settings like the home, school, workplace, and athletic field, it is in the day-to-day events that the motivated and emotional brain is stimulated into action. In the hunger example, it was the act of dieting, or food deprivation, that stirred the ghrelin hormone into action. In the feeling-good example, an unexpectedly positive life event stimulates the dopamine release that stirs the brain events that eventually lead to a positive mood state. While knowledge of how the brain works helps understand motivation and emotion, we still need to link the events in our lives to brain activation. The final section of this chapter returns to this discussion of how day-to-day events stir neurotransmitters and hormones, and hence brain structures, into action.

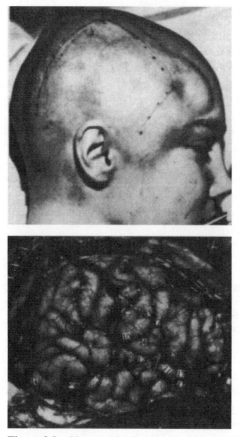

Figure 3.2   Photograph of an Exposed Human Cortex
Source: In *The Excitable Cortex in Conscious Man,* by W. Penfield, 1958, England: Liverpool University Press.

LOOKING INSIDE THE BRAIN

Researchers have several ways of looking inside the brain to see what is going on during motivational and emotional states. The first way is the old-fashioned way, a surgeon's view (discussed below). The second way is purely high technology, the fMRI (discussed subsequently).

Imagine suffering chronic pain, visiting the doctor, and learning that if the pain is to be alleviated then surgery is required. During the surgery, part of your cerebral cortex—the outside layers of the brain—is exposed, as illustrated in Figure 3.2. Sawing through the skull to get to the brain is still a widely used approach (to remove a brain tumor, for instance), though less invasive procedures are being developed and tested. For instance, surgeons now can insert a tiny camera into the nostril or into an incision behind the ear and take a look via a remote computer screen. But, imagine today that you are participating in the more traditional surgery.

As you prepare for the surgery, you learn that the operation needs to be performed while you are awake! This is so because the surgeon needs to coordinate her site stimulations with your specific perceptions and responses. At first, the surgeon touches the surface of your cortex with a tiny, thin probe that emits an extremely mild electrical current. (Since the brain has no pain receptors, the brain stimulation is actually painless.) When she touches the first area you suddenly and unintentionally move your finger, and then, after she repositions the probe, you make a Humphrey Bogart–like flinch of the mouth. You do not understand what is going on, and the movements are occurring outside of your intentional control. The surgeon stimulates your brain, and your body rather automatically moves. Suddenly, the pain stops as the surgeon electrically stimulates your brain stem. Before dismissing the story as science fiction, consider that it is based on two actual studies (Hosobuchi, Adams, & Linchitz, 1977; Penfield, 1958).

The cerebral cortex shown in Figure 3.2 is largely associated with cognitive functions like thinking, planning, and remembering. If the surgeon continued to probe more deeply (as we will soon do), she would eventually come in contact with the limbic system—the part of the brain that is intricately involved in motivation and emotion.

The current gold standard for looking deeply inside the brain is the functional MRI (fMRI). The MRI (magnetic resonance imaging) takes a detailed snapshot—an electronic photograph—of the structure of the brain as the person lies down inside the massive machine with its head-fitting pads, huge magnet, and computer attachments. As the person lies down and experiences some motivational and emotional state, the machine detects changes in blood oxygenation caused by brain activity. Over time, the fMRI produces a videotaped version of moment-to-moment brain activity during a motivational or emotional episode.

The anatomical location of several key brain structures related to motivation and emotion appears in Figure 3.3. The figure is the sort of photograph that can be produced by a MRI. Several of the structures in the figure exist within the limbic system, the so-called inner lobe of the brain that surrounds the brain stem and lies beneath the cortex (Nauta, 1986). The key limbic brain structures include the hypothalamus, amygdala, hippocampus, septal area, ventral tegmental area, and the fibers than connect these structures into a communication network (Isaacson, 1982; see Figure 3.3).

One way researchers can know which particular brain sites are associated with which particular motivational and emotional states can be determined by reviewing the fMRI. The individual might be food deprived (i.e., hungry), asked to recall a memory in which he or she felt afraid, or might be told to expect a forthcoming positive event like a monetary reward. As the person's motivation and emotion changed, so would the activity of his or her brain. And the fMRI can pick up those changing brain states to confirm that this is what the brain does during hunger, this is what the brain does during fear, this is what the brain does during the anticipation of a positive event, and so on. The principal brain structures involved in motivation and emotion appear in Table 3.2.

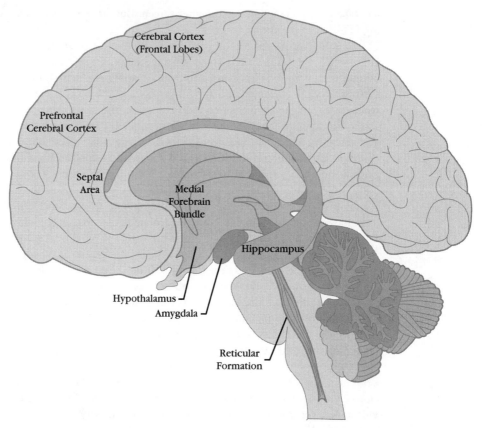

Figure 3.3   Cross Section of the Brain Showing the Anatomic Position of the Key Brain Structures Involved in Motivation and Emotion

BRAIN-GENERATED APPROACH VS. AVOIDANCE

When you imagine what motivation looks like in your mind, you probably imagine someone who shows great effort. But another fundamental dimension underlying motivation and emotion is approach versus avoidance. Much of the brain's activity is organized around generating an excitatory "Yes, I want to" readiness to approach or an inhibitory "No, I don't want do" readiness to avoid.

In this section, the key motivational and emotional brain structures listed in Table 3.2 have been organized around those associated with generating approach and those associated with generating avoidance. The section below highlights the key motivational and emotional role played by (1) two approach-oriented structures—hypothalamus and medial forebrain bundle, (2) two avoidance-oriented structures—amygdala and hippocampus, (3) the prefrontal cerebral cortex, which is associated with both approach- and avoidance-motivation, and (4) one arousal-associated structure—the reticular formation.

Table 3.2   Motivational and Emotional States Associated with Specific Brain Structures

Brain Structure	Associated Motivational or Emotional Experience
Approach-Oriented Structures	
Hypothalamus	Pleasurable feelings associated with feeding, drinking, mating
Medial forebrain bundle	Pleasure, reinforcement
Septal area	Pleasure center associated with sociability, sexuality
Cerebral cortex (Frontal lobes)	Making plans, setting goals, formulating intentions
Left prefrontal cerebral cortex	Approach motivational and emotional tendencies
Avoidance-Oriented Structures	
Right prefrontal cerebral cortex	Withdraw motivational and emotional tendencies
Amygdala	Detecting and responding to threat and danger (e.g., via fear, anger, and anxiety)
Hippocampus	Behavioral inhibition system during unexpected events
Arousal-Oriented Structure	
Reticular formation	Arousal

Hypothalamus

The hypothalamus is a small brain structure that comprises less than 1% of the total volume of the brain. Despite its small size, it is a motivational giant. The hypothalamus exists as a collection of 20 neighboring and interconnected nuclei that serve separate and discrete functions. Through the stimulation of its 20 separate nuclei, the hypothalamus regulates a range of important biological functions, including eating, drinking, and mating (via the motivations for hunger, satiety, thirst, and sex; Table 3.2). Chapter 4 will detail the role of the hypothalamus in regulating these physiological needs. As featured in Chapter 4, hypothalamic stimulation generates wants for, and the pleasures associated with, water, food, and sexual partners. But here the discussion centers on the role of the hypothalamus in the regulation of both the endocrine system and autonomic nervous system. By regulating these two systems, the hypothalamus is able to regulate the body's internal environment (e.g., heart rate, hormone secretion) so to adapt optimally to the environment (e.g., cope with a stressor).

The hypothalamus controls the pituitary gland—the endocrine system's so-called "master gland" (Agnati, Bjelke, & Fuxe, 1992; Pert, 1986). Anatomically, the hypothalamus is immediately north of the pituitary gland, and it regulates the pituitary gland by secreting hormones into the tiny capillaries that connect the hypothalamus to the pituitary gland. The pituitary gland, in turn, regulates the endocrine system. So, the pituitary gland regulates the endocrine (hormonal) system, while the hypothalamus regulates the pituitary gland. For instance, to increase arousal, the hypothalamus stimulates the pituitary gland to send hormones through the bloodstream to stimulate the adrenal glands to release its hormones (epinephrine, norepinephrine) that trigger the well-known "fight or flight" response.

The hypothalamus also controls the autonomic nervous system. The autonomic nervous system (ANS) includes all neuronal innervations into body organs that are under involuntary control (e.g., heart, lungs, liver, intestines, musculature). It is divided into the excitatory sympathetic system that accelerates bodily functions and alerts the body (as through an increased heart rate) and the inhibitory parasympathetic system that facilitates rest, recovery, and digestion following bodily stress and emergency. So, the autonomic nervous system begins at the hypothalamus (the hypothalamus is the ANS's head ganglion, or starting point) and extends its nerves throughout the body by innervating its many organs.

When we experience an important change in the environment (e.g., threat, opportunity), the hypothalamus has two major means to regulate the body's reaction and thereby cope effectively with the environmental change. On the one hand, the hypothalamus can generate arousal (sympathetic activation) or relaxation (parasympathetic activation) by stimulating the ANS. On the other hand, the hypothalamus can stimulate the endocrine system by stimulating the pituitary gland to release hormones into the bloodstream.

Medial Forebrain Bundle

The medial forebrain bundle is a relatively large collection of pathway-like fibers that connect the hypothalamus to other limbic structures, including the septal area, mammillary bodies, and the ventral tegmental area. The medial forebrain bundle is so closely connected to the hypothalamus that many argue that the lateral hypothalamus and the medial forebrain bundle fibers that pass through it cannot be dissociated—that is, they are pretty much the same thing (Isaacson, 1982). In terms of motivation, the medial forebrain bundle is as close to a "pleasure center" in the brain as we have. If an animal is equipped with a tiny electronic backpack like the one shown in Figure 3.4, and if researchers use a laptop

Figure 3.4 Rat with an Electronic Backpack Capable of Delivering a Mild Electrical Stimulation to the Brain via Remote Control

computer to stimulate the animal's medial forebrain bundle, then the animal will repeat whatever behavior it was doing during a stimulation of its medial forebrain bundle. That is, stimulation of the medial forebrain bundle creates pleasure and leads animals to act as if they have just received positive reinforcement, much in the same way as if they had just received actual reinforcement, such as their favorite food. By stimulating the medial forebrain bundle at the right time, researchers can, for instance, motivate/reinforce an animal to learn how to navigate a maze (Talwar et al., 2002).

In humans, stimulating the medial forebrain bundle does not produce intense pleasure and ecstasy but, instead, generally positive feelings (Heath, 1964), as implied by the following clinical observation of schizophrenic patients who received such electrical brain stimulation:

> *The patients brightened, looked more alert, and seemed to be more attentive to their environment during, or for at least a few minutes after, the period of stimulation. With this basic affective change, most subjects spoke more rapidly, and content was more productive; changes in thought were often striking, the most dramatic shifts occurring when prestimulation associations were pervaded with depressive affect. Expressions of anguish, self-condemnation, and despair changed precipitously to expressions of optimism and elaborations of pleasant experiences, past and anticipated (Heath, 1964, p. 224).*

Amygdala

The amygdala (meaning almond-shaped) is a collection of interconnected nuclei associated with separate functions. Overall, the amygdala detects and responds to threatening events, though each of its different nuclei serves a different function. Stimulation of one part of the amygdala generates emotional anger, while stimulation of another part generates emotional fear and defensive behavior (Blandler, 1988). So, the amygdala regulates the emotions involved in self-preservation, such as fear, anger, and anxiety. Consequently, impairment of the amygdala will produce striking changes, including an overall tameness, affective neutrality, a lack of emotional responsiveness, preference for social isolation over social affiliation, a willingness to approach previously frightening stimuli, and an impaired ability to learn that a stimulus signals positive reinforcement or punishment (Aggleton, 1992; Kling & Brothers, 1992; Rolls, 1992). The amygdala is also involved in the perception of other people's emotions, facial expressions, and in our own mood, especially negative emotional information (Adolphs et al., 1994; LeDoux, Romanski, & Xagoraris, 1989; Rolls, 1992). Thus, the amygdala processes emotional information (Hamann et al., 2002).

The amygdala also plays a key role in the learning of new emotional associations (Gallagher & Chiba, 1996). For instance, the amygdala allows us to learn to fear environmental dangers (Davis, 1992). We experience fear through bodily reactions like heart rate acceleration, muscular tension, behavioral freezing, and "fear face" facial expressions. As shown in Figure 3.6, as the person encounters potentially fearful objects in the environment, amygdala stimulation occurs and activates neighboring brain structures (e.g., hypothalamus, VTA) that instigate the coordinated fear response, including rapid breathing (Harper et al., 1984), heart rate acceleration (Kapp et al., 1982), high blood pressure (Morgenson & Calaresu, 1973), as well as hormonal discharge and emotional facial

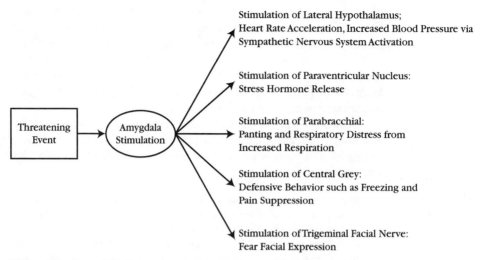

Figure 3.5   Amygdala Connections to Express Fear in Response to a Threatening Event

expressions (Davis, Hitchcock, & Rosen, 1987). As one point of illustration, a rat with a lesioned amygdala will crawl all over a sleeping cat and even nibble playfully on the cat's ear (Blanchard & Blanchard, 1972). What is missing from the fearless rat is its capacity to generate the hard-wired amygdala-coordinated fear response, as shown in the right-hand side of Figure 3.5. Without an amygdala, the rat lacks the means to respond emotionally to the cat, and it also lacks the capacity to learn to fear the cat when it wakes up and acts in a threatening way. When humans have their amygdala removed (to control epileptic seizures, for instance) they become calm, docile, and emotionally indifferent, even in the face of provocation (Aggleton, 1992; Ramamurthi, 1988).

The amygdala has an interesting anatomical relationship with other brain areas. The amygdala sends projections to almost every part of the brain, though only a small number of projections return information back to the amygdala. This imbalance helps explain why emotion, especially negative emotion, generally overpowers cognition more than cognition overpowers emotion. Hence, a lot of fear and anger messages get blurted out while relatively few messages of reason and rationality return back to calm the amygdala.

Septo-Hippocampal Circuit

The septo-hippocampal circuit involves the integrated action of several limbic structures, including the septal area, hippocampus, cingulate gyrus, fornix, thalamus, hypothalamus, and mammillary bodies (see Figure 3.3). While it is a limbic circuit, the septo-hippocampal circuit also includes cerebral cortex interconnections. Hence, a good deal of cognitive activity from memory and imagination are input into the circuit. The septo-hippocampal circuit therefore forecasts the emotion associated with upcoming events in terms of both anticipated pleasure and anticipated anxiety (Gray, 1982).

The hippocampus operates as a "comparator" that constantly compares incoming sensory information with expected (from memory) events (Smith, 1982; Vinogradova, 1975). If a person goes about his or her everyday activity and encounter events and circumstances that match with those that could be expected from memory, then the hippocampus functions in an "okay" checking mode. For example, if you come home and expect to find your front door locked and Rover greeting you at the other side of the door, and sure enough, the door is locked and Rover greets you merrily, then what you expected to happen matches with what did actually happen. In this scenario of confirmed expectations, the septo-hippocampus does not send out an anxious motivational state (because events are unfolding as expected—things are okay). On the other hand, if events do not unfold as expected—the door is not locked or Rover is nowhere to be found, the hippocampus acts in a "not okay" mode. When functioning in not-okay mode, the hippocampus activates the septo-hippocampal circuit, generates an anxiety-ridden motivational state (high attention, arousal) that takes control over behavior.

Anti-anxiety drugs (e.g., alcohol, barbiturates) produce their calming effects by essentially quieting (turning off) the not-okay checking mode of the septo-hippocampal circuit (Gray, 1982). The brain's natural anti-anxiety chemicals are the endorphins, as endorphins turn off the hippocampus's "not-okay" control mode. Disappointment, failure, punishment, and novelty all stimulate the hippocampus to instigate anxiety-ridden behavioral inhibition ("not-okay" mode). Active coping attempts with environmental stressors, when successful, generate the release of endorphins. The endorphin release shuts down the septo-hippocampal circuit, instigates anxiety-relief, and give rise to positive counterfeelings (Gold & Fox, 1982; Gold et al., 1980; Sweeney et al., 1980). This complex action of anxiety and expected punishment being countered by pleasure and expected reward requires the integrated functioning of a limbic circuit, as some structures in the circuit regulate anxiety (hippocampus) while different structures in that same circuit regulate pleasure and positive affects associated with sex and sociability (septal area; MacLean, 1990).

Reticular Formation

The reticular formation plays a key role in arousal and in the process of awakening the brain's motivational and emotional concerns. The reticular formation is a cluster of neurons about the size of your little finger within the brain stem (see Figure 3.6). It consists of two parts: the ascending reticular activating system and the descending reticular formation. The reticular activating system projects its nerves upwards in the brain to alert and arouse the cortex, while the descending reticular formation projects its nerves downward to regulate muscle tonus. Figure 3.6 uses a cat responding to a noise to illustrate that it is the reticular activating system that wakes, alerts, and arouses the cortex so it can process the incoming information. Once aroused, the alert cortex processes the incoming information (e.g., makes a decision about what to do) and, a second or two later, responds appropriately.

Prefrontal Cortex and Affect

The limbic system receives incoming sensory stimulation (sights, smells, tastes) that activate rather automatic emotional reactions. In addition, however, the limbic system receives a good deal of input from the cerebral cortex. Because this is true, stimulation of the cortex can indirectly generate emotional states. The prefrontal lobes of the cerebral cortex lie immediately behind the forehead. One lobe is on the right side of the brain,

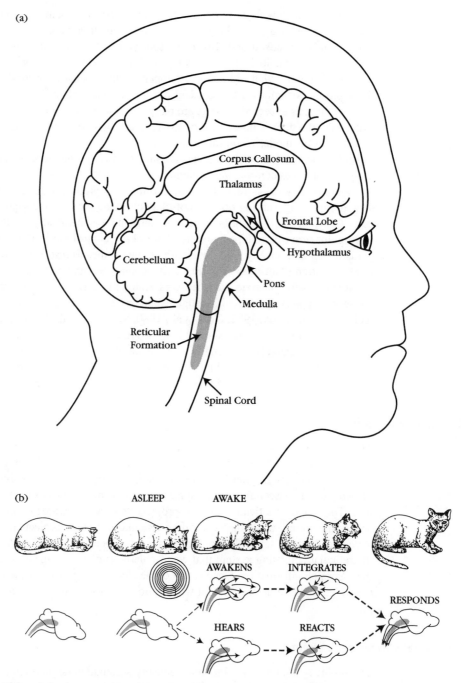

Figure 3.6   Anatomy (a) and Function (b) of the Reticular Formation

Source: Adapted from *The Reticular Formation,* by J.D. French, 1957, *Scientific American, 196,* 54–60.

while the other is one the left side. This right-left distinction is important because their activation generates qualitatively different emotional tones.

The prefrontal cortex houses a person's goals (Miller & Cohen, 2001). These goals routinely compete against one another (goal to eat vs. goal to lose weight), and the two lobes of the prefrontal cortext wash these goals in a bath of emotion (Davidson, 2003). Thoughts that stimulate the right prefrontal cortex generate negative feelings, whereas thoughts that stimulate the left prefrontal cortex generate positive feelings (Gable, Reis, & Elliot, 2000; Sackeim et al., 1982). For instance, the sight of fear-provoking snakes lights up the right prefrontal cortex on a PET scan like a Christmas tree (Fischer et al., 2002; see their Figure 2, p. 238). The ensuing negative emotion then strongly colors which goals the person does and does not pursue.

In addition, basic personality differences exist between people, as some have especially sensitive right prefrontal lobes that leave them highly vulnerable to negative emotionality, while others have especially sensitive left prefrontal lobes that leave them highly vulnerable to positive emotionality (Gable, Reis, & Elliot, 2000). Personality psychologists generally agree that two broad dimensions of personality exist. The first captures how sensitive versus insensitive a person is to incentives and the experience of positive emotion (i.e., extraversion); the second captures how sensitive versus stable a person is to threats, punishments, and the experience of negative emotion (i.e., neuroticism; Eysenck, 1991). Brain researchers use different terms from personality psychologists and refer to these personality dimensions as the behavioral activation system (BAS) and the behavioral inhibition system (BIS, respectively Carver & White, 1994). To get an idea for these two dimensions of personality, consider your own reactions to the questionnaire items listed in Table 3.3. The first four items ask how sensitive you are to avoidance-oriented motivations (i.e., how sensitive is the person's "behavior inhibition system"). The last six items ask how sensitive you are to approach-oriented motivations, emotions, and behaviors, broken down into the three different subscales of reward responsiveness, drive, and fun seeking (i.e., how sensitive is the person's "behavior approach system").

These two broad personality dimensions have a neurobiological basis. Some people show greater activity in their left prefrontal lobe ("left-side asymmetry") while others show greater activity in the right prefrontal lobe ("right-side asymmetry"). People with relatively sensitive right prefrontal lobes—those who show greater right side asymmetry—score high on the BIS items in Table 3.3, and they show a greater sensitivity to punishment, negative emotion, avoidance-oriented behaviors. People with relatively sensitive left prefrontal lobes—those who show greater left-side asymmetry–score high on the BAS items in Table 3.3, and they show a greater sensitivity to reward, positive emotion, and approach-oriented behaviors.

The correlation between people's scores on the BAS and BIS questionnaires and their prefrontal lobe asymmetry is important because the extent of people's asymmetry corresponds to their typical emotionality (BAS vs. BIS; Sutton & Davidson, 1997). That is, even without exposure to a live event, people show a personality-like style to be overly sensitive to negative or to positive emotionality. Hence, how relatively active a person's left prefrontal lobe is serves as a biological foundation of a personality oriented toward an eagerness and approach orientation, and how relatively active a person's right prefrontal

Table 3.3   Behavioral Inhibition System (BIS) and Behavioral Activation System (BAS) Questionnaire Items

---

BIS Items

1. If I think something unpleasant is going to happen I usually get pretty "worked up."
2. Criticism or scolding hurts me quite a bit.
3. I feel pretty worried or upset when I think or know somebody is angry at me.
4. I feel worried when I think I have done poorly at something.

BAS Items

5. When I get something I want, I feel excited and energized.[a]
6. When good things happen to me, it affects me strongly.[a]
7. When I want something, I usually go all-out to get it.[b]
8. I go out of my way to get things I want.[b]
9. I will often do things for no other reason that they might be fun.[c]
10. I crave excitement and new sensations.[c]

Note: BIS = Behavioral Inhibition System; BAS = Behavioral Activation System. In completing the questionnaire, respondents are asked to agree or disagree with each item using a 1 to 7 response scale (1 = strongly disagree, 7 = strongly agree). The BAS scale consists of three subscales: reward responsiveness (denoted by [a] above), drive (denoted by [b] above), and fun seeking (denoted by [c] above). The actual BIS/BAS Questionnaire contains 20 items, 7 BIS items and 13 BAS items, so the table shows only a part of the full questionnaire.

Source: Adapted from *Behavioral Inhibition, Behavioral Activation, and Affective Responses to Impending Reward and Punishment: The BIS/BAS Scales,* by C.L. Carver and T.L. White, 1994, *Journal of Personality and Social Psychology, 67,* 319–333. Copyright 1994 by American Psychological Association. Adapted with permission.

lobe is serves as a biological foundation of a personality oriented toward anxiety and an avoidance orientation.

But this research goes further. It identifies the sources of a person's emotionality as in the (1) hedonic tone brought out by the life event (reward brings positive emotionality, punishment brings negative emotionality); (2) person's dispositional BAS and BIS sensitivities (BAS brings positive emotionality, BIS brings negative emotionality); and (3) interaction between these two sources as negative life events stimulate some people's BIS more than it stimulates other people's BIS (i.e., people with greater right-side asymmetry) and positive life events stimulate some people's BAS more than it stimulates other people's BAS (i.e., people with greater left-side asymmetry).

NEUROTRANSMITTER PATHWAYS IN THE BRAIN

Neurotransmitters act as chemical messengers within the brain's central nervous system. Neurons communicate with one another through neurotransmitters, as an information-sending neuron releases a neurotransmitter so that its neighboring neuron can pick up that neurotransmitter and hence receive the message. A "neurotransmitter pathway" is a term that refers to a cluster of neurons that communicate with other neurons by using one particular neurotransmitter. The four motivationally relevant neurotransmitter pathways are: dopamine—which generates good feelings associated with reward (Montague, Dayan, & Sejnowski, 1996); serotonin—which influences mood and emotion (Schildkraut, 1965);

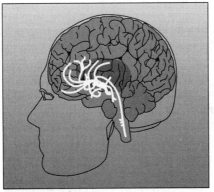 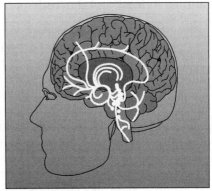

Dopamine pathways   Serotonin pathways

Figure 3.7 Two Neurotransmitter Pathways

Source: From *Mapping the Mind,* by R. Carter, 1998, Berkeley: University of California Press. Published by arrangement with Weidenfeld & Nicolson.

norepinephrine—which regulates arousal and alertness (Heimer, 1995; Robbins & Everitt, 1996); and endorphin—which inhibits pain, anxiety, and fear by generating good feelings to counter these negative feelings (Wise, 1989).

The anatomy of the serotonin and dopamine pathways appear in Figure 3.7. The dopamine pathway is particularly important to understanding motivation and emotion, as its primary motivational function is to generate positive feelings—an experience of pleasure or reward (Ashby, Isen, & Turken, 1999).

Dopamine

Dopamine release generates good feelings. As people go throughout their day, some level of dopamine is always present in the brain. But as people encounter a variety of events, those that signal reward and the anticipation of pleasure trigger neurons in the dopamine pathway to release dopamine into the synapses (Bozarth, 1991; Phillips, Pfaus, & Blaha, 1991). Such a dopamine release triggers an emotional positivity, and the resulting positive affect produces enhanced functioning, such as creativity and insightful problem solving (Ashby, Isen, & Turken, 1999).

The finding that dopamine release generates positive feelings is a significant finding because, as people go throughout their day, they have many choices of what to do and what not to do. Part of the "want" to pursue one course of action over another is regulated by information provided by dopamine output from the ventral tegmental area (VTA). The VTA releases dopamine into other brain sites (e.g, prefrontal cortex) and the pattern of release is predictable in proportion to which the person expects and actually receives reward from a particular course of action. When events unfold in ways that are better than expected, an increased dopamine release serves as information that the particular course of action is producing more reward than it was anticipated to deliver. When events unfold in ways that are worse than expected, a decreased dopamine release serves as information that a particular course of action is producing less reward than it was anticipated to deliver (Montague, Dayan, & Sejnowski, 1996).

Dopamine Release and the Anticipation of Reward

Stimuli that foreshadow the imminent delivery of rewards trigger dopamine release in the brain (Mirenowicz & Schultz, 1994). Pleasure is the result of a rush of dopamine in the reward system. When you smell someone baking chocolate chip cookies in the oven, dopamine release occurs. It is not the eating of the cookies that causes the brain to release dopamine but is, instead, the anticipation of a rewarding meal that triggers dopamine release. Because dopamine release occurs with the anticipation of reward, it therefore participates in the preparatory phases of motivated behavior, including, for instance, an erection that precedes sexual activity or heightened attention to the kitchen upon the smell of chocolate chip cookies. For this reason, we often experience more pleasure in thinking about engaging in sex or eating cookies than we do when actually engaging in sex or munching on the cookies. If things go better than expected during the mating or eating, however, then the dopamine release continues and so does its corresponding positive state of feeling good.

As a person moves through his or her environment, a variety of stimuli invariably impinge upon the senses (e.g., seeing different people, hearing laughter, examining different fruits at the farmer's market). Some of those events are biologically significant to the person (i.e., those related to hunger, thirst, mating), and when they foreshadow the possibility of reward, dopamine release occurs and motivates the person to prepare to take action to secure the environmental event. If dopamine release did not occur, we would not perceive any of the events that surround us as attractive, and we would not prepare ourselves to approach them.

Biology of Reward

Dopamine release not only signals the prospect of forthcoming reward, dopamine release also teaches us which events in the environment are rewarding. That is, dopamine release explains the biology of reward. If an environmental event is to acquire—and to continue to maintain—incentive motivational properties, then dopamine release needs to occur (Beninger, 1983). Dopamine release is greatest when rewarding events occur in ways that are unpredicted—wow, I'm surprised how nice that flower smells—or underpredicted—wow, that flower smells much nicer that I thought it would (Mirenowicz & Schultz, 1994). Hence, it is not so much the occurrence of a rewarding event that generates good feelings as it is the occurrence of unpredicted or unexpected reward. Dopamine release following unexpected reward allows people to learn that event's motivational significance. And because dopamine release defines an event as a rewarding event, the person learns that this event, when encountered in the future, will likely produce a rewarding experience. Thus, activation of the dopamine pathway plays a significant role in the biology of reward.

The evidence that stimulation of the dopamine pathway creates an experience of reward comes from studies on intracranial self-stimulation and drug self-administration (Figure 3.8) (Bozarth, 1991). Researchers can implant an electrode into an animal's brain that, when stimulated, can either send a mild electrical current to stimulate that brain structure (intracranial stimulation) or deliver a small dosage of a particular drug (drug administration). In either case, animals are placed into a cage in which they can down-press the lever with their front paws. Pressing the lever activates a microswitch that either administers the mild electrical stimulation or the small drug dosage. Because the animal controls when the brain is stimulated (because it is the animal's choice to press down the lever or not), the animal can engage in intracranial self-stimulation and/or drug self-administration. Research on intracranial self-stimulation shows that animals will press the lever to stimulate brain structures associated with dopamine release. Research with drug self-administration shows that animals will press the lever to receive psychostimulant drugs like amphetamine and cocaine (Roberts, Corcoran, & Fibiger, 1977). Because animals engage in intracranial self-stimulation and drug self-administration when the implants are located in the dopamine pathway, researchers infer that dopamine release is pleasurable and rewarding.

Dopamine and Motivated Action

Dopamine release is associated with two brain events. First, dopamine release generates positive feelings, as discussed above. But, dopamine release also activates voluntary goal-directed approach responses. The dopamine pathway includes an interface with the body's

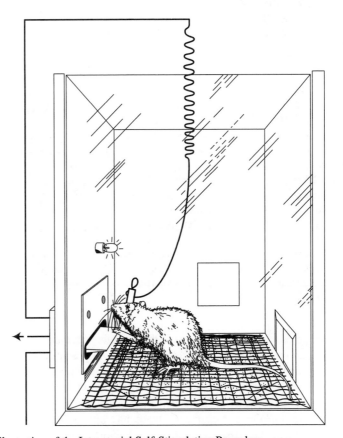

Figure 3.8   Illustration of the Intracranial Self-Stimulation Procedure

Note. When the rat presses down on the lever, the lever press activates a microswitch to send a mild electrical impulse to be sent through the wire into the rat's brain via an implanted electrode. With such a procedure, the rat has the means to deliver self-induced stimulation to its brain.

Source: From *Pleasure Centers in the Brain,* by J. Olds, 1956, *Scientific American, 195,* 105–106.

| BOX 3 | *How and Why Antidepressant Drugs Alleviate Depression* |

Question: Why is this information important?

Answer: To understand how anti-depression drugs work to alleviate depression.

Each of us wages a lifelong struggle against depression. Aversive, stressful events inevitably come our way, as experiences of loss, rejection, criticism, financial woe, failure, too much to do, neglect, being stood up, hassle, and disappointment represent the flow of human experience. These events affect our ongoing bodily biochemistry and, when they deplete our biochemical resources, can leave us vulnerable to depression. Most of us cope well most of the time, but each of us nonetheless remains vulnerable to the feeling that we just might crack under the barrage of stress and disappointment.

Depression is a complex psychological disorder associated with two main types of responsiveness to the environment. On the one hand, exposures to disappointment and uncontrollable stress make demands on the limbic system that gradually robs us of brain serotonin. Serotonin deficiency leaves us vulnerable to depression (Kramer, 1993; Weiss & Simson, 1985).

The popular antidepressant drugs (e.g., Prozac, Zoloft, Paxil) are SSRIs, or selective serotonin-reuptake inhibitors. These antidepressants work on the premise that depression is caused by low serotonin turnover in the serotonin pathways. Even when highly stressed, brain serotonin remains in these pathways, but it is not readily available for usage. During stressful life events, serotonin is released into the synapse but it also quickly returns (experiences reuptake) back to the sending neuron. To reverse depression, the antidepressant needs to increase brain–serotonin transmission and turnover, and it does so by preventing reuptake and making greater use of the available serotonin (rather than allowing it to be re-stored via re-uptake). The antidepessant acts to restore serotonin release and activity back to normal.

The second type of depression is associated with a diminished capacity to experience pleasure and positive feelings. Low dopamine levels can leave the person vulnerable to apathy, boredom, poor concentration, and little initiative to embrace the day. In contrast, dopamine release and activity within the brain's dopamine pathway generates good feelings, positive affect, and essentially leaves the person primed to a positive mood (Ashby, Isen, & Turken, 1999). Some antidepressants work by increasing dopamine receptors' responsiveness and thereby by restoring the person's capacity to experience pleasure and positive emotions (Willner et al., 1991). Drugs of abuse (e.g., cocaine, amphetamines) also work by enhancing dopamine activity in the brain. Cocaine, for instance, works by inhibiting dopamine re-uptake (Di Chiara, Acquas, & Carboni, 1992).

Overall, depression has two faces—serotonin deficiency that leaves the person less able to cope with life's stress, and dopamine deficiency that leaves the person less ready to anticipate and experience pleasure. Knowing this, pharmacological researchers can design drugs to help as each of us wages our lifelong struggle against depression. And motivational researchers can design and implement intervention programs to maintain and regulate people's naturally-occurring levels of serotonin and dopamine.

muscular/motor system via the nucleus accumbens, which is the brain structure involved in the release of locomotion involved in goal-directed behavior (Kelley & Stinus, 1984). Thus, stimulation of the dopamine pathway increases the likelihood of approach behavior (Morgenson, Jones, & Yim, 1980)—partly because good feelings create approach motivation and partly because activation of the motor system releases goal-directed approach behavior. Once dopamine release has initiated approach behavior toward the rewarding event, the person's approach behavior continues and more often than not actually increases in vigor until the goal is attained. To continue the example of the chocolate chip cookies, dopamine release generates not only positive feelings but also the motivated search behavior necessary to find and consume the desired food.

Overall, then, as events come and go during the day, the brain detects some of these events as "biologically significant" and releases dopamine that generates good feelings and goal-directed approach behavior. Further, the pleasurable experience of dopamine allows the person to learn which environmental events are to be associated with pleasure and approach and which other environmental events are to be associated with stress and withdrawal. Dopamine release is therefore a neural mechanism by which motivation gets translated into action (Morgenson, Jones, & Yim, 1980).

THE WORLD IN WHICH THE BRAIN LIVES

Brain research generally relies on artificial methods of stimulating the brain's motivational and emotional states (as depicted in Figures 3.2, 3.4, and 3.8). Such research generally applies an mild electrical current or chemical agent (drug, neurotransmitter, hormone) to a particular brain site to investigate the role that brain structure plays in motivation. This research allows us to collect the sort of information summarized in Table 3.2, such that we know that the medial forebrain bundle is a pleasure center, the amygdala is a fear center, and so on for each particular brain structure. What these research studies do not tell us, however, is how day-to-day events in the social world naturally stimulate these brain structures to generate the motivation and emotion we use to adapt to the world around us.

Motivation Cannot Be Separated from the Social Context in Which It Is Embedded

People have needs, such as those for survival, growth, and well-being. And the social world offers an environment full of supports for and threats against these needs. For instance, the weather can be warm and support our well-being, or it can be too cold or too hot and threaten our well-being. A relationship can be warm and nurturing, or it can be cruel and neglecting. The brain is the means by which we generate the motivational and emotional states we need to adapt optimally to the physical and social world around us. So, to answer questions like "How can I motivate myself?" and "How can I motivate others?", we can use our knowledge of the brain to create social environments that function as natural stimulates to the motivated and emotional brain.

For instance, consider the natural stimulants of motivational brain structures discussed throughout the chapter. Food deprivation explained the rise and fall of ghrelin and leptin hormones. Signals of reward and unexpectedly positive events—a pleasant smell, a gift, a humorous movie—explained dopamine release. Alarm clocks and roller-coaster rides aroused the reticular formation. Threats like predators, bullies, enemies, and hostile opponents stimulated the amygdala. Disappointment, failure, punishing toothaches, novelty, and separation from our loved ones stimulated the hippocampus' "not-okay" mode, just as successfully coping with these aversive events stimulated the release of endorphins and a pleasurable return to the "okay" mode. And drugs like cocaine and amphetamines stimulated pleasure centers in the limbic system. What all these examples illustrate is that environmental events in the social world act as the natural stimulators of the brain's basic motivational processes (e.g., pleasure, anxiety, arousal, and mood).

So, while brain researchers conduct studies to artificially stimulate and change animal's motivational states, researchers in the schools, workplace, clinics, and athletic fields know that the individual's motivational state cannot be separated from the social context in which it is embedded. Though we know how the brain generates its motivational states, we also know that the motivation experienced by students, athletes, patients, children, and workers is inherently intertwined with the social context provided to them by their teachers, coaches, doctors, parents, and workplace supervisors. So, this chapter presented the fundamentals of the motivated and emotional brain. The chapters to come will present how the social context provides natural stimulations that stir the motivated and emotional brain into action.

We Are Not Always Consciously Aware of the Motivational Basis of Our Behavior

The study of the motivated brain makes salient one final point about human motivation, namely that we are not always consciously aware of the motivational basis of our behavior. Motives vary in how accessible they are to consciousness and to verbal report. Some motives originate in language structures and the cerebral cortex (e.g., goals) and are thus readily available to our conscious awareness (e.g., "I have a goal to sell three insurance policies today."). For these motives, if you ask a person why he or she selected that particular goal, the person more often than not can confidently list the rational and logical reasons for doing so. Despite the fact that people can frequently provide prompt and satisfying motives to explain their behaviors, some motivated acts are impulsive and the reasons we do what we do are not clear, even to us. Some motives have their origins in nonlanguage structures and are thus much less available to conscious awareness and to verbal report. These are the motives that originate in the emotional limbic structures rather than in the language-based cerebral cortex. These motives exist in our awareness only as urges and appetites.

Many experimental findings can be offered to make the point that motives can and do originate in the unconscious limbic structures rather than in the conscious cerebral cortex. Consider that people who feel good after receiving an unexpected gift are more likely to help a stranger in need than are people in neutral moods (Isen, 1987). People are more sociable on a sunny day than they are on a cloudy day (Kraut & Johnston, 1979). People commit more acts of violence in summer months than at other times of the year (Anderson, 1989). Major league baseball pitchers are more likely to intentionally hit batters on the opposing team when the temperature is hot rather than cold or moderate (Reifman, Larrick, & Fein, 1991). In each of these examples, the person is not consciously aware of why he or she committed the social or antisocial act. Few people, for instance, would say they helped a stranger because they felt good, and few say they commit murder or throw baseballs at the heads of opponents because of the hot temperature. Still, these are conditions that cause motivations. The brief lesson behind these empirical examples is that the motives, cravings, appetites, desires, moods, needs, and emotions that regulate human behavior are not always immediately obvious.

CONCLUSION

A half century ago, a young neuroscientist, James Olds, was doing his routine laboratory work by implanting an electrode in the brainstem of a rat. One fateful day, the electrode Olds was implanting accidentally bent and ended up in another part of the brain. Not knowing that the electrode had bent, Olds stimulated the rat and watched with amazement as the rat suddenly repeated its behavior and continued enthusiastically to return to the part of the cage where the earlier electrical brain stimulation occurred. The rat liked the stimulation. In fact, the rat really, really liked the stimulation. Follow-up studies showed that animals given the opportunity to stimulate themselves would do so (by pressing a lever that would send an electrical current to their own brain; see Figure 3.8). Olds' research would soon confirm that he had accidentally discovered a pleasure center in the rat's brain (Olds & Milner, 1954).

Researchers soon began to intentionally bend their electric probes as they started the field of neuroscience down its path toward understanding the neural basis of pleasure and aversion (Hoebel, 1976; Olds & Fobes, 1981; Wise & Bozarth, 1984). First, specific brain structures such as the septal area, hypothalamus, mammillary bodies, and medial forebrain bundle were identified as important to motivational process (Olds & Olds, 1963). Then, the consensus converged on the idea that motivational experiences (e.g., pleasure, aversion) were not localized in any one specific brain structure but were instead coordinated among many brain areas known as neural circuits, such as those found in the limbic system (Isaacson, 1982). Later research extended the study of brain circuits to include the study of chemical circuits or pathways in which various brain sites communicated through one specific neurotransmitter, such as dopamine. These efforts to map out the motivational significance of specific brain structures, neural circuits, and chemical pathways allowed researchers to understand how the brain creates, maintains, and regulates motivation, emotion, and mood. In the chapters to come, the emphasis will switch to the motivational significance of external events, relationships, and complex environments like classrooms. Hence, the contents of this chapter will allow us to understand the biology and the neuroscience underlying the motivational states yet to be discussed.

SUMMARY

When thinking about the brain, most people focus their attention on its cognitive and intellectual functions, including thinking, learning, and decision making. But the brain is not only an agent of thought, it is further an agent of motivation and emotion. It is the brain that generates cravings, appetites, needs, desires, pleasure, and the full range of the emotions. To illustrate how the brain creates, maintains, and regulates motivational and emotional states, consider the following three principles that organize how motivational researchers study the brain. First, specific brain structures (e.g., hypothalamus, amygdala) generate specific motivational states. Second, biochemical agents (e.g., neurotransmitters, hormones) stimulate these brain structures. Third, day-to-day events (e.g., a letter from a friend, encountering dangerous traffic) are the events in our lives that stir the brain-stimulating biochemical agents into action.

Looking inside the brain with techniques like surgery and fMRI (functional magnetic resonance imaging) yields a map of the anatomical location of several key brain structures related to motivation and emotion. The brain structures associated with positive feelings and approach motivation include the hypothalamus, medial forebrain bundle, septal area, cerebral cortex, and the left prefrontal cortex. The brain structures associated with negative feelings and avoidance motivation include the amygdala, hippocampus, and right prefrontal cortex. For instance, stimulation of the medial forebrain bundle leads people to report positive feelings and animals to behave in ways as if they had just received positive reinforcement. Stimulation of the amygdala leads people to report negative feelings and to show the behavioral activation associated with a coordinated fear response.

Neurotransmitters act as chemical messengers within the brain, and a "neurotransmitter pathway" refers to a cluster of neurons that communicate with other neurons by using one particular neurotransmitter. The four motivationally relevant neurotransmitter pathways are: dopamine, serotonin, norepinephrine, and endorphin. The dopamine pathway is particularly important as its primary motivational function is to generate positive feelings and it explains the biology of reward. As motivationally significant events come and go throughout the day, the brain detects some of these events as "biologically significant" and releases dopamine that generates good feelings and stimulates goal-directed approach behavior. Further, the pleasurable experience of dopamine allows the person to learn which environmental events are to be associated with pleasure and approach and which other environmental events are to be associated with stress and withdrawal. Dopamine release is therefore a neural mechanism by which motivation gets translated into action.

The purpose of this chapter was not to overwhelm the reader with fancy neurophysiological terminology like leptin and septo-hippocampal circuit. Instead, it was to lift the veil of mystery of just what the brain does to generate and maintain motivational and emotional states.

READINGS FOR FURTHER STUDY

ASHBY, F. G., ISEN, A. M., & TURKEN, A. U. (1999). A neuropsychological theory of positive affect and its influence on cognition. *Psychological Review, 106,* 529–550.

CUMMINGS, D. E., WEIGLE, D. S., FRAYO, R. S., BREEN, P. A., MA, M. K., DELLINGER, E. P., & PURNELL, J. Q. (2002). Plasma ghrelin levels after diet-induced weight loss or gastric bypass surgery. *New England Journal of Medicine, 346,* 1623–1630.

DAVIDSON, R. J., & IRWIN, W. (1999). The functional neuroanatomy of emotion and affective style. *Trends in Cognitive Science, 3,* 11–21.

GRAY, J. A. (1994). Three fundamental emotion systems. In P. Ekman & R. J. Davidson (Eds.), *The nature of emotion: Fundamental questions* (pp. 243–247). New York: Oxford University Press.

LEDOUX, J. E. (1994). Emotion, memory and the brain. *Scientific American, 270,* 32–39.

LEDOUX, J. E. (1995). Emotion: Clues from the brain. *Annual Review of Psychology, 46,* 209–235.

SUTTON, S. K., & DAVIDSON, R. J. (1997). Prefrontal brain asymmetry: A biological substrate of the behavioral approach and inhibition systems. *Psychological Science, 8,* 204–210.

WISE, R. A., & ROMPRÉ, P. P. (1989). Brain dopamine and reward. *Annual Review of Psychology, 40,* 191–225.

Part One

Needs

Chapter 4

Physiological Needs

Consider the following proposal: You are invited to participate in an experiment. The researcher promises that you will be paid handsomely for your effort. All you have to do is try to gain 10% of your present body weight. It sounds easy and profitable enough, so you accept. At first, all goes well and you gain 4 pounds in week 1 and two more in week 2. By week 3, however, your appetite wanes, food is losing its appeal, and your body seems to be putting up defenses to counter the weight gain. As you eat surplus food, you are surprised by how uncomfortable you feel. Plus, your active lifestyle has slowed to a sedentary pace, as you exercise less and use elevators more. It becomes increasingly difficult to gain another pound, let alone the nine still needed to achieve your 10% increase. It takes 2 months, but you gain the 10%.

With time, your body weight, appetite, and lifestyle all recover. But, alas, the experimenter has another offer. This time, she wants to see if you can lose 10% of your body weight. Confident in your previous success, you accept and begin a strict diet. While too much food took away your appetite, the food deprivation is just plain miserable. Gone are the body's kind and gentle defenses. This time your body is not fooling around. You feel cranky and irritable, and your appetite is forever at the center of your attention. After 2 months of continual effort, you begin to realize that you might be in over your head on this one. The more you restrain yourself and the more you ignore your bodily cues to eat, the grouchier you feel and the more tempting high-calorie food seems. The constant irritation is also getting in your way of daily functioning. So you telephone the experimenter to call off the study after a month of futility. A return to your normal weight coincides with the departure of your misery and midnight fantasies of pizza and cookies.

After the experiments are over, two things have changed. On the one hand, you have a lot more money. But on the other hand, you think about hunger, eating, and weight control a little differently. Your experience shows that the body has a predispositional, somewhat automated guide to how much it should weigh. The body does, indeed, feature many self-regulatory guides, and when these self-regulatory guides are upset, ignored, or outright rejected, motivational states arise. Such motivational states (e.g., hunger, misery) will continue, and intensify, until the individual acts to correct the upset regulatory guides. Thus, the thesis of the present chapter is that physiological needs, biological systems, motivational states, and behavior act in concert with one another to achieve stable physiological regulation.

A similar study was conducted with animals, and the results appear in Figure 4.1. For the first 30 days, all animals received a normal diet. Starting at day 30 (point #1), some animals were force-fed (line a), some animals were placed on a restricted diet (line c), while other animals continued to receive their normal diet (line b). Three weeks later (day 48; point #2) all animals were returned to their normal diets. As you would expect, the force-fed animals gained a lot of weight during days 30 to 48, while the restricted diet animals lost a lot of weight. With the return of the normal diet (on day 48), the force-fed animals showed little hunger and ate sparingly, while the starved animals showed great hunger and ate voraciously. By day 75, however, the three groups of animals all weighed about the same. That is, irrespective of whether they were force-fed or starved, the animals motivationally adapted to their condition, and these motivational states allowed them eventually to return back to their normal body weights.

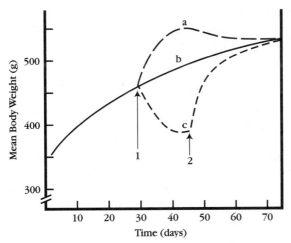

Figure 4.1 Fluctuations in Body Weight Over Time for Force Fed (a), Normally Fed (b), and Food Deprived (c) Animals.

Source: From *The Role of the Lateral Hypothalamus in Determining the Body Weight Set Point*, by R.E. Keesey, P.C. Boyle, J.W. Kemnitz, & J.S. Mitchel, 1976, in D. Novin, W. Wyrwicka, & G. A. Bray (Eds.), *Hunger: Basic mechanisms and clinical implications* (pp. 243–255). New York: Raven Press.

NEED

A need is any condition within the person that is essential and necessary for life, growth, and well-being. When needs are nurtured and satisfied, well being is maintained and enhanced. If neglected or frustrated, the need's thwarting will produce damage that disrupts biological or psychological well being. Motivational states therefore provide the impetus to act before damage occurs to psychological and bodily well being.

Damage can be to the body, so motives arise from physiological needs to avoid tissue damage and to maintain bodily resources (e.g., thirst, hunger, and sex). Damage can be to the self, so motives arise from psychological needs to orient one's development toward growth and adaptation (e.g., self-determination, competence, and relatedness). Damage can also occur to one's relationship to the social world, so motives arise from social needs to preserve our identities, beliefs, values, and interpersonal relationships (e.g., achievement, affiliation, intimacy, and power). Together, physiological, psychological, and social needs provide a range of motives that serve the individual's overall life, growth, and well-being.

Physiological needs involve biological systems such as neural brain circuits, hormones, and bodily organs. When unmet for an extended period, physiological needs constitute life-threatening emergencies and therefore generate motivational states that can dominate consciousness. When gratified, their salience fades, and these needs are forgotten about, at least for a while. Psychological needs involve central nervous system processes. Instead of conforming to a cyclical time course (rise, fall, and rise again) like physiological needs do, psychological needs are forever present in consciousness, at least to a degree. They gain salience in consciousness mostly in the presence of the environmental conditions the individual believes are capable of involving and satisfying these needs. For instance, hanging out with friends makes the need for affiliation salient, while being bossed around frustrates a person's need for autonomy. Two categories of psychological needs exists, and the distinction between psychological and social needs is that the former are innate and inherent in all people, whereas the latter reflect each individual's unique socialization history.

All needs generate energy. How one need differs itself from another is through its directional effects on behavior (Murray, 1937). For instance, a hunger need is different from a thirst need, not in the amount of energy it generates but in its ability to direct attention and action toward seeking out food rather than water. Similarly, a competence need is different from a relatedness need not in the amount of motivation aroused but in the ensuing desire to seek out optimal challenges rather than intimate relationships.

Another way that needs differ from one another is that some generate deficiency motivation whereas others generate growth motivation (Maslow, 1987). With deficiency needs, life goes along just fine until some state of deprivation (i.e., it's been 10 hours since your last meal) activates a need to interact with the world in a way that will quiet the deficit (i.e., consume food). With growth needs, motivational states energize and direct behavior to advance development (seek out challenges, improve interpersonal relationships). The telltale sign to differentiate a deficiency-based need from a growth-based need is by the emotions each generates. Deficiency needs typically generate tension-packed, urgency-laden emotions, such as anxiety, frustration, pain, stress, and relief. Growth needs typically generate positive emotions, such as interest, enjoyment, and vitality.

FUNDAMENTALS OF REGULATION

A half century ago, Clark Hull (1943) created a biologically-based theory of motivation referred to as drive theory (see Chapter 2). According to drive theory, physiological deprivations and deficits (e.g., lack of water, food, and sleep) create biological needs. If the need continues unsatisfied, the biological deprivation becomes potent enough to occupy attention and generate psychological drive. "Drive" is a theoretical term used to depict the psychological discomfort (felt tension and restlessness) stemming from the underlying and persistent biological deficit. Drive energizes the animal into action and directs that activity toward those particular behaviors that are capable of servicing (satisfying) the bodily needs.

Figure 4.2 illustrates the physiological need—psychological drive—behavioral action process. After drinking a glass of water or having breakfast, an individual experiences a satiated (i.e., full) biological condition in which neither thirst nor hunger is of motivational consequence, as depicted in (1). As time goes by, the individual evaporates water and expends calories. With this naturally-occurring loss of water and nutrients, physiological imbalances or deficits begin to accumulate (2). If the physiological imbalances persist and intensify, then continued deprivation produces a bodily need for water or calories (3). In time, the physiological need intensifies enough to produce felt tension and restlessness, which is the psychological drive (4). Once motivated by drive, the person engages in goal-directed action (5). When the thirsty person finds and drinks water, or when the hungry person locates and consumes food, consummatory behavior occurs (6). The water and food intake satisfies and removes the underlying bodily need, which quiets the psychological drive, through a process called drive reduction (7). Following drive reduction, the in-

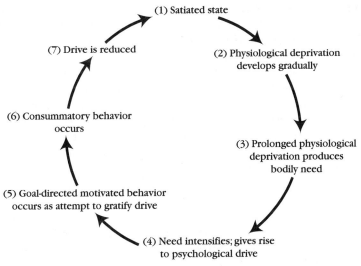

Figure 4.2 Model of Need-Drive-Behavior Sequence

dividual returns to a satiated (i.e., unmotivated) state (1) and the whole cyclical process begins to play itself out again.

The cyclical pattern depicting the rise and fall of psychological drive (Figure 4.2) involves seven core processes: need, drive, homeostasis, negative feedback, multiple inputs/ multiple outputs, intra-organismic mechanisms, and extra-organismic mechanisms.

Physiological Need

Physiological need describes a deficient biological condition. Physiological needs occur with tissue and bloodstream deficits, as from water loss, nutrient deprivation, or physical injury. If neglected, bodily harm or pathology follows. Hence, physiological needs, when unmet and intense, represent life-threatening emergencies.

Psychological Drive

Drive is a psychological, not a biological, term. It is the conscious manifestation of an underlying unconscious biological need. Drive, not the underlying physiological needs per se, has motivational properties. For instance, appetite (psychological drive), not low blood sugar or shrunken fat cells (physiological need), energizes and directs behavior. When salient enough to grab the individual's attention, drive motivationally readies the individual to engage in goal-directed behaviors capable of yielding drive reduction.

Homeostasis

Bodily systems show a remarkable capacity for maintaining a steady state of equilibrium. This is true even as these systems perform their functions and are exposed to widely differing and stressful environmental conditions. The term that describes the body's tendency to maintain a steady state is homeostasis. The bloodstream, for instance, shows a remarkable constancy in its level of water, salt, sugar, calcium, oxygen, temperature, acidity, proteins, and fats (Cannon, 1932, Dempsey, 1951). People constantly face changing external and internal environments, however, and the mere passage of time can bring conditions of deprivation. Or, people eat, drink, and sleep to excess. Hence, bodily systems are inevitably and continually displaced from homeostasis either by changes in environmental conditions or by one's own consummatory behaviors. Homeostasis is essentially the body's ability to return a system (i.e., bloodstream) to its basal state. To do so, bodily systems generate motivational states. Thus, the body has both a tendency to maintain a steady state as well as the means to generate the motivation necessary to energize and direct homeostasis-restoring behaviors.

Negative Feedback

Negative feedback refers to homeostasis' physiological stop system (Mook, 1988). People eat and sleep but only until they are no longer hungry or sleepy. Drive activates behavior; negative feedback stops it.

Without feedback and without a way of inhibiting drive-motivated behavior once the underlying need was satiated, human beings would be like the fabled sorcerer's apprentice (from Dukas's poem popularized by Walt Disney's *Fantasia*; Cofer & Appley, 1964). As the story goes, the apprentice, by imitating the sorcerer, learned how to command a broom to bring a bucket of water. The broom obeyed and brought the apprentice a bucket of water. After a couple of buckets, the apprentice had enough water, but the broom continued to bring bucket after bucket after bucket. Most regrettably, the apprentice forgot to learn how to command the broom to quit bringing water. Were the body unable to inhibit a drive, bodily disaster would result. If people were unable to shut off hunger, they might literally eat themselves to death.

Negative feedback systems actually signal satiety well before the physiological need is fully replenished (Adolph, 1980). At first, people eat and drink rapidly, but the rate of eating and drinking decreases quickly over the course of a meal (Spitzer & Rodin, 1981). As people digest food and water, the body displays an amazing aptitude to estimate how much of the food or water, when transformed and transplanted, is needed to gratify the underlying physiological need. During drinking, for example, the body continuously monitors the volume of fluid ingested on each swallow and uses that information to predict how much water will eventually make its way into the bloodstream and bodily cells. Understanding precisely how the body signals satiety constitutes the study of negative feedback systems.

Multiple Inputs/Multiple Outputs

Drive has multiple inputs, or means of activation. One can feel thirsty, for example, after sweating, eating salty foods, or donating blood, in response to electrical stimulation of a particular brain structure, or at a particular time of day. In much the same way, drive has multiple outlets, or behavioral responses, that satisfy the drive. When cold, a person can put on a jacket, turn up the furnace, engage in vigorous exercise, or shiver. Each of these

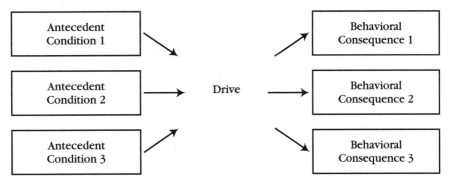

Figure 4.3 Drive as an Intervening Variable

behaviors achieves the same end result—a raised body temperature. The basic idea is that drive arises from a number of different sources (inputs) and motivates a number of different goal-directed behaviors (outputs).

The convergence of multiple inputs with multiple outputs, shown in Figure 4.3, is actually what makes drive such an appealing motivational construct. In theoretical terms, drive is an intervening variable, one that integrates the relationships among several otherwise diverse input and output variables. Pain, as an intervening variable, for example, helps explain what is common among the motivational processes that occur immediately after, for instance, a hammer strikes the hand (Antecedent 1 in the figure), a hand touches a hot stove (Antecedent 2), or a bare foot scrapes across a nail (Antecedent 3) to the time that the person shakes his or her hand frantically (Consequence 1), pours cold water over his or her hand (Consequence 2), or hops around on one foot while holding the injured foot (Consequence 3). Drive, therefore, intervenes between states of deprivation (input stimuli) and restorative goal-directed actions (output responses).

Consider the theoretical advantage of using drive as an intervening variable for connecting multiple inputs with multiple outputs.[1] Imagine that the three inputs in Figure 4.3 were hours of food deprivation, the tempting smell of fresh popcorn, and hanging out at a party with food on every table. Now imagine that the three outputs were amount of calories consumed, latency to begin eating, and probability of eating a meal versus skipping it. Smelling popcorn and attending a party do not cause behaviors like eating a lot of food (amount of calories consumed). We only sometimes eat a lot or eat quickly. Our motivated behavior depends on the intensity of our hunger (drive), not on the lure of popcorn or on the easy availability of the food. For this reason, motivation psychologists focus on the motivational properties of the intervening variable (drive), rather than on the potential motivational properties of hundreds of individual inputs to drive (hours of deprivation, smell of popcorn, plentiful food, and so on).

---

[1]The intervening variable approach depicted in Figure 4.3 applies to all motives, not just to drive. The inputs and outputs for the need for achievement, for instance, could be optimal challenge, rapid feedback, and personal responsibility for one's outcomes (multiple inputs) and persistence in the face of failure, choice of moderately difficult undertakings, and entrepreneurship (multiple outputs).

Intra-Organismic Mechanisms

Intra-organismic mechanisms include all the biological regulatory systems within the person that act in concert to activate, maintain, and terminate the physiological needs that underlie drive. Brain structures, the endocrine system, and bodily organs constitute the three main categories of intra-organismic mechanisms. For hunger, the principle intra-organismic mechanisms include the hypothalamus (brain structure), glucose and insulin hormones (endocrine system), and the stomach and liver (bodily organs). Together, these bodily mechanisms affect one another in ways that explain the physiological events that create, maintain, and terminate the psychological experience of drive. The study of intra-organismic mechanisms is the study of what role brain structures, hormones, and bodily organs play in the rise and fall of physiological needs.

Extra-Organismic Mechanisms

Extra-organismic mechanisms include all the environmental influences that play a part in activating, maintaining, and terminating psychological drive. The principle categories of extra-organismic mechanisms are cognitive, environmental, social, and cultural influences. For hunger, extra-organismic influences include beliefs about calories and goals for losing weight (cognitive influences), the smell of food and the time of day (environmental influences), the presence of others and peer pressure to eat or not to eat (social influences), and sex roles and cultural ideals about desirable and undesirable body shapes (cultural influences). The study of extra-organismic mechanisms is the study of what role cognitive, environmental, social, and cultural influences play in the rise and fall of physiological needs.

THIRST

Our bodies are mostly water—about two-thirds. When our water volume falls by about 2%, we begin to feel thirsty. Dehydration does not occur until the person loses 3% of water volume (Weinberg & Minaker, 1995). Thirst is the consciously experienced motivational state that readies the body to perform behaviors necessary to replenish a water deficit. It is the loss of water, below an optimal homeostatic level, that creates the physiological need that underlies thirst.

Thirst arises as a physiological need because our bodies continually lose water through perspiration, urination, exhalation, and even through bleeding, vomiting, and sneezing (i.e., multiple inputs). Without water replenishment, each of us would die in about 2 days. If you have ever gone more than 24 hours without any water, then you know that the body has effective intra-organismic mechanisms to grab your attention, your full attention, and motivate goal-directed behaviors to find and consume water.

Physiological Regulation

The water inside the human body lies in both intracellular and extracellular fluids. The intracellular fluid consists of all the water inside the cells (approximately 40% of body weight). The extracellular fluid consists of all the water outside the cells in blood plasma and interstitial fluid (approximately 20% of body weight).

Water is water no matter where it is in the body, but the differentiation is important because thirst arises from these two distinct sources. Because thirst arises from both intracellular and extracellular deficits, physiologists endorse the "double-depletion model" of thirst activation (Epstein, 1973). When the intracellular fluid needs replenishment, *osmometric thirst* arises. Cellular dehydration causes osmometric thirst, and cellular hydration stops it. When the extracellular fluid needs replenishment (e.g., after bleeding or vomiting), *volumetric thirst* arises. Hypovolemia (reduction of plasma volume) causes volumetric thirst, and hypervolemia stops it.

Thirst Activation

Consider the standard water deprivation study. Laboratory animals are deprived of water but not food for about 24 hours (Rolls, Wood, & Rolls, 1980). After depriving the animals of water, researchers selectively replace either the intracellular or the extracellular water (using special infusion techniques). The procedure yields three conditions: (1) 24-hour water deprivation followed by intracellular replenishment; (2) 24-hour water deprivation followed by extracellular replenishment; and (3) 24-hour water deprivation with no replenishment (a control group). The amount of water drunk by animals in the third (control) group serves as a standard of normal thirst (indexed by drinking). Rats that received full replenishment of their extracellular fluids drank just a bit less than did the rats that received no replenishment at all. That is, they drank as if they were still very thirsty. Rats that received replenishment of their intracellular fluid drank much less. That is, they drank as if they were mostly full. These results suggest that osmometric thirst is the primary cause of thirst activation. Thirst comes mostly from dehydrated cells.

Thirst Satiety

When people drink, they do not drink forever. Something alerts the body to quit drinking. The negative feedback system is important because the body must not only replenish its water deficits, but it must also prevent drinking so much water that cellular dysfunction occurs and threatens death. In this spirit, animals that are not water deprived do not want to drink, and if forced to do so, they just let the water dribble out the side of their mouths without swallowing it (Williams & Teitelbaum, 1956). Humans, of course, often binge when drinking, but such drinking is regulated by factors other than water, such as taste or alcohol.

During drinking, water passes from the mouth and esophagus to the stomach and intestines and is then absorbed into the bloodstream. Through the process of osmosis, water eventually passes from the extracellular fluids into the intracellular fluids to hydrate the cells. The negative feedback mechanism for this satiety must therefore lie in one (or more) of these bodily sites: mouth, stomach, intestines, bloodstream, and cells.

To locate thirst's negative feedback mechanism(s), physiologists devised a number of experiments. In one, animals drank water, but the experimenters arranged for the water to pass through the mouth but not reach the stomach (or intestines, bloodstream, or cells; Blass & Hall, 1976). The animals, on average, drank four times their normal amount of water, but they did eventually stop drinking. Thus, water passing through the mouth does provide one means of thirst inhibition, albeit a weak one. Later research identified that the mouth's specific stop system was related to the number of swallows during drinking (Mook & Wagner, 1989). After many swallows (but not necessarily after one drinks a large volume of water), drinking stops.

Subsequent studies arranged for animals to drink so that water passed from the mouth to the stomach but not into the intestines, bloodstream, or cells (Hall, 1973). Animals receiving water into their mouths and stomachs drank twice as much as normal. Thus, the stomach, like the mouth, also has a thirst inhibitory mechanism, albeit another weak one. Other studies allowed animals to drink with water passing through the mouth, stomach, and intestines, and into the extracellular fluids (Mook & Kozub, 1968). The water the rats drank, however, was a salt solution. Drinking the salt solution allowed much water into the extracellular fluids but little into the intracellular fluids. (Following the principle of osmosis, salty water does not diffuse into intracellular areas.) These animals drank more than normal. Therefore, the cells themselves must also house a negative feedback mechanism. Hence, water consumption does not fully alleviate thirst and stop drinking unless it eventually hydrates bodily cells (Mook, 1996). When taken as a whole, multiple negative feedback systems for thirst satiety exist—in the mouth, stomach, and cells.

Hypothalamus and Liver

The mouth, stomach, and cells coordinate thirst activation and satiety, but so do the liver, hypothalamus, and specific hormones. The brain (through the hypothalamus) monitors intracellular shrinkage (caused by low-water levels) and releases a hormone into the blood plasma that sends a message to the liver to conserve its water reserves (by producing concentrated, rather than diluted, urine). The kidneys will also release water if the person is low on fluid. While the hypothalamus is managing the involuntary behavior of the liver, it also creates the conscious psychological state of feeling thirsty that directs attention and behavior toward water-replenishing courses of action. It is in the hypothalamus that the psychological experience of thirst originates, enters into consciousness (by sending a message of awareness to the frontal lobes of the neocortex), and generates the motivational urge to drink.

Environmental Influences

Three extra-organismic influences on drinking behavior are the perception of water availability, adherence to drinking schedules, and taste. Animals with water-plentiful environments drink less over the course of a day than do animals with water-restricted environments (Toates, 1979). So to reduce your thirst fill up the refrigerator; to enhance your thirst leave just one beverage in the refrigerator. Animals also acquire and closely adhere to drinking schedules, irrespective of their physiological need for water (Toates, 1979). The most important environmental influence for drinking, however, is taste (Pfaffmann, 1960, 1961, 1982).

Pure water is tasteless and, therefore, offers no incentive value above and beyond water replenishment. When water is given a taste, drinking behavior changes in accordance with the incentive value of the fluid. The incentive values for four tastes appear in Figure 4.4: sweet, sour, salty, and bitter, represented at various stimulus intensities. Using tasteless (pure) water as a baseline (no pleasantness), any taste is slightly pleasant at a

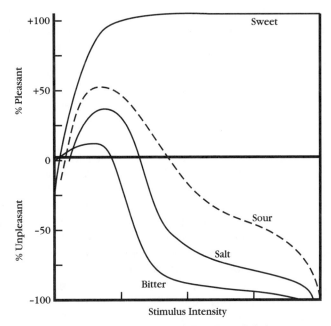

Figure 4.4 Relative Pleasantness of Four Taste Solutions

Source: From *The Pleasures of Sensation,* by C. Pfaffmann, 1960, *Psychological Review,* 67, pp. 253–268.
Copyright 1960 by the American Psychological Association. Reprinted with permission.

very low intensity (even bitter to a small extent). At more substantial intensities, sucrose-flavored (sweet) water is markedly more pleasant than is tasteless water. Tartaric acid (sour), salt, and quinine-flavored (bitter) water are all markedly more unpleasant than tasteless water. So because flavored water has incentive value people overdrink sweet water, homeostatically drink tasteless water, and underdrink sour, salt, and bitter water.[2]

Another extra-organismic influence on drinking behavior is the cultural prescription to drink 8 glasses of water a day. No scientific evidence, however, supports this advice (Valtin, 2002), largely because the typical 2,000-calorie diet already contains the equivalent of about 9 glasses of water (Woods, Bell, & Thorwart, 1999).

When factors such as a sweet taste offer a high incentive value for drinking, human beings drink excessively and sometimes consume dangerously high amounts, biologically speaking (Rolls, Wood, & Rolls, 1980). People often drink soft drinks and tea for their taste alone. For water-based drinks that contain alcohol or caffeine, complications via addictions can emerge. Both alcohol and caffeine, therefore, introduce a number of additional physiological processes that motivate people to drink to excess. Further, a number of social and cultural influences surround the drinking of alcoholic and caffeinated beverages that make drinking behavior more complex than thirst-regulated water consumption.

---

[2]The relationship between taste and drinking behavior is complicated by the fact that water deprivation affects the perception of the taste of water. Water becomes increasingly more hedonically positive (more rewarding) with increased deprivation, and water becomes increasingly more hedonically aversive with water satiation (Beck, 1979; Williams & Teitelbaum, 1956).

Some students on college campuses, for instance, binge drink alcohol in astonishingly large amounts. Some drugs (e.g., ecstasy) can also make people feel intensely thirsty and drink well beyond their physiological need, even to the point of water intoxication and death (Valtin, 2002). Thus, drinking occurs for three reasons: water replenishment, which satisfies physiological needs, sweet taste, and addiction to a substance in the water (and not the water itself).

HUNGER

Hunger is a more complex motive than is thirst. Water loss instigates thirst, and water replenishment satiates it. Hunger, then, might simply involve the cyclical loss and replenishment of food. But hunger only loosely follows a "depletion-repletion" model. Food deprivation does activate hunger and eating (i.e., people eat three meals a day to prevent food deprivation). But hunger regulation involves both short-term daily processes operating under homeostatic regulation (e.g., depletion and repletion of blood glucose and calories) and long-term processes operating under metabolic regulation and stored energy (e.g., fat cells). Hunger and eating are further affected, and substantially so, by cognitive, social, and environmental influences, so much in fact that an understanding of hunger and eating requires (1) short-term physiological models, (2) long-term physiological models, and (3) cognitive-social-environmental models (Weingarten, 1985).

Two models occupy hunger researchers' attention. The first is a short-term model in which immediately available energy (blood glucose) is constantly monitored. This is the glucostatic hypothesis, and it does a good job accounting for the onset and termination of hunger and eating. The second model is a long-term one in which stored energy (fat mass) is available and is used as a resource for supplementing glucose-monitored energy regulation. This is the lipostatic model, and it does a good job showing how fat stores contribute a second layer of complexity onto hunger and eating.

Short-Term Appetite

Short-term hunger cues regulate the initiation of meals, the size of meals, and the termination of meals. The glucostatic hypothesis argues that blood-sugar levels are critical to hunger—when blood glucose drops, people feel hunger and want to eat (Campfield et al., 1996; Mayer, 1952, 1953).

Cells require glucose to produce energy, so after a cell uses its glucose to carry out its functions a physiological need for glucose arises.[3] The bodily organ that monitors level of blood glucose is the liver, and when blood glucose is low the liver sends an excitatory signal to the lateral hypothalamus (LH), the brain center responsible for generating the psychological experience of hunger (Anand, Chhina, & Singh, 1962; Wyrwicka, 1988). Stimulation of the LH is important, because its stimulation will lead animals to overeat and, if stimulation is continued, to obesity (Elmquist, Elias, & Saper, 1999).

---

[3]Blood glucose is not the full story in the onset of hunger, as diabetics will tell you because they often have both high glucose and high hunger. While diabetics have high blood glucose, what they need (and do not have) is high cellular glucose. Diabetics need insulin because insulin (the hormone diabetics lack) increases cell membrane permeability so that glucose can flow freely from the bloodstream into the cells (Schwartz et al., 2000). In the presence of insulin, blood glucose can then become cellular glucose.

The brain structure involved in the termination of meals is the ventromedial hypothalamus (VMH). When stimulated, the VMH acts as the brain's satiety center—that is, the VMH is short-term appetite's negative feedback system; Miller, 1960). Without a VMH, animals become chronic overeaters that double their body weight (Stevenson, 1969). How the VMH gets stimulated in the first place is by the liver's detection of high levels of glucose (Russek, 1971; Schmitt, 1973), stomach distensions (bloated stomach) during eating (Moran, 2000), and the release of the gut peptide cholecystokinin (CCK; Woods, Seeley, Porte, & Schwartz, 1998).

According to the glucostatic hypothesis, appetite rises and falls in response to changes in plasma glucose that stimulate the LH to increase hunger and stimulate the VMH to decrease hunger. Hence, low glucose levels activate the LH with a hunger signal, whereas high blood glucose levels activate the VMH with a negative feedback signal. Other intra-organismic mechanisms also regulate the rise and fall of hunger. The LH, for instance, contains specialized neurons that respond to the sight and taste of food, and these specialized neurons become activated only when the animal is already somewhat hungry (Rolls, Sanghera, & Roper-Hall, 1979). Hormones also stimulate the LH and VMH, as discussed in the opening vignette to Chapter 3 in which plasma ghrelin stimulates the LH (and hunger) while plasma leptin stimulates the VMH (and satiety). Leptin, for instance, is the hormone secreted into the blood by fat cells to produce satiety (Campfield, Smith, & Burn, 1996, 1997b; Spiegelman & Flier, 2001). The LH also manufactures appetite-boosting peptides called orexins (which is the Greek word for appetite; Sakurai et al., 1998). Orexins are powerful appetite boosters, and when injected into the brain of rats, the animals will eat three to six times more than control rats.

Findings such as these with ghrelin and orexins are very exciting to drug researchers trying to find ways to stimulate appetite in humans, such as people going through chemotherapy (Woods et al., 1998). Findings such as these with leptin are even more exciting to drug researchers as they try to find ways to suppress appetite in humans, such as people trying to reverse obesity (Campfield, Smith, & Burn, 1998).

Appetite also rises and falls in response to nonbrain-based cues, as hunger arises from both brain and peripheral (nonbrain) bodily cues. These peripheral bodily cues include the mouth (Cabanac & Duclaux, 1970), stomach distensions (Deutsch, Young, & Kalogeris, 1978; McHugh & Moran, 1985), and body temperature (Brobeck, 1960). (Because cold temperatures stimulate hunger, restauranteurs routinely run their air conditioners on full blast.) The chief nonbrain-based regulator of hunger is the stomach. It empties itself at a calorie-constant rate (about 210 calories per hour), so appetite returns more quickly after a low-calorie meal than after a high-calorie meal (McHugh & Moran, 1985). With a full stomach, people report no hunger; with a stomach that is 60% empty, people report a hint of hunger; and with a stomach that is 90% empty, people report maximum hunger, even though some food remains in the stomach (Sepple & Read, 1989).[4]

---

[4]Deutsch and Gonzalez (1980) further find that the stomach signals not only food volume information but food content information as well. This pair of researchers removed specific nutrients from an animal's food and found that the animal responded by eating foods that had those particular nutrients and refusing foods without those nutrients. Thus the stomach monitors food content and food volume, and both food content and food volume regulate hunger and its satiety.

Long-Term Energy Balance

Like glucose, fat (adipose tissue) also produces energy. And like the body monitors its glucose levels rather precisely, it also monitors its fat cells rather precisely (Faust, Johnson, & Hirsch, 1977a, 1977b). According to the lipostatic (lipo = fatty; static = equilibrium) hypothesis, when the mass of fat stored drops below its homeostatic balance, adipose tissue secretes hormones (e.g., ghrelin) into the bloodstream to promote weight gain motivation that increases food intake (Borecki et al., 1995; Cummings et al., 2002; Wren et al., 2001). Alternatively, when the mass of fat stored increases above its homeostatic balance, adipose tissue secretes hormones (e.g., leptin) into the bloodstream to reduce food intake and promote weight loss motivation (Harvey & Ashford, 2003; Schwartz & Seeley, 1997). Because fat stores are relatively stable and enduring sources of energy, the lipostatic hypothesis illustrates the body's neurohormonal system for smoothing out the otherwise short-term fluctuations in energy balance from blood glucose levels.

A spin-off of the lipostatic hypothesis is the set-point theory (Keesey, 1980; Keesey et al., 1976; Keesey & Powley, 1975; Powley & Keesey, 1970). Set-point theory argues that each individual has a biologically determined body weight or "fat thermostat" that is set by genetics either at birth or shortly thereafter. Genetics create individual differences in the number of fat cells per person. In set-point theory, hunger activation and satiety depend on the size (not the number) of one's fat cells, which vary over time. When fat cell size is reduced (e.g., through dieting), hunger arises and persists until feeding behavior allows the fat cells to return to their natural (set-point) size. Hunger therefore is the body's means of defending its genetic set point (Bennett, 1995; Rosenbaum et al., 1997).

The lipostatic hypothesis reflects long-term enduring factors (e.g., genetics, metabolic rates) that regulate the balance between food intake, energy expenditure, and body weight. As to genetics, people inherit relatively consistent metabolic rates (biochemical processes that convert stored energy into expendable energy). People also inherit a number of fat cells and a homeostatic set-point for how extended (full) those fat cells should be. While these regulatory processes are relatively constant over time, they can and do change. Set point rises with age, metabolism drops following prolonged caloric restriction (as during a diet), and a chronic excess of food intake can lead to an increase in both fat cell size (lipogenesis) and fat cell number (adipogenesis) (Kassirer & Angell, 1998; Keesey, 1989; Mandrup & Lane, 1997).

A comprehensive model that combines short-term and long-term influences on appetite appears in Figure 4.5. The two solid vertical lines represent the glucostatic hypothesis of short-term appetite in which hunger motivates food intake while food intake satiates hunger. The box immediately above food intake illustrates that, in addition to hunger, environmental influences stimulate food intake. Once consumed, food is either used as energy to be expended during physical activity (Hunger → Energy Expenditure) or stored in adipose tissue as fat (Hunger → Fat Stores). The dashed line represents the lipostatic hypothesis of long-term appetite in which high-fat stores satiate hunger while low-fat stores excite hunger.

Environmental Influences

Environmental influences that affect eating behavior include the time of day, stress, and the sight, smell, appearance, and taste of food. Eating behavior increases significantly, for instance, when an individual confronts a variety of foods, a variety of nutrients, and a va-

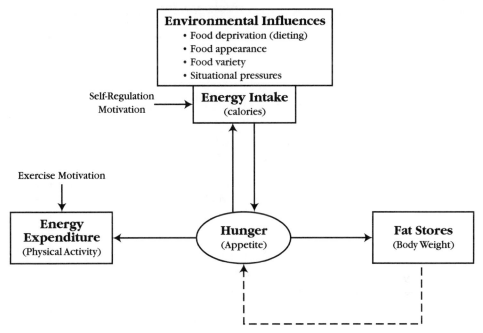

Figure 4.5   Comprehensive Model of Hunger Regulation

riety of tastes (Rolls, 1979; Rolls, Rowe, & Rolls, 1982). The mere availability of food variety encourages more eating than does a monotonous diet (Sclafani & Springer, 1976). Even when the individual has only one type of food (e.g., ice cream), variety in the number of flavors available increases food intake (Beatty, 1982). Food availability (e.g., a lot of different foods sitting out on a table at a party) and large portion sizes also lead people to overeat (Hill & Peters, 1998). For food availability, for instance, people nibble here and there when a lot of different foods are sitting out on a table at a party. Each new food brings a new taste, and hence can initiate eating in a way that is independent of hunger. For large portion sizes, people eat more when the meal is "super-sized" than when it is not.

Eating is often a social occasion. People eat more when they are in the presence of others (who are also eating) than when they are alone (Berry, Beatty, & Klesges, 1985; deCastro & Brewer, 1991). People who are trying to diet are also more likely to relapse when they are in the presence of others who are eating (Grilo, Shiffman, & Wing, 1989). One demonstration of this social facilitation effect involved an experiment with the help of college students participating in an ice-cream tasting experiment. Half the students ate alone, whereas the other half ate in a group of three. Ice-cream eaters also had either one or three flavors from which to choose (a variety manipulation). Table 4.1 lays out the results: Males and females ate more in both the presence of others and in the presence of variety.

Situational pressure to eat or to diet serves as another environmental influence on eating behavior. Binging on food, for instance, is an acquired behavioral pattern under substantial social control (Crandall, 1988). It often occurs in small groups, such as athletic

Table 4.1   Ice-Cream Intake (in Grams) for Students Alone Versus in Group and With One Versus Three Flavors

	Social setting			
	Alone		Three-person group	
	Number of flavors		Number of flavors	
	1	3	1	3
Males	113.8	211.1	245.6	215.6
Females	76.9	137.7	128.5	170.8

Source: From *Sensory and Social Influences on Ice Cream Consumption by Males and Females in a Laboratory Setting,* by S. L. Berry, W. W. Beatty, and R. C. Klesges, 1985, *Appetite, 6,* pp. 41–45.

teams (Crago et al., 1985) and cheerleading squads (Squire, 1983), partly because small groups develop and enforce norms about what is appropriate behavior. Deviation from these norms typically results in some form of interpersonal rejection and a reduction in popularity. If eating is an important behavior for the group, then group pressure can become an even more potent eating signal than one's physiology. Also eating is an important behavior in the lives of children, and children prefer the same foods eaten by those they admire (Birch & Fisher, 1996).

Restraint-Release Situations

Much in the same way that social pressures can interfere with and override physiological regulation, dieting too can interfere with and override physiological guides. By dieting, the dieter attempts to bring eating behavior under cognitive, rather than under physiological, control (e.g., "I will eat this much at this time," rather than "I will eat when hungry"). More often than not, however, dieting paradoxically causes subsequent binging. The dieter becomes increasingly susceptible to disinhibition (or "restraint release"), especially under conditions of anxiety, stress, alcohol, depression, or exposure to high-calorie foods (Greeno & Wing, 1994; Polivy & Herman, 1983, 1985). One study, for example, found that people on a diet ate less ice cream than people not dieting, as you would expect, but dieters actually ate more than nondieters when everyone first drank a 15-ounce milkshake. After the dieters drank the high-calorie food, they became increasingly vulnerable to binging (Herman, Polivy, & Esses, 1987), a phenomenon known as restraint release and a pattern of binging described as counterregulation (Polivy & Herman, 1985). For dieters, there is truth in the advertising slogan, "You can't eat just one."

Counterregulation describes the paradoxical pattern displayed by dieters who eat very little when just nibbling but who eat very much after consuming a large, high-calorie "preload" (Herman & Mack, 1975; Polivy, 1976; Ruderman & Wilson, 1979; Spencer & Fremouw, 1979; Woody et al., 1981). But consuming high-calorie food is only one of many conditions that unleash dieters' binging. Depression also triggers a dieter's restraint release. For instance, depressed dieters typically gain weight, whereas people who are not dieting and are depressed typically lose weight (Polivy & Herman, 1976a). The same pattern holds for anxiety as anxious dieters eat more than anxious people not dieting (Baucom & Aiken, 1981). Conditions that threaten one's ego (e.g., failure at an easy task, making a speech before an evaluative audience) produce the same paradoxical effect in which restrained eaters eat more than do unrestrained eaters (Heatherton, Herman, & Polivy, 1991). Alcohol has this same restraint-release effect on dieters as well (Polivy & Herman, 1976b). Taken as a whole, research on social facilitation, social pressure, and restraint-release documents that eating behavior can and often does move away from physiological regulation and toward some type of counterproductive nonphysiological regulation, such as social, cognitive, or emotional regulation (Polivy & Herman, 1985).

Cognitively-Regulated Eating Style

As illustrated by the glucostatic and lipostatic hypotheses, the body defends its weight. Sometimes, however, people come to the conclusion that their physiologically regulated body weight does not measure up well to their personal or cultural aspirations. Rather like a civil war, people decide that it is time for the mind, or will, to begin the revolution to take over and regulate body weight. The revolt begins as cognitive controls try to supplant, or override, physiological controls. Successful dieting (in terms of weight-loss goals) requires that the dieter first deaden his or her responsiveness to internal cues (e.g., feeling hungry or full) and second substitute conscious cognitive controls for unconscious physiological ones (Heatherton, Polivy, & Herman, 1989). The big problem, however, is that cognitive controls do not feature a negative feedback system. Dieters are therefore highly vulnerable to bingeing when situational events interfere with cognitive inhibitions (e.g., the presence of others, depression, anxiety, alcohol, intake of high-calorie preloads).

Weight Gain and Obesity

Obesity is a medical term that describes a state of increased body weight (adipose tissue) that is of sufficient magnitude to produce adverse health consequences, including an increased risk of heart disease, diabetes, respiratory problems, some cancers, and premature death (Stevens et al., 1998). A whopping 65% of American adults are overweight with 35% of all adults qualifying as obese or as morbidly obese (Yanovsky & Yanovsky, 2002). Unfortunately, little or no research supports the claim that weight loss produces health benefits (Blackburn, 1995), as the cure for obesity (i.e., weight loss) might very well be worse than the condition (Kassirer & Angell, 1998). Therefore, instead of concentrating on encouraging weight loss, most obesity researchers emphasize prevention (adults in their 20s and 30s often gain a lot of weight) and the cultivation of a healthier lifestyle that centers on exercise (see Box 4).

Figure 4.5 showed a comprehensive model of energy intake and energy expenditure. This figure can also be used to show that weight control is a function of balancing (or imbalancing) the ratio of "food intake" to "energy expenditure." If people take in more en-

---

BOX 4   *Obesity Therapy: Reversing Self-Regulation Failure*

Question: Why is this information important?

Answer: Because self-regulation failure has created a national epidemic of obesity.

Body weight and obesity are a lot like the weather: Everybody talks about it, but no one seems to do much about it. One reason people are talking so much about obesity is because it has become nothing less than a national epidemic in the United States and is threatening to become a global epidemic (WHO, 1998). Among adults in the United States, two-thirds are overweight (Hill & Peters, 1998). So the majority of us are overweight—not obese necessarily but getting there nonetheless. And we seem to be getting there quicker each year. Currently, 35% of the U.S. population is obese, and that compares to rates of 33% in 1997, 23% in 1995, 15% in 1980, 14% in 1974, and 13% in 1962 (Taubes, 1998). As you can see, the rates of obesity are rapidly rising (Flegel et al., 1998).

These numbers are based on the measure of body mass index (BMI), which is calculated by dividing the person's weight in kilograms by his height in meters squared. A BMI between 18 and 25 is constitutes normal; over 25 is overweight; and over 30 is obese (Yanovski & Yanovski, 2002). By this measure, a

5 feet, 10 inch (1.78 m) individual would be considered overweight at 175 pounds (80 kg) and obese at 210 pounds (95 kg).

To prevent weight gain and obesity, one has to know its origins (Jeffrey & Knauss, 1981; Rodin, 1982). Obesity, which is basically just an excess surplus of body fat, is a multi-faceted phenomenon that integrates both genetic (Foch & McClearn, 1980; Price, 1987; Stunkard, 1988) and environmental (Grilo & Pogue-Geile, 1991; Jeffrey & Knauss, 1981) causes and influences. Some environmental influences associated with obesity, for instance, include child-rearing (Birch, Zimmerman, & Hind, 1980) and child-feeding (Klesges et al., 1983) practices, low socioeconomic status (Sobal & Stunkard, 1989), high-fat content in the diet (Sclafani, 1980), lack of exercise (Stern & Lowney, 1986), and stress (Greeno & Wing, 1994). Clearly, genetic factors, such as metabolic efficiency, number of fat cells, liver disorders, and hypothalamic sensitivity (Hill, Pagliassotti, & Peters, 1994), are important as some bodies are more genetically predisposed to hoard their fat resources than are other bodies.

Our collective genes have not changed substantially in the last quarter century in which the obesity rates

---

ergy (eat) than they expend through physical activity, they will gain weight; if people expend more calories (physical activity) than they consume (food intake), they will lose weight. Other than surgery (see Cummings et al., 2001), the only two ways people can prevent or reverse weight gain and obesity are to decrease eating to a point of taking in fewer calories than expended during physical activity (e.g., self-regulation motivation in Figure 4.5) or increase physical activity to a point of expending more calories than one takes in during eating (e.g., exercise motivation in Figure 4.5). These two motivations are discussed in Box 4 and in later chapters. These two motivations—self-regulation of food intake and exercise motivation—are important to mention here because eating and exercising involve voluntary behaviors rather than physiological regulatory processes. Physiological regulatory processes (as described above) affect hunger motivation, and hunger motivation is notoriously difficult to gain conscious control over (see the section on Restraint Release). The optimistic point to make is that voluntary behaviors like exercising are not so difficult to gain conscious control over. So motivating oneself to regulate body weight can be effective to the extent that the person focuses his or her motivation on energizing and directing voluntary behaviors like exercising.

have shot through the roof. The primary culprits are a culturally engineered environment that promotes overeating on the one hand and physical inactivity on the other hand (Hill & Peters, 1998). Environments in the United States offer easily available food (when considered in historical context), large portion size of meals, and high-fat meals (Hill & Peters, 1998). Environments encourage physical inactivity by reducing people's requirement for physical exertion, as through advances in transportation and technology (including television, computers, and electronic games). And unfortunately, increased food intake and decreased physical activity are inextricably linked, such that the heavier we get, the more bothersome physical exercise, even walking, becomes.

Pharmaceutical (drug) companies are hard at work trying to create drugs to stimulate weight loss and other drugs to combat weight gain and obesity (Yanovski & Yanovski, 2002). But these drugs have proven difficult to create. For instance, consider leptin therapy. Recall that leptin (the Greek word for "thin") is a hormone that stimulates satiety and the motivation to terminate a meal. So leptin therapy makes sense, but it does not work because people quickly develop a resistance to leptin (El-Haschimi et al., 2000).

If we do not yet have drugs that can help combat our national epidemic of obesity, then we are left with trying to regulate the long-term balance between energy intake (eating) and energy expenditure (exercise). But gaining control over these behaviors is not easy and is often unsuccessful for reasons that surprise us. For instance, fasting rarely works because is it associated with a major reduction in energy expended, with decreased metabolism, and with restraint release. Fasting is also problematic because it relies on cognitive rather than physiological cues for hunger and satiety and because it drops the individual below set-point weight status (Lowe, 1993).

One optimistic finding is that intense physical activity can mitigate the detrimental effects of overeating and protect against weight gain (Birch et al., 1991). Thus, exercise motivation seems centrally important in the effort to reverse the obesity epidemic. To affect the long-term balance between energy intake and energy expenditure, it is the physical activity component of the equation than can be readily altered and subjected to the sort of interventions programs offered by fitness gurus and motivational psychologists.

SEX

In lower animals, sexual motivation and behavior occur only during the female's ovulation period (Parkes & Bruce, 1961). During ovulation, the female secretes a pheromone and its scent stimulates sexual advances from the male. For the male, injections of testosterone (a hormone) can further increase his sexual behavior. Hence, in the lower animals, sex conforms to the cyclical physiological need → psychological drive process shown in Figure 4.2: Time passes, biological need emerges and stimulates psychological drive, and its ensuing consummatory behavior satiates both the psychological drive and the biological need.

Physiological Regulation

Human sexual behavior is influenced, but not determined, by hormones. The sex hormones are the androgens (e.g., testosterone) and estrogens, and their release into the bloodstream (from the adrenal gland) is controlled by the hypothalamus. These hormones rise at times like a woman's ovulation period and fall as the person ages past young adulthood into adulthood and old age (Guay, 2001). At age 40, for instance, men's testosterone levels decline by about 1% each year. In both men and women, sexual desire and the hormones that underlie it decline steadily beginning in the mid-20s (Laumann, Paik, & Rosen, 1999) such that the hormones and sexual desire of a 40 year old are about half of that of a 20 year old (Zumoff et al., 1995). Though present in both sexes, androgens contribute to the sexual motivation of males, and estrogens contribute to the sexual motivation of females (Money et al., 1976). Even for females, however, androgens play the key role in regulating sexual motivation, with decreases in testosterone (as with aging) foreshadowing decreased sexual desire and increases in testosterone (as with androgen replacement therapy) reviving sexual desire (Apperloo et al., 2003; Davis, 2000; Guay 2001; Munarriz et al., 2000; Tuiten et al., 2000).

Men and women experience and react to sexual desire very differently (Basson, 2001). In men, the correlation between physiological arousal and psychological desire is quite high. For instance, the correlation between men's erectile response and their self-reported desire is very high (Meston, 2000). So men's sexual desire can be predicted and explained in the context of their sexual arousal. In the presence of a sexual arousal trigger (e.g., stimulation from a sexual partner), men show a triphasic sexual response cycle: desire, arousal, orgasm (Masters & Johnson, 1966; Segraves, 2001). The triphasic sexual response cycle that describes men's sexual motivation so well—the traditional sex response cycle—appears in the upper half of Figure 4.6. In this model, sexual desire emerges rather spontaneously from an arousal trigger, and that rising sexual desire then generates accompanying physiological and psychological arousal (in the form of sexual thoughts, fantasies, and a consciously-felt urge to be sexual). Such sexual arousal enables orgasm, and with orgasm the traditional response cycle ends with a relatively quick resolution period that returns the person to a baseline state.

In women, the correlation between physiological arousal and psychological desire is quite low. For instance, the correlation between women's vaginal lubrication and their self-reported desire is low to nonexistent (Meston, 2000). So women's sexual desire cannot be predicted and explained in the context of their physiological need (e.g., estrogen, testosterone) or arousal (e.g., genital engorgement). Instead, women's sexual desire is highly responsive to relationship factors, such as emotional intimacy (Basson, 2001, 2002). The intimacy-based model of sexual desire that describes women's sexual motivation so well appears in the lower half of Figure 4.6. In this alternative model, high emotional intimacy anticipates sexual desire. It is emotional intimacy (not genital engorgement) that takes women from a state of sexual neutrality to a state of being open and responsive to sexual stimuli. In this context, sexual motivation and behavior reflect closeness and a desire to share with one's partner more than it does an underlying physiological need (Basson, 2003). In this alternative model, sex begins with intimacy needs (not with sexual desire). Further, sexual desire leads to and enhances long-term relationship intimacy (rather than to resolution, as in the traditional sex response cycle).

Facial Metrics

Many stimuli arise from a sexual partner—chemical (smell), tactile (touch), auditory (voice), and visual (sight, appearance). The physical attractiveness of a potential partner is perhaps the most potent external stimulus that affects sexual motivation. Western cultures

Traditional Sex Response Cycle

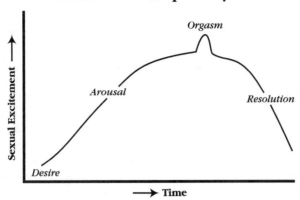

Alternative Sex Response Cycle

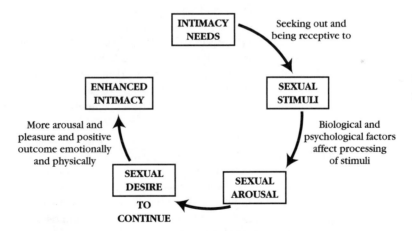

Figure 4.6 Two Models of the Sex Response Cycle: Traditional (Upper) and Alternative (Lower)

Source: From *Using a Different Model for Female Sexual Response to Address Women's Problematic Low Sexual Desire,* by R, Basson, 2001, *Journal of Sex and Marital Therapy, 27,* 395–403.

generally rate a slim body build for women as attractive (Singh, 1993a, 1993b). But such standards vary from one culture to the next, largely because these standards are acquired through experience, socialization, and cultural consensus (Mahoney, 1983). That said, some physical characteristics are viewed as universally attractive, including health (e.g., clear skin; Symons, 1992), youthfulness (Cunningham, 1986), and reproductive capacity (Singh, 1993a).

Both men and women rate slim females as attractive. Women's perceptions of male attractiveness, however, have little consensus as to what body shapes or body parts are seen as attractive (Beck, Ward-Hull, & McLear, 1976; Horvath, 1979, 1981; Lavrakas, 1975). The main predictor of women's rating of men's bodies is waist-to-hip ratio (WHR, a measure that ranges typically from 0.7 to 1.0; it is calculated via the narrowest circumference of the waist divided by the widest circumference of the hips/buttocks). Women rate moderately slim WHRs in males as most attractive (Singh, 1995).

The study of people's judgments of the attractiveness of facial characteristics is called *facial metrics* (Cunningham, 1986; Cunningham, Barbee, & Pike, 1990; Cunningham et al., 1995). Consider the face—and its facial-metric parameters—shown in Figure 4.7. The questions that link facial metrics with the study of sexual motivation are, "On what dimensions do faces vary from each other, and which of those dimensions determine which faces are attractive?" Interestingly, different cultures show an impressive convergence in terms of which facial characteristics are considered attractive and which are not.

Faces vary considerably, and Figure 4.7 illustrates 24 different structural characteristics (e.g., eye size, mouth width, cheekbone prominence). Three categories explain which faces are judged attractive: neonatal features, sexual maturity features, and expressive features. Neonatal features correspond to those associated with the newborn infant, such as large eyes and a small nose, and are associated with attractive nonverbal messages of youth and agreeableness (Berry & McArthur, 1985, 1986). Sexual maturity features correspond to those associated with postpubescent status, such as prominent cheekbones and, for males, thick facial and eyebrow hair, and are associated with attractive nonverbal messages of strength, status, and competency (Keating, Mazur, & Segall, 1981). Expressive features such as a wide smile/mouth and higher-set eyebrows are means to express positive emotions such as happiness and openness (McGinley, McGinley, & Nicholas, 1978).

Thus, a look at a person's facial features cues up a perception of that person's youthfulness/agreeableness, strength/status, and happiness/openness. It is in these perceptions, which are based on implicit facial metric ratings, that a person makes a judgment of how attractive that person's face is. This conclusion raises an interesting slant on the question of whether or not beauty is in the eye of the beholder. In one sense it is not, because facial metric ratings are objective features of faces that yield pan-cultural consensus as to which faces are beautiful. In another sense, however, it is, because a face is beautiful to the extent that the perceiver sees (and subjectively values) youthfulness, status, or happiness-openness. It is youthfulness, status, and happiness-openness that are beautiful, and faces just happen to be a conduit to communicate that information about the person.

Facial metrics research proceeds by showing dozens of different faces of men and women (via a slide projector) to a group of opposite-sex heterosexual individuals (or same-sex homosexual individuals; Donovan, Hill, & Jankowiak, 1989). The individuals judge each face on a variety of dimensions (e.g., how attractive? how desirous as a sexual partner?), and the experimenters painstakingly measure each face on all the facial-metric dimensions listed in Figure 4.7. With these data in hand, the researchers investigate the

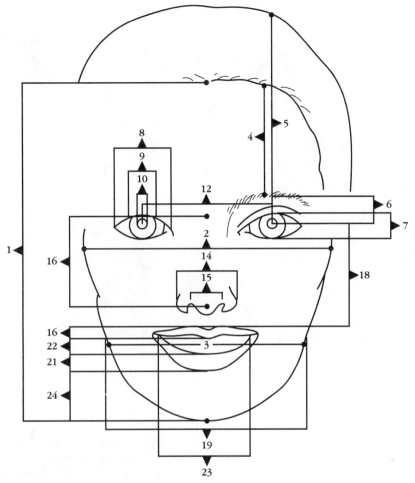

1, Length of face, distance from hairline to base of chin; 2, Width of face at cheekbones, distance between outer edges of cheekbones at most prominent point; 3, Width of face at mouth, distance between outer edges of cheeks at the level of the middle of the smile; 4, Height of forehead, distance from eyebrow to hairline; 5, Height of upper head, measured from pupil center to top of head estimated without hair; 6, Height of eyebrows, measured from pupil center to lower edge of eyebrow; 7, Height of eyes, distance from upper to lower edge of visible eye within eyelids at pupil center; 8, Width of eyes, inner corner to outer corner of eye; 9, Width of iris, measured diameter of eye; 10, Width of pupil, measured diameter of center of eye; 11, Standardized width of pupil, calculated as a ratio of the width of the pupil to the width of the iris (not shown); 12, Separation of eyes, distance between pupil centers; 13, Cheekbone width, an assessment of relative cheekbone prominence calculated as difference between the width of the face at the cheekbones and the width of the face at the mouth length of the face (not shown); 14, Nostril width, width of nose at outer edges of nostrils at widest point; 15, Nose tip width, width of protrusion at tip of nose, usually associated with crease from nostril; 16, Length of nose, measured from forehead bridge at level of upper edge of visible eye to nose tip; 17, Nose area, calculated as the product of the length of nose and width of nose at the tip length of the face (not shown); 18, Mid-face length, distance from pupil center to upper edge of upper lip, calculated by subtracting from the length of face the height of forehead, height of eyebrows, width of upper lip, height of smile, width of lower lip, and length of chin; 19, Width of cheeks, calculated as an assessment of facial roundness based on the measured width of face at mouth; 20, Thickness of upper lip, measured vertically at center; 21, Thickness of lower lip, measured vertically at center; 22, Height of smile, vertical distance between lips at center of smile; 23, Width of smile, distance between mouth inner corners; 24, Length of chin, distance from lower edge of lower lip to base of chin.

Figure 4.7   Male and Female Facial-Metric Parameters

Source: From *Measuring the Physical in Physical Attractiveness: Quasi-Experiments on the Sociobiology of Female Facial Beauty,* by M. R. Cunningham, 1986, *Journal of Personality and Social Psychology, 50,* pp. 925–935. Copyright 1986 by the American Psychological Association. Reprinted with permission.

Figure 4.8 Seven Faces that Vary in Their Facial Metrics (and Hence in Their Attractiveness)

correlations that emerge between attractiveness ratings and the various facial characteristics. To get a more personal feel for such an experiment, look at the seven different faces in Figure 4.8, and you will probably perceive in milliseconds that some of the faces are more attractive than are other faces. Given such different attractiveness perceptions, the question is, Why? Why is one face in Figure 4.8 more attractive than is another face in Figure 4.8? Answering this "why?" question requires breaking down each face by the 24 facial metrics introduced in Figure 4.7.

Facial metrics predict attractiveness ratings for the faces of women (Cunningham, 1986), men (Cunningham, Barbee, & Pike, 1990), different cultures (Cunningham et al., 1995), and different ages (Symons, 1992). For women's faces, the facial metrics most associated with physical attractiveness are the neonatal features (large eyes, small nose, small chin). Sexual maturity (cheekbone prominence and thinness) and expressive characteristics (eyebrow height and smile height and width) also add positively to attractiveness ratings of women's faces. For men's faces, the facial metrics most associated with physical attractiveness are the sexual maturity features (thick eyebrows and prominent chin length). Expressive features (smile height and width) also add to attractiveness ratings of men's faces.

Sexual Scripts

A sexual script is one's mental representation of the step-by-step sequence of events that occur during a typical sexual episode (Gagnon, 1974, 1977; Simon & Gagnon, 1986). A sexual script, not unlike a movie script, includes specific actors, motives and feelings of those actors, and a set of appropriate verbal and nonverbal behaviors that should success-fully conclude with sexual behavior. In its essence, the sexual script is the individual's story line of what a typical sexual encounter involves. The young male learns to coordi-nate his sexual script to coincide with the three linear stages in the sex response cycle of desire (excitement), arousal, and orgasm (see Traditional Sex Response Cycle in Figure 4.6). The pairing of a sexual (cognitive) script with desire-arousal-orgasm cycle is helped along by masturbatory fantasies.

For females the coordination of sexual script and physical activity is looser, partly be-cause fewer females masturbate in early adolescence but mostly because women's sexual arousal is steeped more in relationship factors than it is in physical activity. Further, for females, the content of emerging sexual scripts contains little material that is sexual (from the male point of view). The sexual content of the female is more likely to include events such as falling in love (rather than participating in sex).

With dating, both the male and female sexual scripts gain the opportunity of transi-tioning themselves from independent, fantasy-based scripts to an interpersonal, team-like script. When the couple fails to coordinate their sexual scripts, their sexual episodes will likely be fraught with distress, conflict, anxiety, and sexual performance is awkward and unsuccessful. But when workable sequences of sexual behavior become coordinated and conventionalized and focused as much on the other as on oneself, the couple's sexual scripts begin to have an adaptive, additive, and reeducative character that brings sexual and relational satisfaction (Simon & Gagnon, 1986).

In addition to harboring sexual scripts to guide their sexual episodes, people also harbor sexual schemas, or cognitive representations of their sexual selves (Anderson & Cyranowski, 1994). Sexual schemas are beliefs about the sexual self that are derived from past experiences that feature both positive approach-oriented thoughts and behaviors as well as negative avoidance-oriented thoughts and behaviors. Hence, a person's sexual self includes an inclination to experience sexual desire and sexual participation (positive ap-proach aspects) and also an inclination to experience anxiety, fear, conservatism, and sex-ual inhibition (negative avoidance aspects). Positive elements of sexual schemas promote sexual desire and arousal; negative elements of sexual schemas inhibit sexual desire and arousal (Anderson & Cyranowski, 1994). These green-light (positive approach aspects) and red-light (negative avoidance aspects) elements of a person's sexual schema are im-portant because sexual arousal is always a product of competing excitatory (desire) and inhibitory (anxiety) tendencies (Janssen, Vorst, Finn, & Bancroft, 2002).

Sexual Orientation

A key component of postpubescent sexual scripts is the establishment of sexual orienta-tion, or one's preference for sexual partners of the same or other sex. Sexual orientation actually exists on a continuum, as about one-third of all adolescents have participated in at least one homosexual act (with more boys than girls having done so; Money, 1988). The sexual orientation continuum therefore extends from exclusively heterosexual through a bisexual orientation and continues to an exclusively homosexual orientation. Most adoles-cents rather routinely commit to a heterosexual orientation, but about 4% of males and 2% of females do not, and these percentages are higher if one includes a bisexual orientation.

Though still far from conclusive, research suggests that sexual orientation is not a choice; it is something that happens to the adolescent rather than something that is more deliberate or results from soul-searching (Money, 1988). Part of the explanation for why people develop a homosexual orientation or a heterosexual orientation is genetic (see the twin studies by Bailey & Pillard, 1991; Bailey et al., 1993) and part of the explanation is environmental. Unfortunately, this literature is characterized more by rejected hypotheses than by confirmed ones. For instance, there is little evidence to support the idea that homosexuality emanates from a domineering mother and weak father (Bell, Weinberg, & Hammersmith, 1981) or from exposure to an older same-sex seducer (Money, 1988). The most promising research frontiers in understanding sexual orientation are those in genetics (Bailey & Pillard, 1991; Hamer et al., 1993) and in the prenatal hormonal environment (Berenbaum & Snyder, 1995; Kelly, 1991; Paul, 1993). As to the prenatal hormonal environment, early hormonal exposure (androgens, estrogens) affects subsequent sexual behavior and orientation.

One way people learn their sexual orientation (rather than intentionally choose it), for instance, occurs through a self-observational genital-arousal response to attractive men and women. Among men, heterosexual men show an erectile response to attractive women but not to attractive men, while gay men show an erectile response to attractive men but not to attractive women. Men's genital response to same and opposite sex individuals is therefore one reliable way in which they come to learn about their sexual orientation. Among women, however, heterosexual, bisexual, and lesbian women do not show such a discriminating pattern of association between genital and subjective arousal when looking at attractive men and attractive women.

Evolutionary Basis of Sexual Motivation

Sexual motivation and behavior have an obvious evolutionary function and basis (reproduction and the survival of the species). In an evolutionary analysis, men and women are hypothesized to have evolved distinct psychological mechanisms that underlie their sexual motivations and mating strategies (Buss & Schmitt, 1993). Compared to women, men have shorter-term sexual motivations, impose less stringent standards, value sexual accessibility cues such as youth, and value chastity in mates. Compared to men, women value signs of a man's resources (spends money, gives gifts, lives an extravagant lifestyle), social status and ambition, and promising career potential (Buss & Schmitt, 1993).

Evolutionary psychologists start with the assumptions that sexual behavior is strongly constrained by genes and that genes determine one's mating strategies at least as much as (and often more so) does rational thought. Further, genes keep the evolutionary message simple: men want young, attractive mates; women want powerful, high-status mates.[5] Men's and women's different mate-selection preferences appear in Table 4.2 (Sprecher, Sullivan, & Hatfield, 1994). The data confirm that, essentially, men find physical attrac-

---

[5]Some differences emerge when examining the preference of homosexuals (Bailey et al., 1994), as homosexual (like heterosexual) males rate the physical attractiveness of their partners as very important but, unlike heterosexual males, they do not show a strong preference for younger partners and are not as prone to sexual jealousy.

Table 4.2   Gender Differences in Mate Preferences

Variable	Men	Women	Gender Difference?
Physical Appearance			
Is good-looking	3.59	2.58	Yes, greater preference for men
Age			
Is younger than me by 5 years	4.54	2.80	Yes, greater preference for men
Is older than me by 5 years	4.15	5.29	Yes, greater preference for women
Earning Potential			
Holds a steady job	4.27	5.38	Yes, greater preference for women
Earns more than me	5.19	5.93	Yes, greater preference for women
Has more education than me	5.22	5.82	Yes, greater preference for women
Other Variables			
Has been married before	3.35	3.44	No significant gender difference
Has children	2.84	3.11	Yes, greater preference for women
Is of a different religion than me	4.24	4.31	No significant gender difference
Is of a different race than me	3.08	2.84	Yes, greater preference for men

Note. The possible range for each score was 1 (not at all) to 7 (very willing to marry someone who. . .).

Source: From "Mate Selection Preferences: Gender Differences Examined in a National Sample," by S. Sprecher, Q. Sullivan, and E. Hatfield, 1994, *Journal of Personality and Social Psychology, 66,* pp. 1074–1080. Copyright 1994 by the American Psychological Association. Adapted with permission.

tiveness and youth important in selecting women partners, whereas women find earning potential important in selecting men partners. These data come from asking thousands of unmarried 19- to 35-year-old African-American (36%) and white (64%) men and women the following question: "How willing would you be to marry someone who . . . ," and then from asking each participant to respond on a scale ranging from 1 (not at all willing) to 7 (very willing). The table's right-hand column summarizes verbally where gender differences do and do not exist.

To appreciate men's and women's different mating strategies, open the local newspaper (or online dating service website) to view the personal ads (Baize & Schroeder, 1995; Harrison & Saeed, 1997; Wiederman, 1993). Men look for something akin to a trophy wife/mate. In turn, the more attractive the women is, the more she demands from a potential mate in terms of status and wealth. In turn, the higher the man's social status and wealth, the more he expects in terms of a woman's looks.

Although these conclusions are blatantly and undeniably sexist, they nonetheless represent the expressed preferences of men and women. Such preferences might not be consistent with cultural aspirations, but they are consistent with evolutionary aspirations. This sexist mating strategy hypothesis might be limited, however, only to some, not to all, people. It seems that "likes attract," as women who think a lot about their appearance do strongly prefer men of high status, just as do men who think a lot about their wealth and status are very picky about a woman's youth and looks (Buston & Emlen, 2003). However, when men and women value in themselves factors other than status and attractiveness (e.g., family commitment, sexual fidelity), then they prefer mates with these characteristics more than mates with high status or attractiveness.

People also have multiple mating strategies, as they consider first the "necessities" and then the "luxuries" in mate preferences (Li, Bailey, Kenrick, & Linsenmeier, 2002). At the "must have" necessities level, men value physical attractiveness and women value status and resources. As they consider possible mates, men really want to know first that a women is at least average in physical attractiveness and women want to know first that a man is at least average in social status. Both sexes also rate intelligence and kindness as necessities in their possible mates. If the potential mate passes the so-called test at the necessities level, then men and women begin to consider luxuries like a sense of humor, liveliness, creativity, and an exciting personality. The conclusion of the matter is that men and women possess mating budgets (men have some level of status to spend, women have some level of attractiveness to spend) and these mating budgets are first spent on securing the minimal necessities—must be at least average on intelligence, kindness, and, depending on sex, status or attractiveness), next spent on acquiring a sufficient level of these necessities, and finally spent on luxuries that might make for more interesting interactions but which hold little reproductive value (Kenrick, Groth, Trost, & Sadalla, 1993).

FAILURES TO SELF-REGULATE PHYSIOLOGICAL NEEDS

Trying to exert conscious mental control over our physiological needs often does more harm than good. Still, we try.

People try to control their appetites—their hunger, weight, drinking of alcohol and coffee, sexual impulses, chronic back pain, and the like. Such appetites can at times overwhelm us, and in this experience of being overwhelmed, we look for ways to override our physiological needs in favor of mental control. When mental states regulate physiological needs, self-regulation occurs. But when biological urges overwhelm mental control, self-regulation failure occurs (Baumeister, Heatherton, & Tice, 1994).

People fail at self-regulation for three primary reasons (Baumeister, Heatherton, & Tice, 1994). First, people routinely underestimate how powerful a motivational force biological urges can be when they are not currently experiencing them (Loewenstein, 1996). That is, when we are not feeling hungry, we tend to forget how motivated to eat we can be when hungry.

Second, people can lack standards, or they have inconsistent, conflicting, unrealistic, or inappropriate standards (Karoly, 1993). For instance, many people have extreme (unrealistic) standards for thinness or conflicting standards with the body type they are born with versus the body type they would like to have (Brownell, 1991). Fragile (i.e., unrealistic) mental controls are easily overwhelmed by natural biological forces.

Finally, people fail at self-regulation because they fail to monitor what they are doing as they become distracted, preoccupied, overwhelmed, or intoxicated (Kirschenbaum, 1987). Alcohol, for instance, reduces self-awareness and self-monitoring, and intoxicated people become more likely to do things outside of their normal mental control (Hull, 1981). Thus, even when people have realistic and appropriate standards to cognitively regulate their physiological needs, they are still nonetheless highly prone to being overwhelmed by pent-up biological forces once they are distracted away from attending to these standards.

What all these mishaps have in common is two things: (1) underappreciating how potent and attention-getting physiologically- and biologically-based motives can be and

(2) losing control over one's attention. Self-regulation is often a competition between biological forces and cognitive controls. Mental control that focuses on realistic standards, long-term goals, and on monitoring what one is doing generally leads to self-regulation success (Baumeister, Heatherton, & Tice, 1994). But self-regulation via mental control requires diligent effort and is therefore a vulnerable and unreliable strategy.

SUMMARY

Thirst, hunger, and sex are physiological needs. The anchor for the chapter was Hull's biologically based drive theory (Figure 4.2). According to drive theory, physiological deprivations and deficits give rise to bodily need states, which in turn give rise to a psychological drive, which motivates the consummatory behavior that results in drive reduction. Then, time goes by, the physiological deprivations recur, and the cyclical process repeats itself. In outlining the regulatory process for thirst, hunger, and sex, the chapter introduced seven fundamental processes: physiological need, psychological drive, homeostasis, negative feedback, multiple inputs and outputs, negative feedback, intra-organismic influences, and extra-organismic influences.

Thirst is the consciously experienced motivational state that readies the person to perform behaviors necessary to replenish a water deficit. Its activation and satiety is rather straightforward, biologically-speaking. Water depletion inside (intracellular thirst) and outside (extracellular thirst) the cells activate thirst. Water restoration satiates thirst, especially when injested water hydrates the cells. Drinking behavior (that is not necessarily related to thirst) is influenced further by extra-organismic variables, such as water availability, sweet taste, addictions to alcohol and caffeine, and cultural prescriptions such as "drink eight glasses of water per day."

Hunger and eating involve a complex regulatory system of both short-term (glucostatic hypothesis) and long-term (lipostatic hypothesis, including set-point theory) regulation. According to the glucostatic hypothesis, glucose deficiency stimulates eating by activating the lateral hypothalamus, whereas glucose excess inhibits eating by activating the ventromedial hypothalamus. According to the lipostatic hypothesis, shrunken fat cells initiate hunger, whereas normal or larger fat cells inhibit it. Eating behavior (that is not necessarily related to hunger) is influenced further by environmental incentives such as the sight, smell, and taste of food, the presence of others, and by situational pressures such as a group norm. These environmental factors sometimes interfere with and compete against physiological factors. Dieting, for instance, represents a person's attempt to supplant involuntary physiological controls for eating with voluntary cognitive controls. Such a cognitively regulated eating style has implications associated with bingeing, restraint release, weight gain, and obesity.

Sexual motivation rises and falls in response to a host of factors, including hormones, external stimulation, external cues (facial metrics), cognitive scripts, sexual schemas, and evolutionary presses. Despite these many factors, sexual motivation in the human male is relatively straightforward as desire reflects physiological forces such as a linear triphasic sexual response cycle (desire-arousal-orgasm), a close correlation between erectile response and psychologically felt desire, relatively homogenous sexual scripts, and stereotypical mating preferences and strategies. Sexual motivation in women is more complex, as women's sexual response cycle is often not linear, revolves around emotional intimacy needs, the correlation between genital response and psychological desire is low, and sexual scripts and sexual schemas are heterogeneous. Research on the determinants of sexual orientation points to the importance of genetics, prenatal developmental influences, and the idea that people discover and become aware of their sexual orientation rather than deliberately choose it.

Trying to exert conscious mental control over our physiological needs often does more harm than good. People fail to self-regulate their bodily appetites for three primary reasons—namely, they (1) underestimate how powerful a motivational force biological urges can be when they are not currently experiencing them, (2) lack standards or have inconsistent standards, and (3) fail to monitor what they are doing, as they become distracted from their cognitive regulation and default to their pent-up physiological needs.

READINGS FOR FURTHER STUDY

Thirst

TOATES, F. M. (1979). Homeostasis and drinking. *Behavior and Brain Sciences, 2*, 95–102.

VALTIN, H. (2002). "Drink at least eight glasses of water a day." Really? Is there scientific evidence for "8 × 8"? *American Journal of Physiology: Regulatory, Integrative, and Comparative Physiology, 283*, R993–R1004.

Hunger

CRANDALL, C. S. (1988). Social cognition of binge eating. *Journal of Personality and Social Psychology, 55*, 588–598.

KEESEY, R. E., & POWLEY, T. L. (1975). Hypothalamic regulation of body weight. *American Scientist, 63*, 558–565.

POLIVY, J., & HERMAN, C. P. (1985). Dieting and binging. *American Psychologist, 40*, 193–201.

SPIEGELMAN, B. M., & FLIER, J. S. (2001). Obesity and the regulation of energy balance. *Cell, 104*, 531–543.

Sex

BASSON, R. (2001). Human sex-response cycles. *Journal of Sex and Marital Therapy, 27*, 33–43.

CUNNINGHAM, M. R. (1986). Measuring the physical in physical attractiveness: Quasi-experiments on the sociobiology of female facial beauty. *Journal of Personality and Social Psychology, 50*, 925–935.

HARRISON, A. A., & SAEED, L. (1977). Let's make a deal: An analysis of revelations and stipulations in lonely heart advertisements. *Journal of Personality and Social Psychology, 35*, 257–264.

Chapter 5

Psychological Needs

Imagine visiting a lake for the afternoon, a lake at a campground or state park for instance. As you lie on the shore soaking up the sun's rays, you notice a young girl playfully skipping stones across the water's surface. Before each toss, she studiously inspects piles of stones to find the flattest one. With stone in hand, she puts all her effort into the toss. Each time a rock skips according to plan, she smiles and her enthusiasm grows. Each dud brings a somber expression but also increased determination. At first, she tries only to make each stone skip once off the water's surface. After some practice and several big smiles, she moves on to develop three or four finely-tuned techniques—one very long skip, short skips with many hops, and so forth. And she pretends to throw others, the big and heavy stones, like hand grenades, because these splashes look like explosions in her imagination. Despite her family's fish fry currently going on, her rock skipping continues.

The child is at play. For her, an urban child, the lake is a relatively novel setting. It allows her to use her imagination in a way that is different from every day. As she plays, she feels excited and entertained. Each rock and each toss provides her with a different, surprising result. Each attempt challenges her skills and gives her an experience that is somehow deeply satisfying. In tossing rocks and in using her imagination, she feels competent, she feels free, she learns, and she develops skills. Such behavior is more than frivolous play. It is integral to healthy development. The lake setting provides the child with an opportunity to learn to enjoy an activity solely for the experience and the fun it provides.

Like play, settings like sports, hobbies, school, work, and travel also offer opportunities for people to engage in activities capable of involving and satisfying their psychological needs. This chapter examines the motivational significance of three psychological needs: autonomy, competence, and relatedness. The theme throughout the chapter is that when people find themselves in environments that support and nurture their psychological needs, then positive emotions, optimal experience, and healthy development follow.

PSYCHOLOGICAL NEEDS

People and animals are inherently active. As children, we push and pull things; we shake, throw, carry, explore, and ask questions about the objects that surround us. As adults, we continue to explore and to play. We play games, solve mysteries, read books, visit friends, undertake challenges, pursue hobbies, surf the Web, build new things, and do any number of activities because these activities are inherently interesting and enjoyable things to do.

When an activity involves our psychological needs, we feel interest. When an activity satisfies our psychological needs, we feel enjoyment. So, we feel and are aware of our sense of interest and enjoyment (i.e., "I play tennis because it's fun"), but the underlying motivational cause of engaging our environment is to involve and satisfy our psychological needs. Playing games, solving mysteries, and undertaking challenges are interesting and enjoyable things to do precisely because they provide an arena for involving and satisfying our psychological needs.

Psychological needs are an important addition to our analysis of motivated behavior. As discussed in the last chapter, physiological needs for water, food, and so on emanate from biological deficits. This sort of motivated behavior is essentially reactive, in the sense that its purpose is to react against and alleviate a deficit bodily condition. Psychological needs are of a qualitatively different nature. Energy generated by psychological needs is proactive. Psychological needs promote a willingness to seek out and to engage in an environment that we expect will be able to nurture our psychological needs.

Need Structure

Types of needs exist. These types can be organized within a need structure, as illustrated in Figure 5.1. Physiological needs (thirst, hunger, sex) are inherent within the workings of biological systems (Chapter 4). Psychological needs (autonomy, competence, relatedness) are inherent within the strivings of human nature and healthy development (this chapter). Social needs (achievement, intimacy, power) are internalized or learned from our emotional and socialization histories (Chapter 7).

The distinction between physiological and psychological needs is a relatively easy one to make, but the distinction between psychological and social needs is more subtle. Psychological needs (autonomy, competence, relatedness) exist within human nature and are, therefore, inherent in everyone. Three such organismic needs are autonomy, competence, and relatedness. Social needs arise from our unique personal experiences and thus vary considerably from one person to the next. The social needs we acquire (achievement, affiliation, intimacy, power) depend on the type of social environment in which we were raised, currently live in, and attempt to create for our future self.

Organismic Approach to Motivation

The three psychological needs reviewed in this chapter are sometimes referred to as organismic psychological needs (Deci & Ryan, 1991). Organismic theories get their name from the term *organism*, an entity that is alive and in active exchange with its environment (Blasi, 1976). The survival of any organism depends on its environment because the environment offers resources like food, water, social support, and intellectual stimulation. And all organisms are equipped to initiate and engage in exchanges with their environment as all organisms possess skills and the motivation to exercise and develop those skills. Organismic theories of motivation acknowledge that environments constantly change and,

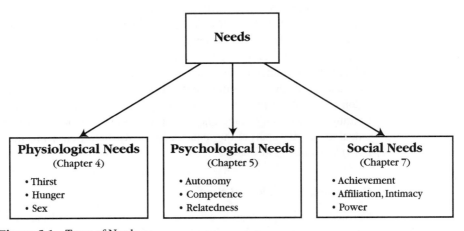

Figure 5.1 Types of Needs

hence, organisms need flexibility to adjust to and accommodate those changes. Organisms also need environmental resources to grow and to actualize their latent potentials. To adapt, organisms must learn to substitute a new response for a previously successful but now outdated one (because the environment changed), and organisms must grow and develop so that new skills, new interests, and new ways of adjusting emerge. The whole focus concerns how organisms initiate interactions with the environment and how organisms adapt, change, and grow as a function of those environmental transactions.

The opposite of an organismic approach is a mechanistic one. In mechanistic theories, the environment acts on the person and the person reacts. For instance, environments produce heat, and the person responds in a predictable and automatic way—by sweating. Sweating leads to water loss, and when the biological systems detect the loss, thirst arises rather automatically (i.e., mechanistically). Chapter 4 discussed these biologically rooted needs. Subsequent chapters will discuss other relatively mechanistic motives (e.g., reinforcement in Chapter 6; the TOTE unit in Chapter 8). In each of these approaches, you will see that the person and the environment relate in a one-way relationship such that the environment acts and the person reacts.

Person-Environment Dialectic

Organismic theories reject such one-way portrayals (environment → person) and instead emphasize the person-environment dialectic (Deci & Ryan, 1991; Reeve, Deci, & Ryan, 2003). In dialectic, the environment acts on the person and the person acts on the environment. Both the person and the environment constantly change.

The person acts on the environment out of an intrinsic motivation to seek out and affect changes in it, and the environment places demands on the person to adjust and accommodate to it (Deci & Ryan, 1985a). The outcome of the person-environment dialectic is an ever-changing synthesis in which the person's needs are fulfilled by the environment, and the environment produces in the person new forms of motivation. The person-environment dialectic appears in Figure 5.2.

The organismic approach to motivation begins with the assumption that the organism is inherently active. Psychological needs, interests, and integrated values are the source of that inherent activity (Deci & Ryan, 1985a). This inherent activity appears as the upper arrow in Figure 5.2. The person-environment dialectic also assumes that environmental events affect the individual, as environments offer challenges, feedback, opportunities to choose, interesting activities, and supportive relationships that sometimes nurture and involve, but other times neglect and frustrate, the individual's psychological needs, interests, and preferences. Environments also offer prescriptions ("do this"), proscriptions ("don't do that"), aspirations to well-being (the "American dream"), as well as goals and priorities ("You should want this; you need to value that"), and various roles for the individual to accept as part of the socialized self (teacher, spouse, receptionist) that affect the individual's inner motivational resources for the better and for the worse.

Organismic Psychological Needs

Consider why people want to exercise and develop their skills, such as walking, reading, swimming, driving, making friends, and hundreds of other such competencies. In part,

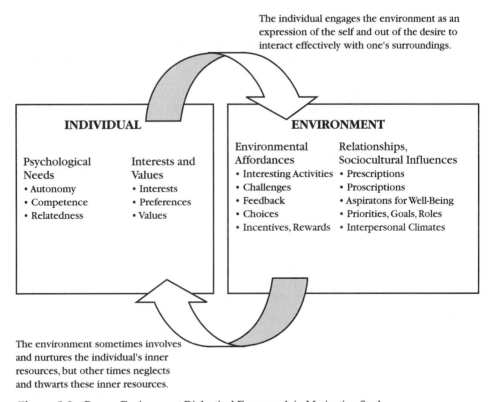

Figure 5.2   Person-Environment Dialectical Framework in Motivation Study

these competencies emerge maturationally, but mostly they emerge through opportunities and affordances from the environment (Gibson, 1988; White, 1959). Organismic psychological needs provide the motivation that supports such initiative and learning (Deci & Ryan, 1985a; White, 1959). As illustrated in the chapter's opening with the young girl skipping rocks, children best illustrate how organismic psychological needs motivate the exercise and development of skills. Endlessly, young children motor about from one place to another without any apparent motivation other than just wanting do something better than they did it the time before (because of the need for competence). Further, children desire to experiment with the world on their own terms as they want to decide for themselves what to do, how to do it, when to do it, and whether to do it at all (because of the need for autonomy). And which activities, skills, and values children regard as important depends on the attitudes, values, and emotional climates offered to them by the important people in their lives (because of the need for relatedness).

Collectively, the organismic psychological needs of autonomy, competence, and relatedness provide people with a natural motivation for learning, growing, and developing. Whether they experience such learning, growing, and healthy development depends on whether the environments support or frustrate the expression of their needs for autonomy, competence, and relatedness.

AUTONOMY

When deciding what to do, we desire choice and decision-making flexibility. We want to be the one who decides what to do, when to do it, how to do it, when to stop doing it, and whether or not to do it at all. We want to decide for ourselves how to spend our time. We want to be the one who determines our actions, rather than have some other person or some environmental constraint force us into a particular course of action. We want our behavior connected to, rather than divorced from, our interests, preferences, wants, and desires. And we want our behavior to arise out of and express our preferences and desires. We want the freedom to construct our own goals, we want the freedom to decide what is important and what is and is not worth our time. In other words, we have a need for autonomy.

Behavior is autonomous (or self-determined) when our interests, preferences, and wants guide our decision-making process to engage or not to engage in a particular activity. We are not self-determining (i.e., our behaviors are determined by others) when some outside force pressures us to think, feel, or behave in particular ways (Deci, 1980). Formally, autonomy (self-determination) is the need to experience choice in the initiation and regulation of behavior, and it reflects the desire to have one's choices rather than environmental events determine one's actions (Deci & Ryan, 1985a).

Three experiential qualities work together to define the subjective experience of autonomy: perceived locus of causality, perceived choice, and volition, as shown in Figure 5.3.

Perceived locus of causality (PLOC) refers to an individual's understanding of the causal source of his motivated actions (Heider, 1958). PLOC exists within a bipolar continuum that ranges from internal to external. This continuum reflects the individual's perception that her behavior is initiated by a personal (internal PLOC) or by an environmental (external PLOC) source. For instance, why read a book? If the reason why you read is some motivational agent within the self (interest, value), then you read out of an internal PLOC. However, if the reason why you read is some motivational agent in the environment (upcoming test, the boss), then you read out of an external PLOC. Some prefer to use the terms "origins" and "pawns" to communicate the distinction between a person whose behavior emanates from an internal versus an external PLOC (deCharms, 1976, 1984; Ryan & Grolnick, 1986). Origins "originate" their own intentional behavior.

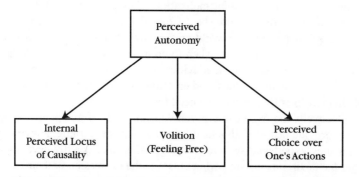

Figure 5.3   Three Subjective Qualities within the Experience of Autonomy

"Pawn," a metaphor taken from the game of chess, captures the experience we feel when powerful people push us around in much the same way that employers boss around their workers, military sergeants command privates, and parents order their children to behave.

Volition is an unpressured willingness to engage in an activity (Deci, Ryan, & Williams, 1995). It centers on how free versus coerced people feel while they are doing what they want to do (e.g., playing, studying, talking), and also how free versus coerced they feel while avoiding what they do not want to do (e.g., not smoking, not eating, not apologizing). Volition is high when the person engages in an activity and feels free and feels that one's actions are endorsed fully by the self—saying, essentially, "I freely want to do this" (Deci & Ryan, 1987; Ryan, Koestner, & Deci, 1991). The opposite of volition and feeling free is feeling pressured and coerced into action. In addition to being pressured by the environment, people sometimes create within themselves a pressure-fueled motivation to force themselves into action—saying, essentially, "I *have* to do this" (Ryan, 1982; Ryan, Mims, & Koestner, 1983; Ryan, Koestner, & Deci, 1991).

Perceived choice refers to that sense of choice we experience when we find ourselves in environments that provide us with decision-making flexibility that affords us with many opportunities to choose. The opposite of perceived choice is that sense of obligation we experience when we find ourselves in environments that rigidly and inflexibly push us toward a prescribed course of action. For instance, when children are given choices within their schoolwork (Cordova & Lepper, 1996), when nursing-home residents are given decision-making power in how to schedule their daily activities (Langer & Rodin, 1976), and when patients communicate with flexible (not authoritarian) doctors (Williams & Deci, 1996), the children, residents, and patients all feel that their behavior flows from a sense of choice. But not all choices are the same and not all choices promote autonomy (Reeve, Nix, & Hamm, 2003). A choice among options offered by others fails to tap into and involve the need for autonomy (e.g., "Do you want to listen to country music or to classical music?"; Overskeid & Svartdal, 1996; Schraw, Flowerday, & Reisetter, 1998). Instead, only when people have a choice over their actions (e.g., "Do you even want to listen to music?") do they experience a sense of autonomy (Cordova & Lepper, 1996; Reeve et al., 2003).

Supporting Autonomy

Environments, external events, social contexts, and relationships all vary in how much versus how little they support a person's need for autonomy. Some environments involve and nuture our need for autonomy, while others neglect and frustrate this need (recall Fig. 5.2). For instance, when the environment imposes a deadline, it interferes with autonomy, but when it provides opportunities for self-direction, it supports autonomy. Relationships, too, can sometimes support and other times thwart our need for autonomy, as when a coach bosses athletes around (undermining their autonomy) or when a teacher listens carefully to her students and uses that information to give students opportunities to work in their own way and at their own pace (supporting their autonomy). Social contexts and cultures in general also vary in how much versus how little they support people's autonomy, as is illustrated when the military commands its personnel, the church decides what parishioners should and should not do, or the day care goes out of its way to support children's interests and initiatives. When environments, relationships, social contexts, and cultures successfully involve and satisfy people's need for autonomy, these environments are referred to as autonomy-supportive; when environments, relationships, social contexts, and cultures neglect, frustrate, and interfere with people's need for autonomy, these environments are referred to as controlling (Deci & Ryan, 1987).

Autonomy-supportive environments encourage people to set their own goals, direct their own behavior, choose their own ways of solving problems, and basically pursue their own interests and values. In doing these things, autonomy support catalyzes the person's intrinsic motivation, curiosity, and desire for challenge (Deci, Nezlak, & Sheinman, 1981; Ryan & Grolnick, 1986). What autonomy-supportive environments are not, however, are environments that are permissive, neglecting, indulging, or laissez-faire (Ryan, 1993). Rather, when people work to create autonomy-supportive environments for others (for their children, students, workers, athletes, etc.), they work hard to identify and support the others' interests, needs, and strivings.

The opposite of an autonomy-supportive environment is a controlling one. Controlling environments essentially ignore people's need for autonomy and instead pressure them to comply with a pre-arranged and externally-prescribed way of thinking, feeling, or behaving. So what gets supported in a controlling environment is not the person's autonomy but an agenda that is external to that person, such as what the teacher wants the student to do, what the manager wants the worker to do, or what the coach makes the athlete do while practicing her sport. Instead of supporting people's autonomy, controlling environments control people's behavior.

When people create autonomy-supportive or controlling environments for others, they adopt a particular motivating style. As shown in Box 5, a person's motivating style toward others can be understood along a continuum that ranges from highly controlling to highly autonomy supportive (Deci, Schwartz, Sheinman, & Ryan, 1981; Reeve et al., 1999). A controlling style generally motivates others by first communicating an agenda in terms of what the other person should think, feel, and do and then by offering extrinsic motivators and pressuring language to shape others toward that agenda. In contrast, an autonomy-supportive style motivates by identifying and supporting the other person's interests, preferences, and autonomous self-regulation. Motivating style is an important construct because people benefit when others support their autonomy rather than control their behavior in that, when they have their autonomy supported, people experience greater intrinsic motivation, perceived competence, mastery motivation, and positive emotion, and they also display greater learning, performance, and persistence (Deci & Ryan, 1987; Grolnick & Ryan, 1987; Patrick, Skinner, & Connell, 1993; Reeve, 2002; Vallerand, Fortier, & Guay, 1997).

Just how people go about creating and establishing autonomy-supportive environments for others involves four essential ways of relating to others (see Deci, 1995; Deci, Connell, & Ryan, 1989; Deci et al., 1994; Koestner et al., 1984; McCombs & Pope, 1994; Reeve, 1996; Reeve, Deci, & Ryan, 2003), as discussed below.

Nurtures Inner Motivational Resources

People with autonomy-supportive motivating styles motivate others by nurturing their inner motivational resources. That is, when they seek to encourage initiative in others, they do so by identifying their interests, preferences, and competencies. Once identified, they find ways

BOX 5   *Your Motivating Style*

Question: Why is this information important?

Answer: To gain insight on your own motivating style toward others.

How do you try to motivate others? What do you say? What would you do? What do teachers do? What do parents do? What do work supervisors do? What do athletic coaches and personal trainers do? What do psychologists, clergy, military sergeants, and authors of self-help books do? People vary widely in the motivating style they rely on (Deci, Schwartz, Scheinman, & Ryan, 1981), but consider your own style. The following is one of the vignettes from the *Problems in Schools Questionnaire*, a questionnaire used to assess interpersonal motivating style (Deci, Schwartz, Scheinman, & Ryan, 1981; Flink, Boggiano, & Barrett, 1990; Reeve, Bolt, & Cai, 1999). Which of the four ways of solving Jim's problem with listlessness in elementary school makes sense to you, and which ways do not?

Jim is an average student who has been working at grade level. During the past 2 weeks, he has appeared listless and has not been participating during reading group. The work he does is accurate, but he has not been completing assignments. A phone conversation with his mother revealed no useful information. The most appropriate thing for Jim's teacher to do is:

1. Impress upon him the importance of finishing his assignments since he needs to learn this material for his own good.

2. Make him stay after school until the day's assignments are done.

3. Let him know that he doesn't have to finish all of his work now and see if she can help him work out the cause of the listlessness.

4. Patiently support and value the participation and work he does show.

The first two options express a preference to endorse a relatively controlling style, while the last two options express a preference to endorse a relatively autonomy-supportive style.

To get a more concrete sense of what behaviors you rely on when motivating others, try the following exercise. Take on the role of a tutor. Try to teach someone how to drive a car, play the piano, paint, wash clothes, say basic phrases in a foreign language, or just about anything. The question soon becomes just what to say and what to do to motivate the other person. How do you encourage initiative in the other person? How do you solve the motivational problems the other person shows? People with a controlling style generally take charge and ask the other person to follow their agenda. People with an autonomy-supportive style generally listen carefully to what the other person's interests and needs are and then create ways to express those inner motivational resources within the learning activity.

Another exercise would be to watch from a distance as an expert provides instructions to a novice. For instance, watch a golf professional try to teach someone how to play golf or watch a school psychologist help an aggressive child develop her social skills. How specifically do they go about the task of energizing and directing the behavior of the other—what do they say and do?

In thinking about which of the four alternatives you favored on the *Problems in Schools* questionnaire and in observing yourself as you try to motivate another person, you can begin to learn about your own motivating style. Hopefully, the guidelines in the present chapter will enable you to expand your own motivating style to include some autonomy-supportive strategies.

to allow others to behave in ways that express those interests, preferences, and competencies. In a school setting, for instance, an autonomy-supportive teacher will coordinate the day's lesson plan with students' expressed interests, preferences, sense of challenge, and competencies. A controlling teacher, in contrast, will forgo students' inner motivational resources and instead rely on extrinsic motivators like incentives, consequences, directives, assignments, and deadlines to gain the students' pawn-like compliance.

Relies on Informational Language

At times the people we try to motivate are listless, other times they perform poorly, and at other times, they behave inappropriately. People with an autonomy-supportive motivating style treat listlessness, poor performance, and inappropriate behavior as motivational problems to be solved rather than as targets for criticism (Deci, Connell, & Ryan, 1989). Instead of pressuring people into doing what they should or have to do, an autonomy-supportive communication style addresses the problem with flexible and informational language. For example, a coach might say to her athlete, "I've noticed that your scoring average has declined lately; do you know why this might be?" In contrast, people with a controlling style use a pressuring, rigid, and "no nonsense" communication style that says that the other person should, must, ought to, or has to do a certain thing (e.g., "Johnny, you should try harder," or "You must finish the project before the end of the day."). Informational language helps others diagnose the cause of their listlessness, poor performance, or misbehavior, and it communicates feedback to identify points of improvement and progress (e.g., "I've noticed a new liveliness in your writing style lately.") while it resists critical, judgmental, negative feedback (e.g., "Your workmanship is sloppy").

Promotes Valuing

In trying to motivate others, we sometimes ask them to engage in tasks that are relatively uninteresting things to do. For instance, parents ask children to clean their rooms, teachers ask students to follow the rules, coaches ask their athletes to run laps around the track, and doctors ask their patients to take their medicine in a timely fashion. To motivate others on uninteresting tasks, people with an autonomy-supportive style communicate the value, worth, meaning, utility, or importance of engaging in these sorts of behaviors, as in "It is important that you follow the rules because we need to respect the rights of everyone in the class. By following the rules, you are respecting others" (Koestner et al., 1984). Promoting valuing means using a "because" phrase to explain why the uninteresting activity is worth the other's time and effort. People with controlling motivating styles, however, do not take the time to explain the use or importance in engaging in these sorts of activities, saying things like, "Just get it done" or "Do it because I told you to do it." The logic in communicating a rationale is that the person who hears it is more likely to internalize and voluntarily accept the externally-imposed rules, constraints, and limits. Once internalized ("Yeah, flossing is a pain, but it keeps plaque off my teeth and that's a worthwhile thing to do."), people put forth voluntary effort in even uninteresting (but important) activities (Reeve et al., 2002).

Acknowledges and Accepts Negative Affect

Sometimes the people we try to motivate show little motivation and express negative affect about having to engage in tasks that they do not find to be interesting. They sometimes show "attitude" and other times display a resistance to having to do things like cleaning their rooms, following rules, running laps, and being nice. People with an autonomy-supportive style listen carefully to these expressions of negative affect and resistance and accept them as valid reactions to being asked to engage in an activity that seems, to them, uninteresting and not worthwhile. Essentially, autonomy-supportive individuals say "okay," and then work collaboratively with the other person to solve the underlying cause of the negative affect and resistance. People with controlling styles make it clear that such expressions of negative affect and resistance are unacceptable, saying things like, "My way or the highway" and "Shape up or ship out, bucko." Instead of working collaboratively with the unmotivated others, those with controlling motivating styles try to change the other person's negative affect into something more acceptable, saying "Wipe that smirk off your face, and do what I told you to do." That is, people with autonomy-supportive styles try to solve the motivational problem and they use the other's expressions of negative affect to help them do so, while people with controlling motivating styles try to overwhelm the other's negative affect as they seek compliance and obedience (rather than motivation).

Moment-to-Moment Autonomy Support

The four characteristics listed above illustrate a general autonomy-supportive motivating style. In addition, when people create autonomy-supportive environments for others, they typically do so by exhibiting characteristic moment-to-moment behaviors. Consider, for instance, specific interactions such as teachers motivating students during a particular lesson or a doctor trying to motivate a patient during a 10-minute office visit. Several studies have used a teacher-student paradigm in which they first assessed whether the teacher has an autonomy-supportive or controlling style and then asked the teacher to teach the student during an instructional episode. The researchers observed how each teacher tried to motivate the student. As shown in Table 5.1, the left-hand column shows what autonomy-supportive teachers characteristically say and do when they try to motivate students, while the right-hand column shows what controlling teachers characteristically say and do when they try to motivate students (based on Deci et al., 1982; Reeve & Jang, 2003; Reeve, Bolt, & Cai, 1999).

When taken as a whole, the behaviors listed above reveal a motivating style associated with promoting high autonomy in others: listen carefully, share learning materials,

Table 5.1   What Autonomy-Supportive and Controlling People Say and Do to Motivate Others

What Autonomy-Supportive People Say and Do	What Controlling People Say and Do
* Listen carefully	* Hold/Hog learning materials
* Allow others time to talk	* Show correct answers
* Provide rationale	* Tell correct answers
* Encourage effort	* Speak directives, commands
* Praise progress, mastery	* Should, must, have to statements
* Ask others what they want to do	* Ask controlling questions
* Respond to questions	* Seem demanding
* Acknowledge the others' perspective	

create opportunities for others to talk and to work in their own ways, communicate rationale for uninteresting endeavors, ask others what they want to do, respond to questions, offer hints, encourage effort, praise progress and improvement, and acknowledge the other person's perspective.

Benefits of an Autonomy-Supportive Motivating Style

The motivating styles teachers, parents, coaches, therapists, doctors, and workplace managers use have strong implications for the subsequent development, engagement, high-quality learning, optimal functioning, performance, and well-being of the students, children, athletes, clients, patients, and employees they try to motivate. This list in the two columns below details the positive outcomes people experience when others support their autonomy rather than control their behavior. Though the outcomes are different, the reason why the outcomes are more positive with autonomy-supportive, rather than controlling, styles is the same—namely, because autonomy-supportive motivators involve and nurture the other's need for autonomy while controlling motivators neglect and frustrate the other's need for autonomy. In the list below, the positive outcome appears on the left-hand side while an illustrative reference appears on the right-hand side (so the interested reader can pursue for additional information).

Positive Outcome Experienced from an Autonomy-Supportive Motivating Style	Supportive Reference(s)
Developmental Gains	
Greater perceived competence	Ryan & Grolnick, 1986
Higher self-esteem	Deci et al., 1981
Enhanced sense of self-worth	Ryan & Grolnick, 1986
Engagement Gains	
Greater engagement	Reeve et al., 2002
Positive emotional tone	Patrick, Skinner, & Connell, 1993; Ryan & Connell, 1989
Stronger perceptions of control	Boggiano & Barrett, 1985
Preference for optimal challenge	Shapira, 1976; Boggiano, Main, & Katz, 1988
Pleasure from optimal challenge	Harter, 1974, 1978b
High-Quality Learning	
Greater flexibility in thinking	McGraw & McCullers, 1979
Enhanced conceptual learning	Benware & Deci, 1984; Boggiano et al., 1993
More active information processing	Grolnick & Ryan, 1987
Greater creativity	Amabile, 1985; Koestner et al., 1984
Optimal Functioning	
Maintenance of behavioral change	Williams et al., 1996
Long-term retention	Ryan et al., 1997

| Lower attrition/dropout; higher retention | Hardre & Reeve, 2003; Vallerand, Fortier, & Guay, 1997 |

Performance Gains

| Improved performance | Miserandino, 1996; Boggiano et al., 1993 |
| Higher achievement | Flink, Boggiano, & Barrett, 1990; Flink et al., 1992 |

The positive outcomes that arise in response to having one's autonomy supported occur because autonomy support, and autonomy-supportive relationships in general, provide people with the "psychological nutriments" they need to satisfy their psychological needs (Ryan, 1995, p. 410). These experiences of psychological need satisfaction energize the person's inherent growth potentials introduced in Figure 5.2 in ways that promote psychological growth, intrinsic motivation, meaningful learning, and social development (Ryan & Deci, 2000a).

Two Illustrations

Consider one study whose purpose was to predict which high-school students would and would not drop out of school (Vallerand, Fortier, & Guay, 1997). Students reported the extent to which they felt autonomy support versus control from their parents, teachers, and

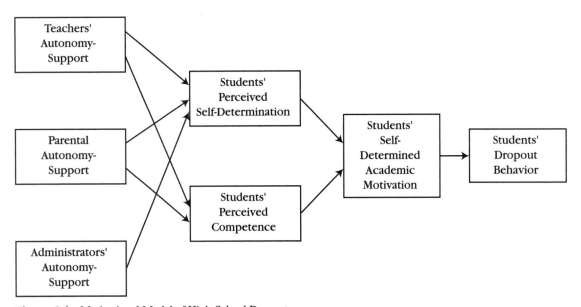

Figure 5.4   Motivational Model of High-School Dropouts
Source: Adapted from *Self-Determination and Persistence in a Real-Life Setting: Toward a Motivational Model of High School Dropout,* by R. J. Vallerand, M. S. Fortier, and F. Guay, 1997, *Journal of Personality and Social Psychology, 72,* 1161–1172. Copyright 1997 by American Psychological Association. Adapted with permission.

school administrators. How autonomy-supportive versus controlling a social world each high-school student lived in was then used to predict how much or how little perceived autonomy and perceived competence each student felt while in school. How self-determining (and how competent) the student felt toward school then predicted how the quality of their academic motivation (autonomous versus controlled) which predicted whether each student actually dropped out or not.

In a second study, researchers asked schoolchildren to paint while the teacher acted in either an autonomy-supportive or controlling way. In both conditions, teachers imposed a list of constraints (rules) children needed to following during the painting, including instructions to not mix the paints, to clean off the brushes before switching to a new color of paint, and to paint only on a particular piece of paper (Koestner et al., 1984). Some children painted under these conditions imposed on them by a controlling teacher. This teacher used controlling, pressuring language that told children to follow the rules. Other children painted under autonomy-supportive conditions. This teacher used informational language that communicated the rationale for each rule so the children could understand why the constraints were important and worth following. After all children painted, the researchers measured the quality of their motivation and scored their artwork on various dimensions, and these results appear in Table 5.2. Children who painted under autonomy-supportive conditions enjoyed the painting more, were more intrinsically motivated to paint (see "free choice behavior"), and produced artwork that was creative, technically good, and of high quality. What this finding shows is that when the social context supports people's need for autonomy, rather than frustrates this need, the quality of people's motivation and performance flourishes.

Table 5.2 Children's Motivational Benefits from Autonomy-Supportive (rather than Controlling) Rules

Dependent Measure		Rules Communicated in a Controlling Way	Rules Communicated in a Autonomy-Supportive Way
Enjoyment	M	4.87	5.57
	(SD)	(0.99)	(0.65)
Free choice behavior	M	107.7	257.1
	(SD)	(166.0)	(212.6)
Creativity	M	4.80	5.34
	(SD)	(1.16)	(1.17)
Technical Goodness	M	4.88	5.90
	(SD)	(0.87)	(1.28)
Quality	M	4.84	5.62
	(SD)	(0.68)	(1.06)

Notes. M = Mean, SD = Standard Deviation; Free choice = Intrinsically motivated behavior; All mean differences are significantly different, $p < .05$.

Source: Adapted from *Setting Limits on Children's Behavior: The Differential Effects of Controlling Versus Informational Styles on Intrinsic Motivation and Creativity,* by R. Koestner, R. M. Ryan, F. Bernieri, and K. Holt (1984). *Journal of Perosnality, 52,* 233–248.

COMPETENCE

Everyone wants and strives to become competent. Everyone desires to interact effectively with their surroundings, and this desire extends into all aspects of our lives—in school, at work, in relationships, and during recreation and sports. We all want to develop skills and improve our capacities, talents, and potential. When we find ourselves face-to-face with a challenge, we give the moment our full attention. When given the chance to grow our skills and talents, we all want to make progress. When we do so, we feel satisfied, even happy. In other words, we have a need for competence.

Competence is a psychological need that provides an inherent source of motivation for seeking out and putting forth the effort necessary to master optimal challenges. Optimal challenges are developmentally-appropriate challenges, such that only some aspects of school, work, or sports successfully test a person's skills at exactly that point that is most appropriate for that person's current level of skill or talent. When we engage in a task with a level of difficulty and complexity that is precisely right for our current skills, that is when we feel the strongest interest and the greatest involvement of the need for competence. Defined formally, competence is the need to be effective in interactions with the environment, and it reflects the desire to exercise one's capacities and skills and, in doing so, to seek out and master optimal challenges (Deci & Ryan, 1985a).

Involving Competence

The situations we find ourselves in can involve and satisfy our need for competence, or they can neglect and frustrate this need. The key environmental conditions that involves our need for competence are optimal challenge and optimal structure, and the key environmental condition that satisfies our need for competence is positive feedback.

Optimal Challenge and Flow

To determine the conditions that create enjoyment, Mihaly Csikszentmihalyi (1975, 1982, 1990) interviewed and studied hundreds of people he presumed knew what it felt like to have fun: rock climbers, dancers, chess champions, basketball players, surgeons, and others. Later, he studied more representative samples, including working professionals, high-school students, assembly-line workers, groups of the elderly, and people who generally sat at home and watched television. Irrespective of which sample he studied, Csikszentmihalyi found the essence of enjoyment could be traced to the "flow experience." Flow is such a pleasurable experience that the person often repeats the activity with the hope of experiencing flow again and again (Csikszentmihalyi & Nakamura, 1989).

Flow is a state of concentration that involves a holistic absorption in an activity. It occurs whenever a person uses his or her skills to overcome some challenge. The relationship between task challenge and personal skill appears in Figure 5.5. The figure identifies the emotional consequences that arise from the different pairings of challenge and skill. When challenge outweighs skill (skill is low; challenge is high), performers worry that the

demands of the task will overwhelm their skills. Being overchallenged threatens competence, and that threat manifests itself emotionally as worry (if moderately overchallenged)
or anxiety (if highly overchallenged). When challenge matches skill (challenge and skill
are both at least moderately high), concentration, involvement, and enjoyment rise. If
challenges and skills are perfectly matched, the experience is one of flow. When skill outweighs challenge (skill is high; challenge is low), task engagement is characterized by
reduced concentration, minimal task involvement, and emotional boredom. Being under-
challenged neglects competence, and that neglect manifests itself emotionally as indiffer-
ence or boredom.

Being overchallenged or overskilled produces emotional problems and suboptimal
experience, but the worst profile of experience actually emanates from the pairing of low
challenge and low skill (the lower left-hand corner of Figure 5.5). With both challenge
and skill low, literally all measures of emotion, motivation, and cognition are at their lowest levels—the person simply does not care about the task (Csikszentmihalyi, Rathunde,
& Whalen, 1993). Flow is therefore a bit more complicated than just the balance of challenge and skill because balancing low skill and low challenge produces apathy. A more
accurate description of how challenge relates to skill is that flow emerges in those situations in which both challenge and skill are moderately high or high (Csikszentmihalyi &
Csikszentmihalyi, 1988). With this qualification in mind, another way to look at Figure

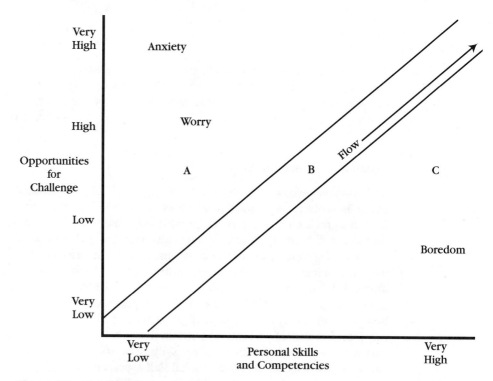

Figure 5.5 Flow Model

Source: Adapted from *Beyond Boredom and Anxiety: The Experience of Flow in Work and Play,* by
M. Csikszentmihalyi, 1975, San Francisco: Jossey-Bass.

5.5 is to divide it into four quadrants in which the upper-left quarter represents conditions for worry and anxiety, the lower-left quarter represents conditions for apathy, the lower-right quarter represents conditions for boredom, and the upper-right quarter represents conditions for flow.

The hypothetical case of three individuals, A, B, and C, also appears in Figure 5.5, as each individual performs a moderately difficult, moderately complex task. A, B, and C differ only in their levels of personal skill brought to the task. Given a moderately difficult task, unskilled person A will worry because his skills cannot match the demands and challenges of the task, somewhat skilled person B will experience flow because his skills equally match with the demands and challenges of the task, and highly skilled person C will be bored because her skills exceed the demands and challenges of the task. To alleviate worry, person A has two options: decrease task difficulty or increase personal skill. To alleviate boredom, person C has two options: increase task difficulty or decrease personal skill (through self-handicapping, for instance). To alter the challenge, persons A and C can manipulate task difficulty by solving easier or harder math problems, choosing an easier or harder jigsaw puzzle, or selecting a more or less proficient partner in an athletic contest. Persons A and C might also change the rules of the task by, for instance, solving the jigsaw puzzle with a partner or within a time limit, or allowing the baseball hitter additional or fewer strikes. As to manipulating skills, persons A and C can practice to increase skills, or they can impose handicaps to effectively decrease skills, such as running a race with ankle weights or playing left-handed if one normally plays right-handed. People engage in these sort of strategies—increase or decrease task difficulty and increase or decrease personal skill—according to flow theory, because they want their task participation to involve and satisfy their need for competence.

For a concrete example, consider three friends on a snow-skiing outing. Ski slopes offer different difficulty levels such that some slopes are relatively flat (beginner slopes), some are fairly steep (intermediate slopes), and others are downright death-defying (advanced slopes). If the skiers have different levels of skill, Figure 5.5 predicts that the emotional experience will vary for each skier on each slope. The novice skier will enjoy the beginner slopes but will experience mostly worry on the intermediate slopes and serious anxiety on the advanced slopes. Because the novice's skill level is so low, she might ski all day and experience only a hint of flow. The average skier will enjoy the intermediate slopes but will experience mostly boredom on the beginner slopes and worry on the advanced slopes. The professional will most likely enjoy the advanced slopes but will experience mostly mind-numbing boredom on the beginner slopes and some boredom on the intermediate slopes. Each skier, however, can experience flow on each slope by intentionally adjusting level of personal skill or level of slope difficulty. For example, a skier might increase skill by taking lessons or decrease skill by handicapping (i.e., using only one ski, using shorter skis, skiing backwards); the skier might increase slope difficulty by confronting moguls or decrease slope difficulty by going at a very slow speed. The fact that people can adjust both level of skill and level of task difficulty means that people can establish the conditions for optimal challenge and, hence, create the conditions under which they can involve the need for competence and experience flow.

The most important practical implication of flow theory is the following: Given optimal challenge, *any* activity can be enjoyed. Doing electrical work, writing papers, debating issues, sewing, analyzing a play, mowing the lawn, and other such activities do not necessarily make the top of most people's list of must-do activities, but the balance of skill with challenge adds the spice of flow—concentration, absorption, enjoyment, and optimal experience. Consistent with the idea that optimal challenge gives rise to flow, Csikszentmihalyi found in a pair of studies that students enjoyed doing homework and working on part-time jobs more than they enjoyed viewing (challengeless) television programs (Csikszentmihalyi, Rathunde, & Whalen, 1993). And people actually experience flow more often at work than they do during their leisure (Csikszentmihalyi, 1982).

Generally speaking, people want optimal challenges that will involve (rather than neglect or overwhelm) the need for competence and set up the conditions for flow. But people are motivationally complex, and sometimes people actually enjoy being overchallenged (Stein et al., 1995). With very high challenge, people sometimes see in a task a potential for gain, growth, and personal improvement. The perception of improvement and progress can be enjoyable, at least until the hope for gain gives way to the reality of being overwhelmed. Also under other conditions, people sometimes enjoy very low levels of challenge (Stein et al., 1995). Generally speaking, people enjoy feedback that confirms they have a skill level that is above and beyond the challenge of the task. Easy success can generate some level of enjoyment, especially in the early stages of task engagement when performers harbor the most doubts as to how their performances will go. The quality of enjoyment that easy success breeds, however, is a defensive and relief-based type of enjoyment. This type of enjoyment might keep anxiety at bay, but it does little to nurture the psychological need for competence. Instead, it is success in the context of optimal challenge that involves and nurtures the need for competence and therefore generates sincere, need-satisfying enjoyment (Clifford, 1990).

Interdependency Between Challenge and Feedback

Everyone is challenged every day. In school, teachers put examinations in front of students. At work, projects and assignments test a person's writing, creativity, and teamwork skills. On the drive home, the interstate challenges both our patience and our driving skills. If the car breaks down, our automotive repair skills will be put to the test. In the gym, the proficiency of an opponent or the weight of a barbell challenges athletic skills. These situations set the stage for challenge. But setting the stage for challenge is not the same thing as creating the psychological experience of being challenged. One additional ingredient still needs to be tossed into the equation—performance feedback. Confronting a test, project, or contest invites challenge, but a person does not *experience* challenge until she begins to perform and receive the first glimpse of feedback. It is at that point— facing a challenge and receiving initial performance feedback—that people report the psychological experience of being challenged (Reeve & Deci, 1996).

Failure Tolerance

The problem with optimal challenge, motivationally speaking, is that when people face moderately difficult tasks, they are as likely to experience failure and frustration as they are to experience success and enjoyment. In fact, one hallmark of optimal challenge is that success and failure are equally likely. Thus, the dread of failure can squash the competence need-involving qualities of optimal challenge. If intense, the dread of failure can motivate avoidance behaviors so that people go out of their way to escape being challenged (Covington, 1984a, 1984b).

Before people will engage freely in optimally challenging tasks, the social context must tolerate (and even value) failure and error making (i.e., adopt a performance climate rich in "failure tolerance" or "error tolerance"; Clifford, 1988, 1990). Optimal challenge implies that considerable error making is essential for optimizing motivation (Clifford, 1990). Error tolerance, failure tolerance, and risk taking rest on the belief that we learn more from failure than we do from success. This helps explain why people feel greater competence in autonomy-supportive and failure tolerant environments than they do in controlling and failure intolerant environments (Deci et al., 1981).

Failure produces opportunities for learning because it has its constructive aspects when people identify its causes, try new strategies, seek advice and instruction, and so on. When our environment—in school, at work, and in sports—tolerates failure and sincerely values the contribution it can make to our learning and developing, then we, as performers, experience an emotional green light for listening fully to the desire the need for competence generates in us to seek out and attempt to master optimal (rather than easy) challenges (Clifford, 1984, 1990).

Structure

Structure is the clear communication of what the environment expects the person to do to achieve desired outcomes. People have an opportunity to involve their need for competence in an activity when they receive guidance (Hokoda & Fincham, 1995; Nolen-Hoeksema et al., 1995) and consistent, sensitive, and responsive feedback (Hokoda & Fincham, 1995; Skinner, 1986) as they exercise their skills to meet challenges and to solve problems. When providing competence-involving structure, one person directly models, explains, coaches, and teaches the other. During these interactions, the first person explains problem-solving strategies, communicates clear expectancies, helps the other regulate negative emotions, gives insight on repairing or preventing negative outcomes, offers task-oriented attributions for setbacks, and administers consequences in ways that are consistent, predictable, and contingent on the other's actions (Connell, 1990; Connell & Wellborn, 1991; Skinner & Belmont, 1993). Overall, what people who are providing structure to others are doing is providing (1) information about the pathways to desired outcomes and (2) support and guidance for pursuing these pathways (Connell & Wellborn, 1991; Skinner, 1991, 1995; Skinner, Zimmer-Gembeck, & Connell, 1998).

Supporting Competence

Positive Feedback

Whether individuals perceive their performance to be competent or incompetent is often an ambiguous undertaking. To make such an evaluation, a performer needs feedback. Feedback comes from one (or more) of the following four sources (from Boggiano & Ruble, 1979; Dollinger & Thelen, 1978; Grolnick, Frodi, & Bridges, 1984; Koestner, Zuckerman, & Koestner, 1987; Reeve & Deci, 1996; Schunk & Hanson, 1989):

- Task itself
- Comparisons of one's current performance with one's own past performances

- Comparisons of one's current performance with the performance of others
- Evaluations of others

In some tasks, competence feedback is inherent in the performance of the task itself, as in successfully logging onto the computer (or not), repairing a machine (or not), or throwing a strike or a ball (in baseball). In most tasks, however, performance evaluation is more ambiguous than a right-versus-wrong performance outcome. In performing social skills, artistic talents, or other such tasks, our own past performances, peer performances, and the evaluations of other people (rather than the task itself) supply the information necessary to make an inference of competence versus incompetence. As for our own past performances, the perception of progress is an important signal of competence (Schunk & Hanson, 1989), just as the perception of a lack of progress signals incompetence. As to the performance of our peers, doing better than others signals competence whereas doing worse than others signals incompetence (Harackiewicz, 1979; Reeve & Deci, 1996; Reeve, Olson, & Cole, 1985). As for the evaluation of other people, praise and positive feedback bolsters perceptions of competence, whereas criticism and negative feedback deflates it (Anderson, Manoogian, & Reznick, 1976; Blank, Reis, & Jackson, 1984; Deci, 1971; Dollinger & Thelen, 1978; Vallerand & Reid, 1984).

In summary, performance feedback in its various forms—task-generated, self-generated, social comparisons, and other-generated—supplies the information individuals need to formulate a cognitive evaluation of their perceived level of competence. When these sources of information converge on an interpretation of a job well done, we experience positive feedback that is capable of satisfying the psychological need for competence.

Pleasure of Optimal Challenge and Positive Feedback

To confirm that people do indeed derive pleasure from optimal challenge, Susan Harter (1974, 1978b) gave school-age children anagrams of different difficulty levels and monitored each student's expressed pleasure (through smiling) upon solving each anagram. (An anagram is a word or phrase such as *table*, with its letters rearranged to form another word or phrase, as in *bleat*.) In general, anagram-solving success produced greater smiling and higher enjoyment than did failure (Harter, 1974), suggesting that mastery in general gratifies the competence need. In addition, however, some anagrams were very easy (three letters), some were easy (four letters), others were moderately difficult (five letters), and still others were very hard (six letters). As the anagrams increased in difficulty, it took students longer and longer to solve them, as expected, but the critical measure in the study was how much the children smiled after solving the anagrams of different levels of difficulty (Harter, 1978b). A curvilinear inverted-U pattern emerged in which children rarely smiled after solving the easy and very easy problems, they smiled most following success on the moderately difficult problems, and they smiled only modestly following success on the very hard problems. The central point is that children experience the greatest pleasure following success in the context of moderate challenge. In the words of the children, "The fives were just right. They were a challenge, but not too much challenge," and "I liked the hard ones because they gave you a sense of satisfaction, but the really hard ones were just too frustrating" (Harter, 1978b, p. 796).

RELATEDNESS

Everyone needs to belong. Everyone desires social interaction. Everyone wants friends. We all go out of our way to form and maintain warm, close, affectionate relationships with others. We all want others to understand us for who we are as individuals, and we want others to accept and to value us. We want others to acknowledge us and to be responsive to our needs. We want relationships with others whom really and honestly care for our well-being. We want our relationships to be reciprocal, as we want to form not only close, responsive, and caring relationships but we also want the other person to want to form these same sort of relationships with us. This desire for relationships with individuals extends to relationships with groups, organizations, and communities too. In other words, we have a need for relatedness.

Relatedness is the need to establish close emotional bonds and attachments with other people, and it reflects the desire to be emotionally connected to and interpersonally involved in warm relationships (Baumeister & Leary, 1995; Fromm, 1956; Guisinger & Blatt, 1994; Ryan, 1991; Ryan & Powelson, 1991; Sullivan, 1953). Because we need relatedness, we gravitate toward people who we trust to care for our well-being, and we drift away from those who we do not trust to look out for our well-being. What people are essentially looking for within need-satisfying relationships is the opportunity to relate the self authentically to another person in a caring and emotionally meaningful way (Ryan, 1993). Relatedness is an important motivational construct because people function better, are more resilient to stress, and report fewer psychological difficulties when their interpersonal relationships support their need for relatedness (Cohen, Sherrod, & Clark, 1986; Lepore, 1992; Ryan, Stiller, & Lynch, 1994; Sarason et al., 1991; Windle, 1992).

Because we need relatedness, social bonds form easily (Baumeister & Leary, 1995). Given an opportunity to engage others in face-to-face interaction, people generally go out of their way to create relationships (Brewer, 1979). The emergence of friendships and alliances seems to require little more than proximity and spending time together (Wilder & Thompson, 1980). The more people interact and the more people spend time together, the more likely they are to form friendships. Once social bonds are formed, people are generally reluctant to break them. When we move, when we graduate from school, and when others take their leave of us, we resist the breakup of the relationship. We promise to write and to telephone, we cry, we exchange addresses and phone numbers, and we plan a future occasion to get back together.

Involving Relatedness: Interaction With Others

Interaction with others is the primary condition that involves the relatedness need, at least to the extent that those interactions promise the possibility of warmth, care, and mutual concern. Starting a new relationship seems to be an especially easy way to involve the need for relatedness. Consider, for instance, the relatedness-involving potential of the following events, each of which promises an entry into new social relationships: first dates, falling in love, childbirth, fraternity or sorority pledging, and starting anew in school or in employment. Generally speaking, people seek emotionally positive interactions and interaction partners, and in doing so they gain the opportunity to involve the psychological need for relatedness.

Satisfying Relatedness: Perception of a Social Bond

Although interaction with others is sufficient for involving the relatedness need, relatedness-need satisfaction requires the creation of a social bond between the self and another (or between the self and the group). To be satisfying, that social bond needs to be characterized by the perceptions that the other person (1) cares about my welfare and (2) likes me (Baumeister & Leary, 1995). But more than caring and liking, the relationships that deeply satisfy the need for relatedness are those steeped in the knowledge that one's "true self"—one's "authentic self"—has been shown and deemed to be important in the eyes of another person (Deci & Ryan, 1995; Rogers, 1969; Ryan, 1993).

Relationships that do not involve caring, liking, accepting, and valuing do not satisfy the need for relatedness. People who are lonely, for instance, do not lack frequent social contact. They interact with others as frequently as do nonlonely people. Rather, those who feel lonely lack close, intimate relationships (Wheeler, Reis, & Nezlek, 1983). When it comes to relatedness and relationships, quality is more important than quantity (Carstensen, 1993).

Marriages, which are clearly close relationships, are not always emotionally satisfying. Some marriages, though full of social interaction, are full of conflict, stress, and criticism and basically make the other person's life more difficult than it otherwise would be. Alternatively, supportive marriages, those rich in mutual care and liking, are the emotionally satisfying relationships that lead people to feel happy (Coyne & DeLongis, 1986). Further, youths' relationships with their parents follow the same pattern in that to keep youths' depression at bay, parent-youth relationships not only need to exist, but they also need to be supportive (Carnelley, Pietromonaco, & Jaffe, 1994). Having one's relatedness need satisfied, as opposed to neglected, promotes vitality and well-being (Ryan & Lynch, 1989), and it lessens loneliness and depression (Pierce, Sarason, & Sarason, 1991; Windle, 1992). Emotions like sadness, depression, jealousy, and loneliness exist as telltale signs of a life lived in the absence of intimate, high-quality, relatedness-satisfying relationships and social bonds (Baumeister & Leary, 1995; Williams & Solano, 1983).

Communal and Exchange Relationships

We involve ourselves in many relationships, some of which are more need satisfying than are others. The distinction between communal and exchange relationships captures the essence of relationships that do (communal) and do not (exchange) satisfy the relatedness need (Mills & Clark, 1982).

Exchange relationships are those between acquaintances or between people who do business together. Communal relationships are those between persons who care about the welfare of the other, as exemplified by friendships, family, and romantic relationships. What distinguishes exchange from communal relationships are the implicit rules that guide the giving and receiving of benefits, such as money, help, and emotional support (Clark, Mills, & Powell, 1986). In exchange relationships, no obligation exists between interactants to be concerned with the other person's needs or welfare. As they say in the movie *The Godfather*, "It's business." In communal relationships, both parties care for the needs of the other, and both feel an obligation to support the other's welfare. Only communal relationships satisfy the relatedness need.

In communal relationships, people monitor and keep track of the other's needs, regardless of any forthcoming opportunities for reciprocity or material gain (Clark, 1984; Clark & Mills, 1979; Clark, Mills, & Powell, 1986; Clark et al., 1987). For instance, people involved in communal (as compared to exchange) relationships frequently check up on the needs of the other (Clark, Mills, & Powell, 1986), resist keeping track (or score) of individual inputs into joint projects (Clark, 1984), provide help when the other feels distressed (Clark et al., 1987), and experience tangible economic gifts as *detrimental* to how friendly, relaxed, and satisfying forthcoming interactions are likely to be (Clark & Mills, 1979). On this latter point, consider the emotional discomfort you might feel after providing a ride home to a close (communal) friend and, upon arrival, were handed $10 for the favor (Mills & Clark, 1982).

Internalization

Internalization refers to the process through which an individual transforms a formerly externally prescribed regulation or value into an internally endorsed one (Ryan, Rigby, & King, 1993). For instance, a person might internalize the value of education or internalize the utility of brushing one's teeth. As a process, internalization reflects the individual's tendency to voluntarily adopt and integrate into the self the values and regulations of other people (or society).

Relatedness to others provides the social context in which internalization occurs (Goodenow, 1993; Grolnick, Deci, & Ryan, 1997; Ryan & Powelson, 1991). When a person feels emotionally connected to and interpersonally involved with another, he or she believes the other person is truly looking out for his or her welfare, relatedness is high, and internalization occurs willingly. When a person feels emotionally distant from and interpersonally neglected by another, relatedness is low and internalization rarely occurs. For instance, children who have a positive relationship with their parents will generally internalize their parents' ways of thinking and behaving. Children with stormy or nonexistent relationships with their parents will generally reject their parents' ways of thinking and behaving and search for a value system elsewhere.

High relatedness does not guarantee that internalization will occur. For internalization to occur, the individual must also see the value, meaning, and utility in the other's prescriptions ("do X, believe Y") and proscriptions ("don't do X, don't believe Y"). To internalize a value or to internalize a way of behaving, the person needs to understand why the value or way of acting has merit, as in "Now, why is it important that I brush my teeth?" Therefore, relatedness is a necessary (but not sufficient) condition for internalization and cultural transmission to occur. Internalization flourishes in relationships that provide a rich supply of (1) relatedness need satisfaction and (2) satisfying rationale for why the others' prescriptions and proscriptions will benefit the self.

PUTTING IT ALL TOGETHER: SOCIAL CONTEXTS THAT INVOLVE AND SATISFY PSYCHOLOGICAL NEEDS

Specific aspects of the social context are noteworthy in their capacity to involve and satisfy the psychological needs. For illustration, Table 5.3 summarizes the prototypical events that involve the needs of autonomy, competence, and relatedness as well as the prototypical events that satisfy these three needs. When involved in activities that offer opportunities for self-direction, optimal challenge, and frequent social interaction, people typically experience need involvement and feel interested in what they do. When involved in activities that offer autonomy support, positive feedback, and communal relationships, people typically experience need satisfaction and feel enjoyment in what they do.

Engagement

The motivational model of engagement (see Figure 5.7) illustrates in a comprehensive way the contribution that relationships and social contexts have for psychological needs (Connell, 1990; Connell & Wellborn, 1991; Skinner & Belmont, 1993). Engagement is a

Table 5.3   Environmental Factors that Involve and Satisfy the Psychological Needs

Psychological Need	Environmental Condition that Involves the Need	Environmental Condition that Satisfies the Need
Autonomy	Opportunities for self-direction	Autonomy support
Competence	Optimal challenge	Positive feedback
Relatedness	Social interaction	Communal relationships

term that captures the intensity and emotional quality people show when they initiate and carry out activities, such as learning in school or practicing skills in music or sports. When highly engaged, people behave in ways that are active and that allow them to express positive emotion; when highly disengaged, people behave in ways that are passive and that cause them to express negative emotion (Patrick, Skinner, & Connell, 1993). Specifically, when people are highly engaged in what they are doing, they show high levels of the following (Wellborn, 1991):

- Attention
- Effort
- Persistence
- Verbal participation
- Positive emotion

Jim Connell and Ellen Skinner explain the conditions under which people show high and low engagement by tracing the origin of engagement to the three psychological needs. Specifically, they argue that (1) autonomy support enhances engagement because it involves and satisfies the need for autonomy, (2) structure enhances engagement because it involves and satisfies the need for competence, and (3) involvement enhances engagement because it involves and satisfies the need for relatedness.

Autonomy support refers to the amount of freedom one person gives to another so that he can find the means to connect his behavior (in school, at work, during athletic practice) to personal goals, interests, and values. The opposite of autonomy support is coercion or being controlled. How autonomy support expresses itself is summarized in Figure 5.7, but the four key elements are nurtures inner motivational resources, relies on informational language, promotes valuing, and acknowledges and accepts expressions of negative affect.

Structure refers to the amount and clarity of information one person, such as a teacher or coach, provides to another regarding the best ways to achieve desired skills and behavioral outcomes. The opposite of structure is chaos or confusion. How structure expresses itself is summarized in Figure 5.7. Some examples include communicating clear expectations, providing optimal challenges, and offering skill-building and information-rich performance feedback.

Involvement refers to the quality of the interpersonal relationship between two people, such as a teacher and a student, and also each person's willingness to dedicate psychological resources (e.g., time, interest, attention) to the other. The opposite of involvement is rejection or neglect. How involvement expresses itself is summarized in Figure 5.7. Some examples include expressing affection and truly enjoying time spent together.

What Makes for a Good Day?

Experiences that involve and satisfy psychological needs generate positive emotion and psychological well-being (Ryan & Deci, 2001; Reis et al., 2000). Simply put, on our good days, the events in our lives work to involve and satisfy our psychological needs. On our

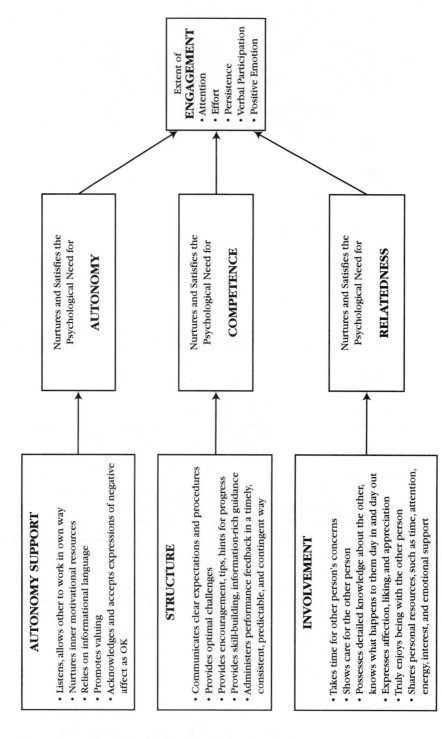

Figure 5.7 Engagement Model to Illustrate the Motivational Significance of Autonomy Support, Structure, and Involvement

126

bad days, the events in our lives work to neglect and frustrate these needs. So psychological need satisfaction predicts and explains when we do and do not have "a good day."

To study day-to-day fluctuations in well-being, one group of researchers asked college students to keep a daily diary of their moods (joyful, angry) and well-being (vitality, symptomatology). The researchers predicted that good days are those in which one's psychological needs are met (Sheldon, Ryan, & Reis, 1996). Circumstances partly dictated when people had their good days, as people had their best days on weekends, for instance. But people also had their best days when they experienced higher levels of daily competence and daily autonomy. (Unfortunately, the researchers did not include a measure of daily relatedness.) For instance, as people spent their days attending classes, talking with friends, and playing the cello, the more effective they felt (daily competence) and the more internal was their perceived locus of causality (daily autonomy) during these activities, the greater was their positive affect and vitality and the lesser was their physical symptomology like a headache.

These findings are especially important because they confirm that psychological needs provide the psychological nutriments necessary for good days and positive well-being (Sheldon, Ryan, & Reis, 1998). Consider an ordinary trip to the gym to exercise. Imagine at the end of the workout that you completed a questionnaire asking how enjoyable the hour was, why you came to exercise, how challenging the workout was and how much you improved, and what was the quality of the social interaction during the hour. Notice that these questions correspond to the psychological needs for autonomy, competence, and relatedness. In the study, the greater the exercisers reported experiencing autonomy, competence, and relatedness, the greater was the exerciser's enjoyment (Ryan et al., 1997). In contrast, people who exercised for other motives (appearance, body image) enjoyed the experience less and worked out for a briefer time. A study with the elderly in nursing homes found much the same result in that the more self-determining and interpersonally related residents felt each day, the greater was their vitality and well-being and the less was their distress (Kasser & Ryan, 1999).

If you will recall from the chapter's opening vignette in which the young girl was skipping stones across the surface of the lake, then the point is worth repeating that she was doing more than merely playing. She was also engaging in the sort of daily activity that provides her with the psychological nutriments she needs to promote her development and well-being. The same can be said for us as we play musical instruments, read books, and hang out with our friends to nourish our psychology with a daily dosage of autonomy, competence, and relatedness.

Vitality

One way people experience a good day is through a subjective experience of vitality. For instance, consider the following three sentences (Ryan & Frederick, 1997):

- I feel alive and vital.
- Sometimes I feel so alive I just want to burst.
- I feel energized.

When people have days that allow them to feel autonomous, competent, and interpersonally related, they are significantly more likely to agree with these statements (Kasser & Ryan, 1993, 1996; Sheldon, Ryan, & Reis, 1996). Psychological need involvement and satisfaction offers us the psychological nutriments we need to feel vital and well.

SUMMARY

The study of the three psychological needs of autonomy, competence, and relatedness relies on an organismic approach to motivation, an approach to motivation that makes two core assumptions. First, people are inherently active. Second, in the person-environment dialectic, the person uses inherent psychological needs to engage in the environment and the environment sometimes supports but other times neglects and frustrates these inner resources. The picture that emerges in an organismic approach to motivation is that human beings possess a natural motivation to learn, grow, and develop in a way that is healthy and mature, and they do so when environments involve and support their psychological needs.

Autonomy is the need to experience choice in the initiation and regulation of one's behavior, and it reflects the desire to have personal choices, rather than environmental events, determine one's actions. When self-determined, behavior emanates from an internal perceived locus of causality, feels free, and flows out of a sense of choice over one's actions. The extent to which an individual is able to involve and satisfy his or her need for self-determination depends a good deal on how supportive and nurturing (i.e., autonomy supportive) versus neglecting and frustrating (i.e., controlling) his or her relationships and environment are perceived to be. An autonomy-supportive motivating style is one that nurtures inner motivational resources, relies on informational language, promotes valuing, and acknowledges and accepts expressions of negative affect as okay. People whose behavior is self-determined, as opposed to controlled by others, show positive outcomes, including gains in learning, emotion, performance, persistence, and achievement.

Competence is the need to effectively interact with the environment. It reflects the desire to exercise one's capacities and skills and, in doing so, to seek out and master optimal challenges. The need for competence generates the motivation to want to develop, improve upon, and refine personal skills and talents. The principal environmental event that involves the competence need is optimal challenge. When personal challenge and environmental skill are both relatively high, people experience flow, which is a psychological state characterized by maximal enjoyment, intense concentration, and full absorption in the task. The principal environmental event that satisfies the competence need is positive feedback. The more environments satisfy people's need for competence, the more willing people are to seek out and try to master optimal challenges that allow them opportunities to develop and grow.

Relatedness is the need to establish close emotional bonds and attachments with other people, and it reflects the desire to be emotionally connected to and interpersonally involved with others in warm, caring relationships. Mere interaction with others is a sufficient condition for involving the need for relatedness. To satisfy relatedness, however, a person needs to confirm that the emerging social bonds with other people involve both caring and liking. A communal relationship represents the type of relationship capable of satisfying the relatedness need. Relatedness to others is important because it provides the social context that supports internalization, which is the process through which one person takes in and accepts as his or her own another person's belief, value, or way of behaving.

An engagement model of motivation (Figure 5.7) illustrates how relationships and social contexts successfully involve and satisfy (or neglect and frustrate) the psychological needs for autonomy, competence, and relatedness. Collectively, autonomy support, structure, and involvement are important aspects of the social context because they provide the means through which environments can involve and satisfy people's psychological needs. When people experience psychological need satisfaction, they experience the psychological nutriments (psychological needs) necessary for active engagement, having "a good day", subjective experiences of vitality, and psychological well-being.

READINGS FOR FURTHER STUDY

Psychological Needs

RYAN, R. M. (1995). Psychological needs and the facilitation of integrative processes. *Journal of Personality, 63*, 397–427.

SHELDON, K. M., RYAN, R. M., & REIS, H. T. (1996). What makes for a good day? Competence and autonomy in the day and in the person. *Personality and Social Psychology Bulletin, 22*, 1270–1279.

RYAN, R. M., & DECI, E. L. (2000). Self-determination theory and the facilitation of intrinsic motivation, social development, and well-being. *American Psychologist, 55*, 68–78.

Self-Determination

DECI, E. L., & RYAN, R. M. (1987). The support of autonomy and the control of behavior. *Journal of Personality and Social Psychology, 53*, 1024–1037.

RYAN, R. M., & GROLNICK, W. S. (1986). Origins and pawns in the classroom: Self-report and projective assessments of individual differences in children's perceptions. *Journal of Personality and Social Psychology, 50*, 550–558.

VALLERAND, R. J., FORTIER, M. S., & GUAY, F. (1997). Self-determination and persistence in a real-life setting: Toward a motivational model of high school dropout. *Journal of Personality and Social Psychology, 72*, 1161–1172.

Competence

HARTER, S. (1978a). Effectance motivation reconsidered: Toward a developmental model. *Human Development, 21*, 34–64.

HARTER, S. (1978b). Pleasure derived from optimal challenge and the effects of extrinsic rewards on children's difficulty level choices. *Child Development, 49*, 788–799.

Relatedness

BAUMEISTER, R. F., & LEARY, M. R. (1995). The need to belong: Desire for interpersonal attachments as a fundamental human motivation. *Psychological Bulletin, 117*, 497–529.

KASSER, V. G., & RYAN, R. M. (1999). The relation of psychological needs for autonomy and relatedness to vitality, well-being, and mortality in a nursing home. *Journal of Applied Social Psychology, 29*, 935–954.

Chapter 6

Intrinsic Motivation and Types of Extrinsic Motivation

PUTTING IT ALL TOGETHER: MOTIVATING OTHERS ON UNINTERESTING ACTIVITIES

SUMMARY

READINGS FOR FURTHER STUDY

Each year more than a half million Americans suffer injuries from automobile accidents, many of which cause fatalities. Fortunately, drivers and passengers have a way to drastically reduce their probability of suffering serious injuries—namely, by wearing seat belts (Henry et al., 1996). Despite convincing data that seat belts save lives and despite our society's consensus that wearing a seat belt is a desirable behavior, all too many people still drive without buckling up.

To reverse seat-belt apathy, the government tried national advertising campaigns to encourage seatbelt compliance. These educational campaigns failed miserably. One study, for instance, reported that a nationwide multimedia advertising campaign increased seat belt usage by 0.1% of drivers (Robertson et al., 1974). Promoters next tried to offer attractive incentives to riders who buckled up (Elman & Killebrew, 1978; Geller, 1988; Geller, Casali, & Johnson, 1980; Geller et al., 1987). The logic behind these incentive-based programs is that if people cannot find the motivation within themselves to buckle up, then perhaps the offer of an attractive incentive will give them the motivation they lack.

For instance, consider the seat-belt sweepstakes program tested at a Virginia university (Rudd & Geller, 1985). To conduct the sweepstakes, researchers placed posters like the one in Figure 6.1 on bulletin boards in campus classrooms and lecture halls. Campus radio stations also announced the sweepstakes. In the conduct of the sweepstakes, campus police recorded all license-plate numbers of the drivers they saw wearing a (shoulder) seat belt. Those numbers were entered into a raffle of weekly prizes, which ranged in value from $20 to $450. To be eligible to win the prizes, drivers therefore had to first engage in the desired behavior—wear a seat belt. During the 3 weeks of the sweepstakes, campus seat-belt usage doubled.

Offering an attractive incentive for compliant behavior represents one strategy of extrinsic motivation. A second strategy is to offer an aversive incentive. This strategy is different, but the logic is the same: If people cannot find the motivation within themselves to buckle up, then perhaps the threat of an aversive consequence (e.g., a ticket) will give them the motivation they lack. With seat-belt usage, the aversive stimulus is typically a harsh-sounding buzzer, bright or flashing panel light, or an ignition interlock system (Geller et al., 1980). All automobiles now offer at least one of these aversive stimuli, and the buzzer, light, or locking system continues until the driver complies and fastens the seat belt. Thus, people buckle up not in the name of safety and saving their lives but simply to prevent or escape from something irritating. This kind of irritating incentive leads people to buckle up even better than the prospect of an attractive incentive (Geller et al., 1980).

Researchers have yet another extrinsic motivational strategy up their intellectual sleeves—namely, provide drivers with prompts to buckle up. An extrinsic prompt to engage in the desired behavior could be a road sign like, "Buckle Up, Stay Safe," or a researcher in the parking lot of a supermarket saying, "Remember to buckle your safety

Figure 6.1 Campus Poster to Advertise the Seatbelt Sweepstakes

Source: From "A University-Based Incentive Program to Increase Safety Belt Use: Towards Cost-Effective Institutionalization," by J. R. Rudd and E. S. Geller, 1985, *Journal of Applied Behavior Analysis,* 18, pp. 215–226. Copyright 1985, *Journal of Applied Behavior Analysis.* Reprinted by permission.

belt" (Austin, Alvero, & Olson, 1998; Cox, Cox, & Cox, 2000; Engerman, Austin, & Bailey, 1997; Gras et al., 2003). Such prompts raised drivers' seat-belt compliance from about 70% to about 90%. Over the years, the government, researchers, and automobile engineers essentially solved the nation's problem with seat-belt apathy.

The discussion throughout this chapter follows the spirit of the seat-belt sweepstakes, obnoxious buzzer, and signage prompt studies by addressing the question of how external events generate motivational states. Like the seat-belt sweepstakes, any number of familiar incentive programs present the same incentive-based appeal—programs such as frequent-flyer programs, token economies, academic honor rolls, perfect attendance certificates, pay-for-performance programs, end-of-the-year bonus checks, school grades, reading-incentive programs (e.g., Learn to Earn, Book It!), rebate credit cards, or frequent-usage cards that offer discounts issued by places such as restaurants and hotels. People do not necessarily want to engage in the behaviors required of them. Rather, the motivation for the behavior comes from wanting the incentive. Basically, people do what they need to do to get the incentives they desire. Because incentives and rewards exert such a strong and reliable effect on behavior, people working in applied settings have embraced extrinsic motivation as a strategy for solving people's motivational problems.

Practically every environment we find ourselves in discriminates between desirable and undesirable behaviors. Further, practically every environment rewards us in one way or another for performing those desired behaviors and punishes us for performing those undesired behaviors. For instance, while driving, desirable behaviors including staying on your side of the road, driving 30 miles per hour on city streets, and making sure your exhaust pipe is not billowing out a cloud of black smoke. If drivers forego such desirable behaviors, the environment will rather quickly deliver an array of punishers, such as honks of the horn, speeding tickets, and steely-eyed stares from people with pro-environment bumper stickers. As a result, we generally follow our hedonistic tendencies (approach pleasure, avoid pain) and engage in those courses of action that we believe will produce reward and prevent punishment. Over time, we learn which behaviors generally bring us pleasurable consequences and which other behaviors bring us aversive consequences.

In the previous chapters on needs, motivation arose from inner sources—physiological and psychological needs. These needs explained why people ate and drank, sought out optimal challenges and intimate relationships, and so on. To propose that people eat and drink and that people seek out challenges and relationships because of their needs to do so, however, recognizes only part of the story. A person might also engage in these same behaviors out of an environmentally-created reason to do so. Some examples of such extrinsic motivators include money, grades, praise, privileges, and the approval of others. A fruitful and comprehensive analysis of motivated behavior, according to the behavior theorists that will be introduced in this chapter (Baldwin & Baldwin, 1986; Skinner, 1938, 1953, 1986), requires that we add the analysis of how environmental incentives and consequences promote in us a sense of "want to."

INTRINSIC AND EXTRINSIC MOTIVATIONS

Needs generate motivational states within us. Causal observation of day-to-day behavior, however, suggests that our needs are sometimes silent, or at least somewhere on the back burner of consciousness. In schools, students are sometimes apathetic and disinterested in the school's curriculum. At work, employees are sometimes listless and slow to apply themselves. In hospitals, patients sometimes feel little desire to exercise and are reluctant to take their medicines. Such observations suggest that people do not always generate their own motivation from within. Instead, people sometimes turn passive and look to the environment to supply motivation for them. In school, teachers see this lack of inner motivation and, in response, they use grades, stickers, praise, recess privileges, and threats of doom to motivate their students. At work, employers use paychecks, bonuses, surveillance, competitions, and threats of termination to motivate their employees. In the hospitals, doctors use orders, appeals to please loved ones, and implicit threats (e.g., "If you don't exercise more, then. . . .) to motivate their patients. Such are the external events that constitute the incentives and consequences that generate extrinsic motivation.

Experience teaches us that there are two ways to enjoy an activity: intrinsically or extrinsically. Consider activities like playing the piano, using the computer, or reading a book. On the one hand, the pianist may become interested and begin to enjoy piano playing because it is an opportunity to involve and satisfy psychological needs like competence. The musician plays the piano to have fun, to exercise and develop valued skills, and to feel free and self-determined. On the other hand, the same piano-playing behavior can be enjoyed because it is an opportunity to make money, to win prizes and trophies, to impress others, or to earn a college scholarship. Any activity, in fact, can be approached with either an intrinsic or an extrinsic motivational orientation (Amabile, 1985; Pittman, Boggiano, & Ruble, 1983; Pittman, Emery, & Boggiano, 1982; Pittman & Heller, 1988; Ryan & Deci, 2000b).

Intrinsic Motivation

Intrinsic motivation is the innate propensity to engage one's interests and to exercise one's capacities and, in doing so, to seek out and master optimal challenges (Deci & Ryan, 1985a). It emerges spontaneously from psychological needs, personal curiosities, and innate strivings for growth. When people are intrinsically motivated, they act out of interest, "for the fun of it," and for the sense of challenge the activity at hand provides. This behavior occurs spontaneously and is not done for any instrumental (extrinsic) reason. Functionally, intrinsic motivation provides the innate motivation to pursue one's interests and to exert the challenge-seeking effort necessary to develop one's skills and capacities.

People experience intrinsic motivation because they have psychological needs within themselves. Psychological needs, when they are involved and nurtured during an activity, spontaneous yield the sense of satisfaction people feel while engaging in interesting activities. Intrinsic motivation comes from feeling competent and feeling self-determined during an activity. When people engage in tasks and feel competent and self-determining, they express their intrinsic motivation by saying, "That's interesting," "That's fun," or "I enjoy doing that." For instance, interest and feeling free can spark the desire to read a book, and enjoyment and feeling competent can involve a person in a challenging crossword puzzle for hours.

Extrinsic Motivation

Extrinsic motivation arises from environmental incentives and consequences (e.g., food, money). Instead of engaging in an activity to experience the inherent satisfactions it can bring (as with intrinsic motivation), extrinsic motivation arises from some consequence that is separate from the activity itself. Whenever we act to gain a high academic grade, win a trophy, make a quota, impress our peers, or beat a deadline, our behavior is extrinsically motivated. That is, because we desire attractive consequences and because we desire to avoid unattractive consequences, the presence of incentives and consequences creates within us a sense of wanting to engage in those behaviors that will produce the sought-after consequences.

Extrinsic motivation arises from a "Do this and you will get that" motivation, and it exists as an "in order to" motivation (as in, "Do this in order to get that"). The "this" is the requested behavior, and the "that" is the extrinsic incentive or consequence. It is also a "what's in it for me?" type of motivation. So extrinsic motivation is an environmentally created reason to initiate or persist in an action.

Often, intrinsically and extrinsically motivated behaviors look precisely the same. Just as the intrinsically motivated person reads a book, paints a picture, or goes to school or work, the extrinsically motivated person does so as well. Therefore, it is difficult to casually observe someone and know whether he or she is intrinsically or extrinsically motivated. The essential difference between the two types of motivation lies in the source that energizes and directs the behavior. With intrinsically motivated behavior, the motivation emanates from psychological needs and spontaneous satisfaction the activity provides; with extrinsically motivated behavior, the motivation emanates from incentives and consequences made contingent on the observed behavior.

Types of Extrinsic Motivation

Traditionally, motivation researchers viewed extrinsic motivation as the motivational opposite from intrinsic motivation (deCharms, 1968; Deci, 1975). Contemporary researchers now, however, recognize varied types of extrinsic motivation (Ryan & Deci, 2000a, 2000b). Some types of extrinsic motivation still correspond to environmentally-engineered forms of motivation, but other types exist within the person and therefore represent self-endorsed motives that are carried out volitionally (freely). The next section focuses on extrinsic motivation in the traditional sense, while the chapter's final two sections focus on extrinsic motivation in the more contemporary sense.

INCENTIVES AND CONSEQUENCES

The study of extrinsic motivation revolves around the language and perspective of operant conditioning. The term *operant conditioning* refers to the process by which a person learns how to operate effectively in the environment. Operating effectively in one's environment means learning and engaging in those behaviors that produce attractive consequences (e.g., gaining approval, earning money) and also in those behaviors that prevent unattractive consequences (e.g., being rejected, getting fired).

To communicate how incentives and consequences motivate behavior, proponents of operant conditioning (Baldwin & Baldwin, 1986) offer the following conceptualization of behavior:

$$S : R \rightarrow C$$

In this three-term model, S, R, and C stand for situational cue (i.e., incentive), behavioral response, and consequence, respectively. The colon between S and R shows that the situational cue sets the occasion for (but does not cause) the behavioral response. The arrow between R and C shows that the behavioral response causes a consequence. Having the attention of a group of friends (S), for instance, does not cause a storyteller to recite jokes (R), but the group does serve as a situational cue to set the occasion for storytelling ($S : R$). Once told, the jokes cause the friends' reactions (C), such that the telling of the jokes causes the audience's subsequent laughter or ridicule ($R \rightarrow C$).

Incentives

An incentive is an environmental event that attracts or repels a person toward or away from initiating a particular course of action. Incentives always precede behavior (i.e., S : R), and, in doing so, they create in the person an expectation that attractive or unattractive consequences are forthcoming. Some positive incentives might include a smile, an inviting aroma, the presence of friends and colleagues, an envelope that looks like it holds a check, and an icon at the bottom of a computer screen that reads "you have mail." Some negative incentives might include a grimace, a spoiled smell, the presence of enemies or competitors, junk mail, and a grinding noise from the computer that indicates it is about to crash.

Incentives do not cause behavior. Instead, they affect the likelihood of whether or not a response will be initiated. The incentive is the situational cue that signals the likelihood that a behavior will or will not produce rewarding or punishing consequences, and this knowledge about a stimulus' incentive value is learned through experience. Car noises do not bring heart-stopping fear to people until that noise has proven in the past to be a reliable predictor that disaster is right around the bend. Similarly, the sight of a particular person is not an attractive or aversive incentive until experience teaches us that this person probably brings ridicule and rejection (we learn that this person is an aversive incentive) or humor and friendship (we learn that this person is an attractive incentive). It is this learning process (this "conditioning") that shapes our goal-directed behavior, as positive incentives cue approach behavior while negative incentives cue avoidance behavior.

These examples might appear to confound what constitutes an incentive and what constitutes a consequence. Both are external events that direct behavior, but two important differences exist. Incentives differ from consequences on the basis of (1) when each occurs and (2) how it motivates behavior. Incentives precede behavior ($S : R$) and excite or inhibit the initiation of behavior. Consequences follow behavior ($R \rightarrow C$) and increase or decrease the persistence of behavior.

What Is a Reinforcer?

From a practical point of view, defining a reinforcer is easy. It is any extrinsic event that increases behavior. If you get a fat check for going to work, then practical experience teaches you that the fat check is obviously a reinforcer, as you keep coming to work so long as the fat checks keep coming your way.

From a theoretical point of view, however, the definition of a reinforcer is more difficult. Theoretically, a reinforcer must be defined in a manner that is independent from its effects on behavior. The problem with defining a reinforcer solely in terms of its effects on behavior is that its definition becomes circular: The cause produces the effect (reinforcers cause increased behavior), but the effect justifies the cause (increased behavior means it must be a reinforcer). Hence, in practice, the only way to identify a reinforcer is to actually give it and then wait and see if the reinforcer will increase behavior. Researchers and practitioners, however, have no means of identifying a reinforcer *before* using it. The challenge is therefore to know ahead of time that the reinforcer will work—that is, what will increase behavior (Timberlake & Farmer-Dougan, 1991).

Another challenge is to explain why the reinforcer will work: Why would anyone expect this external event to increase another person's behavior? To get out of this circular quagmire, the researcher needs to select an extrinsic event never used before on a particular person (e.g., candy bar, field trip to the zoo) and know a priori whether it will or will not increase the sought-after desired behavior. In the history of motivation research, each of the following noncircular definitions of what constitutes a positive reinforcer has been offered:

1. **Stimulus that decreases drive** (Hull, 1943). Food increases behavior because it decreases hunger.
2. **Stimulus that decreases arousal** (Berlyne, 1967). A drug increases behavior because it calms anxiety.
3. **Stimulus that increases arousal** (Zuckerman, 1979). A rock concert increases behavior because it stimulates and excites.
4. **Attractive environmental object** (Skinner, 1938). Money increases behavior because people value money.
5. **Hedonically pleasurable brain stimulation** (Olds, 1969). Electrical stimulation of the medial forebrain bundle increases behavior because it is pleasurable.
6. **Opportunity to perform a high-frequency behavior** (Premack, 1959). A person completes her homework in order to gain the opportunity to watch television.

The advantage of these definitions of a reinforcer, as compared to the "anything that increases behavior" definition, is that the researcher can explain, in advance, *why* the stimulus will increase behavior.

From a more practical perspective, consider one study that used various reinforcers to encourage an 8-year-old to wear an orthodontic device (Hall et al., 1972). The parents quickly observed that the child had little intrinsic motivation to wear the device, so they sought to create in the child an extrinsic motivation to wear the gear. As shown in Figure 6.2, the parents kept track of the percentage of time their child wore the orthodontic device (five observations per day at random times, such as at breakfast, when leaving for school). Wearing the orthodontic device constituted the desired behavior, at least from the parent's point of view. In the first week (with no positive reinforcer), the child wore the device 25% of the time. The parents then began to praise their child each time they saw him wearing the orthodontic gear. With praise, the child wore the gear 36% of the time. For the next two weeks, the parents administered a delayed monetary reward. Each time the parents saw the child wearing the gear, they promised 25 cents at the end of the month. With money on the line, compliance increased to 60% of the time. For a two-week period, the parents next administered an immediate, on-the-spot, 25-cent reward for any observed compliance. Wearing the gear zoomed to 97%. For the next 5 days, the child received no positive reinforcers for compliance. Wearing dropped to 64%. Finally, for 2 weeks, the parents reintroduced the immediate 25-cent reward, and the child's compliance returned to 100%.

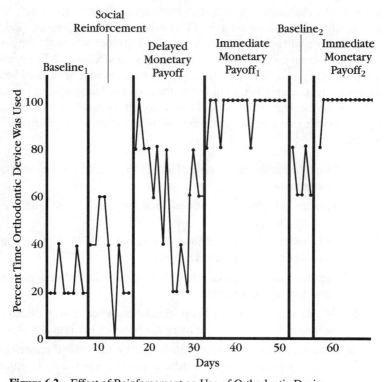

Figure 6.2   Effect of Reinforcement on Use of Orthodontic Device

Source: From "Modification of Behavior Problems in the Home With a Parent as Observer and Experimenter," by R. V. Hall, S. Axelrod, L. Tyler, E. Grief, F. C. Jones, and R. Robertson, 1972, *Journal of Applied Behavior Analysis, 5,* pp. 53–64. Copyright 1972 by the *Journal of Applied Behavior Analysis.* Reprinted with permission.

This study highlights two considerations about the nature of reinforcers. First, reinforcers vary in their quality. Money worked better than praise. For this child, money was a higher-quality reward than was praise. Second, the immediacy at which a reinforcer is delivered partly determines its effectiveness. Money given immediately was more effective than the same amount of money promised at some time in the future.[1]

---

[1] In addition to quality and immediacy, four other characteristics of a reward determine what is or is not a reinforcer. First, a reinforcer can be effective for one person but not for another, suggesting that the person/reinforcer fit is as important as is any particular characteristic of the reinforcer per se. Attention and candy might prove effective for young children (and ineffective for adults), whereas a job promotion and stock options might prove effective for adults (and ineffective for young children). Second, the same reinforcer can be effective for a person at one time but ineffective at another time. A cup of coffee might increase behavior early in the morning, but it may prove ineffective at night. Third, reinforcers vary in their intensity. Money is typically an effective reinforcer but only if considered to exceed some threshold of intensity. A penny is typically not effective as a reinforcer. Lastly, the rewards that administrators (e.g., parents, teachers, employers, therapists, coaches) think will work best often do not correspond to what their recipients actually find to be reinforcing (Green et al., 1988; Pace et al., 1985; Smith, Iwata, & Shore, 1995). For example, a parent might give a child a big hug, thinking the child highly values hugging, though the child might rather have a bowl of chocolate pudding. Thus, six considerations determine a positive reinforcer's effectiveness: (1) its quality; (2) its immediacy; (3) the person/reinforcer fit; (4) the recipient's need for that particular reward; (5) its intensity; and (6) the recipient's perceived value of the reinforcer.

Consequences

There are two types of consequences: reinforcers and punishers. Among reinforcers, there are two types—positive and negative.

Positive Reinforcers

A positive reinforcer is any environmental stimulus that, when presented, increases the future probability of the desired behavior. Approval, paychecks, and trophies operate as positive reinforcers that occur after saying thank you, working a 40-hour week, and practicing athletic skills. What makes the approval, paycheck, or trophy a positive reinforcer is its capacity to increase the probability that the behaviors of being polite, working hard, or practicing for hours will recur in the future. That is, the person who receives the positive reinforcer becomes more likely to repeat the behavior than the person who receives no such attractive consequence for the same behavior. Additional positive reinforcers in the culture include money, praise, attention, grades, scholarships, approval, prizes, food, awards, trophies, public recognition, and privileges.

Negative Reinforcers

A negative reinforcer is any environmental stimulus that, when removed, increases the future probability of the desired behavior. Like positive reinforcers, negative reinforcers increase the probability of behavior. Unlike positive reinforcers, negative reinforcers are aversive, irritating stimuli. The shrill ring of the alarm clock is an aversive, irritating stimulus. Stopping the ringing is negatively reinforcing when it increases the probability that the would-be sleeper gets out of bed. In the same way, medicine that removes headache pain is a negative reinforcer that increases the sufferer's willingness to take this same medicine in the future (i.e., removing pain negatively reinforces the act of taking headache medicine). Additional negative reinforcers in the culture include whining, nagging, crying, surveillance, deadlines, time limits, a pet's incessant meowing or barking, and all sorts of pain.

It is relatively easy to visualize the approach behavior motivated by positive reinforcers. But a couple of examples will help illustrate how negative reinforcers motivate escape and avoidance behaviors. Escape removes a person from the aversive stimulus; avoidance prevents the aversive stimulus from occurring in the first place (Iwata, 1987). Consider how people escape from the sound of the alarm clock by getting out of bed, escape from the car buzzer by buckling a seat belt, and escape from the whining child by leaving the room. Once we discover which behaviors are effective in removing us from the noise, buzzer, or whining, we tend to repeat these same escape maneuvers when the noise, buzzer, or whining return. To prevent the aversive stimuli from occurring in the first place, however, people learn to get out of bed early (to avoid the noise), to buckle up before starting the car (to avoid the buzzer), and to stay away from the child (to avoid hearing the whines). Escape behaviors are reactive against aversive stimuli; avoidance behaviors are proactive in preventing our encountering them again.

One illustration that nicely captures how a negative reinforcer motivates escape and avoidance behaviors is the wearing of a postural harness (Azrin et al., 1968), shown in

Figure 6.3. An automated shoulder harness to discourage postural slouching sends off a 55-dB tone whenever slouching at the shoulders occurs. Slouching sets off the aversive tone. To escape it, the wearer must adjust his or her posture accordingly. Noise termination negatively reinforces the escape behavior of thrusting back the shoulder blades. To avoid hearing the tone, the wearer must maintain correct posture by keeping his shoulders thrust backward. The motivation stems not from wanting good posture but, rather, from not wanting to hear that irritating blast of noise. For all 25 adults using such a postural harness in one study, a marked improvement in posture occurred. The postural harness (like a crying baby or a yelling drill sergeant) communicates a nice metaphor for illustrating extrinsic motivation, as the source of motivation (the 55-dB noise) clearly lies outside the individual—literally on the person rather than in him or her.

The front view in the upper sketch shows the signal component worn around the neck. A wire runs from the component, under the arm, and to the posture switch on the back, which is shown in the lower sketch. The posture switch is attached by the shoulder straps, which are adjusted for the desired posture. Outer garments are worn over the assembly and thereby conceal it from view.

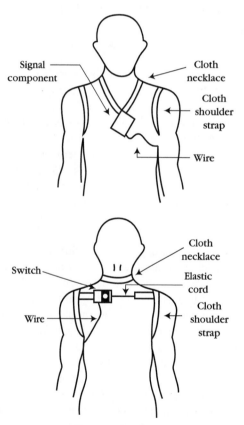

Figure 6.3 Front and Rear View of Person Wearing Postural Harness

Source: From "Behavioral Engineering: Postural Control by a Portable Operant Apparatus," by N. H. Azrin, H. Rubin, F. O'Brien, T. Ayllon, and D. Roll, 1968, *Journal of Applied Behavior Analysis, 2,* pp. 39–42. Copyright 1968 by the *Journal of Applied Behavior Analysis.* Reprinted with permission.

Punishers

A punisher is any environmental stimulus that, when presented, decreases the future probability of the undesired behavior. Criticism, jail terms, and public ridicule operate as punishers that occur after dressing sloppily, stealing another person's property, and endorsing antisocial attitudes. What makes the criticism, a jail term, or public ridicule a punisher is its capacity to decrease the probability that the behaviors of careless dressing, stealing property, and voicing antisocial attitudes will recur in the future. That is, the person who receives the punisher is less likely to repeat the behavior than is the person who receives no such aversive consequence for doing the same thing.

From a behaviorist's point of view, the idea is this: You can engage in the undesirable behavior and suffer the aversive (punishing) consequence, or you can not engage in the undesirable behavior and be spared the aversive (punishing) consequence. That is, you can continue to dress sloppily, steal people's property, or endorse antisocial attitudes, but you will have to pay the price of doing so (in the form of criticisms, jail terms, and public ridicule).

Some confusion exists in discriminating punishers from negative reinforcers because both utilize aversive stimuli. For instance, when parents reprimand children for not cleaning their room, do the parents administer a negative reinforcer or a punisher? The reprimand is a punisher if its intent is to suppress the child's future room cluttering behavior. Punishers say, "Stop it!" The reprimand is a negative reinforcer, however, if the child dutifully cleans the room to escape from or to avoid the reprimand before it occurs. Negative reinforcers say, "Do it!" Punishers decrease (undesirable) behavior; negative reinforcers increase (escape and avoidance) behavior.

When most people think of punishers, what comes to mind are negative punishers. All negative punishers involve the administration of an aversive stimulus for suppressing future behavior. They are very commonly used in the culture. But there is a second type of punisher—a positive punisher. Positive punishers involve removing positive consequences for suppressing future behavior. A synonym for positive punishers is "response cost," as people who engage in undesirable behavior lose some personal resource—the cost of doing the undesirable behavior. Examples include a suspended driver's license to suppress drunk driving, a toy taken away from a child to suppress a temper tantrum, a child not allowed the privilege of watching a favorite television show to suppress ill manners, a $200 ticket to suppress parking in a handicapped space, a $5 fee to suppress using a live teller at the bank, and being grounded to suppress staying out past curfew.

Does Punishment Work?

The use of punishers is ubiquitous. To control other people's behavior, we often resort to using punishers. We criticize, we give cold looks, we complain, we take privileges away, we spank, and utilize dozens of other extrinsic events to get other people to stop doing whatever undesirable behavior they are doing. But research shows that punishment is an ineffective motivational strategy. So, punishment is popular but ineffective, basically. But why is punishment so widely used? Here are five reasons (Gershoff, 2002):

1. To deter the undesirable behaviors in the future.
2. To gain immediate compliance to stop the undesirable behavior.

3. To serve as "just rewards"—they are somehow fair.

4. To express a negative emotional state (e.g., frustration, anger).

5. To do *something* about the undesirable behavior (and cannot come up with any better strategy).

These reasons communicate why people punish others. But the question still remains whether or not punishment works. That is, does the administration of punishers following people's undesirable behavior subsequently decrease the future probability that the other person will engage in the undesirable behavior? Generally speaking, punishment does not work (Baldwin & Baldwin, 1986). Worse, punishment reliably generates a number of worrisome and unintentional "side effects," including negative emotionality (crying, screaming, feeling afraid), impaired relationship between punisher and punishee, and negative modeling of how to cope with undesirable behavior in others.

Perhaps one of the most controversial uses of punishment is corporal punishment, or spanking (Gershoff, 2002). Figure 6.4 addresses the question of does corporal punishment work? Parents (and others) spank their children for one or more of the five reasons listed above, but mostly they spank to gain the child's immediate compliance to stop the undesirable behavior. Typically, this is spanking's intended consequence. The dashed line in Figure 6.4 means that spanking does *not* produce this effect. The figure also identifies a number of unintended consequences of corporal punishment. The solid line in Figure 6.4 means that spanking does produce these effects. Spanking does foreshadow the child showing aggression, antisocial behavior, poor mental health, poor moral internalization, and an impairment of the parent-child relationship, and spanking does foreshadow the child, as an adult, showing aggression, poor mental health, and abuse as an adult.

Looking over the consequences of corporal punishment, one sees little merit in spanking children as a motivational strategy (Gershoff, 2002). It actually does more harm that good. Spanking does not yield its intentional consequence, while it does yield a flurry of unintentional and undesirable consequences. If spanking does not work, then what does? What works in the effort to deal with other people's undesirable behavior at a motivational level is an approach that fosters a positive relationship with the parent, enhanced well-being in the child, and an increased desire to internalize the parent's values, prescriptions, and proscriptions. The final section of this chapter presents such strategies.

HIDDEN COSTS OF REWARD

The research on the distinction between intrinsic and extrinsic motivation began with this question: "If a person is involved in an intrinsically interesting activity and begins to receive an extrinsic reward for doing it, what happens to his or her intrinsic motivation for that activity?" (Deci & Ryan, 1985a, p. 43). For example, what happens to the motivation of the student who reads for the fun of it after she begins to receive money from her parents for reading? One might suppose that rewarding reading behavior with a monetary prize would add to her motivation. Common sense argues that if a person enjoys reading and is also financially rewarded for it, then the intrinsic (enjoyment) and extrinsic (money) motivations should sum to produce some sort of super-motivation. And if you ask people to make predictions about what happens to a person's motivation under these conditions, increased motivation is what most people will predict (Hom, 1994).

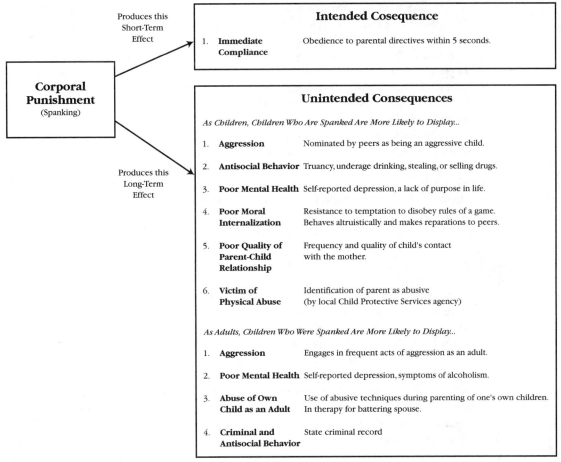

Figure 6.4   Immediate and Long-Term Consequences of Corporal Punishment (Spanking)

Source: From "Corporal Punishment by Parents and Associated Child Behaviors and Experiences: A Meta-Analytical and Theoretical Review," By E.T. Gershoff, 2002, *Psychological Bulletin, 128,* 539–579. Copyright 2002 by American Psychological Association. Adapted by permission.

Increased motivation, however, generally does not occur. Rather, the imposition of an extrinsic reward for an intrinsically interesting activity typically undermines (has a negative effect on) future intrinsic motivation (Condry, 1977; Deci, Koestner, & Ryan, 1999; Kohn, 1993; Lepper, Greene, & Nisbett, 1973). The reward's adverse effect on intrinsic motivation is termed a "hidden cost of reward" (Lepper & Greene, 1978) because our society typically regards rewards as positive contributors to motivation (Boggiano et al., 1987). People use rewards expecting to gain the benefit of increasing another person's motivation and behavior, but in doing so, they often incur the unintentional and hidden cost of undermining that person's intrinsic motivation toward the activity.

Extrinsic rewards can have positive effects on motivation and behavior, as discussed earlier with the seat belt, the postural harness, and the orthodontic gear examples. But extrinsic forms of motivation almost always come with a price—with hidden costs.

The need for autonomy (Chapter 5) provides one way for understanding the hidden costs of reward (Deci & Ryan, 1987). When experimental participants are paid (Deci, 1972), promised an award (Lepper et al., 1973), promised a toy (Lepper & Greene, 1975), threatened with a punisher (Deci & Casio, 1972), given a deadline (Amabile, DeJong, & Lepper, 1976), given a directive (Koestner et al., 1984), involved in competitive pressure (Reeve & Deci, 1996), or watched over as they work (i.e., surveillance; Pittman et al., 1980), these participants gradually lose their perception of autonomy and show decreased intrinsic motivation. In other words, a person's perceived locus of causality (Chapter 5) gradually becomes less and less internal and more and more external (deCharms, 1984). What was once "play" becomes "work." When rewards are at stake, people read less and less out of interest and more and more for money or grades. Basically, coercing individuals to engage in a task, even when using unquestionably attractive rewards like money, instigates a shift in their understanding of why they choose to engage in that task from one of autonomy to one of environment.

Early experiments by Mark Lepper and his colleagues nicely illustrate the hidden costs of extrinsic rewards (Greene & Lepper, 1974; Lepper & Greene, 1975, 1978; Lepper, Greene, & Nisbett, 1973). Preschool children with a high interest in drawing were grouped into one of three experimental conditions: expected reward, no reward, and unexpected reward. In the expected reward group (extrinsic motivational orientation), children were shown an extrinsic reward—an attractive Good Player certificate featuring the child's name and a big blue ribbon—and asked if they wanted to draw in order to win the reward. Children did find this reward to be an attractive one. In the no reward group (intrinsic motivational orientation), children were simply asked if they wanted to draw. In the unexpected reward group, children were asked if they wanted to draw, but they unexpectedly received the Good Player certificate after drawing. One week later, the experimenters provided the children with another opportunity to draw during their free time. During this second week, children who drew in order to win the certificate (expected reward group) spent significantly less time drawing than did children in the other two groups. In effect, children in the expected reward group lost their intrinsic interest in drawing. The no reward and unexpected reward groups showed no such interest decline. The interest maintenance of the unexpected reward group is important because it shows that the extrinsic motivational orientation (rather than the reward per se) caused children's decreased interest in drawing.

In interpreting these findings, one might feel a bit of skepticism and muse over the fact that the sample of participants included preschoolers, the experimental task was drawing, and the reward was an artificial certificate. Perhaps one might then conclude that the findings have little to do with more complex adult motivations. These findings, however, have been replicated using adults, different tasks, and different rewards (see Deci, Koestner, & Ryan, 1999). In accepting the generality of the negative effects (i.e., "the hidden costs") of an extrinsic motivational orientation (Deci et al., 1999a; Deci & Ryan, 1985a; Kohn, 1993; Lepper & Greene, 1978; Rummel & Feinberg, 1988; Sutherland, 1993), one might turn the tables and ask whether rewards always decrease intrinsic motivation. This is precisely what psychologists questioned next. After three decades of research, the conclusion is that extrinsic rewards do generally undermine intrinsic motivation, but not always (Deci et al., 1999; Eisenberger, Pierce, & Cameron, 1999; Rummel &

Feinberg, 1988; Wiersma, 1992). In particular, two factors explain which types of rewards decrease intrinsic motivation: expectancy and tangibility.

Expected and Tangible Rewards

People often engage in behaviors in order to receive a reward. In doing so, people expect to receive a reward if they engage in a particular behavior. If, however, the person engages in the behavior with no such knowledge of a reward yet still receives a reward once the task is completed, then the reward is an unexpected one. The earlier study with children drawing for Good Player certificates (Lepper, Greene, & Nisbett, 1973) showed that reinforcers decrease intrinsic motivation only when the person expects that her task engagement will yield a reward. The telltale sign that a person expects a reward for task participation is an if-then or in-order-to orientation, such as, "If I read this book, then I can watch TV." Expected rewards undermine intrinsic motivation, while unexpected rewards do not (Greene & Lepper, 1974; Orlick & Mosher, 1978; Pallak et al., 1982).

A second factor in understanding which rewards undermine intrinisic motivation and which do not is the distinction between tangible and verbal rewards. Tangible rewards, such as money, awards, and food, tend to decrease intrinsic motivation, whereas verbal (i.e., intangible) rewards, such as praise, do not (Anderson, Manoogian, & Reznick, 1976; Blank, Reis, & Jackson, 1984; Cameron & Pierce, 1994; Deci, 1972; Dollinger & Thelen, 1978; Kast & Connor, 1988; Koestner, Zuckerman, & Koestner, 1987; Sansone, 1989; Swann & Pittman, 1977). In other words, rewards that one can see, touch, feel, and taste generally decrease intrinsic motivation, whereas verbal, symbolic, or abstract rewards do not.

Implications

The two limiting factors of expectancy and tangibility suggest that rewards decrease intrinsic motivation only when they are expected and tangible. This conclusion is a sort of good news/bad news message. The good news is that extrinsic rewards can be used in a way that does not put intrinsic motivation at risk. The bad news is that our society so often relies on expected and tangible rewards to motivate others. Money, bonuses, paychecks, prizes, trophies, scholarships, privileges, grades, gold stars, awards, honor-roll lists, incentive plans, recognition, food, frequent-flyer miles, and so on are ubiquitous incentives and consequences in Western societies (Kohn, 1993). In practice, therefore, it is not so comforting to say that only expected and tangible extrinsic rewards will decrease intrinsic motivation because so many rewards are presented in an expected and tangible way.

Expected, tangible rewards actually put more at risk than just intrinsic motivation (Condry, 1977, 1987; Deci & Ryan, 1987; Kohn, 1993). Extrinsic reinforcers not only decrease intrinsic motivation, they also interfere with both the process and quality of learning. During a learning activity, extrinsic rewards distract the person's attention away from learning and toward getting a reward. Rewards shift the learner's goals away from attaining mastery in favor of attaining extrinsic gain (Harter, 1978b; Pittman, Boggiano, & Ruble, 1983; Shapira, 1976). Extrinsically motivated learners are also more prone to a negative emotional tone (e.g., frustration; Garbarino, 1975) and less prone to positive emotion (e.g., enjoyment; Harter, 1978b; Ryan & Connell, 1989; Skinner & Belmont, 1993). Further, extrinsically motivated learners are relatively passive information processors (Benware & Deci, 1984).

Rewards interfere with the quality of learning by narrowing the would-be learner's attention toward only memorizing factual information at the expense of gaining a conceptual understanding of the material (Benware & Deci, 1984; Boggiano et al., 1993; Flink, Boggiano, & Barrett, 1990). Rewards further put at risk a learner's flexibility in her way of thinking and problem solving (as she tries to produce a right answer quickly rather than discover an optimal solution; McGraw & McCullers, 1979). Expected, tangible rewards also undermine creativity (Amabile, 1985; Amabile, Hennessey, & Grossman, 1986), as people are more creative when they draw and write out of interest than when they draw and write for rewards. And when rewards are involved, learners typically quit as soon as some reward criterion is attained (e.g., reading only the 100 pages required for the test). When rewards are not involved, learners generally persist until curiosity is satisfied, interest is exhausted, or mastery is attained (Condry, 1977; Condry & Chambers, 1978). Thus, not only is intrinsic motivation potentially at risk with the use of expected and tangible rewards, but so is the quality of the learning process (e.g., preference for challenging work, attention, emotional tone, conceptual understanding, cognitive flexibility, and creativity).

A final point is that rewards interfere with the development of autonomous self-regulation (Lepper, 1983; Ryan, 1993). When the social environment tells people what to do and also provides expected and tangible rewards for doing it, people have little difficulty regulating their behavior in rewarding ways. But schools, families, places of work, and other settings often value autonomous self-regulation (i.e., initiative, intrinsic motivation). Learning to depend on rewards can forestall the development of self-regulatory abilities. For instance, students who do not receive rewards for engaging in their academic activities show a close connection between what they are interested in doing and how they spend their time, while children who do receive rewards for engaging in their academic activities show no connection between what they are interested in doing and how they spend their time (Joussemet et al., 2003). This finding occurs because the later students' behavior is regulated by other people's rewards, not by their own interests. If the environment does not offer incentives and consequences, then people with little autonomous self-regulation will have a difficult time finding the needed motivation within themselves.

Benefits of Incentives and Rewards

Rewards sometimes undermine intrinsic motivation, interfere with learning, and forestall autonomous self-regulation. Recognizing this, researchers have tried to use rewards in ways that minimize their detrimental effects. One way to do this, as discussed earlier, is to use rewards that are unexpected and verbal (e.g., praise) and refrain from using those that are expected and tangible (e.g., bribes). A second means is to limit the use of extrinsic motivators to tasks that have social importance but very little intrinsic appeal. That is, if a person has little or no intrinsic motivation to engage in a task in the first place, then intrinsic motivation is not likely to be put at risk by extrinsic rewards (because there is little or no intrinsic motivation present in the person to undermine).

This latter concern raises the interesting question of whether extrinsic motivators will have hidden costs on tasks that are not at all interesting. In other words, if a person has no intrinsic motivation toward the task to undermine, they how can extrinsic motivators undermine their intrinsic motivation? Indeed, research shows that the negative impact of extrinsic rewards on intrinsic motivation is limited to interesting activities (Deci, Koestner, & Ryan, 1999), as extrinsic rewards have no effect—not an undermining effect, not a faciliating effect—on a person's intrinsic motivation for uninteresting tasks. Thus, research currently suggests no reason for using, and no reason for avoiding, the use of rewards when others are faced with having to engage in an uninteresting task.

Incentives and reinforcers have their benefits. Rewards can make an otherwise uninteresting task seem suddenly worth pursuing. So long as the reward is attractive enough, rewarded individuals will engage in almost any task. Children will eagerly wash dishes if it means that doing so will gain them a new toy. This is typically not so with unrewarded children, because washing dishes is just not an intrinsically interesting thing to do for most people. Without a reward at stake, those dishes stay piled in the sink. In applied settings, behaviorists often promise rewards if their clients perform behaviors like homework, being on time, showing assertiveness, attending a group discussion, and participating in that same group discussion. They do so because their experience tells them that, without a reward at stake, their clients will not engage in these sorts of low-interest behaviors. Consider the value of extrinsic motivators in the following instances in which researchers used rewards to increase socially important but intrinsically uninteresting tasks:

- Developing daily living skills, such as dressing (Pierce & Schreibman, 1994)
- Improving children's reading fluency (Eckert et al., 2002)
- Getting motorists to stop at stop signs (Van Houten & Retting, 2001)
- Preventing drunk driving (Geller, Altomari, & Russ, 1984)
- Participating in recycling (Brothers, 1994; Austira et al., 1993) and energy conservation (Staat, Van Leeuwen, & Wit, 2000)
- Motivating young children to start their homework (Miller & Kelley, 1994)
- Teaching autistic children to initiate peer conversations (Krantz & McClannahan, 1993)
- Preventing undesirable behaviors such as thumbsucking (Ellingson et al., 2000) and biting and poking (Fisher et al., 1993)
- Teaching self-control to children with ADHD (Binder, Dixon, & Ghezzi, 2000)
- Increasing the elderly's participation in physical activities (Gallagher & Keenan, 2000)

In each of these examples, an argument can be made that the society's concerns for promoting desirable behavior from its citizens outweighs the concerns for preserving or protecting the individual's autonomy, intrinsic motivation, quality of learning, and autonomous self-regulation. Therefore, is it fine and well to use extrinsic motivators when another person's intrinsic motivation is low, right? Not necessarily. Consider the following four reasons not to use extrinsic motivators, even for intrinsically uninteresting endeavors (Kohn, 1993):

1. Extrinsic motivators still undermine the quality of performance and interfere with the process of learning.

2. Using rewards distracts attention away from asking the hard question of why another person is being asked to do an uninteresting task in the first place.

3. There are better ways to encourage participation than extrinsic bribery (e.g., consider autonomy-supportive environments).

4. Extrinsic motivators still undermine the individual's long-term capacity for autonomous self-regulation.

Let's look a bit closer at this last issue—namely, that extrinsic motivators undermine people's long-term capacity for autonomous self-regulation. One area in which people dish out a steady stream of extrinsic motivators to regulate the behavior of others is in the area of special education (e.g., mental retardation, learning disabilities). While many special education practitioners find utility in administering a steady stream of extrinsic motivators to externally regulate the behavior of people with disabilities, others favor the effort to promote people's long-term capacity for autonomous self-regulation (Algozzine et al., 2001). Instead of asking people with, say, mental retardation to react to the incentives and consequences strategically offered by others, the effort is to help promote self-determination in their lives. For instance, individuals with disabilities are taught skills like self-advocacy and choice making. The idea is to empower people with disabilities to first voice their interests and preferences and then exercise choices that express those preferences. After learning such skills, researchers observed individuals with disabilities in naturalistic settings such as public restaurants in which they acted on their preferences, such as for beverages (Belfoire, Browder, & Mace, 1994) and foods (Cooper & Browder, 1998). Empowered with greater autonomous self-regulation in their lives (rather than regulated externally by extrinsic motivators), these individuals showed enhanced functioning and well-being.

When all is said and done, many people believe that extrinsic motivators simply carry too high a psychological cost in terms of intrinsic motivation, the process of learning, the quality of learning, and autonomous self-regulation. But such a conclusion turns out to be more of the beginning of the story on extrinsic motivators than it does the story's end, as explained in the next section on cognitive evaluation theory.

COGNITIVE EVALUATION THEORY

When people use external events as incentives and consequences, they generally seek to create in others an extrinsic motivation for engaging in that activity. Much of the spirit behind the use of an extrinsic motivator is therefore to shape, influence, or outright control another person's behavior. Sometimes the attempt to control is obvious (e.g., using money to bribe a child to wear orthodontic gear; see Figure 6.2), but other times it is more seductive (e.g., giving free soft drinks at a bar to anyone agreeing to be a designated driver; Brigham, Maier, & Goodner, 1995). Thus, one potential purpose behind almost any extrinsic motivator is to control another person's behavior—that is, to increase some desirable behavior (or to decrease some undesirable behavior). But there is a second purpose. Incentives and consequences also provide feedback that informs the person about her competence at the task. Rewards such as money, awards, good grades, academic scholarships, and verbal praises not only function to increase behavior (i.e., control behavior) but also to communicate a message of a job well done (i.e., inform competence).

Cognitive evaluation theory asserts that *all* external events have both a controlling aspect and an informational aspect (Deci & Ryan, 1985a). The theory presumes that people have psychological needs for autonomy and competence (Chapter 5) and that the controlling aspect of an external event affects the need for autonomy whereas its informational aspect affects the need for competence. Formally, cognitive evaluation theory exists as the set of three propositions shown in Table 6.1.

Propositions 1 and 2 repeat two themes expressed in Chapter 5. According to Proposition 1, external events that promote an internal perceived locus of causality (PLOC) promote intrinsic motivation because these events involve or satisfy the need for autonomy. External events that promote an external PLOC promote extrinsic motivation because these events neglect the need for autonomy and instead establish an if-then contingency between a behavior and a forthcoming consequence. Proposition 1 therefore asks, "Is the purpose of the extrinsic event to control another person's behavior?" If not, autonomy and intrinsic motivation will be preserved; if so, then autonomy and intrinsic motivation will be undermined as extrinsic motivation replaces intrinsic motivation.

According to Proposition 2, events that increase perceived competence promote intrinsic motivation, whereas events that decrease perceived competence undermine this motivation. Hence, the more an external event communicates positive effectance information, the more likely it is to satisfy the need for competence and increase intrinsic motivation. Proposition 2 therefore asks, "Is the purpose of the extrinsic event to inform another person's sense of competence?" If so, perceived competence and intrinsic motivation will

Table 6.1   Cognitive Evaluation Theory

Proposition 1

External events affect a person's intrinsic motivation when they influence the perceived locus of causality (PLOC) for that behavior. Events that promote a more external PLOC will decrease intrinsic and increase extrinsic motivation, whereas those that promote a more internal PLOC will increase intrinsic and decrease extrinsic motivation.

Proposition 2

External events affect a person's intrinsic motivation for an optimally challenging activity when they influence the person's perceived competence. Events that promote greater perceived competence will enhance intrinsic motivation, whereas those that diminish perceived competence will decrease intrinsic motivation.

Proposition 3

Events relevant to the initiation and regulation of behavior have three potential aspects, each with a functional significance. The informational aspect facilitates an internal PLOC and perceived competence, thus enhancing intrinsic motivation. The controlling aspect facilitates an external PLOC, thus undermining intrinsic motivation and promoting extrinsic motivation. The amotivating aspect facilitates perceived incompetence, thus undermining intrinsic motivation and promoting amotivation. The relative salience of these three aspects to a person determines the functional significance of the external event.

Source: Adapted with permission from *Intrinsic Motivation and Self-Determination in Human Behavior*, by E. L. Deci and R. M. Ryan, 1985a, New York: Plenum. Copyright 1985, Plenum Press.

rise and fall to the extent that the external event communicates positive versus negative effectance information.

The contribution that the first two propositions offer for understanding the motivational significance of incentives and consequences is this: They focus attention not only on how an extrinsic event affects *behavior* but, in addition, on how it affects people's *psychological needs*.

Proposition 3 ties together the first two propositions into a full theoretical statement. According to Proposition 3, the relative salience of whether an event is mostly controlling or mostly informational determines its effects on intrinsic and extrinsic motivation. Relatively controlling events undermine intrinsic motivation (via their effect on autonomy) and promote extrinsic motivation. Relatively informational events increase intrinsic motivation (via their effect on competence). It is in Proposition 3 that the usefulness of cognitive evaluation theory becomes apparent. The reader can use cognitive evaluation theory to predict the effect that any extrinsic event will have on intrinsic and extrinsic motivations, as discussed more fully in Box 6. The essential question becomes, Why am I giving another person this external event—Is my purpose to control his behavior, or is my purpose to inform his competence?

Two Examples of Controlling and Informational Events

Any external event—praise, money, grades, a scholarship, surveillance, deadlines, interpersonal competition, etc.—can be administered in a relatively controlling way or in a relatively informational way.

Praise

Consider how praise functions as an extrinsic event sometimes to control another's behavior and sometimes to inform her competence about a job well done. A supervisor using praise, for instance, might communicate praise in an informational way, saying, "Excellent job, your productivity increased by 10%." The supervisor might, however, communicate praise in a controlling way, saying, "Excellent job, you did just as you should." Tagging phrases such as "you should," "you must," "you have to," and "you ought to" onto the praise gives the feedback a tone of pressure (Ryan, 1982). In contrast, providing clear, specific, and competence-diagnosing feedback typically gives praise a highly informative function (Brophy, 1981). For example, the praise, "Excellent job, I noticed that you greeted the customer warmly and with a sincere tone in your voice," speaks informatively to an employee's sense of competence in a way that a simple and vague, "Excellent job," does not. The conclusion is that the motivational effect is not in the praise per se but in the way it is administered (Deci & Ryan, 1985a).

Competition

A second illustration of how the same external event can be relatively controlling or relatively informational is interpersonal competition (Reeve & Deci, 1996). When the social context puts a good deal of pressure on winning (with its evaluative audience, coaches, peers, newspaper reporters, championship trophies, career implications), competitors usually compete with a sense of contingency, pressure, and a sense of doing the work for

BOX 6 *Predicting How* Any *External Event Will Affect Motivation*

Question: Why is this information important?

Answer: So that you can predict, in advance, what effect *any* external event will have on motivation.

When teachers put stickers on children's homework, they hope the stickers will motivate the children to work hard. When employers give end-of-the-year holiday bonuses, they hope the money will motivate the workers to work hard. And when street panhandlers wash the windows of a person's car at a traffic stop, they hope the driver will give them some money. The logic is: Since stickers, money, and favors are good, the children's, workers,' and drivers' motivation will probably respond in a positive way.

Why a reward is given is at least as important as what is given. A sincere pat on the back can enhance motivation even more than can a big fat check, if the check has strings attached to it. Basically, the purpose behind the reward ("Why is this person giving me this reward?") is more important than is the reward itself.

Understanding how any external event affects another person's motivation is the domain of cognitive evaluation theory. The theory can be articulated in the accompanying flowchart.

To make sense of the figure, first write in the blank line (on the left) any external event. A teacher, for instance, might be interested in the motivational effects of external events like stickers, grades, praise, tests, or deadlines. Next, working from left to right, determine the external event's purpose, or functional significance. Is the external event being used to control behavior, or is it being used to inform competence? In particular, which of these two aspects is the relatively more salient one? Is the purpose behind the event (i.e., its "functional significance") mostly about controlling behavior or mostly about communicating competence?

If the external event is used largely to control behavior, then its motivational effect will be to decrease self-determination, decrease intrinsic motivation, and increase extrinsic motivation. If the external event is not used to control behavior, then it will not decrease self-determination, not decrease intrinsic motivation, and not increase extrinsic motivation. If the external event is used to communicate a job well done, then its motivational effect will be to increase competence and hence intrinsic motivation. When the external event communicates a job poorly done, however, its motivational effect will be to decrease competence and hence intrinsic motivation.

Notice that in predicting how any external event will affect another person's motivation, the critical question is not what the external event is, but rather, why one person administers it to another.

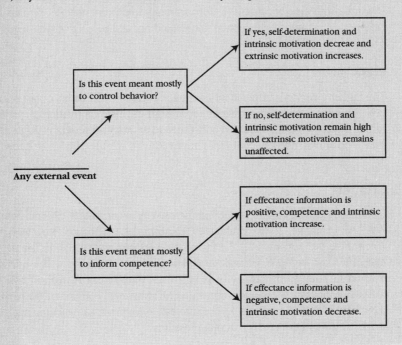

others. When experienced in such a controlling way, competition decreases intrinsic motivation because competitors care relatively little about the task itself and relatively much about the reward of winning (Deci et al., 1981; Vallerand, Gauvin, & Halliwell, 1986). The point of the competition ceases to be about the game or sport but, instead, becomes about winning. However, when the social context places little emphasis on winning (recreational competition, no audience present, no trophy or scholarship for winning, an autonomy-supportive coach), then competition's informational aspect can emerge as relatively more salient. Through its outcome and through competitors' perceptions of making progress in their skills, competitive situations can provide a useful arena for sending a message of competence to competitors. Winning and making progress increase intrinsic motivation, while losing and the failure to make progress decrease it (McAuley & Tammen, 1989; Reeve, Olson, & Cole, 1985). But when the interpersonal competition focuses highly on winning, then the message of high competence gets overwhelmed by the message of pressure. In fact, winning in a controlling context does not increase intrinsic motivation (Reeve & Deci, 1996). Thus, for intrinsic motivation to flourish, both competence and autonomy must be high (Fisher, 1978), and for both competence and autonomy to be high, an external event needs to be presented in both a noncontrolling and informational way.

Benefits of Facilitating Intrinsic Motivation

Intrinsic motivation is a natural motivation that emerges spontaneously out of people's needs for competence and autonomy. So external events cannot create intrinsic motivation in others but, instead, can be used to support and facilate the intrinsic motivation they already have. Hence, the judicious use of external events can facilitate and encourage not only people's extrinsic motivation but also their intrinsic motivation. Intrinsic motivation is worth promoting because it leads to so many important benefits to the person, including persistence, creativity, conceptual understanding, and subjective well-being.

Persistence

The higher a person's intrinsic motivation, the greater will be his or her persistence on that task. This increased persistence effect of high intrinsic motivation plays itself out in different ways, including increased adherence to an exercise program (Ryan et al., 1997) and increased attendance and continuing motivation in school (Hardre & Reeve, 2003).

Creativity

Controlling external events undermine creativity, as creativity declines when one is being watched (Amabile, 1983), evaluated (Amabile, 1979), bossed (Koestner et al., 1984), or when there are rewards at stake for expert performance (Amabile, Hennessey, & Grossman, 1986). In contrast, intrinsic motivation enhances creativity. The role of intrinsic motivation in stimulating creativity is so robust that Teresa Amabile (1983) proposed the following Intrinsic Motivation Principle of Creativity: "People will be most creative when they feel motivated primarily by the interest, enjoyment, satisfaction, and challenge of the work itself—rather than by external pressures."

Conceptual Understanding/High-Quality Learning

A third benefit of intrinsic motivation is its capacity to enhance learner's conceptual understanding during a learning activity. When intrinsic motivation is high, learners show a greater flexibility in their way of thinking (McGraw & McCullers, 1979), are more active information processors (Grolnick & Ryan, 1987), and learn in a way that is conceptual rather than rote (Benware & Deci, 1984; Boggiano et al., 1993; Grolnick & Ryan, 1987). When intrinsically motivated, learners think about and integrate information in a flexible and less rigid way; when externally regulated (e.g., by a test), learners become more rigid in their way of thinking as their attention narrows to focus specifically to factual and rote information (i.e., on getting the right answer).

Optimal Functioning and Well-Being

People experience optimal function and positive well-being when they pursue goals that reflect intrinsic motivation (e.g., competence, relatedness, autonomy in life) rather than when they pursue goals that reflect extrinsic motivation (e.g., financial success, social recognition, physical image). That is, those who pursue intrinsic motivation in life show greater self-actualization and subjective vitality, less anxiety and depression, greater self-esteem, higher-quality relationships with friends and intimates, watch less television, and use drugs such as alcohol and cigarettes less (Kasser & Ryan, 1996, 2001).

SELF-DETERMINATION THEORY

One of the themes of motivation presented in Chapter 1 was that motivation varies not only in intensity but also in its type. This chapter points out the utility in making the distinction between intrinsic and extrinsic motivations. In addition, types of extrinsic motivation exist (Deci & Ryan, 1985a, 1991; Rigby et al., 1992; Ryan & Deci, 2000a, 2000b).

The self-determination continuum of motivation appears in Figure 6.5. According to self-determination theory, three distinct types of motivation exist: amotivation, extrinsic motivation, and intrinsic motivation. These types of motivation can be organized along a continuum of self-determination or perceived locus of causality. On the far left-hand side is amotivation, which literally means "without motivation," a state in which the person is neither intrinsically nor extrinsically motivated (e.g., a drop-out student, disillusioned athlete, or apathetic marriage partner). In the middle of the figure are four types of extrinsic motivation, which can be distinguished from one another on the basis of their degree of self-determination: external regulation (not at all self-determined), introjected regulation (somewhat self-determined), identified regulation (mostly self-determined), and integrated regulation (fully self-determined). On the far right-hand side, intrinsic motivation reflects the individual's full endorsement of self-determination and pertains to all those instances in which a person's psychological needs generate a motivation to act. Overall, the self-determination continuum varies from amotivation or unwillingness, to passive compliance, to active personal commitment, to interest/enjoyment (Ryan & Deci, 2000b).

Identifying types of motivation is important because the amount of self-determination within any motivational state has a substantial effect on what people feel, think, and do (Gottfried, 1985; Grolnick & Ryan, 1987; Ryan & Connell, 1989; Vallerand et al., 1992).

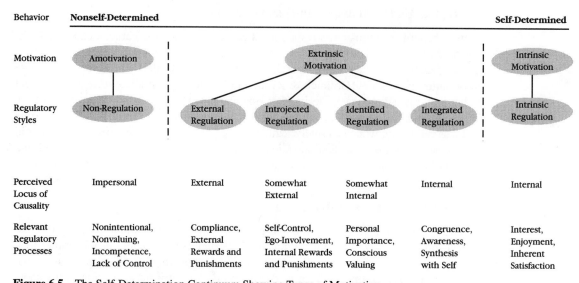

Behavior	**Nonself-Determined**					**Self-Determined**

Figure 6.5 The Self-Determination Continuum Showing Types of Motivation

Source: Ryan, R. M., & Deci, E. L. (2000a). Self-determination theory and the facilitation of intrinsic motivation, social development, and well-being. *American Psychologist, 55,* 68–78. Copyright 2000 by American Psychological Association. Reprinted by permission.

Notice that the four types of extrinsic motivation vary greatly in the degree to which the person experiences them as autonomous or as self-determined. People engage in external and introjected regulation largely out of compliance and because they have to (i.e., they are being controlled), while people who engage in identified and integrated regulation do so largely because they want to and choose to (i.e., they act autonomously). For instance, school-age children were asked what motivated their academic behaviors (e.g., "Why do you do your homework?" and "Why do you try to do well in school?"), and researchers later assessed their school-related emotion, effort, and performance (Ryan & Connell, 1989). Students' reasons reflected various amounts of perceived self-determination that ranged from very little ("because it's the rule; I have to"), through a little self-determination ("because I would feel guilty if I didn't"), to much self-determination ("because it is important to me") to full self-determination ("because it's fun, I enjoy it"). The more self-determined students' motivations were, the more effort they put forth, and the more they achieved. School children with little self-determination put forth minimal effort and achieved poorly. So some types of extrinsic motivation (e.g., identified regulation) generate more productive forms of motivation than do other types of extrinsic motivation (e.g., external regulation).

These findings show the importance of making distinctions among types of extrinsic motivation, and they generalize not only to the students' motivation toward school but also to the efforts exerted by individuals in an alcohol-treatment program (Ryan, Plant, & O'Malley, 1995), in a weight-loss program (Williams et al., 1996), in a relationship (Blais et al., 1990), in adhering to exercise (Ryan et al., 1997), in political participation (Koestner et al., 1996), and to religious participation (Ryan, Rigby, & King, 1993). In each case, the type of motivation mattered, and the more self-determined it was the more positive were the outcomes the person experienced.

Types of Extrinsic Motivation

Although intrinsic motivation is an important type of motivation, most of the activity people do during the day is not intrinsically motivated. Instead, personal responsibility, social demands, and the request of others guide much of what we do. In practice, all types of extrinsic motivation involve the pairing of an extrinsic contingency with some requested behavior. The added external contingency functionally creates an extrinsic motivation to perform the activity that the activity itself cannot generate, as in "Do this in order to get that" in which the "this" is an uninteresting activity and the "that" is an extrinsic contingency. Table 6.2 features an illustration of the sort of external contingencies that promote each of the four types of extrinsic motivation, using the example of recycling.

External Regulation

External regulation is the prototype of nonself-determined extrinsic motivation. Externally-regulated behaviors are performed to obtain a reward or to satisfy some external demand. For the person who is externally regulated, the presence versus absence of extrinsic motivators (e.g., rewards, threats) regulates the rise and fall of motivation. A person who is externally regulated typically has a difficult time beginning a task unless there is some external prompt to do so. A student, for instance, begins to study only when a test is upcoming or begins to write a term paper only when the deadline nears. Without the test or the deadline, the student lacks the motivation necessary to study or to write. With external regulation, the person has not internalized a voluntary willingness to perform the activity (studying, writing) for its own sake. With no internalization, the person simply waits for incentives and pressures in the environment to provide a reason to act. Relative to the other three types of extrinsic motivation, people who are motivated through external regulation show poor functioning and poor outcomes (Deci & Ryan, 1987; Kohn, 1993; Ryan & Connell, 1989; Ryan & Deci, 2000b).

Table 6.2   Four Types of Extrinsic Motivation, Illustrated by Different Reasons of "Why I Recycle"

Type of Extrinsic Motivation	External Contingency At Stake	The reason I recycle is. . .	Illustrative Quotation
External Regulation	Incentives, consequences	"to get a consequence."	"I recycle to make 5 cents on each can."
Introjected Regulation	Avoid guilt, boost self-esteem	"because I should."	"I recycle because I ought to, if I am going to feel good (rather than guilty) about myself."
Identified Regulation	Valuing, sense of importance	"because it is important."	"I recycle because it is important for a cleaner environment."
Integrated Regulation	Value congruence	"because it reflects my values."	"I recycle because it reflects and expresses who I am and what I believe."

Introjected Regulation

Introjected regulation involves taking in, but not truly accepting or self-endorsing, other people's demands to think, feel, or behave in a particular manner. Introjected regulation is essentially being motivated out of guilt and the "tyranny of the shoulds" (Horney, 1937). In essence, the person, acting as a proxy for the external environment, emotionally rewards himself for performing other-defined good behavior (feel proud) and emotionally punishes himself or herself for performing other-defined bad behavior (feel shamed or guilty). Therefore, partial internalization has occurred, but the internalization is kept at an arm's length, so to speak, instead of being really integrated into the self in an authentic and volitional way. The telltale sign that only partial (rather than full) internalization has occurred is because the person feels such high tension and pressure in carrying out the introjected-motivated behavior (e.g., "I just *have to* study tonight!). With introjected regulation, the person carries another person's (or society's) prescriptions inside his or her head to such an extent that the introjected voice, not the self per se, generates the motivation to act. Notice, however, that introjected regulation does include the changing of internal structures because the behavior is regulated not by explicit external contingencies but rather by internalized representations of those contingencies (i.e., a parent's voice, cultural expectations). For instance, employees might come to work on time or may resist stealing office supplies not because they choose to be punctual or honest, but because being late or dishonest would produce the punishing feelings of guilt and shame, whereas being on time or honest would produce the positively reinforcing feelings of pride and approval.

Identified Regulation

Identified regulation represents mostly internalized and self-determined extrinsic motivation. With identified regulation, the person voluntarily accepts the merits and utility of a belief or behavior because that way of thinking or behaving is seen as personally important or useful. Thus, if a student comes to believe that extra work in mathematics is important (e.g., it has utility for a career in science) or if an athlete comes to believe that extra practice on his or her backhand is important, the motivation to study and to practice are extrinsic but freely chosen. Extra work in mathematics or in tennis is extrinsic because these behaviors are instrumental to other aims (a career as a scientist, tennis pro), yet they are freely chosen because they are perceived to be useful and valuable for one's life. Exercise and cooperation provide two additional examples of identified regulation. Many people exercise religiously and cooperate freely with others not because they enjoy jogging or sharing, but because they value what such behaviors can do for them and for their relationships with others. Because these ways of thinking and behaving are valued and deemed as personally important, people internalize/identify with them and, by internalizing them, these ways of thinking and behaving become self-determined.

Integrated Regulation

Integrated regulation constitutes the most self-determined type of extrinsic motivation. While internalization is the process of taking in a value or a way of behaving, integration is the process through which individuals fully transform their identified values and behaviors into the self (Ryan & Deci, 2000a). It is as much a developmental process as it is a type of motivation, because it involves the self-examination necessary to bring new ways of thinking, feeling, and behaving into an unconflicted congruence with the self's pre-existing ways of thinking, feeling, and behaving. That is, integration occurs as otherwise isolated identifications (e.g., "recycling newspapers is not fun, but I want to do it anyway because it is important for the environment.") into coherence and congruence with the existing values of the self (e.g., "I value the environment very much."). The more the person integrates internalized ways of thinking and behaving into the larger self-system, the more his or her extrinsically-motivated actions become self-determined.

Because it is the most self-determined type of extrinsic motivation, integrated regulation is associated with the most positive outcomes, such as prosocial development and psychological well-being (Ryan & Deci, 2000a). The general conclusion from empirical investigations of the self-determination theory continuum of types of motivation is that the more self-determined one's extrinsic motivation is, the better one functions, as with school achievement (Ryan & Connell, 1989) and greater psychological well-being (Sheldon & Kasser, 1995).

PUTTING IT ALL TOGETHER: MOTIVATING OTHERS ON UNINTERESTING ACTIVITIES

People face a difficult motivational problem when they attempt to motivate others to engage in uninteresting, but worthwhile, activities. Examples of such undertakings might include parents asking their children to wash their hands before dinner, teachers asking students to complete a worksheet of difficult math problems, and workplace managers asking workers to be polite to rude customers. The first solution to such a motivational problems is, typically, to use an incentive to prompt the other person into doing what ever it is you want them to do, as with a parent saying, "If you wash your hands then you'll get ice cream for dessert; if you don't wash you hands then there will be no dessert." In this case, the want of the ice cream motivates compliance, not the intrinsic appeal or the personal valuing of washing one's hands. The problem with using expected and tangible rewards is that they yield only compliance, low-quality learning, minimal functioning (poorly washed hands), and a dependence on further external regulation. The hope, however, is that we can somehow come up with motivational strategies that yield initiative, high-quality learning, creative functioning, and autonomous self-regulation.

The reason so many people use external contingencies to motivate others is that in pairing an external contingency (reward, deadline) with an uninteresting activity they hope to redefine that activity away from something "not worth doing" toward something "worth doing." That is, the added external contingency creates a motivation to engage in the activity that the activity itself cannot generate (because it is so uninteresting). Recognizing that external contingencies generally promote controlling forms of extrinsic motivation associated with poor functioning, researchers have tested the extent to which a noncontrolling external contingency could promote a self-determined form of extrinsic motivation that is associated with enhanced functioning. One such contingency is the provision of a rationale—a verbal explanation of why putting forth effort during the activity might be a useful thing to do (Deci et al., 1994; Newby, 1991; Reeve et al., 2002). Here are three illustrations:

- A parent explains to a child why raking the leaves is an important thing to do:

"Raking the leaves is important because we need to clean the yard of its leaves to make way for the Halloween trick-or-treaters tonight."

- An engineering professor explains why his students need to read their dry textbook before the next class:

    "Reading pages 310–325 tonight is important because you are all going to build something and the information you need to build it is in the textbook on pages 310–325."

- A medical doctor explains why exercising is important for her patient:

    "Exercising three times a week is important because it will significantly decrease your susceptibility to a heart attack."

Consider two studies that offered participants a rationale for why engaging in a relatively uninteresting activity was "something worth doing"—was something worth the effort. In the first, researchers asked participants to engage in a very uninteresting vigilance task (pressing the space bar on a keyboard whenever a light appeared on the computer screen) either with or without the following rationale (Deci et al., 1994, p. 127):

"Doing this activity has been shown to be useful. We have found that those subjects who have done it have learned about their own concentration. This has occurred because the activity involves focused attention which is important in concentration. For example, this is the type of task that air traffic controllers use in order to enhance their signal detection abilities."

In the second, researchers asked preservice teachers (college students preparing to become elementary- and secondary-grade teachers) to engage in a foreign-language lesson (learning Chinese) either with or without the following rationale (Reeve et al., 2002, p. 189):

"The reason we are asking you to try hard during the conversational Chinese lesson is because it is useful. Today's lesson offers you the opportunity to gain a skill that will be very handy when you become a classroom teacher. By being able to say 'Hello' and 'What is your name?' in Chinese, you will be communicating a message of care and inclusion to the Chinese-speaking students who will very soon be in your classes."

After hearing a rationale or not, participants in both studies then spent about a half hour with their activity while the experimenters monitored their self-determined motivation (with a questionnaire) and their effort (with behavioral observation). Results from the study with preservice teachers learning the conversational Chinese lesson appear in Figure 6.6. The offering of the rationale ("Reason to try") did allow the preservice teachers to find value in the lesson—to experience the identification experience that underlies identified regulation—and the greater they identified with the lesson's value, the greater effort they invested during the lesson. The line from Pre-Lesson Identified Regulation to the Identification Experience is also important in that it shows that preservice teachers showed individual differences in how important and useful they found the Chinese lesson to be (some thought it was a waste of their time, others thought it was a worthwhile thing to do). Hence, effort during the lesson came from identified regulation (the identification experience), and identified regulation during the lesson came partly from the experimenter-provided rationale as to why the lesson was worth the effort (Reason to Try) and partly from the preservice teachers' preexisting identified regulation toward learning Chinese.

The reason an externally-provided rationale works as a motivational strategy during an uninteresting activity is because it can spark some degree of valuing, internalization, and identified regulation. Internalization occurs as the person comes to agree, "You say

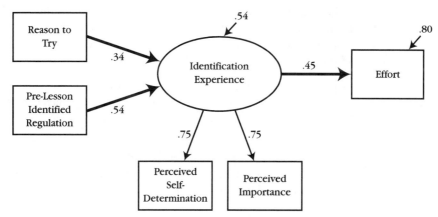

Figure 6.6 Structural Equation Model to Show that the Presence of a Rationale Enhanced Participants' Effort (by Cultivating a Motivation-Rich Identification Experience)

Source: From "Providing a Rationale in an Autonomy-Supportive Way as a Strategy to Motivate Others During an Uninteresting Activity," by J. Reeve, H. Jang, P. Hardre, & M. Omura, 2002, *Motivation and Emotion, 26,* 183–207. Copyright 2002, Plenum Press.

this activity is a useful thing to do. You might be right; this activity might indeed be useful to me." The more fully a person transforms an externally-prescribed regulation into an internally-endorsed one, the more self-determined will be the person's subsequent motivation and behavior (i.e., effort). Both investigations above also found that to help another person "take on" (internalize) the externally-provided rationale as his or her own required not only an articulation of why the activity is useful but also the presence of autonomy-supportive facilitating conditions such as noncontrolling language and the acknowledgment of negative feelings in being asked to engage in what might be a boring activity. Thus, how you say the rationale (noncontrolling, acknowledge negative affect) is as important as why you say the activity is useful to the other person.

The motivational strategy of providing a rationale applies best to those activities that truly are uninteresting things to do. But a boring task does not always have to be a boring task. While people are engaging (or asked to engage) in relatively uninteresting activities (doing homework, washing clothes, driving cross-country), people can engage in a number of strategies to foster interest, even during boring tasks (Sansone et al., 1992; Sansone & Smith, 2000). For instance, enhancing the challenge offered by the activity so as to test one's personal skill can potentially increase intrinsic motivation and flow. People can decrease boredom by adding variety and stimulation to the performance of a repetitive activity. People can also mentally change the context (use fantasy) such that instead of reading about how to motivate others on uninteresting tasks you might add your imagination and instead think about how to get your roommate to wash those dirty dishes in the sink tonight. To make a math-learning computer software program more interesting to elementary grade students, one group of researchers transformed a rather rote mathematics exercise on fractions into a "Space Quest" game in which students needed to solve fractions to save the planet from aliens. Solving fractions within the Space Quest fantasy game was more interesting and fun (and produced better learning) than solving fractions within the more traditional presentation of such a task (Cordova & Lepper, 1996).

The last strategy to try to motivate others during uninteresting activities is to use incentives and consequences, but to administer them in a way that is highly informational and not at all controlling (Box 6). So, overall, practitioners have three effective options to choose from as they try to motivate others during uninteresting activities:

1. Promote identified regulation (and internalization) by acknowledging that the task may be uninteresting but by also articulating its importance, personal use, or "hidden value" in terms of why it is a worthwhile thing to do.

2. Promote interest by translating the boring task into something more interesting to do (via challenge, variety, or a fantasy context).

3. Promote competence and preserve self-determination by administering extrinsic rewards in a highly informational and noncontrolling way.

SUMMARY

Extrinsic motivation arises from an environmentally created reason to initiate an action. External events like money and frequent-flyer miles generate extrinsic motivation to the extent that they establish a "means to an end" contingency in the person's mind, in which the means is the behavior (going to work, flying a particular airline) and the end is some attractive consequence (money, frequent-flyer points). It is not that people develop a desire to engage in behaviors like working or flying a particular airline. Instead, people want to do whatever it is that the environment will reward them for doing.

The study of extrinsic motivation revolves around the three central concepts of incentives, reinforcers, and punishers. An incentive is an environmental event that attracts or repels a person toward or away from a particular course of action. A positive reinforcer (money) is any environmental event that, when presented, increases the probability of that behavior in the future. A negative reinforcer (alarm clock noise) is any environmental event that, when presented, increases the probability of that behavior in the future. A punisher (parking ticket) is any environmental event that, when presented, decreases the probability of that behavior in the future. The chief differences between incentives and consequences are (1) when each occurs and (2) how each motivates behavior. Incentives precede behavior and excite or inhibit the initiation of action; consequences follow behavior and increase or decrease the persistence of behavior.

While extrinsic events can have positive effects on motivation and behavior, they can also produce serious detrimental effects as captured in the phrase, "hidden costs of reward." Incentives and consequences that are expected and tangible typically undermine motivation by decreasing autonomy, interfering with the learning process, and undermining people's development of their own autonomous self-regulation.

Cognitive evaluation theory provides a way for predicting the effects that any extrinsic event will have on motivation. The theory explains how an extrinsic event (e.g., money, grade, deadline) affects intrinsic and extrinsic motivations, as mediated by the event's effect on the psychological needs for competence and autonomy. When an extrinsic event is presented in a relatively controlling way (i.e., given to gain compliance), it increases extrinsic motivation but decreases intrinsic motivation because of its detrimental effects on autonomy. When an extrinsic event is presented in a relatively informational way (i.e., given to communicate a message of a job well-done), it increases intrinsic motivation because of its favorable effect on competence. Hence, whether an extrinsic event is motivationally constructive or destructive depends on the relative salience of its controlling and informational aspects. The art of motivating others with external events therefore becomes the effort to present incentives and rewards in ways that are both noncontrolling and information-rich.

Self-determination theory expands the distinction between intrinsic versus extrinsic motivation into a continuum of types of motivation. Four types of extrinsic motivation exist. External regulation reflects the least self-determined type of extrinsic motivation, and externally-regulated behaviors are performed to obtain a reward or to satisfy some external demand. Introjected regulation reflects some self-determination because the person acts as if he was carrying other peoples' rules and commands inside his head to such an extent that the introjected voice generates self-administered rewards and punishments. Identified regulation represents mostly internalized extrinsic motivation, as the person has identified with the personal importance of an externally-prescribed way of thinking or behaving and has thus accepted it as his or her own way of thinking or behaving. Integration is the most self-determined type of extrinsic motivation, and it involves the self-examination necessary to bring new ways of thinking and behaving into congruence with the preexisting ways of thinking and behaving. The four types of extrinsic motivation are important because the more self-determined is the person's extrinsic motivation (integrated regulation, identified regulation), the greater is his or her functioning in terms of performance, social development, and psychological well-being.

The chapter ends with the problem of motivating others during uninteresting activities. Three recommendations to do this reflect the types of motivation highlighted in the chapter. The first motivational strategy is to promote identified regulation (and internalization) by providing a rationale that articulates why the activity is useful or important to the person. The second motivational strategy is to promote interest by translating the boring task into something more interesting to do via adding challenge, variety, or a fantasy context. The third motivational strategy is to use extrinsic incentives and rewards but to do so in a way that promotes competence and preserves autonomy by administering rewards in a highly informational and noncontrolling way.

READINGS FOR FURTHER STUDY

Extrinsic Motivation

ELMAN, D., & KILLEBREW, T. J. (1978). Incentives and seat belts: Changing a resistant behavior through extrinsic motivation. *Journal of Applied Social Psychology, 8*, 73–83.

HALL, R. V., AXELROD, S., TYLER, L., GRIEF, E., JONES, F. C., & ROBERTSON, R. (1972). Modification of behavior problems in the home with a parent as observer and experimenter. *Journal of Applied Behavior Analysis, 5*, 53–64.

GERSHOFF, E. T. (2002). Corporal punishment by parents and associated child behaviors and experiences: A meta-analytic and theoretical review. *Psychological Bulletin, 128*, 539-579.

Hidden Costs of Rewards

DECI, E. L., KOESTNER, R., & RYAN, R. M. (1999). A meta-analytic review of experiments examining the effects of extrinsic rewards on intrinsic motivation. *Psychological Bulletin, 125*, 627–668.

HOM, H. L., JR. (1994). Can you predict the overjustification effect? *Teaching of Psychology, 21*, 36–37.

LEPPER, M. R., & GREENE, D. (1975). Turning play into work: Effects of adult surveillance and extrinsic rewards on children's intrinsic motivation. *Journal of Personality and Social Psychology, 31*, 479–486.

Self-Determination Theory

KOESTNER, R., RYAN, R. M., BERNIERI, F., & HOLT, K. (1984). Setting limits on children's behavior: The detrimental effects of controlling versus informational styles on intrinsic motivation. *Journal of Personality, 52*, 233–248.

RYAN, R. M., & CONNELL, J. P. (1989). Perceived locus of causality and internalization: Examining reasons for acting in two domains. *Journal of Personality and Social Psychology, 57*, 749–761.

RYAN, R. M., & DECI, E. L. (2000). Intrinsic and extrinsic motivations: Classic definitions and new directions. *Contemporary Educational Psychology, 25*, 54–67.

RYAN, R. M., & DECI, E. L. (2000). Self-determination theory and the facilitation of intrinsic motivation, social development, and well-being. *American Psychologist, 55*, 68–78.

Chapter 7

Social Needs

Imagine driving down the interstate for hours and hours. The monotony grows and grows. To defend against the monotony, your mind and imagination begin to wander. Glancing at the passing countryside, you see houses and farms. Horses run outside one farm, and you imagine what it would be like to race in the Kentucky Derby. You imagine going neck and neck with the best jockeys in the world. Of course, you win and the crowd goes wild. Having conquered the racing world, your thoughts turn to the examination you took before leaving town. You blew it, and that subpar performance gnaws at you, pressing you to figure out ways to improve. Next time you conclude that you will budget your time more efficiently. Hopeful in your plan, you begin to dream of the days when you will graduate and become a physician. You think about working in the laboratory, making important scientific advancements, and perhaps discovering the cure for cancer or AIDS. Yours will be a grand career.

The driving and monotony continue. A song on the radio reminds you that your friends are now 600 miles behind. You feel the loss, and the sense of separation reminds you of the trivial argument with your partner just before you left. You imagine all the things that you could do to make things right again—make a telephone call, send an apologetic e-mail, or, better yet, turn the car around and surprise your partner with an impromptu visit. As you pass a high school, you remember how comfortable it was to hang out with your high-school friends. It was the best of times, and you smile and laugh. Your laughing draws the attention of a passerby, and for a moment, you wonder what it would be like to get to know her and learn about her life and her interests. What does she do? Where is she going? What does she believe? Who is she?

Still, the driving continues. A car zooms by at 90 miles per hour. For some reason, you feel that the other driver has somehow made you look bad, as he drives so fast and you so slow. And the way the driver darted in front of you seemed unnecessarily aggressive, in a posturing sort of way. Offended, you feel an impulse to yell at him and flash your bright lights in his rearview mirror. To restrain yourself, you mutter some tough-sounding name-calling, turn up your shirt collar, and put on your sunglasses to look cool. But since it is dark, you put the sunglasses away, and your thoughts wander to what it would be like to drive down the road in a convertible and to have people see you talking on a cell phone. Maybe you could drive one of those high-sitting, all-terrain, superpowered vehicles. You like the thought of being rich and respected by others.

Fantasies of winning a race, doing well in competition, becoming a better student, and accomplishing something unique like a cure for a disease are achievement-related thoughts. Thoughts of separation and goals to make amends for a broken relationship, be with close friends, and establish new friendships are affiliation- and intimacy-related thoughts. Impulses of assertiveness and concerns over status and reputation arise from power-related thoughts. Generally, as the mind wanders, our needs have a way of working their way into consciousness to affect our thoughts, emotions, and desires. The thoughts that freely pop into one's mind tell the story of which social needs are particularly important to that person.

ACQUIRED NEEDS

This chapter discusses two categories of acquired psychological needs: social needs and quasi-needs. None of us is born with a need for achievement, a need for power, a need for money, a need for a high grade-point average, or a need for a new car that will impress our friends. Yet each of us develops many such strivings, at least to a degree. Personal experience, socialization opportunities and demands, and our unique developmental history teach us to expect more positive emotional experiences in some situations than in other situations. Experiences teach us to associate positive emotional experience with some domains (e.g., opportunities for achievement, affiliation, intimacy, power), and the anticipation of a positive emotional experience in these domains leads us to organize our lifestyle around these experiences. Over time, because of these repeating emotional experiences, we acquire preferences for those particular situations, hobbies, and careers that involve and satisfy the social need or needs we acquire and value. Some of us learn to prefer and enjoy situations that challenge us with explicit standards of excellence (i.e., achievement needs). Others learn to prefer and enjoy situations that afford relationship opportunities (i.e., affiliation and intimacy needs). Still others learn to prefer and enjoy situations that allow them to exercise influence over others (i.e., power needs).

People harbor a multitude of needs, including physiological, psychological, social, and quasi-needs. What is common among the needs discussed in this chapter—the social and quasi-needs—is that they have social (rather than innate) origins. Social needs originate from preferences gained through experience, socialization, and development. These needs come to exist within us as acquired individual differences—as part of our personality. Quasi-needs are more ephemeral, and include situationally induced wants, such as the immediate need for money, self-esteem, an umbrella when it rains, and so on.

To keep the different types of needs separate from one another, Table 7.1 summarizes the definitions for each type. Recall from Chapter 4 that the general definition of need is as follows: Any condition of the person that is essential and necessary for life and growth, such that its nurturance produces well-being, while its thwarting produces damage. Given that general definition, the table lists the specific needs that represent four need subcategories.

The emphasis in this chapter is on those social needs that come to act like personality characteristics: achievement, affiliation, intimacy, and power. This chapter traces the social origins of each of these needs and discusses how each need, once acquired, manifests itself in thought, emotion, action, and lifestyle. The analysis of the four social needs of achievement, affiliation, intimacy, and power constitutes most of the chapter, but another class of more ephemeral needs also energizes and directs behavior—quasi-needs.

Table 7.1   Four Types of Needs and Their Definitions

Type of need	Definition, with examples
Physiological	A biological condition within the organism orchestrating brain structures, hormones, and major organs to regulate and correct bodily imbalances that are essential and necessary for life, growth, and well-being. Examples include thirst, hunger, and sex.
Psychological	An innate psychological process that underlies the desire to seek out interactions with the environment to gain experiences that promote psychological vitality, growth, and well-being. Examples include autonomy, competence, and relatedness.
Social	An acquired psychological process that grows out of one's socialization history that activates emotional responses to a need-relevant incentive. Examples include achievement, affiliation, intimacy, and power.
Quasi	Ephemeral, situationally induced wants that create tense energy to engage in behavior capable of reducing the built-up tension. Examples include the desire for money at the store, a Band-Aid after a cut, and an umbrella in the rain.

Quasi-Needs

Quasi-needs are situationally induced wants and desires that are not actually full-blown needs in the same sense that physiological, psychological, and social needs are. Quasi-needs are so called because they resemble true needs in some ways. For instance, they affect how we think, feel, and act (i.e., affect cognition, emotion, and behavior). A set of quasi-needs that commonly gains the attention of college students is that for money, a secure job, and a career plan that is capable of gaining the approval of one's parents. Day-to-day circumstances remind us of our needs for money, job, and approval, and events like shopping, job interviewing, and a visit home keep these situationally-induced wants in the forefront of our attention. And these quasi-needs, more often than not, have a sense of urgency about them that can, at times, dominate consciousness and perhaps overwhelm and displace other needs.

Quasi-needs originate from situational demands and pressures. Whenever a person satisfies a situational demand or pressure, the quasi-need fades away. When a bill arrives in the mail, we need money. After being rejected, we need self-esteem. Upon seeing a store item on sale, we need to possess it. As we age into our late 20s, we need to get married, and so on. Once we get the money, self-esteem, store item, or marriage, however, the situation is such that we no longer need more money, self-esteem, items, or marriage proposals. (Some situational pressures, like a need for money or relief from back pain, however, can endure for a reasonably long period of time.) The fact that quasi-needs disappear once we get what we want, however, is the telltale sign that the need is not a full-blown need. It is not a condition that is essential and necessary for life, growth, and well-being (the definition of a need). Rather, it is something we introject from the environment for a time and something that has more to do with the pressures in the environment than it does the needs of the individual. Any change to the environment leads to a corresponding change in our quasi-need (i.e., if it stops raining, our need for an umbrella fades).

Quasi-needs originate from situational events that promote a psychological sense of tension, pressure, and urgency within us. Hence, quasi-needs are deficiency-oriented and situationally reactive. Quasi-needs are what we lack, yet need, from the environment in a rather urgent way. For example, when a situation pressures and stresses a person in some way, the person may say he or she needs a vacation, needs to make a good grade on a test, needs to get a haircut, needs to find her lost car keys, needs a piece of paper to write on, needs a friend to talk to, needs to get a job, and so on in response to the situational pressures one faces in the moment. The strength of a quasi-need—its potency to gain attention and demand an action—is largely a function of how pressuring and demanding the environment is (e.g., "I just *have* to find my car keys!"). It is this situationally induced psychological context of tension, pressure, and urgency that supplies the motivation for the quasi-need.

Social Needs

Humans acquire social needs through experience, development, and socialization. In an extensive investigation of how people acquire social needs, one group of researchers sought to determine the child-rearing antecedents of adult needs for achievement, affiliation, and power (McClelland & Pilon, 1983). The researchers initially scored the parental practices of mothers and fathers of 78 five-year-old boys and girls. When the children grew to the age of 31, the researchers assessed the social needs of each adult to see which early socialization experiences, if any, would predict adults' social needs.

Only a few child-rearing antecedents emerged as significant, but the few that did illustrate some early origins of social needs. Adults high in the need for achievement generally had parents who used a strict feeding schedule and severe toilet training practices (high standards). Adults with high needs for affiliation generally had parents who used praise (rather than authority or coercion) as a socialization technique. Adults with high needs for power generally had parents who were permissive about sex and aggression (e.g., permissive about masturbation, fighting).

The finding that few child-rearing experiences predict adult motives suggests that social needs are not set at an early age and, instead, change over time. For instance, some occupations foster achievement strivings more than do other occupations, because they provide opportunities for moderate challenges, independent work, personal responsibility for outcomes, and rapid performance feedback. People in such achievement-congenial occupations (e.g., entrepreneurs) show marked increases in their achievement strivings over the years compared to people in achievement-noncongenial occupations (e.g., nursing; Jenkins 1987). As to developing power strivings, workers in jobs that require assertiveness (e.g., sales) show increases in the need for power over the years (Veroff et al., 1980). Social contexts, like the family and work environments that surround us, therefore, influence the needs we acquire.

Once acquired, we experience social needs as emotional and behavioral potentials that are activated by particular situational incentives (Atkinson, 1982; McClelland, 1985). That is, when an incentive associated with a particular need is present (e.g., a date is an intimacy incentive, an inspirational speech is a power incentive), the person high in that particular social need experiences emotional and behavioral activation (i.e., feels hope, seeks interaction). Experience teaches each of us that we will acquire certain positive emotional

Table 7.2   Incentive that Activates Each Social Need's Emotional and Behavior Potential

Social need	Incentive that activates each need
Achievement	Doing something well to show personal competence
Affiliation	Opportunity to please others and gain their approval
Intimacy	Warm, secure relationship
Power	Having impact on others

reactions in response to some incentives rather than others (McClelland, 1985). The need-activating incentive for each social need appears in Table 7.2.

How Social Needs Motivate Behavior

Social needs arise and activate emotional and behavioral potential when need-satisfying incentives appear. For instance, depending on one's unique constellation of acquired social needs, a school test might activate emotional fear and behavioral avoidance, whereas a school dance might activate emotional hope and behavioral approach. For another person who has a different constellation of social needs, the same test might bring emotional hope and behavioral approach, while the dance cues up only emotional fear and behavioral avoidance. With social needs, people react to events like tests and school dances by learning the incentive value (positive or negative) of the objects around them. When these objects appear, they activate patterns of emotion and behavior associated with their social needs.

Social needs are mostly reactive in nature. They lie dormant within us until we encounter a potentially need-satisfying incentive that brings the social need to the front of our attention in terms of our thinking, feeling, and behaving. In addition, however, people also learn to anticipate the emergence of need-relevant incentives. People learn rather quickly that particular occupations, organizations, and recreational events, for example, are primarily opportunities for doing well and demonstrating personal competence, for pleasing others and gaining their approval, for participating in warm and secure relationships, or for having an impact on others. Thus, people gain and rely on personal knowledge of their social needs to gravitate toward environments that are capable of activating and satisfying their needs. The person high in achievement strivings might enter business to become an entrepreneur or a stockbroker, while the person high in power strivings might enter management, run for a local political office, or take up a hobby that offers opportunities for exerting influence over others.

ACHIEVEMENT

The need for achievement is the desire to do well relative to a standard of excellence. It motivates people to seek "success in competition with a standard of excellence" (McClelland et al., 1953). Standard of excellence is a broad term that encompass (following Heckhausen, 1967):

- Competitions with a task (e.g., solving a jigsaw puzzle, writing a persuasive essay)
- Competitions with the self (e.g., running a race in a personal best time, improving one's GPA)

- Competitions against others (e.g., winning a competition, becoming the class valedictorian)

What all types of achievement situations have in common is that the person has encountered a standard of excellence and has been energized by it, largely because he or she knows that the forthcoming performance will produce an emotionally meaningful evaluation of personal competence.

When facing standards of excellence, people's emotional reactions vary. Individuals high in the need for achievement generally respond with approach-oriented emotions such as hope, pride, and anticipatory gratification. Individuals low in the need for achievement, however, generally respond with avoidance-oriented emotions such as anxiety, defense, and the fear of failure. People's behavioral responses to standards of excellence also vary. When confronting a standard of excellence, people show differences in choice, latency, effort, persistence, and the willingness to take personal responsibility for the ensuing success/failure outcomes (Cooper, 1983). High-need achievers, compared to low-need achievers, choose moderately difficult to difficult versions of tasks instead of easy versions (Kuhl & Blankenship, 1979; Slade & Rush, 1991); they quickly engage in achievement-related tasks rather than procrastinate or avoid them altogether (Blankenship, 1987); they show more effort and better performance on moderately difficult tasks because pride energizes them (Karabenick & Yousseff, 1968; Raynor & Entin, 1982); they persist more in the face of difficulty and failure on moderately difficult tasks (Feather, 1961, 1963); and they take a personal responsibility for successes and failures rather than seeking help or advice from others (Weiner, 1980).

Standards of excellence therefore offer people two-edge swords. Sometimes these standards excite us, and we react with approach emotion and behavior. Othertimes, however, these standards of excellence bring us anxiety, and we react with avoidance emotion and behavior.

Origins of the Need for Achievement

Researchers set out decades ago on a journey to discover the parenting-style roots of children's needs for achievement. The hope was to explain the social determinants of the high- versus low-need achiever's personality. As research progressed, it became increasingly clear that the need for achievement was a multifaceted phenomenon steeped not in a single trait but in a range of social, cognitive, and developmental processes.

Socialization Influences

Strong and resilient achievement strivings arise, in part, from socialization influences (Heckhausen, 1967; McClelland & Pilon, 1983). Children develop relatively strong achievement strivings when their parents provide the following: independence training (e.g., self-reliance, autonomy), high performance aspirations, realistic standards of excellence (Rosen & D'Andrade, 1959; Winterbottom, 1958), high ability self-concepts (e.g., "This task will be easy for you"), a positive valuing of achievement-related pursuits (Eccles-Parsons, Adler, & Kaczala, 1982), explicit standards for excellence (Trudewind, 1982), a home environment rich in stimulation potential (e.g., books to read), a wide scope of experiences such as traveling, and exposure to children's readers rich in achieve-ment imagery (e.g., *The Little Engine That Could*; deCharms & Moeller, 1962). After years of investigation, the effort to identify the childhood socialization practices of high-need achievers was only partly successful, however, largely because longitudinal findings began to show that achievement strivings change a great deal from childhood to adulthood and that adult achievement strivings often changed from one decade to the next (Jenkins, 1987; Maehr & Kleiber, 1980).

Cognitive Influences

As the cognitive revolution of the 1970s and 1980s swept over motivation study, re-searchers turned their attention to the cognitive underpinnings of an achievement way of thinking (Ames & Ames, 1984). Some ways of thinking are more achievement-related than are other ways of thinking, including the following:

- Perceptions of high ability
- Mastery orientation
- High expectations for success
- Strong valuing of achievement
- Optimistic attributional style

Perceptions of high ability facilitate both persistence (Felson, 1984; Phillips, 1984) and performance (Hansford & Hattie, 1982; Marsh, 1990). A mastery orientation (com-pared to a helpless orientation) leads people to choose moderately difficult tasks and to re-spond to difficulty by increasing rather than decreasing their effort (Dweck, 1986, 1999; Elliot & Dweck, 1988). Expectations for success breed approach-oriented behaviors such as seeking out optimal challenges (Eccles, 1984a) and performing well (Eccles, 1984b; Volmer, 1986). Valuing achievement in a particular domain predicts persistence in that do-main (Eccles, 1984b; Ethington, 1991). An optimistic attributional style fosters positive emotions like hope and pride following successes and keeps negative emotions like fear and anxiety at bay (Weiner, 1985, 1986). Thus, when conditions in the home, school, gymnasium, workplace, and therapeutic setting promote high ability beliefs, a mastery orientation, expectations for success, a valuing of achievement, and an optimistic attribu-tional style, these conditions provide the cognitive soil for cultivating an achievement way of thinking.

Developmental Influences

The identification of cognitive influences on achievement behavior led researchers to study how these ways of thinking develop over a person's life span (Heckhausen, 1982; Parsons & Ruble, 1977; Ruble et al., 1992; Stipek, 1984; Weiner, 1979). Achievement-related beliefs, values, and emotions all show predictable developmental patterns (Stipek, 1984). Young children are notorious amateurs in estimating their actual abilities. They hold unrealistically high ability beliefs (Nicholls, 1979; Stipek, 1984), do not lower their ability beliefs following failure (Parsons & Ruble, 1977), and ignore their poor perfor-mance in relation to their peers (Ruble, Parsons, & Ross, 1976). During middle childhood, however, children increasingly pay attention to peer performance comparisons, and by late childhood, they rely on a fuller gamut of information to construct relatively realistic ability beliefs: self-evaluations, peer evaluations, teacher evaluations, and parental evaluations (Felson, 1984; Nicholls, 1978, 1979; Rosenholtz & Rosenholtz, 1981; Ruble et al., 1992; Stipek, 1984). As to values, young children value the approval of others very much, while they care very little about achievement per se (Stipek, 1984). Achievement-related values need to be internalized, such as when parents place a high or low value on achievement (Eccles-Parsons et al., 1982) and one's occupational career places a high or low value on achievement (Waterman, 1988). As to emotions, children are not born with pride or shame. Neither is an innate emotion. Instead, pride emerges from a developmental history of success episodes ending in mastery; shame emerges from a developmental history of failure episodes ending in ridicule (Stipek, 1983). That is, our developmental history teaches us to be pride-prone or shame-prone when we face standards of excellence.

Atkinson's Model

Two theoretical approaches dominate the understanding of achievement motivation: classical and contemporary (Elliot, 1997). The classical view is Atkinson's model of achievement behavior, which includes the dynamics-of-action model. The contemporary view is a cognitive approach that centers on the goals people adopt in achievement situations.

Each approach will be discussed in turn, but what is common between the two is that they share the same portrayal of achievement motivation as an inherent struggle of approach versus avoidance. All of us experience standards of excellence as a two-edged sword: Partly we feel excitement and hope and anticipate the pride of a job well done; partly we feel anxiety and fear and anticipate the shame of possible humiliation. Thus, achievement motivation exists as a sort of balance between the emotions and beliefs underlying the tendency to approach success versus the emotions and beliefs underlying the tendency to avoid failure.

John Atkinson (1957, 1964) argued that the need for achievement only partly predicts achievement behavior. Achievement behavior depends not only on the individual's dispositional need for achievement but also on his or her task-specific probability of success at a task and the individuals incentive value for succeeding at that task. For Atkinson, some tasks had high probabilities for success, whereas others had low probabilities for success. Also, some tasks offered greater incentive for success than did others. For instance, consider the classes you are presently taking. Each course has its own probability of success (e.g., a senior-level advanced calculus course is generally harder than is an introductory-level physical education class) and its own incentive value for success (e.g., doing well in a course in your major is generally valued more than doing well in a course outside of your major).

Atkinson's theory features four variables: achievement behavior and its three predictors—need for achievement, probability of success, and incentive for success. Achievement behavior is defined as the tendency to approach success, abbreviated as Ts. The three determining factors of Ts are (1) the strength of a person's need for achievement (Ms, motive to succeed), (2) the perceived probability of success (Ps), and (3) the incentive value of success at that particular activity (*Is*). Atkinson's model is expressed in the following formula:

$$Ts = Ms \times Ps \times Is$$

Tendency to Approach Success

The first variable in the equation, *Ms*, corresponds to the person's need for achievement. The variable *Ps* is estimated from the perceived difficulty of the task and from the person's perceived ability at that task. The variable *Is* is equal to $1 - Ps$. So, if the probability of success is .25, the incentive for success at that task would be .75 ($1.00 - 0.25$). That is, incentive value for success during difficult tasks is high while it is low during easy tasks. To make sense of the behavioral tendency to approach success (*Ts*), consider a high-school wrestler who is scheduled to wrestle two different opponents this week. The first opponent is last year's state champion (*Ps* = .1) so he consequently has a strong incentive to beat the champ (*Is* = $1 - Ps$, which = .9). The second opponent is his equal (*Ps* = .5) so he consequently has a moderate incentive to succeed (*Is* = .5). If we use an arbitrary number like 10 to characterize the wrestler's dispositional need for achievement (*Ms*), Atkinson's theory predicts the wrestler will experience the greater achievement motivation for the second wrestler (*Ts* = 2.50, because $10 \times .5 \times .5 = 2.50$) than for the first wrestler (*Ts* = 0.90, because $10 \times .1 \times .9 = 0.90$), because optimal challenge (*Ps* = .5) provides the richest motivational combination of expectancy of success and incentive for success.

Tendency to Avoid Failure

Just as people face standards of excellence with a need for achievement (*Ms*), so too do people face standards of excellence with a motive to avoid failure (Atkinson, 1957, 1964). The tendency to avoid failure motivates the individual to defend against the loss of self-esteem, the loss of social respect, and the fear of embarrassment (Birney, Burdick, & Teevan, 1969). The tendency to avoid failure, abbreviated *Taf*, is calculated with a formula that parallels that for *Ts*:

$$Taf = Maf \times Pf \times If$$

The variable *Maf* represents the motive to avoid failure, *Pf* represents the probability of failure (which, by definition, is $1 - Ps$), and *If* represents the negative incentive value for failure (*If* = $1 - Pf$). Thus, if an individual has a motive to avoid failure of, say, 10, then the tendency to avoid failure on a difficult task (*Pf* = .9) can be calculated as 0.90 (*Maf* $\times$ *Pf* $\times$ *If*, which = $10 \times .9 \times .1 = 0.90$).

Combined Approach and Avoidance Tendencies

Atkinson conceptualized *Ms* as a motivational force to seek out achievement situations and *Maf* as a motivational force to escape from (or be anxious about) achievement situations. Thus, to engage in any achievement task is to enter into a risk-taking dilemma in which the person struggles to find a balance between the attraction of pride, hope, and social respect on the one hand versus the repulsion of shame, fear, and social humiliation on the other hand. When Ts is greater than Taf, the person approaches the opportunity to test personal competence against the standard of excellence, but when Taf is greater than Ts, the person hesitates or avoids the opportunity altogether. Atkinson's complete formula for predicting the tendency to achieve (Ta) and hence for displaying achievement-related behaviors (i.e., choice, latency, effort, persistence) is as follows:

$$Ta = Ts - Taf = (Ms \times Ps \times Is) - (Maf \times Pf \times If)$$

Although the model can appear to be overwhelming at first, in actuality one needs to know only three variables: the individual's approach motive (Ms), the individual's avoidance motive (Maf), and probability of success (Ps) on the task at hand. Notice that Is, Pf, and If are all calculated solely from the value of Ps [if $Ps = .3$, then $Is = .7$, $Pf = .7$, and $If = .3$].

If you work through a couple of numerical examples, you will find two general principles that underlie the numerical value for Ta. First, Ta is highest when Ts is greater than Taf and lowest when Taf is greater than Ts (a personality factor). Second, Ta is highest when Ps equals .5 and lowest when Ps is around .9 (task is too easy to generate an incentive to succeed) or .1 (task is too difficult to be motivating). To make sense of how the numbers fit together to predict approach versus avoidance behavior, consider the hesitant child trying to decide if he wants to take a chance and ride the huge pony at the city's petting zoo. If Ms equals 2, Maf equals 5, and Ps equals .2, then Ta would equal an avoidance-biased number (i.e., negative number) of −0.48 because of the following formula:

$$Ta = 0.32 - 0.80 = [(2 \times .2 \times .8) - (5 \times .8 \times .2)]$$

Achievement for the Future

Not all achievement situations are alike, as some have implications that affect one's future achievement efforts, whereas others have implications only for the present (Raynor, 1969, 1970, 1974). For example, a track athlete tries to win a race not only to experience the pride of a moment's accomplishment, but a win in today's race might lead to invitations to other important track meets, such as qualifying for the state championships or gaining a college scholarship. "Future achievement orientation" refers to an individual's psychological distance from a long-term achievement goal (e.g., winning the state championship). The importance of future achievement orientation is that, other things being equal, any achievement goal perceived far away in time receives less approach-versus-avoidance weight than does a goal in the very near future. Thus, achievement behavior is a function of not only Ms, Ps, Is, Maf, Pf, and If, but also whether the present achievement will lead toward some future achievement. From this point of view, achievement behavior is a series of steps in a path, and those achievement situations that are psychologically near have more impact on Ta than those that are psychologically far (Gjesme, 1981).

Dynamics-of-Action Model

In the dynamics-of-action model, achievement behavior occurs within a stream of on-going behavior (Atkinson & Birch, 1970, 1974, 1978). The stream of behavior is determined largely by three forces: instigation, inhibition, and consummation.

Instigation causes a rise in approach tendencies and occurs by confronting environmental stimuli associated with past reward (i.e., anything that cultivates an increased hope for success). Instigation is the same as *Ts*.

Inhibition causes a rise in avoidance tendencies and occurs by confronting environmental stimuli associated with past punishment (i.e., anything that cultivates an increased fear of failure). Inhibition is the same as *Taf*. Therefore, instigation and inhibition are synonyms for *Ts* and *Taf*. The one new variable in the dynamics-of-action model is consummation.

Consummation refers to the fact that performing an activity brings about its own cessation (e.g., running, eating, drinking, sleeping, reading this book). Adding consummatory forces allows achievement behavior to be understood as dynamic (changing over time) instead of episodic or static. For instance, your achievement strivings during any one college class change as the class progresses throughout the semester week-after-week and as you study more hours, attend more classes, and receive feedback about your performances. After 16 weeks, people often feel that they are about done with that class saying, "Okay, thanks, but that's enough."

The four panels in Figure 7.1 portray achievement behaviors over time (Blankenship, 1987). Each panel shows the individual's behavioral preference for an achievement task (a task that arouses both hope for success and fear of failure) and for a nonachievement task (an emotionally neutral task). The four panels correspond to four imaginary people with different levels of instigative and inhibitory forces. Panel 1 shows behavior with high instigation and low inhibition (*Ms > Maf*). Panel 2 shows behavior with high levels of both instigation and inhibition (*Ms = Maf,* and both are high). Panel 3 shows behavior with low levels of both instigation and inhibition (*Ms = Maf,* and both are low). Panel 4 shows behavior with low instigation and high inhibition (*Ms < Maf*).

Notice that in this example all four individuals, represented in the four separate panels of the figure, begin interacting first with the nonachievement-related activity (e.g., watching television). The question then becomes, "How much time passes until each person starts to engage the achievement task (e.g., studying)? The individual in panel 1 (i.e., high need for achievement) shows the shortest latency for engaging the achievement task (i.e., the quickest achievement behavior), while the individual in panel 4 (i.e., low need for achievement, or high fear of failure) shows the longest latency for engaging the achievement task. The person in panel 4 basically procrastinates. Once achievement behavior has begun, it tends to consume itself, and the individual will eventually return to the nonachievement-related task, which over time will also consume itself (i.e., you can only watch so much television). The motive profiles (*Ms* in relation to *Maf*) explain not only latency to initiate achievement behavior but also its persistence, once begun.

Three important messages are communicated in Figure 7.1:

1. Latency to initiate an achievement task varies with motive strengths (i.e., a quick latency is associated with a high *Ms*).

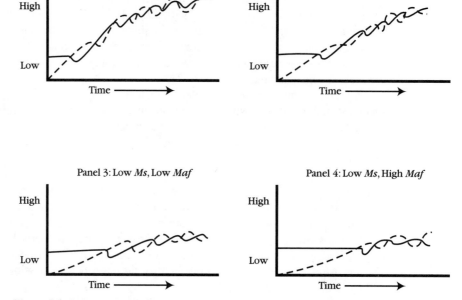

Figure 7.1 Streams of Behavior for People High and Low in *Ms* and *Maf*

Source: From "A Computer-Based Measure of Resultant Achievement Motivation," by V. Blankenship, 1987, *Journal of Personality and Social Psychology, 53*, pp. 361–372. Copyright 1987 by the American Psychological Association. Adapted with permission.

Note: Dashed line represents tendency strength to engage the achievement-related task; solid line represents tendency strength of nonachievement task.

2. Persistence on an achievement task varies with motive strengths (i.e., long persistence is associated with a low *Maf*).

3. Tendencies to pursue achievement and nonachievement tasks rise because of facilitating emotional and environmental incentives and fall because of consummatory forces and inhibitory fears.

Conditions That Involve and Satisfy the Need for Achievement

Three situations are particularly noteworthy for their ability to involve and satisfy the need for achievement: moderately difficult tasks, competition, and entrepreneurship (McClelland, 1985).

Moderately Difficult Tasks

High-need achievers (*Ms* > *Maf*) outperform low-need achievers (*Maf* > *Ms*) on moderately difficult tasks. High-need achievers do not, however, outperform low-need achievers on easy or difficult tasks (Karabenick & Yousseff, 1968; Raynor & Entin, 1982). Performance on a moderately difficult task activates in the high achiever a set of positive emotional and cognitive incentives not socialized into the low achiever. Emotionally, moderately difficult tasks provide an arena for best testing skills and therefore experiencing emotions like pride and satisfaction. Cognitively, moderately difficult tasks provide an arena for best diagnosing one's level of ability, and high-need achievers constantly seek information to diagnose their abilities (Trope, 1975, 1983). Hence, moderately challenging tasks provide a mixture of pride from success and information to diagnose abilities, a mixture that motivates high-need achievers more than it does low-need achievers (Atkinson, 1981; Trope & Brickman, 1975).

Competition

Interpersonal competition captures much of the risk-taking dilemma involved in achievement settings. It generally promotes positive emotion, approach behavior, and improved performance in high-need achievers but negative emotion, avoidance behaviors, and debilitated performance in low-need achievers (Covington & Omelich, 1984; Epstein & Harackiewicz, 1992; Ryan & Lakie, 1965; Tauer & Harackiewicz, 1999). Consider that high-need achievers in general seek diagnostic ability information (Trope, 1975), seek opportunities to test their skills (Epstein & Harackiewicz, 1992; Harackiewicz, Sansone, & Manderlink, 1985), value competence for its own sake (Harackiewicz & Manderlink, 1984), are attracted to activities that allow for self-evaluation (Kuhl, 1978), and enjoy opportunities to demonstrate or prove their ability (Harackiewicz & Elliot, 1993). Competition offers all these attributes and is therefore attractive to high-need achievers (Harackiewicz & Elliot, 1993). For low-need achievers, competition's evaluative pressures arouse mostly anxiety and avoidance (Epstein & Harackiewicz, 1992).

Entrepreneurship

David McClelland (1965, 1987) finds that high-need achievers often display the behavioral pattern of entrepreneurship. He assessed the need for achievement in a group of college students and then waited 14 years to check on the occupational choices they made. Each occupation was classified as either entrepreneurial (e.g., founder of own business, sales, stockbroker) or not entrepreneurial (e.g., office manager, service personnel). Results confirmed that most entrepreneurs were high-need achievers in college, while most low-need achievers were not entrepreneurs. Entrepreneurship appeals to the high-need achiever because it requires taking moderate risks and assuming responsibility for one's successes and failures. Entrepreneurship also provides concrete, rapid performance feedback (e.g., moment-to-moment profits and losses—as from sales or the rise and fall of the stock market), feedback that generates emotions like pride and satisfaction, and feedback that allows one to diagnose personal competence and rate of improvement on a continual basis. High-need achievers prefer just about any occupation that offers challenge, personal responsibility, and rapid performance feedback (Jenkins, 1987; McClelland, 1961).

Achievement Goals

Atkinson's model treats achievement behavior as a choice: Accept and approach the standard of excellence, or reject and avoid it. The model seeks to understand whether a person will approach success or avoid failure, and if so, with what intensity, latency, and persistence that choice will be pursued. Contemporary researchers, however, have become increasingly interested in *why* a person shows achievement behavior, not so much in *whether* achievement behavior occurs.

In daily life, we often do not so much seek out standards of excellence as we have them forced upon us. That is, we are asked, and often required, to approach a standard of excellence put before us, as happens at school (a test), at work (a sales quota), in sports (an opponent), and so on. In these sort of settings, contemporary achievement motivation researchers ask why people adopt one type of achievement goal over another type.

The two main achievement goals are performance goals and mastery goals. With performance goals, the person facing the standard of excellence seeks to demonstrate or prove competence; with mastery goals, the person seeks to develop or improve competence (Ames & Archer, 1988; Dweck, 1986, 1990; Nichols, 1984; Spence & Helmreich, 1983). Performance goals generally cultivate a norm-based evaluation of one's competence, and these goals focus the performer's attention on the demonstration of ability relative to that of others. Achieving a performance goal means doing better than others. Mastery goals generally cultivate a self-based (or task-based) evaluation of one's competence, and these goals focus the performer's attention on developing competence and mastering the task. Achieving a mastery goal means making progress.

The distinction between performance and mastery goals is important because the adoption of mastery goals in an achievement context (e.g., in school, at work, in sports) is associated with positive and productive ways of thinking, feeling, and behaving, whereas the adoption of performance goals in an achievement context is associated with relatively negative and unproductive ways of thinking, feeling, and behaving (Dweck, 1999; Dweck & Leggett, 1988; Harackiewicz & Elliot, 1993; Spence & Helmreich, 1983). When people adopt mastery goals, compared to when they adopt performance goals, they usually do the following:

- Persist longer at the task (Elliot & Dweck, 1988)
- Prefer challenging tasks they can learn from rather than easy tasks on which they can demonstrate high ability (Ames & Archer, 1988; Elliot & Dweck, 1988)
- Use conceptually-based learning strategies such as relating information to existing knowledge rather than superficial learning strategies such as memorizing (Meece, Blumenfeld, & Hoyle, 1988; Nolen, 1988)
- Increase effort in the face of difficulty rather than turn passive or quit (Elliot & Dweck, 1988)
- Are less susceptible to learned helplessness deficits (Stipek & Kowalski, 1989)
- Are more likely to be intrinsically rather than extrinsically motivated (Heyman & Dweck, 1992)
- Perform better (Spence & Helreich, 1983)
- And are more likely to ask for help and information from others that will allow them to continue working on their own (Newman, 1991)

Educational psychologists find the concept of achievement goals to be helpful in understanding students' classroom-based achievement motivation (Ames & Archer, 1988). Part of the reasons achievement goals appeal to educators is that teachers exert a relatively strong influence over the types of achievement goals students adopt. For instance, in one study with elementary-grade children, students were asked to agree or disagree with questions assessing the extent to which their teachers promoted mastery goals ("The teacher pays attention to whether I am improving," and "Making mistakes is part of learning") or performance goals ("I work hard to get a high grade," and "Students feel bad when they do not do as well as others"). The researchers then assessed students' learning strategies, willingness to be challenged, and attitude toward the class. Students with mastery goals, compared to students with performance goals, used relatively sophisticated rather than superficial learning strategies, were attracted to challenge rather than threatened by it, and enjoyed the class more (Ames & Archer, 1988). This pattern of findings helps explain why people with mastery goals outperform people with performance goals. Overall, the different ways that students with mastery goals and students with performance goals construe the classroom climate appears in Table 7.3.

Integrating Classical and Contemporary Approaches to Achievement Motivation

The classical (Atkinson's theory) and contemporary (achievement goals) approaches to achievement motivation can be combined and integrated into a single comprehensive model (Elliot, 1997). In the integrated model, mastery goals and two different types of achievement performance goals exist: performance-approach and performance-avoidance. Mastery goals emanate from a person's perceived competence on the task at hand. Performance-approach goals emanate from a person's need for achievement (*Ms*). Performance-avoidance goals emanate from a person's fear of failure (*Maf*).

Table 7.3   Manifestations of Mastery and Performance Goals in the Classroom Context

Climate dimension	Mastery goal	Performance goal
Success defined as	Improvement, progress	High grades, high normative performance
Value placed on	Effort, learning	Normatively high ability
Reasons for satisfaction	Working hard, challenge	Doing better than others
Teacher oriented toward	How students are learning	How students are performing
Views errors or mistakes as	Part of learning	Anxiety eliciting
Focus of attention	Process of learning	Own performance relative to others' performance
Reasons for effort	Learning something new	High grades, performing better than others
Evaluation criteria	Absolute progress	Normative

Source: From "Achievement Goals in the Classroom: Students' Learning Strategies and Motivation Processes," by C. Ames and J. Archer, 1988, *Journal of Educational Psychology, 80*, pp. 260–267. Copyright 1988, American Psychological Association. Reprinted by permission.

Note: The table can be interpreted by selecting one classroom climate dimension of interest and then reading across the row for how students with mastery goals rate—what they believe, what they are likely to say—on that dimension and then for how students with performance goals rate on that dimension.

The overlap within the classical and contemporary approaches occurs within the relationship between *Ms, Maf,* and *Ps* and the types of goals the person adopts. The classical achievement motivation constructs (*Ms, Maf,* and *Ps*) serve as antecedent conditions that influence the specific type of goals the person takes in a given achievement setting. For instance, the relationships between *Ms, Maf,* and *Ps* to the three types of achievement goals appears in Figure 7.2. People high in the need for achievement tend to adopt performance-approach goals, people high in the fear of failure tend to adopt performance-avoidance goals, and people with high competency expectancies tend to adopt mastery goals. The figure shows the results from an actual study that tracked the achievement strivings, achievement goals, course grades, and intrinsic motivation toward a college course (Elliot & Church, 1997).

The need for achievement served as an antecedent for adopting mastery and performance-approach goals, the fear of failure served as an antecedent for adopting performance-approach and performance-avoidance goals (i.e., performance goals in general), and competency expectancies served as an antecedent for adopting mastery and performance-approach goals and for rejecting performance-avoidance goals (notice the negative sign for ≈14). Further, once these types of achievement goals were adopted, mastery goals increased intrinsic motivation, whereas performance-avoidance goals decreased it; performance-approach goals increased performance, whereas performance-avoidance goals decreased it (Elliot & Church, 1997). To communicate a better understanding of just what performance-approach and performance-avoidance goals are, sample items from the Achievement Goal Questionnaire (Elliot & Church, 1997) appear in Table 7.4.

Integrating the classical and contemporary approaches to achievement motivation overcomes the shortcomings of each individual approach (Elliot, 1997). The problem with the classical approach is that general personality dispositions (*Ms, Maf*) do a poor job predicting achievement behavior in specific settings. In other words, general personality factors are not necessarily the regulators of achievement behavior in specific life domains like school, sports, and work. A person might show strong achievement strivings at work yet only the fear of failure in social situations. The problem with the contemporary approach is that a person is potentially left wondering where these different types of achievement goals come from in the first place. In other words, if you know a basketball

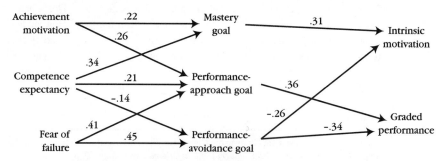

Figure 7.2 Antecedents and Consequences of the Three Achievement Goals

Source: From "A Hierarchical Model of Approach and Avoidance Achievement Motivation," by A. J. Elliot and M. A. Church, 1997, *Journal of Personality and Social Psychology, 72,* pp. 218–232. Copyright 1997, American Psychological Association. Reprinted with permission.

Table 7.4   Two Items From Each Scale of the Achievement Goals Scale

---

MASTERY GOAL

1. I desire to completely master the material presented in this class.
2. In a class like this, I prefer course material that really challenges me so I can learn new things.

PERFORMANCE-APPROACH GOAL

1. My goal in this class is to get a better grade than most of the students.
2. I want to do well in this class to show my ability to my family, friends, advisors, and others.

PERFORMANCE-AVOIDANCE GOAL

1. I just want to avoid doing poorly in this class.
2. My fear of performing poorly in this class is often what motivates me.

Source: From "Approach and Avoidance Motivation and Achievement Goals," by A. J. Elliot, 1999, *Educational Psychologist, 34,* pp. 169–189.

player has a performance-approach goal (e.g., to have the highest scoring average on the team), the question remains as to why he or she adopted that particular achievement goal rather than another. Together, the two theories can predict achievement behavior in specific situations (using achievement goals) and can explain from where these achievement goals arise (using personality dispositions and competence perceptions).

How the classical and contemporary approaches have been integrated can be illustrated through a second reading of Figure 7.2. It models the developmental relationships between personality factors (left-hand side) and specific achievement goals (middle of the figure):

$$Ms \quad \rightarrow \quad \text{performance-approach goals}$$
$$Maf \quad \rightarrow \quad \text{performance-avoidance goals}$$
$$\text{competence perceptions} \quad \rightarrow \quad \text{mastery goals}$$

The left-hand side of the figure shows that achievement needs (*Ms, Maf*) prompt the person to adopt one type of goal over another. The right-hand side shows that it is the type of achievement goal (rather than *Ms, Maf, Ps*, per se) that predicts achievement-related outcomes (i.e., intrinsic motivation, quality of performance).

Avoidance Motivation and Well-Being

So far the discussion on achievement motivation has focused attention mostly on the "approach" side of achievement. But the fear of failure drives people to regulate their behavior in all sorts of ways that interfere with performance, persistence, and emotionality (Birney, Burdick, & Teevan, 1969; Elliot & Sheldon, 1997; Schmalt, 1982). That is, the fear of failure (*Maf*) prompts people to adopt performance-avoidance goals, such as trying to avoid performing poorly, and these avoidance-oriented goals lead people to underperform, quit quickly, and lose interest in what they are doing, whether the task is solving anagrams (Roney, Higgins, & Shah, 1995) or performing in school (Elliot & Church, 1997; Elliot & Harackiewicz, 1996).

BOX 7   *Reducing Achievement Anxiety*

Question: Why is this information important?

Answer: So you can reduce anxiety and poor performance in achievement situations.

How much anxiety do you feel while taking tests in school, while competing in athletics, while making a presentation at work, or while working on a project such as repairing something? Whenever we face a standard of excellence—a task that we know will end with a success/failure evaluation from both self and an audience of others—we feel a blend of enthusiasm and a desire to participate mixed in with anxiety and a desire to avoid it all. The athlete running a race, for example, is both eager to test her skills but also hesitant because she might embarrass herself.

The easiest way to reduce anxiety in achievement settings is to change the content of your thoughts. Just before running the race, for instance, an eager runner thinks, "I want to finish the race in under 10 minutes," while the anxious runner thinks, "I'm afraid I'll finish the race is last place" (Schmalt, 1999). Notice that these thoughts mirror the performance-approach and performance-avoidance goals listed in Table 7.3. To the extent that the runner (or test-taker, presenter, etc.) could change his performance goal from one of avoidance ("don't blow it") to one of approach ("do something special"), he would significantly decrease felt anxiety. Performance would improve as well.

Can control over achievement anxiety really be that simple? Can it really be that straightforward—change your goals and you change your anxiety? Well, no, for two reasons. First, changing the way you think is not as easy as it might first sound. Thoughts are often deeply rooted. Second, achievement situations themselves generate anxiety—time deadlines, presence of an audience, task difficulty, and so on. And our own

dispositional neuroticism (emotional instability) further contributes to our anxiety.

But achievement anxiety comes in two forms: cognitive worry and physiological upset ("hyperemotionality"). The good news is that physiological hyper-emotionality does *not* undermine performance in achievement settings; only cognitive worry does (Elliot & McGregor, 1999). The primary cause of worry in achievement settings are performance avoidance goals. That is, the roots of worry are performance-avoidance goals like, "I just want to avoid making a mistake." So in a sense, these avoidance goals *are* that straightforward. Change your achievement goals and you change your achievement anxiety.

In trying to reduce worry-based anxiety, some productive advice is to change performance-avoidance goals into performance-approach (or mastery) goals. The arousal-based anxiety may remain (e.g., you may still feel nervous or pumped up standing in front of an evaluative audience), but the worry-based anxiety that really debilitates performance will fade in proportion to which performance-avoidance goals are successfully translated into approach-oriented goals.

The preceding advice is precisely the procedure used in experiments on how achievement goals affect motivation, anxiety, and performance. One group of participants is randomly given a performance-approach goal, "Demonstrate you have high ability." A second group of participants is randomly given a performance-avoidance goal, "Don't do worse than others." The first group experiences less anxiety than does the second group (Elliot, 1999; Elliot & Harackiewicz, 1996; Elliot & McGregor, 1999). Experiments such as these make it clear that experimenters can change the contents of our thoughts. To reduce personal anxiety in achievement situations, the performers merely needs to do the same to himself and change the contents of his thoughts.

Such a relationship (fear of failure → performance-avoidance goals → maladjusted coping style in achievement settings) has important implications for personal adjustment and mental health. One team of researchers measured college students' fears of failure and the extent to which they endorsed performance-avoidance goals. They then assessed the students on a host of well-being measures, such as self-esteem, personal control, vitality, life satisfaction, and subjective well-being. The more each student feared failure, the more likely the student would adopt performance-avoidance goals. And the more avoidance goals each student harbored, the poorer his well-being on all five of these measures (Elliot & Sheldon, 1997). The primary reason well-being suffered was that in trying so hard to avoid poor performances, students regulated their day-to-day behavior in ways that produced dissatisfaction, negative affect, and little enjoyment or fulfillment. Always trying to avoid embarrassing oneself, even when successfully accomplished, takes its toll on well-being. Example of this process appears in Box 7.

A follow-up investigation showed that additional dispositional characteristics predispose people to adopt performance-avoidance goals, including neuroticism and poor life skills (e.g., poor social skills, poor time management; Elliot, Sheldon, & Church, 1997). People high in the fear of failure, high in neuroticism, and low in life-skill competence tended to adopt performance-avoidance goals. For instance, some common performance-avoidance goals might be to avoid being a boor at parties, avoid being lonely, and avoid smoking or drinking. Trying to avoid doing something turns out to be a hard thing to do, relative to trying to do something (e.g., be friendly at parties). When people pursue avoidance goals, they generally perceive that they make little progress in the effort, and it is this perception of a lack of progress that leads to dissatisfaction, negative affectivity, and diminished interest. Such motivational and emotional states, when experienced over time, chip away at and eventually undermine subjective well-being (e.g., self-esteem, personal control, vitality, life satisfaction).

This line of research is particularly important because it shows rather convincingly that mastery goals are not necessarily more productive goal orientations than are performance goals. Instead, the pursuit of approach-oriented goals—be they mastery or performance goals—produces a self-regulatory style that is more positive and productive than the pursuit of performance-avoidance goals. Both mastery and performance-approach goals facilitate achievement and positive life outcomes, whereas performance-avoidance goals undermine them (Sansone & Harackiewicz, 2000).

Implicit Theories

Generally speaking, the way people think about their personal qualities like intelligence and personality can be characterized in one of two ways (Dweck, 1999). Some people see personal qualities as fixed and enduring characteristics. Other people, in contrast, see personal qualities as malleable characteristics that can be increased with effort. The first implicit theory applies to "entity theorists," people who believe they (and others) are endowed with fixed, enduring qualities. The thinking is "you either have it, or you don't" in that some people are smart and motivated while other people are not. The second implicit theory applies to "incremental theorists," people who believe they (and others) are endowed with malleable, changing qualities. The thinking is "the more you try and the more you learn, the better you get" in that all people can become smarter and more motivated, at least in proportion to their effort.

As an illustration, consider whether you agree or disagree with the following statements (Dweck, 1999):

- Your intelligence is something about you that you cannot change very much.

- You can always greatly change how intelligent you are.

Entity theorists will generally agree with the first statement but disagree with the second. Entity theorists believe people have a fixed amount of intelligence, personality, or motivation. In other words, characteristics exist as entities or traits that dwell within the person. Incremental theorists will generally agree with the second statement but disagree with the first. Incremental theorists believe personal qualities are something that people cultivate through effort and learning. While they realize that some people are high while other people are low in these qualities, incremental theorists believe that instruction, guidance, effort, learning, and experience increase and improve these qualities.

Implicit theories are important to achievement strivings because they guide the type of goals people pursue (Dweck, 1999; Dweck & Elliot, 1983; Elliot & Dweck, 1988). In achievement situations, entity theorists generally adopt performance goals. People who adopt performance goals are concerned with looking smart and with not looking dumb. That is, they are concerned with performing well, especially while others are watching. The goal is therefore to use performance as the means to prove that one has much of a desirable characteristic (i.e., intelligence). In contrast, incremental theorists generally adopt mastery goals in achievement situations. People who adopt mastery goals are concerned with mastering something new or different and with learning or understanding something new. That is, they are concerned with learning and improving as much as they can. The goal is therefore to use task engagements to improve—to get smarter by learning something new or important.

Both types of goals—performance and mastery—are common in the culture, and both encourage achievement (Elliot & Church, 1997; Harackiewicz et al., 1997). But typically, social settings like the workplace, sports field, and classroom pit these two goals against one another and ask (force) workers, athletes, and students to pick one goal over the other. People are often asked to choose between courses of action that allow them to:

- Look smart and competent but at the sacrifice of learning something new.
- Learn something new, useful, or important, but at the sacrifice of looking smart or competent.

For instance, when college students select "elective" courses, they sometimes choose a course in which they can be assured of doing well, looking smart, avoiding errors, and impressing others, or they sometimes choose a course in which they hope will teach them something new, provide opportunities to learn, and an arena to grow their skills. When given such a choice (at school, at work, in sports, etc.), about half of the population will, on average, select a performance goal while the other half will select a mastery goal.

Different Implicit Theories Mean Different Achievement Goals

When entity and incremental theorists face achievement situations, they prefer different achievement goals. This is important because the type of achievement goal one pursues (performance versus mastery) predicts that person's subsequent motivation, emotion, and performance (Ames & Archer, 1988; Stipek & Kowalski, 1989).

A series of studies with elementary-school, middle-school, and college students (Dweck & Leggett, 1988; Mueller & Dweck, 1997) assessed students' entity versus incremental theories, using questions based on Dweck's (1999) statements on intelligence (listed previously). The researchers then asked the students to choose between tasks that were either:

1. Fun and easy, easy enough so mistakes would not occur, or
2. Hard, new, and different—confusion and mistakes could occur, but the student would probably learn something useful.

The more students endorsed an entity theory, the more they chose the performance opportunity (#1 above). The more students endorsed an incremental theory, the more they chose the learning opportunity (#2 above).

Therefore, like achievement strivings (*Ms, Maf*), implicit theories (entity, incremental) predict the type of achievement goal the individual chooses to pursue—performance or mastery. But do implicit theories cause achievement goal choices? To answer this causation question, researchers manipulated participants' implicit theory beliefs by asking them to read an informative booklet that provided rather convincing (and true) evidence to support either an entity or an incremental theory of intelligence. The booklet offered passages about the intelligence of notable individuals (including Albert Einstein, Helen Keller, and the child Rubik's Cube champion) as either a fixed and inborn trait or as an malleable and acquired talent. Participants were randomly assigned to read either the entity-touting or the incremental-touting booklet. All participants were then given a choice between a performance-approach goal (task is hard enough to show that you are smart), a performance-avoidance goal (task is easy enough so that you won't get many wrong), or a mastery goal (task is hard, new, and different so that you can learn from it). As shown in Table 7.5, students who read the passage supporting an entity view of intelligence were significantly more likely to pursue a performance goal (81.8%) rather than a mastery goal (18.2%), whereas students who read the passage supporting an incremental view of intelligence were significantly more likely to pursue the mastery goal (60.9%) rather than a performance goal (39.1%). These results communicate two conclusions. First, implicit theories are malleable and can be changed (as per the booklets). Second, implicit theories cause people to pursue either performance or mastery goals (as per the results in Table 7.5).

Table 7.5   Effect of Implicit Theories (Entity, Incremental) on Achievement Goal Choice (Performance-Approach, Performance-Avoidance, Mastery)

	Goal Choice		
Implicit theory	Performance-avoidance goal	Performance-approach goal	Mastery Goal
Entity (n = 22)	50.0	31.8	18.2
Incremental (n = 41)	9.8	29.3	60.9

Note. Numbers represent percentages, and the two rows add to 100%.

Source: From "A Social-Cognitive Approach to Motivation and Personality." By C. S. Dweck and E. L. Leggett, 1988, *Psychological Review, 95,* pp. 256–273. Copyright 1988 by American Psychological Association. Reprinted by permission.

Meaning of Effort

For an entity theorist, the meaning of effort is "the more you try, the dumber you therefore must be." High effort means low ability. High effort is, in fact, evidence that the performer lacks ability. For an incremental theorist, the meaning of effort is that it is a tool, the means by which people turn on and take advantage of their skills and abilities. High effort means the unleashing of potential and ability. Consider your own reaction to the following:

> *You see a puzzle in a science magazine and it's labeled "Test your IQ!" You work on it for a very long time, get confused, start over and over, and finally make progress, but very slowly, until you solve it. How do you feel? Do you feel sort of dumb because it required so much effort? Or, do you feel smart because you worked hard and mastered it? (Dweck, 1999).*

The self's interpretation of the meaning of effort is most important in a motivational analysis of behavior when the individual faces a difficult task (Dweck, 1999). What one needs when facing a difficult task is high effort. But marshaling forth high effort possesses a motivational dilemma for the entity theorist. High effort is needed, but high effort is precisely that which signals low ability, which is precisely the sort of thing an entity theorist wants most to avoid. Entity theorists do not really believe that high effort will be effective, even on difficult tasks. So on difficult endeavors, they tend to adopt maladaptive motivational patterns by (1) withholding effort, (2) engaging in self-handicapping to protect the self, and (3) never really understanding or appreciating what effort expenditures can do for them in life (Dweck, 1999; Stipek & Gralinski, 1996; Zuckerman, Kieffer, & Knee, 1998). Incremental theorists, however, do understand the utility of effort—effort is that which becomes learning. Incremental theorists experience no conflict between the effort challenging tasks require and their willingness to roll up their sleeves and engage in effortful and persistent work.

Negative feedback works much the same way as does a difficult task in terms of its effect on entity and incremental thinking (Hong, Chiu, Dweck, Lin, & Wan, 1999). When given negative feedback, entity thinkers attribute their poor performance to low ability. With such an attribution to low ability, entity thinkers withdraw from the task rather than invest the effort in remedial action to master it. On the other hand, when given negative feedback, incremental thinkers attribute their poor performance to not trying hard enough. With such an attribution to low effort, incremental thinkers take remedial action that serves as a highly adaptive motivational pattern to failure and to negative feedback. The bottom line is that difficult tasks, negative feedback, and especially effort mean different things to entity and incremental thinkers. One meaning system, that which is embraced by incremental thinkers, is significantly more motivationally adaptive than is the other.

AFFILIATION AND INTIMACY

In its early study, the need for affiliation was conceptualized as, "establishing, maintaining, or restoring a positive, affective relationship with another person or persons" (Atkinson, Heyns, & Veroff, 1954). According to this definition, the need for affiliation is not the same construct as extraversion, friendliness, or sociability. In fact, the early investigators noted that persons high in the need for affiliation were often less popular than persons low in affiliation strivings (Atkinson, Heyns, & Veroff, 1954; Crowne & Marlowe, 1964; Shipley & Veroff, 1952). Rather than being rooted in extraversion and popularity, the need for affiliation is rooted in a fear of interpersonal rejection (Heckhausen, 1980). People with high-need affiliation interact with others to avoid negative emotions, such as fear of disapproval and loneliness, and typically experience much anxiety in their relationships. People high in the need for affiliation come across not as extraverted, friendly, or sociable but, instead, as "needy."

As they try to calm their anxieties, these high-need people monitor whether others disapprove of them and spend time seeking reassurance from others, a pattern of behavior that explains why they come across as needy. The need for affiliation then can be thought of as the need for approval, acceptance, and security in interpersonal relations.

The more contemporary view of affiliation strivings recognizes its two facets: the need for approval and the need for intimacy. This dual view of affiliation strivings answers the criticism that the former conceptualization was too heavy on rejection anxiety and too light on affiliation interest, the more positive aspect of the need for affiliation (Boyatzis, 1973; McAdams, 1980).

The call for a more positive conceptualization of affiliation strivings (i.e., intimacy motivation) was answered by giving attention to the social motive for engaging in warm, close, positive interpersonal relations that hold little fear of rejection (McAdams, 1980, 1982a, 1982b; McAdams & Constantian, 1983; McAdams, Healy, & Kraus, 1984). The intimacy motive reflects a concern for the quality of one's social involvement. It is a willingness to "experience a warm, close, and communicative exchange with another person" (McAdams, 1980).

A profile of how the need for intimacy expresses itself appears in Table 7.6. An individual with a high need for intimacy thinks frequently about friends and relationships; writes imaginative stories about positive affect-laden relationships; engages in self-disclosure, intense listening, and frequent conversations; identifies love and dialogue as especially meaningful life experiences; is rated by others as warm, loving, sincere, and nondominant; and tends to remember episodes involving interpersonal interactions.

Table 7.6   Profile of High Intimacy Motivation

Category	Description
Thoughts	Of friends, of relationships
Story Themes	Relationships produce positive affect, reciprocal dialogue, expressions of relationship commitment and union, and expressions of interpersonal harmony
Interaction Style	Self-disclosure
	Intense listening habits
	Many conversations
Autobiography	Themes of love and dialogue are mentioned as personally significant life experiences
Peer Rating	Individual rated as warm, loving, sincere, nondominant
Memory	Enhanced recall with stories involving themes of interpersonal interactions

The full picture of affiliation strivings includes a theoretical conceptualization that includes both its positive aspects—the need to engage in warm, close, positive relations (intimacy need), and its negative aspects—the anxious need to establish, maintain, and restore interpersonal relations (affiliation need). These positive and negative aspects affect the extent to which people live happy, well-adjusted lives. One group of researchers, for instance, assessed young adults' needs for affiliation and intimacy and found that after two decades of living, the men with high needs for intimacy were happier—better adjusted in work and marriage—than the men with low needs for intimacy (McAdams & Vaillant, 1982). An energizing growth quality exists within the need for intimacy.

Conditions That Involve the Affiliation and Intimacy Needs

The principal condition that involves the need for affiliation is the deprivation from social interaction (McClelland, 1985). Conditions such as loneliness, rejection, and separation raise people's desire, or social need, to be with others. Hence, the need for affiliation expresses itself as a deficiency-oriented motive (the deficiency is a lack of social interaction). In contrast, the desire, or social need, for intimacy arises from interpersonal caring and concern, warmth and commitment, emotional connectedness, reciprocal dialogue, congeniality, and love (McAdams, 1980). The need for intimacy expresses itself as a growth-oriented motive (the growth opportunity is enriching one's relationships). In the words of Abraham Maslow (1987), the need for affiliation revolves around "deprivation-love," whereas the need for intimacy revolves around "being-love."

Fear and Anxiety

Social isolation and fear-arousing conditions are two situations that increase a person's desire to affiliate with others (Baumeister & Leary, 1995; Schachter, 1959). Under conditions of isolation and fear, people report being jittery and tense, feeling as if they are suffering and are in pain, and seeing themselves as going to pieces. To reduce such anxiety and fear, humans typically adopt the strategy of seeking out others (Rofé, 1984). When afraid, people desire to affiliate for emotional support and to see how others handle the emotions they feel from the fear object. For example, imagine camping out in the wilderness and hearing a sudden loud noise in the middle of the night. The sudden, unexplained noise might produce fear. While feeling fear and anxiety, people seek out others, partly to see if others seem as afraid and partly to gain emotional and physical support. Having other people around while anxious is comforting, but our confidants can be practical allies as well, at least to the extent that they can help us clarify the threatening situation, provide coping strategies, and help carry out our attempts at coping (Kirkpatrick & Shaver, 1988; Kulik, Mahler, & Earnest, 1994).

Stanley Schachter (1959) tested the fear-affiliation relationship. He created two experimental conditions, one of high anxiety and one of low anxiety. All participants were told that they were about to receive some electric shocks (the fear object). The experimenter told participants in the high-anxiety group that they were going to receive intense shocks: "These shocks will hurt, they will be painful." The experimenter told participants in the low-anxiety group that they were going to receive very mild shocks that "will not in any way be painful" and would feel more like a tickle than a shock. (Of course, no participant was ever shocked.) The experimenter announced that there would first be a 10-minute wait, and he asked participants if they preferred to wait alone, with another participant, or did not care one way or the other. Most high-anxiety participants wanted affiliation (to wait with another person), whereas most low-anxiety participants preferred to wait alone or did not care one way or the other.

A second investigation found that anxious people's desires to affiliate applied only to those instances in which each person was anxious for the same reason (i.e., they faced the same threat). Hence, the old adage "misery loves company" must be qualified as "misery loves miserable company." The popularity of mutual support groups, for example, for alcoholics, unwed mothers, patients suffering a particular illness, and people facing particular adjustment problems, provides some confirming testimony to the human tendency to seek out others with similar problems or conditions when afraid or anxious.

Development of Interpersonal Relationships

In an apparent effort to initiate new friendships, people with a high need for intimacy typically join social groups, spend time interacting with others, and when friendships are started, form stable, long-lasting relationships, compared to people with a low need for intimacy (McAdams & Losoff, 1984). As relationships develop, high-need intimacy individuals come to know more personal information and history about their friends (McAdams & Losoff, 1984; McAdams, Healy, & Krause, 1984). And they report being more and more satisfied as their relationships progress, whereas individuals with a low need for intimacy report being less and less satisfied with their developing relationships (Eidelson, 1980). Individuals with a high need for intimacy perceive the tightening bonds of friendship as need involving and as emotionally satisfying, whereas those with a low-need intimacy perceive the tightening bonds of friendship as stifling and as an entrapment.

Maintaining Interpersonal Networks

Once a relationship has been established, individuals with a high need for affiliation strive to maintain those relationships by making more telephone calls, writing more letters, and paying more visits to their friends than do those with a low need for affiliation (Lansing & Heyns, 1959). Those with a high need for intimacy also spend more time in telephone conversations (Boyatzis, 1972) and more time writing letters and participating in face-to-face conversations, compared to those with a low need for intimacy (McAdams & Constantian, 1983).

One study asked persons with high and low needs for intimacy to keep a logbook over a two-month period on which they were to record 10 twenty-minute friendship episodes (McAdams, Healy, & Krause, 1984). Those with a high need for intimacy reported more dyadic (versus larger group) friendship episodes, more self-disclosure, more listening, and more trust and concern for the well-being of their friends. Even when thinking and talking about strangers, high-intimacy-need persons treat others differently than do low-intimacy-need persons, as they use more positive adjectives when describing others and they avoid talking about others in negative terms (McClelland et al., 1982).

During face-to-face interactions, high-intimacy-need persons laugh, smile, and make eye contact more frequently than do low-intimacy-need persons (McAdams, Jackson, &

Kirshnit, 1984). Such laughing, smiling, and looking lead others to rate high-intimacy-need persons as relatively warm, sincere, and loving human beings (McAdams & Losoff, 1984).

Satisfying the Affiliation and Intimacy Needs

Because it is largely a deficit-oriented motive, the need for affiliation, when satisfied, brings out emotions like relief rather than joy. When interacting with others, people high in the need for affiliation go out of their way to avoid conflict (Exline, 1962), avoid competitive situations (Terhune, 1968), are unselfish and cooperative (McAdams, 1980), avoid talking about others in a negative way (McClelland, 1985), and resist making imposing demands on others (McAdams & Powers, 1981). High-need-for-affiliation individuals prefer careers that provide positive relationships and support for others (the helping professions; Sid & Lindgren, 1981), and they perform especially well under conditions that support their need to be accepted and included (McKeachie et al., 1966). When told that others will be evaluating them, high-need-for-affiliation people experience relatively high levels of anxiety via a fear of rejection (Byrne, 1961). Social acceptance, approval, and reassurance constitute the need-satisfying conditions for people high in the need for affiliation.

Because it is largely a growth-oriented motive, people satisfy the need for intimacy through achieving closeness and warmth in a relationship. Hence, people high in the need for intimacy more frequently touch others (in a nonthreatening way; McAdams & Powers, 1981), cultivate deeper and more meaningful relationships (McAdams & Losoff, 1984), find satisfaction in listening and in self-disclosure (McAdams, Healey, & Krause, 1984), and look, laugh, and smile more during interaction (McAdams, Jackson, & Kirshnit, 1984). Relatedness within a warm, close, reciprocal, and enduring relationship constitutes the need-satisfying condition for people high in the need for intimacy.

POWER

The essence of the need for power is a desire to make the physical and social world conform to one's personal image or plan for it (Winter & Stewart, 1978). People high in the need for power desire to have "impact, control, or influence over another person, group, or the world at large" (Winter, 1973).

Impact allows power-needing individuals to establish power.

Control allows power-needing individuals to maintain power.

Influence allows power-needing individuals to expand or restore power.

Such power strivings often center around a need for dominance, reputation, status, or position. High-need-for-power individuals seek to become (and stay) leaders, and they interact with others with a forceful, take-charge style. When asked to recall the peak experiences in their lives, individuals high in the need for power report life events associated with strong positive emotions that occurred as a result of their impact on others, such as being elected to a leadership position or receiving applause from an audience (McAdams, 1982b).

David Winter (1973) provides two scenarios that illustrate power strivings. In the first scenario, research participants watched a film of an authority figure giving an influential speech (John F. Kennedy's presidential inaugural address), and in the second scenario, another set of participants watched a hypnotist ordering students to behave in particular ways as an audience watched. After having his participants view one of these two scenarios, Winter scored the arousal of their power strivings. As expected, these groups scored higher in power strivings (by writing stories rich in power-related imagery) than did a comparison group who did not view the film or hypnosis session (Winter, 1973).

Others have performed experiments that essentially replicated this procedure, but in addition to measuring power strivings, they added measures of mood and physiological arousal (Steele, 1977). As high-need-for-power individuals listened to inspirational speeches, their moods became significantly more lively and energetic and their physiological arousal (measured by epinephrine/adrenaline) showed a striking increase. Based on these findings, the opportunity to involve one's power strivings fills the power-needing individual with a vigor that can be measured via fantasy, mood, and psychophysiological activation (Steele, 1977).

Conditions That Involve and Satisfy the Need for Power

Four conditions are noteworthy in their capacity for involving and satisfying the need for power: leadership, aggressiveness, influential occupations, and prestige possessions.

Leadership and Relationships

People with a high need for power seek recognition in groups and find ways for making themselves visible to others, apparently in an effort to establish influence (Winter, 1973). Power-seeking college students, for example, write more letters to the university newspaper, and power-seeking adults willingly take risks in achieving public visibility (McClelland & Teague, 1975; McClelland & Watson, 1973). They are also more likely to put in hours at a public radio station, presumably in pursuit of an impact on an audience of listeners (Sonnenfield, 1974, cited in McClelland, 1985). They argue more frequently with their professors, and they show an eagerness in getting their points across in the classroom (Veroff, 1957). In selecting their friends and coworkers, power-striving individuals generally prefer others who are not well known and are thus in a position to be led (Fodor & Farrow, 1979; Winter, 1973). When hanging out with their friends, they prefer small groups over dyads, and they adopt an interpersonal orientation that takes on more of a tone of influence than it does a tone of intimacy (McAdams, Healey, & Krause, 1984).

In dating relationships, high-need-for-power men generally fare poorly (Stewart & Rubin, 1976). And they fare no better in marriage, as they generally make poor husbands, at least from the spouse's point of view (McClelland, 1975). In both dating and marriage, high-need-for-power women do not suffer the same poor outcomes that men do, apparently because they resist using interpersonal relationships as an arena for satisfying their power needs (Winter, 1988).

To test the influence of the need for power on tendencies toward leadership, experimenters arranged to have a group of strangers interact with each other for a short time (Fodor & Smith, 1982; Winter & Stewart, 1978). Power-seeking individuals talked more and were judged to have exerted more influence. However, the power-seeking individuals were not the best liked, nor were they judged to have contributed the most to getting the job done or for coming to a satisfactory conclusion. In fact, groups that had high-need-for-power leaders were the ones that produced the poorest decisions. These groups exchanged less information, considered few alternative strategies, and reached poorer final decisions than did groups with a leader low in the need for power. These findings suggest that power-seeking leaders attempt to make others follow their personal plan, even though their assertiveness and leadership style are often detrimental to group functioning.

Aggressiveness

If the need for power revolves around desires for impact, control, and influence over others, aggression ought to be one means for both involving and satisfying power needs. To some extent, the relationship between the need for power and aggression holds true, as men high in power strivings get into more arguments and participate more frequently in competitive sports (McClelland, 1975; Winter, 1973). However, the relationship between the need for power and aggression is diluted because society largely controls and inhibits people's acts of overt aggression. For this reason, aggressive manifestations of the need for power largely express themselves as impulses to (rather than actual acts of) aggression. Males and females with high needs for power report significantly more impulses to act aggressively (McClelland, 1975). When asked, "Have you ever felt like carrying out the following: yelling at someone in traffic, throwing things around the room, destroying furniture or breaking glassware, or insulting clerks in stores?" individuals high in the need for power report significantly more impulses to carry out these acts (Boyatzis, 1973). When asked if they had carried out such behaviors, those with a high need for power did not actually act on their impulses any more or less than did those with a low need for power.

Societal inhibitions and restraints largely constrain the power-seeking person's expression of aggression, but when societal inhibitions are removed, high-need-for-power men are more aggressive than are their low-need-for-power counterparts (McClelland, 1975; McClelland et al., 1972; Winter, 1973). Alcohol is one socially acceptable means of gaining a release from societal inhibitions, and power-seeking men do indeed act relatively more aggressively after drinking (McClelland et al., 1972). Alcohol also likely contributes to individuals' aggressiveness by making them feel more powerful. Similarly, because men get feelings of power from drinking, men with the highest need for power drink the most (McClelland et al., 1972). When life becomes stressful and frustrating, high-need-for-power individuals sometimes seek alcohol as a means for inflating their sense of control (Cooper et al., 1995). Similarly, power-seeking men, but not power-seeking women, frequently respond to stress and setbacks by inflicting abuse on their intimates (Mason & Blankenship, 1987). This research suggests that people can not only increase power through reputation, prestige, and leadership, but they can also create the perception of heightened power through strategies such as drinking alcohol, risk-taking, gesturing and posturing, using abusive language, using drugs, and driving very fast.

Influential Occupations

People high in the need for power are attracted to occupations such as business executives, teachers/professors, psychologists, journalists, clerics, and international diplomats (Winter, 1973). Each of these occupations shares a common denominator in that the person in the occupational role is in the position to direct the behavior of other people in accordance with some preconceived plan (Winter & Stewart, 1978). People in some of these professions speak to and influence audiences (teachers, journalists, clergy), others have inside information they use to influence others (psychologists, diplomats), while others have a professional status that allows them to tell others what to do (business executives). Further, these careers equip the individual with the rewards and punishments necessary for sanctioning the behavior of others. The teacher, cleric, and diplomat, for instance, all have the means for rewarding and punishing other people's compliance or disobedience (through grades, heavenly rewards, and deal making). The journalist can sanction the behavior of others through editorial means. The business executive administers orders and schedules and enforces them through salaries and wages, bonuses, and job security. Thus, people can involve and satisfy their power strivings through the job they choose.

Prestige Possessions

People high in the need for power tend to amass a collection of power symbols, or "prestige possessions" (Winter, 1973). Among college students, individuals high in the need for power are more likely than others to possess a car, wine glasses, a television set, a stereo, wall hangings, carpeted floor, and so on. They are also more likely to put their name on their dormitory room door. Older, power-seeking individuals are more likely to own a rifle or pistol, a convertible car, or a truck that exudes status and power (McClelland, 1975).

Leadership Motive Pattern

A special variant of the need for power is the leadership motive pattern (McClelland, 1975, 1985; McClelland & Burnham, 1976; Spangler & House, 1991). Leadership motivation consists of a threefold pattern of needs: (1) high need for power, (2) low need for intimacy/affiliation, and (3) high inhibition (McClelland, 1982). Thus, the leadership motive pattern features individuals who desire to exercise influence, are not concerned with being liked, and are well controlled or self-disciplined. For instance, the stereotypical military commander or traditional father figure fits this leadership motive pattern rather well.

Such a constellation of high power, low affiliation, and self-control generally results in effective leaders and managers (Spangler & House, 1991). The characteristic of an internally controlling style (i.e., high inhibition) is important because managers who are high in power, low in affiliation, and high in inhibition are generally productive, successful, and rated highly by workers (McClelland & Burnham, 1976). In contrast, managers who are high in power, low in affiliation, but low in inhibition are often unproductive, unsuccessful, and rated lowly by workers. Apparently, an internally controlling style leads power-striving managers to internalize characteristics associated with effective management: respect for institutional authority, discipline, self-control, and a concern for just rewards (McClelland, 1975, 1985). So power needs to be complimented by self-disciplined inhibition (power under control) if one is to be an effective leader.

Effectiveness of U.S. Presidents

The leadership motive provides a framework for assessing the effectiveness of U.S. presidents (Spangler & House, 1991; Winter, 1973, 1987). Winter coded the thematic content of each president's inaugural address for the social needs of achievement, affiliation, and power and used these scores to predict presidential effectiveness. Presidents generally considered strong by historians—Kennedy, Truman, Wilson, and both Roosevelts—scored relatively high on power needs and relatively low on affiliation needs.

Five variables defined presidential effectiveness: direct presidential actions (e.g., entering and avoiding war), perceived greatness, performance on social issues, performance on economic issues, and international relations. To assess each president's needs for power, affiliation, and inhibition, the researchers coded their inaugural speeches, presidential letters, and other speeches. The leadership motive pattern of high power, low affiliation, and high inhibition correlated significantly with all five measures of effectiveness. Apparently, when the United States elects a candidate with personal dispositions consistent with the leadership motive pattern, the nation is electing someone into office who will probably perform quite well, given the rather unique demands and challenges of the office. So how well or poorly each of the Presidents in Figure 7.3 fared in terms of presidential effectiveness was rooted, in part, in the quality of their leadership motive pattern.

The leadership motive pattern also predicts when leaders will engage in war and when leaders will pursue peace (Winter, 1993). Of course, war has many nonpsychological causes, but on the psychological side, historical research shows that when leaders express a motive profile of high power and low affiliation, the probability of subsequent war increases. Using British history, British–German World War I communications, and U.S.–Soviet communications during the Cuban Missile Crisis as his database, Winter found that the motive patterns expressed in speeches foreshadow the coming war-versus-peace decisions. When power imagery rose, war became a historically more likely event. When power imagery fell, war was less likely and ongoing wars tended to end. When affiliation imagery rose, war became a historically less likely event. When affilia-

Figure 7.3   Recent United States Presidents

tion imagery fell, war was more likely to begin (Winter, 1993). According to this research, if you want to forecast whether or not a nation will enter into, avoid, and exit a war, read the speeches of the day and look for changes in whether the leaders are promoting influence (power) or are promoting relationships (affiliation).

SUMMARY

Acquired psychological needs include both quasi-needs and social needs. Quasi-needs are situationally induced wants and desires that arise out of a psychological context of tension and urgency to meet some specific environmental demand, such as needing a high grade-point average or needing money. Social needs are more enduring. They arise from the individual's personal experiences and unique developmental, cognitive, and socialization histories. Once acquired, social needs act as emotional and behavioral potentials activated by situational incentives. The need-activating incentive for each of the four social needs are as follows: For achievement, doing something well to show personal competence; for affiliation, an opportunity to please others and gain their approval; for intimacy, a warm, secure relationship; and for power, having impact on others.

The need for achievement is the desire to do well relative to a standard of excellence. When facing standards of excellence, people's emotional reactions vary. High need for achievement individuals generally respond with approach-oriented emotions (e.g., hope) and behaviors, whereas low need for achievement individuals (high fear of failure) generally respond with avoidance-oriented emotions (e.g., anxiety) and behaviors. High-need achievers therefore choose moderately difficult tasks, quickly engage in achievement-related tasks, put forth more effort and perform better on moderately difficult tasks, persist in the face of difficulty and failure, and take a personal responsibility for successes and failures. The dynamics-of-action model adds that any stream of on-going achievement behavior is determined not only by the need for achievement (instigation), fear of failure (inhibition), but also by the achievement behavior itself (consummation).

According to Atkinson's classical model of achievement, behavioral approach versus avoidance is a multiplicative function of the individual's need for achievement, probability of success, and incentive for success (i.e., $Ts = Ms \times Ps \times Is$), as well as the individual's fear of failure, probability of failure, and incentive to avoid failure (i.e., $Taf = Maf \times Pf \times If$). This formula predicts approach versus avoidance behaviors rather well in situations such moderately difficult tasks, interpersonal competition, and entrepreneurship.

Three types of achievement goals exist: performance-approach, performance-avoidance, and mastery. The need for achievement predicts the adoption of performance-approach goals, fear of failure predicts performance-avoidance goals, and high competency expectancies predict mastery goals. Mastery and performance-approach goals are generally associated with achievement and positive outcomes, whereas performance-avoidance goals are not.

Implicit theories reveal whether people think their personal qualities are fixed and enduring (entity theorists) or are malleable and can be increased (incremental theorists). Implicit theorists are important because they predict the type of goals people choose to pursue, as entity theorists generally adopt performance goals whereas incremental theorists adopt learning goals. Entity and incremental theorists also interpret the meaning of effort differently. Entity theorists generally believe that high effort means low ability: "The more you try, the dumber you must be." Incremental theorists generally believe that effort is the means by which learning occurs and skills develop. When facing difficult tasks or negative feedback, incremental theorists show the relatively more adaptive motivational style in that they understand the utility of effort and show a willingness to roll up their sleeves and engage in effortful and persistent work.

Affiliation strivings have two facets: the need for affiliation (rejection anxiety) and the need for intimacy (affiliation interest). The need for affiliation involves establishing, maintaining, and restoring relationships with others, mostly to escape from and to avoid negative emotions such as disapproval and loneliness. The need for intimacy is the social motive for engaging in warm, close, positive interpersonal relationships that produce positive emotions and hold little threat of rejection. Depriving people of the opportunity for social interaction is the principal condition that involves the need for affiliation, and social acceptance, approval, and reassurance constitute its need-satisfying conditions. Engaging in, developing, and maintaining warm, close relationships involve the need for intimacy, and individuals with high intimacy needs are more likely to join social groups, spend time interacting with others, and form stable, long-lasting relationships that are characterized by self-disclosure and positive affect expressed through looking, laughing, and smiling. Participating in these warm, reciprocal, and enduring relationships constitutes the condition that satisfies the need for intimacy.

The need for power is the desire for making the physical and social world conform to one's personal image for it. High-need-for-power individuals strive for leadership and recognition in small groups, experience frequent impulses of aggression, prefer influential occupations, and amass prestige possessions. A special variant of the need for power is the leadership motive pattern, which consists of the threefold pattern of needs involving high need for power, low need for intimacy, and high inhibition. Leaders, managers in the workplace, and U.S. presidents who possess constellations of needs consistent with the leadership motive pattern (high power, low affiliation, high inhibition) generally perform well as leaders and are rated by others as effective.

READINGS FOR FURTHER STUDY

Need for Achievement

ATKINSON, J. W. (1964). A theory of achievement motivation. *An introduction to motivation* (240–268). Princeton, NJ: D. Van Nostrand.

ELLIOT, A. J. (1999). Approach and avoidance motivation and achievement goals. *Educational Psychologist, 34,* 169–189.

ELLIOT, A. J., & CHURCH, M. A. (1997). A hierarchical model of approach and avoidance achievement motivation. *Journal of Personality and Social Psychology, 72,* 218–232.

ELLIOT, A. J., & SHELDON, K. M. (1997). Avoidance achievement motivation: A personal goals analysis. *Journal of Personality and Social Psychology, 72,* 218–232.

HONG, Y., CHIU, C., DWECK, C. S., LIN, D. M.-S., & WAN, W. (1999). Implicit theories, attributions, and coping: A meaning system approach. *Journal of Personality and Social Psychology, 77,* 588–599.

McCLELLAND, D. C. (1965). Achievement and entrepreneurship: A longitudinal study. *Journal of Personality and Social Psychology, 1,* 389–392.

Needs of Affiliation and Intimacy

McADAMS, D. P., JACKSON, R. J., & KIRSHNIT, C. (1984). Looking, laughing, and smiling in dyads as a function of intimacy motivation and reciprocity. *Journal of Personality, 52,* 261–273.

McADAMS, D. P., & LOSOFF, M. (1984). Friendship motivation in fourth and sixth graders: A thematic analysis. *Journal of Social and Personal Relations, 1,* 11–27.

Need for Power

SPANGLER, W. D., & HOUSE, R. J. (1991). Presidential effectiveness and the leadership motive profile. *Journal of Personality and Social Psychology, 60,* 439–455.

STEELE, R. S. (1977). Power motivation, activation, and inspirational speeches. *Journal of Personality, 45,* 53–64.

Part Two

Cognitions

Chapter 8

Goals

Mirrors don't lie. Lately, your mirror has been saying you added a few pounds. It is time, you decide, to lose 10 pounds and get back on the road to physical fitness. You want to take action, but what? When? How?

Jogging seems sensible, so you start. At first, jogging is new, even fun, as you enjoy the outdoors and sense of accomplishment. A week goes by, but you do not lose much weight. You begin to wonder how much exercise is enough exercise. Another week goes by and the pressures of everyday living increase and compete for your time and attention. Each day you find it more difficult to find the time and to mobilize the energy to exercise. After a month of lackluster progress, jogging is history.

Months later, strolling through a used bookstore, you happen across the book *Aerobics* (Cooper, 1968). You still think exercising and getting into shape are important, so you flip through its pages. Its critical feature is a point system. Page after page, the book lists several different aerobic activities, such as running, swimming, and cycling. For each exercise, the system lists a distance, a performance time, and a number of aerobic points earned for that particular distance and time. For example, under running, joggers who run one mile in 8 minutes earn 5 aerobic points. Under cycling, cyclists who bike for 2.5 miles in 12 minutes earn 5 aerobic points. A few pages later, the book provides a personal progress chart with space for writing in the date, the exercise, its distance and duration, number of points earned, and cumulative points earned for each week. According to *Aerobics*, a person needs to earn 30 aerobic points per week to increase physical fitness and to decrease weight.

Now, you have a goal. No longer are you going to "do your best." Now you are going to earn 30 aerobic points per week. You start the week bent on earning 30 points, but your body protests that 20 is enough. Because you cannot quite earn the 30 points, you find yourself devising point-increasing strategies (e.g., treadmill in the morning instead of "when I feel like it"). By the end of the third week, you earn the 30 points and feel the warm glow of accomplishment. After a month, you boldly decide to try for 40 points per week. You now have a new goal. It will take more effort, more persistence, and an improved exercise strategy. But because you achieved your earlier goal and because your stamina has increased, you feel up to the lifestyle change. Eagerness replaces apathy. As the new week begins, you wake up saying, "Today, I'm going to earn 10 aerobic points—I'm going to run 2 miles in 16 minutes on the treadmill at the university gym this morning before my classes."

Another widely-used weight-loss program illustrates these same motivational processes. Dieting is an ambiguous task much in the same way that exercise is an ambiguous task—how much can I eat? Is my goal high enough? How do I know whether or not I am making any progress? In order to translate general, long-term dieting goals into specific day-to-day action, this popular weight loss program recommends each person consume foods within a daily point range, depending on the person's current weight. A daily points goal for a person of 180 pounds might be, for example, between 22 and 27 points. The daily points range is important because all foods have a points value, depending on the food's number of calories, grams of fat, and grams of fiber (e.g., two pancakes = 6 points). The basic idea is that the person starts each day with a "range of points" goal. The dieter is to plan his or her food choices to eat at least the minimum number of points (to maintain metabolism) but no more than the maximum number of points (to lose weight). Vigorous daily activity (exercise) can increase one's daily points range. The idea is to focus not on a vague, ambiguous diet but, instead, to focus on a difficult and specific goal, carefully keep track of food points consumed, and accomplish this food points goal day after day.

COGNITIVE PERSPECTIVE ON MOTIVATION

This chapter asks how and why mental events such as goals mobilize effort and increase commitment to a long-term course of action. The first part of the chapter focuses on making plans and goals, while the second half focuses on formulating intentions for actually carrying out those plans and goals. The next two chapters focus on different mental events that can also function as causal determinants to action (Gollwitzer & Bargh, 1996). Among the more heavily researched motivational agents in the cognition → action sequence are the following:

Chapter 8

- Plans (Miller, Galanter, & Pribram, 1960)
- Goals (Locke & Latham, 2002)
- Implementation intentions (Gollwitzer, 1999)
- Mental simulations (Taylor et al., 1998)
- Self-regulation (Zimmerman, 2000)

Chapter 9

- Personal control beliefs (Peterson, Maier, & Seligman, 1993)
- Self-efficacy (Bandura, 1986)
- Attributions (Weiner, 1986)
- Explanatory style (Peterson & Seligman, 1984)

Chapter 10

- Self-concept (Markus, 1977)
- Possible selves (Markus & Nurius, 1986)
- Personal strivings (Sheldon & Elliot, 1999)
- Dissonance (Harmon-Jones & Mills, 1999)
- Values (Brophy, 1999)

As we will see, cognitive mental events like goals and expectancies can function as a "spring to action," a moving force that energizes and directs action in purposive ways (Ames & Ames, 1984). The first motivational spring to action studied by cognitive motivational psychologists was "plan."

PLANS

The contemporary cognitive study of motivation began when a trio of psychologists—George Miller, Eugene Galanter, and Karl Pribram—investigated how plans motivate behavior (1960). According to these pioneers, people have mental representations of the ideal states of their behavior, environmental objects, and events. In other words, people have in mind what an ideal tennis serve looks like (ideal behavior), what an ideal birthday gift would be (ideal environmental object), and what constitutes an ideal night on the town (ideal event). People are also aware of the present state of their behavior, environment, and events. That is, people have the knowledge of their current tennis serve (present behavior), gift (present object), and evening itinerary (present event).

Any mismatch perceived between one's present state and one's ideal state instigates an experience of "incongruity," which has motivational properties. Suffering incongruity, people formulate a plan to remove that incongruity (Miller et al., 1960; Newell, Shaw, & Simon, 1958). Hence, the essential motivational process underlying a plan is as follows: People have knowledge of both their present and ideal states and any perceived incongruity between the two makes people uncomfortable enough to formulate and act on a plan of action to remove the incongruity so that the present state will change and become the ideal state. The incongruity acts as the motivational "spring to action" (provides energy), and the plan is the cognitive means for advancing the present state toward the ideal state (provides direction).

The cognitive mechanism by which plans energize and direct behavior is the test-operate-test-exit (TOTE) model, as illustrated in Figure 8.1 (Miller, Galanter, & Pribram, 1960). *Test* means to compare the present state against the ideal. A mismatch between the two (incongruity) springs the individual into action. That is, the mismatch motivates the individual to *operate* on the environment via a planned sequence of action. That is, when you look in the mirror to check if your hair looks okay, you "test" or compare the way your hair presently looks in the mirror against the way you want your hair ideally to look. If the hair looks okay, you say "fine" and walk away from the mirror. But if you see a mismatch between your present hair and your ideal hair, then it is time to "operate" via a plan of action—you comb your hair, take a shower, use hair spray, or just wear a hat. After a period of action, the person again *tests* the present state against the ideal. If the feedback

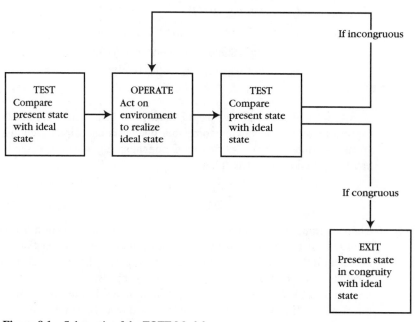

Figure 8.1 Schematic of the TOTE Model

reveals that the incongruity continues to persist, then the person continues to *operate* on the environment (T-O-T-O-T-O, and so on). In daily life, T-O-T-O-T-O looks like, to continue the bad hair day example, as: Look in mirror—Comb your hair—Look in the mirror for feedback—Comb your hair some more—Look in the mirror again—Comb you hair some more, and so on. As long as the incongruity persists, action ("operate") continues. If and whenever the present matches the ideal, the person *exits* the plan.

Consider a second example of the TOTE model. A painter takes an easel to a waterfall, paints the scenery, compares the canvas to the waterfall, and notices that the two are quite dissimilar. Because the canvas does not yet show a satisfactory representation of the waterfall, the painter operates on the painting to reflect on the canvas the ideal picture in her mind. The painter continually compares (tests) the painting on the canvas to its ideal in her mind. As long as incongruity persists, the painting continues (T-O-T-O-T-O, and so on). Only when the actual and ideal paintings match does the painter exit the plan and cease to paint. The ever-repeated process of comparing the present versus the ideal, followed by incongruity-reducing behavioral adjustments, is a common feature of everyday life.

Overcoming bad hair days and painting waterfalls illustrate the moment-to-moment influence plans have on our motivated behavior—getting started, putting forth effort, persisting over time, and eventually stopping. Dozens of additional illustrations of plans as springs to action are possible, including removing items from a "to do" list, repairing a broken object until it is fixed, driving to a destination, revising a poem or term paper, shopping, saving money for a trip, moving the lawn's high grass, cleaning a sink full of dirty dishes, reading this chapter, and so on.

Plans can also be long-term. For instance, how satisfied are you currently with the present state of your career/occupation? Marital status? Capacity to speak a foreign language? Events happen in life that make us aware of the incongruities that exist between our present states and our ideal states. Our friends, for instance, might get an "ideal" job, marriage partner, or opportunity to travel or live abroad. When these incongruities cause enough discomfort to stir us into action (as we say to ourselves, "I want the ideal state more than I want my present state"), we formulate plans of action and start down the road of long-term planning and T-O-T-O-T-O.

Corrective Motivation

The plan → action sequence portrays individuals as (1) detecting present-ideal inconsistencies, (2) generating a plan to eliminate the incongruity, (3) instigating plan-regulated behavior, and (4) monitoring feedback as to the extent of any remaining present-ideal incongruity. Most contemporary researchers (Campion & Lord, 1982; Carver & Scheier, 1981, 1982, 1990, 1998), however, no longer view plans as so fixed, static, and mechanical. Rather, plans are adjustable and subject to revision. Given an incongruity between present and ideal, the individual's plan is as likely to change and undergo modification as is his behavior. The emphasis on modifiable plans is important because it presents human beings as active decision makers who choose which process to follow (Carver & Scheier, 1981, 1982):

- Act ("Operate") to achieve the ideal state
- Change and revise an ineffective plan

From this point of view, any present-ideal incongruity does not instigate an automatic discrepancy-motivated action sequence. Rather, incongruity gives rise to a more generalized "corrective motivation" (Campion & Lord, 1982).

Corrective motivation activates a decision-making process in which the individual considers many ways for reducing the present-ideal incongruity: Change the plan, change behavior (increase effort), or withdraw from the plan altogether. That is, plan-directed behavior is a dynamic, flexible process in which corrective motivation energizes the individual to pursue the most adaptive course.

Corrective motivation also involves emotion (Carver & Scheier, 1990, 1998). When people progress toward their ideal states at rates equal to their expectations, they feel little emotion. When people progress toward their ideal states at slower-than-expected rates, however, the persistent and salient discrepancy produces negative emotions such as anxiety, frustration, or despair. When people progress toward their ideal states at faster-than-expected rates, discrepancy reduction produces positive emotions such as enthusiasm, hope, excitement, and joy. Thus, plans motivate actions, and the person's subsequent evaluations of progress generate emotions.

When a person realizes that a present state-ideal state incongruity exists, devising a good plan for removing or reducing this incongruity is only the first half of the battle. Actually carrying out the plan is the other half because people all too often encounter problems (e.g., situational constraints, personal inadequacies) while trying to translate their plans into action. After discussing the motivational significance of both plans and goals, this chapter will return to the sticky issue of enacting plans and achieving goals in the section, "Implementation Intentions."

Discrepancy

Incongruity is a fundamental motivational principle. The more cognitive psychologists worked with present state versus ideal state mismatches to study plans and corrective motivation, the more they came to see "discrepancy" as a core motivational construct. The basic idea behind discrepancy is straightforward and can be represented by the magnitude of the arrow below that shows the difference or mismatch between one's present state and one's ideal state.

Present   Ideal
State   State

Present state represents the person's current status of how life is going. The ideal state represents how the person wishes life was going. When the present state falls short of the hoped-for ideal state, a discrepancy is exposed. It is the discrepancy (rather than the ideal state per se) that has motivational properties. Discrepancy creates the sense of wanting to change the present state so that it will move closer and closer toward the ideal state. Here are 12 everyday illustrations of discrepancies between what currently is (present state) and what we wish would be (ideal state). For instance, people who are stuck in traffic (present state) wish they were instead driving without interference (ideal state), and the awareness of the mismatch creates a want that motivates people to take action necessary to remove the rather bothersome discrepancy.

Present State	**Ideal State**
Stuck in traffic	Driving without interference
The job you have	The job you want
How skillful you are	How skillful the guy on television is
Current quality of a relationship	How good the relationship could be
Current GPA	GPA needed to make the Dean's List
Messy, cluttered desktop	Clean, well-organized desktop
Suffering headache pain	Not suffering headache pain
Excluded from a club	Included as a member
Making $6 an hour	Making $10 an hour
Having 200 more miles to drive	Being there
10 laps to run around the track	0 laps to run
250 more pages to read in this book	0 pages to read

This list represents a dozen ways for saying essentially the same thing. In these and all other instances of discrepancy, the person envisions possible circumstances that are different from present circumstances. The awareness of the mismatch between "that which presently is" and "that which is desired" creates a sense of incongruity that produces motivational consequences. Therefore, when people ask themselves, "What can I do to increase motivation?" those who study discrepancy-based motivation have a very practical answer: Basically, create an ideal state in your mind. Or, more precisely, create a present state–ideal state discrepancy.

Two Types of Discrepancy

Two types of discrepancies exist (Bandura, 1990; Carver & Scheier, 1998). The first is *discrepancy reduction*, which is based on discrepancy-detecting feedback. Some aspect of the environment (e.g., a boss, scholarship, athletic opponent) provides feedback about the person's naturally-occurring performance that informs the performer of any existing difference between current performance level and an ideal performance level. For instance, at work, the supervisor might tell the salesperson that 10 sales are not enough; 15 sales are needed. Likewise, a student might read in a brochure that his current 2.0 GPA is not enough for scholarship eligibility; a 3.0 GPA is needed. In essence, the environment brings some standard of excellence (an ideal state) to the person's awareness and asks, essentially, "are you currently performing at this desired level"? The 12 present state–ideal state discrepancies listed above all illustrate this discrepancy reduction process, as the person sees an adjacent open lane of traffic, sees the ideal jobs other people have, sees how skilled the actors on television appear to be, sees how high quality other people's relationships are, and so on.

The second type of discrepancy is *discrepancy creation*. Discrepancy creation is based on a "feed-forward" system in which the person looks forward and proactively sets a future, higher goal. The person deliberately sets a higher goal—an ideal state that does not yet exist except in the performer's mind—and does not require feedback from a boss or a scholarship to impose it. For instance, the salesperson might, for whatever reason, decide to try for 15 sales in one week instead of the usual 10, and the student might decide to try for a 3.0 GPA. Thus, the person creates a new, higher goal to pursue.

In both cases—discrepancy reduction and discrepancy creation—it is the discrepancy (or incongruity) that provides the motivational basis for action. But two important distinctions between discrepancy reduction and discrepancy creation exist: (1) Discrepancy reduction corresponds to plan-based corrective motivation (discussed in the previous section), whereas discrepancy creation corresponds to goal-setting motivation (discussed in the next section); and (2) discrepancy reduction is reactive, deficiency overcoming, and revolves around a feedback system, whereas discrepancy creation is proactive, growth pursuing, and revolves around a "feed-forward" system. As discussed next, goal setting is first and foremost a discrepancy-creating process (Bandura, 1990).

GOALS

A goal is whatever an individual is striving to accomplish (Locke, 1996). When people strive to earn $100, make a 4.0 GPA, sell 100 boxes of Girl Scout cookies, or go undefeated in an athletic season, they engage in goal-directed behavior. Like plans, goals generate motivation by focusing people's attention on the discrepancy (or incongruity) between their present level of accomplishment (no boxes of cookies sold) and their ideal level of accomplishment (100 boxes sold by the end of the month). Researchers refer to this discrepancy between present level of accomplishment and ideal level of accomplishment as a "goal-performance discrepancy" (Locke & Latham, 1990). Goal-performance discrepancies follow a proactive, discrepancy creation process.

Performance

Generally speaking, people with goals outperform those without goals (Locke, 1996; Locke & Latham, 1990, 2002). And generally speaking, the same person performs better when she has a goal than when she does not have a goal. So people who create goals for themselves and people who accept the goals other set for them, perform better than those who do not create or accept such goals.

Consider one study in which elementary-grade students performed sit-ups for 2 minutes (Weinberg et al., 1988). Some students set a goal for themselves as to how many sit-ups they would accomplish during the 2 minutes (goal-setting group), while others simply completed sit-ups without a predetermined goal (no-goal group). After 2 minutes of exercise, the goal-setting students finished significantly more sit-ups than did the no-goal students. In effect, the presence of a goal motivated exercisers more than did the absence of a goal. The first group of elementary-grade students were not any healthier or athletic than the other group of students. Instead, the presence of a goal energized and directed their sit-up performance in a way that the absence of a goal did not.

The same result can be found in any number of other studies, as people with goals outperform people without goals, such as in trying to lift weights, learn text information, sell products, shoot archery, conserve natural resources, tolerate pain, study for tests, and lose weight [see Locke & Latham's (1990) Table 2.5, which lists 88 different tasks]. As a point of illustration, loggers with goals cut more trees than do loggers without goals (Latham & Kinne, 1974), word-processing operators with goals typed more and faster than did word-processing operators without goals (Latham & Yukl, 1976), and truck drivers with goals increased the number of trips they made each day relative to truck drivers with no goals (Latham & Baldes, 1975).

Goal setting generally enhances performance, but the type of goal one sets is a key determinant in the extent to which a goal translates into performance gains. As to types of goals, goals vary in how difficult they are and goals vary in how specific they are.

Goal Difficulty

Goal difficulty refers to how hard a goal is to accomplish. As goals increase in difficulty, performance increases in a linear fashion (Locke & Latham, 1990; Mento, Steel, & Karren, 1987; Tubbs, 1986). Relative to goals such as scoring 80 on a test, running a mile in 10 minutes, and making one new friend, more difficult goals would be scoring 90 on a test, running a mile in 8 minutes, and making three new friends. The more difficult the goal, the more it energizes the performer. This is so because people exert effort in proportion to what the goal requires of them. That is, easy goals stimulate little effort, medium goals stimulate moderate effort, and difficult goals stimulate high effort (Locke & Latham, 2002). Effort responds to goal difficulty.

Goal Specificity

Goal specificity refers to how clearly a goal informs the performer precisely what he is to do. Telling a performer to "do your best" sounds like goal setting, but it is actually only an ambiguous statement that does not make clear precisely what the person is to do (Locke & Latham, 1990). On the other hand, telling a writer to have a first draft in 1 week, a revised draft in 2 weeks, and a final manuscript in 3 weeks specifies more precisely what the writer is to do and when she is to do it. Translating a vague goal into a specific goal typically involves restating the goal in numerical terms. Goal specificity is important because specific goals reduce ambiguity in thought and variabilty in performance. As to ambiguous thought, a vague goal like "study hard" might be interpreted as "read the chapter" by one student but as "read the chapter, take notes, review it, and form a study group to discuss it" by a second student. As to variable performance, a vague goal (e.g., "work quickly" or "read a lot") produces a relatively wide range of performances compared to giving a group of performers a specific goal (e.g., "complete the task in the next 3 minutes" or "read 100 pages"), which produces a relatively narrow range of performances (Locke et al., 1989).

Difficult, Specific Goals Enhance Performance

Goals do not always enhance performance. Only those goals that are difficult and specific do so (Locke et al., 1981). The reason difficult, specific goals increase performance while easy and vague ones do not is a motivational reason. Difficult goals energize the performer, and specific goals direct her toward a particular course of action (Earley, Wojnaroski, & Prest, 1987). Therefore, goals need to be difficult to create energy, and goals need to be specific to focus direction.

Difficult goals energize behavior, which is to say that they increase the performer's effort and persistence. Output of effort is directly proportional to the perceived demands of the task (Bassett, 1979; Locke & Latham, 1990). The harder the goal, the greater the effort expended in accomplishing it (Earley, Wojnaroski, & Prest, 1987; Bandura & Cervone, 1983, 1986). Difficult goals increase persistence because effort continues and continues until the goal is reached (LaPorte & Nath, 1976; Latham & Locke, 1975). The athlete trying for 45 sit-ups, for example, keeps performing sit-up after sit-up until all 45 are done. Goals also decrease the probability that the performer will be distracted away from the task or will give up prematurely (LaPorte & Nath, 1976). The exerciser with a "45 sit-ups" goal is more likely to keep going past 30, 35, and 40 situps than is the exerciser with a lesser goal or with a "do my best" goal. With a goal in mind, performers quit the task when the goal is accomplished, not when they get bored, frustrated, tired, or distracted.

Specific goals direct attention and strategic planning. Specific goals focus the individual's attention toward the task at hand and therefore away from tasks that are incidental (Kahneman, 1973; Locke & Bryan, 1969; Rothkopf & Billington, 1979). Goals tell the performer where to concentrate and what specifically to do (Klein, Whitener, & Ilgen, 1990; Latham, Mitchell, & Dossett, 1978; Locke et al., 1989). In studies with students reading texts, for instance, readers with specific goals spent significantly more time looking at their text during a study session than did readers with ambiguous goals, who were more likely to let their eyes wander around the room (Locke & Bryan, 1969; Rothkopf & Billington, 1979). Specific goals also prompt performers to plan a strategic course of action (Latham & Baldes, 1975; Terborg, 1976), and specific goals lead people to use their task knowledge and strategies (Smith, Locke, & Barry, 1990). The weight loss program discussed earlier illustrates this point as the dieter needs to invest a good deal of knowledge and deliberate planning into the creation of a strategic plan if he or she is going to successfully limit the day's food intake to 25 points. Also, with a specific goal in mind, a performer who is unable to accomplish a goal on a first attempt will tend to drop that strategy and revise it by creating a new and improved strategy (Earley & Perry, 1987; Earley, Wojnaroski, & Prest, 1987).

Goals generate motivation, but motivation is only one of the causes underlying performance. Performance also depends on factors that are not motivational, such as ability, training, coaching, and resources (Locke & Latham, 1984). Because these factors also contribute to the quality of performance, no one-to-one correspondence exists between goals and performance. Thus, if two performers have comparable ability, training, coaching, and resources, then performers with difficult and specific goals will likely outperform performers without such goals. This is an important practical point because when difficult, specific goals fail to enhance performance, one might be well advised to focus on factors that are not motivational and that relate to increasing ability (via instruction, practice, role models, videotaped-performance feedback) or resources (via supplying equipment, books, tutors, computers, money).

Feedback

Difficult, specific goals enhance performance by energizing effort and persistence and by directing attention and strategy. One additional variable is crucial in making goal setting effective: feedback (Erez, 1977). Goal setting translates into increased performance only in the context of timely feedback that documents the performer's progress in relation to the goal (Locke et al., 1981). Feedback, or knowledge of results, allows people to keep track of any progress toward their goal. In other words, a performer needs both a goal *and* performance feedback to maximize performance (Bandura & Cervone, 1983; Becker, 1978; Erez, 1977; Strang, Lawrence, & Fowler, 1978; Tubbs, 1986).

Without feedback, performance can be emotionally unimportant and uninvolving. A runner can have a goal to run a mile in 6 minutes, a dieter can have a goal to lose 10 pounds, and a student can have a goal of mastering a subject matter. But if the runner, dieter, and student never gain access to a stopwatch, scale, or examination, respectively, then all the running, dieting, and studying have no way for informing the performer of her progress toward goal attainment. But feedback is just information. Feedback needs a goal (a standard of performance) so that the person can judge performance as poor (below goal), okay (at goal), or excellent (above goal).

The combination of goals with feedback produces an emotionally meaningful mixture: Goal attainment breeds emotional satisfaction, while goal failure breeds emotional dissatisfaction (Bandura, 1991). Both satisfaction and dissatisfaction have motivational properties. Felt satisfaction contributes favorably to the discrepancy-creating process. When feedback shows the individual that he is performing at or above goal level, the individual feels satisfied and competent, competent enough perhaps to create a higher, more difficult goal (the discrepancy-creation process; Wood, Bandura, & Bailey, 1990). Felt dissatisfaction contributes favorably to the discrepancy-reducing process (Matsui, Okada, & Inoshita, 1983). When performance feedback shows the individual that he is performing below goal level, the individual feels dissatisfied and becomes keenly aware of the goal-performance discrepancy, enough perhaps to marshal greater efforts in eliminating the goal-performance incongruity (the discrepancy-reduction process; Bandura & Cervone, 1983, 1986). Feedback therefore provides the emotional punch that brings the goal-setting process to life within experiences of felt satisfaction and felt dissatisfaction.

The core motivational elements of the goal-setting process appear in summary form in Figure 8.2. The left-hand side of the figure explains why goals enhance performance—namely, because people with goals work harder, longer, smarter, and with more focus (i.e., increased effort, persistence, strategic planning, and attention). The right-hand side explains the motivational process that arise out of feedback in one's progress to remove the goal-performance discrepancies (i.e., discrepancy reduction, new discrepancy creation).

Goal Acceptance

In addition to goals needing to be (1) difficult and specific, and (2) coupled with feedback, a third condition is necessary before goals translate into performance gains: goal acceptance (Erez & Kanfer, 1983). Goal acceptance is a critical variable when goal setting takes place within an interpersonal relationship in which one person attempts to provide another person with a goal. For instance, a coach might ask an athlete to run 2 miles in 12 minutes, a parent might ask a child to wash the dishes each Monday evening, or a priest might ask parishioners to tithe 10% of their income to the church. Goal acceptance involves the person's decision either to accept or reject the goal. It varies on a continuum from total acceptance of the externally imposed goal to total rejection (Erez & Zidon, 1984). Only internalized (i.e., accepted) goals improve performance (Erez, Earley, & Hulin, 1985). They do so because goal acceptance breeds goal commitment.

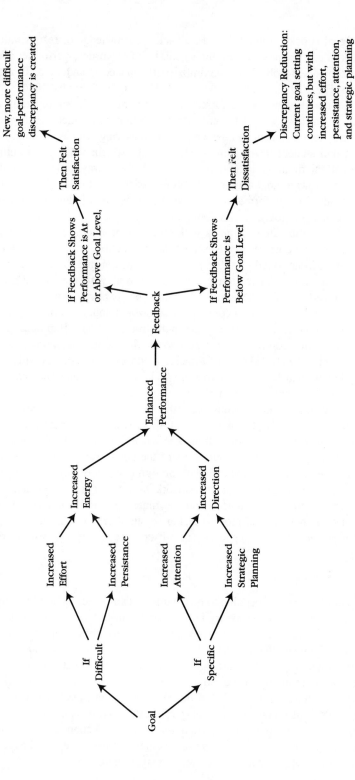

Figure 8.2   Summary of the Goal-Setting Process

If the person fully accepts another person's externally imposed goal ("Okay, coach, I'll do it, I will run 2 miles in 12 minutes."), the goal-setting process illustrated in Figure 8.2 proceeds as diagrammed (Erez & Zidon, 1984). If the goal is rejected, however, the goal-setting process does not proceed as diagrammed and, in fact, a negative relationship often exists between the externally set goal and the person's ensuing performance. With difficult and specific—but rejected—goals, the person generally puts forth little or no effort.

Four factors determine whether an externally set goal will be accepted or rejected:

- Perceived difficulty of the imposed goal
- Participation in the goal-setting process
- Credibility of the person assigning the goal
- Extrinsic incentives

As to the perceived difficulty of the imposed goal, goal acceptance is inversely related to goal difficulty. As the person contemplates whether or not to accept the imposed goal, he or she first evaluates its perceived difficulty. Easy-to-accomplish goals generally breed goal acceptance, whereas difficult goals breed goal rejection (Erez, Earley, & Hulin, 1985). When parents tell their child to bring home a report card with all As, for instance, the child evaluates the likelihood of attaining such a goal before accepting it. When the imposed goal is perceived to be relatively easy, the student will tend to think, "Okay, that's reasonable; I'll give it a try." When the imposed goal is perceived to be quite difficult, the student will tend to think, "Ugh . . . oh, that's impossible; I won't even try."

The second factor that affects goal acceptance is the extent to which the performer participates in the goal-setting process. Participation refers to how much say (input) the performer has in the goal he or she is to pursue. If the performer sets the goal himself or herself, it is readily accepted. With an externally imposed goal, however, an interpersonal negotiation process ensues in which the performer's goal acceptance is at stake. In general, performers reject goals that others try to force on them (Latham & Yukl, 1975), but they accept assigned goals when others listen carefully to their point of view and also provide a clear rationale for the goal (Latham, Erez, & Locke, 1988; Latham & Saari, 1979).

Credibility of the person assigning the goal refers to how trustworthy, supportive, knowledgeable, and likeable the performer perceives this person to be. A person with little credibility comes across as authoritarian, manipulative, and pejorative when assigning goals. All other things being equal, performers are more likely to accept and internalize goals assigned to them by credible others who have the performer's well-being in mind (Locke & Latham, 1990; Oldham, 1975). In the world of work, one way workplace leaders increase their credibility to workers is by providing a compelling vision for the future of the company (Turner, Barling, & Zacharatos, 2002).

When extrinsic incentives and rewards are contingent on goal attainment, a performer's goal acceptance increases in proportion to the perceived benefits of attaining the goal (Locke & Latham, 1990). Incentives such as money, public recognition, and scholarships contribute positively to a performer's willingness to accept a goal regardless of its difficulty, origin, or the credibility of the person assigning the goal. Overall, goal acceptance is highest when goals are perceived to be easy or only moderately difficult, are self-set (or are at least negotiated to the performer's satisfaction), are assigned by credible and trustworthy others, and promise forthcoming personal benefit. When these conditions are met, goal acceptance sets the stage for productive goal-directed performance, as summarized in Figure 8.2.

Criticisms

Goal setting has its advantages, but it also has its cautions and pitfalls (Locke & Latham, 1984). Goal setting is associated with two cautions and three pitfalls.

Goal-setting theory (Locke & Latham, 1990, 2002) developed within the fields of business, management, the world of work, sales, and the bottom line (profit). Goal-setting theory is therefore more about enhancing performance (worker output) than it is about enhancing motivation per se. Hence, the first caution associated with goal setting is that its purpose is to enhance performance, not necessarily motivation for its own sake. The second caution is that goal setting works best when tasks are relatively uninteresting and require only a straightforward procedure (Wood, Mento, & Locke, 1987), as shown with tasks such as adding numbers (Bandura & Schunk, 1981), typing (Latham & Yukl, 1976), proofreading (Huber, 1985), assembling nuts and bolts (Mossholder, 1980), and sit-ups (Weinberg, Bruya, & Jackson, 1985). Goal setting aids performance on uninteresting, straightforward tasks by generating motivation that the task itself cannot generate (because it is so boring on its own). On tasks that are inherently interesting and require creativity or problem solving, goal setting does not enhance performance (Bandura & Wood, 1989; Earley, Connolly, & Ekegren, 1989; Kanfer & Ackerman, 1989; McGraw, 1978).

Goal setting is associated with three pitfalls that limit its utility in applied settings—namely, stress, opportunities for failure, and putting creativity and intrinsic motivation at risk. The logic behind goal setting is to increase performance demands so the performer's effort, persistence, attention, and strategic planning improve from lackluster to a more intense level. Sometimes, however, overly challenging goals ask performers to perform at a level that exceeds their capabilities. Overly challenging goals stress performers (concern one; Csikszentmihalyi, 1990; Lazarus, 1991a). Difficult goals also create an explicit, objective performance standard and therefore open the door to the possibility of failure. Failure feedback yields distressing consequences that are emotional (e.g., feelings of inadequacy), social (e.g., loss of respect), and tangible (e.g., financial). The third pitfall is that goals are sometimes administered in ways that are controlling, pressure-inducing, and intrusive and thus can undermine creativity and intrinsic motivation by interfering with autonomy, cognitive flexibility, and personal passion for one's work (Amabile, 1998; Harackiewicz & Manderlink, 1984; Hennessey & Amabile, 1998; Mossholder, 1980; Vallerand, Deci, & Ryan, 1985).

Long-Term Goal Setting

A student who wants to become a doctor or an athlete who wants to win an Olympic event exemplify individuals involved in long-term goal setting. To accomplish a distant goal, the performer first has to attain several requisite short-term goals. Would-be doctors first have to make a high GPA as undergraduates, get accepted into a medical school, raise or borrow a great deal of money, probably move to a different city, graduate from medical school, complete an internship, join a hospital or partnership, and so forth, all before they can begin their careers as doctors. Thus, goals can be short-term or long-term, or a series of short-term goals linked together into one long-term goal. No significant difference in performance emerges among performers with short-term, long-term, or a mixture of short- and long-term goals (Hall & Byrne, 1988; Weinberg et al., 1985; Weinberg et al., 1988), though all outperform performers with no goals.

Instead of affecting performance per se, goal proximity affects persistence and intrinsic motivation. As for persistence, many would-be doctors and Olympians eventually forfeit their long-term goals because of a lack of positive reinforcements along the way. During all those years of studying and practicing, the goal of actually being a doctor or Olympian never materialize. Because the long-term goal striver receives insufficient opportunities for performance feedback and positive reinforcement, his or her persistence would benefit from setting a series of short-term goals that chain together to eventually end in the long-term target goal. Short-term goals provide repeated commitment-boosting opportunities for reinforcement following goal attainment that long-term goals cannot provide (Latham, Mitchell, & Dossett, 1978). Short-term goals also provide repeated opportunities for feedback that allows the performer to evaluate performance as being at, above, or below the goal. An athlete trying for a long-term goal such as winning the state championship receives little day-to-day feedback as compared to the athlete trying for a short-term goal such as winning a contest each week.

Several researchers assessed the impact that short-term and long-term goals have on intrinsic motivation (Bandura & Schunk, 1981; Harackiewicz & Manderlink, 1984; Mossholder, 1980; Vallerand, Deci, & Ryan, 1985). On uninteresting tasks, short-term goals create opportunities for positive feedback, the experience of making progress, and a means of nurturing a sense of competence, which enhances intrinsic motivation (Vallerand, Deci, & Ryan, 1985). On interesting tasks, however, only long-term goals facilitate intrinsic motivation. For the highly interested performer, short-term goals are experienced as superfluous, intrusive, and controlling. People who enjoy an activity typically already feel competent at that task, so their sense of competence is not in question and does not benefit much from goal-setting feedback. Hence, the only effect a short-term goal can have on an interesting task is a negative one. In contrast, people prefer to pursue long-term goals in their own way, and this sense of self-determination explains why long-term goals can increase intrinsic motivation (Manderlink & Harackiewicz, 1984; Vallerand et al., 1985).

One final point on long-term goals is that they typically exist as complex cognitive structures (Ortony, Clore, & Collins, 1988). Short-term goals can be thought of as specific behavioral targets, such as to lose 5 pounds, to find a job, or to make 10 consecutive free throws. To think of long-term goals as cognitive lattice structures, Figure 8.3 illustrates the long-term goal of an aspiring concert pianist (Ravlin, 1987). At the top of the goal lattice structure are the pianist's most abstract (and long-term) goals, and at the bottom are the most concrete (and short-term) goals. Each aspiration is interconnected with each other in the sense that each shares in the musician's overall long-term goal of becoming a concert pianist. Further, each aspiration is connected in a causal flow in which the achievement of a short-term goal increases the probability of attaining the next short-term goal, whereas the failure to achieve one goal decreases the probability of attaining another.

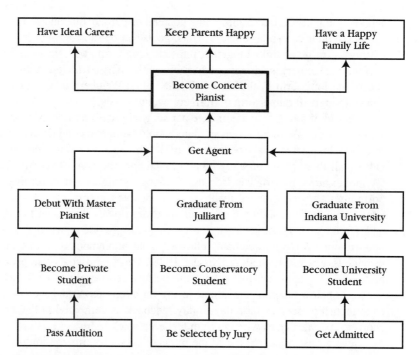

Figure 8.3 A Long-Term Goal as a Complex Cognitive Lattice Structure

Source: From "A Computer Model of Affective Reactions to Goal-Relevant Events," by S.B. Ravlin, 1987, in an unpublished master's thesis, University of Illinois-Urbana-Champaign. As cited in *The Cognitive Structure of Emotions,* A. Ortony, G.L. Clore, and A. Collins (Eds.), 1998. Cambridge: Cambridge University Press.

Personal Strivings

Personal strivings are "what a person is typically or characteristically trying to do" (Emmons, 1989). These strivings represent what an individual is characteristically aiming to accomplish in his day-to-day behavior and over the course of his life (Emmons, 1986, 1996). Personal strivings are not goals per se but, instead, exist as superordinate aspects of the self that organize and integrate the many different goals a person seeks. Thus, personal strivings reflect general personality dispositions, whereas goals reflect situationally specific objectives. For instance, a person striving "to be physically attractive" might express that striving in a (1) school-specific goal to dress in the current fashion, (2) gym-specific goal to exercise, or (3) store-specific goal to purchase a magazine with tips on how to be physically attractive. Personal strivings exist at a personality level and act as a source of generating the person's daily goals.

To provide a concrete illustration of personal strivings, one person's self-reported strivings appear in Table 8.1. This woman's strivings are organized around concerns about profession (becoming a teacher, become better at my job), personality (being more independent, being more open-minded), relationships (finding a partner, not being so mean), emotion regulation (improving attitude, remaining calm), and well-being (being healthy, losing weight, having more money, traveling more).

Table 8.1   One Individual's Personal Strivings

---

 1. Become a teacher
 2. Have a better attitude
 3. Become more independent
 4. Stay healthy
 5. Lose weight
 6. Have more money
 7. Remain calm
 8. Find a decent partner
 9. Become better at my job
10. Become more open-minded
11. Travel more often
12. Not be so mean

Note: To produce these personal strivings, 12 blank lines were listed down the left-hand side of the page, which began with the following instructions:

> A personal striving is an objective that you are typically trying to accomplish or attain. Personal strivings can be either positive or negative. In other words, a personal striving can be an objective that you typically approach and strive to attain, or it can be an objective that you typically strive to avoid. For instance, a striving you might approach and strive to attain might be "Be a fun person to be around." A striving you might strive to avoid might be "Quit smoking cigarettes."

Personal Growth and Subjective Well-Being

All personal strivings are not equal when it comes to their implications for the person's well-being. Instead of striving for what they are interested in and what they value, people often strive for extrinsic reasons such as social pressure or out of an expectation of what they should do (Sheldon & Kasser, 1998). Those goals that are not endorsed by the self are as likely to generate conflict in the person as they are to enhance effort, persistence, attention, and strategic planning (Sheldon & Elliot, 1999; Sheldon & Houser-Marko, 2001). The type of personal strivings that cultivate personal growth and subjective well-being are those that seek greater autonomy, competence, or relatedness in the person's life (Sheldon, 2001).

Why this is so can be illustrated by an analogy to nutrition (Kasser & Ryan, 2001). Personal strivings that seek greater autonomy, competence, and relatedness in one's life are those that seek to satisfy one's innate psychological needs (see Chapter 5). Striving for these sort of goals acts like a diet of apples, while strivings for extrinsic aspirations acts like a diet of chocolate cake. Extrinsically-oriented personal strivings (money, fame) are irrelevant to people's innate psychological needs and therefore do not serve to promote personal growth or subjective well-being, sort of like a diet of chocolate cake. Intrinsically-oriented personal strivings (autonomy, competence, relatedness) are highly relevant to people's psychological needs and therefore do serve to promote personal growth and subjective well-being, sort of like a diet of apples. People who strive in ways to satisfy their psychological needs (rather than to attain extrinsic rewards) are more likely to keep going in their goal-striving efforts, which is more likely to lead them to goal progress or to goal attainment. That, in turn, is like eating apples and creating the psychological experiences in one's life that lead to personal growth and psychological well-being.

Further, well-being neither follows from nor depends upon actually attaining one's goals or personal strivings. That is, people who attain high levels of popularity, money, and awards are not more psychologically well than are those who do not attain these same sort of goals. Rather, subjective well-being comes from the content of what one is trying to do (Emmons, 1996; Sheldon & Elliot, 1998). When people strive for autonomy, competence, and relatedness aspirations, they are able to create a meaning in their lives that fosters positive affect and subjective well-being. When people strive for chocolate cake (popularity, money, awards), people divorce their strivings from personal meaning in such a way that leads to negative affect, alienation, and subjective distress, and this is true even for those people who actually attain their strivings for popularity, money, and awards (Kasser & Ryan, 2001). Subjective well-being is more about what one is striving for than it is about what one actually attains.

IMPLEMENTATION INTENTIONS

Goal setting seems so promising, so ripe with potential, as a motivational intervention strategy for helping people accomplish the sort of things they wish to accomplish (see Box 8). The self-help books in the mega bookstores agree, as they advise readers to set goals and to focus their full attention on these goals. If you want to make better grades, lose 10 pounds, save a ton of money, or be successful in love and work, then you must visualize the goal you want. Think it—be it, they say. Focus on it, visualize it, see the new you with goal in hand. Unfortunately, motivational processes are not that simple. The gap between goal-directed thinking and goal-direction action can be a wide one.

Mental Simulations: Focusing on Action

Consider a series of studies designed explicitly to test the advice to "visualize success" (Taylor et al., 1998). In these studies, participants either (1) focused on the goal they wished to attain, (2) focused on how to attain the goal, or (3) did not focus on anything in particular (a control group). Focusing on the goal actually interfered with goal attainment! Focusing one's attention on the goal itself actually backfired as a motivational strategy. Focusing on how to accomplish the goal, however, did facilitate goal attainment. These data are important because (1) they draw out the distinction between the content of a goal (what one is striving for) and the process of goal striving (the means one uses to attain the goal), and (2) once a goal has been set, it does not inevitably and automatically translate itself into effective performance.

Salespeople know the following trick well: Ask someone to imagine having and using an item, and that person will become significantly more likely to later actually go out of her way to have and use that item (as in "Just imagine sitting in this beauty, driving it home, and parking this fine machine right in front of your home. Can you see it? Can you feel it?"). In an experimental demonstration of what salespeople already know, researchers asked members of a community to imagine owning and using cable-television service (Gregory, Cialdini, & Carpenter, 1982). These community members were asked to

---

| BOX 8 | *Setting Goals and Implementing Action* |

Question: Why is this information important?

Answer: To translate the goals you value into effective action.

What would you like to accomplish? Would you like to increase the number of friends you have? Increase your GPA? Decrease your weight? One means for attaining the objectives you seek is goal setting. Effective goal setting entails following and then implementing these sequential procedures:

1. Identify the objective to be accomplished.
2. Define goal difficulty.
3. Clarify goal specificity.
4. Specify how and when performance will be measured.

For instance, consider the goal of getting in shape (to continue the example introduced in the beginning of the chapter). In numerical terms, getting in shape could be represented by earning aerobic points through jogging. A numerically-stated goal would be to earn 30 points per week. Thirty aerobic points constitutes a sufficiently difficult goal. To clarify goal specificity, the goal setter next needs to articulate the specifics of those 30 points (e.g., "I'll run on the treadmill 4 days a week, 20 minutes at a time.") To specify how and when performance will be assessed, the goal setter might decide to keep a written log to monitor how many aerobic points his efforts earn each day and each

week. At the end of each week, the test will be to earn 30 aerobic points, and at the end of the month, the test will be to earn 120 aerobic points.

Identifying the goal gets you halfway home. The other half is to generate goal-attainment strategies and to specify the necessary implementation intentions, as in how and when you will:

1. Get started.
2. Persist, even in the face of difficulties.
3. Resume, even after disruptions.

Getting started means specifying when, where, how, and for how long all this treadmill pounding will occur. You might decide, for instance, to run at 8:00 each morning at the university's gym on a treadmill for 20 minutes each day, including a warm-up and cool-down. An implementation intention for persistence and resumption might anticipate having to cut back on running time during exams, papers, and home football games but then doubling up the next week.

Given this goal-setting process and the forethought to formulate implementation intentions, the would-be jogger has both a plan of action (goal) and a plan of when, where, and how that goal-directed behavior will unfold (implementation intention). This is just one example, but you might be surprised by how readily these procedures generalize to other domains that might be important to the objectives you seek.

---

visualize the positive events related to the service (a mental simulation of using the service). Compared to nonvisualizers (a control group), those who worked through the mental simulation of using the service were indeed significantly more likely to subscribe for the service (Taylor et al., 1998).

Mental simulations are not fantasies of success or episodes of wishful thinking. Drawing out the difference between the content of a goal and the process for attaining that goal is an important distinction because visualizing fantasies of success (i.e., wishful thinking) do not produce productive behavior (Oettingen, 1996). Focus on the rich you, the thin you, or the married you does not get you very far. Instead of focusing on outcomes (i.e., on goal content), mental simulations focus on planning and problem solving. This sort of effort does produce productive goal-directed action. To illustrate this point, imagine hearing one of the two following instructions (Pham & Taylor, 1999):

Outcome-Simulation (Focus on the Goal)

In this exercise, you will be asked to visualize yourself getting a high grade on your psychology midterm and asked to imagine how you would feel. It is very important that you see yourself getting a high grade on the psychology midterm and have that picture in your mind.

Process-Simulation (Focus on the Implementation Intentions)

In this exercise, you will be asked to visualize yourself studying for the midterm in such a way that would lead you to obtain a high grade on the midterm. As of today and for the remaining days before the midterm, imagine how you would study to get a high grade on your psychology midterm. It is very important that you see yourself actually studying and have that picture in your mind.

The first set of instructions basically asked students to rehearse experiencing the joy of success, while the second set of instructions basically asked students to engage in planning and problem solving. Compared to a no-simulation control group, students in the outcome-simulation condition actually studied less and made poorer scores on the test. Students in the process-simulation condition studied more and made better test scores. Focusing on success might cultivate hope, but it does not promote productive goal-striving behavior. To facilitate action, people need to mentally simulate a goal process—the means by which they will accomplish the objective they seek.

Formulating Implementation Intentions

When people fail to realize the goals they set for themselves, part of the problem can be explained by how people set goals (i.e., Is the goal difficult? specific? accepted? paired with feedback?). The other part of the problem, however, is simply that people fail to act on the goals they set for themselves (Orbell & Sheeran, 1998).

Imagine that you have set a goal, such as making a 4.0 GPA, reading this book, or saving $100 this month. How do you bridge the gap between goal and action? Should you focus on the content of the goal (visualize the 4.0 you) or on the means by which the goal is to be accomplished (the steps you need to take)? Should you spend time planning how to attain your goal, or would planning just be a waste of time and what you should really do is just get started? As discussed above, planning how to attain a goal turns out to be an integral part of the goal-performance relationship (Gollwitzer, 1996, 1999).

A key reason people fail to attain their goals is that they often fail to develop specific action plans for how they will attain their goals. They fail to specify when they will initiate their goal-directed action, and they fail to specify how they will ensure their goal-directed persistence in the face of distractions and interruptions (Gollwitzer, 1999). In contrast, when people with goals also specify implementation intentions, they strongly increase their chance of eventually goal attainment (Aarts, Dijksterhuis, & Midden, 1999; Brandstatter, Lengfelder, & Gollwitzer, 2001; Gollwitzer & Schaal, 1998; Oettingen, Honing, & Gollwitzer, 2000).

Planning how to carry out a goal allows the performer to overcome the inevitable volitional problems associated with goal-directed behavior. Once a goal is set and committed to, the following volitional problems emerge:

- Getting started, despite daily distractions
- Persisting, in spite of difficulties and setbacks
- Resuming, once a disruption occurs

Planning how to carry out a goal involves deciding on when, where, how, and for how long one is to act. An implementation intention is such a plan—when, where, how, and for how long goal-directed action will occur. For example, in forming implementation intentions for goal-directed behavior, the performer decides to do X when situation Y is encountered (Gollwitzer, 1996). In planning an implementation intention, an anticipated future encounter ("When I encounter situation Y, . . .") is linked to specific goal-directed behavior (". . . I intend to do X").

The study of implementation intentions is the study of how goals, once set, are effectively acted on (Gollwitzer & Moskowitz, 1996). Implementation intentions are an important part of understanding motivation because it is one thing to set a goal, yet another to actually accomplish it. To set and attain a goal, one needs solutions to the sort of volitional problems listed above. All goals take time, but time has a way of opening the door to distractions, difficulties, and interruptions. The act of setting implementation intentions is the effort to close the door on volitional problems. In effect, implementation intentions buffer performers against falling prey to volitional problems.

In the first experiment on implementation intentions, experimenters asked college students going home for the Christmas holidays how they planned to spend their time and what they wanted to get done (e.g., write a paper, read a book, solve a family conflict; Gollwitzer & Brandstatter, 1997). The experimenters asked half of the students to form explicit implementation intentions for their goal by asking them to pick a specific time and a specific place in which to carry out the goal-directed action. The other half of the students were not asked to specify a time and a place for their goal-directed behavior. When students returned, a majority of students in the implementation intentions group had indeed attained their goal, while only a minority of students in the control group had attained their goal. Plus, the more difficult the goal was to accomplish, the more important the forming of implementation intentions were to completion rates.

The motivational effect of an implementation intention is to link goal-directed behavior to a situational cue (i.e., to a time and place) so that goal-directed behavior is carried out automatically, without conscious deliberation or decision making. With an implementation intention in mind, the presence of the cue facilitates the goal-direction action being implemented swiftly and effortlessly. In other words, once an intention is formed (e.g., "From December 27 through 29, I'll go to the university library and write a 10-page paper on topic X by working from 1:00 until 5:00 each afternoon"), the mere presence of the anticipated situational cue (December 27 rolls around) automatically initiates goal-directed action. When no such intention is formed, the person's good intention to write the paper may suffer the same fate as a typical New Year's resolution.

Implementation intentions facilitate goal-directed behavior in two ways: getting started and finishing up. Getting started with goal-directed behavior is a volitional problem when people let good opportunities to pursue their goals pass by, as in "I had all day to read the chapter, but I just never sat down and read it." Finishing up is a volitional problem when people get interrupted, distracted, and face difficulties, as in "I started to read the chapter, but then the phone rang and I never did get back to the book."

Goal Pursuit: Getting Started

Some people exercise every day at a certain time in the afternoon; some people read steadily and persistently when they are in the library; some people always stop completely at stop signs; and some people go to church each Sunday. Frequent and consistent pairings of particular situations with particular behaviors lead to strong links between the situation and the behavior. Creating an implementation intention for a new behavior in a new situation is essentially this same effect (Gollwitzer, 1996). Implementation intentions set up environment-behavior contingencies that lead to automatic, environmental control of behavior: "Implementation intentions create habits" (Gollwitzer, 1999).

Deciding in advance when and where a person will enact her goal-directed behavior facilitates getting started. Women who wrote down when and where they would conduct a breast self-examination actually did so 100% of the time during the next month, whereas women who simply had the goal of conducting a breast self-examination did so only 53% of the time (Orbell, Hodgkins, & Sheeran, 1997). Similar results occurred when these same procedures were carried out with the goals of eating healthy foods (Verplanken & Faes, 1999), taking vitamin pills (Sheeran & Orbell, 1999), and resuming an active lifestyle following surgery (Orbell & Sheeran, 2000). These studies make it clear that attaining goals requires not only effective goal setting but also a pre-action period in which one decides when, where, and how that goal will be implemented.

Goal Pursuit: Persisting and Finishing

Once started in the pursuit of a goal, people often face circumstances that were more difficult than they expected. They encounter distractions and demands on their time, and they also get interrupted and face the prospect of getting started all over again. But implementation intentions, once set, facilitate persistence and reengagement during goal pursuit.

Implementation intentions facilitate persistence by helping people anticipate a forthcoming difficulty and therefore form an intention of what they will do once the difficulty comes their way. For instance, a woman with a weekend goal of meeting at least one new person can anticipate that, when the weekend comes, she will feel anxious and discouraged. Anticipating this, she can remind herself of the need to meet people and also ask her friends for their encouragement in meeting her goal. Such preparatory planning does indeed help people's subsequent persistence and goal attainment (Koestner et al., 2002).

Implementation intentions create a type of close-mindedness that narrows one's field of attention to include goal-directed action but to exclude distractions. For instance, students were placed in front of a computer terminal and asked to solve a series of attention-demanding mathematical problems while distracting video clips of television commercials played at random times on a television monitor mounted just above the computer screen. Some of the students were asked to form an implementation intention (i.e., as soon as the commercial came on, students told themselves to ignore it), while others were not. Students who formed the implementation intention prior to solving the mathematics problems solved more problems than did students who did not form the distraction-inhibiting intention (Schaal & Gollwitzer, 1999). Without an implementation intention, students were highly vulnerable to distraction.

Implementation intentions also help people finish up uncompleted goals. Workers who began to write a letter of correspondence were interrupted, and half of the workers were then asked to form an implementation intention while the other half were not. When the two groups of workers returned to their desks, those with an intention to finish the letters upon their return (implementation intention) were indeed more likely to complete their unfinished business than were those who were similarly interrupted but who did not harbor an implementation intention to cope with the interruption.

Whether the problem is getting started or finishing up, taking the time necessary to plan how, when, where, and for how long one will carry out goal-directed behavior improves the performer's chance of realizing the goal. Of course, setting the goal is a crucial part of the goal-performance relationship, but the addition of implementation intentions helps close the gap that often exists between setting a goal and actually carrying it out. The full how-to process of setting goals and implementing action is summarized in Box 8.

SELF-REGULATION

Cognitive events like goals and implementation intentions allow people to translate their thoughts into motivated action. All the striving and planning within the goal-setting process takes place over time, and during this time people constantly reflect on how things are going. Such metacognitive monitoring of the on-going goal setting process is referred to as self-regulation (Zimmerman, 2002). As people attempt to get started and to maintain their goal-directed strivings, they mentally step back to monitor and evaluate the overall goal-setting and goal-striving process. Self-regulation is therefore the mental act of monitoring and evaluating one's on-going effort to attain the goals one seeks.

The interrelationships among goal-setting, implementation intentions, performance, and self-regulation appear in Figure 8.4 (based on Zimmerman, 2000). Self-regulation is an ongoing, cyclical process. It involves forethought, action, and reflection. Forethought involves goal setting and strategic planning, including implementation intentions. Following such preperformance forethought, the individual engages the task and begins to perform and receive feedback. It is during this time that the person experiences goal-performance feedback discrepancies and becomes aware of various obstacles, difficulties, distractions, and interruptions. With this information in hand, the performer reflects on how its going in terms of self-monitoring and self-evaluating. Self-reflection leads to more informed forethought prior to the next performance opportunity. The ongoing, cyclical nature of self-regulation is apparent when self-reflection on one's performance leads to new and improved forethought.

A second illustration of how the self-regulatory process of monitoring and evaluating fit into the overall goal-setting process appears in Table 8.2. Once a person sets a goal and formulates an implementation intention to carry out goal-directed action, the person also steps back to monitor the goal-performance discrepancy (Is the discrepancy being reduced?) and evaluates how well the performance is going. The table illustrates these interrelationships by using the examples of a student, a tennis player, and a stage actor.

Self-regulation is both a self-observational and a self-evaluation process in which the person monitors performance and compares it with a goal state. Careful, consistent, and

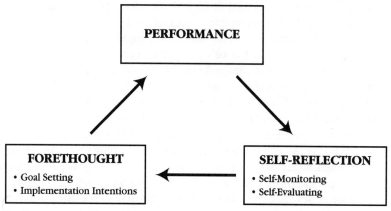

Figure 8.4   Cyclical Phases of Self-Regulation

objective self-monitoring makes self-evaluation possible. Once done, self-evaluation adds to the overall goal-setting and implementation intentions processes by supplying the means by which one attains information about goal progress. A tennis player that lands 80% of her first serves in the serving court realizes that she is making progress and is ahead of her goal level. This perception of progress creates the sense of satisfaction depicted in Figure 8.1 and therefore supplements discrepancy with the second motivational process of satisfaction-dissatisfaction.

Table 8.2   Illustration of Self-Regulatory Processes (Monitoring, Self-Evaluation) of a Student, Tennis Player, and Stage Actor

Goal	Implementation Intentions	Self-Regulation	
		Monitoring	Self-Evaluation
Student			
Learn 3 new motivational concepts in Chapter 8	From 7–10 P.M. this evening, read the chapter and take notes	Identify the 3 motivational concepts in the notes taken	Critique quality of those notes to see if one really understands these concepts
Tennis Player			
Land 70% of first serves	This Thursday, 2–4 P.M. at the university courts, hit 100 serves	Write down on a notepage the number of serves in or out	Critique performance as to whether at least 70% of serves landed in the service area
Stage Actor			
Increase voice volume while on stage	During tonight's rehearsal, increase voice volume at the beginning of each new turn to talk	Audiotape the rehearsal and later play it back that evening	Play audiotape while sitting in the back row of the theatre to see if it is easy to hear

Developing More Competent Self-Regulation

Everyone engages in self-regulation, but some people do it better than others (Winne, 1997). Self-regulatory processes need to be acquired, especially when the performer pursues a goal in an unfamiliar area (Schunk & Zimmerman, 1997). Gains in self-regulatory competence generally occur within a social learning process and at an observational level in which a relative novice in the domain observes the behavior and verbalizations from an expert model. The novice then begins to imitate the expert model, and in doing so, receives social guidance and feedback as to the effectiveness of his imitative behaviors. Following a history of social guidance and feedback, the novice begins to internalize the standards of excellence endorsed by the model. The person becomes self-regulating in the domain when he no longer needs the expert model and can self-regulate in terms of self-monitoring and self-evaluating.

As shown in Figure 8.5, self-regulation involves the capacity to carry out the full goal-setting process on one's own (Schunk & Zimmerman, 1997). Developing self-regulatory skills involves three phases. First, the person is unable to regulate his or her behavior and unable to carry out the goal-setting process, because it involves goals, planning, implementation intentions, and strategies to cope with distractors and disruptions in an unfamiliar domain. Gains in self-regulation at this level occur from observing an expert. Figure 8.6 illustrates this first phase as the young dancer observes her mentor. Second, observation leads to imitation, as the person participates in a social learning process by taking on the self-regulatory skills of an expert model. Observation leads to imitation, and imitation in turn leads to internalization and the roots of effective self-regulation. Third, the person is able to competently regulate his or her behavior and carry out the goal-setting and performance-monitoring process on his or her own. For instance, in learning how to become a competent and self-regulated writer, the novice observes and emulates the expert writer's style and standards, learns to set goals and formulate implementation intentions, restructures the physical environment to facilitate writing, solicits feedback and tips about writing, and acquires the means to monitor and evaluation one's own work (Zimmerman & Risemberg, 1997).

The model depicted in Figure 8.5 shows that effective self-regulation progresses through the following four developmental phases: observation, imitation, self-control, and

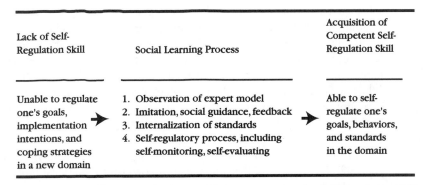

Figure 8.5   Summary of the Social Learning Process to Acquire Self-Regulation Skill

Figure 8.6 Acquiring Self-Regulation Skill by First Observing and Imitating an Expert Model

self-regulation. But, in some sense, self-regulation is only the beginning of expertise. Building expertise is a very time-consuming process that requires not only the intensive mentoring described above but also countless hours of practice on one's own (Ericsson, Krampe, & Tesch-Romer, 1993; Ericsson & Charness, 1994). Independent practice is very important, but the thesis in the self-regulation literature is that people can acquire, develop, and master complex skills more quickly and more expertly if they have the benefit of a tutor who models how to set goals, develop strategies, formulate implementation intentions, monitor performance, and evaluate (on one's own) how the on-going goal-performance-feedback process.

To summarize, consider a saying of the Chinese: "Start with your master, finish with yourself." The study of self-regulation adds how that translational process from master to self of developing more competent self-regulation occurs.

SUMMARY

The cognitive perspective on motivation focuses on mental processes as causal determinants to action. Thus, the cognitive study of motivation concerns itself with the cognition → action sequence. This chapter discusses the motivational significance of six elements in the cognition → action sequence: plans, goals, personal strivings, implementation intentions, mental simulations, and self-regulation.

Plans, goals, and personal strivings rely on discrepancy as their driving motivational force to action. Cognitive discrepancies explain motivation by highlighting how mismatches between the person's present state versus ideal state energize and direct action. Two types of discrepancies exist: discrepancy reduction and discrepancy creation. Discrepancy reduction captures the essence of plans, whereas discrepancy creation captures the essence of goals and the goal-setting process.

People are readily aware of the present state of their behavior, their environment, and the status of the events in their lives. People also envision ideal states for these same behaviors, environments, and events. When a present-state-versus-ideal-state mismatch exists, incongruity (or discrepancy) produces a general corrective motivation that gives rise to plan-directed behavior capable of reducing (or removing) the discrepancy. For instance, a student might say, "My work desk sure is a mess. I would like the desk to be clean and well-organized. That discrepancy is sort of bothering me, so I'll make a plan how I can change my desk from clutter to clean." When discrepancies generate corrective motivation, people either generate a plan that will advance their present behavior up to its ideal or they revise the plans to reverse the ideal state down to something closer to the present state. Corrective motivation also has emotional implications, as people who make slower than expected progress toward their plans experience negative emotions like frustration, whereas people who make faster than expected progress experience positive emotions like enthusiasm.

Goals are the objectives people strive to accomplish. Goals that are both difficult and specific generally improve performance, and they do so by producing motivational effects: Difficult goals mobilize effort and increase persistence, while specific goals direct attention and promote strategic planning. Two conditions are necessary before goals will enhance performance: feedback and goal acceptance. With feedback, a performer can evaluate his or her performance as being at, above, or below the level of the goal standard. Performing below goal level generates dissatisfaction that underlies a desire to improve; performing above goal level generates satisfaction that underlies a willingness to set more difficult goals in the future. Goal acceptance refers to the process in which the performer accepts another person's assigned goal as his own.

Personal strivings constitute the superordinate goals people try to accomplish. Personal strivings are important not only because they organize and foreshadow a person's underlying goal system, but also because they foreshadow a person's emotional well-being. Well-being is more about what one strives for than it is about what one actually obtains in life. For example, performance and well-being are highest when personal strivings revolve around intrinsic aspirations like those related to psychological needs for autonomy, competence, and relatedness, rather than the extrinsic aspirations like those related to social pressure and expectations of what they should do like popularity, money, and awards.

Once a goal has been set, it does not inevitably and automatically translate itself into effective performance. This is so because people have trouble getting started and because people have trouble persisting and finishing when they encounter inevitable distractions and interruptions. In the effort to translate their goals into action, performers benefit from formulating implementation intentions that specify a plan as to when, where, how, and for how long one is to act. People who set implementation intentions in advance of their goal-directed action are significantly more likely to attain or complete their goals than are people who do not set implementation intentions. Implementations have positive effects on goal striving by helping performers overcome the volitional problems associated with getting started, persisting in the face of difficulties, and resuming goal-direction action once interrupted. These intentions essentially delegate the control of goal-directed action to merely encountering anticipated situational cues (e.g., "When I encounter situation X, I will do Y.").

Self-regulation involves the person's metacognitive monitoring of how his or her goal-setting progress is going. As people attempt to get started and to maintain their goal-directed strivings, they mentally step back to monitor and evaluate the process. Self-monitoring is a self-observational and a self-judgment process in which the person compares present performance with the goal state. Self-regulatory processes, such as self-monitoring and self-evaluation, are often acquired through a social learning process in which a novice observes, imitates, and then internalizes the competent self-regulatory skills of an expert model.

READINGS FOR FURTHER STUDY

Plans

CAMPION, M. A., & LORD, R. G. (1982). A control systems conceptualization of the goal-setting and changing process. *Organizational Behavior and Human Performance, 30,* 265–287.

CARVER, C. S., & SCHEIER, M. F. (1990). Origins and functions of positive and negative affect: A control-process view. *Psychological Review, 97,* 19–35.

Goals

EMMONS, R. A. (1991). Personal strivings, daily life events, and psychological and physical well-being. *Journal of Personality, 59,* 453–472.

EREZ, M., EARLEY, P. C., & HULIN, C. L. (1985). The impact of participation on goal acceptance and performance: A two-step model. *Academy of Management Journal, 28,* 50–66.

LOCKE, E. A. (1996). Motivation through conscious goal setting. *Applied and Preventive Psychology, 5,* 117–124.

LOCKE, E. A., & LATHAM, G. P. (2002). Building a practically useful theory of goal setting and task motivation: A 35-year odyssey. *American Psychologist, 57,* 705–717.

TUBBS, M. E. (1986). Goal setting: A meta-analytic examination of the empirical evidence. *Journal of Applied Psychology, 71,* 474–483.

Implementation Intentions

GOLLWITZER, P. M. (1999). Implementation intentions: Strong effects of simple plans. *American Psychologist, 54,* 493–503.

GOLLWITZER, P. M., & BRANDSTATTER, V. (1997). Implementation intentions and effective goal pursuit. *Journal of Personality and Social Psychology, 73,* 186–199.

KOESTNER, R., LEKES, N., POWERS, T. A., & CHICOINE, E. (2002). Attaining personal goals: Self-concordance plus implementation intentions equals success. *Journal of Personality and Social Psychology, 83,* 231–244.

Self-Regulation

SCHUNK, D. H., & ZIMMERMAN, B. J. (1997). Social origins of self-regulatory competence. *Educational Psychologist, 32,* 195–208.

ZIMMERMAN, B. (2002). Attaining self-regulation: A social cognitive perspective. In M. Boekaerts, P. R. Pintrich, & M. Zeidner's (Eds.), *Handbook of self-regulation* (pp. 13–39). San Diego, CA: Academic Press.

Chapter 9

Personal Control Beliefs

What does the future have in store for you? Will you graduate from college? Will your classes be interesting? Will you pass this course? Will you find this ninth chapter interesting? Will the chapter address important topics, or will it present topics that are only dry and confusing? This winter, will you catch the flu? When you apply for your next job, will you get it? Will you fall in love? Will you fall out of love? If you were to go on a blind date or to meet your mate's parents, would these strangers like you? Will you find someone to share your life with, as in marriage? When you drive to school or work tomorrow, will you get stuck in traffic? Will you get a parking ticket? When you turn the car's ignition key, will the car start on the first try? Will you live to see your 50th birthday?

How able are you to cope with what the future has in store? Do you have what it takes to graduate? If you bomb your first exam in this course, can you mount a comeback and still do well in the course? Can you use a computer to write a term paper? What would happen if you tried to shop online—would it go well? In relationships, can you make another person laugh? Can you cheer up your friends when they feel depressed? Can you defuse arguments? Could you be the life of a party? If a bully insults and pesters you, could you handle the situation? Can you run 3 miles without stopping to rest? Okay, how about 1 mile? Can you sing? Could you hit a golf ball on your first try? Could you hit the golf ball if an audience was watching?

Our expectancies of what will happen and our expectancies of how well we can cope with what happens have important motivational implications. Imagine how motivationally problematic your college experience would be if you expected not to graduate, not to pass a particular course, not to get a job after graduation, and not to understand the professor or this book. Imagine how motivationally problematic your interpersonal relationships would be if you expected others not to like you, not to care about your welfare, or to express only hostility. What if you expected that everyone you met would reject you? Imagine how motivationally problematic your athletic participation would be if you expected only to fail and to embarrass yourself in front of others. Imagine how difficult it would be to muster the motivation to run three miles if you knew beforehand that you could not do so.

MOTIVATION TO EXERCISE PERSONAL CONTROL

The focus throughout this chapter is the motivation to exercise personal control over what happens to you. To some extent, environments are predictable, and to some extent, people are able to figure out how to exert control over the predictable aspects of the environment. In predicting what will happen and in trying to influence what happens, people try to make desirable outcomes more likely and undesirable outcomes less likely. By exercising personal control in this way, people attempt to improve their lives and also the lives of others.

The desire to exercise personal control is predicated on a person's belief that they have the power to produce favorable results. When people believe they (1) "have what it takes" to influence their environment and (2) the environment will be responsive to their influence attempts, then they will indeed try to make things happen for the better—they will be motivated to exercise personal control.

The strength with which people try to exercise personal control can be traced to the strengths of their expectancies of being able to do so. Expectancy is a subjective prediction of how likely it is that an event will occur. That event can be an outcome (e.g., losing 10 pounds) or a course of action that brings the outcome to pass (e.g., running 20 minutes on a treadmill without having a heart attack). When politicians enter an election or athletes enter a competition, they appraise the likelihood that they will win. Before people leap across a creek or tell a risqué joke, they appraise the likelihood of landing on solid ground. In anticipating events and outcomes, people rely on their past experiences and personal resources to make forecasts about what the future holds and how they will cope with what is to come.

Two Kinds of Expectancy

Two types of expectancies exist: efficacy expectations and outcome expectations (Bandura, 1977, 1986, 1997; Heckhausen, 1977; Peterson, Maier, & Seligman, 1993). An efficacy expectation (see Figure 9.1) is a judgment of one's capacity to execute a particular act or course of action. An outcome expectation (see Figure 9.1) is a judgment that a given

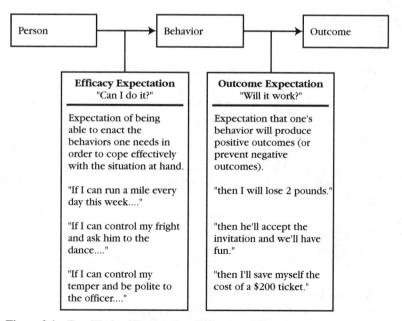

Figure 9.1   Two Kinds of Expectation: Efficacy and Outcome

action, once performed, will cause a particular outcome. Efficacy expectations estimate the likelihood that an individual can behave in a particular way; outcome expectations estimate how likely it is that certain consequences will follow once that behavior is enacted.

For an illustration of efficacy and outcome expectations, consider the political candidate who wants to win an election and believes that by giving a convention speech she can will the election. Efficacy expectations pertain to her confidence that she can do what it takes to give a competent speech. Outcome expectancies pertain to her beliefs that once she gives her competent speech, then people will listen, be persuaded by her oratory, and vote for her in the election. The two expectancies are, essentially, "I can do it" (efficacy expectation) and "What I do will work" (outcome expectation).

Efficacy and outcome expectations are separate, causal determinants to the initiation and regulation of behavior (Bandura, 1991). Consider the different expectancies that might run through a surgeon's mind in preparing for an operation. The extent to which the surgeon engages in that operation depends on (1) his efficacy expectation that he can successfully perform the surgery with excellence and (2) his expectation that the surgery, once enacted, will produce certain physical, psychological, emotional, financial, and social benefits for himself and for his patient.

Both efficacy and outcome expectations must be reasonably high before behavior becomes energetic and goal-directed. Thus, an analysis of efficacy and outcome expectancies allows us to understand people's reluctance to engage in activities such as public speaking, dating, athletics, and job interviews. To address a group, date, compete, or interview, the person must not only be confident in his efficacy to execute these behaviors but he must also be reasonably assured that an effective performance will pay off (i.e., will lead to desired outcomes). Take away either of these positive forecasts and reluctance and avoidance become rather logical ways of acting.

SELF-EFFICACY

Efficacy expectations center on questions such as the following: Can I perform well on this particular task? If things start to go wrong during my performance, do I have the resources within me to cope well and turn things around for the better? But efficacy expectations and self-efficacy are not quite the same thing. Self-efficacy is a more generative capacity in which the individual organizes and orchestrates his skills to cope with the demands and circumstances he faces. It is the capacity to use one's personal resources well under diverse and trying circumstances. Formally, self-efficacy is defined as one's judgment of how well (or poorly) one will cope with a situation, given the skills one possesses and the circumstances one faces (Bandura, 1986, 1993, 1997).

Self-efficacy is not the same as "ability." Competent functioning requires not only possessing skills (i.e., ability), but also the capacity to translate those skills into effective performance, especially under trying and difficult circumstances. A snow skier might have wondrous slalom, mogul, and downhill racing skills but still perform dismally if the wind blows, the snow ices, or the slopes are crowded with clumsy skiers who keep falling. Self-efficacy is that generative capacity in which the performer improvises ways to best translate personal abilities into effective performance. Self-efficacy is just as important a determinant of competent functioning as is ability because performance situations often are stressful, ambiguous, and unpredictable, and as one performs, circumstances *always* change (Bandura, 1997).

Consider that most of us can drive a car rather well on the interstate as most of us rate very high on abilities such as steering, braking, negotiating traffic, reciting traffic laws, and finding our destinations. But self-efficacy becomes important when circumstances rise to test our abilities, as when driving in an unreliable car on an unfamiliar road with poorly marked streets, during a snowstorm, or as monster trucks whiz by splashing slush that covers the windshield. Even highly skilled drivers sometimes perform dismally because circumstances change in stressful and overwhelming ways. Under trying circumstances, the driver must have what it takes to keep arousal in check, to think clearly in deciding between options, to avoid perils, and perhaps to negotiate or show leadership in enlisting the assistance of the passenger. The same self-efficacy analysis applies to academic test taking (Bandura et al., 1988), athletic performance (Feltz, 1992), self-defense (Ozer & Bandura, 1990), gender role conduct (Bussey & Bandura, 1999), health-promoting behaviors (Bandura, 1998), and collective agency for solving social problems (Bandura, 1997).

The opposite of efficacy is doubt. For the driver who doubts his or her capacity to cope, then surprises, setbacks, and difficulties will create anxiety (Bandura, 1988), confusion (Wood & Bandura, 1989), negative thinking (Bandura, 1983), and aversive physiological arousal and bodily tension (Bandura et al., 1985). Imagine the unfolding of events that might occur when the self-doubt of an otherwise skilled driver comes face to face with surprises, setbacks, and difficulties. Perhaps an unexpected storm begins (surprise), or the windshield wipers fail (setback), or ice forms on the road (difficulty). Under such trying conditions, doubt can interfere with effective thinking, planning, and decision making to cause anxiety, confusion, arousal, tension, and distress that can spiral performance toward disaster. Of course, surprises, setbacks, and difficulties may not produce poor performance, just as skill, talent, and ability may not produce excellent performance. Rather, extent of self-efficacy (versus self-doubt) is the motivational variable that determines the extent to which a performer copes well (versus poorly) when her skills and abilities are stressed.

Consider the more extended example of trying to present oneself as socially competent as during a job interview, auditioning for a part in a play, or going on a first date. In a self-efficacy analysis, the skills involved in interviewing, auditioning, and dating and the situational demands placed on the performer are complex and multidimensional. The following list describes an adolescent on a first date (Rose & Frieze, 1989) by listing some task demands (left) as well as the skills needed to successfully cope with those demands (right).

Dating Demand	**Dating Skill**
Ask for a date	Assertiveness
Make a plan to do something interesting	Creativity
Arrive on time at date's house	Punctuality
Relate warmly to parents or roommates	Sociability
Joke, laugh, and talk	Sense of humor
Impress date	Salesmanship
Be polite	Social etiquette
Understand how other feels	Empathy

Dating Demand	**Dating Skill**
Be responsive to the other's needs	Perspective taking
Kiss goodnight	Romance

As the adolescent contemplates the date, he asks what specific events will take place. What skills will be needed to perform well? If things go unexpectedly wrong, can he make the necessary corrective adjustments? How does he expect to feel during the date and during each specific event? In this hypothetical situation, the adolescent expects that the overall task at hand will require a dozen or so different skills, such as assertiveness, sociability, and so on. The adolescent also has some expectation of how effectively he can execute each of these skills, and those expectancies might range from woefully incompetent to highly competent. These expectations represent the heart and soul of self-efficacy beliefs: Just how effective will I be when the situation calls for me to be assertive? When I try to be assertive, will I feel mostly confidence or mostly doubt? Are my skills hardy enough to get the evening back on track if things go wrong (e.g., parents turn out to be very difficult to relate to)? Just how much social doubt and anxiety the adolescent feels in this particular situation can be predicted by a self-efficacy analysis of his perceived efficacy expectations in each of the 10 task-related demands.

Further, once we know the adolescent's expectancies of efficacy versus doubt in coping with these task demands, we can predict his motivation to go on the date versus avoid it. Boiled down to its essence, self-efficacy predicts the motivational balance between wanting to try on the one hand and anxiety, doubt, and avoidance on the other.

Sources of Self-Efficacy

Self-efficacy beliefs do not just occur out of the blue; they have causes. Self-efficacy beliefs arise from (1) one's personal history in trying to execute that particular behavior, (2) observations of similar others who also try to execute that behavior, (3) verbal persuasions (pep talks) from others, and (4) physiological states such as a racing heart versus a calm one.

Personal Behavior History

The extent to which a person believes she can competently enact a particular course of action stems from her personal history of trying to enact that course of action in the past (Bandura, Reese, & Adams, 1982). People learn their current self-efficacy from their interpretations of past attempts to execute the same behavior. Past attempts to enact the behavior judged as competent raise self-efficacy, whereas past attempts judged as incompetent lower self-efficacy. For instance, as a child prepares to ride a bicycle, her personal history of being able to actually carry out the cycling behavior on past occasions functions as firsthand information about self-efficacy in the present encounter. How important any one behavioral enactment is to future efficacy depends on the strength of the performer's preexisting expectation. Once one's personal behavior history has produced a strong sense of efficacy, an occasional incompetent enactment will not change self-efficacy much (or an occasional competent enactment will not raise a strong sense of inefficacy much). If the performer is less experienced (i.e., lacks a behavioral history), however, each new competent or incompetent enactment will have greater effect on future efficacy. Of the four sources of self-efficacy, personal history is the most influential (Bandura, 1986).

Vicarious Experience

Vicarious experience involves observing a model enact the same course of action the performer is about to enact (e.g., "You go first, I'll watch."). Seeing others perform masterfully raises an observer's own sense of efficacy (Bandura et al., 1980; Kazdin, 1979). This is so because seeing similar others perform the same behavior initiates a social comparison process (e.g., "If they can do it, so can I."). But vicarious experience works the other way as well, as observing someone perform the same behavior clumsily lowers our own sense of efficacy (e.g., "If they can't do it, what makes me think I can?"; Brown & Inouye, 1978). The extent to which a model's enactment affects our own efficacy depends on two factors. First, the greater the similarity between the model and the observer, the greater the impact the model's behavior will have on the observer's efficacy forecast (Schunk, 1989a). Second, the less experienced the observer is at the behavior (a novice), the greater the impact of the vicarious experience (Schunk, 1989b). Thus, vicarious experience is a potent source of efficacy for relatively inexperienced observers who watch similar others perform.

Verbal Persuasion

Coaches, parents, teachers, employers, therapists, peers, spouses, friends, audiences, clergy, authors of self-help books, infomercials, inspirational posters, happy-face stickers, and songs on the radio often attempt to convince us that we can competently execute a given action—despite our entrenched inefficacy—if we will just try. When effective, pep talks persuade the performer to focus more and more on personal strengths and potentials and less and less on personal weaknesses and deficiencies. Pep talks shift a performer's attention from sources of inefficacy to sources of efficacy. But verbal persuasion goes only so far if it is contradicted by direct experience. Its effectiveness is limited by the boundaries of the possible (in the mind of the performer) and depends on the credibility, expertise, and trustworthiness of the persuader. Individuals also give themselves pep talks, usually in the form of self-instruction, that can boost efficacy, at least for a little while (Schunk & Cox, 1986). Verbal persuasion works to the extent that it provides the performer with enough of a temporary efficacy boost to generate the motivation necessary for another try (Schunk, 1991).

Physiological State

Fatigue, pain, muscle tension, mental confusion, and trembling hands are physiological signals that the demands of the task currently exceed the performer's capacity to cope with those demands (Taylor et al., 1985). An abnormal physiological state is a private, yet attention-getting, message that contributes to one's sense of inefficacy. An absence of tension, fear, and stress, on the other hand, heightens efficacy by providing firsthand bodily feedback that one can indeed cope adequately with task demands (Bandura & Adams, 1977). The causal direction between efficacy and physiological activity is bidirectional:

Inefficacy heightens arousal and heightened arousal feeds perceived inefficacy (Bandura et al., 1988). Physiological information communicates efficacy information most when initial efficacy is uncertain (one is performing a task for the first time). When efficacy is relatively assured, people sometimes discount, or even reinterpret, their physiological cues as a positive source of efficacy, as in "I'm pumped up for this" (Carver & Blaney, 1977).

As people face challenging and difficult circumstances and ready themselves to carry out a course of action, these are the four sources of information they rely on to forecast their sense of efficacy during the performance. For a concrete illustration, consider the child at the county swimming pool waiting her turn in line to jump off the high diving board. How eager (motivated) she will be to do so depends on how well she has been able to negotiate the jump in the past, how well or ineptly the divers in the line before her are able to dive, the conversation of encouragement versus doubt and ridicule she hears from her friend standing in line with her, and the message of panic versus "cool, calm, and collected" her heart sends her as she stands six feet above the water looking down. By itself, none of this information determines her efficacy or her diving forecasts. Instead, through reflective thought, she selects information to attend to, weighs each's importance, and eventually integrates the multiple (and sometimes contradictory) sources of information into an overall self-efficacy judgement (Bandura, 1997).

While integrating these multiple sources of self-efficacy information into a single judgment is a complex process, the first two sources of efficacy information—personal behavior history and vicarious experience—are generally the stronger sources of efficacy beliefs (Schunk, 1989a). The relative potency of the different sources of efficacy information is important because of its implications for therapeutic strategies for designing motivational interventions for persons with low self-efficacy beliefs. Personal behavior history and vicarious experience are promising therapeutic possibilities, while verbal persuasion and regulating physiological states serve as supplemental opportunities to alter pessimistic self-efficacy beliefs.

Self-Efficacy Effects on Behavior

Once formed, self-efficacy beliefs contribute to the quality of human functioning in multiple ways (Bandura, 1986, 1997). Generally speaking, the more people expect that they can adequately perform an action, the more willing they are to put forth effort and persist in facing difficulties when activities require such action (Bandura, 1989; Bandura & Cervone, 1983; Weinberg, Gould, & Jackson, 1979). In contrast, when people expect that they cannot adequately perform the required task, they are not willing to engage in activities requiring such behavior. Instead, they slacken their effort, prematurely settle for mediocre outcomes, and quit in the face of obstacles (Bandura, 1989). More specifically, self-efficacy beliefs affect (1) choice of activities and selection of environments, (2) extent of effort and persistence put forth during performance, (3) the quality of thinking and decision making during performance, and (4) emotional reactions, especially those related to stress and anxiety. The four sources of efficacy and the four effects of strong versus weak self-efficacy beliefs are organized in summary form in Figure 9.2.

Sources of Self-Efficacy   *Effects of Self-Efficacy*

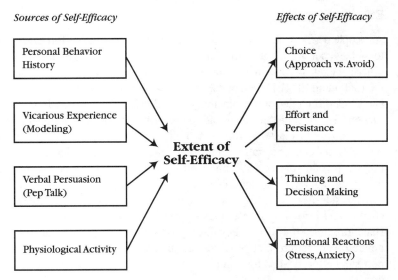

Figure 9.2   Sources and Effects of Self-Efficacy Beliefs

Choice: Selection of Activities and Environments

People continually make choices about what activities to pursue and which environments to spend time in. In general, people seek out and approach with excitement those activities and situations that they feel capable of adjusting to or handling, while people shun and actively avoid those activities and situations that they see as likely to overwhelm their coping capacities (Bandura, 1977, 1989). In a self-efficacy analysis, a person will often choose to avoid tasks and environments as a self-protective act for guarding against the possibility of being overwhelmed by their demands and challenges. If the student expects a math class or a foreign language class to be overwhelming, confusing, and frustrating, doubt overwhelms efficacy and produces an avoidance decision, such as withdrawing from class discussions or not enrolling in the class in the first place. The same doubt-plagued avoidance choices apply to social opportunities, like dating, dancing, participating in sports, selecting (or avoiding) a particular musical instrument, and career paths pursued and shunned.

Avoidance choices exert a profound, detrimental, long-term effect on this person's development (Bandura, 1986). Weak self-efficacy beliefs set the stage for people to shun participating in activities and therefore contribute to their own arrested developmental potentials (Holahan & Holahan, 1987). When people shun an activity out of doubt over personal competence, they participate in the self-destructive process of retarding their own development. Further, the more they avoid such activities, the more entrenched self-doubt becomes because doubters never get the chance to prove themselves wrong and never give themselves opportunities to observe expert models or receive instruction, assistance, or advice. Such a pattern of avoidance progressively narrows people's ranges of activities and settings (Bandura, 1982; Betz & Hackett, 1986; Hackett, 1985).

Effort and Persistence

As people perform, self-efficacy beliefs influence how much effort they exert as well as how long they put forth that effort in the face of adversity (Bandura, 1989). Strong self-efficacy beliefs produce persistent coping efforts aimed at overcoming setbacks and difficulties (Salomon, 1984). Doubt, on the other hand, leads people to slacken their efforts when they encounter difficulties or give up altogether (Bandura & Cervone, 1983; Weinberg, Gould, & Jackson, 1979). Self-doubt also leads performers to settle prematurely on mediocre solutions.

In trying to master complex activities, learning is always fraught with difficulties, obstacles, setbacks, frustrations, rejections, and inequalities, at least to a degree. Self-efficacy plays a pivotal role in facilitating effort and persistence not because it silences doubt following failure and rejection (because these are expected, normal emotional reactions). Instead, self-efficacy leads to a *quick recovery* of self-assurance following such setbacks (Bandura, 1986). Using examples of persistent writers, scientists, and athletes, Albert Bandura argues that it is the resiliency of self-efficacy in the face of being pounded by uninterrupted failure that provides the motivational support necessary in continuing the persistent effort needed for competent functioning and the development of expertise (Bandura, 1989).

Thinking and Decision Making

People who believe strongly in their efficacy for solving problems remain remarkably efficient in their analytic thinking during stressful episodes, whereas people who doubt their problem-solving capacities think erratically (Bandura & Wood, 1989; Wood & Bandura, 1989). To perform their best, people must first use memories of past events to predict the most effective course of action. They must also analyze feedback to assess and to reassess the merit of their plans and strategies. Further, they must then reflect upon performance, remembering which courses of action were effective and which were not. A strong sense of efficacy allows the performer to remain task focused, even in the face of situational stress and problem-solving dead ends. In contrast, self-doubt distracts decision makers away from such task-focused thinking as attention shifts to the deficiencies of the self and the overwhelming demands of the task. In short, doubt deteriorates, whereas efficacy buffers, the quality of a performer's thinking and decision making during a performance.

Emotionality

Before performers begin an activity, they typically spend time thinking about how they will perform. Persons with a strong sense of efficacy attend to the demands and challenges of the task, visualize competent scenarios for forthcoming behaviors, and react to task challenges and feedback with enthusiastic effort, optimism, and interest. Persons with a weak sense of efficacy, however, dwell on personal deficiencies, visualize the formidable obstacles they face, and react to challenges and feedback with pessimism, anxiety, and depression (Bandura, 1986). Once performance begins and things start to go awry, strong self-efficacy beliefs keep anxiety at bay. People who doubt their efficacy, however, are quickly threatened by difficulties, react to setbacks with distress, and see their attention drift toward personal deficiencies.

Life in general brings any number of potentially threatening events (e.g., examinations, public performances, physical and psychological threats), and perceived self-efficacy plays a central role in determining how much stress and anxiety such events bring to any individual performer. Rather than existing as a fixed property of events, "threat" always depends on the relationship a person has to the task (Folkman & Lazarus, 1985; Lazarus & Folkman, 1984). Knowing that one's coping abilities cannot handle an event's perceived demands conjures up thoughts of disaster, emotional arousal, and feelings of distress and anxiety (Bandura, 1983; Bandura, Reese, & Adams, 1982; Bandura et al., 1985; Lazarus, 1991a).

More optimistically, when people plagued with self-doubt undergo therapy-like conditions to enhance their coping capabilities, the intimidating event that once conjured up such an avalanche of doubt, dread, and distress no longer does so (Bandura & Adams, 1977; Bandura et al., 1980; Bandura et al., 1982; Ozer & Bandura, 1990). As self-efficacy increases, fear and anxiety slip away. Self-efficacy researchers go so far as to say that the root cause of anxiety is low self-efficacy (Bandura, 1983, 1988). So any increase in efficacy means a corresponding decrease in anxiety.

Empowerment

Two practical points about self-efficacy are important to highlight. First, self-efficacy beliefs come from personal behavior history, vicarious experiences, verbal persuasion, and physiological states (e.g., Figure 9.2). What makes this a practical point is that it means high self-efficacy beliefs can be acquired and changed. Second, the level of self-efficacy predicts ways of behaving that can be called "competent functioning" or "personal empowerment" (e.g., overcoming avoidance-based fears, putting forth high effort, persisting in the face of adversity, thinking clearly and exercising control during performance). Thus, once enhanced, self-efficacy expectations provide the cognitive-motivational foundation underlying personal empowerment.

Empowerment involves possessing the knowledge, skills, and beliefs that allow people to exert control over their lives. One example of self-efficacy as empowerment can be found in learning to defend oneself against intimidation and threats from abusive others (Ozer & Bandura, 1990). When threatened, people typically feel anxious, stressed, vulnerable, at risk, and in danger. To empower oneself, people need more than just skills and the knowledge of what to do. People also need self-efficacy beliefs so they can (1) translate their knowledge and skills into effective performance when threatened and (2) exert control over intrusive negative thoughts.

In one study, researchers trained a group of women over a 5-week period in self-defense and emotion-management skills. The women felt very afraid for their safety when going out at night because they feared being overpowered by the threats and dangers of night life in San Francisco. The researchers first asked the women to watch expert models defend themselves against assailants (using vicarious experience) and then asked the women to master the modeled behavior while hearing support and encouragement from peers (using verbal persuasion) during simulated attacks (Ozer & Bandura, 1990). The women then enacted the behaviors they had seen modeled and received coaching and corrective feedback as needed (personal behavior history). With each successive week, women's self-efficacy beliefs to control interpersonal threats behaviorally and intrusive negative thinking cognitively soared. Once empowered, the women felt less vulnerable and began to engage in activities that were once thought to be too risky (e.g., outdoor exercise, evening recreation, travel to different parts of town). In other words, empowerment occurred as efficacy and engagement replaced doubt and avoidance.

One of the women voiced her empowerment by saying, "I feel freer and more capable than ever. I now make choices about what I will or won't do based on whether or not I want to, not whether or not it is frightening to me" (Ozer & Bandura, 1990). Understandably, the reader might wonder whether the women's increased confidence led them to behaving recklessly and served to put them in harm's way. This did not happen. Instead, the women's generalized avoidance was replaced by flexible, adaptive, confident behavior. Such a program would seemingly be effective in practically any activities that people avoided out of a fear of having their skills overwhelmed by situational challenges and demands.

Empowering People: Mastery Modeling Program

A formal program to empower people through self-efficacy training is to employ a mastery modeling program. In a mastery modeling program an expert in the skill area works with a group of relative novices to show them how to cope with an otherwise fearsome situation. In the example above, professionals empowered women self-defense skills. In the school, teachers might use a mastery modeling program to empower children with reading skills, computer skills, or cooperative learning skills. On the athletic field, coaches might empower athletes with defensive skills and resilient confidence to cope with whatever offense next week's opponent might try. In the hospital, therapists might empower lonely clients with social skills and resilient confidence in social situations with strangers.

In a mastery modeling program, the expert model walks the group of novices through the following seven steps:

1. Teacher identifies component skills involved in effective coping and measures students' efficacy expectation on each component skill.

2. Teacher models each component skill.

3. Students emulate each modeled skill. Teacher provides corrective feedback, as needed.

4. Students integrate the separate component skills into an overall simulated performance. Teacher introduces mild obstacles so students will need to use all the separate skills during the simulated performance.

5. Students participate in cooperative learning groups. One student gives a simulated performance while peers watch. As they watch, peers provide encouragement and tips. Students take turn until each student performs multiple times.

6. Students perform individually in a near-naturalistic situation that features numerous and realistic difficulties, obstacles, and setbacks while teacher provides modeling and corrective feedback.

7. Teacher models confident demeanor and arousal-regulating techniques.

The mastery modeling program is a formal procedure to utilize the four sources of self-efficacy as a means to advance from anxious novices to confident masters of the craft. By having students perform each skill and receive corrective feedback from the teacher, the student builds efficacy through a personal behavior history. By watching the expert perform (step 2) and by watching similar peers perform (step 5), the student builds efficacy through vicarious experience. By hearing peers' encouragement and tips (step 5), the student builds efficacy through verbal persuasion. By observing and imitating the teacher's ways of handling performance-debilitating arousal (step 7), the student builds efficacy through physiological calmness.

PERSONAL CONTROL BELIEFS

Personal control beliefs reflect the degree to which an individual believes she causes desirable outcomes and prevents aversive ones (Peterson, Maier, & Seligman, 1993). When personal control beliefs are strong and resilient, the individual perceives a strong causal link between actions and outcomes. When personal control beliefs are weak and fragile, the individual perceives that personal initiatives and actions produce little effect on what happens. Trying seems pointless.

Mastery Versus Helpless Motivational Orientations

People learn to react to failure to control the events and outcomes in their lives in different ways. A mastery motivational orientation refers to a hardy, resistant portrayal of the self during encounters of failure. With a mastery motivational orientation, the person responds to failure by remaining task-focused and by being bent on achieving mastery in spite of difficulties and setbacks (Diener & Dweck, 1978, 1980). On the other hand, a helpless motivational orientation refers to a fragile view of the self during encounters of failure. With a helpless motivational orientation, the person responds to failure by giving up and withdrawing, acting as if the situation were out of her control (Dweck, 1975; Dweck & Repucci, 1973).

Most people perform well and stay task-focused when working on easy problems and when performing well. When tasks turn difficult and challenging, however, the motivational significance of mastery versus helpless motivational orientation becomes clear. Mastery-oriented persons seize challenges and become energized by setbacks. Helpless-oriented persons shy away from challenges, fall apart in the face of setbacks, and begin to question and then outright doubt their ability. On those occasions in which success feedback slips into failure feedback, mastery-oriented individuals increase their efforts and change their strategies (Diener & Dweck, 1978, 1980). Under these same conditions, helpless-oriented individuals condemn their abilities and lose hope for any future successes (Dweck, 1975; Dweck & Repucci, 1973). In sum, during failure feedback, helpless-oriented children focus on why they are failing (low ability), whereas mastery-oriented children focus on how they can remedy the failure (effort, strategy; Diener & Dweck, 1978).

The different reactions to failure feedback for mastery-oriented and failure-oriented performers emanate from a different meaning of failure (Dweck, 1999). Mastery-oriented individuals do not see failure as an indictment of the self. Instead, these individuals, during setbacks and failures, might say things like, "The harder it gets, the harder I need to try"; "I love a challenge"; and "Mistakes are my friend." Failure feedback is, generally speaking, just information. Because mastery-oriented persons recognize that failure feedback is telling them they need more effort, better strategies, and more resources, these individuals typically perform better and more enthusiastically in the face of failure. Helpless-oriented individuals see failure as an indictment of the self. They see failure as a sign of personal inadequacy, one that in turn leads them toward a state of despair.

Perhaps the reader might think the term "helpless" is a bit strong, but research by Carol Dweck (1975) suggests that it is not. When failure rears its ugly head, helpless-oriented people might start to say things like, "I'm no good at things like this" and "I guess I'm not very smart." In other words, they denigrate their abilities and even their self-worth (Diener & Dweck, 1978). Their emotions quickly turn negative, and they start to show unusual ways for dealing with their rising anxiety and doubt, such as acting silly or trying to change the task or its rules (Diener & Dweck, 1978). Their problem-solving strategies collapse into simply making wild guesses or picking answers for random reasons. The self-denigration, negative mood, and immature strategies signal the presence of helplessness, but the telltale sign of helplessness is how quickly and how emphatically the performer gives up (Dweck, 1999).

LEARNED HELPLESSNESS

As efficacy expectancies underlie self-efficacy, outcome expectancies underlie learned helplessness. When people engage in a task, some outcome is typically at stake. During such task engagement, people make a subjective forecast of how controllable versus uncontrollable the outcome at stake is. For controllable outcomes, a one-to-one relationship exists between behavior (what a person does) and outcomes (what happens to that person). For uncontrollable outcomes, a random relationship exists between behavior and outcomes (e.g., "I have no idea what effect, if any, my behavior will have on what happens to me.").

When people expect desired outcomes (e.g., making friends, getting a job) or undesired outcomes (e.g., preventing illness, being fired from a job) are independent of their behavior, they develop a "learned helplessness" over attaining or preventing those outcomes. Learned helplessness is the psychological state that results when an individual expects that life's outcomes are uncontrollable (Mikulincer, 1994; Seligman, 1975).

Boiled down to its essentials, learned helplessness can be understood by the strength of the perceived relationship between the person's behavior and the person's subsequent fate, or outcome, as represented in Figure 9.3. The relationship between one's behavior and one's outcomes can be very high, as represented by a solid and bold arrow between what one does and what outcomes one experiences. The bold solid arrow between behavior and outcomes graphically represents a mastery orientation. In contrast, the relationship between one's behavior and one's outcomes can be nonexistent, as represented by the dashed and thin arrow between what one does and what outcomes one experiences. The thin dashed arrow between behavior and outcomes graphically represents a learned helplessness orientation. With learned helplessness, one's behavior exerts little or no influence over one's outcomes. Instead, other factors outside one's control determine the outcomes, as represented by the bold solid arrow between outside influences and one's outcomes.

Mastery Orientation

Figure 9.3   Illustration of the Relationship between Behavior and Outcomes, According to a Mastery Orientation and According to Learned Helplessness

For example, a job applicant experiencing learned helplessness might perceive that while his behaviors during the job interview (acting professionally, demonstrating skills, answering questions well) have nothing to do with whether or not he is hired by the company, he may perceive that factors outside his control (e.g., poor economy, "who you know," skin color) determine whether he is hired. Because his behaviors do not control the outcome and because outside, uncontrollable influences do control the outcome, then the job applicant presumes that he is helpless to influence the hiring decision.

Learning Helplessness

Helplessness is learned. Consider the following experiment with three groups of dogs that were administered either (1) inescapable shock, (2) escapable shock, or (3) no shock (control group) (Seligman & Maier, 1967). Dogs in the two shock groups were placed into a sling and given mild 5-second electric shocks once a day for 64 consecutive days. In the inescapable shock group, the shocks occurred randomly, and no response could terminate the shock. Whether the dog barked, howled, or thrashed about frantically, the shock continued for its full 5 seconds. In other words, the shock was inescapable. The outcome (shock) was uncontrollable. In the escapable shock group, the dogs could terminate the shock. If the dog pressed a button mounted on the wall (placed just in front of their snouts), the shock stopped. The dogs therefore had a response available to escape the shock—push the button. The outcome (shock) was controllable. In the no-shock control group, dogs were placed into a sling just like the dogs in the other two conditions were but they received no shocks.

Exposure to inescapable shock, escapable shock, or no shock constituted the first phase—the learning phase—of the two-phase experiment. In the second phase, the dogs in each group were all treated the same. Each dog was placed into a shuttle box in which its two compartments were separated by a wall partition of elbow height. The two compartments were the same size and similar in most respects, except the first compartment had a grid floor through which a mild electrical shock could be delivered while the second compartment was safe from shock. To illustrate the procedure, the top half of Figure 9.4 (a) shows a dog in the sling (during phase 1), and the lower half of the figure (b) shows the dog in the shuttle box (during phase 2; Carlson, 1988). On each trial during phase 2, the dogs were placed into the grid floor compartment and a mild shock was delivered. The onset of this shock was always preceded by a signal (a dimming of the light on the wall). After the lights were dimmed, the electric shock followed 10 seconds thereafter. If the dog jumped over the partition, it escaped the shock. So, for all the dogs, the shock was both predictable and preventable (i.e., controllable) during the second phase of the study. If the dog failed to jump over the partition within 10 seconds, however, the electric shock started and continued for one minute.

A summary of the study's procedure and results appears in Table 9.1 (Seligman & Maier, 1967). The dogs in both the escapable shock and no shock groups quickly learned how to escape the shock in the shuttle box. When shocked, these dogs ran about franti-

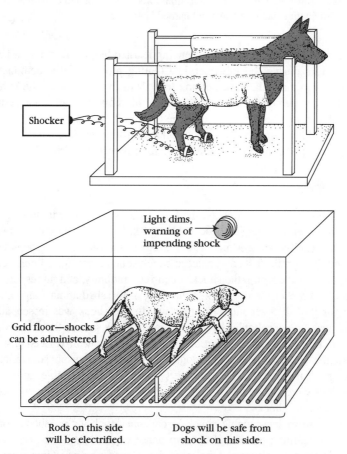

Figure 9.4 Apparatus Used in the Seligman and Maier Experiment on Learned Helplessness

Source: From Discovering Psychology by N.C. Carlson, 1988. Boston, MA: Allyn and Bacon. Copyright 1988 by Pearson Education. Reprinted by permission.

Table 9.1 Results of a Prototypical Learned Helplessness Study

Experimental condition	Phase 1	Phase 2	Results
Inescapable Shock	Received shock, no coping response could terminate the shock	Received an escapable shock	Failed to escape from the shock
Escapable Shock	Received shock, pressing nose against button could terminate shock	Received an escapable shock	Quickly learned to escape shock by jumping over barrier
Control, No Shock	Received no shocks	Received an escapable shock	Quickly learned to escape shock by jumping over barrier

cally at first and rather accidentally climbed, fell, scrambled, or jumped over the barrier. That is, through trial and error, the dogs learned that if they somehow overstepped the barrier, they could escape the shock. After only a few trials, these dogs jumped over the barrier to safety as soon as the warning light dimmed. These dogs learned mastery over the very stressful conditions. These dogs learned how to control (prevent) the shock.

The dogs in the inescapable shock group behaved very differently. When shocked, these dogs at first behaved as the other dogs did by running about frantically and howling. However, unlike the dogs in the other two groups, these dogs soon stopped running around and, instead, whimpered until the trial (and shock) terminated. After only a few trials, these dogs gave up trying to escape and passively accepted the shock. On subsequent trials, the dogs failed to make any escape movements at all. What these dogs learned in the sling—that the onset, duration, intensity, and termination of the shock (in phase 1) were all beyond their control—had a carryover effect in the shuttle box: The dogs perceived that escape was beyond their control. These dogs learned helplessness in the very stressful conditions.

The startling generalization that emerged from this study is that whenever animals are placed in a situation in which they perceive they have little or no control, they develop the expectation that their future actions will have little or no effect on what happens to them. This learned expectation that one's voluntary behavior will not effect desired outcomes is the heart of learned helplessness.

Application to Humans

The early experiments on learned helplessness used animals as research participants mostly because the uncontrollable events used in these studies included traumatic events, such as electric shock. Later studies found ways to test the extent to which helplessness applied to humans (Diener & Dweck, 1978, 1980; Dweck, 1975; Hiroto, 1974; Hiroto & Seligman, 1975; Mikulincer, 1994; Peterson et al., 1993). In Donald Hiroto's (1974) experiment, irritating noise constituted the aversive, traumatic stimulus event. The results with humans paralleled the results with dogs (see Table 9.1) in that participants in the inescapable noise group sat passively and were unwilling to attempt an escape from the noise, whereas participants in the escapable and no-noise groups learned quickly to escape the noise (by operating a lever). Humans too learned helplessness.

To demonstrate how learned helplessness operates, try to solve problems that vary in how controllable they are: Can you solve academic problems? relationship problems? financial problems? health problems? If your car broke down on the highway, would you try to cope or would you turn passive? How about a migraine headache?

Looking at the sequence of four cards shown in Figure 9.5, consider an experiment in which the participant's task is to figure out which feature the experimenter is looking for—triangle or square, dot or star, shaded or white. A series of 10 cards appear in sequential order and the participant's task is to identify which feature is being tracked. On the first card, he simply guesses "left" or "right," and the experimenter replies "correct" or "incorrect." The same procedure occurs for the following nine cards. For instance, a person who is tracking the hypothesis of "square" would choose right, right, left, and right (in the four cards shown in Figure 9.5).

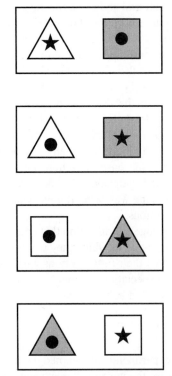

Figure 9.5 Sample of a Problem Used in the Study of Learned Helplessness with Humans
Source: From "An Analysis of Learned Helplessness: Continuous Changes in Performance, Strategy, and Achievement Cognitions Following Failure," by C. I. Diener and C. S. Dweck, 1978, *Journal of Personality and Social Psychology, 36,* pp. 451–462. Copyright 1978 by the American Psychological Association. Reprinted with permission.

Now imagine that in one condition, the experimenter (or a computer program) provided authentic feedback such that the participant could, with concentration and effort, use the feedback provided to figure out the answer to the problem. In other words, the problem is controllable, at least with concentration and effort. In a second condition, however, the feedback was random and bogus. With random feedback, the participant could try all the hypotheses in the world and only gain a sense of confusion and frustration for the effort. After several of these problems, the second phase of the study begins as all participants (in both conditions) are asked to solve some moderately difficult problems (e.g., multiplication problems, six-letter anagrams). The consistent finding is that people exposed to solvable problems in the first phase of the study solve significantly more problems in the second phase than do people exposed to unsolvable problems in the first phase (Diener & Dweck, 1978). It is not so much how smart and clever the participant is that matters; instead, it is how responsive and controllable is the environment while one attempts to solve problems. People who learned mastery (from the contingent feedback) performed well, while people who learned helplessness (from the random feedback) performed dismally.

Components

Learned helplessness theory features three components: contingency, cognition, and behavior (Peterson et al., 1993). Collectively, these three components explain the motivational dynamics that unfold as experience teaches people to expect that the events in their lives will be beyond their personal control.

Contingency

Contingency refers to the objective relationship between a person's behavior and the environment's outcomes. The environment can be the home, classroom, workplace, sports field, hospital, interpersonal relationship, psychology laboratory, and so on. Contingency exists on a continuum that ranges from outcomes that occur on a random, noncontingent basis (i.e., uncontrollable outcomes) to outcomes that occur in perfect synchronization with a person's voluntary behavior (i.e., controllable outcomes). That is, how contingent any one environment is can be scored on a continuum that ranges from 0 (uncontrollable outcomes) to 1 (controllable outcomes).

Take a moment to ask yourself what your own experiences have taught you about contingency in the following situations: getting a traffic ticket, getting a job in your hometown, winning a tennis match against a rival, winning the state lottery, catching the flu during winter, getting cancer from smoking cigarettes, gaining weight over the holidays, and graduating from college. To characterize the contingency inherent in each of these situations, ask yourself the following: "To what extent does the average person's voluntary, strategic behavior influence the outcomes that occur in these settings?" That is, how much influence does voluntary coping behavior (from people in general, not from you in particular) exert on avoiding a traffic ticket, avoiding the flu, getting a job, winning a contest, winning the lottery, escaping cancer, preventing weight gain, and obtaining a college degree?

Cognition

A good deal of cognitive intervention takes place between the actual, objective environmental contingencies that exist in the world and a person's subjective understanding of personal control in such environments. Mental events distort the relationship between objective contingencies and subjective understandings of personal control, and these events therefore create some margin of error between objective truth and subjective understanding.

Three cognitive elements are particularly important: biases (e.g., the "illusion of control"); attributions (explanations of why we think we do or do not have control); and expectancies, which are the subjective personal control beliefs we carry over from past experiences into our current situation. To illustrate the importance of cognition, ask two people who experience the same environmental contingency why they avoided a traffic ticket, avoided the flu, got a job, and so on. People's outcome beliefs (and hence their replies to your question) stem not only from the objective information about the world (i.e., contingency) but also from each person's unique biases, attributions, and expectancies. Hence, to understand learned helplessness, we need to pay attention not only to objective environmental contingencies (how controllable outcomes really are) but also to subjective personal control beliefs (how controllable the person thinks those outcomes are).

Behavior

Just as contingency exists on a continuum, coping behavior to attain or to prevent outcomes also exists on a continuum. In a traumatic event, for instance, people's voluntary coping behavior varies from very passive to very active.

Coping responses can be lethargic and passive, or coping responses can be active and assertive. Lethargy, passivity, and giving up typify a listless, demoralized effort that characterizes the behavior of the helpless individual (recall the passive behavior of the dogs in the inescapable shock group). Alertness, activity, and assertiveness characterize people who are not helpless (who have some expectation of control). To illustrate passive behavior as a component of learned helplessness, consider once again the situations listed earlier (driving on the highway, job hunting, competing against an opponent). Consider your own passive-to-active coping behaviors in the face of such situations and potential outcomes. The job hunter who quits reading newspaper advertisements, revising her résumé, telephoning prospective employers, and rising early and enthusiastically in the morning to look for a job manifests the listless, demoralized coping behavior that characterizes helplessness.

Effects of Helplessness

Learned helplessness occurs when people expect that their voluntary behavior will produce little or no effect on the outcomes they strive to attain or avoid. How the mental event that is learned helplessness generates behavioral passivity is through its affect on three kinds of deficits: motivational, learning, and emotional (Alloy & Seligman, 1979). Collectively, this set of expectancy-induced deficits causes passive, helpless behavior.

Motivational Deficits

Motivational deficits consist of a decreased willingness to try. Motivational deficits become apparent when a person's willingness to emit voluntary coping responses decreases or disappears altogether. Typically, when people care about an outcome and when the environment is at least somewhat responsive in delivering those outcomes, they act enthusiastically and assertively in bringing about those outcomes. For instance, at the beginning of a season, an athlete might practice diligently and persistently, but after a series of athletic defeats (victory becomes an uncontrollable outcome), willingness to practice wanes. The athlete begins to wonder if the time spent practicing is really worth it. In the learned helplessness experiment described in the preceding paragraphs, the experimenters asked participants why they did not try to terminate an unpleasant noise in the second phase of the study (Thornton & Jacobs, 1971). Approximately 60% of the participants (from the inescapable noise group) reported that they felt little control over the noise so did not see the point in trying to terminate the noise, saying "Why try?" Thus, "Why try?" characterizes the motivational deficit in learned helplessness.

Learning Deficits

Learning deficits consist of an acquired pessimistic set that interferes with one's ability to learn new response-outcome contingencies. Over time, exposure to uncontrollable environments cultivates an expectancy in which people believe that outcomes are generally independent of their actions. Once expectancies take on a pessimistic tone, the person has a very difficult time learning (or, more precisely, re-learning) that a new response can affect outcomes. This pessimistic set essentially interferes with, or retards, the learning of future response-outcome contingencies (Alloy & Seligman, 1979).

When students first learn the results from learned helplessness experiments, they frequently wonder why dogs in the inescapable groups do not learn in the second phase of the experiment that jumping over the barrier terminates the shock. Like a laid-off worker who has given up applying for a new job, you want to yell (to the dog): "Jump! Jump! C'mon boy, just jump!"

Consider, however, what the human subjects learned during the first phase of the earphone session with the inescapable noise blast. The first time they heard the noise, they flinched and jumped, and the second time, they manipulated the lever. Perhaps they perceived that on some trials turning their heads or shifting their weight from side to side coincided with the turning off of the noise. But on later trials, they again turned their heads or shifted their weight, but the noise persisted for its programmed 5 seconds. Gradually, they learned that no response turned off the noise in a reliable way. They tried everything, but nothing worked. Consequently, when they entered the second phase of the experiment and happened to move the now-working lever, any positive outcome (turning off the noise) comes across as a "successful accident" and unworthy of being tried again (as were head turning, lever turning, weight shifting, and so forth in the first phase). Compared to the participants in the escapable noise and control groups who quickly learned to discriminate between responses that worked and responses that did not work, participants in the inescapable noise groups had an unusually difficult time learning an effective coping response.

Emotional Deficits

Emotional deficits consist of affective disruptions in which lethargic, depressive emotional reactions occur in situations that call for active, assertive emotion. In the face of trauma, the natural and typical human response is one of highly mobilized emotion (e.g., fear, anger, assertiveness, frustration). When afraid, people struggle vigorously to overcome, escape, counteract, or do whatever is necessary to cope effectively. Over time, however, an unrelenting onslaught of environmental unresponsiveness leads people to view coping as futile. Once fear-mobilized emotionality is believed to be unproductive, depression-related emotionality takes its place. Once the person becomes convinced that there is nothing that can be done to escape the trauma, the resulting expectation makes energy-mobilizing emotions less likely and makes energy-depleting emotions (e.g., listlessness, apathy, depression) more likely.

Helplessness and Depression

Some clinical psychologists view learned helplessness as a model of naturally occurring unipolar depression (Rosenhan & Seligman, 1984; Seligman, 1975). Learned helplessness and depression are similar in that the same expectations cause both: The individual expects that bad events will occur, and there is nothing she can do to prevent their occurrence (Rosenhan & Seligman, 1984). Learned helplessness and depression also share common symptoms (passivity, low self-esteem, loss of appetite) and therapeutic intervention strategies (time, cognitive behavior modification).

Using the learned helplessness model to understand the etiology of unipolar depression touched off a flurry of research that brought both strong criticism (Costello, 1978; Depue & Monroe, 1978) and strong support (Seligman, 1975). One of the most exciting findings to emerge is that depressed individuals sometimes see the events in their lives as less controllable than do individuals who are not depressed. Such a finding led researchers to wonder whether the depressive tendency of individuals to see their worlds as uncontrollable might be the core cause of unipolar depression. Perhaps the root of depression lies in a depressed individual's inability to recognize that he has more control over his life outcomes than he knows.

Depressed and nondepressed college students (as assessed by a questionnaire) performed a task in which they pushed a button on some trials and did not push it on other trials (Alloy & Abramson, 1979). With a button push, a green light sometimes came on. The point of the study was for the participant to estimate what proportion of time the green light came on. The experimenters controlled the light—whether it came on and when it came on. For one group, the green light came on 75% of the time and only when the button was pressed. This was the high-control group. For a second group, the green light came on when the button was pressed 75% of the time, but the light also came on 50% of the time when no button was pushed. This was the low-control group. In a final group, the green light came on when the button was pressed 75% of the time, but it also came on 75% of the time when the participants did not push the button. This was the no-control group (because the light came on at the same rate regardless of the participant's button pressing).

Results were most surprising (see Figure 9.6). Depressed individuals accurately judged how much control they had over each situation, as did nondepressed individuals except in one condition, namely in the no-control situation (Alloy & Abramson, 1979). The depressed individuals accurately judged that they had no control in this condition. The light came on in a random way, and they knew it. The nondepressed individuals were the ones who misperceived how much control they had—they overestimated their perceived control.

A second study tested the idea that people who are not depressed have an "illusion of control" (Alloy & Abramson, 1982). An illusion of control is evident whenever individuals overestimate the extent of control over events (Langer, 1975). In the experiment's first phase, participants completed a button-pressing task and were told that a buzzer noise was either controllable or uncontrollable. In the second phase, participants either succeeded (won money for each trial they exerted control over) or failed (lost money for each trial they did not control). In actuality, outcomes in the second phase occurred randomly so that the participant had no control over her outcomes whatsoever. The experiment tested the judgments of control after success and failure feedback for both depressed and nondepressed individuals. Results appear in Figure 9.7. Depressed individuals in all groups and nondepressed individuals in the controllable-noise groups accurately judged the extent of their control over the win-and-lose problems. The interesting group was the nondepressed individuals who received positive feedback over the uncontrollable outcomes. When they won on an uncontrollable task, these individuals showed a strong illusion of control.

The most interesting conclusion to draw from Lauren Alloy and Lyn Abramson's (1979, 1982) research is that depressed people are *not* more prone to learned helplessness deficits. Rather, it is the individuals who are not depressed who sometimes believe they have more personal control than they actually have (Taylor & Brown, 1988, 1994). Though the conclusion might sound startling, depressed persons' memories for the positive and

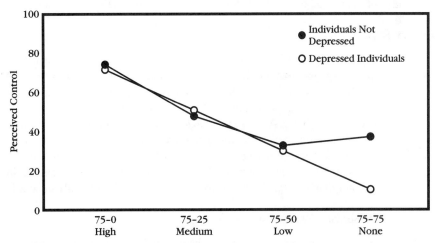

Figure 9.6   Perceived Control Judgments for Depressed and Nondepressed Individuals

Source: From "Judgments of Contingency in Depressed and Nondepressed Students: Sadder but Wiser?" by L.B. Alloy and L.T. Abramson, 1979, *Journal of Experimental Psychology: General*, 108, pp. 441–485. Copyright 1979 by the American Psychological Association. Adapted with permission.

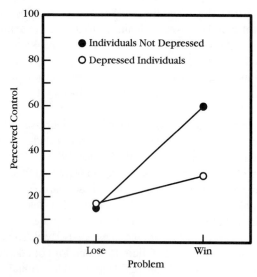

Figure 9.7   Perceived Control for Depressed and Nondepressed Individuals After Winning and Losing

Source: From "Judgments of Contingency in Depressed and Nondepressed Students: Sadder but Wiser?" by L.B. Alloy and L. T. Abramson, 1979, *Journal of Experimental Psychology: General, 108,* pp. 441–485. Copyright 1979 by the American Psychological Association. Adapted with permission.

negative events in their lives are balanced and equal, whereas the memories of the nondepressed persons harbor biases for recalling more of the positive events (Sanz, 1996). While people often misjudge the control they have over the events in their lives (Abramson & Alloy, 1980; Alloy & Abramson, 1979, 1982; Langer, 1975; Nisbett & Ross, 1980), most of the misjudging is done by nondepressed individuals, not by those who are depressed.

Explanatory Style

Explanatory style is a relatively stable, cognitively based personality variable that reflects the way people explain the reasons why bad events happen to them (Peterson & Barrett, 1987; Peterson & Park, 1998; Peterson & Seligman, 1984). Bad events happen to everyone, but people explain these setbacks with attributions that vary in their locus, stability, and controllability. An *optimistic explanatory style* manifests itself as the tendency to explain bad events with attributions that are external, unstable, and controllable (e.g., "I lost the contest because my opponent cheated.") A *pessimistic explanatory style* manifests itself as the tendency to explain bad events with attributions that are internal, stable, and uncontrollable (e.g., "I lost the contest because I'm physically uncoordinated.").

Pessimistic Explanatory Style

Academic failures, poor physical health, and subpar job performance are common. They happen to us all. Some of us react to such failures by increasing effort and by trying even harder than before. Others react by giving up. A pessimistic explanatory style predisposes people toward the latter response—giving up—in times of failure and setbacks.

When a student with a pessimistic style faces such educational frustrations and failures (e.g., disappointing grades, unintelligible lectures, confusing textbooks), she typically responds with a passive, fatalistic coping style that leads to decreased effort and increasingly poor grades (Peterson & Barrett, 1987). As to job performance, one vocation with more than its share of frustrations, failures, and rejections is selling life insurance because only a small percentage of potential clients ever buy a policy. One pair of researchers assessed life insurance agents' explanatory styles and recorded which agents performed well or poorly and which agents stayed on the job or quit (Seligman & Schulman, 1986). The attributionally pessimistic agents were more likely to quit, and those who continued to work performed significantly worse than did their more optimistic peers.

Overall, a pessimistic explanatory style is associated with academic failure (Peterson & Barrett, 1987), social distress (Sacks & Bugental, 1987), physical illness (Peterson, Seligman, & Vaillant, 1988), impaired job performance (Seligman & Schulman, 1986), depression (Beck, 1976), and even electoral defeat in presidential elections (Zullow et al., 1988). Individuals with a pessimistic explanatory style generally make lower grades in college, speak less with nonresponsive (uncontrollable) partners, quit work, suffer depression, and consider suicide.[1]

Optimistic Explanatory Style

The illusion of control is an attributional phenomenon that, over time, fosters an optimistic explanatory style. People with an optimistic explanatory style tend to take substantial credit for their successes but accept little or no blame for their failures (e.g., "Its not my fault that I am unemployed, divorced, broke, and had a car accident last month. I am, however, responsible for my team winning the softball game last night."). As you might expect, depressed individuals rarely have an optimistic style and are not vulnerable to the illusion of control (Alloy & Abramson, 1979, 1982).

Equipped with the self-serving bias of an illusion of control, people with an optimistic explanatory style readily ignore negative self-related information, impose distorting filters on incoming information, and interpret positive and negative outcomes in self-protecting ways. Attributing failure to an external cause allows the individual to discount the self-related meaning of the failure. In the same spirit, negative life outcomes are blamed on others, bad luck, and the environment in general. Externalizing failure therefore immunizes the individual against any detrimental effect of failure. Over time, a history of internalizing successes and externalizing failures breeds an enduring belief that one has more control over fate than is actually the case, even if what is needed is a full repertoire of excuses, denials, and self-deceptions (Lazarus, 1983; Sackeim, 1983; Tennen & Affleck, 1987).

In one sense, an optimistic explanatory style is delusional, and the extent to which a person harbors an optimistic explanatory style does indeed correlate with narcissism

---

[1]Care must be exercised in interpreting these correlational data, however, as it certainly could be the case that poor grades, nonresponsive partners, and difficulties at work lead individuals toward adopting a pessimistic style. Thus, one can say that a pessimistic style and mental and physical well-being correlate negatively, but one cannot say assertively that a pessimistic style causes mental and physical distress. Researchers continue to investigate the causal status of a pessimistic explanatory style in coping with life's setbacks (Peterson, Maier, & Seligman, 1993).

(John & Robins, 1994). Narcissists hold a grandiose sense of self-importance, tend to exaggerate their talents and achievements, and expect to be recognized as superior without commensurate achievements (Kohut, 1971; Millon, 1990; Westen, 1990). But most of us are not narcissists. For most of us (depressives and narcissists aside), an optimistic explanatory style is functionally an asset, because a "mentally healthy person appears to have the enviable capacity to distort reality in a direction that enhances self-esteem, maintains beliefs in personal efficacy, and promotes an optimistic view of the future" (Taylor & Brown, 1988).

Criticisms and Alternative Explanations

The learned helplessness model is not without its critics (Costello, 1978; Weiss, Glazer, & Pohorecky, 1976; Wortman & Brehm, 1975). The central question under debate is just what causes helplessness. In the learned helplessness model, helplessness follows from a cognitive event, namely the expectation of a response → outcome independence. But, learned helplessness experiments induce participants with trauma, and it could be that traumatic events themselves (e.g., shocks, noise blasts, unsolvable problems) induce helplessness. Through clever and sophisticated research designs (i.e., triadic design with a yoking procedure), researchers found that it was indeed the learned expectation, not the trauma itself, that produces helplessness (Weiss, 1972).

Other researchers argue that the expectation of failure, rather than the expectation of uncontrollability per se, induces helplessness. But investigators' clever research designed showed that failure, more often that not, actually produces a positive motivation (a phenomenon discussed in the next section under "Reactance Theory") and that it is the expectation of uncontrollability, not the expectation of failure, that causes learned helplessness deficits (Winefield, Barnett, & Tiggemann, 1985).

Yet a third possibility is that uncontrollable events induce helplessness deficits not because they are uncontrollable but because they are unpredictable (Winefield, 1982). It is extremely difficult, and probably impossible, to separate uncontrollability from unpredictability, and research shows that predictability does indeed mitigate learned helplessness deficits. The conclusion is that uncontrollability is a necessary, but not a sufficient, condition for inducing learned helplessness deficits. For sufficiency, uncontrollability must coincide with unpredictability (Tiggemann & Winefield, 1987). When life's rejections, losses, failures, and setbacks are perceived to be *both* uncontrollable and unpredictable, people are highly vulnerable to learned helplessness.

One alternative explanation for why people turn passive and give up in the face of uncontrollable outcomes is that people are actually motivated to remain passive. People are motivated to be passive if they sense that active responding will only make matters worse (Wortman & Brehm, 1975). In the face of a hurricane (an uncontrollable, unpredictable event), for example, it is possible that people are passive and helpless because they believe that negative outcomes will be more likely when they respond compared to when they do not respond. If this is the case, passivity is actually an enlightened strategic coping response that minimizes trauma. For a second example, imagine the socially anxious person who does not voluntarily engage in social interaction because of a belief that she will only make matters worse by initiating conversations. Perhaps this person is correct. By intentionally not initiating interactions, the anxious person may very well avoid making

BOX 9   *Is Personal Control Always Good?*

Question: Why is this information important?

Answer: Because we live in the age of personal control, which leads one to wonder, "Is personal control always good?"

We live in the age of personal control. Indeed, the title of three books featured in this chapter are *Self-Efficacy: The Exercise of Control* (Bandura, 1997), *Learned Helplessness: A Theory for the Age of Personal Control* (Peterson, Maier, & Seligman, 1993), and *The Psychology of Hope: You Can Get There from Here* (Snyder, 1994). In chapter 13, two more books will be featured: *Individual Differences and the Development of Perceived Control* (Skinner, Zimmer-Gembeck, & Connell, 1998) and *Desire for Control: Personality, Social, and Clinical Perspectives* (Burger, 1992). This is indeed the age of personal control. But is the seeking and gaining of personal control really all it's cracked up to be? Is more always better?

Generally speaking, people very much want control. Most of us overestimate how much control we have in situations, are optimistic about our ability to achieve control in these situations, believe we have more skill and greater ability than we actually have, and underestimate how vulnerable we are to overpowering circumstances (Lewinsohn et al., 1980; Seligman, 1991; Taylor & Brown, 1988, 1994; Weinstein, 1984, 1993). And generally speaking, people benefit from their perceptions of control in terms of psychological and physical well-being (Bandura, 1997; Rodin & Langer, 1977; Seligman, 1991). The conclusion

seems to be the following: Having control is good, and the more control you have, the better (Evans, Shapiro, & Lewis, 1993; Shapiro, Schwartz, & Astin, 1996; Thompson, 1981).

This conclusion presumes, however, that the world is a controllable place. Sometimes people unrealistically desire control, their skills and abilities are not up to par, and they find themselves in uncontrollable situations. In this light, control for all situations seems delusional. When you lack skill and live in an uncontrollable world, desiring too much control (i.e., a "control freak") can lead to anxiety, depression, and physical illness (e.g., cardiovascular hyperactivity, Shapiro et al., 1996).

Consider the figure below. People harbor personal control beliefs (i.e., psychological control factors). They bring these beliefs (self-efficacy, mastery orientation, hope) into situations that vary in how controllable and predictable they are. Some situations match the person's control beliefs, while others do not. Person-environment matches, rather than personal control beliefs per se, predict positive well-being and physical health outcomes. And person-environment mismatches, rather than personal vulnerability beliefs, predict physical illness and mental irregulation. The two-part conclusion is that (1) people sometimes want too much control for their own good, and (2) control is adaptive and beneficial when environments are controllable but it can be maladaptive when environments offer little opportunity for control (Shapiro et al., 1996).

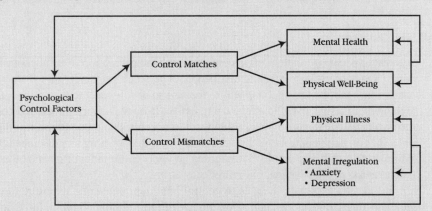

Source: Adapted from "Controlling Ourselves, Controlling Our World: Psychology's Role in Understanding Positive and Negative Consequences of Seeking and Gaining Control," by D.H. Shapiro Jr., C.E. Schwartz, and J.A. Astin, 1996, *American Psychologist, 51*, pp. 1213–1230. Copyright 1996 by the American Psychological Association. Adapted with permission.

circumstances worse (by keeping secret her lack of social skill). Thus, looked at in a different light, passivity can be, in some circumstances, a strategic coping response rather than a motivational deficit. This question of whether the exercise of personal control is always desirable is addressed in Box 9.

A second interpretation of helplessness argues that helplessness might fundamentally be a physiological, rather than a cognitive, phenomenon (Weiss, 1972). When animals experience inescapable shock, they experience a significant decline in the neurotransmitter norepinephrine (Weiss, 1972, Weiss et al., 1976; Weiss, Stone, & Harrell, 1970). Depletion of brain norepinephrine has been repeatedly associated with helplessness and giving-up responses (Weiss et al., 1976). Even when humans spend time solving difficult problems, they deplete their levels of brain glucose. With a low level of glucose to fuel the brain's activity, people have a difficult time mustering the motivation they need to solve problems. And when people eat high carbohydrate/low fat foods (e.g., bread, pasta), their motivation to solve problems rebounds with the corresponding rise in their brain glucose. What is changing in these examples is brain chemistry rather than cognitive expectations.

REACTANCE THEORY

Why do people sometimes do precisely the opposite of what they are told to do? Why do people sometimes resist another person's well-intended favor? Why does propaganda frequently backfire? These are the questions posed by reactance theorists (Brehm, 1966; Brehm & Brehm, 1981). Any instruction, any favor, any advice, no matter how well intended, has the potential to interfere with people's expected freedoms in making up their own minds. When children do precisely what they were told not to do, when gift recipients are more resentful than thankful, and when the targets of propaganda do the opposite of the source's intention, each performs a countermaneuver aimed at reestablishing a threatened sense of freedom. The term reactance refers to the psychological and behavioral attempt at reestablishing ("reacting" against) an eliminated or threatened freedom.

Reactance and Helplessness

A threat to personal freedom often coincides with the perception of an uncontrollable outcome. Reactance theory predicts that people experience reactance only if they expect to have some control over what happens to them. And people react to a loss of control by becoming more active, even hostile and aggressive. Both reactance and learned helplessness theories therefore focus on how people react to uncontrollable outcomes. But the two theories suggest that people act in very different ways. Recognizing this discrepancy, Camille Wortman and Jack Brehm (1975) proposed an integrative model of reactance and learned helplessness, which is shown in Figure 9.8.

If a person expects to be able to control important outcomes, exposure to uncontrollable outcomes arouses reactance (Wortman & Brehm, 1975). Thus, in the first few trials in a learned helplessness experiment, the person should show vigorous opposition to the uncontrollable environment. Recall that the dogs in the inescapable shock group in the learned helplessness studies first howled, kicked, and generally thrashed about for several

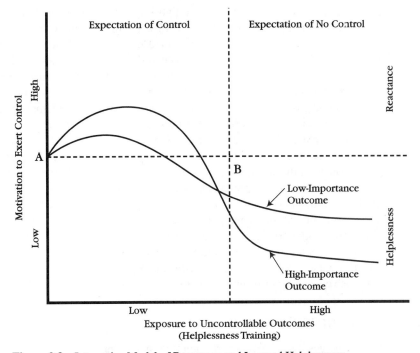

Figure 9.8 Integrative Model of Reactance and Learned Helplessness

Source: From "Responses to Uncontrollable Outcomes: An Integration of Reactance Theory and the Learned Helplessness Model," by C. B. Wortman and J. W. Brehm, 1975, in L. Berkowitz (Ed.), *Advances in Experimental Social Psychology* (Vol. 8, pp. 277–336): New York: Academic Press. Copyright 1975 Academic Press.

trials before eventually becoming helpless. The two lines graphed between points A and B in Figure 9.8 represent reactance responses. These active, assertive coping efforts usually pay off in life as they enable people and animals to reestablish their lost sense of control. Over time, however, if the environment continues to be uncontrollable, people eventually learn that all attempts at control are futile. Once a person becomes convinced that reactance behaviors exert little or no influence over the uncontrollable situation, he shows the passivity of helplessness. The lines graphed to the right of point B represent helplessness responses.

The critical difference in predicting whether an individual will show reactance or helplessness is the perceived status of the uncontrollable outcome. As long as the person perceives that coping behavior can effect outcomes, reactance behaviors persist. It is only after the person perceives a response-outcome independence (i.e., the unequivocal loss of a behavioral freedom) that he slips into helplessness. The critical information needed to interpret the relationships depicted in Figure 9.8 appears at the top of the figure, labeled "Expectation of Control" and "Expectation of No Control." Expectations of control foster reactance; expectations of no control foster helplessness.

Notice also that the figure shows two curved lines, one denoting the relationship between perceived control and motivation for a low-importance outcome and the other depicting the same relationship for a high-importance outcome. Reactance and helpless responses are exaggerated on those outcomes that the person most cares about and values, while reactance and helplessness are muted on low-importance outcomes (and may be zero for outcomes that have no importance to the person whatsoever; Mikulincer, 1986).

For an illustration of reactance and helplessness responses, consider the following experiment (Mikulincer, 1988). One group of participants worked on one unsolvable problem, a second group worked on a series of four unsolvable problems, and a third group did not work on any problems (control group). Mario Mikulincer reasoned that exposure to one unsolvable problem would produce reactance and actually improve performance, while repeated exposure to unsolvable problems would produce helplessness and impair performance. In the second phase of the experiment, all participants worked the same set of solvable problems. As predicted, participants given one unsolvable problem performed the best, participants given four unsolvable problems performed the worst, and participants not given any problems performed in between these two groups. This finding provides strong support for the ideas that (1) both reactance and helplessness arise from outcome expectancies; (2) reactance is rooted in perceived control, while helplessness is rooted in its absence; (3) a reactance response precedes a helplessness response; and (4) reactance enhances performance whereas helplessness undermines it.

PUTTING IT ALL TOGETHER: HOPE

Hope emerges out of a two-part cognitive motivational system. When people have both the motivation to work toward their goals and when people know ways to achieve those goals, they experience hope (Snyder, 1994; Synder et al., 1991). The first part of hope involves high agency, or the "can do" belief relating to a person's confidence in their capacity to accomplish the goals they set for themselves. The second part of hope involves clear pathways, or the belief that one has multiple pathways to those goals.

In reference to the terminology used so far in this chapter, agency represents self-efficacy and pathways represents mastery over helplessness. Together, high self-efficacy supports confidence while a mastery motivational orientation supports optimism. A glance back to Figure 9.1 shows how efficacy and outcomes work together and when both are positive the overall emotional experience is one of hope. The integration of confidence in one's self and optimism over one's outcomes nurtures and explains hope.

Central to the experience of hope is pathway thinking, or the belief that one can generate viable routes to desired goals, as people say to themselves, "I'll find a way to get this done" (Snyder, Lapointe, Crowson, & Early, 1998). The athlete preparing for a match or the salesperson trying to close a sale feels hope only when she can generate at least one, and often more than one, workable routes to the desired goal (scoring points, making a sale). Multiple pathways are important because environmental obstacles (opponent's strategy, competitor's products) often close off one pathway. Closing a pathway to a goal does not diminish hope if the performer has a number of alternative pathways to the goal. All goals have obstacles to their eventual attainment, so hope follows from knowing that one has more pathways to a goal that the environment has obstacles.

Agentic thinking within the experience of hope reflects the performer's perceived capacity to use those pathways to reach the goal, as people say to themselves, "I can do this" and "I am not going to let these obstacles stop me" (Snyder et al., 1998). As one pursues a pathway to a goal, agentic thinking ("Yes, I can do this") functions as the antidote or counterforce to environmental obstacles ("No, you will not be able to do this."). Hopeful thinking emerges only out of both agentic and pathways thinking (Snyder, 1994).

In college, high-hope freshers achieve higher GPAs and are more likely to graduate from college 5 years later than are low-hope freshers (Snyder et al., 2002). During athletic performance, high-hope track athletes outpeform low-hope athletes during stressful competitions (even after controlling for ability; Curry, Snyder, Cook, Ruby, & Rehm, 1997). Facing physical illnesses (e.g., chronic pain, blindness), high-hope patients remain appropriately energized and focused on finding pathways to cope with their illness (Elliott, Witty, Herrick, & Hoffman, 1991; Jackson et al., 1998). And when stressed, high-hope persons generate more strategies to cope with the stressor and endorse greater belief that they will use the various coping options available to them (Snyder, 1994).

Why do high-hope individuals outperform and outcope their low-hope counterparts? High-hope persons (Snyder, 1994; Snyder et al., 1998; Snyder et al., 2002):

1. Establish specific and short-term, rather than vague and long-term, goals.
2. Set mastery (learning), rather than performance, achievement goals.
3. Rely on internally self-set goals, rather than on externally, other-set goals.
4. Engage goals with intrinsic, rather than extrinsic, motivation.
5. Are less easily distracted by external obstacles or by task-irrelevant (distracting) thoughts and negative feelings.
6. Generate multiple pathways and pursue other avenues when stumped rather than stick stubbornly with one approach.
7. Have reservoirs of internally-generated determination ("I will get this done"; "Keep going!").
8. See more meaning in their lives as they reflect back on their lifelong progress in constructing and attaining valued goals.

From a cognitive-motivational point of view, high hope individuals tap into their motivational resources of confidence and high self-efficacy and also optimism and a mastery motivational orientation. In doing so, they find the motivational support to overcome life's obstacles and achieve the sort of coping and competent functioning shown in the eight outcomes listed above.

SUMMARY

The motivation to exercise personal control over one's outcomes in life emanates from the expectations people harbor as to how much or how little influence they have in producing desired events and in preventing undesired events. As people try to control events, they learn expectancies about their control. Expectations come in two types: efficacy and outcome. Efficacy expectations are forecasts about one's capacity to competently enact a particular course of action (e.g., "Can I do it?"). Outcome expectancies are forecasts that a particular outcome will be achieved (or prevented) once a given action is adequately executed (e.g., "Will it work?"). Before people are willing to exert strong coping efforts to exert personal control, both efficacy and outcome expectancies must be reasonably high.

Self-efficacy is the individual's belief that he "has what it takes" to marshal together the resources needed to cope effectively with the diverse and potentially overwhelming demands of a situation. Self-efficacy arises from (1) personal behavior history of trying to execute that particular course of action in the past, (2) observations of similar others as they execute the same behavior, (3) verbal persuasions (or pep talks) from others, and (4) physiological states such as an abnormally fast versus calm heartbeat. Once formed, self-efficacy effects the performer's (1) choice of activities and selection of environments (approach versus avoidance), (2) extent of effort and persistence, (3) the quality of thinking and decision making, and (4) emotional reactions, especially those related to stress and anxiety. Because self-efficacy beliefs can be acquired and because self-efficacy beliefs enable such productive ways of thinking, feeling, and behaving, self-efficacy serves as a model for personal empowerment. People who participate in therapy-like conditions (e.g., a mastery modeling program) to build stronger and more resilient self-efficacy beliefs respond by showing flexible, adaptive, and confident engagements with the world. Gains in self-efficacy counter and vanquish anxiety, doubt, and avoidance.

Learned helplessness is the psychological state that results when an individual expects that events in her life are uncontrollable. Helplessness is learned. As people learn that their behavior exerts a stronger influence over their outcomes than do outside influences, they learn a mastery motivational orientation. As people learn that their behavior exerts little or no influence over their outcomes while outside influences actually control what happens to them, they learn a helpless motivational orientation.

Learned helplessness theory relies on three fundamental components in explaining helplessness effects: contingency, cognition, and behavior. Contingency refers to the objective relationship between a person's behavior and the environment's positive or negative outcomes. Cognition includes all those mental processes (e.g., biases, attributions, expectancies) that the individual relies on to translate objective environmental contingencies into subjective personal control beliefs. Behavior refers to the person's voluntary coping behavior, and it varies along a continuum that extends from active and energetic to passive and withdrawing. Once it occurs, helplessness produces profound disruptions in motivation, learning, and emotion. The motivational deficit is a decreased willingness to engage in voluntary coping responses; the cognitive deficit is a pessimistic learning set that interferes with learning future response-outcome contingencies; and the emotional deficit involves the emergence of energy-depleting emotions such as depression to replace naturally occurring energy-mobilizing emotions such as frustration.

Reactance theory, like the learned helplessness model, explains how people react to uncontrollable life events. In short, expectations of controllability foster reactance, while expectations of uncontrollability foster helplessness. When confronting a situation that is difficult to control, individuals show an initial reactance response by becoming increasingly assertive in their psychological and behavioral attempts to reestablishing control. If reactance efforts fail to reestablish personal control, individuals then show a subsequent helplessness response.

Together, strong self-efficacy and strong mastery motivation combine to give people a confidence and optimism during encounters with the motivational problems they face. In doing so, hope integrates the personal control beliefs literature by showing how agentic thinking (self-efficacy) and pathway thinking (mastery vs. helplessness) function together to provide energy and direction for one's coping efforts. High-hope individuals, who possess resilient self-efficacy and strong mastery motivation, outperform and outcope low-hope individuals in domains such as academics, athletics, and physical illness.

READINGS FOR FURTHER STUDY

Self-Efficacy

BANDURA, A. (1988). Self-efficacy conception of anxiety. *Anxiety Research, 1,* 77–98.

BANDURA, A. (1989). Human agency in social cognitive theory. *American Psychologist, 44,* 1175–1184.

OZER, E. M., & BANDURA, A. (1990). Mechanisms governing empowerment effects: A self-efficacy analysis. *Journal of Personality and Social Psychology, 58,* 472–486.

Learned Helplessness

ALLOY, L. B., & ABRAMSON, L. V. (1982). Learned helplessness, depression, and the illusion of control. *Journal of Personality and Social Psychology, 42,* 1114–1126.

DIENER, C. I., & DWECK, C. S. (1978). An analysis of learned helplessness: Continuous changes in performance, strategy, and achievement cognitions following failure. *Journal of Personality and Social Psychology, 36,* 451–462.

MIKULINCER, M. (1986). Motivational involvement and learned helplessness: The behavioral effects of the importance of uncontrollable events. *Journal of Social and Clinical Psychology, 4,* 402–422.

Reactance

MIKULINCER, M. (1988). The relationship of probability of success and performance following unsolvable problems: Reactance and helplessness effects. *Motivation and Emotion, 12,* 139–153.

WORTMAN, C. B., & BREHM, J. W. (1975). Responses to uncontrollable outcomes: An integration of reactance theory and the learned helplessness model. In L. Berkowitz (Ed.), *Advances in experimental social psychology* (Vol. 8, pp. 277–336). New York: Academic Press.

Hope

SNYDER, C. R., SHOREY, H. S., CHEAVENS, J., PULVERS, K. M., ADAMS, V. H. III, & WIKLUND, C. (2002). Hope and academic success in college. *Journal of Educational Psychology, 94,* 820–826.

SNYDER, C. R., HARRIS, C., ANDERSON, J. R., HOLLERAN, S. A., IRVING, L. M., SIGMON, S. T., YOSHINOBU, L., GIBB, J., LANGELLE, C., & HARNEY, P. (1991). The will and the ways: Development and validation of an individual differences measure of hope. *Journal of Personality and Social Psychology, 60,* 570–585.

Chapter 10

The Self and Its Strivings

How have you been lately? Reflecting back on the last month, how many days have been happy ones? At school or work, how lively and satisfied have you felt? How are your relationships going? Are they providing you with experiences that leave you energized and fulfilled, or have they left you feeling mostly bland or frustrated? How are your personal finances? How is your health?

In the spirit of these questions, consider whether you agree or disagree with each of the following statements:

1. Many of my personal qualities trouble me enough that I wish I could change them.
2. I feel isolated and frustrated in interpersonal relationships.
3. When making important decisions, I rely on the judgments of others.
4. Often I am unable to change or improve my circumstances.
5. My life lacks meaning.
6. I have a sense of personal stagnation that often leaves me bored.

These six statements represent facets of psychological well-being. These are, in order, *self-acceptance*—positive evaluations of oneself; *positive interpersonal relations*—close, warm relationships with others; *autonomy*—self-determination; *environmental mastery*—sense of effectance in mastering circumstances and challenges; *purpose in life*—a sense of meaning that gives one's life a sense of direction and purpose; and *personal growth*—harboring a developmental trajectory characterized by improvement and growth (Ryff, 1989, 1995; Ryff & Keyes, 1995; Ryff & Singer, 2002). Your response on each of these dimensions reflects a distinct contour of self-functioning and psychological well-being. To be well psychologically is to possess positive self-regard, positive relationships with others, autonomy, environmental mastery, a sense of purpose, and a trajectory of growth.

Pursuing these qualities is the province of the self. And your answers to these questions reveal how well or how poorly the self is doing its job.

Table 10.1 describes these six dimensions of self-functioning in greater detail. The self benefits in terms of well-being by making progress in any one of these areas, but the self which is able to make progress in a number of these dimensions benefits particular well.

THE SELF

In a motivational analysis of the self and its strivings, three problems take center stage (Baumeister, 1987):

1. Defining or creating the self.
2. Relating the self to society.
3. Discovering and developing personal potential.

In the quest to define or create the self, we wonder about who we are, how others see us, how similar and how different we are from others, and whether we can become the person we want to be. In the quest to relate the self to society, we contemplate how we want to relate to others, what place we wish to occupy in the social world, and what soci-

Table 10.1   Six Dimensions of Psychological Well-Being

Self-Acceptance

High scorer: possesses a positive attitude toward the self; acknowledges and accepts multiple aspects of self, including good and bad qualities; feels positive about the past.

Low scorer: feels dissatisfied with self; is disappointed with what has occurred in past life; is troubled about certain qualities; wishes to be different than what he or she is.

Positive Relations with Others

High scorer: has warm, satisfying, trusting relationships with others; is concerned about the welfare of others; capable of strong empathy, affection, and intimacy; understands give-and-take of human relationships.

Low scorer: has few close, trusting relationships with others; finds it difficult to be warm, open, and concerned about others; is isolated and frustrated in interpersonal relationships; is not willing to make compromises to sustain important ties with others.

Autonomy

High scorer: is self-determining; is able to resist social pressures to think and act in certain ways; regulates behavior from within; evaluates self by personal standards.

Low scorer: is concerned about the expectations and evaluations of others; relies on judgments of others to make important decisions; conforms to social pressures to think and act in certain ways.

Environmental Mastery

High scorer: has a sense of mastery and competence in managing the environment; controls complex array of external activities; makes effective use of surrounding opportunities; is able to choose or create contexts suitable to personal needs and values.

Low scorer: has difficulty managing everyday affairs; feels unable to change or improve surrounding context; is unaware of surrounding opportunities; lacks sense of control over external world.

Purpose in Life

High scorer: has goals in life and a sense of directedness; feels there is meaning to present and past life; holds beliefs that give life purpose; has aims and objectives for living.

Low scorer: lacks a sense of meaning in life; has few goals or aims; lacks a sense of direction; does not see purpose in the past; has no outlooks or beliefs that give life meaning.

Personal Growth

High scorer: has a feeling of continued development; sees self as growing and expanding; is open to new experiences; has sense of realizing his or her potential; sees improvement in self and behavior over time; is changing in ways that reflect more self-knowledge and effectiveness.

Low scorer: has a sense of personal stagnation; lacks sense of improvement or expansion over time; feels bored and uninterested with life; feels unable to develop new attitudes or behaviors.

Source: From, Possible selves in adulthood and old age: A tale of shifting horizons, by C. D. Ryff, 1991, *Psychology and Aging, 6,* 286–295. Copyright 1991 by the American Psychological Association. Reprinted by permission.

etal roles are (and are not) available to us. In the quest to discover and develop the self, we explore what does and does not interest us, we internalize the values of those we respect, we strive to create meaning, we seek to discover and develop our talents, and we devote our time to developing some skills and relationships while we choose to ignore others.

Defining or creating the self shows how *self-concept* energizes and directs behavior. Some aspects of self-definition are simply ascribed to us (e.g., gender). Other aspects, however, must be gained through achievement and through acts of choice (e.g., career, friends, values). This responsibility makes our lifelong quest to define and create the self a motivational struggle.

Relating the self to society shows how *identity* energizes and directs behavior. In some respects, society is rigid in the roles it encourages or even allows individuals to pursue. In other respects, however, society is flexible. It gives the individual some choice and even some responsibility in determining one's relationships to others (e.g., partners) and to society (e.g., careers). These acts of choice and internalization of responsibility make the effort to relate the self to society a motivational struggle.

Discovering and developing the potential of the self is also a motivational struggle, one that reflects *agency*. Agency means that an agent (the self) has the power and intention to act. It reveals the motivation inherent within the self. Hence, agency communicates a natural motivational force that originates from within the person rather than from within the environment or culture. This developing sense of agency makes the potential of the self a motivational struggle.

The Problem with Self-Esteem

Before discussing self-concept, identity, and agency, it will be helpful to pause and challenge a cornerstone belief that many people endorse: Namely, the best way to increase another person's motivation is to increase his self-esteem. Teachers, employers, and coaches consistently and enthusiastically say that the way to motivate students, workers, and athletes is to increase their self-esteem. Make them feel good about who they are. Then watch as all sorts of wonderful things unfold.

Increasing self-esteem is a fine objective. It is, after all, correlated positively with being happy (Diener & Diener, 1996). The problem with boosting self-esteem as a motivational intervention, however, is that "there are almost no findings that self-esteem causes anything at all. Rather, self-esteem is caused by a whole panoply of successes and failures. . . . What needs improving is not self-esteem but improvement of our skills [for dealing] with the world" (Seligman, quoted in Azar, 1994). In other words, in the relationship between self-esteem and self-functioning, self-esteem is not a causal variable. In that spirit, one pair of researchers concluded that self-esteem "is mainly a consequence of cumulative achievement-related successes and failures and that it does not have a significant impact on later achievement" (Helmke & van Aken, 1995). These same researchers went on to argue for the merits of a "skill-development model" as the best way to build strong and resilient self-concepts in elementary-grade children.

The critical point to notice that is embedded within these two quotations is the direction of the causal effect between self-esteem and achievement/productivity/self-functioning. Self-esteem and achievement are correlated positively with one another (Bowles, 1999; Davies & Brember, 1999). However, increases in self-esteem do *not* produce corresponding increases in achievement; rather, increases in achievement produce corresponding increases in self-esteem (Byrne, 1984, 1986, 1996; Harter, 1993; Helmke & van Aken, 1995; Marsh, 1990; Scheier & Kraut, 1979; Shaalvik & Hagtvet, 1990). Self-esteem reflects how life it going, but it is not the source of motivation that allows people to make life go well. In conclusion, there is simply no evidence that boosting people's self-esteem will improve their functioning (Baumeister et al., 2003).

Low self-esteem is no bargain. People low in self-esteem tend to suffer unusually high levels of anxiety. The chief benefit of high self-esteem is that it buffers the self against depression (Alloy & Abramson, 1988) and anxiety (Greenberg et al., 1992; Solomon, Greenberg, & Pyszczynski, 1991). Thus, low self-esteem leaves the person vulnerable to the suffrages of anxiety. But just because low self-esteem is bad does not mean that attempts to inflate self-esteem are good. In fact, inflated self-esteem clearly has a dark side. People with inflated self-views are significantly more prone to aggression and acts of violence when their favorable self-views are threatened (Baumeister, Smart, & Boden, 1996). For instance, when people with very high self-esteem perceive they have just been publicly ridiculed or "dissed," they become unusually prone to acts of retaliatory aggression. For these two reasons—gains in self-esteem do not cause anything good, and threats to an inflated self-view is a prelude to retaliatory violence—the crusade to boost self-esteem is overrated.

If the above logic is true, then it is worth asking how the "self-esteem movement" got started in the first place. The movement owes its roots to 1986 when the state of California decided to boost the self-esteem of all state residents as a strategy to reduce school failure, welfare dependency, crime, unwanted pregnancy, and drug addiction. The thinking was that virtually all psychological problems were traceable to a person's low self-esteem (Branden, 1984). Following this lead (without any empirical evidence to support it), self-esteem boosting programs exploded on the scene in the form of programs like Upward Bound, Head Start, Early Training Project, and perhaps that classroom pep rally you went through in school yourself ("I *am* somebody!"). By the time empirical research caught up with these programs to test their effectiveness, results showed that these programs failed miserably to curb the sort of social problems identified by the California state legislatures (Baumeister et al., 2003).

In the end, the best conclusion to offer is that self-esteem is like happiness. Trying to be happy does not get you very far. Rather, happiness is a byproduct of life's satisfactions, triumphs, and positive relationships (Izard, 1991). In the same spirit, self-esteem exists as an end product of the self's adaptive and productive functioning. It is a byproduct of successfully measuring up to personal aspirations and to culturally mandated norms (Josephs, Markus, & Tafarodi, 1992). The same holds true for the six aspects of psychological well-being introduced earlier—self-acceptance, positive interpersonal relationships, autonomy, environmental mastery, purpose in life, and personal growth. Each is largely a byproduct of other pursuits. This chapter is about those "other pursuits." The motivationally significant pursuits of the self are (1) defining or creating the self (self-concept), (2) relating the self to society (identity), and (3) discovering and developing the self's potential (agency).

SELF-CONCEPT

Self-concepts are individuals' mental representations of themselves. Just as people have mental representations of other people (what teenagers are like), places (what the city of Chicago is like), and events (what Mardi Gras is like), people also have mental representations of themselves (what I am like). The self-concept is constructed from experiences and from reflections on those experiences.

To construct a self-concept, people attend to the feedback they receive in their day-to-day affairs that reveals their personal attributes, characteristics, and preferences. The building blocks people use to construct and define the self come from specific life experiences, such as the following:

- During the group discussion, I felt uncomfortable and self-conscious.
- On the school field trip to the zoo, I did not talk very much.
- At lunch, I avoided sitting with others.

During times of reflection, people do not remember their thousands of individual life experiences. Rather, people aggregate their experiences into general conclusions. Over time, people translate their multitude of specific experiences into a general representation of the self (e.g., given my inhibited experiences in groups, at the zoo, and during lunch, I perceive myself as "shy"). It is this general conclusion ("I'm shy"), rather than the specific experiences (in the preceding list), that people readily remember and use as building blocks for constructing and defining the self-concept (Markus, 1977).

Self-Schemas

Self-schemas are cognitive generalizations about the self that are domain-specific and are learned from past experiences (Markus, 1977, 1983). The earlier generalization of being shy exemplifies a self-schema. Being shy is both domain-specific (relationships with others) and learned from past experiences (during group discussions, field trips, lunchroom conversations). Being shy does not represent the self-concept, but it does represent the self in one particular domain, relationships with others.

In athletics, a high-school student constructs a domain-specific self-schema by looking back on the week's experiences and recalling his last-place finish in a 100-meter dash, his abandonment of a mile run because of exhaustion, and his repeated crashes into the bar during the high jump competition. In a different domain such as school, however, the same student might recall scoring well on a test, answering all the questions the teacher asked, and having a poem accepted for a school publication. Eventually, if the experiences in athletics and if the experiences in the classroom are consistent and frequent enough, the student will generalize a self that is, for the most part, incompetent in athletics but skillful in school. These generalizations (athletically inept; intellectually smart) constitute additional self-schemas in different domains (like being shy in the domain of interpersonal relationships).

The self-concept is a collection of domain-specific self-schemas. Which self-schemas are involved in the definition of the self-concept are those life domains that are most important to the person (Markus, 1977). The major life domains in early childhood, for instance, typically include cognitive competence, physical competence, peer acceptance, and behavioral conduct (Harter & Park, 1984). In adolescence, the major life domains generally include scholastic competence, athletic competence, physical appearance, peer acceptance, close friendships, romantic appeal, and behavioral conduct or morality (Harter, 1990). By college, the major life domains include scholastic competence, intellectual ability, creativity, job competence, athletic competence, physical appearance, peer acceptance, close friendships, romantic relationships, relationships with parents, morality, and sense of humor (Harter, 1990; Neemann & Harter, 1986). What this litany of major life domains shows is the range of self-schemas any one person is likely to possess at different stages in his or her life cycle. The specific life domains vary from one person to the next, but these domains illustrate the typical age-related structure of the self-concept (Harter, 1988; Kihlstrom & Cantor, 1984; Markus & Sentisk, 1982; Scheier & Carver, 1988).

Motivational Properties of Self-Schemas

Self-schemas generate motivation in two ways. First, self-schemas, once formed, direct an individual's behavior that elicits feedback that is consistent with the established self-schemas. That is, because a person sees himself or herself as shy, that person directs his or her future behavior in interpersonal domains like meetings and conversations in ways that produce feedback that confirms the person's "I'm shy" self-view. Shy people want to act in shy ways and thus receive social feedback that they are shy, just like humorous people want to act in humorous ways and receive social feedback that they are humorous. This is so because self-schemas direct behavior in ways that confirm our established self-view. In contrast, feedback that is inconsistent with the established self-schema produces a motivational tension. In short, when people behave in self-schema consistent ways, they experience a comfort from the consistency and from the self-confirmation; when people behave in self-schema inconsistent ways, they experience tension from the inconsistency and from the self-disconfirmation.

The basic idea behind the motivation for self-schema consistency is that if a person is told she is introverted when she believes she is extraverted, that contradictory feedback generates a motivational tension. The tension motivates the self to restore consistency. An extravert who receives feedback that she is an introvert directs her behavior toward proving that she is indeed an extravert. Therefore, people behave in self-schema-consistent ways to prevent feeling an aversive motivational tension. If prevention does not work, then people behave in ways to restore their self-schema consistency.

Second, self-schemas generate motivation to move the present self toward a desired future self. Much like goal setting's discrepancy-creating process (chapter 8), an ideal possible self initiates goal-directed behavior. Thus, the student who wants to become an actor initiates whatever actions seem necessary for advancing the self from being a "student" to becoming an "actor." "Student" constitutes the present self, while "actor" constitutes the ideal self.

Seeking ideal possible selves is a fundamentally different motivational process than is striving to maintain a consistent self-view. Seeking possible selves is a goal-setting process that invites self-concept development (see section: Possible Selves), whereas seeking a consistent self-view is a verification process that preserves self-concept stability (see section: Consistent Self).

Consistent Self

Once an individual establishes a well-articulated self-schema in a particular domain, he generally acts to preserve that self-view. Once established, self-schemas become increasingly resistant to contradictory information (Markus, 1977, 1983).

People preserve a consistent self by actively seeking out information consistent with their self-concept and by ignoring information that contradicts their self-view (Swann,

1983, 1985, 1999; Tesser, 1988). It is psychologically disturbing to believe one thing is true about the self yet be told that the reverse is actually the case. Imagine the turmoil of the career politician who loses a local election or the turmoil of the star athlete who does not get drafted into the professional ranks. Inconsistency and contradiction generate an emotional discomfort that signals that consistency needs to be restored. It is this negative affective state that produces the motivation to seek self-confirmatory, and to avoid self-disconfirmatory, information and feedback.

To ensure that other people see us as we see ourselves, we adopt self-presentational signs and symbols that announce who we are (or think we are). Examples of such signs and symbols include the appearances we convey in our physical selves through clothes, dieting, weightlifting, cosmetic surgery, and even our possessions and the kinds of cars we drive. We also use external appearances to communicate to others our political preferences, social status, sexual preferences, and so forth. For instance, the person wearing a Green Bay Packers jacket sends a self-presentational message to others along the lines of, "I am a sports enthusiast and an athlete." A bumper sticker on one's automobile might communicate a similar message. In doing so, the person strives to develop a social environment that will feedback self-confirmatory information.

Further, in the name of self-schema preservation, we intentionally choose to interact with others who treat us in ways that are consistent with our self-view, and we intentionally avoid others who treat us in ways that are inconsistent with our self-view, a process referred to as "selective interaction" (Robinson & Smith-Lovin, 1992; Swann, Pelham, & Krull, 1989). By choosing friends who confirm our self-view and by keeping our distance from those who contradict that self-view, we make self-confirmatory feedback more likely and we make self-disconfirmatory feedback less likely. Selective interaction explains why we choose our interaction partners—our friends, roommates, tutors, teachers, teammates, spouses, and so on—namely, because we use social interactions to maintain and verify our self-view (Swann, 1987). Selective interaction also explains why people tend to break up a relationship in which the other person sees the self differently than one sees oneself, as in divorce (De La Ronde & Swann, 1998; Katz, Beach, & Anderson, 1996; Schafer, Wickram, & Keith, 1996). By marrying one person rather than another, the individual selects an interaction partner who will be a source of self-consistent feedback; and by divorcing a marriage partner, the individual might be removing a source of self-discrepant feedback.

Despite preventive efforts, self-discrepant feedback does sometimes occur (as it did for the career politician and star athlete). The first line of defense in the effort to maintain a consistent self is to distort that information until it loses its status as discrepant information. In the face of discrepant self-schema feedback, the individual may ask if the feedback is valid, if the source of the feedback is trustworthy, and how important or relevant this feedback is (Crary, 1966; Markus, 1977; Swann, 1983). For example, a student with a self-view of being intelligent but who fails a college course might functionally discredit that feedback by arguing against (1) its validity (i.e., the student scored as unintelligent only because she was too busy to focus), (2) the professor's judgment (i.e., the student thinks her professor is a nitwit), and (3) its importance or relevance (i.e., the student feels it is not what she knows, but who she knows that is important). People also counter disconfirming feedback with compensatory self-inflation (Greenberg & Pyszczynski, 1985), self-affirmation (Steele, 1988), and a barrage of new behaviors to prove one's actual self-view (e.g., "No, no; here let me show you...."; Swann & Hill, 1982). What all these means for maintaining self-concept consistency have in common is that they marshal forward counter-examples and counter-explanations to essentially discredit the otherwise self-discrepant feedback. Once invalidated, self-discrepant feedback can be ignored and the self-view preserved.

An individual's confidence that his self-schema is valid and true constitutes "self-concept certainty" (Harris & Snyder, 1986; Swann & Ely, 1984). When high, self-concept certainty anchors stable self-schemas. Discrepant feedback rarely changes a self-schema. When low, however, discrepant feedback can eventually instigate self-schema change. Conflict between an uncertain self-schema and discrepant feedback instigates a "crisis self-verification" (Swann, 1983, 1999): How do we verify the accuracy of our self-view, given contradictory feedback and an uncertain self-view? People resolve the self-verification crisis by seeking out additional domain-relevant feedback (Swann, 1983), a sort of "best two out of three to break the tie" approach for figuring out who they are.

The rather complicated self-verification process appears in Figure 10.1. Individuals start with a representation of self (a self-schema) and a preference for self-confirmatory feedback, as illustrated at the top of the figure. So most everyday feedback takes place only between the two uppermost boxes in Figure 10.1 (Preference for Self-Confirmatory Feedback → Routine Self-Verification). Things begin to get complicated only after the

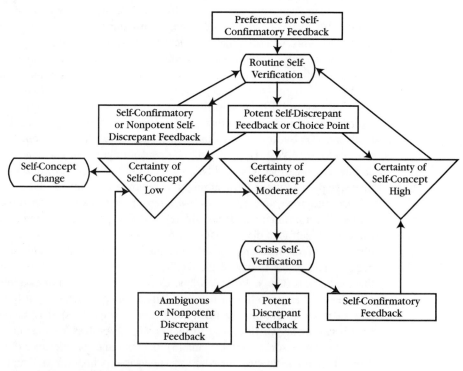

Figure 10.1 Processes Underlying Self-Verification and Self-Concept Change

Source: From "Bringing Social Reality Into Harmony With Self," by W. B. Swann Jr., 1983, in J. Suls and A. Greenwald (Eds.), *Psychological Perspectives on the Self* (Vol. 2, pp. 33–66). Hillsdale, NJ: Lawrence Erlbaum.

appearance of self-discrepant social feedback ("Potent Self-Discrepant Feedback" in Figure 10.1). People handle mild self-discrepant information rather well (Swann & Hill, 1982), as discussed earlier with the marshaling forward of counter-evidence. The two arrows between Routine Self-Verification and Self-Confirmatory or Nonpotent Self-Discrepant Feedback play themselves out in daily life as people discredit discrepant feedback and marshal forward compensatory self-affirmations. Mild self-discrepant feedback is therefore rather easily integrated into routine self-verification. The effect of potent (strong) disconfirming feedback on self-schema change, however, is not so easily integrated. The effect of potent disconfirming feedback depends on self-concept certainty (the three triangles in the middle of the figure). When self-concept certainty is low (triangle on the left), potent feedback *can* overwhelm preexisting self-schemas and instigate self-concept change. When self-concept certainty is high (triangle on the right), however, potent feedback is evaluated as only one piece of information in the context of a lifetime of historical information (e.g., "I was outgoing this time, but I was not outgoing on 100 occasions in the past; therefore, I still think I am shy, all things considered.").

The most interesting case, developmentally speaking, occurs when self-concept certainty is moderate (triangle in the middle). When self-concept certainty is moderate and the person faces potent self-discrepant feedback (as did the politician and athlete), the individual experiences the self-verification crisis. During a self-verification crisis, the individual suspends judgment and seeks out additional feedback. If the additional feedback is very convincing, the self-verification crisis does not change the self-view but instead lowers self-concept certainty. It is the lowered self-concept certainty that makes the person vulnerable to subsequent self-concept change in the future. Notice, for instance, that the only path to "Self-Concept Change" is from low self-concept certainty (as shown on the far left side of the figure). If the additional feedback is self-confirming, the "best two out of three tie" is broken in favor of the preexisting self-view and the self-verification crisis ends by strengthening self-concept certainty.

Before self-schemas change, (1) self-concept certainty must be low and (2) self-discrepant feedback must be potent and unambiguous—that is, difficult to discredit (Swann, 1983, 1985, 1987). Though self-concept can change, it is worth repeating that self-concept change is the exception rather than the rule. The rule is routine self-verification, a process that leads to a portrait of the self as an artitect of its own design so to speak—the self creates, builds, and maintains itself (McNulty & Swann, 1994).

Possible Selves

Self-schemas sometimes change in response to social feedback. But it is much more likely that self-schemas change by a second, more proactive and intentional way. Self-schema change can occur through a deliberate effort to advance the present self toward a desired future possible self. Possible selves represent individuals' ideas of what they would like to become and also what they are afraid of becoming (Markus & Nurius, 1986; Markus & Ruvolo, 1989). Some hoped-for selves might include, for instance, the successful self, the creative self, the rich self, the thin self, or the popular self; some feared selves might include the unemployed self, the disabled self, the overweight self, or the rejected self.

Possible selves are mostly social in origin, as the individual observes the selves modeled by others (Markus & Nurius, 1986). The individual sees the current self as his or her "present state" and sees the role model as a desired, future "ideal self." Seeing the discrepancy, the individual makes an inference that he or she could become, just like the successful role model became, that desired self. For instance, a child might watch performers in a musical and aspire to be a singer. Possible selves do not always arise from our observations of positive models, though, as a person might read in the newspaper of massive job layoffs and fear that she too could become unemployed. In this case, the individual sees the current self as his or her "present state" and sees the unsuccessful role model as an undesired future "feared self."

Possible selves represent the future self. The motivational function of a possible self therefore operates like that of a goal (or personal striving). A possible self provides the individual with an attractive incentive for which to strive. It can therefore act as a potent impetus for action by energizing effort and persistence and by directing attention and strategic planning (see Chapter 8).

Possible selves add an important piece of the puzzle in understanding how the self develops. Possible selves are essentially mental representations of attributes, characteristics, and abilities that the self does not yet possess (e.g., "I would like to become a physician, though I don't know much about human anatomy or surgical techniques."). When the self does not have the evidence or feedback to confirm the emerging possible self, one of two outcomes follows (Markus, Cross, & Wurf, 1990). On the one hand, an absence of supportive evidence (or the presence of disconfirming feedback) will lead the self to reject and abandon the possible self. On the other hand, the possible self can energize and direct action so that the attributes, characteristics, and abilities of the self actually and do begin to materialize (Cross & Markus, 1994; Nurius, 1991; Oyserman & Markus, 1990). Thus, the possible self's motivational role is to link the present self with ways to become the possible (ideal) self. Hence, an individual pursuing a possible self relies little on the present self-schema and much on the hoped-for self, possibly asking questions such as the following: If I am going to become my possible self, then how should I behave? What activities should I pursue? What education do I need? (Cantor et al., 1986; Markus & Nurius, 1986; Markus & Wurf, 1987).

The notion of possible selves portrays the self as a dynamic entity with a past, present, and future (Cantor et al., 1986; Day et al., 1994; Ryff, 1991). The individual without a possible self in a particular domain lacks an important cognitive basis for developing abilities in that domain (Cross & Markus, 1994). An individual who can envision a possible self in the domain engenders feelings of competence and acts to attain the future view of self (Cross & Markus, 1994, 1999; Markus, Cross, & Wurf, 1990). Perhaps, the reader can look back at his or her own effort devoted to college courses and ask the following: To what extent did a possible self relate to each course I completed or dropped, to each book I have or have not read, and to each lecture I attended or skipped? The presence of a possible self creates a proactive motivation to develop the self in goal-directed ways.

To illustrate that positive selves play a positive role in the development of the self over the life span, researchers asked young adults (average age, 19), middle-aged adults (average age, 46), and old-aged adults (average age, 73) to rate their present self, future self, past self, and ideal self along the six dimensions of well-being listed earlier in Table 10.1 (Ryff, 1991). The data for the first of these dimensions—self-acceptance—appear in Figure 10.2. Young adults rated their present self-acceptance higher than their past self-acceptance, showing improvement in self-acceptance from adolescence (past self) to young adulthood (present self). They rated their ideal self-acceptance even higher, showing a

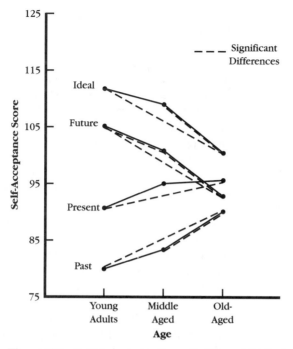

Figure 10.2 Self-Acceptance Scores for Young, Middle-Aged, and Old-Aged Adults According to the Past, Present, Future, and Ideal Selves

Source: From, Possible selves in adulthood and old age: A tale of shifting horizons, by C. D. Ryff, 1991, *Psychology and Aging, 6,* 286–296. Copyright 1991 by the American Psychological Association. Reprinted by permission.

large "present self—ideal self" discrepancy. Because they had such an optimistic ideal self, young adults forecast very high self-acceptance during their middle age (future self). These data show that the embracing of a positive ideal self does seem to lead young adults to improve their well-being during adolescence (present self > past self) and to anticipate improvement in their well-being in the years to come (future self > present self).

Middle-age adults showed a very similar pattern of developmental growth (see Figure 10.2). The findings for older adults were different. Older adults did not harbor such optimistic ideal selves. Because they did not embrace a large "present self—ideal self" discrepancy to develop the self in goal-directed ways, they rated their past, present, and future self (in terms of self-acceptance) similarly. Overall, these data show that when people visualize and pursue positive possible future selves, they are able to construct a goal-directed vision for themselves that motivates developmental improvement and progress over the years (Ryff, 1991).

COGNITIVE DISSONANCE

Most people harbor a rather favorable view of themselves. Most people see themselves as competent, moral, and reasonable. Such a self-view is represented cognitively as a set of beliefs about the self. Sometimes, however, people engage in behavior that leaves them feeling stupid, immoral, and unreasonable. For instance, people smoke cigarettes, toss litter, tell white lies, neglect to recycle, fail to wear condoms during sex, drive their cars recklessly, skip classes, act rudely toward strangers, and engage in other such hypocritical conduct. When beliefs about who the self is and what the self does are inconsistent (i.e., believing one thing, yet actually behaving in the opposite way), people experience a psychologically uncomfortable state referred to as "cognitive dissonance" (Aronson, 1969, 1992, 1999; Festinger, 1957; Gerard, 1992; Harmon-Jones & Mills, 1999).

With cognitive consistency, two beliefs are consonant when one belief follows from the other (being a moral person and telling the truth). With cognitive dissonance, two beliefs are dissonant when the opposite of one belief follows from the other (being a moral person but lying). Just how psychologically uncomfortable cognitive dissonance is depends on its magnitude. When intense and uncomfortable enough, dissonance takes on motivational properties, and the person begins to seek ways to eliminate, or at least reduce, the dissonance.

Imagine the following scenario of a woman whose sense of self includes pro-environmental beliefs. She believes in clean water, clean air, clean land, energy conservation, and nature preservation. And she believes that polluted air, polluted land, energy consumption, and overdevelopment are immoral and unreasonable. Her pro-environmental beliefs are all consonant with one another (i.e., believing in clear water is consistent with believing in nature preservation). But suppose she reads an article in the newspaper that says that automobile exhaust fumes are rapidly and irreversibly depleting the ozone layer. Further, according to the article, used automobile tires are littering the rivers and crowding the landfills. Suppose further that this environmentalist drives her car to work every day, and she needs her car for many additional purposes as well. She loves the environment, but she needs her car. She believes one thing, but she does another. This is an air of hypocrisy, and it is this experience of hypocrisy between self and action that causes dissonance (Aronson, 1999; Fried & Aronson, 1995).

The experience of dissonance is psychologically aversive (Elliot & Devine, 1994). People seek to reduce it, and they do so in one of four ways (Festinger, 1957; Harmon-Jones & Mills, 1999; Simon, Greenberg, & Brehm, 1995):

- Remove the dissonant belief
- Reduce the importance of the dissonant belief
- Add a new consonant belief
- Increase the importance of the consonant belief

Our environmentalist, for instance, might (1) quit driving her car and start riding a bicycle, or she might come to believe that volcano ash, not automobile exhaust, is responsible for the hole in the ozone layer (thereby removing the dissonant belief); (2) trivialize her immoral or unreasonable act of driving by justifying that her driving to work will have no impact on the global condition, especially when considering how much worse pollution is at the factories and refineries (thereby reducing the importance of the dissonant belief; Simon, Greenberg, & Brehm, 1995); (3) read articles that reassure her that science is hard at work and will soon solve the pollution problem, or she might think of how truly enjoyable and useful it is to drive her car (thereby adding a new consonant belief, or two); or (4) think to herself that car exhaust proves that the city needs more bike trails, and the government needs emission-control device laws for all automobiles (thereby increasing the importance of the consonant belief). How resistant to change these beliefs are depends on (1) how close to reality they are (e.g., Will science really find a solution?), (2) how important or central they are to one's view of the self (Simon et al., 1995; Thibodeau & Aronson, 1992), and (3) how much pain and cost must be endured (e.g., How painful will it be to quit driving a car?). Therefore, reality, importance, and personal costs work to support one's current beliefs, while dissonance stirs up a belief system that puts pressure on hypocritical ways of thinking and behaving. It is a psychological competition—reality versus dissonance—with motivational implications.

Dissonance-Arousing Situations

Human beings frequently encounter information that is dissonant with their beliefs and values, and they sometimes engage in behavior that is dissonant with their beliefs and values. Four specific situations illustrate dissonance-arousing circumstances: choice, insufficient justification, effort justification, and new information.

Choice

People often choose between alternatives. In some cases, the choice between alternatives is easy, as the merits of one alternative far outweigh the merits of its rival. In other cases, the choice is not so easy, as both alternatives offer a number of advantages and disadvantages. If a person is choosing between apartments, this person must consider that one might be in a convenient location but expensive while the other might be in an inconvenient location but inexpensive. Once such a difficult choice is made, people experience dissonance. As soon as the choice for one apartment is made, one must face the facts that the chosen apartment has a small kitchen while the rejected apartment had a larger kitchen and was cheaper. Given dissonance (or "post-decision regret"), the person engages in cognitive work to manipulate the relative desirability of the two alternatives. Dissonance is resolved by appreciating the chosen alternative—viewing it more positively, and by depreciating the rejected alternative—viewing it more negatively (Brehm, 1956; Gilovich, Medvec, & Chen, 1995; Knox & Inkster, 1968; Younger, Walker, & Arrowood, 1977). To illustrate this process for yourself, simply ask a person both before and after acting on a difficult choice the following question: "How sure are you that your choice is the correct one?" Whether the choice involves deciding between restaurants, classes, or marriage partners, post-choice decision makers are invariably more confident in the wisdom of their choices than are those still in the decision-making process.[1]

Insufficient Justification

Insufficient justification addresses how people explain their actions for which they have little or no external prompting. For example, people might ask themselves why they donated money to a charity or why they stopped to pick up litter. In one experiment, researchers asked participants to engage in a terribly dull and pointless task (Festinger & Carlsmith, 1959). Afterwards, an experimenter asked each participant to tell a lie to the

---

[1] A good illustration of this phenomenon is the often heard (yet absurd) quote from a person looking back on life, "If I had to live my life over again, I wouldn't change a thing—not where I lived, what school I attended, who I married, which career I pursued, nor anything I said or did."

next hour's participant, saying that the task was really quite entertaining. Half received $1 for the telling (insufficient justification for lying), while the other half received $20 (sufficient justification for lying). After the participants complied (and they all did), a different experimenter asked each participant to rate how interesting the task was. Those with insufficient justification ($1) reported liking the task significantly more than those with sufficient justification ($20). Those paid $20 had little dissonance to wrestle with (i.e., "I know why I lied—to earn the big bucks!"). Those paid a measly dollar, however, had to wrestle the dissonance brought on by deceiving another without good reason (e.g., "I don't know why I lied."). With $1 worth of insufficient justification, however, there exists good reason for changing one's attitude toward a greater liking of the task by actually thinking the task was not that boring: "If the task is not boring, then I didn't lie, did I?"

Effort Justification

During initiation rituals in the military, fraternities, sororities, athletic teams, neighborhood gangs, reality television shows, and other groups, recruits often exert great effort and perform extreme behaviors that must later be justified. Consider the Army private who parachutes out of an airplane as part of boot-camp training. For novice recruits, parachuting is extreme behavior. To justify why they would put their lives on the line like this, privates typically endorse a rather extreme liking for the behavior. Extreme behaviors breed extreme beliefs: "If I did *that*, then I must really *love* this place!" Dissonance theory proposes that the attractiveness of a task increases as a direct function of the magnitude of effort expended to complete it (Aronson & Mills, 1959; Beauvois & Joule, 1996; Rosenfeld, Giacalone, & Tedeschi, 1984). People who engage in extreme behavior need to develop correspondingly extreme values (Aronson, 1988).

New Information

As you listen to the radio, watch television, attend lectures, read the newspaper, and interact with others, you expose yourself to opportunities to contradict your beliefs. One group of researchers followed the Seekers, a cult-like group convinced that their city and the entire western coast of the Americas would be destroyed by a great flood on a specific day (Festinger, Riecken, & Schachter, 1956, 1958). The specific day of cataclysm came and passed rather uneventfully, so the Seekers found their cherished belief of doom unequivocally disconfirmed. Given belief disconfirmation, what were the dissonance-suffering Seekers to do? Some did reject their belief and dropped out of the group. Other Seekers, however, were more rationalizing than rational. They saw the disconfirmation as a test of their commitment to the cause and responded with strong, persistent attempts at proselytizing. By proselytizing, the latter group tried to resolve their dissonance by adding new consonant beliefs (i.e., new people who would agree with their beliefs).

Motivational Processes Underlying Cognitive Dissonance

People engage in all sorts of behaviors that imply that they are incompetent, immoral, or unreasonable. Inconsistency between what one believes (I am competent) and what one does (I acted incompetently) creates the cognitive inconsistency that is dissonance. Being psychologically uncomfortable, people implement various strategies for reducing dissonance (as discussed earlier: remove the dissonant belief, add a new consonant belief, etc.). By changing the number of consonant or dissonant cognitions or by changing the level of importance attached to consonant or dissonant cognitions, people reduce, and sometimes even eliminate, dissonance.

The sequence of events depicted in Figure 10.3 summarizes the psychological processes underlying cognitive dissonance motivation and people's attempts to reduce or eliminate it (Harmon-Jones & Mills, 1999). With cognitive consistency, action flows from the self in ways that are effective and nonconflicting. In the face of dissonance-arousing situational events, like the four discussed above, however, cognitive inconsistency and dissonance motivation arise and motivate changes in ways of believing or behaving. Therefore, dissonance as a motivational state revolves mostly around eliminating a rather ephemeral negative emotional state so that thinking and behaving can proceed in ways that are effective, smooth, and nonconflicting (Gerard, 1992; Harmon-Jones & Mills, 1999; Jones & Gerard, 1967).

Most dissonance researchers portray dissonance motivation through the analogy of pain—the person changes beliefs or behaviors in order to eliminate the aversive, persistent, and uncomfortable experience. But this characterization of an aversive motivational state is not all gloom and doom. Dissonance can be used to accomplish productive social goals too. For instance, using a dissonance framework, researchers have been successful in changing people's attitudes and behaviors toward pro-social causes such as using condoms during sex (Aronson, Fried, & Stone, 1991), conserving natural resources (e.g., water; Dickerson, et al., 1992), and reducing prejudice (Leippe & Eisenstadt, 1994). The conclusion from each of these three experiments may be summarized succinctly as follows: "Saying, or doing, is believing." Beliefs follow from (and act to justify) what one says and does. For instance, if you join your friend while she walks in the multiple sclerosis walk-a-thon, your attitude toward patients with multiple sclerosis will probably start to change for the better (i.e., add a new consonant belief to justify the effort). The fact that you walked in a charity's marathon is effort that needs to be justified, especially if it rained.

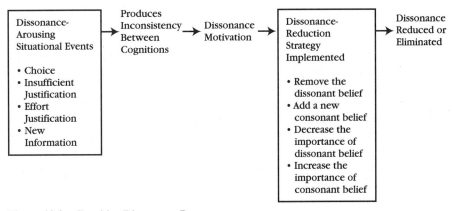

Figure 10.3   Cognitive Dissonance Processes

Self-Perception Theory

An alternative interpretation of cognitive dissonance is that people do not develop and change their beliefs in response to a negative emotional state born in cognitive contradiction (i.e., dissonance) but, rather, from self-observations of their behavior. For example, we eat squid for whatever reason (maybe we did not know it was squid because the restaurant referred to it as calamari) and after doing so we presume that since we ate squid, we must therefore like it. Acquiring or changing attitudes via self-observations of one's own behavior is the basic tenet to self-perception theory (Bem, 1967, 1972; Bem & McConnell, 1970).

Both cognitive dissonance theory and self-perception theory revolve around the tenet that "saying, or doing, is believing." The difference between the two theories is that cognitive dissonance theory argues that beliefs change because of negative affect from cognitive inconsistencies, whereas self-perception theory argues that we simply come to believe whatever we do and say.

The dissonance versus self-perception debate generated a great deal of research (Elliot & Devine, 1994; Fazio, Zanna, & Cooper, 1977, 1979; Ronis & Greenwald, 1979; Ross & Shulman, 1973; Snyder & Ebbesen, 1972; Zanna & Cooper, 1976). The conclusion was that both cognitive dissonance and self-perception theories are correct, but each applies to a different set of circumstances. Self-perception theory applies best to situations in which people's beliefs are initially vague, ambiguous, and weak. In such cases, people do indeed draw inferences from their behavior. For example, suppose you go to the supermarket to buy hand lotion but have little or no brand preference. After you pick brand X instead of brand Y, by chance or because of a coupon, the next time you tend to buy the same lotion. According to a self-perception theory interpretation because you bought brand X the first time, you must, therefore, now prefer that brand. On the other hand, dissonance theory applies best to situations in which people's beliefs are initially clear, salient, and strong. In the domains of the self-concept, for instance, people hold well-entrenched self-views. In those cases, people do indeed experience negative emotion following counter-attitudinal behavior.

IDENTITY

A second major aspect of the self is identity. Identity is the means by which the self relates to society, as it captures the essence of who one is within a cultural context (Deaux et al., 1995; Gecas & Burke, 1995). Of course, people have unique personality traits and strivings, but people also are members of social and cultural groups. These cultures and social groups offer identities to their individual members, and it is within this cultural or social context that people play out a culturally- or socially-defined role. Once a person inhabits a role, the identity directs the person to pursue some behaviors (identity-confirming behaviors) and to avoid other behaviors (identity-disconfirming behaviors).

Five broad parameters of identity include (with illustrative roles in parentheses) relationships (friend, grandfather), vocations (musician, salesperson), political affiliations (Republican, liberal), stigma groups (smoker, homeless person), and ethnic groups (Catholic, Southerner; Deaux et al., 1995). In addition to inhabiting these larger cultural roles, people further find themselves in a host of social roles, such as student, mother, jogger, and poet.

Roles

A role consists of cultural expectations for behavior from persons who hold a particular social position (Gross, Mason, & McEachern, 1958). Each of us holds a number of different social positions (roles), and which role we inhabit at any given time depends on the situation we are in and the people with whom we are interacting. For instance, in a college classroom, you probably assume the role of student as you interact with other students and with a professor. From a sociological point of view, it is not so much that Joe is interacting with Mary, Sue, and Jamar (individuals with unique motives and personalities) as it is that an inhabitant of the "professor" role interacts with several inhabitants of the "student" role. When you leave the classroom and go to your job at the psychology clinic, the role you occupy is very likely to change as you might assume the role of a counselor as you interact with clients. At home, your role and the roles of those you interact with might change yet again as you assume the role of mother (or father) who interacts with a daughter.

While assuming one role rather than another, people change how they act. They change the topic of their conversation, the vocabulary they use, the tone of their voice, and so forth. Even though "Mary" is still the same person, she converses in very different ways when she finds herself in the role of "professor" versus "mother." Behavior varies to such an extent from one role to the next that it makes sense to speak of a person's set of identities rather than his or her identity. Individuals have many identities, and they present to others the particular identity that is most appropriate for the situation. For instance, if you telephone an office, the person who answers your call is likely assuming a role of a receptionist. Figuring out who you are (what role the situation places you in) and who it is you are talking to is a burden placed on the person answering the phone.

Perhaps that sounds silly, but deciding what to say and what to do is actually quite difficult when the identities of the self and others remain in question. Knowing what roles the self and others hold in a given situation tells interactants which behaviors and which ways of interacting are most and least appropriate (Foote, 1951). Once you know that a "client" is telephoning a "receptionist," both people know how to behave, what to say, and how the conversation will go. The client expresses behaviors that are consistent with a client role, and the receptionist expresses behaviors that are consistent with that role.

Sociologists refer to this process of figuring out roles as the "definition of the situation" (Goffman, 1959; Gonas, 1977). Whenever people participate socially, their first task is to define the roles for the self and for others. Once done, social interaction can proceed to the extent that both interactants agree on their identities and on the definition of the situation.

Affect Control Theory

According to affect control theory (Heise, 1979, 1985; MacKinnon, 1994; Smith-Lovin & Heise, 1988), people act differently from one situation to the next because they inhabit different identities. Cultural and social groups offer a wide range of identities, and each of these identities has an expected behavioral profile associated with it. In affect control theory, the multitude of possible identities anyone is likely to inhabit is represented numerically along three dimensions, known as EPA: evaluation (E; level of goodness), potency (P; level of powerfulness), and activity (A; level of liveliness; Osgood, May, & Miron, 1975; Osgood, Suci, & Tannenbaum, 1957). For instance, how good, how powerful, and how lively is a teacher? a lawyer? a drug addict? The important point is that to understand identity-motivated action one does not need to keep track of a hundred different identities; instead, one needs only to know the "EPA profile" of the identity the person currently inhabits.

EPA scores generally range from –4 to +4 and are described as follows: evaluation—bad to good; potency—weak to strong; and activity—quiet to lively. The numbers 0 to 4 describe the extent of that goodness and badness, weakness and strength, quietness and liveliness. Ratings are defined as follows: 0 is "neutral," 1 is "slightly," 2 is "quite," 4 is "extremely," and 4 is "infinitely."

According to U.S. citizens (the reference culture in the examples that follow), the EPA profile for a teacher is 1.5, 1.4, and –0.6. That is, according to the U.S. culture, teachers are considered to be quite good, slightly powerful, and slightly quiet. The EPA profile for a lawyer is 1.0, 1.7, and 0.2 (slightly good, quite powerful, and neither lively nor quiet). The EPA profile for a drug addict is –2.0, –1.7, and 0.7 (quite bad, quite weak, and slightly lively). To capture the flavor of how a multitude of different identies can all be understood in terms of an EPA (evaluation, potency, and activity) profile, consider these 10 identity-related EPA profiles:

Identity	E	P	A	Identity	E	P	A
Alcoholic	−1.6,	−1.6,	−0.5	Musician	1.3,	0.4,	0.3
Baby	2.5,	−2.3,	2.3	Newcomer	0.9,	0.8,	0.2
Beggar	−1.0,	−2.1,	−1.3	Slob	−1.6,	−1.3,	−0.2
Criminal	−1.8,	−0.3,	1.1	Superstar	−1.0,	2.0,	1.8
Daughter	1.5,	−0.3,	1.2	Teammate	1.4,	1.2,	1.4

Trying to represent an identity by a three-dimensional profile might at first appear cumbersome, but once you get the hang of it, there is much to gain. EPA numerical profiles express a culturally agreed-upon common ground (how good, how powerful, and how active) for understanding any and all possible identities within that culture.

Like identities, the cultural meaning of behaviors and emotions can be expressed in EPA profiles. That is, any action a person takes and any emotion a person expresses can be understood in terms of its cultural meaning—its goodness, its potency, and its liveliness. To "assault" someone is extremely bad, slightly powerful, and quite active (EPA = –3.0, 1.2, 2.0). To "hug" someone is quite good, quite powerful, but not too lively (EPA = 2.3, 1.9, –0.2). Illustrative EPA profiles for five behaviors (on the left) and for five emotions (on the right) are as follows:

Behavior	E	P	A	Emotion	E	P	A
Amuse	1.9,	1.3,	1.3	Anger	−0.8,	0.2,	0.7
Command	−0.3,	2.0,	1.0	Disgust	−1.1,	−0.3,	0.2
Double-cross	−2.5,	0.1,	1.0	Fear	−0.8,	−0.9,	−0.2
Flee	−0.2,	−0.6,	1.3	Happiness	1.6,	0.9,	1.3
Work	0.1,	1.0,	0.5	Sadness	−1.3,	−1.1,	−1.0

These EPA profiles come from multiple data collections in which members of the U.S. culture rated the goodness, potency, and liveliness of many identities, behaviors, and emotions (Heise, 1991). Current EPA profile "dictionaries" also exist for the cultures (nationalities) of China, Japan, Korea, Ireland, Canada, and Germany.

Three constructs explain motivational processes in affect control theory, as follows:

Fundamental sentiment: The EPA profile of an identity, as defined by the culture. A "teacher" is 1.5, 1.4, −0.6, for instance.

Transient impression: The EPA profile implied by a person's current behavior. "To amuse" is 1.9, 1.3, 1.3, for instance and is carried out by someone whose identity is quite good, slightly powerful, and slightly active.

Deflection: The discrepancy between the person's fundamental sentiment (who one is according to a societal role) and the person's transient impression (who one appears via a behavioral act). Deflection is calculated mathematically by noting the differences between the two EPA profiles.

A fundamental sentiment is the EPA profile for any one particular identity. When identities participate in social interaction, the behaviors and emotions that occur create a transient impression of who the person is. Thus, if a "teacher" (EPA = 1.5, 1.4, −0.6, which is the fundamental sentiment) "coerces" (EPA = −1.0, 1.4, 0.0) a student, the act of coercing creates a transient impression of who the teacher seems to be: Is this person a teacher (someone with an EPA of 1.5, 1.4, −0.6), or is this person one who coerces (someone with an EPA of −1.0, 1.4, 0.0)? This discrepancy is referred to as a *deflection*. Deflections range from nonexistent (identity-confirming behavior) to very large (identity-violating behavior).

The affect control principle is basically the following: People behave in ways that minimize affective deflection (MacKinnon, 1994). That is, people create new events (behavior) to maintain old meanings (identity). *Deflection acts in the same way as do both self-schema consistency and cognitive dissonance.* To minimize affective deflection, people act in ways that maintain their identities and restore those identities when deflections arise (i.e., the consistent self).

Energy and Direction

You may be wondering what EPA profiles have to do with understanding motivation and emotion. The direction for behavior and emotion comes from fundamental sentiments. The energy for (the intensity of) behavior and emotion comes from deflection. Thus, in affect control theory, motivation and emotion produce (1) identity-confirming (i.e., fundamental sentiment-confirming) behaviors and (2) identity-restoring behaviors.

Identity-Confirming Behaviors

Human beings possess a wide range of potential behaviors, but only a subset of those behaviors are appropriate and expected in any one particular setting. Precisely which behaviors and emotions are most appropriate is determined by the identity the person inhabits. That is, for a friend (EPA = 3.0, 1.5, 0.6), the behaviors that are most appropriate are those the culture assigns a similar EPA profile—help (2.2, 1.5, 0.3) and laugh (2.2, 0.8, 1.0). The numbers 2.2, 1.5, 0.3 and 2.2, 0.8, 1.0 are a little bit different from 3.0, 1.5, 0.6 (the EPA profile for "friend"), but the point is that the behaviors of "help" and "laugh" have EPA profiles that are closer to the EPA profile for "friend" than are other possible behaviors. Hence, help and laugh are behaviors that are most consistent with someone occupying the identity of friend. The point is that when an interaction partner, or society in general, sees you in the role of "friend," then you feel motivated to engage in behaviors like helping and laughing. For a "pest" (EPA = −1.8, −0.5, 1.7), however, the behaviors that are most appropriate are "disrespect" (−2.1, −0.2, 1.1) and "annoy" (−1.6, 0.0, 1.2).

The essence of affect control theory's behavioral predictions in regard to identity-confirming behavior is as follows: Nice identities lead people to behave in nice ways, powerful identities lead people to behave in powerful ways, passive identities lead people to behave in passive ways, and so on. Identities direct behavior. Affect control theory is an identity-maintenance theory (Robinson & Smith-Lovin, 1992). Its prescription for how to motivate others is this: If you want people to be nice, place them into an identity that the culture sees as nice. If you want people to be assertive, place them into an identity that the culture sees as assertive. If a teacher wants her students to show strong initiative and creativity, she might put them into the role of "detectives". An athletic coach can generate extra initiative from an athlete by putting him or her in the role of "team captain" or "coach for a day."

Identity-Restoring Behaviors

When situational events cause deflection from one's identity, the individual initiates restorative actions to bring affectively disturbing events back in line with his established identity (or with his "fundamental sentiments"; MacKinnon, 1994). Consider the EPA of a "mother" (2.7, 1.6, 1.0) versus the EPA of a "mother who scolds her child" (−1.4, 0.9, 1.0). The changes in EPA profile numbers are generated by a computer program[2] (Heise, 1991). A mother who scolds her child becomes less good (2.7 drops to −1.4) and somewhat less powerful (1.6 drops to 0.9). To restore the culturally understood meaning of mother (E = 2.7; P = 1.6), she needs to engage in identity-restoring behavior by either performing a good and powerful behavior (e.g., cuddle her child, EPA = 1.7, 1.0, −0.7) or express a good and powerful emotion (e.g., pride in her child, EPA = 1.5, 0.8, 0.8). What the mother needs to do, if she wants to preserve her identity within the culture, is to counter the identity-disconfirming behavior with a barrage of identity-restoring behaviors and emotional expressions (Smith-Lovin, 1990; Smith-Lovin & Heise, 1988). In doing so, she uses social interaction to reestablish her fundamental sentiment. If she does not engage in such identity-restoring behaviors, her interaction partners will redefine her role away from "mother" to some other identity that better reflects her recent behavior. Hence, identities (fundamental sentiments) motivate identity confirming behaviors, while deflections motivate identity-restoring behaviors.

If a person behaves in an identity-inconsistent way (a teacher scolds a student), he or she can restore the original identity either through restorative behaviors or restorative emotional displays. That is, both behavioral displays and emotional displays create transient impressions of who the person is. Consider how people use strategic emotion displays to restore their identities (Robinson, Smith-Lovin, & Tsoudis, 1994). Emotion displays act as public identity cues such that good people who act bad should show sorrow if they are truly good people (just as bad people who act bad should show no such sorrow if they are truly bad people). If a good person commits a bad act and does not show remorse, an observer is left to wonder whether that person really is a good person or not. Good people should display deep remorse following a deviant act (because the

---

[2] The affect control theory computer program is available at the following internet address: *www.indiana.edu/~socpsy/ACT/.*

identity-behavior deflection should be very high), whereas bad people should display little post-behavior remorse (because the identity-behavior deflection would be too low to generate an identity-restoring emotional display). Notice here that the behavior is known, the emotion is observed, and the underlying identity is the only unknown. The mental calculus is to use the behavior and the emotion to figure out what the underlying character (identity) of the person must be. This is precisely why affect control theory uses all those EPA profile numbers.

Why People Self-Verify

The self prefers feedback that confirms or verifies its self-schemas and social identities. Self-verification theory and affect control theory both assume that the key to smooth interpersonal relationships is the individual's ability to recognize how other people and society in general perceive the self. The self notices how others respond to it and internalizes these social and cultural responses into a self-concept and into a sense of identity. Stable self-concepts and identities play such a central role in the self's negotiation of social reality that the self comes to prefer social feedback that confirms its self-schemas and identities (Swann, 1992a, 1992b). People with positive self-views prefer to hang out with friends who augment positive feedback and buffer negative feedback; people with negative self-views prefer to hang out with friends who buffer positive feedback and augment negative feedback (Robinson & Smith-Lovin, 1992; Swann, 1992a, 1992b; Swann et al., 1990; Swann, Pelham, & Krull, 1989; Swann, Wenzlaff, & Tafarodi, 1992).

People prefer self-verification feedback for cognitive, epistemic, and pragmatic reasons. On the cognitive side, people self-verify because they seek to know themselves (to be true to oneself; Swann, Stein-Servossi, & Giesler, 1992). Following epistemic concerns, people seek self-verfication because verifications of the self bolster perceptions that the world is predictable and coherent (Swann & Pelham, 2002). On the pragmatic side, people self-verify because they wish to avoid interactions that might be fraught with misunderstandings and unrealistic expectations and performance demands; they seek interaction partners who know what to expect from them (Swann, 1992a, 1999; Swann & Pelham, 2002).

BOX 10 | *Reversing Negative Self-Views*

Question: Why is this information important?

Answer: To help the self and others reverse negative self-views.

People generally respond to social feedback in one of two ways (Swann & Schroeder, 1995). First, people generally prefer positive feedback. People like praise and adoration, and when they hear it, the praise just feels good. Second, people prefer self-verifying feedback. People want to hear the truth about themselves. A critical question in contexts such as therapy, friendship, and marriage, is which type of feedback do people prefer more—self-enhancement or self-verification (Swann, 1999)?

Self-verification is a ubiquitous motivation within the strivings of the self-concept. But self-verification does not mean "negative feedback" because people with favorable self-views also seek verification of their goodness. It is just hard to notice self-verification among people with positive self-views because self-enhancement and self-verification feedback will sound just the same (i.e., praise). The motive for self-

(continued)

BOX 10 *Reversing Negative Self-Views* *(continued)*

verification becomes apparent when the person's self-view is negative because self-enhancement (praise) will sound very different from self-verification (criticism; Robinson & Smith-Lovin, 1992).

This chapter provides both the reasons why and the means through which people seek self-verification. But what can a person do to reverse a potentially debilitating negative self-view in another person (or in oneself)? To start with, such a self-appointed therapist would *not* want to make the mistake of underestimating the strength of the motivation to self-verify. Praising someone with a negative self-view leads rather predictably to a reaction along the lines of the following: "I like the favorable evaluation, but I am not sure that it is correct. It sounds good, but . . ." (Swann, Stein-Seroussi & Giesler, 1992). When a person with a negative self-view hears enhancing feedback (e.g., compliment, praise), she may very well be motivated to act in a way that proves the validity of the negative self-view (Robinson & Smith-Lovin, 1992). For instance, Marsha Linehan (1997) uses this logic for explaining why therapists' verbal affirmations are routinely unsuccessful during attempts to change the negative self-views of drug abusers. That is, self-verification strivings often interfere with and compete against therapeutic processes to overcome weaknesses and build strengths.

Figure 10.1 suggested the possible strategy of working to undermine the person's self-concept certainty (instead of working directly on the positivity of the person's self-schema). But the therapist needs to first make sure that the negative self-view is indeed unjustified or incorrect. When people who see themselves as clumsy, stupid, unworthy, and incompetent are in fact incorrect and are overly self-defensive, then a couple of strategies exist to help reconstruct an *unnecessarily* negative self-view.

One strategy that opens up some room for self-concept change is to present extreme self-verification feedback. For instance, Bill Swann (1997) provides the example of challenging an unassertive person's self-view by forwarding the impression that he is a "complete doormat." The hope is that the person will behaviorally resist the extreme version of the identity (e.g., will counter-argue, will show rebuttal "signs and symbols"). He has done the same with extreme conservatives, asking, "Why do you think men always make better bosses than women?"

A second strategy that opens up some room for self-concept change is to gain the self-enhancing support of key interaction partners, such as friends, lovers, relatives, and coworkers. Negative self-views are stabilized by interaction partners that provide a steady stream of negative feedback. There is some truth to the notion that women with low self-esteem marry men who are highly negative and abusive toward them (Buckner & Swann, 1996). Changing a negative self-view therefore involves changing the social feedback one receives day after day. And social interaction partners are the richest source of that social feedback (Swann & Predmore, 1985). Hence, gaining the cooperation and support of the person's key interaction partners is pivotal if one is to reverse a negative self-view. The therapeutic message that the client is loveable and competent can be swiftly and convincingly undone by family members who think little of the client's worth and competence. From this point-of-view, self-views are not merely psychological structures that exist inside of people. Rather, people construct a social world around them and the steady and consistent feedback from their interaction partners is the social process underlying self-concept consistency or change (Swann, 1997, 1999; Swann & Pelham, 2002).

AGENCY

The self presented thus far has been a cognitive and social one. But the self goes deeper than just cognitive structures (self-concept) and social relationships (identity). Within the self is an intrinsic motivation that gives it a quality of agency (Ryan, 1993). Agency entails action (deCharms, 1987). This section presents a view of self "as action and development from within, as innate processes and motivations" (Deci & Ryan, 1991).

The self does not enter into the world tabula rasa—an empty slate—awaiting life experiences to endow it with a self-concept and with cultural identities. Rather, the newborn possesses a rudimentary, nonlanguage-based self that is characterized by inherent needs, developmental processes, preferences, and capacities for interacting with the environment. As the newborn taps into her inborn capacities (e.g., walking, talking, intrinsic motivation), the self begins the lifelong process of discovering, developing, and fulfilling her potential. In doing so, the self begins to advance away from heteronomy (a dependence on others), toward autonomy (a reliance on self), on the way to becoming a "fully functioning person" (Rogers, 1961; Ryan, 1993).

Self as Action and Development from Within

Chapter 5 discussed the organismic psychological needs of autonomy, competence, and relatedness—needs that provide a natural motivational force to foster agency (i.e., initiative, action). Intrinsic motivation is inseparably coordinated with the active nature of the developing self (Deci & Ryan, 1991). It is the source of motivation that underlies agency as it spontaneously energizes people to pursue their interests, seek out environmental challenges, exercise their skills, and develop their talents.

Differentiation and Integration

Differentiation and integration are two processes inherent within agency that guide ongoing motivation and development. Differentiation expands and elaborates the self into an ever-increasing complexity. Integration synthesizes that emerging complexity into a coherent whole, thereby preserving a sense of a single, cohesive self.

Differentiation proceeds as the individual exercises existing interests, preferences, and capacities in such a way that a relatively general and undifferentiated self becomes specialized into several life domains. For an illustration, consider your own history in which you learned that not all computers are alike, not all sports are alike, not all politicians are alike, not all relationships are alike, and not all religions are alike. Minimal differentiation manifests itself in simplicity in which the person has only a unidimensional understanding of a particular domain of knowledge; rich differentiation manifests itself in understanding fine discriminations and unique aspects of a particular life domain. The same holds true for differentiation of the domains of the self-concept. Intrinsic motivation, interests, and preferences motivate the self to interact with the world in such a way that sets the stage for the self to differentiate into an ever-increasing complexity. For instance, the child with an interest in model airplanes skims through catalogues, attends club meetings, talks with peers about model building, subscribes to a topical magazine, experiments with new materials and with various construction techniques, and basically develops specialized skills while learning. It is the self's intrinsic motivation that gives it the agency it needs to skim through catalogues, attend club meetings, talk to peers, etc., and it is ongoing stream of experience that allows the self to differentiate and grow in complexity.

Differentiation does not expand the complexity of the self unabated. Rather, there exists a synthetic tendency to integrate the self's emerging complexity into a single sense of self, into a coherent unity. Integration is an organizational process that brings the self's differentiated parts together. Integration occurs as the self's individual parts (i.e., self-schemas, identities, interests, and so on) are successfully interrelated and organized as mutually complementary. One example of the interplay between differentiation and integration can be found in a study that asked young and old adults to list their possible selves and also what actions they took to realize them (Cross & Markus, 1991). The younger adults listed many more possible selves (showing strong differentiation), while the older adults took more actions to realize specific possible selves (showing more integration). Thus, younger adults explored and experimented with many possible selves, while the older adults, who had completed this experimental and expansive process, focused on a more cohesive, well-defined self (integration).

The notions of agency (via intrinsic motivation), differentiation, and integration argue that the self possesses innate aspects. Psychological needs and developmental processes provide a starting point for the development of the self. As individuals mature, they gain increasing contact with the social context, and some of these aspects of the social world become assimilated and integrated into the self-system. The motivational portrayal of self-development therefore argues strongly against the idea that the self is merely a passive recipient of the social world's feedback (self-schemas) and identities (places in the social order). The self is a recipient of social feedback (hence, self-concept) and the self does exist within an array of social relationships (hence, identifies), but the self also actively develops via its inherent agency. An understanding of the developing self therefore begins by adopting the frame of reference of the individual rather than that of the society (Deci & Ryan, 1991; Ryan, 1993).

Internalization and the Integrating Self

With its inherent needs and emerging interests, preferences, potentials, and capacities, the self is poised to grow, develop, and differentiate. The need for relatedness, however, keeps the individual close to societal concerns and regulations, and the self therefore develops both toward autonomy as well as toward an internalization of society's values and concerns. So behaviors, emotions, and ways of thinking originate not only within the self but also within the social context and society. As a person plays, studies, works, performs, and interacts with others, these other people request that the self comply with particular ways of behaving, feeling, and thinking. Thus, intentional acts (i.e., agency) sometimes arise from the self, but intentional acts also sometimes arise from the guidance and recommendations of others. The process through which individuals take in and accept as their own an externally prescribed way of thinking, feeling, or behaving is referred to as internalization (Ryan & Connell, 1989; Ryan, Rigby, & King, 1993). Internalization refers to the process through which an individual transforms a formerly externally prescribed way of behaving or valuing into an internal one (Ryan et al., 1993).

Internalization occurs for two essential reasons. First, internalization occurs from the individual's desire to achieve meaningful relationships with friends, parents, teachers, coaches, employers, clergy, family, and others. Thus, internalization is motivated by the need for relatedness. Second, internalization occurs from the individual's desire to interact effectively with the social world. Thus, internalization is motivated by the need for competence. Much of what the person internalizes promotes his effective functioning (e.g., go to school, brush your teeth, apologize to others). Such internalization has adaptive interpersonal value for the self, as it promotes greater unity between the self and society, such as in the close relationships between parent and child; and it has adaptive intrapersonal value for the self, as it promotes greater effectance in environmental transactions (Ryan, 1993).

The contribution of agency to a portray the self as action and development from within is to recognize that (1) human beings possess a core self, one energized by innate motivation and directed by the inherent developmental processes of differentiation and integration, and (2) not all self-structures are equally authentic; while some reflect the core self, others reflect and reproduce the society (Deci et al., 1994; Deci & Ryan, 1985a, 1991; Ryan, 1991, 1993; Ryan & Connell, 1989).

Self-worth follows from being open to experience and from valuing the self for who one is. When people are open to experience, they are more honest and self-disclosing during interpersonal interactions, they take more responsibility for their behaviors and are less likely to hide and distort information to deceive others, they engage in fewer activities to escape self-awareness (e.g., television viewing, movies, compulsive behaviors like food and work), they take fewer experience-altering substances, they show less defensiveness (e.g., less denial, less criticisms of others), and they prefer interaction partners that fulfill innate needs rather than partners that promote extrinsic goals such as image and wealth (Hodgins & Knee, 2002; Hodgins, Koestner, & Duncan, 1996; Hodgins, Liebeskind, & Schwartz, 1996; Knee & Zuckerman, 1996, 1998). For example, in a love relationship, an individual developing in the direction of greater autonomy would prefer an intimate connection with a growth-oriented partner rather than a partner with socially desirable physical attributes, wealth, or social status. If the self develops away from greater autonomy, self-worth follows from distorting experience and being valuable for doing particular activities or appearing in certain ways to others (Hodgins & Knee, 2002).

People do not always behave in ways that express the core self. Sometimes environmental conditions do not facilitate integration but, instead, place external pressures on people to behave in ways consistent with social demands. Controlling (pressuring) environmental conditions lead the self to ignore innate needs and preferences and, instead, develop a self-structure around the goal of external validation. Hence, people who pursue external validation of a socially-desirable self might choose a career for the financial wealth, prestige, or social power it offers rather than a career that is more consistent with their intrinsic interests, preferences, and innate needs. People organize their behavior and self-worth around the needs of the core self when the environment supports autonomy and personal agency, and people organize their behavior and self-worth around external validation as an adaptation to an environment that supports neither autonomy nor personal agency and instead promotes extrinsic aspirations.

Self-Concordance

The question asked by the self-concordance model is, How do people decide what to strive for in their lives, and how does this process sometimes goes awry and diminish well-being but other times nurture the self and promote well-being (Sheldon, 2002)? When people decide to pursue goals that are congruent or "concordant" with their core self, they pursue "self-concordant goals."

The self-concordance model appears in Figure 10.4 (Sheldon & Elliot, 1999). The model begins when the person sets a goal for which to strive. For instance, one person might set the goal of getting married, another might set a goal of graduating high school,

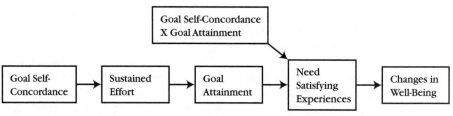

Figure 10.4 The Self-Concordance Model

Source: From, Goal striving, need satisfaction, and longitudinal well-being: The self-concordance model, by K. M. Sheldon & A. J. Elliot, 1999, *Journal of Personality and Social Psychology, 76,* 482–497. Copyright 1999 American Psychological Association. Reprinted by permission.

while yet another might set a goal of quitting smoking. Some goals reflect and emanate out from the core self's needs, interests, and preferences (self-concordant goals), while other goals do not.

Figure 10.5 graphically illustrates this notion that a person's goals may or may not represent the self's inherent needs, interests, and internalized values (see Sheldon & Elliot, 1998). Following self-determination theory (discussed in Chapter 6), intrinsic goals (goals set out of a strong interest) and identified goals (goals set out of a personal conviction, or value) represent self-concordant goals. Self-concordant goals reflect and express the integrated, agentic self. Introjected goals (goal set out of a sense of social obligation—it's what I should or ought do) and extrinsic goals (goals set out of a desire to be praised or rewarded) represent self-discordant goals. Self-discordant goals reflect and express nonintegrated action that emanates out of controlling internal and external pressures.

As shown in Figure 10.4 self-concordant goals generate greater sustained effort (i.e., greater "agency") than do self-discordant goals. Greater effort increases the likelihood of subsequent goal attainment. Goal attainments foster need-satisfying experiences. That is, making progress in one's goals feels good, while failing to make progress feels bad (Carver & Scheier, 1990). But just how need-satisfying any one particular goal attainment is, however, depends on the extent to which the goal is a self-concordant one (see the line connecting "Goal Self-Concordance × Goal Attainment" → Need Satisfying Experience" in Figure 10.4). Attaining self-concordant goals produces need satisfying experiences to a greater degree than does attaining self-discordant goals. Finally, it is this experience of authentic need satisfying experiences that increases well-being (i.e., gains in positive mood, vitality, physical health). That is, attaining self-concordant goals provide the self with psychological nutriments that sustain well-being and agency motivation (Ryan, 1995).

A handy self-test exists to determine whether a personal goal is self-concordant or self-discordant. Self-concordant goals (intrinsic goals, identified goals) emanate out of a sense of ownership—the person is fully aware that the striving is based on a personal interest, need, or value. Accordingly, the desire to pursue self-concordant goals is embedded in a context of positive affect and "wanting to." Self-discordant goals (extrinsic goals, introjected goals) emanate out of a sense of pressure—that the personal striving is based on an obligation to others or to social pressures. Accordingly, the desire to pursue self-discordant goals is embedded in a context of anxiety, pressure, and "having to." In Chapter 5, this distinction was referred to as "perceived locus of causality," as self-concordant goals

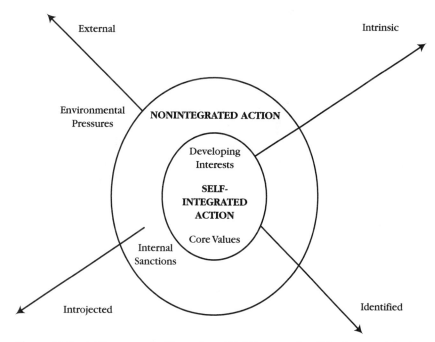

Figure 10.5 A Diagrammatic Illustration of Self-Integrated and Nonintegrated Action

Source: From, Goal striving, need satisfaction, and longitudinal well-being: The self-concordance model, by
K. M. Sheldon & A. J. Elliot, 1999, *Journal of Personality and Social Psycholgy, 76*, 482–497. Copyright 1999
American Psychological Association. Reprinted by permission.

arise from an internal perceived locus of causality while self-discordant goals arise from
an external perceived locus of causality. Thus, self-concordance refers to the sense of
ownership that people have (or do not have) regarding their goals and strivings.

The act of acquiring a sense of ownership in one's personal goals is a crucial developmental task of the self. A self characterized by agency is proactive and self-generates personal initiatives for life-improvement and self-expansion, rather than just being reactive to
the situational and cultural forces that come along. How self-concordance grows developmentally appears in Figure 10.6. The left-hand side of the figure essentially repeats the
self-concordance model depicted earlier in Figure 10.4 (i.e., self-concordant goals → enhanced goal-seeking effort → enhanced goal attainment → need satisfying experiences →
enhanced well-being). But the model in Figure 10.6 extends the self-concordant model
because need satisfying experiences contribute to the development of the self by increasing future self-concordance (Sheldon & Houser-Marko, 2001). That is, psychological
need satisfaction (feeling more self-determined, competent, and related) encourages
greater self-assurance and greater knowledge of the integrated self. Feeling greater self-
awareness and greater self-knowledge, people are increasingly likely to set and pursue
self-concordant goals for themselves in the future. In doing so, they participate in an "upward spiral" in which gains in self-concordance contribute to subsequent gains in well-
being, personal growth, and happiness (Sheldon & Houser-Marko, 2001).

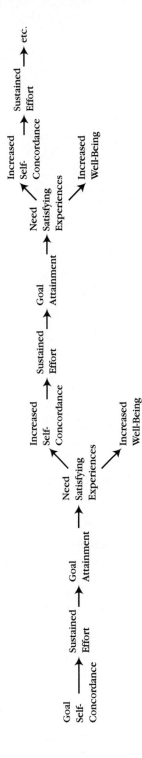

Figure 10.6 Cyclical Path Model for the Self-Concordance Model to Illustrate Developmental Gains in Both Well-Being and Self-Concordance

Note. The "Goal Self-Concordance × Goal Attainment" Box and Its Path/Arrow to "Need Satisfying Experiences" shown in Figure 10.4 has been omitted from this figure for clarity and simplification.

Source: Adapted from Sheldon, K. M., & Houser-Marko, L. (2001). Self-concordance, goal attainment, and the pursuit of happiness: Can there be an upward spiral? *Journal of Personality and Social Psychology, 80,* 152–165. Copyright 2001 American Psychological Association. Adapted with permission.

SUMMARY

Three basic problems occupy the self: defining and creating the self, relating the self to society, and discovering and developing its potential. This chapter presented these problems as self-concept (defining the self), identity (relating the self to society), and agency (developing personal potential). The notions of self-concept, identity, and agency tell the story of how the self generates motivation by highlighting the self's cognitive structures, social relationships, and strivings from within.

Self-schemas are cognitive generalizations about the self that are domain specific and are learned from past experience. The self-concept is a collection of domain-specific self-schemas (e.g., how people mentally represent their personal characteristics in domains such as athletic competence and interpersonal relationships). Self-schemas generate motivation in two ways: the consistent self and the possible self. For the consistent self, self-schemas direct behavior to confirm the self-view and to prevent episodes that generate feedback that might disconfirm that self-view. In other words, behavior is used to verify one's self-concept. Cognitive dissonance theory illustrates one way the consistent self maintains its self-view. The basic tenets of cognitive dissonance theory are that people dislike inconsistency, that the experience of dissonance is psychologically aversive, and that people seek to reduce dissonance by striving to maintain consistency in their beliefs, attitudes, values, and behaviors. For the possible self, the individual observes others and proactively forecasts a view of the future self that the person would like to become. Possible selves generate motivation for developing and growing toward particular aspirations.

Identity is the means by which the self relates to society, and it captures the essence of who the self is within a cultural context. Affect control theory explains how identities motivate behavior such that cultural values (how good, how powerful, how active) direct behavior, while affective deflections (between fundamental sentiments and transient impressions) energize behavior. Once people assume social roles (e.g., mother, bully), their identities direct their behaviors in ways that express the role-identity's cultural value. People with nice identities engage in nice behaviors, just as people with powerful identities engage in powerful behaviors. Thus, a physician is helpful and kind, rather than hostile or cruel, because these behaviors exemplify the good and powerful identity of doctor. When people act in identity-confirming ways, social interactions flow smoothly. When people act in identity-conflicting ways, however, affective deflection occurs to energize identity-restoring courses of action.

The self also possesses motivation of its own, or agency. Agency entails action. Action emerges spontaneously from intrinsic motivation, and its development proceeds through the processes of differentiation and integration. Intrinsic motivation, which is inherent within psychological needs, energizes the self to exercise and develop its inherent capabilities. Differentiation occurs as the self exercises its intrinsic interests, preferences, and capacities to grow and expand the self into an ever-increasing complexity. Integration occurs as these differentiated parts of the self are brought together into a sense of coherence or unity. The process is a dynamic one in which intrinsic motivation, differentiation, integration, and the internalization of social experience all contribute to the ongoing development and growth of the self. The self-concordance model illustrates the motivational and developmental benefits of pursuing life goals that emanate out of the integrated or core self. Self-congruence between one's self and one's goals generates enhanced effort that leads to a greater likelihood of need-satisfying experiences that, in turn, promote both well-being and future gains in self-concordance.

READINGS FOR FURTHER STUDY

Self-Functioning

BAUMEISTER, R. F. (1987). How the self became a problem: A psychological review of historical research. *Journal of Personality and Social Psychology, 52,* 163–176.

RYFF, C. D. (1989). Happiness is everything, or is it? Explorations on the meaning of psychological well-being. *Journal of Personality and Social Psychology, 57,* 1069–1081.

Self-Concept

MARKUS, H. (1977). Self-schemata and processing information about the self. *Journal of Personality and Social Psychology, 35,* 63–78.

SWANN, W. B., JR. (1987). Identity negotiation: Where two roads meet. *Journal of Personality and Social Psychology, 53,* 1038–1051.

Cognitive Dissonance

ARONSON, E. (1992). The return of the oppressed: Dissonance theory makes a comeback. *Psychological Inquiry, 3,* 303–311.

HARMON-JONES, E., & MILLS, J. (1999). An introduction to cognitive dissonance theory and an overview of current perspectives on the theory. In E. Harmon-Jones & J. Mills (Eds.), *Cognitive dissonance: Progress on a pivotal theory in social psychology* (Chapter 1, pp. 3–21). Washington, DC: American Psychological Association.

Identity

MACKINNON, N. J. (1994). Affect control theory. In N. J. MacKinnon's *Symbolic interactionism as affect control* (Chapter 2, pp. 15–40). Albany, NY: SUNY Press.

ROBINSON, D. T., & SMITH-LOVIN, L. (1992). Selective interaction as a strategy for identity maintenance: An affect control model. *Social Psychology Quarterly, 55,* 12–28.

Agency

DECI, E. L., & RYAN, R. M. (1991). A motivational approach to self: Integration in personality. In R. Dienstbier (Ed.), *Nebraska symposium on motivation: Perspectives on motivation* (Vol. 38, pp. 237–288). Lincoln: University of Nebraska.

SHELDON, K. M., & ELLIOT, A. J. (1999). Goal striving, need satisfaction, and longitudinal well-being: The self-concordance model. *Journal of Personality and Social Psychology, 76,* 482–497.

Part Three

Emotions

Chapter 11

Nature of Emotion: Five Perennial Questions

According to Chinese fortune cookies, the great philosophers, the Bible, Roosevelt (FDR) speeches, Vulcans, and the Dalai Lama, emotions like anger and fear rarely pay off. Most of the time, these sources say, emotions lead to destructive results. Emotion researchers, in contrast, generally see all emotions as constructive responses to fundamental life tasks. Anger and fear might feel bad and they might sometimes lead to problematic ways of behaving, but even the hottest of emotions exists as a necessary tradeoff in human's emotion-laden quest for survival.

Emotion researchers are a fair and open minded bunch, so they decided to pack their bags, board an airplane to Dharamsala, and visit the Dalai Lama to hear a second opinion about "destructive emotions" and how to overcome them (see Goleman, 2003). After all, it does make a good deal of sense to think of some emotions as potentially dangerous. You do not want to be in the same car with an anger-prone driver in city traffic who fumes, speeds, weaves in and out, and grips the steering wheel like he is strangling the life out of other drivers' throats. This driver probably could benefit from a chat with the Dalai Lama.

So what wisdom did the Dalai Lama have to offer? A lot, it turns out. Buddhist thought organizes itself around the goal of recognizing and then lessening destructive emotions, particularly the big three of craving, agitation, and hatred. These emotions apparently are those that are most harmful to self and others. They have their place in survival and adapting to threatening situations, but since saber tooth tigers are no longer in the neighborhood, anger, fear, and the like may cost us at least as much as they provide.

Through many years of meditation, Buddhists can translate their craving into contentment, their agitation into calm, and even their hatred into compassion. In the West, people lessen their negative emotions mostly with medicines (e.g., a pill for anxiety, a drug for depression). In the East, those who practice meditation turn their negative emotions into positive ones as anger and resentment can, potentially, be focused into compassion and even into love and respect for the other. Our biology has indeed prepared us to act emotionally to important life events, as everyone feels sad with loss and fear with threat. But a lot happens immediately after the loss or threat before we react, less than a second later, with a destructive or constructive response. Once we know what happens in the brief time that occurs in between our exposure to an important life events and our subsequent emotional reaction, then we will have the means of translating biologically destructive reactions into more constructive responses.

Emotions typically arise as reactions to important situational events. Once activated, they generate feelings, arouse the body into action, generate motivational states, and express themselves publicly. To understand emotions and how they generated motivated action, Chapter 11 discusses the nature of emotion while Chapter 12 discusses emotion's various aspects. Here, Chapter 11 discusses and answers the following five perennial questions in the study of emotion:

1. What is an emotion?
2. What causes an emotion?
3. How many emotions are there?
4. What good are the emotions?
5. What is the difference between emotion and mood?

WHAT IS AN EMOTION?

Emotions are more complex than first meets the eye. At first glance, we all know emotions as feelings. We know joy and fear because the feeling aspect on an emotion is so salient in our experience. It is almost impossible not to notice emotion's feeling aspect when we encounter a threat (fear) or make progress toward a goal (joy). But, in the same way that the nose is only part of the face, feelings are only part of the emotion.

Emotions are multidimensional. They exist as subjective, biological, purposive, and social phenomena (Izard, 1993). In part, emotions are subjective feelings, as they make us feel a particular way, such as angry or joyful. But emotions are also biological reactions, energy-mobilizing responses that prepare the body for adapting to whatever situation one faces. Emotions are also agents of purpose, much like hunger has purpose. Anger, for instance, creates a motivational desire to do what we might not otherwise do, such as fight an enemy or protest an injustice. And, emotions are social phenomena. When emotional, we send recognizable facial, postural, and vocal signals that communicate the quality and intensity of our emotionality to others (e.g., movement of the eyebrows, tone of the voice).

Given the four-part character of emotion, it is apparent that the concept is going to elude a straightforward definition. The difficulty in defining emotion might puzzle you at first because emotions seem so straightforward in everyday experiences. Everyone knows what it is like to experience joy and anger, so the reader might ask, "What's the problem with actually defining emotion?" The problem is the following: "Everyone knows what emotion is, until asked to give a definition" (Fehr & Russell, 1984). None of these separate dimensions—subjective, biological, purposive, or social—adequately defines emotion. One cannot equate a feeling with an emotion any more than one can equate a posed facial expression with an emotion (Russell, 1995). There is simply more to emotion than just a feeling or just an expression. Each of these four dimensions simply emphasizes a different character of emotion. To understand and to define emotion, it is necessary to study each of emotion's four dimensions and how they interact with one another.

Emotion's four dimensions (or components) appear in Figure 11.1. The figure shows four boxes, and each box corresponds to a separate aspect of emotion. The feeling component gives emotion its subjective experience that has both meaning and personal significance. In both intensity and quality, emotion is felt and experienced at the subjective (or "phenomenological") level. The feeling aspect is rooted in cognitive or mental processes.

The bodily arousal component includes our biological and physiological activation, including the activity of the autonomic and hormonal systems as they prepare and regulate the body's adaptive coping behavior during emotion. Bodily arousal and physiological activation are so intertwined with emotion that any attempt to imagine an angry or disgusted person who is not aroused is nearly impossible. When emotional, our body is prepared for

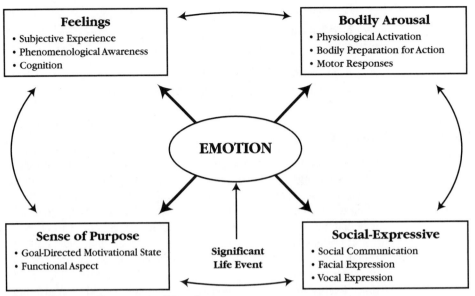

Figure 11.1 Four Components of Emotion

action, and that is true in terms of our physiology (heart rate, epinephrine in the bloodstream) and musculature (alert posture, clenched fist).

The purposive component gives emotion its goal-directed motivational state to take the action necessary to cope with the emotion-causing circumstances one faces. The purposive aspect explains why people benefit from their emotions. The person without emotions would be at a substantial social and evolutionary disadvantage to the rest of us. Imagine, for instance, the physical and social survival handicap of the person without the capacity for fear, embarrassment, interest, or love.

The social-expressive component is emotion's communicative aspect. Through postures, gestures, vocalizations, and facial expressions, our private experiences become public expressions. During the expression of emotion, we nonverbally communicate to others how we feel and how we interpret the present situation. For instance, as a person opens a private letter, we watch their face and listen to the tone of their voice to read their emotions. Emotions therefore engage our whole person—our feelings, bodily arousal, sense of purpose, and nonverbal communications.

Given this introduction to the four components of emotion, we can offer an introductory definition. Emotions are short-lived, feeling-arousal-purposive-expressive phenomena that help us adapt to the opportunities and challenges we face during important life events. Because emotions arise in response to the significant events in our lives, Figure 11.1 includes a path from "significant life event" to "emotion".

Defining emotion is more complicated that a "sum of its parts" definition. Emotion is the psychological construct that unites and coordinates these four aspects of experience into a synchronized pattern. That is why the term "emotion" appears in Figure 11.1 as a separate construct from its individual components. Emotion is that which choreographs the feeling, arousal, purposive, and expressive components into a coherent reaction to an eliciting event. For instance, in the case of fear, the eliciting event might be steep ski slopes, while the reaction includes feelings, bodily arousal, goal-directed desires, and all-too-public nonverbal communications. Thus, the threatened skier feels scared (feeling aspect), is "pumped up" (bodily arousal aspect), strongly desires self-protection (purposive aspect), and shows tensed eyes and pulled-back corners of the mouth (expressive aspect). These synchronized, mutually supportive elements form a pattern of reactivity to an environmental danger that is the emotion of fear.

This definition of emotion highlights how different aspects of experience complement and coordinate with one another (Averill, 1990; LeDoux, 1989). For instance, what people feel correlates with how they move the muscles of their face. As you view and smell rotten food, for instance, the way you feel and the way you wrinkle your nose and scrunch your upper lip are coordinated as a coherent feeling-expressive system (Rosenberg & Ekman, 1994). Similarly, the way you move your face is coordinated with your physiological reactivity, such that lowering your brow and pressing your lips firmly together coincides with increased heart rate and a raised skin temperature (Davidson et al., 1990).

These interrelationships and the inter-coordination among the four different components of emotion are shown graphically in Figure 11.1 by the thin curved lines that connect each aspect of emotion to each of the other three aspects. The two-way arrows communicate that, for instance, changes in feelings influence and co-occur with bodily arousal just as changes in bodily arousal influence and co-occur with feelings.

Figure 11.2 provides a concrete illustration of the otherwise abstract principle shown in Figure 11.1. Sadness is an emotional reaction to an encounter with a significant life event like separation or failure. Using the emotion of distress/sadness as an example, the aversive feeling influences and co-occurs with lethargic bodily arousal, sense of purpose to reverse being separated, and the distinctive sad facial expression. Hence, emotions are the synchronized systems that coordinate feeling, arousal, purpose, and expression so to

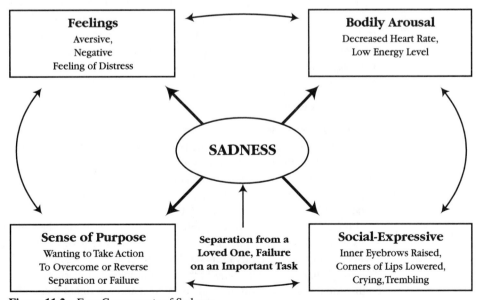

Figure 11.2 Four Components of Sadness

ready ourselves to adapt successfully to life circumstances. "Emotion" is the word psychologists use to name this coordinated, synchronized process.

Relationship Between Emotion and Motivation

Emotions relate to motivation in two ways. First, emotions are one type of motive. Like all other motives (e.g., needs, cognitions), emotions energize and direct behavior. Anger, for instance, mobilizes subjective, physiological, hormonal, and muscular resources (i.e., energizes behavior) to achieve a particular goal or purpose (i.e., directs behavior), such as overcoming an obstacle or righting an injustice. Second, emotions serve as an ongoing "readout" system to indicate how well or how poorly personal adaptation is going. Joy, for instance, signals social inclusion and progress toward our goals, whereas distress signals social exclusion and failure.

Emotion as Motivation

Most emotion researchers agree that emotions function as one type of motive. Some researchers, however, go further. They argue that emotions constitute the *primary* motivational system (Tomkins, 1962, 1963, 1984; Izard, 1991). Throughout the 100-year history of psychology, the physiological drives (hunger, thirst, sleep, sex, and pain) were considered to be the primary motivators (Hull, 1943, 1952). Air deprivation provides one example. Being deprived of air generates a physiological drive that can capture the person's full attention, energize the most vigorous of action, and direct behavior decidedly toward a single purpose. Accordingly, it seems logical to conclude that air deprivation produces a potent and primary homeostatic motive for taking whatever action is necessary in gaining the air needed to reestablish homeostasis (see Chapter 4). Emotion researcher Silvan Tomkins, however, called this reasoning, this apparent truism, a "radical error" (Tomkins, 1970). According to Tomkins, the loss of air produces a strong emotional reaction—one of fear or terror. It is this terror that provides the motivation to act. Thus, the terror, not the air deprivation or the bodily threat to homeostasis, is the causal and immediate source of the panicked, grasping display of motivated behavior. Take away the emotion, and you take away the motivation.

Emotion as a Readout System

Emotions also provide a readout of the status of the person's ever-changing motivational states and personal adaptation status (Buck, 1988). Positive emotions reflect the involvement and satisfaction of our motivational states, while negative emotions reflect the neglect and frustration of our motivational states. Positive emotions also reflect our successful adaptation to the circumstances we face, while negative emotions reflect our unsuccessful adaptation.

From this point of view, emotions are not necessarily motives in the same way that needs and cognitions are but, instead, reflect the satisfied versus frustrated status of motives. Consider sexual motivation and how emotion provides an on-going progress report ("readout") that facilitates some behaviors and inhibits others. During attempts at sexual gratification, positive emotions such as interest and joy signal that all is well and facilitate further sexual conduct. Negative emotion such as disgust, anger, and guilt signal that all is not well and inhibit further sexual conduct. The positive emotions during attempts at involving and satisfying one's motives (i.e., interest, joy) provide a metaphorical green light for continuing to pursue that course of action. Negative emotions during attempts at involving and satisfying one's motives (i.e., disgust, guilt), on the other hand, provide a metaphorical red light for stopping the pursuit of that course of action.

WHAT CAUSES AN EMOTION?

When we encounter a significant life event, an emotion comes to life, as shown in Figure 11.3. As shown below, people's mind (cognitive processes) and body (biological processes) react in adaptive ways to significant life events. That is, encountering a significant life event, activates cognitive and biological processes that collectively activate the critical components of emotion, including feelings, bodily arousal, goal-directed purpose, and expression.

One central question in the study of emotion is, What causes an emotion? Many viewpoints come into play in this causal analysis, including those that are biological, psychoevolutionary, cognitive, developmental, psychoanalytical, social, sociological, cultural, and anthropological. Despite this diversity, understanding what causes an emotion rallies around one central debate: biology versus cognition. In essence, this debate asks whether emotions are primarily biological or primarily cognitive phenomena. If emotions are largely biological, they should emanate from a causal biological core, such as neuroanatomical brain circuits and how the body reacts to significant life events. If emotions are largely cognitive, however, they should emanate from causal mental events, such as subjective appraisals of what the situation means for the person's well-being.

Biology and Cognition

Together, the cognitive and biological perspectives provide a relatively comprehensive picture of the emotion process. Nonetheless, acknowledging that both cognitive and biological aspects underlie emotion begs the question as to which is primary: biological or cognitive factors (Lazarus, 1982, 1984, 1991a, 1991b; Scherer & Ekman, 1984; Zajonc, 1980, 1981, 1984). Those who argue for the primacy of cognition contend that individuals cannot respond emotionally unless they first cognitively appraise the meaning and personal significance of an event: Is the event relevant to well-being? Is it relevant to a loved one's well-being? Is it important? beneficial? harmful? First, meaning is established, and then emotion follows accordingly. Appraisal of meaning causes emotion. Those who

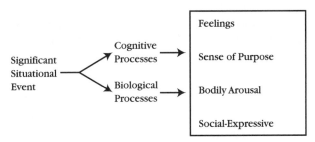

Figure 11.3 Causes of the Emotion Experience

argue for the primacy of biology contend that emotional reactions do not necessarily require such cognitive evaluations. Events of a different sort, such as subcortical neural activity or spontaneous facial expressions, activate emotion. For the biological theorist, emotions can and do occur without a prior cognitive event, but they cannot occur without a prior biological event. Biology, not cognition, is therefore primary.

Biological Perspective

Three representatives for the biological perspective include Carroll Izard (1989, 1991), Paul Ekman (1992), and Jaak Panksepp (1982, 1994). Izard (1984) finds that infants respond emotionally to certain events despite their cognitive shortcomings (e.g., limited vocabulary, limited memory capacity). A 3-week-old infant, for instance, smiles in response to a high-pitched human voice (Wolff, 1969), and the 2-month-old expresses anger in response to pain (Izard et al., 1983). By the time the child acquires language and begins to use sophisticated long-term memory capacities, most emotional events then involve a great deal of cognitive processing. Nonetheless, despite the richness of cognitive activity in the emotion process, Izard (1989) insists that much of the emotional processing of life events remains noncognitive—automatic, unconscious, and mediated by subcortical structures. Infants, because they are biologically sophisticated yet cognitively limited, best demonstrate the primacy of biology in emotion.

Ekman (1992) points out that emotions have very rapid onsets, brief durations, and can occur automatically/involuntarily. Thus, emotions happen to us, as we act emotionally even before we are consciously aware of that emotionality. Emotions are biological because they evolved through their adaptive value in dealing with fundamental life tasks. Ekman, like Izard, recognizes the cognitive, social, and cultural contributions to emotional experience, but he concludes that biology—rather than learning, social interaction, or socialization history—lies at the causal core of emotion.

For Panksepp (1982, 1994), emotions arise from genetically endowed neural circuits that regulate brain activity (e.g., biochemical and neurohormonal events). Panksepp acknowledges that it is more difficult to study the hidden recesses of brain circuits than it is to study verbally labeled feelings. He insists, however, that brain circuits provide the essential biological underpinning for emotional experience. For instance, we (and other animals) inherit a brain-anger circuit, a brain-fear circuit, a brain-sadness circuit, and a few others. The rationale in supporting Panksepp's biological perspective comes from three important findings:

1. Because emotional states are often difficult to verbalize, they must therefore have origins that are noncognitive (not language-based).

2. Emotional experience can be induced by noncognitive procedures, such as electrical stimulation of the brain or activity of the facial musculature.

3. Emotions occur in infants and nonhuman animals.

Cognitive Perspective

Three representatives of the cognitive perspective include Richard Lazarus (1984, 1991a, 1991b), Klaus Scherer (1994a, 1994b, 1997), and Bernard Weiner (1986). For each of these theorists, cognitive activity is a necessary prerequisite to emotion. Take away the cognitive processing, and the emotion disappears.

Lazarus argues that without an understanding of the personal relevance of an event's potential impact on personal well-being, there is no reason to respond emotionally. Stimuli appraised as irrelevant do not elicit emotional reactions. For Lazarus (1991a, 1991b), the individual's cognitive appraisal of the meaning of an event (rather than the event itself) sets the stage for emotional experience. That is, a car passing you in traffic is not likely to call up your fear unless its way of passing leads you to think that your well-being has in some way been put at risk. The emotion-generating process begins not with the event itself and not with one's biological reaction to it, but instead, with the cognitive appraisal of its meaning.

Scherer (1994a, 1997) agrees with Lazarus that some life experiences produce emotions, whereas other life experiences do not. Scherer identifies several specific cognitive appraisals that generate emotional experiences, including: Is the event good or bad? Can I cope successfully with this situation? and Is this event okay on a moral level? Answers to these questions of how we appraise the situation we face constitute the sort of cognitive processing that gives rise to emotions.

In his attribution analysis of emotion, Weiner (1986) concentrates on the information processing that takes place after life outcomes occur. That is, attribution theory focuses on the thinking and personal reflection we engage in following life's successes and failures. Following a success, believing that it was caused by the self produces one emotion (pride) while believing that same success was caused by a friend produces a different emotion (gratitude). Notice that both the outcome and the life event might be the same, but if the attribution is different then so is the emotional experience. Thus, attributions, not the event or the outcome, gives life to the emotion.

The most direct benefit to extract from the cognition versus biology debate is that both sides clearly state their respective positions. Once introduced to the thinking from both sides, the following now be asked: Which side is correct? Or, which side is more correct? Emotion psychologists have struggled for answers to this question, and two answers have emerged.

Two-Systems View

One answer to the "What causes emotion?" question is that both cognition and biology cause emotion. According to Buck (1984), human beings have two synchronous systems that activate and regulate emotion.

One system is an innate, spontaneous, physiological system that reacts involuntarily to emotional stimuli. A second system is an experience-based cognitive system that reacts interpretatively and socially. The physiological emotion system came first in humankind's evolution (i.e., the limbic system), whereas the cognitive emotion system came later as human beings became increasingly cerebral and increasingly social (i.e., the neocortex). Together, the primitive biological system and the contemporary cognitive system combine to provide a highly adaptive, two-system emotion mechanism.

The two-systems view appears in Figure 11.4 (Buck, 1984). The lower system is biological and traces its origins to the ancient evolutionary history of the species. Sensory information is processed rapidly, automatically, and unconsciously by subcortical (i.e., limbic) structures and pathways. The second system is cognitive and depends on the unique social and cultural learning history of the individual. Sensory information is

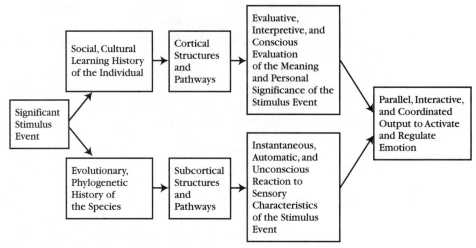

Figure 11.4   Two-Systems View of Emotion

processed evaluatively, interpretatively, and consciously by cortical pathways. The two emotion systems are complementary (rather than competitive) and work together to activate and regulate emotional experience.

Robert Levenson (1994a) takes the two-systems view of emotion a bit farther by hypothesizing how the biological and cognitive emotion systems interact. Instead of existing as parallel systems, the two systems influence one another. Panksepp (1994) adds that some emotions arise primarily from the biological system, whereas other emotions arise primarily from the cognitive system. Emotions such as fear and anger arise primarily from subcortical neural command circuits (from subcortical structures and pathways in Buck's terminology). Other emotions, however, cannot be well explained by subcortical neural circuits. Instead, they arise chiefly from personal experience, social modeling, and cultural contexts. This category of emotions arises primarily from appraisals, expectancies, and attributions (from cortical structures and pathways in Buck's terminology).

Chicken-and-Egg Problem

Robert Plutchik (1985) sees the cognition versus biology debate as a chicken-and-egg quandary. Emotion should not be conceptualized as cognitively caused or as biologically caused. Rather, emotion is a process, a chain of events that aggregate into a complex feedback system. The elements in Plutchik's feedback loop are cognition, arousal, feelings, preparations for action, expressive displays, and overt behavioral activity (i.e., recall the multidimensional aspects of emotion from Figures 11.1 and 11.2). One possible representation of Plutchik's emotion feedback loop appears in Figure 11.5. The feedback system begins with a significant life event and concludes with emotion. Mediating between event and emotion is a complex interactive chain of events. To influence emotion, one can intervene at any point in the feedback loop. Change the cognitive appraisal from "this is beneficial" to "this is harmful," and the emotion will change. Change the quality of the arousal (as through exercise, a drug, or an electrode in the brain), and the emotion will change. Change bodily expression (e.g., the facial musculature, bodily posture), and the emotion will change, and so on.

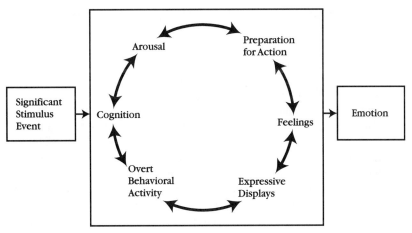

Figure 11.5   Feedback Loop in Emotion

Plutchik's solution to the cognition-biology debate enters into the complex world of dialectics, in which each aspect of emotion is both cause and effect and the final outcome is due to the dynamic interplay among the six forces in the figure. The most important theme to extract from a chicken-and-egg analysis is that cognitions do not directly cause emotions any more than biological events do. Together, cognition, arousal, preparation for action, feelings, expressive displays, and overt behavioral activity constitute the cauldron of experience that causes, influences, and regulates emotion. Others echo this emotion-as-a-process view by emphasizing that all emotional experiences exist as episodes that occur over time (Scherer, 1994b). Over time, the different components of emotion rise and fall and exert continuous influences on one another.

Comprehensive Biology-Cognition Model

Emotions are complex (and interactive) phenomena. As with most complexities, it makes sense to work on one piece of the puzzle at a time. Generally speaking, biologists, ethologists, and neurophysiologists focus mostly on the biological aspects of emotion, whereas cognitive psychologists, social psychologists, and sociologists focus mostly on its cognitive, sociocultural aspects. This is precisely the organizational scheme adopted in the next chapter, Chapter 12. It discusses first the biological aspects of emotion and then the cognitive aspects. The chapter also adds an additional section on the social and cultural contributions to emotional experience.

HOW MANY EMOTIONS ARE THERE?

The cognition-biology debate indirectly raises another important question: How many emotions are there? A biological orientation emphasizes primary emotions (e.g., anger, fear) and downplays the importance of secondary or acquired emotions. A cognitive orientation acknowledges the importance of the primary emotions, but it stresses that much of what is interesting about emotional experiences arises from individual, social, and cultural experiences. Hence, the interesting and important story in emotion lies in the complex (secondary, acquired) emotions. Ultimately, any answer to the "How many emotions are there?" question depends on whether one favors a biological or a cognitive orientation.

Biological Perspective

The biological perspective typically emphasizes several primary emotions, with a lower limit of two (Solomon, 1980) or three (Gray, 1994) to an upper limit of ten (Izard, 1991). Each biological theorist has a very good reason for proposing a specific number of emotions, though each proposal is based on a different emphasis. Eight major research traditions in the biological study of the emotions appear in Figure 11.6. The figure identifies the number of emotions suggested by the empirical findings within that tradition, it explains the rationale on which the theorist proposes that number of emotions, and it offers a supportive reference citation for further reading.

Richard Solomon (1980) identifies two hedonic, unconscious brain systems that exist such that any pleasurable experience is automatically and reflexively opposed by a counter-aversion experience, just as any aversive experience is automatically and reflexively opposed by a counter-pleasurable process (e.g., fear is countered by, and quickly replaced by, the "opponent process" of euphoria, as during sky diving). Jeffrey Gray (1994) proposes three basic emotions rooted in separate brain circuits: the behavioral approach system (joy), the fight-or-flight system (anger/fear), and the behavioral inhibition system (anxiety). Jaak Panksepp (1982) proposes four emotions—fear, rage, panic, and expectancy—based on his finding of four separate neuroanatomical, emotion-generating pathways within the limbic system. Nancy Stein and Tom Trabasso (1992) stress the four emotions of happiness, sadness, anger, and fear because these emotions reflect reactions to life's essential pursuits: attainment (happiness), loss (sadness), obstruction (anger), and uncertainty (fear). Silvan Tomkins (1970) distinguishes six emotions—interest, fear, surprise, anger, distress, and joy—because he finds six distinct patterns of neural firing produce these different emotions (e.g., rapid increase in rate of neural firing instigates surprise). Paul Ekman (1992, 1994a) proposes six distinct emotions—fear, anger, sadness, disgust, enjoyment, and contempt—because he finds that each of these emotions is associated with a corresponding universal (cross-cultural) facial expression. Robert Plutchik (1980) lists eight emotions—anger, disgust, sadness, surprise, fear, acceptance, joy, and anticipation—because each one corresponds to an emotion-behavior syndrome common to all living organisms (e.g., fear corresponds to protection). Finally, Carroll Izard (1991) lists ten emotions on the basis of his differential emotions theory: anger, fear, distress, joy, disgust, surprise, shame, guilt, interest, and contempt.

Each of these eight research traditions agree that (1) a small number of basic emotions exists, (2) basic emotions are universal to all human beings (and animals), and (3) basic emotions are products of biology and evolution. Where the eight traditions diverge is in their specifications of what constitutes the precise biological core that orchestrates emotional experience.

Cognitive Perspective

The cognitive perspective asserts firmly that human beings experience a greater number of emotions than the 2 to 10 highlighted by the biological tradition. Cognitive theorists grant that, yes of course, there are only a limited number of neural circuits, facial expressions,

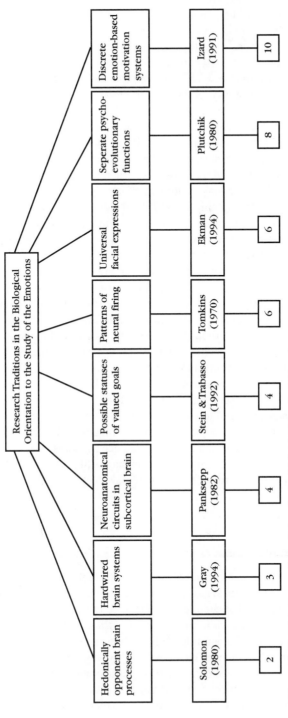

Figure 11.6 Eight Research Traditions in the Biological Study of Emotion

and bodily reactions (e.g., the fight-or-flight reaction). They point out, however, that several different emotions can arise from the same biological reaction. For instance, a single physiological response, such as a rapid rise in blood pressure, can serve as the biological basis for anger, jealousy, or envy. High blood pressure and an appraisal injustice produce anger; high blood pressure and an appraisal that an object should be the self's rather than another's produce jealousy; and high blood pressure and an appraisal that another is in a more favorable position than is the self produce envy. For cognitive theorists, human beings experience a rich diversity of emotion because situations can be interpreted so differently (Shaver et al., 1987) and because emotion arises from a blend of cognitive appraisal (Lazarus, 1991a), language (Storm & Storm, 1987), personal knowledge (Linville, 1982), socialization history (Kemper, 1987), and cultural expectations (Leavitt & Power, 1989).

Nine research traditions within the cognitive study of the emotions appear in Figure 11.7. The figure explains the rationale on which each theorist proposes that emotions come to life, and it offers a supportive reference citation for further reading. The figure shows that all cognitive theorists answer the "How many emotions are there" question with the same answer, namely that an almost limitless number of emotions exist. This is so because all cognitive theorists share the assumption that "emotions arise in response to the meaning structures of given situations; different emotions arise in response to different meaning structures" (Frijda, 1988). How the cognitive theories of emotion differ is in how they portray the way people generate and interpret the meaning of a situation. The situation can provide the context to interpret one's aroused state (Schachter, 1964), the individual can interpret his own aroused state (Mandler, 1984), and people can be socialized to interpret their aroused state (Kemper, 1987). In addition, people make appraisals of whether their relationship to the environment affects their personal well-being (Lazarus, 1991a), the meaning and memories of the situations they face (Fridja, 1993), and their attributions of why good and bad outcomes occurred (Weiner, 1986). And emotional experiences are embedded deeply within language (Shaver et al., 1987), socially constructed ways of acting (Averill, 1982), and social roles like "cheerleader" and "bully" (Heise, 1989).

Reconciliation of the Numbers Issue

Everyone—biologically and cognitively minded researchers—agrees that there are dozens of emotions. The debate therefore centers on whether some emotions are more fundamental or more basic than are others (Ekman & Davidson, 1994). A middle-ground perspective is to argue that each basic emotion is not a single emotion but rather a *family* of related emotions (Ekman, 1994a). For instance, anger is a basic emotion, but anger is also a family of emotions that includes hostility, rage, fury, outrage, annoyance, resentment, envy, and frustration. Similarly, joy is a basic emotion, but joy is also a family of emotions that includes amusement, relief, satisfaction, contentment, and pride in achievement. Each member of a family shares many of the characteristics of the basic emotion—its physiology, its subjective feeling state, its expressive characteristics, and so on (recall Figure 11.2). There are a limited number of these basic emotion families rooted in biology and evolution (as argued by the biologically-minded theorists in Figure 11.6), but also a number of variations of these basic emotions via learning, socialization, and culture (as argued

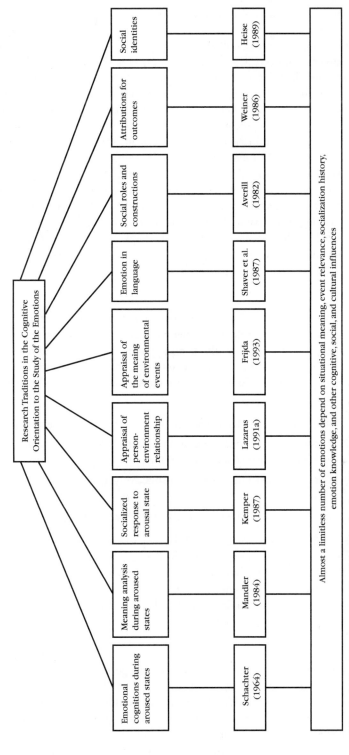

Figure 11.7 Nine Research Traditions in the Cognitive Study of Emotion

by the cognitively-minded theorists in Figure 11.7). At least five such emotion families exist: anger, fear, disgust, sadness, and enjoyment (Ekman, 1992, 1994a).

Emotion families can also be understood from a more cognitive perspective. An analysis of the English language led one group of researchers to conclude that emotion knowledge involves five basic emotion prototypes: anger, fear, sadness, joy, and love (Shaver et al., 1987). According to this group of researchers, people learn increasingly finer distinctions within the causes and consequences of these five basic emotions. For instance, a young child's emotional repertoire might include only anger, fear, sadness, joy, and love, but, after a good deal of experience and socialization, the child learns that different situations give rise to different variations of the basic emotion. For instance, it takes learning, experience, and socialization to understand the varieties of fear—alarm, shock, fright, horror, terror, panic, hysteria, mortification, anxiety, nervousness, tension, uneasiness, apprehension, worry, dread, and perhaps others. Thus, fear is the basic emotion, while the other variations are acquired as secondary emotions.

Basic Emotions

Any answer to the question of how many emotions there are forces one to commit to a level of specificity (Averill, 1994), which means that emotions can be conceptualized at a general level such as the family or prototype (e.g., anger) or at a situation-specific level (e.g., hostility, envy, frustration). In this section, emotions are considered at a general level. The so-called basic emotions are those that meet the following criteria (Ekman & Davidson, 1994):

1. Are innate rather than acquired or learned through experience or socialization.
2. Arise from the same circumstances for all people (personal loss makes everyone sad, irrespective of their age, culture, and so on).
3. Are expressed uniquely and distinctively (as through a universal facial expression).
4. Evoke a distinctive and highly predictable physiological patterned response.

Some researchers argue against the idea of basic emotions (Ortony & Turner, 1990), and others offer a list of basic emotions that is different from the one presented here. Despite this diversity of opinion, no list of basic emotions would vary far from including the six presented here: fear, anger, disgust, sadness, joy, and interest (from Ekman, 1992; Ellsworth & Smith, 1988a; Izard, 1991; Shaver et al., 1987; Weiner, 1986).

Fear

Fear is an emotional reaction that arises from a person's interpretation that the situation he or she faces is dangerous and a threat to one's well-being. Perceived dangers and threats can be psychological or physical. The most common fear-activating situations are those rooted in the anticipation of physical or psychological harm, a vulnerability to danger, or an expectation that one's coping abilities will not be able to match up to forthcoming circumstances. The perception that one can do little to cope with an environmental threat or danger is at least as important a source of fear as is any actual characteristic of the threat/danger itself (Bandura, 1983). Fear is therefore mostly about a perceived vulnerability to being overwhelmed by a threat or danger.

Fear motivates defense. It functions as a warning signal for forthcoming physical or psychological harm that manifests itself in autonomic nervous system arousal (as in the flight part of the fight-or-flight response). The individual trembles, perspires, looks around, and feels nervous tension to protect the self. It is through the experience of fear that our emotion system tells us of our vulnerability (often in no uncertain terms). Protection motivation manifest itself either through escape or withdrawal from the object(s). Fleeing puts physical (or psychological) distance between the self and that which is feared. If fleeing is not possible, fear motivates coping, as by being quiet and still.

On a more positive note, fear can provide the motivational support for learning new coping responses that remove the person from encountering danger in the first place. Few highway drivers in a torrential rainfall, for instance, need to be reminded to pay attention to the slippery road (fear activates coping efforts), and experienced drivers are better at coping with such a danger than are novice drivers (fear facilitates the learning of adaptive responses). Fear therefore warns us of our vulnerability, and it also facilitates learning and activates coping.

Anger

Anger is a ubiquitous emotion (Averill, 1982). When people describe their most recent emotional experience, anger is the emotion that most often comes to mind (Scherer & Tannenbaum, 1986). Anger arises from restraint, as in the interpretation that one's plans, goals, or well-being have been interfered with by some outside force (e.g., barriers, obstacles, interruptions). Anger also arises from a betrayal of trust, being rebuffed, receiving unwarranted criticism, a lack of consideration from others, and cumulative annoyances (Fehr et al., 1999). The essence of anger is the belief that the situation is not what it should be; that is, the restraint, interference, or criticism is illegitimate (de Rivera, 1981).

Anger is the most passionate emotion. The angry person becomes stronger and more energized (as in the fight part of the fight-or-flight response). Anger also increases people's sense of control (Lerner & Keltner, 2001). Anger makes people more sensitive and attuned to the injustices of what other people do (Keltner, Ellsworth, & Edwards, 1993), and the fight and sense of control are directed at overcoming or righting the illegitimate restraint. This attack can be verbal or nonverbal (yelling or slamming the door) and direct or indirect (destroying the obstacle or just throwing objects about). Other common anger-motivated responses are to express hurt feelings, talk things over, conciliate, or avoid the other person altogether (Fehr et al., 1999). When people do act out their anger, research shows a surprising success rate (Tafrate, Kassinove, & Dundin, 2002). Anger often clarifies relationship problems, energizes political agendas, and spurs a culture to change for the better, as occurred with the civil rights movement, the women's suffrage movement, and American's national response to the September 11th terrorists attacks (Tavris, 1989). In all these cases of anger serving a positive function, however, it is almost always the assertive, nonviolent expression of anger that pays off rather than its violent expression, because anger can serve an important alerting function ("Take me seriously!") that leads others to a deeper understanding of the other person and the anger-causing problem.

Anger is not only the most passionate emotion, it is also the most dangerous emotion, as its purpose is to destroy barriers in the environment. About one-half of anger episodes include yelling or screaming, and about 10% of anger episodes lead to aggression (Tafrate et al., 2002). When anger prompts aggression, it produces needless destruction and injury, as when we shove a rival, curse at a teammate, or thoughtlessly damage property. An anger-fueled temper also dramatically increases the person's likelihood of a heart attack. But, again, one a more positive note, anger can be a productive emotion. Anger is productive when it energizes vigor, strength, and endurance in our efforts to cope productively as we change the world around us into what it should be. And people (e.g., politicians) who express anger generally get more respect and status following a wrong than do people who express sadness or guilt (Tiedens & Linton, 2001). When circumstances change from what they should not be (injustice) to what they should be (justice), anger appropriately fades away (Lerner, Goldberg, & Tetlock, 1998).

Disgust

Disgust involves getting rid of or getting away from a contaminated, deteriorated, or spoiled object. Just what that object is depends on development and culture (Rozin, Haidt, & McCauley, 1993; Rozin, Lowery, & Ebert, 1994). In infancy, the cause of disgust is limited to bitter or sour tastes. In childhood, disgust reactions expand beyond distaste to include psychologically-acquired revulsions and generally any object deemed to be offensive (Rozin & Fallon, 1987). By adulthood, disgust arises from our encounters with any object we deemed to be contaminated in some way, as in bodily contaminations (poor hygiene, gore, death), interpersonal contaminations (physical contact with undesirable people), and moral contaminations (child abuse, incest, infidelity). Cultural learning determines much of what the adult considers a bodily, interpersonal, or moral contamination, but people from most cultures rate disgusting things as those that are of animal origin and spread to contaminate other objects (e.g., a dead roach touching your food triggers core disgust and pretty much contaminates the whole plate, emotionally speaking).

The function of disgust is rejection. Through disgust, the individual actively rejects and casts off some physical or psychological aspect of the environment. Consider these environmental invasions that the person, through the disgust emotion, seeks to reject (Rozin, Lowery, & Ebert, 1994): eating something bitter (bad taste), smelling ammonia or rotten meat (bad smell), eating an apple with a worm in it (contaminated food), watching a medical dissection (body violation), thinking about someone engaged in incest (moral violation), and sleeping in a hotel bed on which the linens have not been changed (interpersonal contamination).

Because disgust is phenomenologically aversive, it paradoxically plays a positive motivational role in our lives as the wish to avoid disgusting objects motivates us to learn the coping behaviors needed to prevent encountering (or creating) conditions that produce disgust. Therefore, because people wish to avoid putting themselves into disgusting situations, they change personal habits and attributes, discard waste and sanitize their surroundings, and reappraise their thoughts and values. They wash the dishes, brush their teeth, take showers, and exercise to avoid an out-of-shape or "disgusting" body.

Sadness

Sadness (or distress) is the most negative, aversive emotion. Sadness arises principally from experiences of separation or failure. Separation—the loss of a loved one through death, divorce, circumstances (e.g., travel), or argument—is distressing. In addition to being separated from the ones we love, we also experience separation from a place (hometown) and from a valued job, position, or status. Failure, too, leads to sadness, as in failing an examination, losing a contest, or being rejected from a group's membership. Even failure outside of one's volitional control can cause distress, as in war, illness, accidents, and economic depression (Izard, 1991).

Because it feels so aversive, sadness motivates the individual to initiate whatever behavior is necessary to alleviate the distress-provoking circumstances before they occur again. Sadness motivates the person to restore the environment to its state before the distressing situation. Following separation, the rejected lover apologizes, sends flowers, or telephones in an effort to repair the broken relationship. Following failure, a performer practices to restore confidence and to prevent the re-occurrence of a similar failure. That is, because we feel sad, we are more likely to apologize and to offer reparations. Unfortunately, many separations and failures cannot be restored. Under hopeless conditions, the person behaves not in an active, vigorous way but in an inactive, lethargic way that essentially leads to withdrawal.

One beneficial aspect of sadness is that it indirectly facilitates the cohesiveness of social groups (Averill, 1968). Because separation from significant people causes sadness and because sadness is such an uncomfortable emotion, its anticipation motivates people to stay cohesive with their loved ones (Averill, 1979). If people did not miss others so much, then they would be less motivated to go out of their way to maintain social cohesion. Similarly, if the student or athlete did not anticipate the possibility of suffering failure-induced distress, she would be less motivated to prepare and practice. So, while sadness feels miserable, it can motivate and maintain productive behaviors.

Threat and Harm

The themes that organize the otherwise diverse emotions of fear, sadness, anger, and disgust are threat and harm. When threatening or harmful events are forecast or anticipated, we feel fear. During the struggle to fight off or to reject the threat or harm, we feel anger and disgust. Once the threat or harm has occurred, we feel sadness. In response to threat and harm, fear motivates avoidance behavior—fleeing the threat. Anger motivates fighting and vigorous counterdefense. Disgust motivates rejection of the bad event or object. Sadness leads to inactivity and withdrawal and is effective when it leads one to give up coping efforts in situations that he cannot flee from, reject, or fight against. Hence, fear, anger, disgust, and sadness work collectively to endow the individual with an emotion system to deal effectively with all aspects of threat and harm.

Joy

The events that bring joy include desirable outcomes—success at a task, personal achievement, progress toward a goal, getting what we want, gaining respect, receiving love or affection, receiving a pleasant surprise, or experiencing pleasurable sensations (Ekman &

Friesen, 1975; Izard, 1991; Shaver et al., 1987). The causes of joy—desirable outcomes related to personal success and interpersonal relatedness—are essentially the opposite of the causes of sadness (undesirable outcomes related to failure and separation/loss). How joy affects us also seems to be the opposite of how sadness affects us. When sad, we feel lethargic and withdrawn; when joyous, we feel enthusiastic and outgoing. When sad, we are often pessimistic; when joyous, we turn optimistic.

The function of joy is twofold. First, joy facilitates our willingness to engage in social activities. Smiles of joy facilitate social interaction (Haviland & Lelwica, 1987), and if the smiles keep coming, then they help relationships form and strengthen over time (Langsdorf et al., 1983). Few experiences are as potent and as rewarding as are the smile and interpersonal inclusion. Joy is therefore a social glue that bonds relationships, such as infant and mother, lovers, coworkers, and teammates. Second, joy has a "soothing function" (Levenson, 1999). It is the positive feeling that makes life pleasant and balances life experiences of frustration, disappointment, and general negative affect. Joy allows us to preserve psychological well-being, even in the face of the distressing events that come our way. Joy also has a way of undoing the distressing effects of aversive emotions, as when parents sing and make funny faces to soothe distressed infants and when lovers show affection to soothe away an otherwise conflictual exchange (Carstensen, Gottman, & Levenson, 1995).

Interest

Interest is the most prevalent emotion in day-to-day functioning (Izard, 1991). Some level of interest is ever-present. Because this is so, increases and decreases in interest usually involve a shifting of interest from one event, thought, or action to another. In other words, we typically do not stop and start our interest, but rather, we redirect it from one object or event to another. The life events that direct our attention include those that involve our needs or well-being (Deci, 1992b). Other events that direct our attention are those that instigate a moderate increase in the rate of our cortical neural firing, such as those associated with stimulus change, novelty, uncertainty, complexity, puzzles and curiosities, challenge, thoughts of learning, thoughts of achieving, and acts of discovery (Berlyne, 1966; Izard, 1991).

Interest creates the desire to explore, investigate, seek out, manipulate, and extract information from the objects that surround us. Interest motivates acts of exploration, and it is in these acts of turning things around, upside down, over, and about that we gain the information we seek. Interest also underlies our desire to be creative, to learn, and to develop our competencies and skills (Renninger, Hidi, & Krapp, 1992). A person's interest in an activity determines how much attention is directed to that activity and how well that person processes, comprehends, and remembers relevant information (Hidi, 1990; Renninger et al., 1992; Renninger & Wozniak, 1985; Schiefele, 1991; Shirey & Reynolds, 1988). Interest therefore enhances learning (Alexander, Kulikowich, & Jetton, 1994). It is difficult to learn a foreign language, allocate time to read a book, or engage in most any learning activity without emotional support from interest.

Motive Involvement and Satisfaction

Motive involvement and satisfaction are the themes that unite the positive emotions of interest and joy. When a beneficial event related to our needs and well-being is anticipated, we feel interest. If and when the event materializes into motive satisfaction, we feel joy (or enjoyment). Interest motivates the approach and exploratory behavior necessary for promoting contact with the potentially motive-satisfying event. Interest also prolongs our task engagement so we can put ourselves in a position to experience motive satisfaction. Joy adds to and somewhat replaces interest once motive satisfaction occurs (Izard, 1991). Joy then promotes ongoing task persistence and subsequent reengagement behaviors with the motive-satisfying event. Together, interest and joy regulate a person being fully and voluntarily involved in an activity (Reeve, 1989).

WHAT GOOD ARE THE EMOTIONS?

While feeling the angst inherent in sadness, anger, or jealousy, people understandably ask themselves the following question: "What purpose do emotions serve—what good are they?" It is not uncommon for people who feel aversive emotions to wish that their emotion would just go away and leave them alone. Who wants to feel sad?

Work on the utility or function of emotion began with Charles Darwin's *The Expression of Emotions in Man and Animals* (1872), a less famous effort than his 1859 work on the evolution of species. In his work on emotions, Darwin argued that emotions help animals adapt to their surroundings. Displays of emotion help adaptation much in the same way that displays of physical characteristics (e.g., height) do. For example, the dog baring its teeth in defense of its territory helps it cope with hostile situations (by warding off opponents). Such expressiveness is functional, and emotions are therefore candidates for natural selection.

Coping Functions

Emotions do not just occur out of the blue. They occur for a reason. From a functional point of view, emotions evolved because they helped animals deal with fundamental life tasks (Ekman, 1994a). To survive, animals must explore their surroundings, vomit harmful substances, develop and maintain relationships, attend immediately to emergencies, avoid injury, reproduce, fight, and both receive and provide care giving. Each of these behaviors is emotion produced, and each facilitates the individual's adaptation to changing physical and social environments.

Fundamental life tasks are universal human predicaments, such as loss, frustration, and achievement (Johnson-Laird & Oatley, 1992). The emotion during life tasks energizes and directs behavior in evolution-benefiting ways (e.g., after separation, crying for help proved more effective than did other courses of action). That is, emotion and emotional behavior provide animals with ingrained and automated ways for coping with the major challenges and threats to their welfare (Tooby & Cosmides, 1990).

As shown in Table 11.1, emotions serve at least eight distinct purposes: protection, destruction, reproduction, reunion, affiliation, rejection, exploration, and orientation (Plutchik, 1970, 1980). For the purpose of protection, fear energizes and directs the body for withdrawal and escape. To destroy some aspect of the environment (e.g., enemy, obstacle, restraint), anger prepares the body for attack. To explore the environment, anticipation sparks interest and readies the body for investigation. For every major life task, human beings evolved a corresponding, adaptive emotional reaction. The function of emotion is therefore to prepare us with an automatic, very quick, and historically successful response to life's fundamental tasks.

Table 11.1   Functional View of Emotional Behavior

Emotion	Stimulus Situation	Emotional Behavior	Function of Emotion
Fear	Threat	Running, flying away	Protection
Anger	Obstacle	Biting, hitting	Destruction
Joy	Potential mate	Courting, mating	Reproduction
Sadness	Loss of valued person	Crying for help	Reunion
Acceptance	Group member	Grooming, sharing	Affiliation
Disgust	Gruesome object	Vomiting, pushing away	Rejection
Anticipation	New territory	Examining, mapping	Exploration
Surprise	Sudden novel object	Stopping, alerting	Orientation

Source: From "Functional View of Emotional Behavior," *Emotion: A Psychoevolutionary Synthesis* (p. 289), by R. Plutchik, 1980, New York: Harper & Row. Adapted with permission.

This line of reasoning leads to the following conclusion: There is no such thing as a "bad" emotion. Joy is not necessarily a good emotion, and anger and fear are not necessarily bad emotions (Izard, 1982). *All* emotions are beneficial because they direct attention and channel behavior to where it is needed, given the circumstances one faces. In doing so, each emotion provides a unique readiness for responding to a particular situation. From this point of view, fear, anger, disgust, sadness, and all other emotions are good. This is so because fear optimally facilitates protection, disgust optimally facilitates repulsion of contaminated objects, and so forth. Emotions are therefore positive, functional, purposive, and adaptive organizers of behavior.

Other biologically oriented emotion researchers stress greater flexibility in emotional ways of coping than is otherwise apparent from Table 11.1 (Frijda, 1994). That is, while fear essentially motivates protective behavior, it also readies us for additional and more flexible actions, including preventing the dangerous event from occurring in the first place or suppressing activity until the threat passes. Likewise, anger essentially motivates destructive action, but it also prepares us to enforce social norms or to discourage anger-causing events before they occur (e.g., discourage injustice, restraint, and insults with preparatory behavior like negotiating rules). Individual experience and cultural learning further contribute to how we express our emotional coping. Individual experience and cultural learning over time greatly expand the entries in the "Emotional Behavior" column in Table 11.1. This increased flexibility is important because it makes it clear that emotional responses are more flexible than are reflexes (Scherer, 1984b).

Social Functions

In addition to serving coping functions, emotions serve social functions (Izard, 1989; Keltner & Haidt, 1999; Manstead, 1991). Emotions:

1. Communicate our feelings to others.

2. Influence how others interact with us.

3. Invite and facilitate social interaction.

4. Create, maintain, and dissolve relationships.

Emotional expressions are potent, nonverbal messages that communicate our feelings to others. Through emotional expressions, infants nonverbally communicate what they cannot communicate verbally, as through the face (Fridland, 1992), voice (Scherer, 1986), and emotional behavior in general (Huebner & Izard, 1988). At birth, infants are capable of expressing joy, interest, and disgust; by two months, infants can also express sadness and anger; and by six months, infants can express fear (Izard, 1989). Throughout infancy, interest, joy, sadness, disgust, and anger represent almost 100% of emotion-based facial expressions (Izard et al., 1995). Caregivers reliably recognize and accurately interpret these facial expressions (Izard et al., 1980). Infant facial expressions therefore guide caretakers' emotion-specific care (Huebner & Izard, 1988).

Emotional displays influence how people interact, as the emotional expression of one person can prompt selective behavioral reactions from a second person (Camras, 1977; Coyne, 1976a, 1976b; Frijda, 1986; Klinnert et al., 1983). In a conflict situation over a toy, for instance, a child who expresses anger or sadness is much more likely to keep the toy than is a child who expresses no such emotion (Camras, 1977; Reynolds, 1982). The emotional expression nonverbally communicates to others what one's probable forthcoming behavior is likely to be. If the toy is taken away, the anger-expressing child communicates a probable forthcoming attack, whereas the sadness-expressing child communicates a probable barrage of tears. The signal that one is likely to attack or cry often succeeds in regaining the lost toy (or preventing the toy from being taken in the first place). Hence, in the context of social interaction, emotions serve multiple functions, including informative ("This is how I feel"), forewarning ("This is what I am about to do"), and directive ("This is what I want you to do") functions (Ekman, 1993; Schwartz & Clore, 1983). In this way, emotional expressions communicate social incentives (joy smile), social deterrents (angry face), and unspoken messages (embarrassment face) that smooth and coordinate social interactions (Fernald, 1992; Keltner & Buswell, 1997; Tronick, 1989).

Many emotional expressions are socially, rather than biologically, motivated. This assertion sounds strange because it is generally assumed that people smile when they feel joy and frown when they feel sad. Nonetheless, people frequently smile when they do not feel joy. People sometimes smile when they wish to facilitate social interaction.

Ethologists studying smiling in primates found that chimpanzees use the voluntary smile sometimes to deflect potentially hostile behavior from dominant animals and other times to maintain or increase friendly interactions (van Hooff, 1962, 1972). Just as primates smile (bare their teeth) to appease dominants, young children smile when approaching a stranger, and children are more likely to approach a stranger who smiles than a stranger who does not smile (Connolly & Smith, 1972). Adults who are embarrassed socially are also likely to smile (Kraut & Johnston, 1979). In addition, the smile is a universal greeting display (Eibl-Eibesfeldt, 1972; van Hooff, 1972) that seems to say, nonverbally, "I am friendly; I would like us to be friends." In each of these instances, smiling is socially, rather than emotionally, motivated.

The idea that a smile can be socially motivated leads to the question of whether smiling is typically an emotional expression of joy or a social expression of friendliness

(Fernandez-Dols & Ruiz-Belba, 1995; Kraut & Johnston, 1979). To test this hypothesis, Robert Kraut and Robert Johnston observed people smiling while bowling, while watching a hockey match, and while walking down the street. The researchers wondered whether people smiled more often when engaged in social interaction or when experiencing a joy reaction to a positive event (a good bowling score, a goal for their hockey team, sunny weather). Generally speaking, bowlers, spectators, and pedestrians were more likely to smile socially (to smooth social interactions) than emotionally (in response to positive outcomes).

Why We Have Emotions

Life is full of challenges, stresses, and problems to be solved. Emotions exist as solutions to these challenges, stresses, and problems (Ekman, 1992; Frijda, 1986, 1988; Lazarus, 1991a; Scherer, 1994b). By coordinating and orchestrating feelings, arousal, purpose, and expression (the emotion processes in Figure 11.1), emotions "establish our position vis-à-vis our environment" (Levenson, 1999) and "equip us with specific, efficient responses that are tailored to problems of physical and social survival" (Keltner & Gross, 1999).

Some argue that emotions serve no useful purpose. They argue that emotions disrupt ongoing activity, disorganize behavior, and rob us of our rationality and logic (Hebb, 1949; Mandler, 1984). These emotion researchers grant that while emotions served important evolutionary functions thousands of years ago, they no longer do so in the modern world. This position stands in stark contrast to the assertion that emotions prioritize behavior in ways that optimize adjustment to the demands we face (Lazarus, 1991a; Levenson, 1994a, 1999; Oatley & Jenkins, 1992; Plutchik, 1980). Everyone agrees that emotions affect the way we think, feel, and behave. So, the question hinges on whether emotions are adaptive and functional or whether emotions are maladaptive and dysfunctional.

The reason that both sides of the "functional versus dysfunctional" question makes sense is because both are correct. Emotions exist as both a masterpiece of evolutionary design (as pointed out by emotion theorists) and also as excess baggage in the age of reason (as pointed out by Stoics, Buddhists, and others).

Human emotion operates within a two-system design (Levenson, 1999). The biological core of the emotion system is one that humans share with other animals, and this is the part of the emotion system that evolved to solve fundamental life tasks. Because only a few life tasks are truly fundamental, the emotion system responds in a stereotypical way that recruits and orchestrates a limited but highly appropriate set of responses. This way of responding can be characterized rather like a "time-tested recipe" (to borrow an example from Levenson, 1999). These prototypical ways of responding to fundamental life tasks are the same as those listed in Table 11.1. When situationally appropriate, these automated ways of responding to problems can be highly adaptive. But they can also be situationally inappropriate when activated under other circumstances (e.g., attacking one's opponents is not always the best way to handle a situation). For emotions to be adaptive across many different situations, emotions need to be regulated and controlled.

As Robert Levenson (1999) points out, in the modern world, tigers rarely jump out at us, people rarely steal our food, and beasts rarely threaten to kill our young. Today's threats are on a smaller scale and therefore do not require the same sort of massive mobi-

BOX 11   *Emotion's Role in Development*

Question: Why is this information important?

Answer: To appreciate why Vulcans could never be smarter than humans.

In science fiction (i.e., *Star Trek*), Vulcans are a race of people who deny and reject their emotions. They constantly seek to overcome their emotions. Vulcans are also a very smart race, full of logic, intelligence, and amazing cognitive development. Vulcans accomplish these lofty cognitive attainments, they believe, because they reject their emotions.

Rejecting emotions to enrich cognitive development is more fiction than it is science. The emotion system is a critical ally in the development of the cognitive system. What if the Vulcan infant refused to smile or show spontaneous interest? The poor little guy's quantity and quality of social interaction with caretakers would nose dive. The social smile recruits caregiving and approach by others. Without a constant barrage of smiling, the Vulcan infant would not have the means of gaining a steady stream of stimulation and challenge from others that is necessary for optimal cognitive development, perspective taking, role playing, and rule internalization.

Interest is an emotion that arises from environmental novelty and change. Without interest, the Vulcan would lack an inner motivational resource to explore her physical surroundings—to pick things up, shake them, toss them, and conduct all sorts of little experiments on the world. Infants who express positive emotions like interest and joy bring caretakers close to them, and the relationship with an attachment figure is the infant's springboard for increasing exploration, increasing play, reducing wariness of strangers, and gaining an increased sociability with others outside the infant-caregiver relationship (Colin, 1996).

Anger during the "terrible twos" helps foster the preschool child's sense toward self-reliance (Dunn & Mum, 1987). Imagine the Vulcan child without the capacity for anger when goals were obstructed or blocked. He or she would show little or no protest against restraints and discomforts. He or she would feel little motivation to engage in the thinking and problem solving necessary for figuring out how to cope best to reverse and overcome obstacles.

Sadness, shame, guilt, sympathy, and empathy are emotional ingredients in the development of prosocial behavior. Without the information provided by these emotions, the Vulcan child would be slow to learn what would be wrong with taking a prized toy from another child. Empathy and sadness allow the child ways to understand the deleterious consequences to the other child (Davidson, Turiel, & Black, 1983). Shame and guilt make it painful to violate social rules (shame) and moral standards (guilt). Shame tells the self that one is acting in a way that is inadequate or unacceptable to others (Barrett, 1995). Guilt tells the self that a moral standard is being violated and therefore motivates reparative behaviors that help maintain our relationships with others (Baumeister, Stillwell, & Heatherton, 1995).

Vulcans are known for their abstract thinking, logical reasoning, and a capacity to consider multiple possible future events. In contrast, emotion researchers are known for their studies of how emotional changes facilitate cognitive development (Abe & Izard, 1999; Larson & Asmussen, 1991). One interesting analysis of this process appears in *The Diary of Anne Frank*. Her writings consistently showed that experiences of intense emotion were quickly followed by higher levels of thinking (Haviland & Kramer, 1991). Emotional experiences (e.g., fear, anger, disgust, sadness) contribute motivationally to the adolescent's active mental construction of the self-concept, the discovery of meaning, consideration of ideal and possible selves, and abstract thinking in general. In this way, emotions fuel cognitive development.

The Vulcan solution for coping with emotions is to suppress them. The human solution is to use emotions as allies to cope and adjust in ways that are healthy. Because he had a lifetime of emotional episodes to enrich his cognitive development, Captain Kirk often out-coped Spock.

lization of our emotion systems. Becoming competent in regulating one's emotions generally improves with experience, and it constitutes a lifelong undertaking (Carstensen, 1995; Gross et al., 1997). In the end, whether emotions serve us well depends on how able we are to self-regulate our emotion systems such that we experience regulation *of* emotion rather than regulation *by* emotion (Gross, 1999).

WHAT IS THE DIFFERENCE BETWEEN EMOTION AND MOOD?

A fifth fundamental question on the nature of emotion asks, What is the difference between emotion and mood (Ekman & Davidson, 1994; Russell & Barrett, 1999)? Several distinguishing criteria can be listed (Goldsmith, 1994), but three seem especially telling:

- Different antecedents
- Different action-specificity
- Different time course

First, as to different antecedents, emotions and moods arise from different causes. Emotions emerge from significant life situations and from appraisals of their significance to our well-being. Moods, on the other hand, emerge from processes that are ill-defined and are oftentimes unknown (Goldsmith, 1994). Second, as to different action-specificity, emotions mostly influence behavior and direct specific courses of action. Moods, however, mostly influence cognition and direct what the person thinks about (Davidson, 1994). Third, as to different time course, emotions emanate from short-lived events that last for seconds or perhaps minutes, whereas moods emanate from mental events that last for hours or perhaps days. Hence, moods are more enduring than are emotions (Ekman, 1994a).

Everyday Mood

Most people have about 1,000 waking minutes in their day, but only a few of these actually include a prototypical emotion such as anger, fear, or joy (Clark, Watson, & Leeka, 1989; Watson & Clark, 1994). In contrast, the average person generally experiences an ever-present stream of moods. Though emotions are relatively rare in daily experience, people are always feeling something. What they typically feel is a mood, a way of feeling that often exists as an aftereffect of a previously experienced emotional episode (Davidson, 1994).

Mood exists as a positive affect state or as a negative affect state (i.e., good mood, bad mood; Watson & Tellegen, 1985; Watson, Clark, & Tellegen, 1988). Positive affect and negative affect are not opposite ways of feeling, however. Instead, these two moods are independent—not opposite—ways of feeling (Diener & Emmons, 1984; Diener & Iran-Nejad, 1986). For example, during a job interview, people often report feeling both positive and negative affects simultaneously. The job interviewer typically feels both enthusiastic and nervous at the same time. Positive affect also varies systematically in accordance with the sleep-wake cycle, while negative affect does not (Watson et al., 1999). As shown in Figure 11.8, level of positive affect is quite low upon waking. It increases rapidly throughout the morning, and positive affect continues to rise gradually throughout the afternoon until it hits its peak from 6:00 P.M. to 9:00 P.M. Positive affect then declines rapidly throughout the late evening as it returns to its early-morning low level (Clark, Watson, & Leeka, 1989).

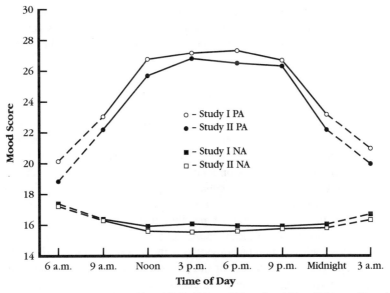

Figure 11.8   Levels of Positive Affect (PA) and Negative Affect (NA) as a Function of Time of Day in Two Studies

Source: From, Diurnal variation in the positive affects, by L.A. Clark, D. Watson, & J. Leeka, 1989, *Motivation and Emotion, 13*, 205–234. Copyright 1989 Plenum Press.

Positive affect reflects pleasurable engagement. It exists as a person's current level of pleasure, enthusiasm, and progress toward goals. People who feel high positive affect typically feel enthusiastic and experience energy, alertness, and optimism, whereas those who feel low positive affect typically feel lethargic, apathetic, and bored.

Negative affect reflects unpleasant engagement. People who feel high negative affect typically experience dissatisfaction, nervousness, and irritability, whereas those who feel low negative affect are calm and relaxed. These feelings of alertness versus boredom (positive affect) and irritability versus relaxation (negative affect), rather than prototypical emotional states like joy and fear, constitute the essential nature of everyday, ongoing affective experience.

Positive and negative affect pertain not only to moods but also to broad cognitive, motivational, biological, and behavioral systems (Clark, Watson, & Mineka, 1994). Positive affect reflects a reward-driven, appetitive motivational system (Fowles, 1988), whereas negative affect reflects a punishment-driven, aversive motivational system (Gray, 1987). Basically, positive affect and a good mood support approach behavior, while negative affect and a bad mood support withdrawal (Watson et al., 1999). The positive affect system has its own neural substrate—dopaminergic pathways. These pathways are activated by the expectancy of desirable events (Wise, 1996; Ashby, Isen, & Turken, 1999). The negative affect system has its own neural substrate—serotonergic and noradrenergic pathways. These pathways are activated by the expectancy of negative outcomes (MacLeod, Byrne, & Valentine, 1996). Again, these findings point to the conclusion that positive and negative affects are more independent ways of feeling than they are emotional or neural opposites. The expectation of desirable events activates dopaminergic pathways that generate positive affect and approach behavior (and does not impact negative affect processes), while the expectation of negative events activates serotonergic and noradrenergic pathways that generate negative affect and withdrawal behavior (and does not impact positive affect processes).

Positive Affect

Positive affect refers to the everyday, low-level, general state of feeling good (Isen, 1987). It is the warm glow that so often accompanies everyday pleasant experiences such as walking in the park on a sunny day, receiving an unexpected gift or good news, listening to music, or making progress on a task. Although we focus on the park scenery, good news, pleasant music, or positive feedback, the mild good feeling arises subconsciously. We may smile more, whistle while we walk, daydream about happy memories, or talk more excitedly, but the positive feelings typically remain outside our conscious attention. In fact, if someone brings the pleasant mood to our attention ("My, aren't we in a good mood today!"), such attention paradoxically is the beginning of the end of the positive affect.

This lack of awareness of the positive affect stands in contrast to the more intense, attention-grabbing positive emotions, such as joy. The purpose of an emotion is to capture attention and direct coping behavior (so the person can adapt to situational demands effectively). Positive affect is more subtle. It affects neither attention nor behavior. Instead, positive affect subtly influences the information processing flow—what we think about, the decisions we make, creativity, judgments, and so on (Isen, 1987, 2002).

Conditions That Make Us Feel Good

People have difficult times explaining why they feel good. If pressed, they typically say that life is generally going well. Mood researchers, on the other hand, have learned which conditions lead people to feel good, and most of these conditions create positive affect in ways such that people remain unaware of the causal source of their good moods (Isen, 1987). Consider these positive affect-inducing experimental manipulations of a small gain, amusement, or pleasure: Find money in the coin-return slot of a public telephone (Isen & Levin, 1972), receive a gift of a bag of candy (Isen & Geva, 1987; Isen, Niedenthal & Cantor, 1992), receive a free product sample (Isen, Clark, & Schwartz, 1976), receive a candy bar (Isen et al., 1985; Isen, Daubman, & Nowicki, 1987), learn that a performance was successful (Isen, 1970), receive a cookie (Isen & Levin, 1972), receive refreshments such as orange juice (Isen et al., 1985), receive positive feedback (Isen, Rosenzweig, & Young, 1991), think about positive events (Isen et al., 1985), experience sunny weather (Kraut & Johnston, 1979), watch an amusing film (Isen & Nowicki, 1981), or rate funny cartoons (Carnevale & Isen, 1986).

Once instigated by an eliciting event (e.g., receiving a small gift), the warm glow of a positive mood continues for up to 20 minutes (Isen, Clark, & Schwartz, 1976). Because we enjoy feeling good, happy people make decisions and act in ways that maintain their good moods for longer than 20 minutes (Forest et al., 1979; Isen et al., 1978). More often than not, however, some rival event or interrupting life task distracts our attention away from the positive affect-inducing event. That is, we lose our positive mood by engaging in neutral and aversive events (e.g., boring work, congested traffic, bad news, a risk turned sour).

Benefits of Feeling Good

Compared to people in a neutral mood, people exposed to conditions that allow them to feel good are more likely to help others (Isen & Levin, 1972), act sociably (i.e., initiate conversations, Batson et al., 1979), express greater liking for others (Veitch & Griffitt, 1976), be more generous to others (Isen, 1970) and to themselves (Mischel, Coates, & Raskoff, 1968), take risks (Isen & Patrick, 1983), act more cooperatively and less aggressively (Carnevale & Isen, 1986), solve problems in creative ways (Isen, Daubman, & Nowicki, 1987), persist in the face of failure feedback (Chen & Isen, 1992), make decisions more efficiently (Isen & Means, 1983), and show greater intrinsic motivation on interesting activities (Isen & Reeve, 2003). Consider two illustrations.

Positive affect facilitates our willingness to help others (Isen & Levin, 1972). A group of researchers conducted a field study at the local mall in which they randomly filled a telephone booth's coin return slot with or without change. Their thinking was that everyone would check the coin slot after making their telephone call and those that found the spare change would feel good while those that found no such spare change would continue to feel their regular day-to-day mood. After each participant left the telephone booth, the researchers arranged to have a young woman walk by and "accidently" drop an armful of books while walking by the participant. If positive affect facilitates helping others, then the participants who received the spare change should be significantly more likely to help the woman than would the participants who did not receive the spare change. Results appear in Table 11.2. People in their normal and regular daily mood (did not receive the spare change) almost never helped (only 1 out of 25 helped). People in a good mood (did receive the spare change) almost always helped (fully 14 out of 16 helped). These results show that a very mild, pleasant feeling dramatically increased people's willingness to help a stranger in need.

Positive affect facilitates cognitive flexibility (Isen, Niedenthal, & Cantor, 1992) and creative problem solving (Estrada, Isen, & Young, 1994, 1997; Isen, Daubman, & Nowicki, 1987). Alice M. Isen and her colleagues (1987) induced positive or neutral affect in groups of college students and then asked them to solve one of two problem-solving tasks requiring creativity—the candle task (Dunker, 1945) or the Remote Associates Test (RAT; Mednick, Mednick, & Mednick, 1964). In the candle task, the participant receives a pile of tacks, a candle, and a box of matches and the instructions to attach the candle to the

Table 11.2 Effect of Positive Affect on Helping Others

Condition	Females		Males	
	Helped	Did Not Help	Helped	Did Not Help
Positive Affect (Did Receive Dime)	8	0	6	2
Neutral Affect (Did Not Receive Dime)	0	16	1	8

Source: From, The effect of feeling good on helping: Cookies and kindness, by A.M. Isen & P.F. Levin, (1972), *Journal of Personality and Social Psychology, 21,* 384–388. Copyright 1972 American Psychological Association. Reprinted by permission.

wall (a cork board) so that the candle can burn without dripping wax on the floor. In the RAT, the participant sees three words (soul, busy, guard) and is asked to generate a fourth word that relates to the other three (in this case, "body"). Positive affect participants solved the creativity-demanding candle task and gave creative (unusual or "remote") associates to the RAT (Isen, Daubmen, & Nowicki, 1987). In contrast, the candle task stumped the neutral affect participants, and they gave routine, stereotypical responses to the RAT. Thus, there are inherent processing advantages conferred by feeling good, as positive affect acts as a resource in solving problems and attaining goals (Aspenwall, 1998).

The explanation as to *how* and *why* positive affect facilitates creativity, decision-making efficiency, sociability, prosocial behavior, persistence, and so on is not as straightforward as it might first appear to be. Being a mood rather than an emotion, positive affect influences cognitive processes, such as memories, judgments, and problem-solving strategies. It therefore influences the contents of working (short-term) memory by biasing what the individual thinks about and what memories and expectations come to mind (Isen, 1984, 1987, 2002). When feeling good, positive affect essentially serves as a retrieval cue to put the spotlight on positive material stored in memory (Isen et al., 1978; Laird et al., 1982; Nasby & Yando, 1982; Teasdale & Fogarty, 1979). As a result, people who feel good have ready access to happy thoughts and positive memories (compared to people who feel neutral). With happy thoughts and pleasant memories salient in one's mind, people show increased creativity, help others more, show persistence in the face of failure, make decisions efficiently, show high intrinsic motivation, and so on.

SUMMARY

This chapter addresses five questions central to understanding the nature of emotion. The first question asks, "What is an emotion?" Emotions have a four-part character in that they feature dimensions of feeling, arousal, purpose, and expression. Feelings give emotions a subjective component that has personal meaning. Arousal includes biological activity such as heart rate that prepares the body for adaptive coping behavior. The purposive component gives emotion a goal-directed sense of motivation to take a specific course of action. The social component of emotion is its communicative aspect, as through a facial expression. Emotion is the psychological construct that coordinates and unifies these four aspects of experience into a synchronized, adaptive pattern.

The second question asks, "What causes an emotion?" Rephrased, this question debates whether emotion is primarily a biological or a cognitive phenomenon. According to the biological perspective, emotions arise from bodily influences such as neural pathways in the brain's limbic system. According to the cognitive perspective, emotions arise from mental events such as appraisals of the personal meaning of the emotion-causing event. Both sides of the biology-cognition debate marshal together an impressive array of evidence to support their positions. Both biology and cognition play a pivotal role in the activation and regulation of emotion, and researchers specify two ways that biology and cognition cause emotion. The first argues for two parallel emotion systems—an innate, spontaneous, and primitive biological emotion system and an acquired, interpretive, and social cognitive emotion system. The second argues that as emotion occurs as a dynamic, dialectical process rather than the linear output of either the biological or cognitive system.

The third question asks, "How many emotions are there?" The answer depends on one's perspective. According to the biological perspective, human beings possess somewhere between 2 and 10 basic emotions. These researchers illustrate how primary emotions emerge from hardwired limbic neural pathways, patterns of neural firing, universal facial expressions, evolutionary functions, and discrete patterns of facial feedback. According to the cognitive perspective, human beings possess a much richer, more diverse emotional repertoire than just the basic emotions. These researchers illustrate how an almost limitless number of secondary emotions are acquired through personal experiences, developmental histories, socialization influences, and cultural rules. Despite this diversity of opinion, most lists of emotion include the six discussed in some depth: fear, anger, distrust, sadness, joy, and interest.

The fourth question asks, "What good are the emotions?" It highlights that emotions serve a purpose. From a functional point of view, emotions evolved as biological reactions that helped us adapt successfully to fundamental life tasks, such as facing a threat. The emotion that arises during an important life task serves a goal-directed purpose that has coping and social purposes. Without a sophisticated emotional repertoire, people would function poorly in their physical and social environments. Still people need to regulate their emotions. Whether emotions serve us well depends on how able we are to experience regulation of emotion rather than regulation by emotion.

The final question asks, "What is the difference between emotion and mood?" Emotions arise in response to a specific event, motivate specific adaptive behaviors, and are short-lived. Moods arise from ill-defined sources, affect cognitive processes, and are long-lived. Mood exists as a positive or as a negative affect state. Positive affect refers to the everyday, low-level, general state of feeling good. When people feel good, they are more sociable, cooperative, creative, persistent during failure, efficient in their decision making, and intrinsically motivated during interesting tasks. Positive affect exerts these effects by affecting cognitive processes such as memories and judgments. As a result, people who feel good have greater access to happy thoughts and positive memories and therefore behave in ways that reflect easy access to happy thoughts (e.g., more creative, more helpful).

READINGS FOR FURTHER STUDY

What Are Emotions?

IZARD, C. E. (1993). Four systems for emotion activation: Cognitive and noncognitive processes. *Psychological Review, 100*, 68–90.

LAZARUS, R. S. (1991). Cognition and motivation in emotion. *American Psychologist, 46*, 352–367.

OATLEY, K., & DUNCAN, E. (1994). The experience of emotions in everyday life. *Cognition and Emotion, 8*, 369–381.

How Many Emotions Are There?

EKMAN, P. (1992). An argument for basic emotions. *Cognition and Emotion, 6*, 169–200.

KEMPER, T. D. (1987). How many emotions are there? Wedding the social and autonomic components. *American Sociological Review, 93*, 263–289.

Functions of Emotion

CARSTENSEN, L. L., GOTTMAN, J. M., & LEVENSON, R. W. (1995). Emotional behavior in long-term marriage. *Psychology and Aging, 10*, 140–149.

KRAUT, R. E., & JOHNSTON, R. E. (1979). Social and emotional messages of smiling: An ethological approach. *Journal of Personality and Social Psychology, 37*, 1539–1553.

TOOBY, J., & COSMIDES, L. (1990). The past explains the present: Emotional adaptations and the structure of ancestral environment. *Ethology and Sociobiology, 11*, 375–424.

Mood and Positive Affect

ISEN, A. M., DAUBMAN, K. A., & NOWICKI, G. P. (1987). Positive affect facilitates creative problem-solving. *Journal of Personality and Social Psychology, 51*, 1122–1131.

WATSON, D., CLARK, L. A., & TELLEGEN, A. (1988). Development and validation of brief measures of positive and negative affect: The PANAS scales. *Journal of Personality and Social Psychology, 54*, 1063–1070.

Chapter 12

Aspects of Emotion

Try to look sad—try to produce a sad facial expression. As you try this, attend to the changing sensations you feel from the movements of your facial musculature. If you just pouted out the lower lip and pulled down the corners of your mouth, then you probably did not feel too sad. So, try this again.

Produce a second sad facial expression. But this time move not only your lower lip and corners of your mouth but also move your eyebrows inward at the same time. Moving your eyebrows inward will take some skill, so pretend that you have a couple of golf tees attached to the inner corners of the eyebrows. Pretend these golf tees are about an inch apart and pointing outward from your face in a parallel way (base of each tee rests on the inner eyebrow with its tip extending outward). Now move your eyebrows inward until the tips of the golf tees touch. Now try to move all three of these muscles together—touch the golf tees together, pout your lower lip, and turn the corners of your mouth down (Larsen, Kasimatis, & Frey, 1992).

Did you feel anything as you were attempting this facial expression? Did you sense a hint of a sad feeling coming on? Did your heart rate drop? Any vague urge to cry? If so, the feeling will be mild because a posed facial expression is not as authentic and emotion-producing as a spontaneous facial expression. But the mild sad feeling via a patterned facial expression is a good way to introduce one of the many aspects of emotion discussed in this chapter—in this case, the "facial feedback hypothesis."

As important life events come our way, these events activate biological and cognitive reactions in us. The resulting biological and cognitive processes generate emotion. And the emotion readies us to cope adaptively with the important life event before us. An outline of the biological and cognitive processes involved in emotion appears in Table 12.1. The first half of this chapter will overview the biological processes in emotion (left-hand side), while the second half of the chapter will overview the cognitive processes in emotion (right-hand side).

BIOLOGICAL ASPECTS OF EMOTION

Emotions are, in part, biological reactions to important life events. The list of biological events in Table 12.1 is important because these entries identify the body's emotion-related biological reactions to important life events. Facing a situation of personal significance (e.g., a threat), the body prepares itself to cope effectively (e.g., gets ready to run) by activating the following: (1) heart, lungs, and muscles (autonomic nervous system); (2) glands and hormones (endocrine system); (3) limbic brain structures such as the hypothalamus (neural brain circuits); (4) neural activity and the pace of information processing (rate of neural firing); and (5) discrete patterns of the facial musculature (facial feedback).

Table 12.1   Biological and Cognitive Aspects of Emotion

Biological Aspects	Cognitive, Social, and Cultural Aspects
1. Autonomic nervous system	1. Appraisals
2. Endocrine system	2. Knowledge
3. Neural brain circuits	3. Attributions
4. Rate of neural firing	4. Socialization history
5. Facial feedback	5. Cultural identities

With these biological systems engaged, the person experiences emotion and is significantly more readied to cope with the impending threat.

Emotion study began about 100 years ago by asking what role the autonomic nervous
system played in the subjective experience of emotion. The first theory of emotion, the
James-Lange theory, asked whether or not the different emotions each had unique bodily
reactions associated with them. We all know that fear and joy feel different, but do fear and
joy also have their own unique bodily reactions? Do our heart, lungs, and hormones behave
one way when we are afraid yet another way when we experience joy? And if so, do these
biological differences explain why the emotions we experience are different? Does the pattern of activity in our heart, lungs, and hormones actually cause the felt fear and felt joy?

James-Lange Theory

Personal experience suggests that we experience an emotion and that the felt emotion is
quickly followed by bodily changes. As soon as we see the flashing red lights and hear the
siren of a police car, fear arises and the feeling of fear subsequently makes our heart race
and our palms sweat. The sequence of events seems to be stimulus → emotion → bodily
reaction. William James (1884, 1890, 1894) argued against this common view. He suggested that our bodily changes do not follow the emotional experience; rather, emotional
experience follows and depends on our bodily and behavioral responses to the flashing
lights and siren sounds. Hence, bodily changes cause emotional experience: stimulus →
bodily reaction → emotion.

James' theory rested on two assumptions: (1) The body reacts uniquely (discriminato-
rily) to different emotion-eliciting events, and (2) the body does not react to nonemotion-
eliciting events. To appreciate James' hypotheses, think of your body's physiological
responses to an unexpectedly cold shower. The physiological reaction—the increased
heart rate, quickened breath, and widened eyes—begins before you have time to think
about why your heart is racing and why your eyes are widening. The body reacts and the
ensuing emotional reactions are on us before we are aware of what is happening. James
argued that such instantaneous bodily reactions occur in discernible patterns, and emotional experience is a person's way of making sense of each different pattern of bodily reactions. If the bodily changes did not occur, then the ensuing emotion would not occur.

The James-Lange theory of emotions quickly became popular, but it also met with
criticism (Cannon, 1927).[1] Critics argued that the sort of bodily reactions James referred
to were actually part of the body's general mobilizing fight-or-flight response that did not
vary from one emotion to the next (Cannon, 1929; Mandler, 1975; Schachter, 1964).[2]
These critics also argued that emotional experience was quicker than physiological reactions. That is, while a person feels anger in a 10th of a second, it takes this person's nervous system a full second or two to activate important glands and send excitatory
hormones through the bloodstream. These critics contended that the role of physiological

---

[1] At the same time James presented his ideas, a Danish psychologist, Carl Lange (1885), proposed essentially the
same (but more limited) theory. For this reason, the idea that emotions emanate from our interpretation of patterns of physiological arousal is traditionally called the James-Lange theory (Lange & James, 1922).

[2] For instance, does a person experience specific emotions after taking a stimulant drug known to induce bodily
changes—increase heart rate, minimize gastrointestinal activity, and dilate the bronchioles? Drug-induced visceral stimulation leads people to feel "as if afraid" or "as if going to weep without knowing why" rather than
afraid or sad per se (i.e., people feel generally aroused but not specifically afraid).

arousal was to augment, rather than cause, emotion (Newman, Perkins, & Wheeler, 1930). Critics concluded that the contribution of physiological changes to emotional experience was small, supplemental, and relatively unimportant. A decade after it was proposed, the first major theory of emotion was in doubt.

Contemporary Perspective

In the face of criticism, James's ideas faded out of favor, and rival theories of emotion emerged and became popular (e.g., see Schachter & Singer, 1962). Nonetheless, his ideas continue to guide contemporary study (Ellsworth, 1994; Lang, 1994), and contemporary research now finds some support for physiological specificity in a few emotions (Buck, 1986; Levenson, 1992; Schwartz, 1986). Paul Ekman, Robert Levenson, and Wallace Friesen (1983), for example, studied whether each of several emotions does or does not have a unique pattern of bodily changes. These researchers recruited people who could experience emotions on command (professional actors) and asked each to relive five different emotions—anger, fear, sadness, joy, and disgust—while the researchers measured for emotion-specific patterns of physiological activity. Distinct differences in heart rate (HR) and skin temperature (ST) emerged. With anger, HR and ST both increased. With fear, HR increased while ST decreased. With sadness, HR increased while ST was stable. With joy, HR was stable while ST increased. And with disgust, both HR and ST decreased. Just as James suspected, different emotions did indeed produce distinguishable patterns of bodily activity.

Persuasive evidence exists for distinctive autonomic nervous system (ANS) activity associated with anger, fear, disgust, and sadness (Ekman & Davidson, 1993; Ekman, Levenson, & Friesen, 1983; Levenson, 1992; Levenson et al., 1991; Levenson, Ekman, & Friesen, 1990; Sinha & Parsons, 1996; Stemmler, 1989). These patterns of ANS activity supposedly emerged because they were able to recruit ways of behaving that proved to be adaptive. For instance, in a fight that arouses anger, increased heart rate and skin temperature facilitate strong, assertive behavior.

Not all emotions have distinct patterns of ANS activity, however. If no specific pattern of behavior has survival value for an emotion, there is little reason for the development of a specific pattern of ANS activity (Ekman, 1992, 1994a). For instance, what is the most adaptive behavioral pattern to jealousy? to joy? hope? For these emotions, no single adaptive activity seems universally most appropriate, as adaptive coping depends more on the specifics of the situation than on the emotion itself. Hence, there is little reason to expect a single pattern of ANS activity to evolve.

In discussing the James-Lange theory of emotion, the fundamental question is whether the physiological arousal causes, or just follows, emotion activation. This question is important because if arousal causes emotion, then the study of physiological arousal becomes the cornerstone study for any understanding of emotion. But if arousal merely follows and augments emotion, physiological activity is therefore much less important—important, but not vital. Contemporary researchers generally agree that physiological arousal accompanies, regulates, and sets the stage for emotion, but it does not cause it directly. The modern perspective is that emotions recruit biological and physiological support to enable adaptive behaviors such as fighting, fleeing, and nurturing. Hence, the autonomic nervous system's role in emotion is to create the optimal biological milieu that will support the adaptive behavior called for by a particular emotion-causing life situation (Levenson, 1994b).

BOX 12 *Affective Computing*

Question: Why is this information important?

Answer: Because it will help you get ready for the coming technology that will read and adapt to your emotions.

The finding that emotions show ANS specificity has intriguing implications for coming technology. If changes in blood pressure and skin temperature can reliably distinguish between the emotions of anger, fear, sadness, joy, and disgust, and if an electronic stethoscope and thermostat can detect these bodily changes, then we can build machines that know how we feel. Machines that read our emotions are not far away.

Imagine electronic sensors built into steering wheels, mobile telephones, and the handles of bicycles, pilot simulators, computer joysticks, and golf clubs that constantly monitor its user's ANS arousal while driving, talking, and so on. Imagine electronic sensors in a device held by audience members during plays, lectures, musical performances, and political debates.

Soon, you will not need to imagine such technology, as scientists in the new field of "affective computing" are hard at work building such devices (Azar, 2000; see also "Soon: Computers that know you hate them," The *New York Times*, January 6, 2000). One particularly interesting invention is the "emotion mouse." It functions like an ordinary computer mouse, except it has special sensors for monitoring heart rate, skin temperature, hand movements, and electrical skin conductance. The computer monitors the data collected by the emotion mouse and analyzes these data as a means to infer the user's emotional state.

If a computer can read a user's emotions, then it gains the capacity to adjust its programming to user's emotionality. A computer game can be made more or less challenging. A tutorial can be adjusted to decrease fear, say by re-presenting familiar information rather than new, stressful information. An online counseling session can provide emotional feedback regarding the feelings of a client at different points in the conversation. Such feedback would be particularly useful during distance counseling (the client is in one place while the therapist is in a different place).

But even the best emotion mouse will still be limited to monitoring only the five emotions of anger, fear, sadness, joy, and disgust (i.e., only the emotions that show ANS specificity). To expand the computer's ability to monitor and analyze additional emotions, another feature could be added—something akin to a video camera built into a computer or hand-held phone to monitor and analyze facial expressions. Such a camera could monitor movements of the user's face—the user's frontalis, corrugators, orbicularis oculi, zygomaticus, nasalis, depressors, orbicularis oris, and quadratus labii (see Figure 12.3). With these facial movements, the computer gains the data necessary for inferring both the presence and the intensity of anger, fear, distress, disgust, joy, interest, and contempt (see Figure 12.5).

Computers can analyze and interpret a user's facial muscles because researchers have already developed an elaborate coding system to do so, called "FACS" for facial action coding system (Ekman & Friesen, 1978). Software based on FACS already exists. Computers using this software are about as accurate as (and much faster than) people who score the same facial movements (Cohn et al., 1999). The ability of computers to instantly recognize people's emotional expressions appears to be only a matter of time (Ekman & Friesen, 1975; Ekman & Rosenberg, 1997).

Specific Neural Circuits

Just as early researchers looked for emotion-specific patterns of physiological activity, contemporary researchers search for emotion-specific patterns in brain activity (Gray, 1994; LeDoux, 1987; Panksepp, 1982, 1986). For instance, Jeffrey Gray's (1994) neuroanatomical findings (with nonhuman mammals) document the existence of three distinct neural circuits in the brain, each of which regulates a distinctive pattern of emotional behavior: (1) a *behavioral approach system* that readies the animal to seek out and interact with attractive environmental opportunities, (2) a *fight-or-flight system* that readies the animal to flee from some aversive events but to defend aggressively against other events, and (3) a *behavioral inhibition system* that readies the animal to freeze in the face of aversive events. These three neural circuits underlie the four emotions of joy, fear, rage, and anxiety.

Neural Activation

Different emotions are activated by different rates of cortical neural firing (Tomkins, 1970). Neural firing refers to the pattern of electrocortical activity (in the brain) at any given time. According to Silvan Tomkins, there are three basic patterns of neural firing: activity increases, activity decreases, or activity remains constant. Whether the rate of neural firing is increasing, decreasing, or constant depends mostly on environmental events. For example, if you are sleeping (a low rate of neural firing, as measured by the electroencephalogram, or EEG) and a cat jumps on your face (a stimulating event), the rate of neural firing will increase. If you are at a rock concert (another stimulating event) and exit to relative quiet, the rate of neural firing will decrease. Other times, neural activity is constant, as in persistent cognitive effort while reading the newspaper.

With these three basic patterns of neural firing, the person is equipped for virtually every important life event. If neural firing suddenly increases, the person experiences one class of emotions—surprise, fear, or interest—with the specific emotion depending on the suddenness of the increased rate of neural firing (i.e., slight increase → interest, moderate increase → fear, and dramatic increase → surprise). If neural firing reaches and maintains a high level, then the constant (and high) neural firing activates either distress or anger, depending on the magnitude of the neural stimulation (i.e., continuously high → distress, continuously very high → anger). Finally, if neural firing decreases, joy is activated, as the individual laughs and smiles with relief. The relationship between each of these changes in the rate of neural firing and its associated emotion appears in Figure 12.1.

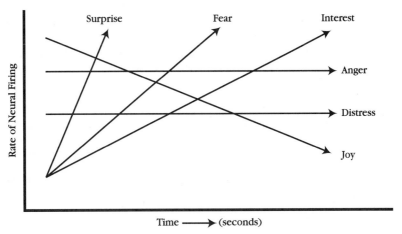

Figure 12.1   Emotion Activation as a Function of Changes in the Rate of Neural Firing

Source: From "Affect as the Primary Motivational System," by S. S. Tomkins (1970) in M. B. Arnold (Ed.), *Feelings and emotions* (pp. 101–110), New York: Academic Press.

Consider the neural activity of an audience watching a horror movie. First, the audience is slowly introduced to the characters, setting, and circumstances of the plot. Exposure to all this new information gradually increases neural firing, and the audience becomes interested. Suddenly, the crazy man with an axe jumps out from behind the bushes, an event that drastically increases the audience's neural firing and activates surprise. Later, the audience watches the protagonist move through the dark forest and seeing strange sights. The audience's neural firing quickens and arouses fear. If the neural firing remains high, it arouse distress. So, the writer makes sure to toss in a joke or two, and the writer makes sure the hero and heroine conquer the crazy man in the end, events that decrease the rate of neural firing and activate joy.

Differential Emotions Theory

Differential emotions theory takes its name from its emphasis on basic emotions serving unique, or different, motivational purposes (Izard, 1991, 1992, 1993; Izard & Malatesta, 1987). The theory endorses the following postulates (Izard, 1991):

1. Ten emotions constitute the principal motivation system for human beings.
2. Unique Feeling: Each emotion has its own unique subjective, phenomenological quality.
3. Unique Expression: Each emotion has its own unique facial-expressive pattern.
4. Unique Neural Activity: Each emotion has its own specific rate of neural firing that activates it.
5. Unique Purpose/Motivation: Each emotion generates distinctive motivational properties and serves adaptive functions.

The 10 discrete emotions that fit these 5 postulates appear in Table 12.2. Each emotion, according to differential emotions theory, operates as a system that coordinates feeling (postulate 2), expression (postulate 3), neural activity (postulate 4), and purpose/motivation (postulate 5) components. Notice how closely these four aspects of emotion correspond to the four aspects of emotion introduced at the start of Chapter 11 (see Figure 11.1).

Differential emotions theory argues that these 10 discrete emotions act as motivation systems that prepare the individual for acting in adaptive ways (Izard, 1989, 1991, 1992).

Table 12.2   Izard's 10 Fundamental Emotions Included in His Differential Emotions Theory

Positive Emotions	Neutral Emotions	Negative Emotions
Interest	Surprise	Fear
Joy		Anger
		Disgust
		Distress
		Contempt
		Shame
		Guilt

Each emotion exists to provide the individual with an organized heuristic for dealing effectively with life tasks and problems that are both important and recurring (e.g., establish social bonds, confront threats).

Seeing the list of emotions in Table 12.2 is likely to conjure up a question such as the following: Where are emotions like jealousy, hope, love, hate, smugness, and worry? Biologically minded theories generally do not count experiences such as these among the basic emotions. Paul Ekman (1992) offers seven reasons to explain why:

1. Emotion families exist such that many nonbasic emotions are experienced-based derivatives of a single basic emotion (e.g., anxiety is a derivative of fear).
2. Many emotion terms actually better describe moods (e.g., irritation).
3. Many emotion terms actually better describe attitudes (e.g., hatred).
4. Many emotion terms actually better describe personality traits (e.g., hostile).
5. Many emotion terms actually better describe disorders (e.g., depression).
6. Some nonbasic emotions are blends of basic emotions (e.g., romantic love blends interest, joy, and the sex drive).
7. Many emotion words refer to specific aspects of a basic emotion (e.g., what elicits the emotion [homesickness] or how a person behaves [aggression]).

Facial Feedback Hypothesis

According to the facial feedback hypothesis, the subjective aspect of emotion stems from feelings engendered by (1) movements of the facial musculature, (2) changes in facial temperature, and (3) changes in glandular activity in the facial skin. Therefore, emotions are "sets of muscle and glandular responses located in the face" (Tomkins, 1962). In other words, emotion is the awareness of proprioceptive feedback from facial behavior.

Upon being introduced to the hypothesis that emotion is facial feedback information, the reader might be a bit skeptical—"C'mon, smiling makes you happy?" But consider the following sequence of events depicted in Figure 12.2 to understand how sensations from the face feed back to the cortical brain to produce emotional experience (Izard, 1991). Exposure to an external (loud noise) or internal (memory of being harmed) event increases the rate of neural firing quickly enough to activate a subcortical emotion program such as fear (#1 in Figure 12.2). The human subcortical brain (limbic system) possesses innate, genetically wired, emotion-specific programs (#2). When activated, these programs send impulses to the basal ganglia and facial nerve to generate discrete facial expressions (#3). Within microseconds of the displayed fear facial expression (#4), the brain interprets the facial feedback proprioceptive stimulation (which muscles are contracted, which muscles are relaxed, changes in blow flow, changes in skin temperature, glandular secretions; #5). This particular pattern of facial feedback is cortically integrated—made sense of—to give rise to the subjective feeling of fear (#6). Only then does the frontal lobe of the cortex become aware of the emotional state at a conscious level. Quickly thereafter, the whole body joins the facial feedback to become involved in the fear emotion as the glandular-hormonal, cardiovascular, and respiratory systems become aroused and amplify and sustain the activated fear experience.

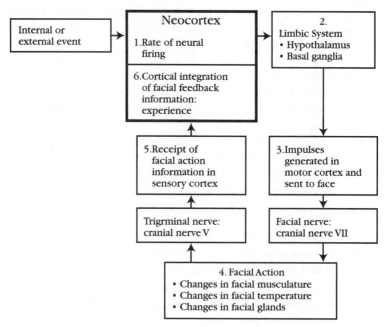

Figure 12.2 Sequence of the Emotion-Activating Events According to the Facial Feedback Hypothesis

Facial feedback does one job: emotion activation (Izard, 1989, 1994). Once an emotion is activated, it is the emotion program, not the facial feedback, that then recruits further cognitive and bodily participation to maintain the emotional experience over time. The person then becomes aware of and monitors not her facial feedback but her changes in heart rate, respiration, muscle tonus, posture, and so on. Nonetheless, it is the facial feedback that activates the chain of events that underlie the emotional experience.

Facial action also changes brain temperature, such that facial movements associated with negative emotion (sadness) constrict breathing, raise brain temperature, and produce negative feelings, whereas facial movements associated with positive emotion (happiness) enhance breathing, cool brain temperature, and produce positive feelings (McIntosh et al., 1997; Zajonc, Murphy, & Inglehart, 1989). To make sense of this result, make a sad facial expression and see if the facial action around the nose does not constrict your air flow a bit. Also, make a joy facial expression and see if that facial action does not encourage and open up air flow from the nose. The changing brain temperatures do have (mild) emotional consequences.

Facial Musculature

There are 80 facial muscles, 36 of which are involved in facial expression. For purposes of exposition, however, the 8 facial muscles shown in Figure 12.3 are sufficient for differentiating among the basic emotions (for more information, see Ekman & Friesen, 1975;

Izard, 1971). The upper face (the eyes and forehead) has 3 major muscles: the frontalis (covers the forehead), corrugator (lies beneath each eyebrow), and orbicularis oculi (surrounds each eye). The middle face has 2 major muscles: the zygomaticus (extends from the corners of the mouth to the cheekbone) and the nasalis (wrinkles the nose). The lower face has 3 major muscles: the depressor (draws the corners of the mouth downward), the orbicularis oris (circular muscle surrounding the lips), and the quadratus labii (draws the corners of the mouth backward).

Patterns of facial behavior produce discrete emotions. Anger, fear, disgust, distress, and joy, for instance, all have a recognizable facial expression. These facial expressions are described muscle-by-muscle in words in Figure 12.3 and also in photographic presentation in Figure 12.4 (Ekman & Friesen, 1975). Two additional emotions are associated with a particular pattern of facial behavior: interest (Reeve, 1993) and contempt (Ekman & Friesen, 1986). The interest expression is illustrated in 18 of the 19 faces shown in Figure 12.5 (all but the boy in the lower right corner). For interest, the orbicularis oculi open the eyelids and the orbicularis oris slightly parts the lips open (notice the unique positions of the eyes and mouth). For contempt, the zygomaticus unilaterally raises the corner of one lip upwards. In contempt, the person "snarls" upwards one side of the mouth.

Test of the Facial Feedback Hypothesis

Feedback from facial behavior, when transformed into conscious awareness, constitutes the experience of emotion (Laird, 1974; Tomkins, 1962, 1963). This is the facial feedback hypothesis (FFH). Investigations to test the validity of the FFH have used two different methodologies, because there are two testable versions of the FFH—the strong version and the weak version (McIntosh, 1996; Rutledge & Hupka, 1985).

In its strong version, the FFH proposes that manipulating one's facial musculature into a pattern that corresponds to an emotion display (e.g., see Figure 12.4) will activate that emotional experience. In other words, frowning the lips and raising the inner eyebrows activates sadness (recall the example at the beginning of this chapter). In empirical tests, an experimenter instructs a participant to contract and relax specific muscles of the face and, with a particular facial expression displayed, complete a questionnaire to assess emotional experience. For example, in one study, participants were instructed to (1) "raise your brows and pull them together," (2) "now raise your upper eyelids," and (3) "now also stretch your lips horizontally, back towards your ears" (Ekman, Levenson, & Friesen, 1983). So posed, the participants were asked about their emotional state (fear, in this case) on a questionnaire. Research has both supported (Laird, 1974, 1984; Larsen, Kasimatis, & Frey, 1992; Rutledge & Hupka, 1985; Strack, Martin, & Stepper, 1988) and refuted (McCaul, Holmes, & Solomon, 1982; Tourangeau & Ellsworth, 1979) the strong version of the FFH. One area of consensus is that a posed facial musculature produces reliable changes in physiological reactions, such as changes in cardiovascular and respiratory rates (Tourangeau & Ellsworth, 1979; Ekman et al., 1983). It is still debated whether the posed facial musculature produces emotional experience, but most studies suggest that it does produce at least a small effect (Adelmann & Zajonc, 1989; Izard, 1990; Laird, 1984; Matsumoto, 1987; Rutledge & Hupka, 1985).

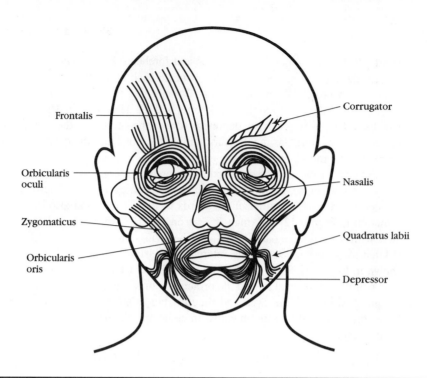

Facial Muscle	Anger	Fear	Disgust	Sadness	Joy
Frontalis (Forehead)	n/a	contracts, producing forehead wrinkles	n/a	n/a	n/a
Corrugator (Eyebrows)	draws eyebrows in and down	raises inner corners of eyebrows	n/a	raises and draws together inner corners of eyelids	n/a
Orbicularis Oculi (Eyes)	tenses lower eyelids upward	raises upper eyelids, tenses lower eyelids	n/a	raises upper inner corner of eyelids	relaxes, showing wrinkles below eyes
Nasalis (Nose)	n/a	n/a	wrinkles nose	n/a	n/a
Zygomaticus (Cheeks)	n/a	n/a	raises cheeks	n/a	1. pulls corners of lip back and up; 2. raises cheeks, showing Crow's feet below eyes
Orbicularis Oris (Lips)	presses lips firmly together	n/a	raises upper lip	n/a	n/a
Quadratus Labii (Jaw)	n/a	pulls lips backward	n/a	n/a	n/a
Depressor (Mouth)	n/a	n/a	n/a	pull corners of lips down	n/a

Figure 12.3 Eight Major Facial Muscles Involved in the Expression of Emotion.

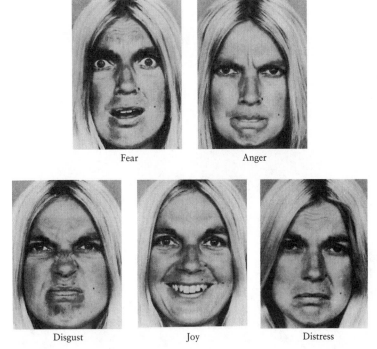

Fear   Anger

Disgust   Joy   Distress

Figure 12.4 Facial Expressions for Five Emotions
Source: From *Unmasking the face*, by P. Ekman and W. V. Friesen, 1975, Englewood Cliffs, NJ: Prentice Hall.

In its weaker (more conservative) version, the FFH proposes that facial feedback modifies the intensity of (rather than causes) the emotion. Thus, managing one's facial musculature into a particular emotional display will augment (exaggerate) but will not necessarily activate (cause) the emotional experience. In other words, if you intentionally smile when you are already joyful, then you will feel a more intense joy. In one experiment, participants either exaggerated or suppressed their spontaneous facial expressions while watching a video, which depicted either a pleasant, neutral, or unpleasant scenario (Zuckerman et al., 1981). Exaggerating naturally occurring facial expressions did augment both emotional and physiological experience, just as suppressing naturally occurring facial expressions softened both emotional and physiological experience (Lanzetta, Cartwright-Smith, & Kleck, 1976).

Unlike its stronger version, the weaker version of the FFH has received a consensus of support (McIntosh, 1996). These results highlight the two-way street between the emotions we feel and the emotions we express: Emotions activate facial expressions, and facial expressions, in turn, feed back to exaggerate and suppress the emotions we feel. Critics content, however, that the contribution of such facial feedback is small and that other factors are more important (Matsumoto, 1987).

Figure 12.5 Eighteen Facial Expressions of Interest
Source: AP/Wide World Photos

Are Facial Expressions of Emotion Universal Across Cultures?

The facial feedback hypothesis assumes that facial expressions are innate. But much facial behavior is surely learned. It is a rare individual who has not learned to express the polite smile and to inhibit the angry face while talking with the boss. But the fact that some facial behavior is learned (and therefore under voluntary control) does not rule out the possibility that facial behavior also has a genetic, innate component, as proposed by the proponents of the FFH.

A series of cross-cultural investigations tested the proposition that human beings display similar facial expressions regardless of cultural differences (Ekman, 1972, 1994b; Izard, 1994). In each of these studies, representatives from diverse nationalities looked at three photographs, each showing a different facial expression (Ekman, 1972,

1993; Ekman & Friesen, 1971; Ekman, Sorenson, & Friesen, 1969; Izard, 1971, 1980, 1994). From these photographs, participants chose, via a multiple-choice format, the photograph they thought best expressed a particular emotion. For example, participants were shown photographs of three faces, one expressing anger, one expressing joy, and one expressing fear. The participants selected the picture they thought showed what a face would look like when the person encountered an injustice or obstacle to a goal (i.e., anger). The research question is whether persons from different cultures would agree on which facial expressions correspond with which emotional experiences. The finding that people from different cultures (different cultures, different languages, different nationalities) match the same facial expressions with the same emotions is evidence that facial behavior is cross-culturally universal (Ekman, 1994b; Ekman & Friesen, 1971; Izard, 1971).[3] This is evidence that emotion-related facial behavior has an innate, unlearned component.

To test yourself as the participants in the cross-cultural experiments were tested, take a look at the photographs shown in Figure 12.6. The photographs show four different expressions of a New Guinea native (someone from a different culture than you). Your task is to identify the face that just encountered a contaminated object (i.e., disgust).

Can We Voluntarily Control Our Emotions?

One intriguing question in emotion research asks, "Can we voluntarily control our emotions?" (Ekman & Davidson, 1994). Can we voluntarily feel happy or voluntarily not be afraid? The difficulty in providing a definitive answer emerges when you recall that emotions have four aspects: feelings, arousal, purpose, and expression. Emotion's multidimensional nature begs the question whether feelings, heart rate and physiological states, motivational desires, and facial expressions are controllable. In trying to answer the more general question, however, some emotions clearly just happen to us, and we therefore cannot be held responsible for the involuntary feelings, physiology, desires, and behaviors that ensue (Ekman, 1992, 1994a).[4] On the other hand, we all have difficulty conjuring up

---

[3]Research with infants supports the idea that facial behavior has a strong innate component (Izard et al., 1980) because presocialized infants show distinct, identifiable facial expressions. Blind children, who lack opportunity to learn facial expressions from others through modeling and imitation, show the same recognizable facial expressions as do children of the same age who can see (Goodenough, 1932). Severely mentally handicapped children, who have difficulty learning new motor behaviors, also show full expressions of the emotions (Eibl-Eibesfeldt, 1971).

[4]Daily experience confirms that we can voluntarily regulate emotions once they happen to us, at least to some extent. Intentionally, we mask and hide our fear before sky diving, and we suppress our boredom while listening to another person's conversation. Because we can regulate our emotions, through inhibition mostly (Levenson, 1994a), we are therefore somewhat responsible for our emotionality (e.g., how angry or sad we get and how long we stay that way). Therefore, the initial onset of an emotion is what is so difficult to control. But our capacity for emotional regulation allows us control over the intensity of the rise and fall of our emotions once they happen to us (Ekman, 1992; Levenson, 1994a).

Figure 12.6 Which Facial Expression Shows Disgust? The photograph of the New Guinea native expressing disgust appears in the lower-right corner. Clockwise from the bottom-left are expressions of anger, joy, and distress.

Source: From "Universal and Cultural Differences in Facial Expression of Emotion," by P. Ekman, 1972, in J. R. Cole (Ed.), *Nebraska Symposium on Motivation* (Vol. 19, pp. 207–283), Lincoln: University of Nebraska Press.

some emotions at will—courage, love, optimism, interest, and so on. It is very difficult to just say, "Okay, I'm now going to feel joy." Instead, you need an exposure to an emotion-generating event capable of conjuring up that specific emotional state. Emotions are largely reactions, and you need some event to react to before conjuring up an emotion.

If emotions are largely biological phenomena that are governed by subcortical structures and pathways, then it makes sense that much of an emotion will escape our voluntary control. If, however, emotions are largely cognitive phenomena that are governed by thoughts, beliefs, and ways of thinking, it makes sense that a good deal of emotional experience can nevertheless be voluntarily controlled, at least to the point that we can voluntarily control our thoughts, beliefs, and ways of thinking. Such a perspective introduces a discussion on the cognitive aspects of emotion.

COGNITIVE ASPECTS OF EMOTION

For those who study emotion from a cognitive, social, or cultural point of view, biological events are not necessarily the most important aspects of emotion. Emotions do emerge from biological processes. But they also emerge from information processing, social interaction, and cultural contexts. For instance, a purely biological analysis with a spotlight on subcortical brain circuits, autonomic and endocrine system activity, and facial expressions does not give one an understanding of emotions such as hope, pride, and alienation. "Disappointment" stems not from ANS activity or changes in facial expressions but, instead, from a cognitive, social, and cultural understanding of not having what you hoped you would have (van Dijk, Zeelengerb, & van der Pligt, 1999). The same could be said for "shame" (not having done what was expected of you) and for many other emotions.

Appraisal

The central construct in a cognitive understanding of emotion is appraisal (Frijda, 1993; Scherer, Schorr, & Johnstone, 2001; Smith et al., 1993). An appraisal is an estimate of the personal significance of an event—is this life event significant? Does this event have implications for my well-being? All cognitive emotion theorists endorse two interrelated beliefs (Frijda, 1986; Lazarus, 1991a; Ortony, Clore, & Collins, 1988; Roseman, 1984; Scherer, 1984a; Smith & Ellsworth, 1985; Weiner, 1986):

1. Emotions do not occur without an antecedent appraisal (cognition) of the event.

2. The appraisal, not the event itself, causes the emotion.

Consider a child who sees a man approaching. Immediately and automatically, the child appraises the meaning of the man's approach as probably "good" or "bad." The appraisal is based on the salient characteristics of the man approaching (gender, facial expression, pace of approach), expectations of who might be approaching, beliefs of what approaching people typically do, and memories of people approaching in the past. It is not the approaching man per se that explains the quality of the child's emotional reaction, but rather, it is how the child thinks the approaching man will affect her well-being that gives life to her emotion. If she sees the approaching man smiling and waving and if she remembers the man as being her friend, then she will likely appraise the event as a good one. If she sees the approaching man ranting and raving and if she remembers the man as being the neighborhood bully, then she will likely appraise the event as a bad one. These appraisals cause her to experience emotion (and physiological bodily changes as well). If the child did not appraise the personal relevance of the approaching man, she would not have had an emotional reaction to the man because events that are irrelevant to well-being do not generate emotions (Lazarus, 1991a; Ortony & Clore, 1989; Ortony, Clore, & Collins, 1988).

Appraisals precede and elicit emotions. Situations and outcomes do not cause emotions in the way that the person's appraisals (interpretations) of those situations and outcomes do. To reinforce this idea, consider the counterintuitive finding that Olympic bronze medallists experience more post-competition happiness than do Olympic silver medallists. For this to be true, the athlete's appraisal of what might have been is at least as important as what situation actually took place (e.g., "I could have won the gold" versus "I could have come up empty"; Medvec, Madey, & Gilovich, 1995). The same sort of cognitive construal also works in emotions such as shame ("If only I weren't . . .") and guilt ("If only I hadn't . . ."; Niedenthal, Tangney, & Gavanski, 1994). Emotions follow appraisals. Change the appraisal, and you change the emotion.

One of the earliest cognitive theorists was Magda Arnold (1960, 1970). She specified how appraisals, neurophysiology, and arousal work together to produce the experience and expression of emotion by focusing on three questions: (1) How does the perception of an object or event produce a good or bad appraisal; (2) how does the appraisal generate emotion; and (3) how does felt emotion express itself in action?

From Perception to Appraisal

According to Arnold, people categorically appraise stimulus events and objects as positive or negative. To substantiate her ideas, Arnold paid particularly close detail to the neurological pathways in the brain. In all encounters with the environment, limbic system brain structures (e.g., the amygdala) automatically appraise the hedonic tone of sensory information. For instance, a harsh sound instantaneously is appraised as intrinsically unpleasant (bad), while the smell of a rose is appraised as intrinsically pleasant (good). Recent neuroanatomical research confirms Arnold's claim that the limbic system (and amygdala in particular) is the focal brain center that appraises the emotional significance of sensory stimuli (LeDoux, 1992a, 1992b). In addition, most stimuli are further appraised cortically by adding information processing and hence expectations, memories, beliefs, goals, judgments, and attributions. Full appraisal therefore draws on both subcortical (limbic system) and cortical interpretations and evaluations.

From Appraisal to Emotion

Once an object has been appraised as good or bad (as beneficial or harmful), an experience of liking or disliking follows immediately and automatically. For Arnold, the liking or disliking is the felt emotion.

From Felt Emotion to Action

Liking generates a motivational tendency to approach the emotion-generating object; disliking generates a motivational tendency to avoid it. During appraisal, the individual relies on memory and imagination to generate a number of possible courses of action in dealing with the liked or disliked object. When a particular course of action is decided upon, the hippocampal brain circuit activates the motor cortex, which leads to behavioral action. Contemporary research adds that the limbic system also has direct access to the muscles that control facial expressions (Holstedge, Kuypers, & Dekker, 1977), autonomic and endocrine system reactions (Kapp, Pascoe, & Bixler, 1984; LeDoux et al., 1988), and general arousal systems (brain stem; Krettek & Price, 1978). Through its effects on these biological systems, emotions produce action.[5]

---

[5]One important feature of Arnold's theory is that emotion is defined in terms of motivation. The tendency to approach or avoid gives the emotion a directional force, while the physiological changes in the muscles and viscera give emotion its energy. A second important feature of Arnold's theory treats emotion as a unitary construct, as she preferred to talk about emotion forces of approach and avoidance, of attraction and repulsion, and of liking and disliking more than she did of specific emotions such as anger, sadness, or pride.

Arnold's ground-breaking appraisal theory of emotion can be summarized as follows:

	Appraisal	Emotion	Action
Life Event	→ Good vs. Bad (Beneficial vs. Harmful)	→ Liking vs. Disliking	→ Approach vs. Withdrawal

Complex Appraisal

Like Arnold, Richard Lazarus emphasized the cognitive processes that intervene between important life events (environmental conditions) and physiological and behavioral reactivity. While following Arnold's ideas as a road map, he expanded her general good/bad appraisal into a more complex conceptualization of the appraisal process (Lazarus, 1968, 1991a; Lazarus & Folkman, 1984). As shown below, "Good" appraisals were conceptualized into several types of benefit, while "Bad" appraisals were differentiated into several types of harm and into several types of threat. Lazarus's (1991a) complex appraisals framework appears in Figure 12.7.

In articulating a more comprehensive view of appraisal, Lazarus pointed out that people evaluate whether the situation they face has personal relevance for their well-being. When well-being is at stake, people then evaluate the potential harm, threat, or benefit they face, as shown above. For Lazarus (1991a), these appraisals take form through questions such as: Is this event relevant to my well-being? Is this event congruent with my goals? How deeply does this event touch my self-esteem? Given these appraisals of per-

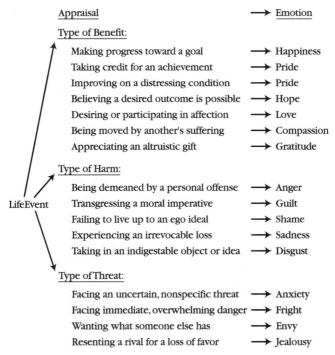

Figure 12.7   Lazarus' Complex Appraisals: Types of Benefit, Harm, and Threat.

sonal relevance, goal congruence, and ego involvement, people appraise situations as particular kinds of harm, as particular kinds of threat, or as particular kinds of benefit (see Lazarus, 1991a, 1994).

The appraisal process does not end with an assessment of personal relevance, goal congruence, and ego involvement. Perceived coping abilities continue to alter how people interpret (appraise) the situations they face (Folkman & Lazarus, 1990; Lazarus, 1991a, 1991b). The person asks himself or herself, can I cope with the potential benefit, threat, or harm I face? Can I bring the benefit into fruition, and can I prevent the harm or threat from happening? Anticipated coping changes the way a situation is appraised (if I can cope with the threat, then it is not really much of a threat). A changed appraisal leads to a changed emotion. Overall, then, people first appraise their relationship to the life event ("primary appraisal") and then they appraise their coping potential within that event ("secondary appraisal").

Primary Appraisal

Primary appraisal involves an estimate of whether one has anything at stake in the encounter (Folkman et al., 1986). The following are potentially at stake in primary appraisal: (1) health, (2) self-esteem, (3) a goal, (4) financial state, (5) respect, and (6) the well-being of a loved one. In other words, primary appraisals ask whether one's physical or psychological well-being, goals and financial status, or interpersonal relationships are at stake during this particular encounter with the environment. As soon as one of these six outcomes is at stake, an ordinary life event becomes a "significant life event" with the potential to generate an emotional reaction. For instance, when driving a car and it swerves on ice, the cognitive system immediately generates the primary appraisal that much is now at stake—personal health, reputation as a skillful driver, a valuable possession (the car), and the physical and psychological well-being of one's passenger.

Secondary Appraisal

Secondary appraisal, which occurs after some reflection, involves the person's assessment for coping with the possible benefit, harm, or threat (Folkman & Lazarus, 1990). Coping involves the person's cognitive, emotional, and behavioral efforts to manage the benefit, harm, or threat. For instance, imagine the coping options for a musician scheduled to perform for an audience. The musician might solicit advice from a mentor, practice throughout the night, find a means of escape, make a plan of action and follow through, copy another musician's style, joke and make light of the event's significance, and so forth. The musician's emotional experience will depend not only on his initial appraisal of the potential benefit, harm, or threat within the evening's performance, but also on his reflection on the potential efficacy of his coping strategies to realize the benefit or to prevent the harm or threat.

Appraisal Model of Emotion

Lazarus's full emotion model appears in Figure 12.8. Given an encounter with the environment—a life event, the individual first makes a primary appraisal pertaining to the event's relevance and personal significance to the self. If the event is not foreseen as a po-

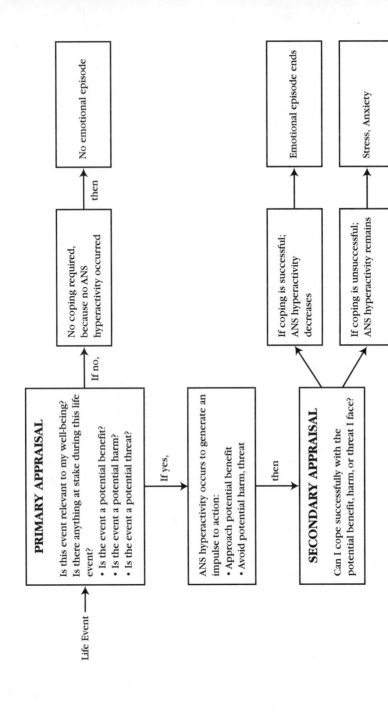

Figure 12.8 Lazarus's Conceptualization of Emotion as a Process

tential benefit, harm, or threat, then it is perceived to be irrelevant to well-being. Hence, no autonomic nervous system (ANS) hyperactivity occurs. The lack of an ANS discharge signals that no coping is required for this particular life event. Benign events fail to generate an emotional episode. If the life event is perceived to be either a potential benefit, a potential harm, or a potential threat, then ANS discharge and hyperactivity occurs to help the person prepare to adapt to the important life event (Tomaka et al., 1993). ANS activation readies the individual to engage in approach or avoidance behavior, and it also activates or prompts secondary appraisal, as the individual considers the extent to which he or she can cope successfully with the life event. ANS activation cues up the need for secondary appraisal. If the individual's approach and avoidance coping efforts are successful, then ANS hyperactivity begins to calm and the emotion-generating event loses its status as an emotional episode because the benefit is realized or the threat or harm dissipates. If coping responses are unsuccessful, however, then ANS hyperactivity continues at a high level and the person experiences stress and anxiety because the benefit slips away or the threat or harm occur.

Motivation

Lazarus's portrayal of emotion is a motivational one. A person brings personal motives (goals, well-being) into a situation. When personal motives are at stake, emotions follow. Further, emotions constantly change as primary and secondary appraisals change. The whole emotion process is characterized not so much by the linear sequence of life event → appraisal → emotion as it is by the ongoing change in the status of one's personal motives. Life events offer potential benefits, harms, and threats to well-being, and ongoing coping efforts have important implications for the extent to which those benefits, harms, and threats are realized. So, the individual's personal motives (goals, well-being) lie at the core of the emotion process and the individual continually makes primary and secondary appraisals about the status of those personal motives as events unfold and coping efforts are implemented.

Lazarus labels his emotion theory as a cognitive-motivational-relational one (Lazarus, 1991b). *Cognitive* communicates the importance of appraisal, *motivational* communicates the importance of personal goals and well-being, and *relational* communicates that emotions arise from one's relationship to environmental threats, harms, and benefits.

Appraisal Process

Following the work of Arnold and Lazarus, cognition-minded theorists continued to develop an increasingly sophisticated understanding of the appraisal process (de Rivera, 1977; Frijda, 1986; Johnson-Laird & Oatley, 1989; Oatley & Johnson-Laird, 1987; Ortony, Clore, & Collins, 1988; Roseman, 1984, 1991; Scherer, 1984a, 1997; Smith & Ellsworth, 1985; Weiner, 1986). Each theorist embraces the life event → appraisal → emotion sequence, but they differ on how many dimensions of appraisal are necessary for explaining emotional experience. Arnold used appraisal to explain two emotions (like and dislike), Lazarus's primary and secondary appraisals explain approximately 15 emotions (see Table 15.2), yet cognitive emotion theorists ultimately seek to use appraisals to explain *all* emotions.

These cognitive theorists believe each emotion can be described by a unique pattern of compound appraisals. A compound appraisal consist of interpreting multiple meanings within an environmental event, such that an event might be both pleasant and caused by the self (hence, pride). Eventually, if one knew the full pattern of the person's appraisals, then it would be a rather straightforward task to predict which ensuing emotion the person would experience.

To explain the full complexity of emotions, theorists have argued for the importance of both (1) compound appraisals and (2) additional dimensions of appraisal. Dimensions of appraisal begin with Arnold's pleasant-unpleasant appraisal and also Lazarus's personal significance and coping potential (primary and secondary appraisals). But a more comprehensive list of appraisals might further add appraisals of the event's unexpectedness and its compatibility with internalized standards (Scherer, 1997). Other appraisals might include appraisals of the event's certainty, one's anticipated effort required, and its legitimacy (Smith & Ellsworth, 1985). It is difficult to say how many dimensions of appraisal exist or which appraisals are most fundamental and which are of only a peripheral importance. The following list of additional appraisals, however, represents the thinking of most cognition-minded emotion theorists (these dimensions are a combination of those proposed by Roseman, 1984, 1991; Smith & Ellsworth, 1985; Scherer, 1984a, 1997):

Arnold's Appraisal:

Pleasantness   Is the event good or bad?

Lazarus' Appraisals:

Personal Relevance   Is the event relevant to personal well-being? Is the event desirable or undesirable?

Coping Ability   Can I cope successfully with the event? How much coping effort will be needed?

Other Possible Appraisals:

Expectancy   Did I expect the event to happen?
Responsibility   Who caused the event—self? Others? Circumstances?
Legitimacy   Is what happened fair? Is it deserved?
Compatibility with the   Is this event okay on a moral level?
  standards of self, society

Consider how a combination of several different appraisals can produce one specific emotion. Anger, for instance, is a combination of the following four appraisals: (1) A valued goal is at stake (personal relevance); (2) the goal was lost (unpleasantness); (3) someone blocked my goal attainment (irresponsibility); and (4) the loss was undeserved (illegitimacy). That is, personal relevance + unpleasantness + irresponsibility + illegitimacy = anger. For a second example, "sentimentality" is a function of the following appraisals: personal relevance, high coping potential, expectancy, pleasantness, and compatibility with standards. Change any one of these appraisals, however, and the experienced emotion will also change. That is, change high coping ability to low coping ability (while keeping the other four appraisals constant) and "sentimentality" changes to "longing."

The ultimate goal of the appraisal emotion theorists is perhaps now apparent. They are hard at work to construct a decision tree in which all possible patterns of appraisal lead to a single emotion (Scherer, 1993, 1997). That is, if the person makes appraisals X, Y, and Z, then emotion A will surely and inevitably follow.

Emotion Differentiation

The strong suit of an appraisal theory of emotion is its ability to explain emotion differentiation processes (e.g., how people experience different emotions to the same event). Figure 12.9 depicts one possible decision tree to show how six appraisal dimensions can differentiate among 17 different emotions (Roseman, Antoniou, & Jose, 1996). The appraisal dimensions are shown on the border of the figure, while the differentiated emotions appear in the boxes inside the figure. The appraisal dimensions on the left side of the figure are responsibility (circumstance-caused, other-caused, self-caused), expectancy (unexpected), and certainty (uncertain, certain). The appraisal dimensions on the top of the figure are goal/need at stake (motive-consistent, motive-inconsistent) and pleasantness (appetitive, aversive). The appraisal dimension on the right side of the figure is coping ability (low versus high). And the appraisal dimension on the bottom is source of the aversive event (noncharacterological, characterological). Admittedly, the figure can be diffi-

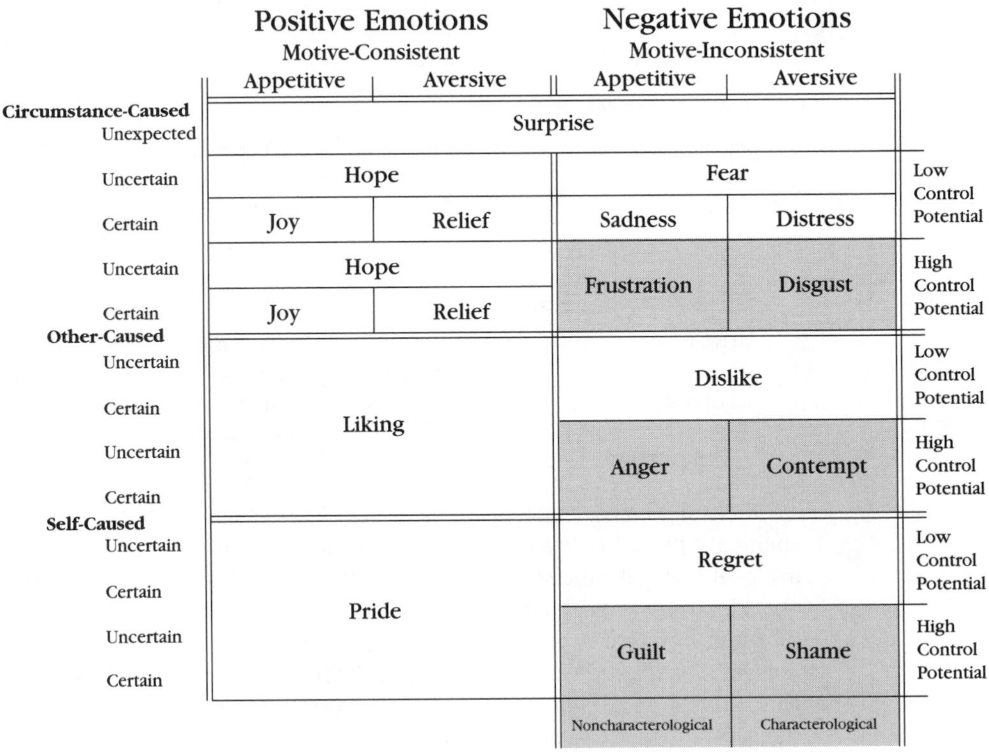

	Positive Emotions Motive-Consistent		Negative Emotions Motive-Inconsistent		
	Appetitive	Aversive	Appetitive	Aversive	
Circumstance-Caused Unexpected	Surprise				
Uncertain	Hope		Fear		Low Control Potential
Certain	Joy	Relief	Sadness	Distress	
Uncertain	Hope		Frustration	Disgust	High Control Potential
Certain	Joy	Relief			
Other-Caused Uncertain	Liking		Dislike		Low Control Potential
Certain					
Uncertain			Anger	Contempt	High Control Potential
Certain					
Self-Caused Uncertain	Pride		Regret		Low Control Potential
Certain					
Uncertain			Guilt	Shame	High Control Potential
Certain					
			Noncharacterological	Characterological	

Figure 12.9 Decision Tree of Six Dimensions of Appraisal to Differentiate Among 17 Emotions

Source: From "Appraisal Determinants of Emotions: Constructing a More Accurate and Comprehensive Theory," by I. J. Roseman, A. A. Antoniou, and P. E. Jose, 1996, *Cognition and Emotion, 10*, pp. 241–277. Reprinted by permission of Psychology Press, Ltd.

cult to follow, but it does get one point across rather well—namely, that in an emotional episode, people engage in a good deal of cognitive appraisal to interpret what is happening to them and as any of these interpretations (appraisals) change so does the person's emotional experience.

An appraisal decision tree such as the one depicted in Figure 12.8 will never predict ensuing emotions correctly 100% of the time (Oatley & Duncan, 1994). Appraisal theorists generally agree that knowing a person's particular configuration of appraisal allows them about a 65 to 70% accuracy rate in predicting people's emotions (Reisenzein & Hofmann, 1993). Four reasons explain why appraisal theory cannot explain emotional reactions with 100% accuracy (Fischer, Shaver, & Carnochan, 1990; Reisenzein & Hofmann, 1993; Scherer, 1997):

1. Processes other than appraisal contribute to emotion (as discussed in the first half of this chapter).

2. While each specific emotion has a unique pattern of appraisals associated with it, the patterns of appraisals for many emotions overlap and create some confusion (e.g., guilt and shame have similar patterns of appraisal).

3. Developmental differences exist among people such that children generally experience basic, general emotions (e.g., joy), whereas socialized adults generally experience a richer variety of appraisal-specific emotions (e.g., pride, relief, gratitude).

4. Emotion knowledge and attributions (the next two topics in this chapter) represent additional cognitive factors beyond appraisal that affect emotion.

Emotion Knowledge

Infants and young children understand and distinguish between only a few basic emotions. They learn to name the few basic emotions of anger, fear, sadness, joy, and love (Kemper, 1987; Shaver et al., 1987). As people gain experience with different situations, they learn to discriminate shades within a single emotion. The shades of joy, for instance, include happiness, relief, optimism, pride, contentment, and gratitude (Ellsworth & Smith, 1988b). The shades of anger include fury, hostility, vengefulness, rage, aggravation, and wrath (Russell & Fehr, 1994). These distinctions are stored cognitively in hierarchies of basic emotions and their derivatives. Thus, the number of different emotions any one person can distinguish constitutes her *emotion knowledge* (Shaver et al., 1987). Through experience, we construct a mental representation of the different emotions and how each individual emotion relates to other emotions and to the situations that produce them.

One person's hypothetical (computer-generated) emotion knowledge appears in Figure 12.10. One level at the top of the figure includes basic emotion categories—love, joy, surprise, anger, sadness, and fear. For this person, these are his or her six basic emotions (or emotion families). With experience, the individual learns shades of these basic emotions (listed on the lower part of the figure). For instance, the individual depicted in the figure understands three shades of love—affection, lust, and longing—and six shades of sadness—suffering, depression, disappointment, shame, neglect, and sympathy. The asterisk in each column of emotion words denotes the prototype within the shades of that emotion.

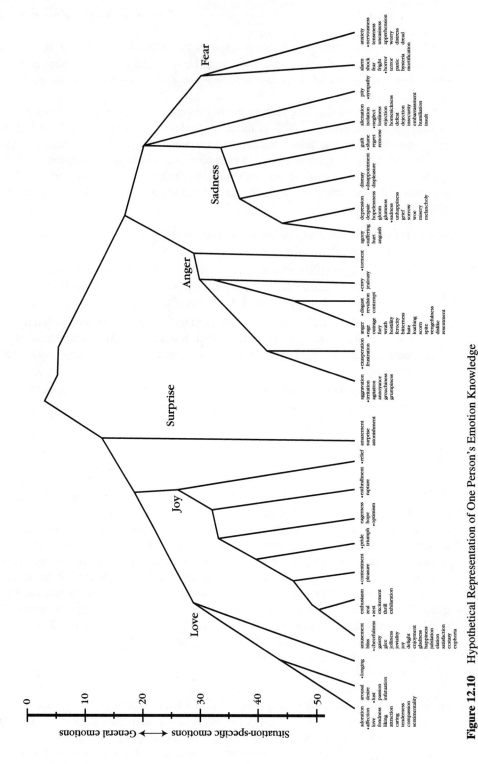

Figure 12.10 Hypothetical Representation of One Person's Emotion Knowledge

Source: From "Emotion knowledge: Further exploration of a prototype approach," by P. Shaver, J. Schwartz, D. Kirson, and C. O'Connor, 1987, *Journal of Personality and Social Psychology, 52,* pp. 1061–1086. Copyright © 1987 by American Psychological Association. Adapted with permission.

Much of the diversity of emotion experience comes from learning fine distinctions among emotions and the specific situations that cause them. Appraisal theorists believe that there are as many emotions as there are cognitive appraisal possibilities of a situation (Ellsworth & Smith, 1988a; Smith & Ellsworth, 1985, 1987). For example, an individual who has just lost out to a rival might potentially experience distress, anger, fear, disgust, and jealousy (Hupka, 1984). One learns that these emotions can coincide and are therefore related to one another (as in the jealousy complex; Hupka, 1984; White, 1981). One also learns that other emotions (e.g., love, joy) are far removed from this cluster of emotional experience. Finally, one learns the differences between shades of anger—the differences among jealousy, hate, irritation, and so on. Eventually, a lifetime of such learning produces a highly personal emotion knowledge. It is this reservoir of emotion knowledge that enables the individual to appraise situations with high discrimination and therefore to respond with situationally appropriate emotions (rather than with general ones). Hence, the finer and more sophisticated one's emotion knowledge is, the greater his or her capacity to respond to each life event with a specialized and highly appropriate emotional reaction.

Attributions

Attribution theory rests on the assumption that people very much want to explain why they experienced a particular life outcome (Heider, 1958; Jones & Davis, 1965; Kelley, 1967, 1973; Weiner, 1980, 1985, 1986). Following an outcome, we ask: Why did I fail that chemistry examination? Why did the Yankees win the World Series? Why did Suzy drop out of school? Why is this person rich while that person is poor? Why didn't I get that job? Why didn't Frank return my telephone call?

An attribution is the reason the person uses to explain an important life outcome (Weiner, 1985, 1986). It is the causal explanation to answer "why?" an outcome occurred. For instance, if we answer the question, "Why did I fail that chemistry test?" by saying, "because I didn't study for it," then "low effort" is the attribution to explain the failure outcome. Attributions are important because the explanation we use to explain our outcome generates emotional reactions. Following positive outcomes, people generally feel happy, and following negative outcomes, people generally feel sad or frustrated. In his attributional theory of emotion, Bernard Weiner (1985, 1986) refers to the outcome-dependent emotional reaction as a "primary appraisal of the outcome." Basic emotions of happy and sad simply follow good and bad outcomes (Weiner, Russell, & Learman, 1978, 1979). Attribution theory proposes that in addition to these primary, outcome-generated emotional reactions, people further explain why they succeeded or failed. Once the outcome has been explained, new emotions surface to differentiate the general happy-sad initial emotional reaction into specific secondary emotions. The attribution of why the outcome occurred constitutes the "secondary appraisal of the outcome." The sequence of events in Weiner's attribution theory of emotion appears in Figure 12.11.

As depicted in Figure 12.11, seven emotions occur in reliable ways as a function of the attributional information-processing flow (Weiner, 1985, 1986; Weiner & Graham, 1989). The attributional roots to the seven emotions are as follows:

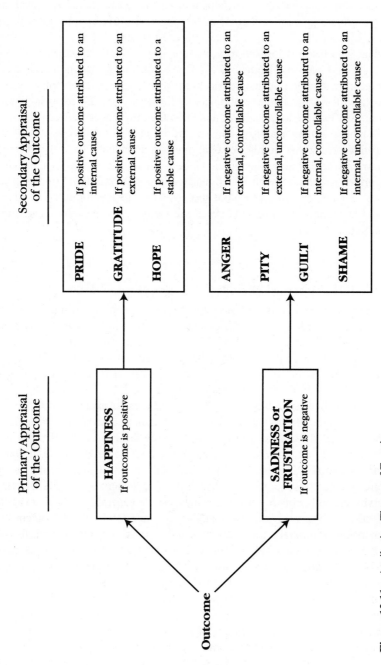

Figure 12.11 Attribution Theory of Emotion

Pride	Attributing a positive outcome to an internal cause. "I succeeded because of my outstanding ability."
Gratitude	Attributing a positive outcome to an external cause. "I succeeded because of help from my teammates."
Hope	Attributing a positive outcome to a stable cause. "I do well in sports because I am athletic by nature."
Anger	Attributing a negative outcome to an external-controllable cause. "I lost because my opponent cheated."
Pity (Sympathy)	Attributing a negative outcome to an external-uncontrollable cause. "I lost my job because of the poor economy."
Guilt	Attributing a negative outcome to an internal-controllable cause. "I lost because I didn't put forth much effort."
Shame	Attributing a negative outcome to an internal-uncontrollable cause. "I was rejected because I am ugly."

Notice that in each of these seven emotions (three positive, four negative), the attributional analysis of why the outcome came to pass is causally prior to the specific emotion. For instance, the fundamental assertion of an attributional analysis of emotion is that if the attribution was to change, then the emotion would change as well (i.e., change the attribution and you change the emotion). If a student feels pride because she feels her ability won her a scholarship and if the student then learns that the real reason she won the scholarship was because of someone's strong support of her application during a meeting, then the experienced emotion flows from pride into gratitude. The outcome is the same (she won the scholarship), but when the attribution changed so did the person's emotional reaction.

Appraisal theorists begin their analysis with relatively simple appraisals, such as whether an event signifies harm, threat, or danger (Lazarus, 1991a). They continue with progressively more complex appraisals, such as legitimacy (Ellsworth & Smith, 1988a). Cognitive theorists then add emotion knowledge to explain further how people make fine-tuned appraisals. In his attributional analysis, Bernard Weiner (1982, 1986) adds yet one more type of appraisal to help explain emotional processes—the post-outcome appraisal of why the outcome occurred. Thus, the role of cognition is not only to appraise the meaning of the life event (appraisal) but also to appraise why the life outcome turned out the way it did (attribution). When taken as a whole, pre-outcome appraisals such as potential benefit, harm, and threat explain some emotional processes, as do post-outcome appraisals (attributions) that explain additional aspects of people's emotional reactions to important life events (Leon & Hernandez, 1998).

SOCIAL AND CULTURAL ASPECTS OF EMOTION

As appraisal contributes to a cognitive understanding of emotion, social interaction contributes to a social understanding of emotion. In addition, the sociocultural context one lives in contributes to a cultural understanding of emotion. Social psychologists, sociologists, anthropologists, and others argue that emotion is not necessarily a private, biological, intrapsychic phenomenon. Instead, they contend that many emotions originate within both social interaction and a cultural context (Averill, 1980, 1983; Kemper, 1987; Manstead, 1991).

Those who study the cultural construction of emotion point out that if you changed the culture you lived in, then your emotional repertoire would also change (Mascolo, Fischer, & Li, 2003). Consider, for instance, the emotional repertoire of people in the United States and China. Chinese infants are less emotionally reactive and expressive than American infants, probably because Chinese parents emphasize and expect emotional restraint whereas American parents emphasize and expect emotional expression.

In the same spirit, Figure 12.12 graphically illustrates the similar and dissimilar basic emotions for people from both cultures. The solid lines to anger, sadness, fear, and happiness illustrate that members of both cultures see essentially the same meaning within these emotional experiences. The dashed lines to shame and love illustrate that members from the two cultures see different meanings within these emotions. For Chinese, love is not a positive emotion. The meaning of love is much closer to "sad love," and it is considered to be a negative emotion. For people in China, shame is considered to be a basic emotion. Thus, people in the United States find meaning in two positive emotions and three negative emotions, while people in China find meaning in one positive emotion and five negative emotions. (The 17 subordinate emotions—jealousy, wrath, disgust, etc.—are from the Chinese participants, not from the American participants.)

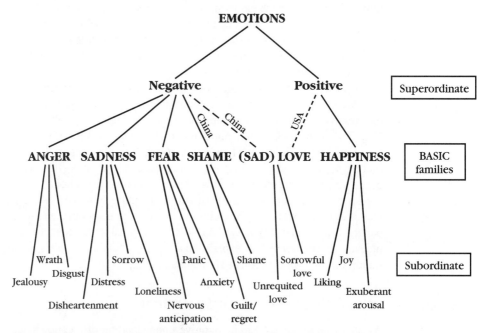

Figure 12.12 Cluster Analysis of Basic Emotion Families in Chinese and English

Source: From Cross-cultural similarities and differences in emotion and its representation: A prototype approach, by P. R. Shaver, S. Wu, & J. C. Schwartz, 1992, in M. S. Clark (Ed.), *Review of Personality and Social Psychology,* Volume 13, pp 231–251. Thousand Oaks, CA: Sage.

If you are an English-speaking reader and are surprised that Chinese-speaking participants understand love ("sad love") as a negative emotion, then the point helps illustrate the cultural basis of emotion. In traditional Chinese culture, parents arrange their children's marriages. Marriages function as the joining of two extended families, in addition to the joining of two people. When one anticipates an arranged marriage, romantic loves takes on meaning as a potentially disruptive force that can separate a son or daughter from his or her parents (Potter, 1988). If embraced, romantic love therefore has the potential to break down the proper respect and deference that sons and daughters are expected to show their parents (Russell & Yik, 1996). The experience of romantic love therefore takes on a negative valence and is better represented by the experience of "sad love."

Those who study the social construction of emotion point out that if you changed the situation you were in, then your emotions would also change. Think about the typical emotions experienced at a playground, at work, at a weekend party, at a sporting event, cleaning the bathroom, during a fistfight, and so on. Situations define what emotions are most appropriate and expected, and because people know which emotions are likely to occur in which settings, they can select a setting and therefore "construct" a particular emotional experience for themselves. If you want to construct joy, for example, you go to a weekend party; if you want to construct disgust, you clean the shower. Also, think about the typical emotions experienced while interacting with someone with superior status (boss, parent), with someone of equal status (friend, spouse), or with someone of inferior status (child, new employee). Status differences between interactants define what emotions are appropriate and expected, and because people know which emotions go with which interactants, they can select interaction partners and therefore "construct" a particular emotional experience. Thus, by strategically selecting which situations to be in and by strategically selecting which people to interact with, each of us has the means to socially construct which emotions we will most likely experience.

Social Interaction

Other people are typically our most frequent source of day-to-day emotion (Oatley & Duncan, 1994). We experience a greater number of emotions when interacting with others than when we are alone.

If you kept track of which events and experiences caused your emotional reactions—another person's action, an action of your own, something you read or saw—you would likely discover that interactions with others triggered most of your emotions (Oatley & Duncan, 1994). Emotions are intrinsic to interpersonal relationships. They also play a central role in creating, maintaining, and dissolving interpersonal relationships, as emotions draw us together and emotions push us apart (Levenson, Carstensen, & Gottman, 1994; Levenson & Gottman, 1983). For instance, joy, sadness, and anger all work to affect the social fabric of relationships. Joy promotes the establishment of relationships. Sadness maintains relationships in times of separation (by motivating reunion). And anger motivates the action necessary to break off injurious relationships.

Other people not only cause emotions to stir in us, but they also affect us indirectly, as through *emotional contagion*. Emotional contagion is "the tendency to automatically mimic and synchronize expressions, vocalizations, postures, and movements with those of another person and, consequently, to converge emotionally" (Hatfield, Cacioppo, & Rapson, 1993a). The three propositions of mimicry, feedback, and contagion explain how, during social interaction, the emotions of others create emotions in us (Hatfield, Cacioppo, & Rapson, 1993b):

Mimicry:	"In conversation, people automatically mimic and synchronize their movements with the facial expressions, voices, postures, movements, and instrumental behaviors of other people."
Feedback:	"Emotional experience is affected, moment to moment, by the activation of and feedback from facial, vocal, postural, and movement mimicry."
Contagion:	"Consequently, people tend to 'catch' other people's emotions."

As we are exposed to the emotional expressions of others, we tend to mimic their facial expressions (Dimberg, 1982; Strayer, 1993), speech style (Hatfield et al., 1995), and posture (Bernieri & Rosenthal, 1991). Once mimicry occurs, the facial feedback hypothesis illustrates how mimicry (of not only the face, but also voice and posture) can affect the observer's emotional experience, and hence lead to a contagion effect.

During social interaction, we not only expose ourselves to emotional contagion effects, but we also put ourselves into a conversational context that provides an opportunity to reexperience and relive past emotional experiences, a process referred to as "the social sharing of emotion" (Rimé et al., 1991). Social sharing of emotional conversations usually take place later in the day and when in the company of intimates (close friend, love partner, teammates). When people share their emotions, they typically do so by recounting the full account of what happened during the emotional episode, what it meant, and how the person felt throughout (Rimé et al., 1991). During such social sharing of emotion, an empathic listener can offer support or assistance, strengthen coping responses, help make sense of the emotional experience, and reconfirm the self-concept (Lehman, Ellard, & Wortman, 1986; Thoits, 1984). It is in these times of sharing our emotions that we build and maintain the relationships that are central to our lives (Edwards, Manstead & McDonald, 1984), such as marital relationships (Noller, 1984).

Emotional Socialization

Emotional socialization occurs as adults tell children what they ought to know about emotion. Emotional socialization occurs among adults as well, but the process is best illustrated when adults interact with children for the explicit purpose of teaching socialization information (Pollak & Thoits, 1989). Adults tell children about the situations that cause emotions, about how emotion expresses itself, and about emotion words or labels for their feelings and behaviors. In turn, children learn that a basic emotion can be differentiated into specific emotions (emotion knowledge; Shaver et al., 1987), that certain expressive displays should be controlled (expression management; Saarni, 1979), and that negative emotions can be manipulated deliberately into neutral or positive emotions (emotion control; McCoy & Masters, 1985). When children learn from adults about emotions, most of what they learn falls under the rubrics of emotion knowledge, expression management, and emotion control.

Consider the socialization that occurs in settings such as daycare centers, preschools, and elementary schools (Denham et al., 1997; Pollak & Thoits, 1989). During a child's emotional episode, a caretaker or teacher might explain the child's feelings, point out the causes of an emotion, and instruct the child about which expressive displays are most appropriate and welcomed and which other expressive displays are not.

Consider an example of emotion knowledge—how adults tell children about the causes of emotion (Pollak & Thoits, 1989):

GIRL (several times):	My mom is late.
STAFF MEMBER:	Does that make you mad?
GIRL:	Yes.
STAFF MEMBER:	Sometimes kids get mad when their moms are late to pick them up.

Consider an example of expression management—how adults tell children to express their emotions (Pollak & Thoits, 1989):

STAFF MEMBER: (While holding a kicking, screaming boy in time-out):	Robert, I see you're very angry.

Consider an example of emotion control—how adults teach children to control their emotional displays (Pollak & Thoits, 1989):
During circle, Alec tried to climb all over John, a volunteer.

JOHN:	If you want to be close, there are some things you could do. . . . You could sit next to me and we could hold hands, or I could put my arm around you, or you could sit on my lap.

Different societies socialize their children's emotions in different ways. Consider, for instance, the different socialization messages communicated by parents of a child in the United States (upper quote) and communicated by parents of a child in China (lower quote):

Three-year-old Danny and his mother are putting together the pieces of a puzzle. Danny places a piece in its correct location. Immediately, he looks up to his mother, smiles, and says "Oh! I did it!" Looking up from her work, his mother smiles and says "You did it!" Danny claps his hands, after which his mother applauds and says, "That's great!"

Mother asks 3-year-old Lin to sing a song for guests. After she finishes, with smiles and exaggerated expressions, the guests say, "Wonderful! You sing nicer than my child!" Mother replies, "Haihao, she is O.K. Her voice is kind of off the tune, though. But she likes to sing." To Lin, "You did all right, but now you need more practice. Play down your success!" (Mascolo, Fischer, & Li, 2003, p. 375).

This pair of quotes depict the different ways in which socialization agents react to children's accomplishments. As these quotes suggest, parents of children in the United States tend to praise their children's accomplishments and encourage positive self-expression. Parents of children in China tend to make effacing remarks to others about their children's efforts. Guests, relatives, and others, however, generally lavish praise on the child, even as they efface their own children. Years of such socialization lead American children to take pride in their accomplishments, and years of such socialization lead Chinese children to harmonize the self with others through self-effacement (Chen, 1993; Stipek, 1999).[6]

Managing Emotions

How people learn to manage their emotions can be seen in professionals who interact frequently, closely, and intimately with the public, such as airline flight attendants (Hochschild, 1983), hair stylists (Parkinson, 1991), and physicians (Smith & Kleinman, 1989). In these fields, socialization pressures to manage one's emotions mostly revolve around a theme of coping with aversive feelings in ways that are both socially desirable and personally adaptive (Saarni, 1997). Physicians, for instance, are not supposed to feel either attraction or disgust for their patients, irrespective of how beautiful or revolting their appearance might be. Therefore, during their medical school training, physicians must learn affective neutrality, a detached concern for their patients.

Imagine being a medical student asked to conduct pelvic, rectal, and breast examinations and perform surgery, dissections, and autopsies. Such situations are clearly emotion-generating life events, but physicians need to learn a professional affective neutrality—even when blood is spewing out an artery or they reach their hands into patients' intestines. How physicians learn such affective neutrality provides insight into how the rest of us learn to manage our emotions too.

For two years, researchers observed and interviewed medical students to identify the emotion-management strategies they learned during medical school to achieve affective neutrality (Smith & Kleinman, 1989). Medical students learned to manage their emotions by internalizing the following five strategies:

Transform the emotional contact into something else.
Mentally transform intimate bodily contact into something qualitatively different, such as a step-by-step procedure.

Accentuate the positive.
Identify the satisfaction in learning or the opportunity to practice medicine.

Use the patient.
Shift awareness of uncomfortable feelings onto the patient, as in projection or blame.

Laugh about it.
Joke about it, as joking exempts the doctor from admitting weakness.

Avoid the contact.
Keep the patient covered, look elsewhere, or hurry through the procedure.

---

[6]Societies clearly socialize their members' emotional experiences and expressions. Still, limits exist as to how much a culture can socialize particular emotions into its constituents. Consider the claim that in some cultures people exchange romantic partners without jealousy. Biology-minded theorists argue that sharing a sexual partner would surely produce jealously, and appraisal theorists might make a similar argument (see Table 12.2). But can people be socialized to not experience jealousy during the exchange of romantic partners? The short answer is, basically, no (Reis, 1986). Cultures *do* vary as to which behaviors signal jealousy, which signs of affection justify jealousy, and how people express jealousy, but the emotional angst of sexual jealousy occurs in all cultures (Reis, 1986). Like many other basic emotions, jealousy is universal, though many of its nuances (causes, expressions) vary from one culture to the next.

These five emotion-management strategies illustrate the culture that is Western medicine. When students rely on that culture for guidance as to how they might manage their emotions, they in effect reproduce the culture for the next generation of students (Smith & Kleinman, 1989).

Consider also hairstylists (Parkinson, 1991). To be professionally successful, hairstylists need to develop an open communication style characterized by expressiveness, affect intensity, empathy, poise, frequent positive facial expressions, and a concealment of negative emotions. Further, the more natural and spontaneous the hairstylist appears to clients, the better the job goes. How do hairstylists learn to manage their emotions in this way? The problem hairstylists face is, essentially, how can they acquire an open interaction style with clients who are often uptight and socially remote (Straub & Roberts, 1987). Part of the job of being a hairstylist is to figure this out, and the ones who do develop these emotion management skills report higher job satisfaction. Hairstylists who fail to develop these emotion management skills report lower job satisfaction.

Flight attendants need to adopt an open interaction style similar to that of the hairstylist. To do so, the flight attendant frequently uses "deep-acting" methods that are not too unlike the methods stage actors use during a two-hour performance. Using deep-acting methods, the flight attendant replaces her natural and spontaneous emotional reactions with an emotional repertoire characterized by constant courtesy to clients (Hochschild, 1983). In all these cases—medical students, hairstylists, and flight attendants—people learn to manage their private, spontaneous feelings and express them in publicly-scripted and socially-desirable ways of acting. Doing so facilitates smooth professional interactions with their clients (Manstead, 1991).

Inferring Identities from Emotional Displays

People react emotionally to the events in their lives, and how people react tells us something about what kind of people they are. In sports, for instance, a popular saying is that the game does not build character; rather, it reveals it. The athlete reveals her character largely through her emotion displays, and these displays function to confirm or to disconfirm one's identity (Heise, 1989). Emotional displays are public expressions ("readouts") of a person's underlying identity.

During social interaction, each person uses emotional expression information to infer the other person's underlying identity and probable future behaviors. Legal trials illustrate this process, as judges and jurors must (1) observe a person they know little about (the defendant), (2) infer his character (identity), and (3) predict what the defendant's likely future behavior will be so that they can make sentencing recommendations if necessary (Robinson, Smith-Lovin, & Tsoudis, 1994). When people speak of their deviant acts (as does a defendant in a court case), their behaviors endow them with a corresponding identity such as thief, murderer, or freeloader. The speaker's emotional expressions signal a confirmation or disconfirmation of that inferred identity. The sobbing, remorseful, grief-stricken thief somehow is a regular sort of guy who got involved in an accident, while the relaxed, cold-hearted thief somehow is a devilish rogue who performed a crime.

Glance at the two photographs in Figure 12.13. Imagine that both men have just admitted to stealing another person's property. The person on the left tells the court of his misdeed while showing little emotion, little remorse. The person on the right, however, tells the court of the same misdeed but with a rich display of remorse. When a person en-

Figure 12.13   Emotional Expressions of Two Defendants on Trial for Theft

gages in a bad act and shows no sign of remorse, the observer infers that this is surely a bad person—a cold, evil monster who needs to be put away for a long time. But when a person engages in a bad act and does show remorse, the observer infers that this person must not be so bad after all—just a regular guy who got involved in an accident (Robinson, Smith-Lovin, & Tsoudis, 1994).

SUMMARY

Three central aspects of emotion exist: biological, cognitive, and social-cultural. The chapter begins with a biological analysis of emotion because emotions are, in part, biological reactions to important life events. They serve coping functions that allow the individual to prepare herself to adapt effectively to important life circumstances. Emotions energize and direct bodily actions (e.g., running; fighting) by affecting (1) the autonomic nervous system and its regulation of the heart, lungs, and muscles; (2) the endocrine system and its regulation of glands, hormones, and organs; (3) neural brain circuits such as those in the limbic system; (4) the rate of neural firing and therefore the pace of information processing; and (5) facial feedback and discrete patterns of the facial musculature.

Research on the biological underpinnings of emotion identify that the activation and maintenance of about 10 different emotions can be understood from a biological perspective: interest, joy, fear, anger, disgust, distress, contempt, shame, guilt, and surprise. For instance, 4 emotions show a unique pattern of autonomic nervous system and endocrine system physiological specificity. Four emotions possess unique anatomical neural circuits in the brain. Differential emotions theory shows that 10 emotions have unique, cross-cultural facial expressions. And 6 emotions are associated with a unique rate of neural firing in the cortex.

The facial feedback hypothesis asserts that the subjective aspect of emotion is actually the awareness of proprioceptive feedback from facial action. The facial feedback hypothesis appears in two forms: weak and strong. According to its strong version, posed facial expressions activate specific emotions, such that smiling activates joy. According to its weak version, exaggerated and suppressed facial expressions augment and attenuate naturally occurring emotion. Although research is mixed on the strong version, evidence confirms the validity of the weaker version. Facial management moderates emotional experience, as people can intensify or reduce their naturally ongoing emotional experience by exaggerating or suppressing their facial actions.

The central construct in a cognitive understanding of emotion is appraisal. Two types of appraisal—primary and secondary—regulate the emotion process. Primary appraisal evaluates whether or not anything important is at stake in a situation—physical well-being, self-esteem, a goal, financial state, respect, or the well-being of a loved one. Secondary appraisal occurs after some reflection and revolves around an assessment of how to cope with a potential benefit, harm, or threat. Appraisal theorists pursue the goal of constructing a decision-tree in which knowing all the different appraisals the person makes during an emotional episode will yield a prediction of which emotion the person must inevitably experience (e.g., something is at stake, it was lost, and it was lost because of an outside and illegitimate force → anger).

Emotion is also embedded in cognition via emotion knowledge and attributions. Emotion knowledge involves learning fine distinctions among basic emotions and learning which situations cause which emotions. Sophisticated emotion knowledge enables the individual to appraise a situation with high discrimination and therefore respond with highly appropriate emotions. An attributional analysis focuses on post-outcome attributions to explain when and why people experience pride, gratitude, or hope following positive outcomes and guilt, shame, anger, and pity following negative outcomes.

In a social and cultural analysis of emotion, other people are our richest sources of emotional experiences. During social interaction, we often "catch" other people's emotions through a process of emotion contagion that involves mimicry, feedback, and, eventually, contagion. We also share and relive our recent emotional experiences during conversations with others, a process referred to as the social sharing of emotion. And the culture socializes its members to experience and express emotions in particular ways. Other people and cultures in general instruct us about the causes of our emotions (emotion knowledge), how we should express our emotions (expression management), and when to control our emotions (emotion management). And how people react emotionally to the events in their lives tells us something about the kind of people they are.

READINGS FOR FURTHER STUDY

Biological Aspects of Emotion

EKMAN, P. (1993). Facial expression and emotion. *American Psychologist, 48*, 384–392.

IZARD, C. E. (1989). The structure and functions of emotions: Implications for cognition, motivation, and personality. In I. S. Cohen (Ed.), *The G. Stanley Hall lecture series* (Vol. 9, pp. 39–73). Washington, DC: American Psychological Association.

LEVENSON, R. W. (1992). Autonomic nervous system differences among emotions. *Psychological Science, 3*, 23–27.

McINTOSH, D. N. (1996). Facial feedback hypotheses: Evidence, implications, and directions. *Motivation and Emotion, 20*, 121–147.

Cognitive Aspects of Emotion

LAZARUS, R. S. (1991). Progress on a cognitive-motivational-relational theory of emotion. *American Psychologist, 46*, 819–834.

LAZARUS, R. S., & SMITH, C. A. (1988). Knowledge and appraisal in the cognition-emotion relationship. *Cognition and Emotion, 2*, 281–300.

SCHERER, K. R. (1993). Studying the emotion-antecedent appraisal process: An expert system approach. *Cognition and Emotion, 7*, 325–355.

SHAVER, P., SCHWARTZ, J., KIRSON, D., & O'CONNOR, C. (1987). Emotion knowledge: Further exploration of a prototype approach. *Journal of Personality and Social Psychology, 52*, 1061–1086.

Cultural Aspects of Emotion

POLLAK, L. H., & THOITS, P. A. (1989). Processes in emotional socialization. *Social Psychology Quarterly, 52*, 22–34.

SMITH, A. C., III, & KLEINMAN, S. (1989). Managing emotions in medical school: Students' contacts with the living and the dead. *Social Psychology Quarterly, 52*, 56–69.

Part Four

Individual Differences

Chapter 13

Personality Characteristics

Are you happy? If researchers followed you around all day for several consecutive days, would they observe someone who is frequently happy? Would they see a person who experiences positive emotion frequently, or only rarely? When you do feel happy, what sort of happiness is it—an intense and deeply felt joy, or is it something more like contentment?

Are you unhappy? Do you suffer emotionally? How frequently during the day are you unhappy? If these same researchers followed you around daily for several more days, would they see someone who suffers emotional distress frequently, or only rarely and only in response to special circumstances? When you do suffer the slings and arrows of negative emotionality, how intensely do you feel your negative emotions? Do your negative emotions affect you only on the surface and only for a short period of time, or do they affect you deeply and for an extended period of time? Is your typical day a roller coaster rise and fall of negative emotions like anxiety, stress, and irritability? Or is your typically day in the experience of negative emotions more like driving through Nebraska?

Researchers actually carry out investigations of experiences such as these by using the "experience-sampling method" (Larson, 1989). In this research, participants carry around an electronic device (e.g., a Palm pilot) that the researchers use to send a signal at various times throughout the day to ask participants to record their emotions and mood at that particular time. When people report their day-to-day emotionality, they generally report high levels of positive emotion and low levels of negative emotion. This pattern of emotion is true for college students (Thomas & Diener, 1990), and it is also true for working mothers juggling multiple roles throughout the day (Williams et al., 1991). Basically, most people are happy (Diener & Diener, 1996). But, one theme that runs throughout the present chapter is that some people are happier than others. And some people are unhappier than others. Just who is happy and who is unhappy can be predicted rather reliably from personality characteristics.

This chapter focuses on three motivational principles related to personality characteristics: (1) happiness; (2) arousal, and (3) control. Any situational event offers the potential to affect all three of these subjective experiences. The personality characteristics presented in this chapter—extraversion, neuroticism, sensation seeking, affect intensity, perceived control, and desire for control—explain why different people have different motivational and emotional states even when they are in the same situation.

Taking an examination, for instance, is typically stressful (unhappy), arousing, and somewhat controllable in terms of its outcome. Consider that all situations vary in their capacity to produce positive or negative emotions in us (e.g., parties are fun, accidents are distressing). All situations vary in how stimulating and arousing they are (e.g., libraries are sedate, rock concerts are stimulating). And, all situations vary in how controllable they are (e.g., losing weight is somewhat under your control and somewhat out of your control). Of particular importance to the present chapter, individuals, too, harbor personality characteristics that affect how they respond to these situations in terms of felt happiness, felt arousal, and perceived control.

One important caution applies throughout the chapter: When the discussion refers to specific individual differences, keep in mind that relatively few people are at either extreme of the characteristics. A few people are sensation seekers, and a few people are sensation avoiders, but most people are somewhere in the middle, as shown graphically in the top half of Figure 13.1. As illustrated, when a large number of people take the Sensation-Seeking Scale (SSS), only a minority (about 15%) score between 15 and 21, the high end of the SSS, and show themselves to be card-carrying sensation seekers. Only a minority (about 15%) score between 0 to 7, the low end of the SSS, which identifies sensation avoiders. The majority (about 70%) score between 7 and 15 (the middle) and are therefore identified as neither sensation seekers nor sensation avoiders. Also, beware of typologies, shown in the lower part of Figure 13.1. Typologies categorize people as one type of personality or the other (e.g., as a sensation seeker or as a sensation avoider). In doing so, typologies oversimplify the contribution of personality processes in motivation. Personality characteristics exist within everyone. It is just that only a few people harbor a high or intense level of the personality characteristic, most people harbor a moderate amount of the personality characteristic, and a few others harbor only a low or mild level of the characteristic.

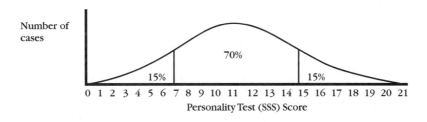

Normal Distribution Curve

Number of
cases

70%

15%   15%

0 1 2 3 4 5 6 7 8 9 10 11 12 13 14 15 16 17 18 19 20 21
Personality Test (SSS) Score

Typology

People are either:

Sensation Seekers (50%)	Sensation Avoiders (50%)

Figure 13.1   Personality Characteristics as Understood within a Normal Distribution versus a Typology

HAPPINESS

Most people are happy, and this is true almost irrespective of their life circumstances (Diener & Diener, 1996). People in low income groups generally say they are happy, people with little formal education generally say they are happy, and people in almost every nation say they are happy. Nevertheless, we all know intuitively that the events in our lives affect our emotions and moods. Is it not true that people who get all the brakes are happier than those who do not?

Consider the happiness of lottery winners and accident victims (Brickman, Coates, & Janoff-Bulman, 1978). These are dramatic life events that produce strong emotions. No doubt exists in saying that winning the lottery is a positive life event, and no doubt exists in saying that suffering an accident that leaves one a quadrapedic is a negative life event. When researchers ask lottery winners and accident victims if they are happy a year after their dramatic life event, people who won large sums of money and people who experience debilitating injuries did not differ much from the average person.

People react strongly to life events, and they react very strongly to events like lottery luck and life-threatening accidents. But they also seem to return back to the same level of happiness they had before the event. When researchers monitored the emotions of spinal-cord injury victims, they found that these person felt very strong negative emotions and only rare positive emotions one week after the accident, as you would expect from the circumstances they faced. Over the next two months, however, the negative emotions decreased while the positive emotions increased. After two months, their positive emotions were stronger and more frequent than were their negative emotions (Silver, 1982).

People seem to have a happiness "set point" (Lykken & Tellegen, 1996). Imagine that you assessed how happy a group of 20-year-olds were and then waited for 10 years to pass so that life events could happen to them all (marriage, career, family, accidents, financial stresses, death of parents, etc.). What you would very likely find when you track down these same people at age 30 is that those who were happy in their 20s are still happy in their 30s and those who were unhappy in their 20s are still unhappy in their 30s. Just like people have a set-point that regulates their body weight (discussed in Chapter 4), people also seem to have a set-point that regulates their happiness and subjective well being (Williams & Thompson, 1993). One group of researchers went so far as to conclude that "It may be that trying to be happier is as futile as trying to be taller" (Lykken & Tellegen, 1996, p. 189). That statement is certainly too strong, but it does get its point across that happiness is as much in our genes and personality as it is in the events in our lives.

Actually, we seem to have two emotional set-points rather than just one. One set-point is for positive emotionality (a happiness set-point). Another is for negative emotionality (an unhappy set-point). Plus, how happy and how unhappy we are turn out to be independent (rather than opposite) indicators of well-being.

The status of our happiness and unhappiness set-points can be explained by individual differences in our personalities. The happiness set point emerges mostly from individual differences in extraversion. The unhappiness set point emerges mostly from individual differences in neuroticism.

Extraversion and Happiness

The personality characteristic associated with "Who is happy?" is extraversion. To define extraversion, personality psychologists discuss its three facets. The first is sociability, or the preference for and enjoyment of other people and social situations. The second is assertiveness, or a tendency toward social dominance. The third is venturesomeness, or a tendency to seek out and enjoy exciting, stimulating situations. Thus extraverts are different from introverts because they have greater tendencies toward sociability, assertiveness, and being exciting (Depue & Collins, 1999; Watson & Clark, 1997).

Emotionally, extraverts are happier than are introverts and they enjoy more frequent positive moods than do introverts (Costa & McCrae, 1980; Diener, Sandvik, Pavot, & Fujita, 1992; Emmons & Diener, 1986; Larsen & Ketelaar, 1991; Lucas & Fujita, 2000; Watson et al., 1992; Williams, 1990). Extraverts are highly sociable, but this does not explain why they are happier. Extraverts are happier whether they live alone or with others, whether they live in large cities or remote rural areas, and whether they work in social or nonsocial occupations. Instead of being more social, extraverts are happier than introverts because they are more sensitive to the rewards inherent in most social situations (Lucas et al., 2000). Being more sensitive to rewards, extraverts are more susceptible to positive feelings than are introverts. Thus, because they have a greater sensitivity to positive feelings, extraverts eagerly approach potentially rewarding situations more than do introverts (Elliot & Thrash, 2002).

Extraverts are happier than introverts because they possess a greater inherent capacity to experience positive emotions. For instance, watch the emotional reactions of an extravert and an introvert when a positive life event happens to them, and you will see something like joy in the extravert but only contentment in the introvert. This differential capacity for positive emotions occurs because extraverts and introverts possess differing levels of sensitivity to an underlying biological motivation system introduced in Chapter 3, the Behavioral Activating System (BAS; Depue & Collins, 1989). So, basically, extraverts have a stronger BAS than do introverts. This brain system detects and regulates signals of reward in the environment. In the BAS, signals of forthcoming reward are the source of positive emotions. Thus, extraverts' emotionality benefits from more frequent and more intense signals of reward that leave them anticipating situations with excitement, feeling happy, and wanting to approach situations.

The motivational function of the BAS is to energize approach-oriented, goal-directed behavior (like sociability, assertiveness, and venturesomeness). For extraverts, signals of reward strongly activate their BAS, while these same environmental signals of reward only mildly activate the BAS of introverts. Extraverts therefore experience a stronger incentive motivational state that energizes and guides their approach behavior. The activated BAS also supplies the extravert with a steady stream of motivational and emotional states such as feelings of happiness, desire, wanting, excitement, enthusiasm, energy, potency, and confidence (Depue & Collins, 1999). Hence, extraverts are more likely to show approach behavior and they are also more likely to enjoy behaviors like talking and acting assertively.

The idea that extraversion is associated with brain functioning (a strong BAS) means that extraversion is a biologically-based individual difference. Support for the idea that extraverts are born, not made, can be found in studies showing that extraversion is heritable (Eaves, Eysenck, & Martin, 1989; Pedersen et al., 1988; Shields, 1976; Viken et al., 1994). For instance, twins who are reared apart in very different environments will score similarly on questionnaires designed to assess extraversion, suggesting that extraversion is based more on genetic factors than it is on environmental factors (Pedersen et al., 1988).

Neuroticism and Suffering

The personality characteristic associated with "Who is unhappy?" is neuroticism. Neuroticism is defined as a predisposition to experience negative affect and to feel chronically dissatisfied and unhappy (McCrae, 1990; Watson & Clark, 1984). Day in and day out, neurotics experience greater stress and more negative emotionality and mood states such as anxiety, fear, and irritability. The opposite of neuroticism is emotional stability. Thus, neurotics' emotionality suffers to a greater extent than do those who are emotionally stable (Bolger & Zuckerman, 1995; Suls, Green, & Hillis, 1998).

Neurotics suffer emotionally. They do so mostly because of their greater capacity to experience negative emotions, but also because disturbed and troubling thoughts so frequently accompany their emotional negativity (McCrae & Costa, 1987). That is, bad life events bring the neurotic not only a bad life event but also a host of upsetting and pessimistic thoughts that have a way of hanging around long after the bad life event is over.

This differential capacity for negative emotions occurs because neurotic and emotionally-stable individuals possess differing levels of sensitivity to the underlying biological motivation system introduced in Chapter 3 as the Behavioral Inhibition System (BIS; Gray, 1987b; Tellegen, 1985). So, basically, neurotics have a stronger BIS. This brain system detects and regulates environmental signals of punishment. In the BIS, signals of forthcoming punishment are the source of negative emotions like fear and anxiety. For this reason, neurotics are more vulnerable and more susceptible to negative emotions (Larsen & Ketelaar, 1991). Thus, neurotics' emotionality suffers from more frequent and more intense signals of punishment that leave them anticipating situations with fear and anxiety, feeling upset and wanting to avoid situations.

The motivational function of the BIS is to energize avoidance-oriented, goal-directed behavior (like escape, withdrawal, and avoidance). For neurotics who are exposed to a potentially punishing situation (e.g., a job interview, taking an exam, being in a noisy house), signals of punishment strongly activate their BIS while these same signals of punishment only mildly activate the BIS of emotionally stable individuals. Neurotics therefore experience a stronger incentive motivational state that energizes and guides their avoidance behavior. The activated BIS also supplies the neurotic with a steady stream of motivational and emotional states such as feelings of fear, anxiety, irritability, distress, hostility, anger, depression, and self-consciousness (McCrae & Costa, 1986). Hence, neurotics are more likely to show avoidance behavior and they are also more likely to suffer emotional distress during behaviors like taking an examination (Bolger, 1990) or arguing with a spouse (Bolger & Schilling, 1991).

Extraverts Are Generally Happy, Neurotics Are Generally Unhappy

Extraversion and neuroticism represent two basic personality dimensions. The personality dimension that predisposes the individual toward a positive emotionality, the behavioral activation system, and an approach temperament is extraversion. The personality dimension that predisposes the individual toward a negative emotionality, the behavioral inhibition system, and an avoidance temperament is neuroticism (Costa & McRae, 1980; McCrae & Costa, 1991; Elliot & Thrash, 2002; Gray, 1982, 1987a, 1987b; Tellegen, 1985).

Several reliable and valid questionnaires exist to measure these personality dimensions, including the NEO PI-R scales (Costa & McRae, 1992), the Big Five Inventory (BFI; John & Srivastrava, 2000), and the Eysenck Personality Questionnaire (EPQ-R; Eysenck, Eysenck, & Barrett, 1985). Based on people's scores on these questionnaires, psychologists can predict with confidence who will be excited, enthusiastic, and happy about being in potentially rewarding situations (i.e., extraverts), and psychologists can predict with confidence who will be inhibited, hesitant, and anxious about being in potentially threatening situations (i.e., neurotics). Psychologists' confidence stems from knowing the following. When extraverts enter a situation, their BAS motivational system generally makes them particularly sensitive to its potentially rewarding aspects and thus they experience the positive emotions it affords and they willing approach it. When neurotics enter a situation, their BIS motivational system generally makes them particularly sensitive to its potentially punishing aspects and thus they experience the negative emotions it affords and they willingly avoid it.

AROUSAL

Arousal represents a variety of processes that govern alertness, wakefulness, and activation (Anderson, 1990). These processes are cortical, behavioral, and autonomic mechanisms. Thus, the activity of the brain (cortical), skeletal muscular system (behavioral), and autonomic nervous system (autonomic) together constitute most of the motivational construct of arousal.

Four principles explain arousal's contribution to motivation:

1. A person's arousal level is mostly a function of how stimulating the environment is.

2. People engage in behavior to increase or decrease their level of arousal.

3. When underaroused, people seek out opportunities to increase their arousal levels, because increases in environmental stimulation are pleasurable and enhance performance while decreases are aversive and undermine performance.

4. When overaroused, people seek out opportunities to decrease their arousal levels, because increases in environmental stimulation are aversive and undermine performance while decreases are pleasurable and enhance performance.

These four principles can be organized collectively into the "inverted-U" relationship between arousal and performance/well-being shown in Figure 13.2. The inverted-U curve, first introduced 100 years ago by Robert Yerkes and John Dodson (1908), helps explain the relationship between felt arousal and people's ensuing motivational and emotional states (Berlyne, 1967; Duffy, 1957; Hebb, 1955; Lindsley, 1957; Malmo, 1959).

Performance and Emotion

The inverted-U curve illustrates that a low level of arousal produces relatively poor performance (lower left). As arousal level increases from low to moderate, both the intensity and the quality of performance improves. As arousal level continues to increase from moderate to high, performance quality and efficiency (but not intensity) decrease (lower right). Thus, optimal performance is a function of being aroused but not too aroused. To make sense of the arousal-performance relationship, recall your personal performance ef-

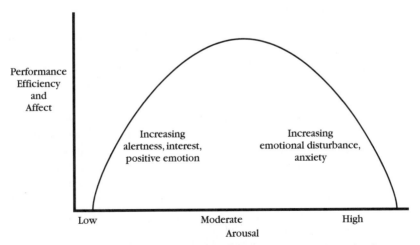

Figure 13.2   The Inverted-U Curve: Relationship between Arousal Level and Performance/Well-Being

Source: From "Drive and the C. N. S.—Conceptual Nervous System," by D. O. Hebb, 1955, *Psychological Review, 62*, pp. 245–254.

ficiency while doing something important—public speaking, competing in athletics, or job interviewing, for instance. When nonchalant and underaroused or when anxious and overaroused, performance tends to suffer. When moderately aroused—alert but not tense—performance tends to be optimal.

A moderate level of arousal coincides with the experience of pleasure (Berlyne, 1967). Low stimulation produces boredom and restlessness; high stimulation produces tension and stress. Both boredom and stress are aversive experiences, and people strive to escape from each. When underaroused and experiencing negative affect, a person will seek out activities that offer increased stimulation, opportunities for exploring something new, and perhaps even risk taking. On the other hand, when arousal is greater than optimal, a person will avoid and is repulsed by further increases in environmental stimulation. When overaroused, increased stimulation, novelty, and risk create negative affect—stress, frustration, and hassle. Overaroused people find themselves attracted to an environmental calm—a vacation, a casual reading of the newspaper, or going for a quiet walk. Thus, the inverted-U curve predicts when increases and decreases in stimulation will lead to positive affect and approach behavior and when they will lead to negative affect and avoidance.

Insufficient Stimulation and Underarousal

Sensory deprivation research illustrates the psychological consequences of being underaroused (Bexton, Heron, & Scott, 1954; Heron, 1957; Zubek, 1969). Sensory deprivation refers to an individual's sensory and emotional experience in a rigidly unchanging environment. In his studies, Woodburn Heron (1957) paid male college students a substantial amount of money per day to lie on a comfortable bed for as many days as they cared to stay (see Figure 13.3). The participant's task was simply to stay in the unchanging environment, with time out for meals and visits to the restroom. To restrict sensory information from touch, participants wore cotton gloves with long cardboard forearm cuffs. They also wore a special translucent visor that restricted their visual information. To restrict auditory information, an air conditioner purred out a steady hum that masked most sounds.

Even on the first day, participants reported an inability to think clearly. As the hours passed, many participants reported experiencing blank periods (running out of things to think of) and others just let their minds wander. Nearly everyone reported dreams and visions while awake. During the study, the sensory-deprived men took a series of arithmetic, anagram, and word association tests after 12, 24, and 48 hours of deprivation. Performance on even simple math problems depreciated quickly. After the second day, computations like $16 \times 65 = ?$ were too difficult to solve. Participants also became increasingly irritable. In fact, Heron found it difficult to keep his irritated participants in the experiment for more than 2 or 3 days, despite the large financial incentive to stay.

Sensory deprivation studies underscore the fact that the brain and nervous system prefer a continual and moderate level of arousal generated by environmental stimulation. Imagine the emotional experiences of zoo animals in cages, inmates in prison cells, the elderly in nursing homes, political prisoners in solitary confinement, long-term patients in hospital wards, and students enduring monotonous lectures. But human beings are not simply passive recipients of whatever stimulation the environment offers. When understimulated, people rely on various cognitive and behavioral means for increasing arousal level (e.g., mental imagery, social interaction). That is, human beings harbor motives for counteracting insufficient stimulation and underarousal.

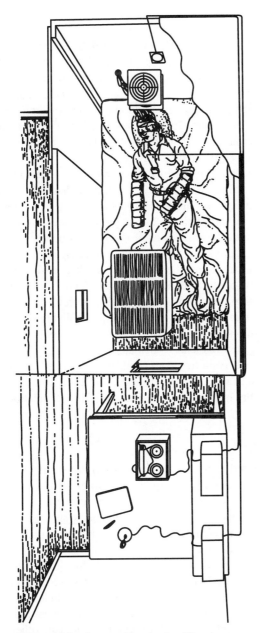

Figure 13.3   Sensory Deprivation Chamber

Source: From "The Pathology of Boredom," by W. Heron, 1957, *Scientific American, 196,* pp. 52–56. Copyright 1957 by *Scientific American.* Adapted with permission from the illustration by Eric Mose.

Excessive Stimulation and Overarousal

Sometimes life is boring, but other times life is stressful. Stress comes from major events, such as divorce, physical injury, and unemployment (Holmes & Rahe, 1967; Iversen & Sabroe, 1989); from daily hassles, such as misplacing or losing things and getting stuck in traffic (DeLongis, Folkman, & Lazarus, 1988; Lazarus & DeLongis, 1983); and from chronic circumstances, such as inadequate child care, overcrowding, or repetitious relationship difficulties (DeLongis et al., 1982; Eckenrode, 1984). Major life events jolt the body's nervous and endocrine systems, whereas daily hassles and chronic circumstances produce a cumulative taxing effect on bodily systems.

Overstimulating, stressful environments upset emotional states, impair cognitive activity, and accelerate physiological processes. Emotional disruption manifests itself in feelings of anxiety, irritability, and anger (Horowitz et al., 1980). Cognitive disruption manifests itself in confusion, forgetfulness, and impaired concentration (Broadbent et al., 1982). Physiological disruption manifests itself in sympathetic nervous system hyperactivity, as through high blood pressure (Seyle, 1956). As a case in point, imagine that your term paper is due in 2 hours and is nowhere near its completion. Your amiability is probably decidedly negative (few overly stressed individuals smile, laugh, and tell jokes), your mental efficiency is probably disturbed (not being able to think straight), and your heart rate, muscle tone, and vulnerability to a headache are probably high and rising.

Because stress and strain are aversive ways of feeling, people generally want to escape from overstimulating environments. When unable to do so, daily functioning is characterized by negative affect, cognitive confusion, performance impairment, and health problems. Fortunately, just as we harbor motives to counteract insufficient stimulation and underarousal, we also harbor motives to counteract excessive stimulation and overarousal.

Credibility of the Inverted-U Hypothesis

The credibility of the inverted-U curve (see Figure 13.2) is not without debate. Rob Neiss (1988) levied four criticisms against the hypothesis, two of which are relevant to motivation and emotion (Anderson, 1990). Neiss' first criticism is that the inverted-U curve is descriptive rather than explanatory. That is, the hypothesis summarizes the relationship between arousal and performance/emotion, but it stops short of explaining *how* arousal facilitates or impairs performance/emotion.

Neiss' second criticism is that even if the inverted-U hypothesis is true, it is still trivial. In other words, the inverted-U hypothesis applies only when arousal levels are extreme, such as in sensory-deprivation studies. Neiss concludes that the inverted-U hypothesis does not apply to everyday affairs in which arousal level changes relatively little. While some motivation psychologists agree with this criticism, others disagree.

To illustrate how the inverted-U hypothesis applies to mundane changes in arousal, college students completed a pair of vocabulary tests under a condition of either leisure or stress (time pressure; Revelle, Amaral, & Turriff, 1976). In addition, before taking the tests, all students took either a 200-mg caffeine pill (equivalent to the caffeine in two cups of coffee) or a placebo pill (no caffeine). The purpose of the time pressure and caffeine manipulations was to create the sort of high stimulation that occurs in everyday life. The experiment had one more important variable: Each student completed a personality survey to differentiate introverts (people who are chronically overaroused) from extraverts (people who are chronically underaroused). Based on the inverted-U hypothesis, the experimenters predicted that (1) overaroused introverts would perform well when relaxed but poorly when stimulated, whereas (2) underaroused extraverts would perform poorly when relaxed but well when stimulated. Results confirmed the predictions. The experiment is important because it shows that the inverted-U hypothesis applies nicely to everyday sources of stimulation—caffeine and time pressure. Moderate everyday arousal is associated with optimal performance and emotion, while being underaroused or overaroused is not.

Sensation Seeking

Human beings differ in their genetic baseline level of arousal and in their reactivity to environmental stimuli. Baseline level of arousal is how aroused a person is without external stimulation. Reactivity refers to one's arousal reaction when exposed to external stimulation.

Sensation seeking is the personality characteristic related to arousal and reactivity. A high sensation seeker prefers a continual external supply of brain stimulation, becomes bored with routine, and is continually in search of ways to increase arousal through exciting experiences. A low sensation seeker prefers less brain stimulation and tolerates routine relatively well. In general, the sensation-seeking construct pertains to the extent to which a person's central nervous system (brain and spinal cord) requires change and variability, as sensation seekers prefer to change activities, change television channels, change drugs, change sexual partners, and so on (Zuckerman, 1994).

Sensation seeking is defined as "the seeking of varied, novel, complex, and intense sensations and experiences, and the willingness to take physical, social, legal, and financial risks for the sake of such experience" (Zuckerman, 1994). Marvin Zuckerman (1994) uses the example of driving very fast after heavy drinking to illustrate a sensation seeker's willingness to take physical risks (injure self or others), social risks (being exposed as a drunk driver), legal risks (being arrested and jailed), and financial risks (being fired from work). Such risks are the price sensation seekers are willing to take to receive the sensations and experiences they seek.

Search for New Experiences

The sensation seeker continually searches for novel experiences—spicy foods (Terasaki & Imada, 1988), switching television programs (Schierman & Rowland, 1985), listening to music with some punch (Litle & Zuckerman, 1986), and so on. One manifestation of the search for new experiences is sex. Compared to sensation avoiders, sensation seekers report a greater frequency and variety (number of partners) in sexual activity (Zuckerman et al., 1972; Zuckerman, Tushup, & Finner, 1976). Sensation seekers report that less of a relationship and less emotional involvement are necessary prerequisites for participation in sexual relations than do sensation avoiders (Hendrick & Hendrick, 1987; Zuckerman et al., 1976). Further, as parents, high sensation seekers set more permissive standards for their children's sexual activity (Zuckerman et al., 1976).

Drugs can also provide the means for a quick arousal boost. Drugs also open the door to new experiences (hallucinations), release inhibitions against risky behavior, and serve as an escape from boredom. Through any or all of these means of altering experiences, drug use functions as a form of sensation seeking (Zuckerman, 1978, 1994; Zuckerman et al., 1972). To substantiate these claims, Zuckerman and his colleagues (1972) asked college students to complete the Sensation-Seeking Scale (SSS) and a questionnaire on their drug and alcohol use. Sensation seekers reported frequent alcohol and drug use. Their search for new experiences also extends into deviance such as vandalism, aggression, stealing, and criminality (Newcomb & McGee, 1991; White, Labourvie, & Bates, 1985; Zuckerman, 1979).

Risk Taking

No one really likes risk per se, which is essentially the forecast that a behavior will produce aversive consequences. The risks related to sensation seeking involve those that are physical, social, legal, or financial. It is not that sensation seekers are attracted to such risks; rather, sensation seekers see sensations and experiences being worth these risks, whereas sensation avoiders do not. Thus, "risk accepting" seems to be a more appropriate term than does "risk taking."

High sensation seekers voluntarily engage in physically risky hobbies, such as motorcycling (Brown et al., 1974), parachuting and skydiving (Hymbaugh & Garrett, 1974), adventuresome travel (Jacobs & Koeppel, 1974), immigration (Winchie & Carment, 1988), cigarette smoking (Zuckerman, Ball, & Black, 1990), downhill skiing (Calhoon, 1988), and gambling (Kuhlman, 1975). In contrast, low sensation seekers show aversive reactivity to risky sources of stimulation (Mellstrom, Cicala, & Zuckerman, 1976). Gambling illustrates some of the sensation seekers' motivation for risk taking, as excitement, rather than money, motivates most people's gambling (Anderson & Brown, 1984).

Sensation seekers' risk taking manifests itself in many areas of life, such as in criminal behavior (shoplifting, selling drugs), minor violations (traffic offenses), finances (gambling, risky businesses), and sports (parachuting; Horvath & Zuckerman, 1993). Fast driving, for instance, offers potential physical, social, legal, and financial risks. Compared to sensation avoiders, sensation seekers report driving fast (well over the posted speed limit) under normal conditions (Arnett, 1991; Clement & Jonah, 1984; Zuckerman & Neeb, 1980), and they do not perceive tailgating (driving close behind the car in front) as risky or as physiologically upsetting (Heino, van der Molen, & Wilde, 1992, as reported in Zuckerman, 1994).

Biological Basis

Biochemical brain events determine how people react to environmental stimulation. So researchers investigate the links between the sensation-seeking trait and biochemical events in the brain. The most reliable finding is that sensation seekers have low levels of monoamine oxidase (MAO; Schooler et al. 1978). MAO is a limbic system enzyme involved in breaking down brain neurotransmitters such as dopamine and serotonin. Dopamine contributes to the experiences of reward and therefore facilitates approach behaviors (Stellar & Stellar, 1985). Serotonin contributes to a biological inhibition, or to the brain's physiological stop system, and therefore inhibits approach behaviors (Panksepp, 1982). Sensation seekers tend to have relatively high levels of dopamine; hence, their biochemistry favors approach over inhibition (Zuckerman, 1994). They also tend to have relatively low levels of serotonin; hence, their biochemistry fails to inhibit them from risks and new experiences.

Affect Intensity

Affect intensity concerns people's capacity to become aroused emotionally. It is defined in terms of the strength with which individuals typically experience their emotions (Larsen & Diener, 1987). Affect-intense individuals experience their emotions strongly and show emotional reactivity and variability across many different emotion-eliciting situations. Affect-stable individuals experience their emotions only mildly and show only minor fluctuations in their emotional reactions from moment to moment or from day to day.

Researchers measure affect intensity with a self-report questionnaire that includes items such as the following: When I feel happy, it is a strong type of exuberance, and When I am nervous, I get shaky all over (Larsen & Diener, 1987). Originally, re-

---

BOX 13   *Arousal and Stress*

Question: Why is this information important?

Answer: To explain why the psychological experiences of perceived control and perceived competence have the capacity to turn off the physiological response to stress.

Environments stimulate and challenge us. Arousal and stress are two motivationally based responses to stimulating, demanding environments. In response to being stimulated and challenged, we try to cope and adapt. That is, meeting your fiance's parents will stimulate and challenge you, and to relate well to your in-laws your heart accelerates and your attention focuses on the task at hand. The bodily responses that allow us to adapt constitute the biological underpinnings of felt arousal and felt stress.

Arousal is mostly a function of how stimulating the environment is. Stress is mostly a function of how demanding and controllable the environment is.

Our bodies respond to stimulating, stressful environments with an acute, short-lived response produced by the sympathetic-adrenal-medullary system. When stimulation is high, the sympathetic-adrenal-medullary system activates the sympathetic nervous system to expend energy (as in the fight-or-flight response). When stimulation is low, the system activates the parasympathetic nervous system to conserve energy (as in resting and digesting food). One key event in the activation of the sympathetic nervous system is the release of epinephrine (or adrenaline). Epinephrine is the catecholamine responsible for increasing heart rate, blood pressure, and respiration rate. People do not experi-

ence an increase level of epinephrine directly, but, instead, they experience an elevated state of bodily activation. It is this state of bodily activation that people experience as being aroused.

Our bodies also respond to stimulating, stressful environments with a chronic, long-lived response produced by the pituitary-adrenocortical system. When demands and challenges are high, the adrenal gland secretes corticosteroids, the most motivationally important of which is cortisol. Unlike epinephrine, which is released into the body in seconds, cortisol is released by the pituitary-adrenocortical system in minutes and hours. As long as the person continues to experience stress, cortisol continues to be released. To the extent that the person copes successfully with the stressing event, cortisol slows or stops altogether. When successful coping inhibits cortisol release, the person has the psychological experience of decreased stress. When unsuccessful coping fails to "turn off" cortisol, the person has the psychological experience of increased stress.

The suppression of cortisol is central to effective coping because elevated cortisol decreases intellectual functioning, alters metabolism, diminishes the immune response, reduces the body's response to infection, and suppresses the reproductive process. For instance, when cortisol is high, people's ability to solve intellectual problems is significantly impaired (Kirschbaum et al., 1996). On a more positive note, a perception of competence, mastery, or control suppresses cortisol (Booth et al., 1989). Thus, the antidote to cortisol and stress is an increase in perceived control.

searchers assessed affect intensity in an interesting, although laborious, way that nicely illustrates people's emotionality over time (Larsen, 1988). Over a period of 80 to 90 consecutive days, respondents completed a daily-mood questionnaire that featured positive (e.g., happy, joyful) and negative (e.g., depressed, worried) mood words. To compute affect intensity, the individual's daily score on the negative mood words was totaled and subtracted from the daily score on the positive mood words total to yield a daily mood. On each consecutive day, the overall daily mood score was plotted on a graph. How much the person's daily mood score deviated from neutral (0) defined her affect intensity. A daily-mood graph for three different people in the experiment appears in Figure 13.4. The daily mood of the affect-intense individual (subject 23) rose and fell rather substantially. Days were very good or very bad. The daily mood of the affect-stable individual (subject 21) hovered continuously around neutral. Days were mostly the same, emotionally speaking. The more typical daily mood graph appears in the center (subject 74) and shows the daily emotionality of a person who was neither affect intense nor affect stable.

For purposes of illustration, imagine that each of the following events, some good and some bad, recently happened to you: You won a scholarship you desperately needed or received a letter from a long-lost friend (positive life events); your automobile had a flat tire or you saw your ex-boyfriend/girlfriend with a new flame (negative life events; Larsen, Diener, & Emmons, 1987). Suppose further that you were asked to rate precisely how good or how bad each event was immediately after it occurred. For example, how good did you feel when you received a letter from your long-lost friend? How bad did you feel when your tire went flat? Just how good or how bad the events were in the lives of affect-intense and affect-stable individuals appear in Figure 13.5. For all bad events (upper figure), affect-intense individuals (black squares) reported a significantly worse negative emotionality than did affect stable individuals. For all good events (lower figure), affect-intense individuals (black squares) reported a significantly more positive emotionality than did affect stable individuals.

Affect-intense and affect-stable individuals do not differ physiologically from one another (Blascovich et al., 1992). Instead, they differ psychologically, as affect-intense individuals are more psychologically sensitive to changes in arousal than are affect-stable individuals. It is almost as if affect-intense persons have a highly sensitive "arousal thermostat" that monitors their arousal increases. Affect-stable individuals on the other hand have a relatively dull and insensitive arousal thermostat (Blascovich et al., 1992).

CONTROL

Many possible personality characteristics could be included under the category of personal control beliefs, including locus of control (Findley & Cooper, 1983; Levenson, 1981; Rotter, 1966), perceived control (Skinner, 1985), causality orientations (Deci & Ryan, 1985b), mastery versus helpless orientations (Diener & Dweck, 1978, 1980), explanatory style (Peterson & Seligman, 1984), desire for control (Burger, 1992), type A behavior pattern (Strube et al., 1987), and self-efficacy (Bandura, 1986; Berry & West, 1993). Two of these personality characteristics, however, adequately capture most of the spirit of control beliefs: perceived control and the desire for control. Perceived control

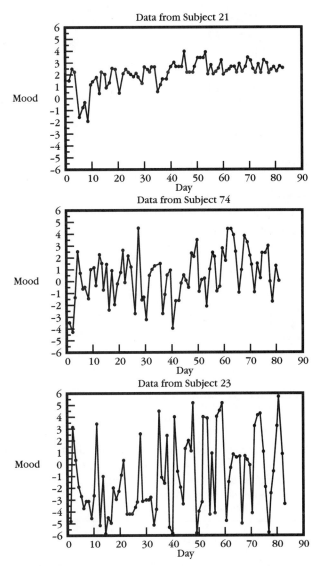

Figure 13.4   Daily Mood Reports Graphed Over 80 Consecutive Days
Source: From "Individual Differences in Affect Intensity," by R. J. Larsen, 1988, paper presented at the annual meeting of the Motivation and Emotion Conference at Nags Head, NC.

concerns differences in people's preperformance expectancies of possessing the needed capacity to produce positive outcomes (Skinner, Zimmer-Gembeck, & Connell, 1998). Desire for control concerns the extent to which people strive to make their own decisions, influence others, assume leadership roles, and enter situations in overly prepared ways (Burger, Oakman, & Bullard, 1983).

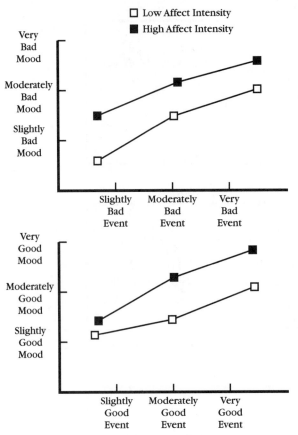

Figure 13.5   Affective Reactions to Good and Bad Events by Affect-Intense and Affect-Stable Individuals

Source: From "Affect Intensity and Reactions to Daily Life Events," by R. J. Larsen, E. Diener, and R. A. Emmons, 1987, *Journal of Personality and Social Psychology, 51*, pp. 803–814. Copyright 1987 by American Psychological Association. Adapted with permission.

Perceived Control

Perceived control refers to the beliefs and expectations a person holds that she can interact with the environment in ways that produce desired outcomes and prevent undesired outcomes (Skinner, 1995; Skinner, Zimmer-Gembeck, & Connell, 1998). In order to perceive that one has control over a given situation, one needs two things to be true. First, the self must be capable of obtaining the available desired outcome. Second, the situation in which one attempts to exercise control needs to be at least somewhat predictable and responsive.

Research on learned helplessness (Chapter 9) shows that as people find themselves in unpredictable, unresponsive environments, they learn that their actions and efforts are futile. But the reverse is not necessarily true. That is, when environments are predictable and responsive people do not necessarily put forth strong effort to exert control over their outcomes. This is true because even structured situations can be difficult to control, as is often the case in education, sports, relationships, and at work. When some barrier like task difficulty separates the person from attractive outcomes (e.g., good grades, fame, marriage, promotion), individual differences in perceptions of control intervene, explaining when and why people willingly put forth the effort necessary to control their fate.

Perceived control beliefs predict how much effort a person is willing to exert (Skinner, 1985; Skinner, Zimmer-Gembeck, & Connell, 1998). When a person with relatively high perceived control faces a reasonably structured situation, he seeks out and selects relatively challenging tasks, sets relatively high goals, and generates sophisticated plans about how to succeed and what to do when progress is slow. With this forethought, a person with high perceived control initiates action, exerts effort, focuses concentration, and persists in the face of difficulty. During performance, the high-perceived-control individual keeps her plans and strategies in mind, maintains positive emotional states, monitors problem-solving strategies, and generates and monitors feedback to adjust or improve relevant skills. Such an engaged focus on the task generally leads to strong performance and makes control over desirable and undesirable outcomes possible. In contrast, when a person with relatively low perceived control faces the same situation, he seeks out and selects relatively easy tasks, sets lower and vaguer goals, and generates simple plans with few fallback strategies. If things go wrong, concentration is likely to wander, confidence is quick to drop, and attention often turns to ruminating over why the task is so difficult. As effort decreases and cognitive and emotional engagements decline, discouragement and passivity set in, and performance suffers accordingly. Over time, such events lead people to become more pessimistic, to reduce their expectations of future control, and to quit making plans and strategies to prevent such a recurrence.

To assess individual differences in perceptions of control, researchers use questionnaires that contain the following items (Skinner, Chapman, & Baltes, 1988):

1. If you decide to sit yourself down and learn something really hard, can you learn it?
2. I'll bet you don't like to get bad grades. Can you do anything to keep from getting any?
3. Let's say: You decide that you're not going to get any problems wrong (like on a math or spelling paper). Can you do it?

From these items (written for elementary-grade students), perceived control appears to be conceptually similar to related constructs, such as perceived competence, self-efficacy, and perceived ability. One difference, however, is that perceived control functions as the antecedent foundation on which these other beliefs are constructed. For instance, perceived control bolsters perceived competence, and perceived competence predicts performance outcomes, such as preference for challenge and positive emotionality (Boggiano, Main, & Katz, 1988). Perceived control is, therefore, a necessary forerunner for constructing beliefs about one's competence, efficacy, and ability. A second difference between perceived control and these other constructs is that perceived control beliefs can emanate from any capacity, not just from one's own competence, efficacy, or ability. For instance, an athlete might perceive high control because of a capacity to solicit assistance from the coach, from teammates, or from the heavens. The belief that one has high control over outcomes therefore means that one has control over whatever it is that controls the outcomes—self, teammates, luck, or the heavens.

Self-Confirming Cycles of High and Low Engagement

Engagement in the effort to gain control over an important outcome exists on a continuum that ranges from disaffection to engagement (Skinner & Belmont, 1993; Wellborn, 1991). When highly engaged, people exert strong and persistent effort and express positive emotion; when disaffected, people behave passively and express negative emotion (Patrick, Skinner, & Connell, 1993). Thus, engagement captures the intensity and emotional quality of a person's participation during somewhat difficult undertakings to control the outcomes that matter to them (Connell & Wellborn, 1991; Skinner, 1991).

Perceived control beliefs influence the individual's engagement, emotion, coping, and challenge-seeking (Boggiano et al., 1988; Skinner, 1995; Skinner, Zimmer-Gembeck, & Connell, 1998). People with high perceived control show relatively high effort, concentrate and pay attention, persist in the face of failure, maintain interest and curiosity in the task, and maintain optimism for future positive outcomes. People with low perceived control show relatively low effort, doubt their capacities, tend to give up in the face of challenge or failure, become discouraged quickly, are prone to passivity, anxiety, and even anger, and appear to simply go through the motions of participating (Skinner, Zimmer-Gembeck, & Connell, 1998). Such patterns of engagement versus disaffection are important because they predict the outcomes people attain. Attained outcomes, in turn, effect performers' postperformance perceptions of control. Hence, engaged effort produces the positive outcomes and postperformance perceptions of high control that produced the engaged effort in the first place. Disaffection (i.e., just passively going through the motions) produces the negative outcomes and postperformance perceptions of low control that produced the disaffected effort in the first place. This is the so-called self-confirming cycle of higher versus lower engagement.

One group of researchers tested the validity of these self-confirming cycles over a four-month period by asking grade-school children to complete short questionnaires (Schmitz & Skinner, 1993). The researchers assessed the children's expected control, extent of engagement, actual performance, perceived performance, and estimates of future control. On each graded assignment, the researchers examined the following relationships: (1) effects of preperformance expected control on subsequent engagement, (2) effects of engagement on actual performance, and (3) effects of performance outcomes on subsequent expectations of control. Results supported the validity of all three effects. Perceived control beliefs contributed positively to effort, which enhanced performance, which fueled further gains in the children's developing perceptions of control (Schmitz & Skinner, 1993). Over the course of many months and years, this self-confirming cycle explains how and why some people develop strong personal control beliefs while others do not.

Desire for Control

Desire for control (DC) reflects the extent to which individuals are motivated to establish control over the events in their lives (Burger, 1992; Burger & Cooper, 1979). High-DC individuals approach situations by asking themselves whether they will be able to control what happens. They are not content to take whatever life throws their way but instead are motivated to influence life and what happens (Burger, 1992). High-DC persons prefer making their own decisions, prepare for situations in advance, avoid dependence on others, and assume leadership roles in group settings. Low-DC persons tend to avoid responsibilities and feel comfortable having others make decisions for them (Burger, 1992; Burger & Cooper, 1979). They prefer to take life as they find it—to wing it.

The scale to assess the desire for control is the DC scale (Burger, 1992; Burger & Cooper, 1979). Two items from the DC scale are the following:

1. I prefer a job where I have a lot of control over what I do and when I do it.
2. I like to get a good idea of what a job is all about before I begin.

What makes the desire for control different from perceived control is that high-desire-for-control individuals want control over their fates irrespective of how much control they currently have and irrespective of how structured or responsive the situation appears to be. Desire for control relates to (i.e., predicts) a variety of experiences and behaviors that are fundamental to personal control beliefs, including learned helplessness, depression, illusion of control, hypnosis, achievement, perceived crowding, stress and coping, interpersonal style with friends health habits, and even an elderly person's choice of a place to die—in control at home or managed by others in a hospital (Burger, 1984, 1992; Burger & Arkin, 1980; Burger & Cooper, 1979; Burger, Oakman, & Bullard, 1983; Burger & Schnerring, 1982; Smith et al., 1984). The common links between desire for control and these behavioral manifestations of personal control are the high desire to, one, establish control and, second, to restore lost control.

Establishing Control

Control is often an issue in our daily conversations and interactions with others. To establish some measure of control over interpersonal conversations (what will be talked about, what attitudes the persons in the conversations hold, what plans will be made), high-DC individuals speak loudly, explosively, and rapidly; they respond quickly to questions and comments; and they interrupt and talk over their partners (Dembroski, MacDougall, & Musante, 1984). High-DC persons also tend to end conversations when they want to, usually after having finished what they wanted to say or after having successfully persuaded the other person of the correctness of the high-DC individual's viewpoint (i.e., after establishing control; Burger, 1990, 1992).

Desiring control is generally adaptive and productive when situations are controllable. Often, however, high-DC individuals want and expect control over events when, in fact, their outcomes are determined by chance. For example, many gambling opportunities such as slot machines, lottery games, and roulette wheels are determined by chance (Burger & Cooper, 1979). Nonetheless, high-DC individuals tend to perceive that they can control such outcomes through personal effort. The *desire* for control feeds into the *illusion* of control (Burger, 1986, 1992).

Achievement situations provide an arena for high-DC individuals' desires to establish control (Burger, 1985). High-DC individuals typically interpret a difficult task as a challenge to their ability to control. Thus, when confronted with a difficult task, the high-DC individual should persist longer than the low-DC individual. To give up on a difficult task is to admit that the task is beyond personal control. To test this idea, Jerry Burger gave students a series of insoluble puzzles and observed how long the high- and low-DC individuals persisted. As predicted, high-DC individuals persisted longer at the puzzles than did the low-DC individuals.

	Aspiration Level	**Response to Challenge**	**Persistance**	**Attributions for Success and Failure**
High DC Compared with Low DC	Select harder tasks; set goals more realistically	React with greater effort	Work at difficult task longer	More likely to attribute success to self and failure to unstable source
High DC Benefit	Higher goals are achieved	Difficult tasks are completed	Difficult tasks are completed	Motivation level remains high
High DC Liability	May attempt goals too difficult	May develop performance-inhibiting reactions	May invest too much effort	May develop an illusion of control

Figure 13.6 Influence of Desire for Control during Achievement-Related Performance

Source: From "Desire for Control and Achievement-Related Behaviors," by J. M. Burger, 1985, *Journal of Personality and Social Psychology, 48,* pp. 1520–1533. Copyright 1985 by American Psychological Association. Adapted with permission.

Figure 13.6 shows a four-step model to illustrate the multidimensional nature of the high-DC individual's quest to establish control in achievement situations (Burger, 1985). High-DC persons select hard tasks because they generally have high aspirations and standards, put forth unusually high effort when challenged, persist at difficult tasks and are slow to give up and move on, and make self-serving and control-enhancing attributions such as taking credit for success while attributing failure to an unstable cause (Burger, 1985, 1992). The desire for control is generally a positive resource in achievement situations. But Figure 13.6 also outlines the desire for control's counterproductive side. Because high-DC individuals strongly desire control, they sometimes attempt overly difficult goals, exhibit a hostile reactance effect with failure, persist too long on tasks that cannot be solved, and develop an illusion of control. What these data show is that the desire for control leads people to overestimate how well they will perform, to overinvest their energies, to persist too long on difficult tasks, and to interpret success and failure feedback in ways that feed an illusion of control.

Losing Control

People sometimes face situations where little control is possible. In circumstances such as overcrowding, military life, nursing homes, hospitals, prison, and living next door to an offensive dump or an ear-pounding airport, little control is possible. Such situations present an obvious plight for the high-DC individual. When their control is threatened or lost altogether, high-DC individuals exhibit distinct reactions, such as distress, anxiety, depression, dominance, and assertive coping (Burger, 1992).

Visiting the dentist's office is one of these low-control situations (Law, Logan, & Baron, 1994). When people with a high DC visit the dentist, the idea of another person using tools on their teeth causes unusually high levels of anxiety, anticipated pain, and distress. Interestingly, a 20-minute stress-inoculation training session immediately before the dental visit can give high-DC individuals the control-coping strategies and responses they desire (Law, Logan, & Baron, 1994).

Crowding is another low-control situation. Crowding, defined by the number of people per square foot, undermines control because one cannot move about freely (Stokols, 1972). Having a lot of other people around, as in dense traffic, overpopulated sidewalks, and long supermarket checkout lines, interferes with anyone's ability to get things done. High-DC individuals are more vulnerable to perceptions of being crowded, and they therefore try to avoid such distressing situations (Burger, 1992).

When people desire control but the environment refuses to afford it, the person becomes vulnerable to learned helplessness and depression. Jerry Burger and Robert Arkin (1980) asked high- and low-DC individuals to participate in a typical learned-helplessness experiment in which they were exposed to harsh, uncontrollable, and unpredictable noise. Compared to low-DC persons, high-DC persons reported higher levels of post-task depression. Further, the magnitude of helplessness and depression varied in proportion to which how important control was for that person in that situation (Mikulincer, 1986). So, in controllable environments, the desire for control works as a motivational asset, but, in uncontrollable environments, the desire for control works as a motivational liability.

SUMMARY

Chapter 1 identified a number of questions in motivation study that are best answered through a study of personality and individual differences. These questions were as follows: For which motives are there individual differences? How do such motivational differences between people arise? and What are the implications of such individual motivational differences? This chapter identified two personality characteristics related to happiness and well being, two personality characteristics related to arousal, and two related to control. In doing so, it explained how these personality differences arise and what implications they have for motivation, emotion, and everyday life.

Two personality characteristics related to happiness are extraversion and neuroticism. The personality characteristic that explains "Who is happy?" is extraversion. Extraverts are happier than are introverts. Extraverts are happy because they have a stronger behavioral activating system (BAS) that makes them highly responsive to signals of reward in the environment. The personality characteristic that explains "Who is unhappy?" is neuroticism. Neurotics suffer emotionally. They do so because they have a stronger behavioral inhibition system (BIS) that makes them highly responsive to signals of punishment in the environment.

Extraversion predisposes the individual toward a positive emotionality, the behavioral activation system, and an approach temperament. Neuroticism predisposes the individual toward a negative emotionality, the behavioral inhibition system, and an avoidance temperament. When extraverts enter a situation, their BAS predisposes them to be particularly sensitive to its potentially rewarding aspects and thus they experience positive emotions and show approach-oriented behavior. When neurotics enter a situation, their BIS predisposes them to be particularly sensitive to its potentially punishing aspects and thus they experience negative emotions and show avoidance-oriented behavior.

Sensation seeking and affect intensity represent two personality characteristics related to arousal and to the inverted-U curve of arousal, performance, and emotion/mood. Sensation seeking is the need for varied, novel, complex, and intense sensations and the willingness to take physical, social, legal, and financial risks for the sake of such experiences. To attain such sensations, sensation seekers seek new experiences, as in sex and drugs, and they engage in risk-accepting behavior, as in gambling. Affect intensity represents the strength with which individuals typically experience their emotions. Affect-intense individuals experience emotions strongly and show emotional hyperactivity in emotion-eliciting situations. Affect-stable individuals experience their emotions only mildly and show only minor fluctuations in their emotional reactions.

Perceived control and the desire for control represent two personality characteristics related to control. Perceived control concerns the capacity to initiate and regulate the behavior needed to gain desirable outcomes and to prevent undesirable ones. When perceived control is strong, people engage in tasks with active coping and positive emotion, and this on-task engagement increases the probability that they will attain the outcomes they seek. But when perceived control is weak, people engage in tasks in only halfhearted ways as they show passivity and negative emotion. This disaffection, in turn, decreases the probability that they will attain the outcomes they seek. Thus, by affecting engagement, perceived control beliefs initiate a self-confirming cycle in which people with high perceived control initiate the effort that produces the positive outcomes that, in turn, increases subsequent perceptions of high control. Desire for control reflects the extent to which people are motivated to control the events in their lives. High-DC individuals approach situations by wanting to control what happens to them, so they strive establish control and to restore it when control is lost or threatened. To establish control, high-DC individuals embrace high standards and aspirations, put forth high effort when challenged, overly persist at difficult tasks, and interpret success/failure feedback in a self-serving and control-enhancing way. When control is threatened or lost, as in visiting the dentist, entering a crowded room, or participating in a learned-helplessness experiment, high-DC individuals exhibit distinct reactions such as distress and depression.

READINGS FOR FURTHER STUDY

Personality and Happiness

BRICKMAN, P., COATES, D., & JANOFF-BULMAN, R. (1978). Lottery winners and accident victims: Is happiness relative? *Journal of Personality and Social Psychology, 36*, 917–927.

COSTA, P. T., & MCCRAE, R. R. (1980). Influence of extraversion and neuroticism on subjective well-being: Happy and unhappy people. *Journal of Personality and Social Psychology, 38*, 668–678.

DUPUE, R. A., & COLLINS, P. F. (1999). Neurobiology of the structure of personality: Dopamine facilitation of incentive motivation and extraversion. *Behavioral and Brain Sciences, 22*, 491–569.

ELLIOT, A. J., & THRASH, T. M. (2002). Approach-avoidance motivation in personality: Approach and avoidance temperament and goals. *Journal of Personality and Social Psychology, 82*, 804–818.

Personality and Arousal

ANDERSON, K. J. (1990). Arousal and the inverted-U hypothesis: A critique of Neiss's reconceptualizing arousal. *Psychological Bulletin, 107*, 96–100.

LARSEN, R. J., & DIENER, E. (1987). Affect intensity as an individual difference characteristic: A review. *Journal of Research in Personality, 21*, 1–39.

ZUCKERMAN, M., BONE, R. N., NEARY, R., MANGELSDORFF, D., & BRUSTMAN, B. (1972). What is the sensation seeker? Personality trait and experience correlates of the Sensation Seeking Scale. *Journal of Clinical and Counseling Psychology, 39*, 308–321.

Personality and Control

BOGGIANO, A. K., MAIN, D. S., & KATZ, P. A. (1988). Children's preference for challenge: The role of perceived competence and control. *Journal of Personality and Social Psychology, 54*, 134–141.

BURGER, J. M. (1985). Desire for control and achievement-related behaviors. *Journal of Personality and Social Psychology, 53*, 1520–1533.

LAW, A., LOGAN, H., & BARON, R. S. (1994). Desire for control, felt control, and stress inoculation training during dental treatment. *Journal of Personality and Social Psychology, 67*, 926–936.

SCHMITZ, B., & SKINNER, E. A. (1993). Perceived control, effort, and academic performance: Interindividual, intraindividual, and multivariate time-series analyses. *Journal of Personality and Social Psychology, 64*, 1010–1028.

Chapter 14

Unconscious Motivation

Imagine accompanying your friend on his visit to a psychiatrist. To begin the session, your friend undergoes hypnosis. Once hypnotized, the psychiatrist suggests that your friend brought a newspaper with him to the session and that once he awakes, he will want to read it. In actuality, your friend brought no newspaper. Further, the therapist suggests that upon his awakening, he will look for the newspaper but will be unable to find it. The therapist tells your friend that, after a couple of minutes of searching, an idea will occur to him that another person has taken his newspaper—that the other person has, in fact, stolen it. The therapist also suggests that your friend's discovery will provoke him to anger. Further, the therapist tells your friend to direct that anger toward the thief. Unfortunately for you, the psychiatrist next tells your friend that you are that thief. The therapist next tells your friend that, in his fit of anger, he will first insist and will then demand that you return his newspaper. To conclude the hypnosis session, the psychiatrist tells your friend that he will forget that the source of all this (mis)information was actually a series of suggestions given to him by the therapist.

Your friend awakens. He begins to chat leisurely about the day's events, and then remarks, "Incidentally, that reminds me of something I read in today's newspaper. I'll show you." Your friend looks around, does not see his newspaper, and begins to search for it. You begin to feel a hint of anxiety because you have been with your friend all day and know that he has neither read nor purchased a paper. Then, suddenly, he turns toward you with piercing eyes. Accusingly, your friend pronounces that you took his newspaper, and he now wants it back. You are starting to think coming along was not such a good idea and rather sheepishly say that you know nothing of the newspaper. But your friend persists. He is truly upset. With his anger piqued, your friend forcefully accuses you of stealing his newspaper. He goes further, saying that you took it because you are too cheap to buy one of your own. To substantiate his accusation, he says someone saw you steal his newspaper and told him about it.

This is no longer funny. Your friend *really* believes you stole his newspaper, and he *really* wants it back.

What does this hypnosis session illustrate (based on Fromm, 1941)? The scenario illustrates that human beings can have thoughts, feelings, and emotions that subjectively feel to be their own but, in fact, have been introjected from another source. Your friend wanted something—to show you an item in the newspaper. He thought something—you stole his newspaper. And he felt something—anger against an alleged thief. But your friend's wants, thoughts, and feelings were not his own in the sense that they did not originate within him. Yet, your friend surely acted as if they were his own. Such a demonstration of the posthypnotic suggestion testifies to the paradox that while we can be sure of what we want, think, and feel, we can also have little idea as to the source of what we want, think, and feel. The whole scenario bears witness to the idea that motivation can arise from a source that lies outside of conscious awareness and volitional intent.

PSYCHOANALYTICAL PERSPECTIVE

In contrast to humanism (Chapter 15), the psychoanalytic approach presents a deterministic, pessimistic image of human nature. Psychoanalysis is deterministic in that it holds that the ultimate cause of motivation and behavior derives from biologically endowed and socially acquired impulses that determine our desires, thoughts, feelings, and behaviors, whether we like it or not. Psychoanalysis is further deterministic in that personality changes little after puberty. Thus, many of the motivational impulses of an adult can be traced to events that took place in childhood. Motivation comes across as something that happens to us, rather than as something one chooses or creates. Psychoanalysis is also relatively pessimistic in tone, as it places the spotlight on sexual and aggressive urges, conflict, anxiety, repression, defense mechanisms, anxiety, and a host of emotional burdens, vulnerabilities, and shortcomings of human nature. It sees anxiety as inevitable and the collapse of personality as a matter of degree rather than as an exceptional event that happens to only some of us. We are all dogged by guilt, anxiety is our constant companion, narcissism and homophobia are common, and distortions of reality are modus operandi. It is not a pretty picture, Freud said, but it is reality nonetheless. In his mind, Freud was not a pessimist; he was a realist.

Psychoanalysis is strangely appealing and wonderfully popular. Part of its appeal is that, in reading psychoanalytic theory, the reader comes face to face with some difficult aspects of human nature. According to psychoanalysis, people "are more interested in getting sexual pleasure than they will admit" and people have "blind rages, wild lusts, and parasitic infantile longings" (Holt, 1989). These difficult, mysterious aspects of human nature present us with a psychological riddle that pulls in our curiosity. Who can resist wanting to learn more about a theory that reveals the secrets of the mind—secret crushes and jealousies, fantasies and desires, memories of things done and not done, and all sorts of hidden intrigue and despair?

Part of the appeal of psychoanalysis is that it makes the unconscious its subject matter. Thus, psychoanalysis willingly goes "where no theory has gone before" (to paraphrase *Star Trek*)—into dreams, hypnosis, inaccessible memories, fantasy, and all the hidden forces that shape our motives and behaviors without our awareness and without our consent. In doing so, psychoanalysis offers a chance to talk about a deeply interesting subject matter—the content of our own private subjective experience and why unwanted desires and fears make their home there.

Psychoanalytic Becomes Psychodynamic

A few decades ago, the terms psychoanalytic and psychodynamic could be used as synonyms. A growing number of scholars, however, found themselves in the uncomfortable position of accepting Freud's ideas about unconscious mental processes but rejecting some of his other ideas, such as his dual-instinct theory of motivation (discussed below). Today, the term psychoanalytic refers to practitioners who remain committed to most traditional Freudian principles, whereas the term psychodynamic refers to the study of dynamic unconscious mental processes. In other words, one can study unconscious mental processes (e.g., prejudice, depression, thought suppression, defense mechanisms) inside or outside the Freudian tradition. That is, many researchers study psychodynamic processes without embracing the psychoanalytic approach. The present chapter is, accordingly, about psychodynamic unconscious motivation and not necessarily about traditional Freudian principles. But to understand the foundation of the psychoanalytical perspective, the chapter begins where Freud began his study of motivation—namely, with his controversial dual-instinct theory.

Dual-Instinct Theory

A physician by training, Sigmund Freud viewed motivation as regulated by impulse-driven biological forces. The human body was seen as a complex energy system organized for the purpose of increasing and decreasing its energies through behavior. Some behaviors increased bodily energy (eating, breathing), and some behaviors depleted energy (working, playing). Some bodily energy was mental energy, and the mind needed mental energy to perform its functions (e.g., thinking, remembering). The mind received this psychic energy from the body's physical energy. The source of all physical energy was biological drive (or instinct), which was a biologically rooted force "emanating within the organism and penetrating to the mind" (Freud, 1915). Hence, instinctual bodily drives explained the source of all motivation.

For Freud, there were as many biological drives as there were different bodily demands (e.g., food, water, sleep). But Freud recognized that there were too many different bodily needs to list. Instead of compiling a taxonomy of bodily drives, Freud (1920, 1923) emphasized two general categories: instincts for life and instincts for death.

The first class of instincts—Eros, the life instincts—are the more easily defined of the two. Eros instincts maintain life and ensure individual and collective (species) survival. Thus, instincts for food, water, air, sleep, and the like all contribute to the life and survival of the individual. These are instincts for self-preservation. Instincts for sex, nurturance, and affiliation contribute to the life and survival of the species, a reproductive emphasis Freud borrowed from Darwin (Ritvo, 1990). These are instincts for species-preservation. In his discussions of the life instincts, Freud gave primary emphasis to sex, though he conceptualized sex quite broadly as "pleasure seeking" (including thumb-sucking, being tickled, being rocked, being caressed, being tossed in the air, rhythmic stimulation, masturbation, and sexual contact; Freud, 1905).

The second class of instincts—Thanatos, the death instincts—push the individual toward rest, inactivity, and energy conservation. An absence of any bodily disturbance could be achieved only through total rest, which was death. In discussing the death instincts, Freud gave primary emphasis to aggression. When focused on the self, aggression manifests itself in self-criticism, sadism, depression, suicide, masochism, alcoholism, drug addiction, and unnecessary risks taking like gambling. When focused on others, aggression manifests itself in anger, hate, prejudice, verbal insult, cruelty, rivalry, revenge, murder, and war. For example, a hostile joke about an ethnic group represented an expression of the Thanatos (Freud, 1905).

These bodily based instinctual drives toward life and death—sex and aggression—provide the energy to motivate behavior. But people did not just impulsively act on their inborn sexual and aggressive energies. Instead, the individual learned from experience to direct his or her behavior toward need-satisfying aims. Through experience, which is a synonym for "psychosexual development," the individual learns defensive reactions for managing her sexual and aggressive energies. One's habitual, learned manner of defense is what Freud meant by the ego, or by "personality." Thus, instinctual drives provide the energy for behavior, while the ego provides its direction—attain biological (instinctual) satisfaction in the most socially appropriate and in the least anxiety-provoking way.

Drive or Wish?

The dual-instinct theory of motivation represents psychoanalysis, circa 1930. Times have changed, and progress has been made. Few contemporary psychoanalysts understand motivation as a function of the dual instinct theory (Kolb, Cooper, & Fishman, 1995; Westen, 1991), and this has been true for several decades (Berkowitz, 1962).

Unlike hunger and thirst, neither sex nor aggression conform to a physiological model of drive. For instance, notice how poorly an analysis of aggression would fit into the cyclical pattern of homeostasis depicted earlier in Figure 4.1: Homeostasis → need →

drive → goal-directed behavior → consummation → return to homeostasis. Physiological deprivation rarely produces aggressive urges, and the urge to aggress does not intensify with the passage of time. Further, consummatory behavior typically fuels and intensifies, rather than satiates and quiets, aggressive desires. Because sex and aggression are so central to Freud's view of motivation and because sex and aggression fit the drive conceptualization so poorly, contemporary psychoanalysts drop the idea of the instinctual drive as their central motivational construct (Holt, 1989).

As a substitute motivational principle, sex and aggression are conceptualized as psychological wishes, rather than as physiological drives (Holt, 1989; Klein, 1967). The reformulated "wish model" is essentially a discrepancy theory of motivation (see chapter 8) and proposes the following: At any time, individuals are aware, consciously or unconsciously, of their present state and, on encountering almost any situation, perceive some more potentially desirable state. For example, a man goes about his daily affairs without any aggressive urge but, upon being insulted, demeaned, dissed, or ridiculed, perceives a potentially more favorable social status than his lowly present one. Consequently, a "present state" versus "ideal state" mismatch occurs, and the aggressive wish arises as motivation to move the present state closer to the ideal state. Contemporary psychoanalysts now propose that psychological wishes, not instinctual drives, regulate and direct human behavior (Holt, 1989). The wish retains all the spirit of Freudian motivation as people wish constantly for ideal states in the sexual and aggressive realms, but it overcomes the contradictory evidence that sex and aggression do not function as physiological drives.

The goal of psychoanalytic therapy has always been to understand the confusing activities of the unconscious and therefore free the ego to deal with reality. To do so, contemporary psychodynamic therapists focus more and more on cognitive and interpersonal forces, and less and less on biological and intrapersonal forces (Wegner, 1989; Westen, 1998). Contemporary psychoanalytic therapists and researchers do not write much about ids and egos, and they do not spend most of their time undertaking archaeological-like expeditions in search of lost memories that will lead to a discovery of the patient's present-day psychopathology (Kolb, Cooper, & Fishman, 1995; Mitchell, 1988; Wachtel, 1993; Westen, 1998). Instead, the contemporary focus is decidedly interpersonal as it centers on helping people recognize, improve upon, or outright run away from problematic interpersonal relationships (Hazan & Shaver, 1987; Loevinger, 1976; Scharff & Scharff, 1995; Westen et al. 1991). For example, a common problem in psychodynamic therapy is recognizing and developing the skills necessary to overcome the chronic tendency to involve oneself in intimate relationships with the wrong kind of person (Greenberg & Mitchell, 1983; Westen et al., 1991).

Contemporary Psychodynamic Theory

Basically, a lot has changed since Freud. Today, four postulates define psychodynamic theory (Westen, 1998). That these principles are contemporary, as opposed to classically Freudian, is important for two reasons. First, psychodynamic thought has had time to put Freud's insightful propositions to empirical tests to see which postulates do, and which postulates do not, stand the objective tests of time and empirical evaluation. Second, most readers will be more familiar with Freud's classical psychoanalysis than they will be with what contemporary psychodynamic theory embraces, a fact that makes it necessary to review the following core postulates (Westen, 1998):

1. The Unconscious.
   Much of mental life is unconscious.

2. Psychodynamics
   Mental processes operate in parallel with one another.

3. Ego Development
   Healthy development involves moving from an immature, socially dependent personality to one that is more mature and interdependent with others.

4. Object Relations Theory
   Mental representations of self and others form in childhood that guide the person's later social motivations and relationships.

The first postulate emphasizes the unconscious. It argues emphatically that thoughts, feelings, and desires exist at the unconscious level. Thus, because unconscious mental life affects behavior, people can behave in ways that are inexplicable, even to themselves.

The second postulate emphasizes psychodynamics. It argues that motivational and emotional processes frequently operate in parallel with one another—people commonly want and fear the same thing at the same time. It is the rule, not the exception, that people have conflicting feelings that motivate them in opposing ways. Hence, people commonly harbor divergent conscious and unconscious racial (Fazio et al., 1995) and gender (Banaji & Hardin, 1996) attitudes that produce simultaneous approach and avoidance behavior.

The third postulate emphasizes ego development. While recognizing the motivational significance of sexual and aggressive energies, ego psychologists focus on how we grow, develop, and leave behind our relatively immature, fragile, egocentric, and narcissistic beginnings in life to become relatively mature, resilient, empathic, and socially responsible beings.

The fourth postulate highlights object relations theory. It argues that stable personality patterns begin to form in childhood as people construct mental representations of the self and others. Once formed, these beliefs about self and others shape enduring patterns of motivation (relatedness, anxiety) that guide the quality of the adult's interpersonal relationships.

THE UNCONSCIOUS

Scientific psychology has had a difficult time with the empirical exploration of the unconscious. After all, if the unconscious is hidden from both private consciousness and public observation, then how can a researcher ever gain access to it? This problem is not an insurmountable one, however, any more than concepts such as electrons are insurmountable to those who study physics. Like unconscious mental processes, electrons, velocity, and the expanding universe are also difficult, but not impossible, to measure and to study scientifically.

Freud believed that the individual must express strong unconscious urges and impulses, though in a disguised form. The unconscious is therefore a "shadow phenomenon" that cannot be known directly but can be inferred only from its indirect manifestations (Erdelyi, 1985). Believing the unconscious constituted the "primary process" while consciousness was but a "secondary process," Freud and his colleagues explored the contents and processes of the unconscious in a number of ways, including hypnosis, free association, dream analysis, humor, projective tests, errors and slips of the tongue, and so-called "accidents" (Exner, 1986; Freud, 1900, 1901, 1905, 1920, 1927; Murray, 1943).

It has been a rocky and emotionally charged 100-year debate, but the conclusion that much of mental life is unconscious is now largely accepted as true (Westen, 1998). Instead of debating whether some of mental life is unconscious, the debate now centers on two different portrayals of the unconscious. The two views can be called the Freudian unconscious and the non-Freudian unconscious. Just as Freud used methods like hypnosis and slips of the tongue, modern-day psychologists use methods like subliminal activation, selective attention, unconscious learning, and implicit memory to study the non-Freudian unconscious (Greenwald, 1992; Kihlstrom, 1987).

The empirical study of the non-Freudian unconscious began with a patient with epilepsy. Because of his seizures, he had his hippocampus removed and, as a result, had amnesia. He was brought into a laboratory for several consecutive days to practice a motor skill. As he walked into the laboratory each new day, he had absolutely no memory of being there before, no memory of the people who worked there, and no memory of the motor skill he practiced each day. Still, he showed rather marked improvement in the motor skill day-after-day. This experiment suggested the existence of an unconscious memory. Non-Freudian cognitive neuroscientists now generally concede that normal people have both types of memory—a conscious memory and an unconscious memory.

One question that separates the two views of the unconscious is whether the unconscious is smart or dumb (Loftus & Klinger, 1992). In the Freudian conceptualization, the unconscious is very smart, every bit as smart as is its conscious counterpart. The unconscious is smart because it uses sophisticated defenses, is complex and dynamic, is flexible, manages complex bodies of knowledge, and knows how to best protect the conscious mind from injury. Those who study the non-Freudian unconscious, however, view the unconscious is dumb. To call the unconscious dumb is to say that it is (compared to the conscious mind) simple, automated, and capable of performing only routine information processing. It carries out habitual or automatic processing, such as that which occurs when driving a car or playing the piano (i.e., unconscious procedural knowledge).

A second question that arises concerns whether the unconscious is motivationally hot and passionate or is only cognitively cold and automated. The Freudian unconscious was hot. It reeked with lust and anger; it was irrational, impulsive, primitive, demanding, and hallucinatory. The non-Freudian unconscious studied by present-day psychologists, however, is cold. It is mechanical and automated as it carries out countless computations and innumerable adjustments during acts like tying your shoes (Greenwald, 1992).

Freudian Unconscious

The division of mental life into what is conscious and what is unconscious is the fundamental premise of psychoanalysis (Freud, 1923). Freud rejected the idea that consciousness was the essence of mental life and therefore divided the mind into three components: conscious, preconscious, and unconscious. The conscious (i.e., "short-term memory" or "consciousness") includes all the thoughts, feelings, sensations, memories, and experiences that a person is aware of at any given time. The preconscious stores all the thoughts, feelings, and memories that are absent from immediate consciousness but can be retrieved into consciousness with a little prompting (e.g., you are aware of but are not currently thinking about your name or what color ink these words are printed in). The most important, and by far the largest, component of mental life is the unconscious. The unconscious is the mental storehouse of inaccessible instinctual impulses, repressed experiences, childhood (before language) memories, and strong but unfulfilled wishes and desires (Freud, 1915, 1923).

To illustrate the view of the unconscious as flexible and strategic (i.e., smart), consider unconscious activity during dreaming. For Freud, daily tensions continually mounted in the unconscious and were vented during dreaming. Because dreams vent unconscious tensions, dreams provided an opportunity for accessing the unconscious' wishful core. Assuming that the person could recall his dreams, dream analysis began by asking the individual to report a dream's story line and ended with the therapist's interpretation of the underlying meaning of the dream. A dream's story line represents its manifest content (its face value and defensive facade), while the symbolic meanings of the events in the story line represent its latent content (its underlying meaning and wishful core). Because the explicit expression of unconscious wishes would be anxiety-provoking (and would therefore awaken the dreamer), the unconscious expresses its impulses through the latent and symbolic, rather than the obvious and manifest.

As one illustration, consider the following dream reported by one of Freud's patients (Freud, 1900):

> *A whole crowd of children—all of her brothers, sisters and cousins of both sexes—were romping in a field. Suddenly they all grew wings, flew away and disappeared.*

The patient first had this dream as a young child and continued to have this same dream repeatedly into adulthood. In the dream, all of the patient's brothers, sisters, and cousins flew away and she alone remained in the field. According to Freud, the dream does not make much sense at the manifest level, and to gain an understanding of its meaning and significance, the analysis must take place within the latent content, using the technique of free association. At the latent level, the dream is (for this particular person) a death wish from the Thanatos. According to Freud, the dreamer is wishing that her brothers, sisters, and cousins would all sprout wings and fly away like a butterfly (a child's view of the soul leaving the body upon death), leaving her to the full attention and affection of her parents.

Before we can conclude that dreams function to vent unconscious wishes, however, we must acknowledge what 20th-century research has discovered since Freud. In addition to serving a venting function, dreams serve (1) *neurophysiological activity* in that the brain stem (not unconscious wishes) produces random neural input for the neocortex to process and make sense of (Crick & Mitchison, 1986); (2) a *memory consolidating function* as memories of the day are moved from short-term into long-term memory (Greenberg & Perlman, 1993); (3) a *stress-buffering or coping function* by providing an opportunity to pair defense mechanisms against threatening events such as job stress (Koulack, 1993); and (4) a *problem-solving function* in that, during dreaming, people process information, organize ideas, and arrive at creative constructions for solving their problems (Winson, 1992). While some evidence supports the idea that dreams provide an outlet for venting wishes and tensions (Fisher & Greenberg, 1996), it is also true that Freud's concept of the dream was too limited. Dreams express unconscious wishes, but dreams are also neurophysiological, cognitive, coping, and problem-solving events that have little to do with unconscious wishes (Fisher & Greenberg, 1996; Levin, 1990; Moffitt, Kramer, & Hoffman, 1993).

Non-Freudian Unconscious

The view of the unconscious that has emerged within modern-day scientific psychology offers an understanding that is quite different from what Freud and his contemporaries talked and wrote about (Greenwald, 1992; Kihlstrom, 1987; Schacter, 1992). This modern research recognizes the existence of unconscious information processing but argues that its analytic (i.e., problem-solving) capabilities are severely limited (Greenwald, 1992) and that its influence on behavior has been overestimated (Jacoby & Kelly, 1992). Much of the non-Freudian unconscious has little to do with motivational processes. Instead, it enacts procedural knowledge (the "how-to knowledge" underlying motor skills), recognizes events as familiar (Roediger, 1990), and acquires the sort of implicit knowledge we gain as when we listen to and remember music.

Subliminal information processing provides a good example in which to discuss these two contrasting views of the unconscious. To subliminally activate unconscious information, a stimulus is presented at a very weak energy level (or for only a very brief duration of time) to an unsuspecting research participant. For instance, while the person looks through a tachistoscope, the phrase "Mommy and I are one" appears for four milliseconds, which is much too brief a time for anyone to report actually seeing anything, much less read, recognize, and comprehend the message. Both the Freudian and the non-Freudian views of the unconscious agree that the information does get processed at an unconscious level. Just what the mind does with that unconscious information is where the two views differ dramatically.

According to the Freudian view, the phrase functions every bit as does a hypnotic suggestion in that it activates deep wishes embedded in the viewer's infant experience with a comforting, protecting, and nurturing mother. Such activation then produces positive effects, such as increased self-esteem and decreased anxiety (Hardaway, 1990; Silverman & Weinberger, 1985). According to the non-Freudian view, however, the idea that the brain can process a complex phrase like "Mommy and I are one" during such a brief exposure is, well, "generous." At best, people can process a single word or perhaps an outline of a figure. In this view, it is asking too much to think that just because people can respond to a subliminal message in some way (i.e., with a gut feeling of recognition) that is a far cry from saying that they will automatically follow its directives.

Consider the sort of subliminal information processing made popular in the 1960s when a marketing executive superimposed briefly flashed messages—"Eat popcorn" and "Drink Coke"—over a film shown at a local theater. Popcorn sales exploded (Morse & Stoller, 1982). Marketers have been trying to send subliminal messages into the minds of the unsuspecting masses ever since, as with department stores' antishoplifting subliminal messages broadcast over the public address system ("If you steal, you will get caught"; Loftus & Klinger, 1992). But researchers have tested whether people act on subliminal messages and found that people do not. People do not behave in ways consistent with the subliminal directive. The unconscious might recognize and understand the message in some way, but acting on the directive is a whole different matter. And therein lies the current controversy—while subliminal marketing messages routinely fail to influence people, subliminal messages, like "Mommy and I are one," can increase self-esteem and decrease anxiety.

One group of researchers tested the validity of widely available subliminal audiotapes designed to enhance memory or boost self-esteem (Greenwald et al., 1991). The audiotapes play subliminal messages (e.g., "You're the best"; "I love you") over relaxing material (e.g., popular music, nature sounds of the forest) to improve the daily listener's self-esteem. The researchers recruited college-aged volunteers who wanted to increase their self-esteem or improve their memory. Each volunteer completed initial measures of their self-esteem and memory, listened daily to the audiotape for 5 weeks, and completed follow-up measures of their self-esteem and memory. In a nutshell, results showed that the audiotapes did not work. Like the "Eat popcorn" and "If you steal, you will get caught" messages, the "I love you" subliminal messages were not processed in a way that affected thoughts or behaviors (Greenwald et al., 1991).

PSYCHODYNAMICS

Freud observed that people often engaged in behavior that they clearly did not wish to do (e.g., ritualized hand washing). Because people sometimes did what they did not want to do, he reasoned that motivation must be more complex than that which follows intentional volition. Conscious volition must have to wrestle with an unconscious counterwill. Following this line of reasoning, Freud conceptualized people as being of two minds: "The mind is an arena, a sort of tumbling-ground, for the struggle of antagonistic impulses" (Freud, 1917). People have ideas and wills, but people also have counterideas and counterwills. When the conscious (ego's) will and the unconscious (id's) counterwill are of roughly equal strength, a sort of internal civil war ensues in which neither is completely satisfied. The mental combatants can be diagramed as follows:

$$\text{Will} \to \leftarrow \text{Counterwill}$$

Freud's depiction of the human mind was one of conflict—idea versus counteridea, will versus counterwill, desire versus repression, excitation versus inhibition, and cathexis (sexual attraction) versus anticathexis (guilt). This clashing of forces is what is meant by the term *psychodynamics*.

For Freud, psychodynamics concerned the conflict between the personality structures of the id and ego (and superego, which is not discussed here). The motivations of the id were unconscious, involuntary, impulse-driven, and hedonistic, as the id obeyed the pleasure principle: Obtain pleasure and avoid pain and do so at all costs and without delay. The motivations of the ego were partly conscious and partly unconscious, steeped in defenses, and organized around the delay of gratification, as the ego obeyed the reality principle: Hold pleasure seeking at bay until a socially acceptable need-satisfying object can be found. Today, psychoanalysts point out that wishes, fears, values, goals, emotions, thoughts, and motives are never in harmony, and mental conflict is an inevitable constant (e.g., one wants and fears the same thing, as during a job interview, a marriage proposal, or in contemplating attending tomorrow's college class in motivation). As a case in point, Drew Westen (1998) points out that children's feelings toward their parents almost *have* to be riddled in conflict since parents provide not only security, comfort, and love but also frustration, distress, and disappointment.

Repression

When most readers think of psychodynamics, what comes to mind are concepts like the id, ego, libido, and the Oedipal complex (Boneau, 1990). But, when Freud himself defined psychodynamics, the central concept was repression (Freud, 1917).

Freud envisioned the unconscious as a vastly overcrowded apartment. The conscious acted as a reception room one enters just prior to entering the public world. And repression served as a metaphorical doorkeeper to check each unconscious thought's identification card to judge whether it was fit to leave the crowded apartment and enter into the public world. Because many motivations reside in the unconscious, people necessarily remain unaware of many of their own motivations. In addition, people go out of their way to remain unaware of the motivations. They do this because they cannot bear to know things about themselves that contradict either their self-view or public opinion. Awareness of one's true motives would generate conflict with either the ideal self or what society regards to be a respectable person. Thus, repression—the metaphorical doorkeeper that checks each thought's ID card—constituted the foundation of psychodynamics (Fromm, 1986).

Repression is the process of forgetting information or an experience by ways that are unconscious, unintentional, and automatic. It is the ego's psychodynamic counterforce to the id's demanding desires. Repression is a defensive process for keeping out of consciousness some otherwise distressing wish, desire, idea, or memory. Without repression, the ego's charge to coordinate the demands of the id, superego, and physical/social reality would be an impossible undertaking. When unconscious thoughts and impulses begin to surface, anxiety emerges as a danger signal. It is this anxiety that moves the unconscious mind to action—to repression and perhaps to other ways of coping as well (Freud, 1926; Holmes, 1974, 1990).

Repression is tremendously difficult to study empirically because you have to ask people about things they do not remember. Studying repression is similar to figuring out whether the light stays on after you close the refrigerator door. Research on repression has not yet produced impressive understandings (Erdelyi & Goldberg, 1979; Erdelyi, 1985, 1990), but research on the related mental control process of suppression has been enlightening.

Suppression

The ability to stop a thought is beyond the human mind. When an unwanted thought or worry comes to mind, people cannot stop and remove the thought or worry. So what people generally try to do is control the intruder via suppression. Suppression is the process of removing a thought by ways that are conscious, intentional, and deliberate (Wegner, 1992). Generally speaking, suppression fails.[1] When we try to suppress a thought, all we get for our trouble is a lesson that we have less control over our thoughts than we care to

---

[1]Suppressing a thought given by an external source (i.e., another person) is that which lies beyond the capacity of the human mind to suppress. People's own, self-generated intrusive thoughts are a different story (Kelly & Kahn, 1994). The number-one strategy that works with self-generated intrusive thoughts is distraction (Wegner, 1989). With familiar intrusive thoughts, people generally have a rich network of thoughts they have used previously to distract themselves from their unwanted thoughts (Kelly & Kahn, 1994). But a psychodynamic rebound effect always occurs when thoughts are generated by an outside agent, like an experimenter saying not to think of a white bear (Wegner et al., 1987) or a friend asking you to keep a secret (Lane & Wegner, 1995). With externally induced intrusive thoughts, people lack the experience they need to suppress them.

admit (Wegner, 1989). Like a balloon held under water, thoughts and emotions can be suppressed for only a while.

Consider the psychodynamics of the following:

- Do not *think* about something.
  (Try not to think about today's dental appointment.)
- Do not *do* something.
  (Try to go all day without smoking a cigarette.)
- Do not *want* something.
  (Try not to want food while on a diet.)
- Do not *remember* something.
  (Try to forget about a deeply humiliating experience.)

When such thoughts enter our consciousness, our thinking halts itself because the thought precedes something that we wish not to happen. That is, the self-instruction of "don't think about that candy bar" precedes the undesired act of eating the candy bar. With the stream of thought interrupted—in fact, halted—the unwanted thought lingers out there in consciousness all by itself with a spotlight on it. We can suppress that thought for a few seconds or perhaps even for a few minutes, but there is a curious tendency for that thought to pop up again (Wegner, 1989; Wegner et al., 1987).

Consider a laboratory experiment in which college students were asked not to think of a white bear (Wegner et al., 1987). Each participant sat alone at a table with a bell on it (like those bells used on hotel counters). For the first 5 minutes, the participant said whatever popped into mind. "Free association" was easy. For the next 5 minutes, however, the participant was asked explicitly not to think of a white bear, but if she did think of the bear, she was to ring the bell as a signal that the unwanted thought had accidentally popped into her mind. The attempt at thought suppression was very difficult. A lot of bell ringing occurred. During a final 5-minute period, the participant once again was to say whatever popped to mind (i.e., free association). In this last period, participants experienced a "rebound effect" in which the thought of the white bear preoccupied their attention. Bell ringing sounded like a hotel desk at check-out time.

These results contradict common sense. Thought suppression not only failed, but it produced an obsessive preoccupation about those white bears (the rebound effect). Thought suppression paradoxically opened the door to thought obsession.

People rely on thought suppression to control their thoughts and actions in practically all areas of life. People rely on thought suppression for behavioral self-control, as in the effort to abstain from eating certain foods (Polivy & Herman, 1985) or consuming addictive substances (Marlatt & Parks, 1982). People rely on thought suppression to keep a secret (Pennebaker, 1990) or to deceive another person (DePaulo, 1992). People rely on thought suppression for self-control over pain (Cioffi, 1991) and fear (Rachman, 1978). And people use thought suppression to avoid making public the inner workings of their mind and its socially offensive wants, desires, and intentions (Wegner & Erber, 1993). People basically rely on thought suppression for seemingly good reasons. Many of our private thoughts would produce public confusion (to put it nicely) if they were allowed to be freely expressed. Thought suppression turns potential social conflict into a private mental struggle of wanted versus unwanted thoughts (Wegner, 1992). We learn quickly that thought suppression can be a social ally in preventing us from just blurting out our thoughts, as sometimes happens when we are stressed (Jacobs & Nadel, 1985) or impaired by drugs or alcohol (Steele & Josephs, 1990).

All this makes for interesting psychodynamics. An unwanted thought pops to mind, so we suppress it. But conscious thought suppression activates an unconscious counterprocess. While the conscious mind is busy suppressing the unwelcomed thought, the unconscious mind is just as busy searching and detecting for the presence of the thought to be suppressed. The unconscious mind keeps vigilant search over whether or not those white bears have returned. The unconscious monitoring process ironically keeps the to-be-suppressed thought activated, which is the very thing that the conscious intention was trying to avoid. With this psychodynamic process in mind, it makes sense why research shows that the act of suppressing produces an uninvited rebound effect of the unwanted thought. Continued suppression actually, in time, builds a rather potent counterforce that drives the unwanted thought toward an obsession (e.g., the dieter who tries not to think of food is vulnerable to thinking only about food; Polivy & Herman, 1985). According to Dan Wegner (1989, 1992), the way out of the thought suppression quagmire is to stop suppressing and, instead, focus on and think about the unwanted thought. Paradoxically, only those unconscious thoughts that we welcome into consciousness are we able to forget (Frankl, 1960).

Do the Id and Ego Actually Exist?

Given the preceding discussion on psychodynamics, an interesting question arises that asks: What does contemporary empirical research have to say about the scientific status of the id and ego? Is the human brain organized such that part exists as a cauldron of innate and impulsive desires and emotions, while another part exists as an executive control center that perceives the world and learns and adapts to it?

The conscious awareness responsible for executive control over mental life is a relatively new evolutionary development that has been structurally superimposed over a primitive and motivationally rich information processing system (Reber, 1992). The limbic structures of the brain—the hypothalamus, thalamus, amygdala, medial forebrain bundle, and so on—are commonly referred to as pleasure-unpleasure brain centers. Electrical stimulation of the brain reveals that some limbic areas are pleasure centers (i.e., septum, lateral hypothalamus, medial forebrain bundle), whereas other limbic areas are unpleasure centers (i.e., thalamus, amygdala, medial hypothalamus; Olds & Fobes, 1981; Stellar & Stellar, 1985; Wise & Bozarth, 1984). The limbic system makes for a pretty fair id. The neocortex qualifies as the brain structure that corresponds to the ego, as it performs all those functions that reflect learning, memory, decision making, and intellectual problem solving. Further, the neural pathways and structures of the neocortex and the limbic systems are intricately interrelated. Unilateral and bidirectional neural interconnections are everywhere throughout the brain. Even within the neocortex itself, and even within the limbic system itself, the interrelationships of how one structure affects the other are many (e.g., the amygdala both excites and inhibits the hypothalamus, the amygdala both excites and is inhibited by the neocortex). The picture that emerges corresponds to a pattern of psychodynamics, of forces and counterforces, of excitations and inhibitions, of limbic system activation and neocortical inhibition.

EGO PSYCHOLOGY

Freud postulated that all psychical energy originated in the id. At birth, the infant was all id, while the ego was only in the beginning processes of formation (Freud, 1923). Throughout infancy, the ego developed from perceiving instincts to curbing them. The id was force; the ego—the personality—developed to fulfill the adaptive role of counterforce.

The neo-Freudians saw ego functioning as much more. Heinz Hartmann (1958, 1964), the "father of ego psychology," saw the ego involved in a process of maturation that made it increasingly independent from its id origins. For Hartmann, the ego, unlike the id, developed through learning and experience. Learning occurred because the child engaged in a tremendous amount of manipulative, exploratory, and experimental activity (such as grasping, walking, and thinking), all of which provided the ego with information about itself and its surroundings. With feedback from its manipulative, exploratory, and experimental activity, the ego began to acquire ego properties—language, memory, intentions, complex ideas, and so on—that facilitated its ability to adapt successfully to the realities, demands, and constraints of the world. Hartmann conceptualized that because of its ability to learn, adapt, and grow, the mature ego was mostly autonomous from the id. Neo-Freudians studied the motivational dynamics of the "autonomous ego."

Ego Development

Defining ego is difficult because it is not so much a thing as it is a developmental process. The essence of ego development is a developmental progression toward what is possible in terms of psychological growth, maturity, adjustment, pro-social interdependence, competence, and autonomous functioning (Hartmann, 1958; Loevinger, 1976). From its infantile origins through its progression toward what is possible, the ego unfolds along the following developmental trajectory (Loevinger, 1976):

- Symbiotic
- Impulsive
- Self-protective
- Conformist
- Conscientious
- Autonomous

During the (infantile) symbiotic stage, the ego is extremely immature and constantly overwhelmed by impulses. The ego is symbiotic in the sense that its welfare depends on and is wholly provided for by its caretaker, not by itself. With language, the symbiotic ego begins to differentiate itself from the caretaker but remains extremely immature. In the impulsive stage, external forces (parental constraints, rules) and not the ego per se, curb the child's impulses and desires. Self-control emerges when the child first anticipates consequences and understands that rules exist. The ego then internalizes these consequences and rules in guiding its self-protective defensive capabilities. During the conformist stage, the ego internalizes group-accepted rules, and the anxiety of group disapproval becomes a potent counterforce against one's impulses. The conscientious ego has a conscience, an internalized set of rules and a pro-social sense of responsibility to others. The conscience functions as a set of internal standards to curb and counter impulses. The autonomous ego is one in which thoughts, plans, goals, and behaviors originate from within the ego and its resources, rather than from id impulses or from other people's (including society's) demands and pressures (Ryan, 1993). The autonomous ego is self-motivating and self-regulating.

Ego development is important to motivation study in two ways. First, the ego develops to defend against anxiety. If the ego is unable to accomplish its task of mediating the demands of the id, superego, and environment, then it experiences anxiety. Anxiety is the emotional reaction in which the ego is "obliged to admit its weakness" (Freud, 1964, p. 78). Strong ego development therefore develops mature defenses against anxiety (as discussed below in the section Ego Defense). Second, the ego develops to empower the person to interact more effectively and more proactively with its surroundings. By growing its sense of competence, the ego gains an increasing capacity to deal effectively with environmental challenges and also to generate its own inner motivation and become self-motivating (as discussed below in the section Ego Effectance).

Ego Defense

The day-to-day existence of the ego is one of vulnerability. The person who walks into class is in a state of vulnerability. The person who goes out on a date is in a state of vulnerability. And the person who tries to learn something new is in a state of vulnerability. The ego is always in a state of vulnerability. Through its defense mechanisms, the ego buffers consciousness against potentially overwhelming levels of anxiety originating from conflict with id impulses (neurotic anxiety), superego demands (moral anxiety), and environmental dangers (realistic anxiety). The role that defense mechanisms play in keeping mental pathology at bay appears in Figure 14.1, which shows that conflict emanating from the environment, id, and superego will create anxiety and, eventually, distress and depression if the conflicts are not defended against. It is the role of the defense mechanisms to play that defensive, protective function. Without the use of defense mechanisms, changes in internal and external reality generate a steady stream of anxieties in our lives. Fourteen such defense mechanisms appear in Table 14.1, along with a definition and example for each (American Psychiatric Association, 1994; A. Freud, 1946; Vaillant, 2000).

Defense mechanisms exist in a hierarchical ordering from least to most mature, from least to most adaptive (Vaillant, 1977, 1992, 1993). At the most immature level, defense mechanisms deny reality or invent an imaginary one. Defense mechanisms such as denial

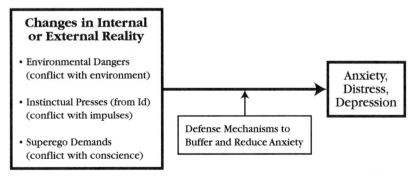

Figure 14.1   Role of Defense Mechanisms in Buffering the Ego from Anxiety-Generating Events

Table 14.1 Ego Defense Mechanisms

Defense Mechanism	Definition (with *EXAMPLE IN ITALICS*)
Denial	Unpleasant external realities are ignored or their acknowledgment is refused. *Preoccupation with work so there is no attention paid to the messages of rejection coming from a problematic personal relationship.*
Fantasy	Gratifying frustrated desires by imaginary and omnipotent achievement. *Imagining oneself to be a courageous national hero who performs incredible feats to win the admiration of all.*
Projection	Attributing one's own unacceptable desire or impulse onto someone else. *The anxiety of "I am failing this course because I am unintelligent" is expressed as "This textbook is stupid" or "The teacher is an idiot."*
Displacement	Releasing one's anxiety against a substitute object when doing so against the source of the anxiety could be harmful. *Discharging pent-up aggressive impulses against a father figure (the boss) onto a more anxiety-manageable object, such as the household dog. The worker kicks the dog as a substitute for the father figure.*
Identification	Taking on the characteristics of someone viewed as successful. *Seeing the nation adore a celebrity and then adjusting one's appearance (hair style, mode of dress, walk) to be loved and treated like the celebrity.*
Regression	Returning to an earlier stage of development when experiencing stress or anxiety. *Using baby talk to gain another's nurturance and sympathy to win an anxiety-provoking argument.*
Reaction formation	Adopting or expressing the strong opposite of one's true feelings or motives. *Expressing and endorsing strong optimism ("Everything will work out just fine") in the face of the grim realities of world hunger, nuclear war, or interpersonal rejection.*
Rationalization	Justifying a disturbing or unacceptable thought or feeling by selecting a logical reason to think or feel that way. *Producing an acceptable reason to justify one's hatred for a particular group of people, such as "because they lie and cheat all the time."*
Anticipation	Forecasting future danger in small steps so to cope with the danger gradually rather than all in one avalanche. *A person anticipates a probable future loss by dealing with the loss one step at a time—making a list of things to do, making a plan, practicing what one will say at different stages of the danger, etc.*
Humor	Capacity to not take oneself too seriously, as in accepting one's shortcoming and talking about it in a socially acceptable way. *A newspaper editorial cartoon exaggerates an anatomical feature of a high-ranking politician that allows readers to laugh at, yet also feel affection for, the authority figure.*
Sublimation	Transforming a socially unacceptable anxiety into a source of energy that produces no adverse consequences and is made socially acceptable—even exciting. *Lust or sexual impulses are channeled into love, sexual foreplay, or work that is creative, scientific, or manual.*

and fantasy are the most immature because the individual fails even to recognize external reality. At the second level of maturity are defenses such as projection in which the person recognizes reality but copes by casting its disturbing aspects away from the self. At the third level of maturity are the most common defenses, including rationalization and reaction formation. These defenses deal effectively with short-term anxiety but fail to accomplish any long-term gain in adjustment (because reality is repressed rather than accommodated). Rationalization, for example, temporarily excuses unacceptable desires, but it fails to provide the means for coping with the problem that produced the anxiety in the first place. Level four defenses are the most adaptive and mature and include mechanisms such as sublimation and humor. Sublimation accepts unconscious impulses but effectively channels these impulses into socially beneficial outlets, such as the creative energy that produces a painting or a poem (making unconscious impulses both socially acceptable and personally productive). Humor is a mature defense because it allows the person to look directly at what is painful or anxiety-provoking and deal with it in a socially acceptable way (Freud, 1905; Vaillant, 2000). Still, like all defenses, humor does not transform reality but instead transforms only the perception of reality (to alleviate subjective distress; Lefcourt & Martin, 1986; Nezu, Nezu, & Blissett, 1988).

To test his ideas that the maturity level of one's defenses reflects ego strength and predicts life adjustment, Vaillant (1977) followed the lives of 56 men over a 30-year period. He interviewed each man in his college-age years, and independent testers classified each man as using predominantly mature (levels 3 and 4) or predominantly immature (levels 1 and 2) defense mechanisms as a personal style against distress and anxiety. The study sought to determine how these two groups of men would fare in life, and the research assessed each man's life adjustment 30 years later in four categories: career, social, psychological, and medical. Ego strength, as indexed by maturity level of defense mechanisms, successfully discriminated men who suffered under the burden of career, social, psychological, and medical problems from those who did not (see Table 14.2). Mature defense mechanisms allowed the men to live a well-adjusted life, show psychosocial maturity, find and keep a fulfilling job, develop a rich and stable friendship pattern, avoid divorce, avoid the need for psychiatric visits, avoid psychopathology and mental illnesses, and so on. A second, similar longitudinal study with both men and woman and also with people from more diverse backgrounds showed that the maturity level of one's defenses predicted—30 years later—income level, job promotions, psychosocial adjustments, social supports, joy in living, marital satisfaction, and physical functioning such as the ability to climb stairs during old age (Vaillant, 2000).

One illustration of how mature defense mechanisms promote well being appears in Figure 14.2 (Cui & Vaillant, 1996). On the horizontal x-axis, the graph shows the extent to which adults in the study used mature defense mechanisms (with 5 representing the most mature defense mechanisms). The y-axis plots the study's dependent measure, depression. The diagonal line with the o's shows the depression scores for those adults who lived very stressful lives (poverty, physical disability, loss of a loved one). The four adults with highly stressful lives and immature defense mechanisms were very likely to experience depression (75%), while the nine adults with equally stressful lives but mature defense mechanisms were essentially inoculated against depression (0%). Adults who did not live stressful lives did not experience depression (as shown by the straight horizontal line with the x's). Thus, depression occurred when people used immature defenses to cope with life

Table 14.2 Relationship Between Maturity of Defense Mechanisms and Life Adjustment

	Predominant Adaptive Style (%)	
	Mature (N = 25)	Immature (N = 31)
Overall adjustment		
1) Top third in adult adjustment	60%	0%
2) Bottom third in adult adjustment	4%	61%
3) "Happiness" (top third)	68%	16%
Career adjustment		
1) Income over $20,000/year	88%	48%
2) Job meets ambition for self	92%	58%
3) Active public service outside job	56%	29%
Social adjustment		
1) Rich friendship pattern	64%	6%
2) Marriage in least harmonious quartile or divorced	28%	61%
3) Barren friendship pattern	4%	52%
4) No competitive sports (age 40–50)	24%	77%
Psychological adjustment		
1) 10+ psychiatric visits	0%	45%
2) Ever diagnosed mentally ill	0%	55%
3) Emotional problems in childhood	20%	45%
4) Worst childhood environment (bottom fourth)	12%	39%
5) Fails to take full vacation	28%	61%
6) Able to be aggressive with others (top fourth)	36%	6%
Medical adjustment		
1) 4+ adult hospitalizations	8%	26%
2) 5+ days sick leave/year	0%	23%
3) Recent health poor by objective exam	0%	36%
4) Subjective health consistently judged excellent since college	68%	48%

N = sample size.

Source: From Adaptation to Life (p. 87), by G. E. Vaillant, 1977, Boston: Little, Brown & Company. Copyright 1977 by George E. Vaillant.

stress. When life was not stressful or when adults used mature defenses, depression was avoided. This same conclusion (mature defenses prevent sickness) was also found in preventing post-traumatic stress disorder after combat (Lee et al., 1995).

Ego Effectance

Ego effectance concerns the individual's competence in dealing with environmental challenges, demands, and opportunities (White, 1959; Harter, 1981). Effectance motivation begins during infancy as an undifferentiated source of ego energy. With its diffuse energy, properties (e.g., grasping, crawling, walking), and acquired skills (e.g., language, penman-

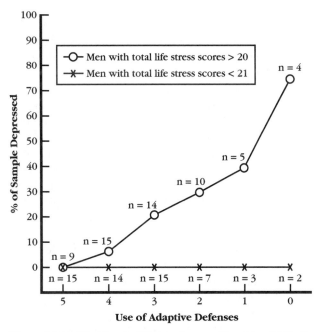

Figure 14.2   Likelihood of Depression as a Function of Life Stress and the Maturity Level of One's Defense Mechanisms

Source: From "The Antecedents and Consequences of Negative Life Events in Adulthood: A Longitudinal Study," by X. Cui & G.E. Vaillant, 1996, *American Journal of Psychiatry, 152,* 21–26. Copyright 1996 American Psychiatric Association. http://psychiatryonline.org. Reprinted by permission.

ship, social skills), the ego attempts to deal satisfactorily with the circumstances and stressors that come its way. In the process of adapting and developing, the undifferentiated ego energy begins to differentiate into specific motives, such as the needs for achievement, affiliation, intimacy, and power (see Chapter 7). Thus begins the development of a variety of separate ego motivations, but the core ego motivation is effectance motivation, or the desire to interact effectively with the environment (see Chapter 5, especially Figure 5.1).

Ego effectance develops into more than just a defensive, reactive coping response to life's demands. As the child exercises skills, she begins to learn how to produce successful change in the environment. The child learns how to use crayons, climb trees, cross streets, hold the attention of adults, feed herself, write letters, make new friends, ride a bicycle, and a hundred other tasks. When successful, such interactions produce a sense of being effective, a perception of competence, and feelings of satisfaction and enjoyment. The ego aggregates these perceptions and feelings into a general sense of competence. The greater the ego's effectance motivation, the greater the person's willingness to use ego properties proactively (not just reactively) by intentionally changing the environment for the better. With each successful transaction with the environment (a friend is made, a tree house is constructed), the ego's effectance motivation grows. The greater the effectance motivation, the stronger the desire to seek out new and challenging interactions with the environment. From this point of view, effectance motivation is a near synonym for "intrinsic motivation," as introduced in Chapter 6.

OBJECT RELATIONS THEORY

The study of unconscious motivation began with a rather single-minded focus on sexual and aggressive drives. Over time, thinking about unconscious motivation became less biological and more interpersonal. Emphasis on the biological need for sexual gratification, for instance, gradually gave way to an emphasis on the psychological need for relatedness (Horney, 1939). Central to the object relations theory are the infant's need for attachment to the caregiver and the adult's subsequent interpersonal connectedness to the important people in his life.

"Object relations" is an awkward term. But the term is less awkward than it might at first appear to be when its etiology is told. Freud used the word "object" to refer to the gratification target of one's individual's drives. Therefore, object relations theory studies how people satisfy their need for relatedness through their mental representations of and actual attachments to social and sexual objects (i.e., other people). Object relations theory studies people's need to be in relationship with others who can satisfy that emotional and psychological need for relatedness.

Objects relations theory focuses on the nature and the development of mental representations of the self and others and on the affective processes (wishes, fears) associated with these representations (Bowlby, 1969; Eagle, 1984; Greenberg & Mitchell, 1983; Scharff & Scharff, 1995; Westen, 1990). In particular, object relations theory focuses on how childhood mental representations of one's caretakers are captured within the personality and persist into adulthood. What persists into adulthood are those mental representations of self and of other significant people (Main, Kaplan, & Cassidy, 1985; van IJzendoorn, 1995). For instance, is the self lovable or unlovable? Is the self worthy of other people's attention and care or unworthy of such affection and investment? Are other people warm and caring or selfish and unreliable? Can other people be trusted? Can you depend on others when you need them to be there for you?

Object relations often stress the impact that parental abuse or neglect has on the infant's emerging representations of self and others (Blatt, 1994; Luborsky & Crits-Christoph, 1990; Strauman, 1992; Urist, 1980). In essence, the bond between mother (caregiver) and child becomes the child's template for self and for other mental representations. When one's primary caretaker is warm, nurturing, responsive, available, and trustworthy, the parental object satisfies the infant's need for relatedness, communicates a message of approval, and nonverbally sends a message about relationships that encourages a secure and affectionate attachment; when one's primary caretaker is cold, abusive, unresponsive, neglectful, and unpredictable, the parental object frustrates the infant's need for relatedness, communicates a message of disapproval, and nonverbally sends a message about relationships that encourages insecurity and anxiety (Ainsworth et al., 1978; Sullivan, 1953).

Positive mental models of one's self predict adult levels of self-reliance, social confidence, and self-esteem (Feeney & Noller, 1990; Klohnen & Bera, 1998). Similarly, as shown in Box 14, secure mental models of others predict the quality of one's adult romantic relationships (Feeney & Noller, 1990; Hazan & Shaver, 1987), including whether that person ever marries and, if so, how long that person stays committed to that marriage (Klohnen & Bera, 1998). Alternatively, a childhood of interpersonal traumas (e.g., physical abuse, serious neglect, sexual molestation) and parental psychopathology (e.g., de-

BOX 14 *Love as an Attachment Process*

Question: Why is this information important?

Answer: To understand how your own early attachments manifest themselves in your current (adult) romantic love relationships.

Consider the following three-item, multiple-choice question. Read each statement carefully, and check the one that best describes you:

____ I find it easy to get close to others. I am comfortable depending on others. I am comfortable having other people depend on me. I don't worry about being abandoned, and I don't worry about someone getting too close to me.

____ I am somewhat uncomfortable being close to others. I find it difficult to trust others completely. I find it difficult to allow myself to depend on others. I become nervous when anyone gets too close, and I get nervous when others want me to be more intimate with them than I feel comfortable being.

____ I find that others are reluctant to get as close as I would like. I worry that others don't really love me or that others don't really want to stay with me. I want to merge completely with others, especially love partners, and this desire sometimes scares people away.

Like object relations theory, attachment theory argues that affectionate bonds develop between infants and their caretakers and that these affectionate bonds, whether positive or negative, carry forward into adulthood, affecting the adult's relationships with lovers (Bowlby, 1969, 1973, 1980). In both object relations theory and attachment theory, infants have a psychological need for relatedness that strongly motivates them to desire close, affectionate bonds with their caregivers. Based on the quality of the care infants receive, they form mental models of how interaction partners relate to them that can be characterized by secure attachment, anxious attachment, or avoidant attachment (Ainsworth et al., 1978).

Which of the three statements above best resonated with your own experience? The three statements characterize, in order, a secure, an avoidant, and an anxious attachment style. About 55% of adults classify themselves as secure, about 20% classify themselves as anxious, and about 25% classify themselves as avoidant, respectively (Hazan & Shaver, 1987; Shaver & Hazan, 1987).

Cindy Hazan and Phillip Shaver (1987) gave the above multiple-choice question to about 600 adults in the Denver, Colorado, area and asked them also to complete questionnaires about their attachment history, beliefs about love, and experiences with a current partner. The three attachment groups experienced adult romantic love very differently.

Securely attached adults experienced love as a trilogy of friendship, trust, and happiness. They accepted and supported their partner, and their relationships endured over the years. Avoidantly attached adults experienced love as an ongoing fear of intimacy and commitment, they often felt jealous, and they reported a marked absence of a positive emotion from the relationship. This is the approach to love heard every 15 minutes on television soap operas, "He is afraid of commitment." Anxiously attached lovers experienced love as an obsession, a desire for constant reunion and reciprocation, as an extreme attraction and an extreme jealousy that produced emotional highs and lows. Obsessive preoccupations might play out well in soap operas, but in real life, they generally lead to "needy, clingy" partners who are troubled by frequent episodes of loneliness and whose relationships are less likely to last than are those of securely attached lovers.

Infant attachment experiences do not just fast-forward into adulthood. Instead, the experiences, emotions, and mental models of childhood spill over and color adult beliefs about love. To articulate how infantile experiences color the adult mind, Freud compared Ancient Rome (the child) with modern-day Rome (the adult; see *Civilization and Its Discontents*, 1958, pp. 15–20). Under the great 21st-century metropolis lie centuries of ruins that have been buried after a repeated series of traumas such as fires, earthquakes, and invasions. Like the metaphor of Ancient Rome, the psychological traumas of infancy, childhood, and adolescence harbor still-smoldering anger, frustration, sadness, craving, longing, and a fear of mistrust and commitment that carry forward into and color subsequent adult mental models of romantic love.

pression, anxiety, substance abuse, violent marital interaction) predict adulthood dysfunctional relationships (Mickelson, Kessler, & Shaver, 1997).

For a concrete example, consider a schematic of one female's mental representation of men, which is depicted in Figure 14.3 (Westen, 1991). The young woman suffered from rather severe depression and social isolation, and she reported a childhood history in which she characterized her parents as openly contemptuous of one another. Her mother constantly spoke of the ways in which she was victimized verbally and sexually by her husband and three sons. In the course of psychotherapy, the woman's mental representation of her expected and actual relationships with men became apparent. Her mental representation, as illustrated in Figure 14.3, contains aspects of a psychological need for relatedness (closeness, sexuality), but it also contains an ample supply of abuse (enslavement), anger and resentment (rejection), and conflict (close with father, yet also rejected by father).

The feelings associated with men are difficult to represent in a figure, but they too are part of the women's object ("men") relations. As you might suspect, the woman's conflicting needs and feelings led her to adopt an interpersonal style toward men that was extremely anxious and full of avoidance.

According to object relations theory, the quality of any one's mental representations of relationships (e.g., Figure 14.3) can be characterized by three chief dimensions:

- unconscious tone (benevolent vs. malevolent)
- capacity for emotional involvement (selfishness/narcissism vs. mutual concern)
- mutuality of autonomy with others

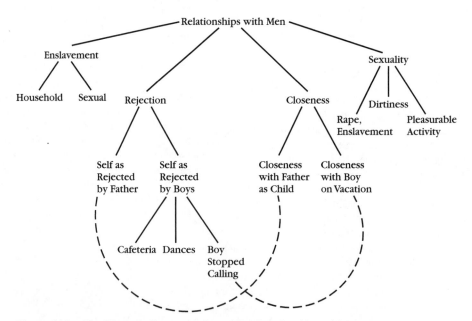

Figure 14.3 One Woman's Representation of Her Relationships with Men

Source: From "Social Cognition and Object Relations," by D. Westen, 1991, *Psychological Bulletin, 109,* pp. 429–455. Copyright 1991 by American Psychological Corporation. Reprinted with permission.

First, mental representations possess an unconscious affective tone (Westen, 1991). This affective coloring of the object world ranges from understanding relationships as good-benevolent versus bad-malevolent. Second, mental representations possess an unconscious capacity for emotional involvement (Westen, 1991). This capacity ranges from a narcissistic, exploitive, and unilateral orientation toward relationships to a more mature relatedness based on mutual concern, respect, and eagerness to invest in the relationship. Third, mental representations possess a capacity for the mutuality of autonomy (Urist, 1980). At its higher level (mutuality of autonomy), objects are viewed as having an autonomous existence vis-à-vis one another, and relationships present no risk to the integrity and autonomy of the participants. At its lower level, objects are viewed in an absence of any sense of people as autonomous agents, and relationships are seen as overpowering threats (Ryan, Avery, & Grolnick, 1985; Urist, 1977).

Research on object relations theory underscores the fundamental motivational significance of people's psychological need for relatedness. When this need is nurtured through warm and responsive care, a person develops positive mental models of himself or herself, of significant others, and of relationships in general. Positive object relations, in turn, enable the person to develop, and to relate to others, in ways that are healthy, growth-oriented, and resistant to psychopathology. When this need for relatedness is frustrated or ignored through cold, rejecting, and unresponsive care, however, a person develops maladaptive mental models that leave him vulnerable to psychopathology and to developing unhealthy and defense-oriented motivational orientations, as illustrated through one woman's defense-oriented representation of men in Figure 14.3.

CRITICISMS

Despite its intrigue, Freud's psychoanalytic contribution to the study of human motivation is plagued by (at least) two criticisms. Contemporary research on psychodynamics has addressed and smoothed over many criticisms but it helps to identify the most important and limiting ones nonetheless, because contemporary researchers still have some more smoothing over to accomplish.

The most devastating criticism against Freud is that many of his concepts are not scientifically testable (Crews, 1996; Eysenck, 1986). Without scientific tests, such concepts are best taken with skepticism and understood metaphorically rather than as credible scientific constructs. In science, theoretical constructs that have not yet stood the test of objective experimentation must remain guilty until proven innocent, invalid until proven valid. For this reason, psychoanalytic thinkers have spent the last 50 years finding ways for testing Freud's ideas and, once done, glean his many ideas into a core set of postulates like the four mentioned earlier in the chapter. Some (but certainly not all) of Freud's ideas have indeed stood the test of empirical validation (Fisher & Greenberg, 1977; Masling, 1983; Silverman, 1976). Other ideas and phenomena have been reinterpreted in ways that do not rely on psychoanalytic concepts (e.g., consider Brown's analysis of the tip-of-the-tongue phenomenon [1991] and Wegner's analysis of mental control [1994]). But on many points about human motivation and emotion, Freud was simply wrong (e.g., his theory of superego formation; Fisher & Greenberg, 1977).

A second criticism is that although psychodynamic theory is a wonderful interpretive device for events that occurred in the past, it is woeful as a predictive device. For instance, suppose a person has a dream about siblings dying (as discussed earlier in the chapter).

For one person, the dream might be best interpreted as a wish for her siblings to die. For a second person, however, the dream might be best interpreted (via reaction formation) as a wish for her siblings to survive. For yet another person, the siblings' deaths or survivals might represent sentiments associated with a third party, for instance, one's own children. All these post hoc (after the fact) interpretations make sense in psychoanalysis. The theory, however, is very poor at predicting a priori (before the fact) that a person will have a dream specifically about siblings sprouting wings and flying off into the sky. For the theory to be predictive, it must allow us to anticipate when a person will or will not have a particular type of dream (or use a particular defense mechanism, or achieve a particular level of ego development, or commit suicide, or do this, or say that, et cetera). A scientific theory must be able to predict what will happen in the future. It is hard to trust a theory that explains only the past. It is even harder to apply such a theory in productive ways to real life settings, such as schools or the workplace.

In the neo-Freudian years, the ego psychologists have taken these criticisms to heart. They respect both the insight of Freud and the criticisms levied against his subjective (nonscientific) methods of data collection. The contemporary study of thought suppression, ego development, defense mechanisms, and effectance motivation, use relatively more rigorous scientific research methods, and relatively more attention to building a theoretical framework that values prediction over post hoc explanations.

SUMMARY

Psychoanalysis makes for a strangely appealing study. By studying the unconscious and by embracing a rather pessimistic view of human nature, psychoanalysis opens the door to study topics such as traumatic memories, inexplicable addictions, anxieties about the future, dreams, hypnosis, inaccessible and repressed memories, fantasies, masochism, repression, self-defeating behaviors, suicidal thoughts, overwhelming impulses for revenge, and all the hidden forces that shape our needs, feelings, and ways of thinking and behaving that we would probably not want our neighbors to know about us. The subject matter of psychoanalysis strangely reflects what seems to be so popular in contemporary movies (hence, in contemporary society): sex, aggression, psychopathology, revenge, and the like.

The father of the psychoanalytic perspective was Sigmund Freud. His view of motivation presented a biologically based model in which the two instinctual drives of sex and aggression supplied the body with its physical and mental energies. Contemporary psychoanalysts, however, emphasize the motivational importance of psychological wishes (rather than biological drives) and of cognitive information processing. The concept of the psychological wish retains the full spirit of Freudian motivation, but it overcomes the contradictory evidence that sex and aggression do not function like physiological drives.

Four postulates define contemporary psychodynamic theory. The first is that much of mental life is unconscious. This postulate argues emphatically that thoughts, feelings, and desires exist at the unconscious level. Thus, because unconscious mental life affects behavior, people can behave in ways that are inexplicable, even to themselves. In contemporary study, some researchers study the smart and motivationally hot Freudian unconscious, while other researchers study the dumb and automated non-Freudian unconscious.

The second postulate of a contemporary psychodynamic understanding of motivation and emotion is that mental processes operate in parallel with one another, such that people commonly want and fear the same thing at the same time. This is the postulate of psychodynamics. It is the rule, not the exception, that people have conflicting feelings that motivate them in opposing ways. Hence, people commonly harbor divergent conscious and unconscious racial attitudes, gender biases, and love/hate (approach/avoidance) relationships with their parents, their jobs, and practically everything else in their lives.

The third postulate is that of ego development. Healthy development involves moving from an immature, socially dependent personality to one that is more mature and socially responsible. According to neo-Freudians, the ego develops motives of its own by moving through the following developmental progression: symbiotic, impulsive, self-protective, conformist, conscientious, and autonomous. To develop and to overcome immaturity and vulnerability, the ego must gain resources and strengths, including resilient defense mechanisms for coping successfully with the inevitable anxieties of life (e.g., ego defense) and a sense of competence that provides a generative capacity for changing the environment for the better (e.g., ego effectance).

The fourth postulate of a contemporary psychodynamic understanding is that mental representations of self and others form in childhood to guide adult social motivations. This is the postulate of object relations. It argues that lifelong personality patterns begin to form in childhood as people construct mental representations of the self, others, and relationships. Once formed, these beliefs form the basis of motivational states (e.g., relatedness, anxiety) that guide the course of the adult's interpersonal relationships. Positive mental models of oneself, for instance, predict adult levels of self-reliance, social confidence, self-esteem, and loving and committed partnerships. Negative mental models, on the other hand, forecast dysfunctional interpersonal relationships.

READINGS FOR FURTHER STUDY

Psychodynamics and the Unconscious

KOLB, J., COOPER, S., & FISHMAN, G. (1995). Recent developments in psychoanalytic technique: A review. *Harvard Review of Psychiatry, 3*, 65–74.

WEGNER, D. M. (1992). You can't always think what you want: Problems in the suppression of unwanted thoughts. In M. P. Zanna (Ed.), *Advances in experimental social psychology* (Vol. 25, pp. 193–225). San Diego: Academic Press.

WEGNER, D. M., SCHNEIDER, D. J., CARTER, S., III, & WHITE, L. (1987). Paradoxical effects of thought suppression. *Journal of Personality and Social Psychology, 53*, 5–13.

WESTEN, D. (1998). The scientific legacy of Sigmund Freud: Toward a psychodynamically informed psychological science. *Psychological Bulletin, 124*, 333–371.

Ego Development

LOEVINGER, J. (1976). Stages of ego development. In *Ego development* (Chap. 2, pp. 13–28). San Francisco: Jossey-Bass.

WHITE, R. W. (1959). Motivation reconsidered: The concept of competence. *Psychological Review, 66*, 297–333.

VAILLANT, G. E. (2000). Adaptive mental mechanisms: Their role in a positive psychology. *American Psychologist, 55*, 89–98.

Object Relations Theory

HAZAN, C., & SHAVER, P. (1987). Romantic love conceptualized as an attachment process. *Journal of Personality and Social Psychology, 52*, 511–524.

WESTEN, D., KLEPSER, J., RUFFINS, S. A., SILVERMAN, M., LIFTON, N., & BOEKAMP, J. (1991). Object relations in childhood and adolescence: The development of working representations. *Journal of Consulting and Clinical Psychology, 59*, 400–409.

Chapter 15

Growth Motivation
and Positive Psychology

Our inborn temperament predisposes us to act in ways that are naturally inhibited and introverted or in ways that are naturally impulsive and extraverted. In a real sense, some of us are natural introverts while some of us are natural extraverts. What makes a person a "natural" is that person's biologically inherited temperament.

But cultures also have ideas about how a person should behave. For instance, the typical college campus culture values extraversion, emotional intensity, and being exciting and entertaining but devalues introversion, emotional calm, and being a wallflower. Thus, each of us hears two messages of how to behave socially—one from our biological temperament and another from cultural priorities. This dual message situation is not much of a problem for extraverts: Just act naturally and the culture will value you. The dual message is a problem, however, for introverts.

Introverts face a dilemma. What happens when biological disposition contradicts socialization preference? What happens when an experience feels right and natural, but the culture devalues anyone who gravitates toward that experience? Should the introvert follow the cultural press and reject his inner nature and try to substitute a more socially acceptable extraverted style in its place?

Over time, all might be well. Introverts who act like extraverts do experience some of the positive emotional benefits of acting in extraverted ways (e.g., having fun at a party; Lucas et al., 2000). And, what is wrong with the individual's effort to be sensitive to, adjust to, and accommodate to her culture? Humanistic psychology is willing to answer that question. It argues that rejecting one's nature in favor of social priorities puts personal growth and psychological well-being at risk.

Imagine yourself in the following experiment (Ford, 1991a): The experiment begins by asking you to self-report your temperament, using questionnaires such as those discussed in Chapter 13 for extraversion, sensation-seeking, and affect intensity. The experimenter also asks for permission to send identical questionnaires to one of your parents (i.e., your primary caretaker), asking him or her to complete each in terms of how you behaved during the preschool ages of 3 to 5 years. The ages 3 to 5 are important because toddlerhood is old enough for temperament to express itself and be observed by parents yet also young enough to precede the heavy socialization that occurs as toddlers begin to ready themselves to venture out of the house. The study's prediction is that adults who express something other than their childhood temperament will show maladjustment. That is, the prediction is that when the culture tries to replace a person's inner nature with a socially valued style—that is, when the culture tries to socialize the introvert into becoming more like an extravert, then what follows is maladjustment—not the hoped-for adjustment.

To index maladjustment, the experimenter also asks you to complete questionnaire measures of anxiety, depression, hostility, feelings of inadequacy, and physical/somatic troubles. To test the humanistic hypothesis, the experimenter computes a discrepancy score of the difference between your expressed temperament as an adult and your parent's rating of your temperament as a child. Results showed the greater the discrepancy, the greater the adult's maladjustment. People who were pressured—willingly or unwillingly—into acting in ways that contradicted their biologically-based temperaments encountered problems.

These findings introduce the theme of this chapter: "If this essential core (inner nature) of the person is frustrated, denied, or suppressed, sickness results" (Maslow, 1968).

To Abraham Maslow's theme, we can add its logical complement: If this essential core is nurtured, appreciated, and supported, health results.

The everyday choice to follow "one's inner nature" versus "cultural priorities" is not a neutral choice. Social preferences and social priorities are communicated to us and strongly enforced as desirable ways of acting by all sorts of supports, including incentives, rewards, approval, love, advertising messages, social demands, rules, norms, expectations, and all the voices we hear each day that tell us what we should, ought to, have to, and must do. Inner guides are more subtle. Unlike the culture around us, inner guides have no organized lobby to persuade us what to do. So, in every day living, our inner guides are relatively quiet while social expectations and cultural priorities are relatively loud.

It is easy to hear the culture's priorities, but it might not be so psychologically healthy to unquestionably following these priorities. For instance, people who choose to devote their lives to the pursuit of the "American dream" (the pursuit of money, fame, and popularity) suffer more psychological distress (anxiety, depression, narcissism) than do people who pursue inner guides like self-actualization. This is true even when those who pursue the American dream do actually attain the money, fame, and popularity they seek (Kasser & Ryan, 1993, 1996). Humanistic psychology plays a key role in motivation by asking people to pause, listen to their inner guides, and consider the potential benefits of coordinating their inner guides (interests, preferences, values) with their day-to-day lifestyle. Research on positive psychology adds that inner guides like meaning, authenticity, and the passion to learn add reservoirs of strength and wellness.

HOLISM AND POSITIVE PSYCHOLOGY

Human motives can be understood from many different perspectives, ranging from the most objective viewpoints of objectivism (Diserens, 1925), behaviorism (Watson, 1919), and logical positivism (Bergmann & Spence, 1941) to the most subjective viewpoints of existentialism (May, 1961), gestalt psychology (Goldstein, 1939; Perls, 1969), and holism (Aristotle, *On the soul*). Along with existentialism and gestalt psychology, holism asserts that a human being is best understood as an integrated, organized whole rather than as a series of differentiated parts. It is the whole organism that is motivated rather than just some part of the organism, such as the stomach or brain. In holism, any event that affects one system affects the entire person. To borrow a phrase from Maslow, it is John Smith who desires food, not John Smith's stomach.

In modern parlance, holism sees little value in a "bottom-up" approach (i.e., focus on specific, individual motives, one at a time, and in relative isolation from one another) and, instead, prefers a "top-down" approach (i.e., focus on general, all-encompassing motives, seeing how the master motives govern the more specific ones). Both the bottom-up and the top-down approaches to motivation study have merit. This chapter, however, highlights the top-down approach (while Chapters 3 and 4 highlight the bottom-up approach).

Holism

Holism derives its name from "whole" or "wholeness" and therefore concerns itself with the study of what is healthy, or unbroken. In contrast, a broken view of personality emphasizes human beings as fragmented sets of structures or forces that oppose one another.

For instance, a broken view speaks of the conflict between an ideal self and an actual self, or the conflict between the biological desire for food and the social demand for a slim figure. In psychoanalytic theory (see Chapter 14), a broken self manifests itself in a sort of psychological competition among the three personality structures of id, ego, and super-ego. In contrast, humanism identifies strongly with the holistic perspective, as it stresses "top-down" master motives, such as the self and its strivings toward fulfillment.

In a nutshell, humanistic psychology is about discovering human potential and encouraging its development. To accomplish this, the humanistic perspective concerns strivings (1) toward growth and self-realization and (2) away from facade, self-concealment, and the pleasing and fulfilling of the expectations of others (Rogers, 1966). In every page authored by humanistic thinkers, the reader can hear a commitment to personal growth as the ultimate motivational force.

Positive Psychology

Positive psychology is a newly emerging field in psychology (Seligman & Csikszentmihalyi, 2000; Snyder & Lopez, 2002). It seeks to articulate the vision of the good life (psychologically speaking), and it uses the empirical methods of psychology to understand what makes life worth living. The goal is to show what actions lead to experiences of well being, to the development of positive individuals who are optimistic and resilient, and to the creation of nurturing and thriving institutions and communities. The subject matter of positive psychology is therefore the investigation of positive subjective experiences such as well-being, contentment, satisfaction, enjoyment, hope, optimism, flow, competence, love, passion for work, hope, courage, perseverance, self-determination, interpersonal skill, talent, creativity, originality, authenticity, future mindedness, wisdom, interpersonal responsibility, good citizenship, altruism, tolerance and civility, a strong work ethic, and the nurturance of others.

Positive psychology is not a subfield of humanistic psychology. It chooses the same subject matter as does humanistic psychology, so the two fields do substantially overlap one another. What sets positive psychology apart from humanistic psychology is not its subject matter but is, instead, its strong reliance on hypothesis-testing, data-based empirical research. Positive psychology is the more scientifically rigorous of the two fields of study.

In a nutshell, positive psychology looks at a person and asks, "What could be?" As a field, positive psychology realizes both that people routinely fall short of "what could be" and also the epidemic-like prevalence of pathologies like depression, substance abuse, apathy, and violence. It further realizes that important role played by the effort to cure or reverse these human pathologies. Mostly, however, positive psychology devotes attention to the proactive building of personal strengths and competencies. To prevent sickness, people need to possess strengths like hope, optimism, skill, perseverance, intrinsic motivation, and the capacity for flow. The question is less "how can we correct people's weaknesses?" and more "how can we develop and amplify people's strengths?" How can families, schools, and corporations develop human strengths? How can these communities foster excellence? Positive psychology seeks to make people stronger and more productive, and positive psychology seeks to actualize the human potential in all of us.

SELF-ACTUALIZATION

Self-actualization is an inherent developmental striving. It is a process, a process of leaving behind timidity, defensive appraisals, and a dependence on others that is paired with the parallel process of moving toward courage to create, realistic appraisals, and autonomous self-regulation. It is "an underlying flow of movement toward constructive fulfillment of its inherent possibilities" (Rogers, 1980). It refers to an ever-fuller realization of one's talents, capacities, and potentialities (Maslow, 1987).

The two fundamental directions that characterize self-actualization as a process are autonomy and openness to experience. *Autonomy* means moving away from heteronomy and toward an ever-increasing capacity to depend on one's self and to regulate one's own behavior (Deci & Ryan, 1991). *Openness* means a way of receiving information and feelings such that neither is repressed, ignored, or filtered, nor distorted by wishes, fear, or past experiences (Mittelman, 1991). So openness indexes the extent of leaving behind timidity and defensive appraisals and moving toward courage to create and realistic appraisals, while autonomy indexes the extent of leaving behind a dependence on others and moving toward autonomous self-regulation.

Hierarchy of Human Needs

The cornerstone of Maslow's understanding of motivation is the proposition that human needs can be organized into five clusters. The arrangement of these need clusters, Maslow felt, was best communicated visually by a hierarchy, as illustrated in Figure 15.1. The first set of needs contains physiological needs, as discussed in Chapter 4. All the other needs in the hierarchy are psychological needs (safety and security, love and belongingness, esteem, and self-actualization).

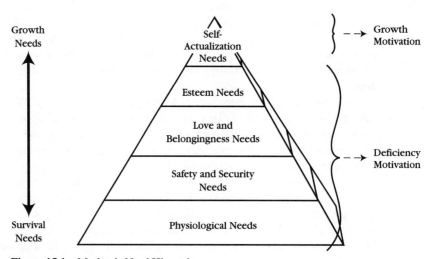

Figure 15.1   Maslow's Need Hierarchy

The hierarchical presentation conveys three themes about the nature of human needs (Maslow, 1943, 1987).

1. Needs arrange themselves in the hierarchy according to potency or strength. The lower the need is in the hierarchy, the stronger and more urgently it is felt.
2. The lower the need is in the hierarchy, the sooner it appears in development. Young people experience only the lower needs in the hierarchy, while older people are more likely to experience the full range of the hierarchy.
3. Needs in the hierarchy are fulfilled sequentially, from lowest to highest, from the base of the pyramid to its apex.

Theme 1 proposes that the survival-based needs (at the bottom of the hierarchy) dominate as the strongest motives, whereas the self-actualization needs (at the top) are the weakest. In theme 1, Maslow wanted to make the point that self-actualization needs are relatively quiet urges that are easily overlooked in the rush of one's day-to-day affairs. Theme 2 communicates that the lower needs (e.g., safety and security) characterize needs typical of nonhuman animals and of children, whereas the higher needs (e.g., esteem) are uniquely human and pertain to adults. Theme 3 stipulates that satisfying lower needs is a prerequisite to satisfying higher needs. Hence, before people seek esteem and peer respect, they must first have physiological, safety, and belongingness needs sufficiently gratified.

Deficiency Needs

Physiological disturbances and needs for safety, belongingness, and esteem are collectively referred to as deficiency needs. Deficiency needs are like vitamins; people need them because their absence inhibits growth and development. The presence of any of the deficiency needs indicated that the individual was in a state of deprivation, whether that state of deprivation involved food, job security, group membership, or social status. Maslow (1971) characterized such deprivation as human sickness, a term he used to connote a failure to move toward growth and actualization.

Growth Needs

Given satisfaction of all deficiency needs, growth needs surface and render the person restless and discontent. The person no longer feels hungry, insecure, isolated, or inferior, but he instead feels a need to fulfill personal potential. Growth needs—or self-actualization needs—provide energy and direction to become what one is capable of becoming: "A musician must make music, an artist must paint, a poet must write, if he is to be ultimately happy. What a man can be, he must be. This need we may call self-actualization" (Maslow, 1943). Putting the sexist language aside, it can be difficult to pinpoint precisely what self-actualization needs are and are not. One can understand physiological needs by thinking of hunger and thirst, but self-actualization is a more abstruse term. It is actually a master motive that coalesces 17 "metaneeds", such as longing for a sense of wholeness, aliveness, uniqueness, and meaning.

One way to discover what self-actualization needs are is to pay attention to the pathological state that arises when the person is deprived of each metaneed (Maslow, 1971). For instance, when deprived of the need for wholeness, the person feels a sense that one's world is falling apart in chaos and disintegration. When deprived of sense of aliveness, the person suffers through a sense of just going through the motions day after day. A man deprived of the need for uniqueness might speculate that his wife could easily find another mate that would be just as good as he. In other words, sometimes it is easier to see people's pathological states of disintegration, deadness, sameness, dishonesty, humorlessness, and despair than it is to see people's actualized states of wholeness, aliveness, uniqueness, truth, playfulness, and meaning.

Research on the Need Hierarchy

Maslow's need hierarchy was, and still is, wildly popular. It has been embraced as a modus operandi in education, business, management, the workplace, psychotherapy, and the health professions of medicine, nursing, and geriatrics (Cox, 1987). The need hierarchy can still be found in practically all introductory psychology textbooks. It also fits so nicely with both personal experience and common sense. Despite its tremendous popularity, research has actually found very little empirical support for the need hierarchy (Wahba & Bridwell, 1976).

One research strategy investigates changes in motivation related to age (Goebel & Brown, 1981). According to Maslow's second theme, the young tend to be occupied with physiological and safety needs, while adults tend to be occupied with esteem and actualization needs, generally speaking. Goebel and Brown (1981) had children, adolescents, young adults, middle-aged adults, and older adults report which needs were most important to them. Age did not predict need importance. For instance, self-actualization ranked lowest (not highest) for older adults. A second research strategy tests the hierarchy's validity using the rank order method (Blai, 1964; Goodman, 1968; Mathes, 1981). In this methodology, participants rank the needs in the order of desirability or importance. In general, the way people rank the needs does not conform to Maslow's predicted order. College students' priorities, for instance, were (in order from least to most important): esteem, security, self-actualization, belongingness, and physical/physiological (Mathes, 1981).

These data involve only self-reports of needs (rather than actually experiencing deprivation directly) but, overall, the pattern of findings casts considerable doubt on the hierarchy's validity. The only finding with some empirical support is the conceptualization of a dual-level (not a five-level) hierarchy. In a dual-level hierarchy, the only distinction is between deficiency and growth needs (Wahba & Bridwell, 1976), and when researchers make this distinction they do find some empirical support for the 2-level hierarchy (Sheldon, Elliot, Kim, & Kasser, 2001). Thus, three conclusions from research on the need hierarchy are to:

1. Reject the five-level hierarchy.
2. Collapse the physiological, safety, belongingness, and esteem needs into the single category of deficiency needs.
3. Hypothesize a simplified, two-level hierarchy distinguishing only between deficiency and growth needs.

Given these conclusions, take a second look at Figure 15.1. In your mind's eye, erase the three horizontal lines that separate the physiological, safety, belongingness, and esteem needs. With these lines eased, you will see one large triangle that includes the full range of the deficiency needs and one small triangle at the top for the self-actualization needs.

Encouraging Growth

Despite enjoying tremendous popularity, research on the hierarchy demonstrated its short-comings. When talking and theorizing about deficiency needs, Maslow made some mistakes. But when talking about growth needs, he was much more in his element and some of his ideas about growth needs have indeed stood the test of time.

Maslow estimated that less than 1% of the population ever reached self-actualization. Because the self-actualization needs were supposedly innate, one is left wondering why everyone does not ultimately self-actualize. In some cases, Maslow reasoned, people fail to reach their potential because of a nonsupportive internal (e.g., chronic back pain) or external (e.g., chronic deprivation from food, shelter) environment. In other cases, the person was responsible for her own lack of growth (i.e., each of us fears our own potential, which Maslow termed the "Jonah complex," after the Biblical character who tried to flee his destiny). Like Maslow, all humanistic thinkers continue to emphasize that the process of self-emergence is an inherently stressful and anxiety-provoking process, because it always makes the person face the insecurities of personal responsibility. When a person works toward self-emergence, she typically feels isolated and, to some degree, alone, or what Erich Fromm called the "unbearable state of powerlessness and aloneness." Facing such insecurity and facing the burden of having personal responsibility for one's freedom and personal growth, many people—like Jonah—seek escape (Fromm, 1941). The popular musical, *The Sound of Music*, illustrates this process for two young identity-seeking adults, as Marie sings "I'll need someone older and wiser showing me what to do" while Peter becomes an automaton within the powerful authoritarian military force of the day.

Maslow recognized the contradiction between his proposition that self-actualization was innate (and therefore operative in all human beings) and his observation that few among us actually gratify self-actualization needs. Ever the counselor and clinician, Maslow (1971) therefore offered several everyday behaviors for encouraging growth, as listed in Table 15.1.

In addition, Maslow stressed the important role of relationships—intimate and fulfilling relationships rather than the all-too-common superficial ones—as the soil for cultivating peak experiences (Hardeman, 1979). Setting up conditions to foster growth in our lives involved not only enacting the sort of behaviors listed in Table 15.2 but also involved engaging ourselves in relationships that support both autonomy and openness.

ACTUALIZING TENDENCY

Humanistic psychology's emphasis on holism and self-actualization can be represented by Carl Rogers's oft-cited quotation: "The organism has one basic tendency and striving—to actualize, maintain, and enhance the experiencing self" (1951). Fulfillment of physiological needs maintains and enhances the organism, as does the fulfillment of needs for be-

Table 15.2 Six Behaviors That Encourage Self-Actualization

1. **Make Growth Choices**

   See life as a series of choices, forever a choice toward progression and growth versus regression and fear. The progression-growth choice is a movement toward self-actualization, whereas the regression-fear choice is a movement away from self-actualization. For instance, enroll in a difficult but skill-building college course rather than in a safe and "easy A" course.

2. **Be Honest**

   Dare to be different, unpopular, nonconformist. Be honest rather than not, especially when in doubt. Take responsibility for your choices and the consequences of those choices. For instance, at a bookstore, pick a book that reflects your personal (but not necessarily popular) interest rather than a book featured on the best seller's list.

3. **Situationally Position Yourself for Peak Experiences**

   Set up conditions to make peak experiences more likely. Get rid of false notions and illusions. Find out what you are not good at, and learn what your potential is by learning what your potentials are not. Use your intelligence. If you are talented and interested in playing the piano, then spend more and more time in that domain and less and less time in more socially-rewarding domains in which you lack talent and interest.

4. **Give Up Defensiveness**

   Identify defenses and find the courage to give them up. For instance, instead of using fantasies to prop up the self and to keep anxiety at bay, drop the indulgent fantasy and get to work on developing the skills needed to actually become that sort of person.

5. **Let the Self Emerge**

   Perceive within yourself and see and hear the innate impulse voices. Shut out the noises of the world. Instead of only looking to others to tell you who to become, also listen to your own personal interests and aspirations of who you want to become.

6. **Be Open to Experience**

   Experience fully, vividly, selflessly with full concentration and total absorption. Experience without self-consciousness, defenses, or shyness. Be spontaneous, original, and open to experience. In other words, stop and smell the roses.

longingness and social status. Further, a motive like curiosity enhances and actualizes the person via greater learning and the development of new interests. Overall, Rogers (1959, 1963) recognized the existence of specific human motives and even the existence of clusters of needs like those proposed by Maslow's hierarchy, but he emphatically stressed the holistic proposition that all human needs serve the collective purpose of maintaining, enhancing, and actualizing the person.

Rogers, like Maslow, believed that the actualizing tendency was innate, a continual presence that quietly guides the individual toward genetically determined potentials. This forward-moving pattern of development was characterized by "struggle and pain," and Rogers offered the following illustration for communicating the self-actualizing tendency's path toward development and growth. The nine-month-old infant has the genetic potential to walk but must struggle to advance from crawling to walking. The struggle to make those first steps inevitably includes episodes of falling and feeling frustrated, hurt, and disappointed. Despite the struggle and pain, the child nevertheless persists toward walking and away from crawling. The pain and disappointment undermine and discourage the child's motivation to walk, but the actualization tendency, "the forward thrust of life," supports the child ever forward. The actualizing tendency is the source of that energy that motivates development "toward autonomy and away from heteronomy" (Rogers, 1959).

All experiences within the struggle and pain of actualizing one's potential are evaluated in accordance with an "organismic valuation process," an innate capability for judging whether a specific experience promotes or reverses growth. Experiences perceived as maintaining or enhancing the person are positively valued. Such growth-promoting experiences are given the metaphorical green light by the organismic valuation process and are subsequently approached. Experiences perceived as regressive are valued negatively. Such growth-blocking experiences are given the metaphorical yellow or red light by the organismic valuation process and are therefore subsequently avoided. In effect, the organismic valuation process provides an experiential feedforward system that allows the individual to coordinate life experiences in accordance with the actualization tendency.

The actualizing tendency motivates the individual to want to undertake new and challenging experiences, and the organismic valuation process provides the interpretive information needed for deciding whether the new undertaking is growth-promoting or not. The feedforward system of the organismic valuation process is an interesting addition to a motivational analysis of behavior as it complements the many feedback systems already discussed (i.e., physiological stop system in Chapter 4, goal-feedback system in Chapter 9). With a feedback system, information follows behavior to affect continuing motivation and subsequent persistence; with a feedforward system, information precedes behavior to communicate a proverbial green, yellow, or red light as to one's *intention* to act and, hence, behavioral initiation (rather than persistence).

Emergence of the Self

The actualizing tendency characterizes the individual as a whole. With the emergence of the self, a person grows in complexity, and the organismic valuation process begins to apply not only to the organism as a whole but also to the self in particular. The most important motivational implication of the emergence of the self is that the actualizing tendency begins to express itself in part toward that portion of the organism conceptualized as the self. This means that the individual gains a second major motivational force in addition to the actualizing tendency, namely the self-actualizing tendency. Notice that actualization and self-actualization are not the same thing (Ford, 1991b), as the actualizing tendency and the self-actualizing tendency can work at odds with one another, as discussed in the next section.

The emergence of the self prompts the emergence of the need for positive regard—approval, acceptance, and love from others. The need for positive regard is of special significance because it makes the individual sensitive to the feedback of others (criticisms and praises). The evaluations and priorities expressed by other people assume a greater importance in one's life. Over time, evaluating the self from other people's points of view becomes a rather automated and internalized process.

Conditions of Worth

Soon after birth, children begin to learn the "conditions of worth" on which their behavior and personal characteristics (the self) are judged as either positive and worthy of acceptance or negative and worthy of rejection. Eventually, because the need for positive regard sensitizes the individual to attend to the acceptances and rejections of others, the child internalizes parental conditions of worth into the self structure. Throughout development, the self structure expands beyond parental conditions of worth to include societal conditions of worth as well. By adulthood, the individual learns from parents, friends, teachers, clergy, spouses, coaches, employers, and others what behaviors and which characteristics are good and bad, right and wrong, beautiful and ugly, desirable and undesirable.

According to Rogers (1959), all of us live in two worlds—the inner world of organismic valuing and the outer world of conditions of worth. To the extent to which one internalizes conditions of worth, these acquired conditions of worth gain the capacity to substitute for, and largely replace, the innate organismic valuation process. When governed by conditions of worth, individuals necessarily divorce themselves from their inherent means of coordinating experience with the actualizing tendency. No longer is experience judged in accordance with the innate organismic valuation process. Rather, experience is judged in accordance with conditions of worth.

Rogers viewed the child's movement toward conditions of worth and away from organismic valuation as antithetical to the development of the actualizing tendency. When the developing individual adheres to conditions of worth, he moves farther away from an inherent ability to make the behavioral choices necessary to actualize the self. The overall process and consequences of adherence to either the organismic valuation process or socialized conditions of worth are summarized in Figure 15.2.

The way not to interfere with organismic valuation is to provide "unconditional positive regard," rather than the "conditional positive regard" that emanates from conditions of worth. If given unconditional positive regard, a child has no need to internalize societal conditions of worth. Experiences are judged as valuable to the extent that they enhance oneself (see upper half of Figure 15.2). If parents approve of, love, and accept their child for who she naturally is (i.e., unconditional positive regard) rather than for who the parents wish her to be (i.e., conditional positive regard), then the child and the child's self-structure will be a relatively transparent representation of her inherent preferences, talents, capacities, and potentialities. A condition of worth arises, however, when the positive regard of another person is conditional—depends on some way of being or some way of behaving (see lower half of Figure 15.2). Here, experiences are judged as valuable to the extent that they are approved of by others.

In the absence of salient conditions of worth, no conflict exists between the actualizing tendency and the self-actualizing tendency, and the two motivational tendencies remain unified (Rogers, 1959). Internalized conditions of self-worth, however, create the potential for motivational conflict. With conditional self-regard, conflict between the actualizing and self-actualizing tendencies creates a tension and internal confusion since some aspects of behavior are regulated by the actualizing tendency, while other aspects of behavior are regulated by the self-actualizing tendency (Ford, 1991b; Rogers, 1959). Self-actualization, when evaluated and directed via conditions of worth rather than organismic valuation, can paradoxically lead a person to develop in a way that is incongruent, con-

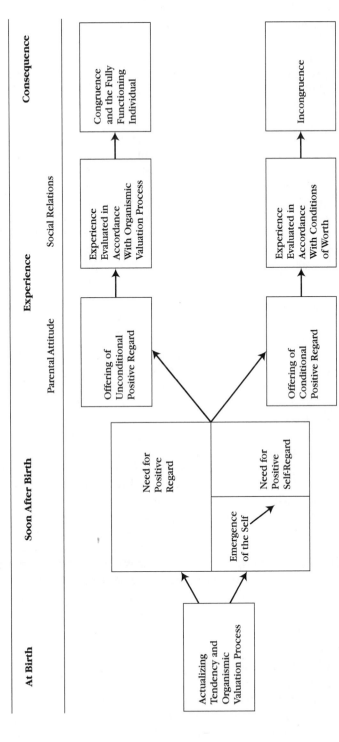

Figure 15.2 Rogerian Model of the Process of Self-Actualization

flicting, and maladaptive (Ford, 1991b). Thus, self-actualization does not necessarily lead to and result in health and growth. Sometimes the pursuit of self-actualization leads to and results in maladjustment, as when conditions of worth define and direct self-actualization processes. Health and growth occur only when the actualizing tendency and the self-actualizing tendency are in synchronization and when all experiences are evaluated internally within the framework of organismic valuation.

Parents, for instance, are placed in difficult positions when their child expresses a somewhat socially undesirable characteristic, such as shyness, moodiness, irritability, or an explosive temper (e.g., recall the chapter's opening vignette). Conditional positive regard implies rejection and retraining for the child's temperament, in the name of promoting social inclusion and popularity. But unconditional positive regard implies acceptance of and support for the child's natural temperament. The difficult position the parents face manifests itself in the dilemma of avoiding psychological costs (e.g., depression) versus avoiding social costs (e.g., peer rejection) to the developing child (Dykman, 1998).

Congruence

Congruence and incongruence describe the extent to which the individual denies and rejects (incongruence) or accepts (congruence) the full range of his personal characteristics, abilities, desires, and beliefs. Psychological incongruence is essentially the extent of discrepancy or difference between "the self as perceived and the actual experience of the organism" (Rogers, 1959). The individual might perceive himself as having one set of characteristics and one set of feelings but then publicly express a different set of characteristics and a different set of feelings. Independence between experience and expression reveals incongruence; coordination between experience and expression reveals congruence.

When people move toward identifying with external conditions of worth, they adopt facades. A facade is essentially the social mask a person wears, and it relates to ways of behaving that have little to do with inner guides and much to do with a social front to hide behind (Rogers, 1961). Consider the unauthentic smile (the social façade of acting very happy and very friendly). Introverts often find themselves wearing the facade of the unauthentic smile on a regular basis, as when they force themselves to smile for hours at a social gathering). Doing so on a regular basis—acting one way yet feeling another way—predicts proneness to maladjustment, including anxiety, depression, self-doubt, and hypo-assertiveness (Ford, 1995). Adopting socially desirable facades carries its psychological costs.

Fully Functioning Individual

According to Rogers, when fully functioning, the individual lives in close and confident relationship to the organismic valuation process, trusting that inner direction. Congruence is a constant companion. Further, the fully functioning individual spontaneously communicates inner impulses both verbally and nonverbally. He or she is open to experience, accepts the experiences as they are, and expresses those experiences in an unedited and authentic manner. To characterize the moment-to-moment experience of the fully functioning individual, Figure 15.3 illustrates the sequential process of a motive's emergence, acceptance, and unedited expression.

BOX 15 *Perfectionism as Conditions of Worth*

Question: Why is this information important?

Answer: It invites you to examine the origins and implications of your own sense of perfectionism.

Nowhere in the industrialized world is the suicide rate higher for young men than it is in New Zealand. The everyday cultural expectations these men face stress inflated standards of masculinity, self-reliance, total emotional control, and unbound excellence in school and sports. From a humanistic perspective, these young men are asked to internalize societal conditions of worth characterized by perfectionism.

High personal standards are not bad. High standards generally cultivate both achievement strivings and good work habits (Frost et al., 1990). The psychological costs of perfectionism become apparent when the individual experiences stressful and negative life events (Blatt, 1995).

In "normal perfectionism," people remain capable of experiencing pleasure and satisfaction in their work (Hamachek, 1978; Timpe, 1989). But perfectionism, like ice cream, comes in flavors, including "self-oriented perfectionism," "socially prescribed perfectionism," and "neurotic perfectionism" (Hewitt & Flett, 1991a, 1991b).

Self-oriented perfectionism features exceedingly high, self-imposed, unrealistic standards that are paired with extreme self-criticism and an unwillingness to accept failure and personal flaws. When the self-oriented perfectionist does experience failure, self-criticism and depression are likely aftershocks.

Socially prescribed perfectionism is rooted in one's belief that other people hold exaggerated and unrealistic expectations for the self that are difficult, if not impossible, to meet—yet must be met if one is to gain acceptance and approval (Hewitt & Flett, 1991a, 1991b).

These imposed standards are not only external to the self but they are also uncontrollable standards. Failure to live up to these external-uncontrollable standards therefore ushers forth a full dosage of anxiety, helplessness, and suicidal thoughts (Blatt, 1995).

When relationships (as with parents and teachers) are supportive and nurturing, both self-oriented and socially prescribed dimensions of perfectionism can facilitate constructive strivings (Nystul, 1984). When relationships are not supportive, however, these two types of perfectionism often collapses into "neurotic perfectionism" (Hamachek, 1978), which is essentially the *intense* need to avoid failure. With neurotic perfectionism, no performance is good enough, and even well-done jobs yield little or no satisfaction. Deep feelings of inferiority throw the individual into an endless cycle of self-defeating, excessive striving accompanied by self-criticism, self-attack, and intense negative feelings. In general, neurotic perfectionism is associated with a wide range of psychopathology—depression (Hewitt & Dyck, 1986; LaPointe & Crandell, 1980), suicide (Adkins & Parker, 1996; Delisle, 1986; Shaffer, 1977), and eating disorders (Brouwers & Wiggum, 1993; Druss & Silverman, 1979; Katzman & Wolchik, 1984).

Neurotic perfectionism grows out of childhood experiences with disapproving parents whose love is conditional on how well the child behaves and performs (Hamachek, 1978). These parents incessantly urge their child to do better. The child never feels satisfied because his behaviors and performances never hit his parents' moving target of being good enough to earn approval and love. The result is a constant quest to avoid mistakes. And, typically, the harsh parental standards become internalized into a self-critical voice that uses the withdrawal of self-love as a means of personal punishment. Such a voice of neurotic perfectionism is the antithesis of organismic valuing.

CAUSALITY ORIENTATIONS

People vary in their understandings of the forces that cause their behavior. Some people adopt a general orientation that their behavior is caused primarily by inner guides and self-determined forces; others adopt a general orientation that their behavior is caused primarily by social guides and environmental incentives. To the extent that individuals habitually rely on internal guides (e.g., needs, interests), individuals have an "autonomy

Emergence	Acceptance	Expression
Onset of innate desire, impulse, or motive $\rightarrow$	Desire, impulse, or motive is accepted "as is" into consciousness $\rightarrow$	Unedited communication of desire, impulse, or motive

Figure 15.3 Fully Functioning as the Emergence, Acceptance, and Expression of a Motive

causality orientation." To the extent that individuals habitually rely on external guides (e.g., social cues), they have a "control causality orientation."

The autonomy orientation involves a high degree of experienced choice with respect to the initiation and regulation of behavior (Deci & Ryan, 1985b). When autonomy-oriented, people's behavior proceeds with a full sense of volition and an internal locus of causality. Needs, interests, and personally valued goals initiate the person's behavior, and needs, interests, and goals regulate her decision in persisting or quitting. In making a choice of college majors or careers to pursue, external factors such as salary and status are not irrelevant influences, but autonomy-oriented individuals pay closer attention to their needs and feelings than they do environmental contingencies and pressures.

The control orientation involves a relative insensitivity to inner guides, as control-oriented individuals prefer to pay closer attention to behavioral incentives and cues that exist either in the environment or inside themselves (Deci & Ryan, 1985b). When control-oriented, people make decisions in response to the presence and quality of incentives, such as extrinsic rewards or concerns over attaining some outcome, such as pleasing others. A central ingredient in the determination of control-oriented people's ways of thinking, feeling, and behaving is a sense of pressure to comply with what is demanded or with what should be done. Environmental factors such as pay and status are very important. When researchers ask control-oriented individuals what they aspire to, their goals center around financial and material success (Kasser & Ryan, 1993).

The General Causality Orientations Scale (Deci & Ryan, 1985b) measures causality orientations by presenting a series of 12 vignettes (short stories). Each vignette presents a situation and lists responses to that situation, one of which is autonomy-oriented and the other of which is control-oriented. (A third scale to assess the impersonal orientation is not discussed here.) For instance, one of the vignettes presents the following situation:

You have been offered a new position in a company where you have worked for some time. The first question that is likely to come to mind is:

I wonder if the new work will be interesting? (Autonomy)

Will I make more money at this position? (Control)

Causality orientations reflect self-determination in personality. Hence, self-determination theory (see Chapter 6) explains the origins and dynamics of causality orientations (Chapter 6; Deci & Ryan, 1985a). The autonomy-oriented personality is characterized by intrinsic motivation and identified regulation, as the forces that cause behavior are personal needs and interests (intrinsic motivation), as well as beliefs and values that have been integrated into the self (identified regulation). The control-oriented personality is characterized by extrinsic regulation and introjected regulation, as the forces that cause behavior are environmental rewards and constraints (extrinsic regulation), and beliefs and values that have been forced onto the self (introjected regulation). Because of its close relationship to self-determination in personality, the autonomy orientation, like self-determination in general, correlates positively with measures of positive functioning, such as self-actualization, ego development, self-esteem, openness to experience, attitude-behavior consistency, and acceptance of one's true feelings (Deci & Ryan, 1985b; Koestner, Bernieri, & Zuckerman, 1992; Scherhorn & Grunert, 1988). This is true in domains as diverse as religion, education, prosocial behavior, and trying to empower the self to make important life changes like losing a lot of weight (Ryan & Connell, 1989; Ryan, Rigby, & King, 1993; Williams et al., 1996).

When people seek to change their behavior, they typically rely on either internal guides (personal goals) or external guides (relationship pressures) to do so. While participating in a weight-loss program, for instance, people can generally rely on both internal and external support for assistance and motivation for changing their behavior (Williams et al., 1996). After the program ends, however, people lose much of their external support (the staff, the structure of the program) for changing their behavior. Researchers therefore reasoned that the more autonomy oriented the participants were, the more likely it was that they would stay in the program from one week to the next, lose weight during the program, and, most importantly, maintain their weight loss after the program ended (i.e., maintain the behavior change). How autonomy-oriented individuals succeeded in maintaining their behavior change appears in Figure 15.4. The more autonomy-oriented the participants were (and the more autonomy supportive the staff-patient interactions were), the more these participants relied on relatively autonomous reasons for losing weight, such as identified regulation ("It is important to my health that I lose more weight") rather than external regulation ("My spouse will divorce me if I don't lose more weight"). Rooting weight loss motivation in autonomous reasons promoted week-to-week attendance, and the more frequently they attended meetings the more successful they were in losing weight and maintaining that weight loss, as indicated in the figure by a decline in their final body mass index (BMI).

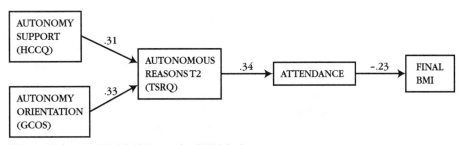

Figure 15.4   Model of Self-Determined Weight Loss

Source: Adapted from "Motivational Predictors of Weight Loss and Weight-Loss Maintenance," by G. C. Williams, V. M. Grow, E. R. Freedman, R. M. Ryan, and E. L. Deci, 1996, *Journal of Personality and Social Psychology, 70*, pp. 115–126. Copyright 1996 by American Psychological Association. Adapted with permission.

GROWTH-SEEKING VERSUS VALIDATION-SEEKING

When people identify with and internalize societal conditions of worth, they do more than just adopt socially desirable facades. Quasi-needs emerge. A quasi-need (see chapter 7) emerges to the extent that the individual *needs* social approval—directly or symbolically—during social interaction. That is, valuing oneself along the lines of societal conditions of worth leads people into processes of validation-seeking. For the person who *needs* the approval of others to feel good about himself or herself, fulfilling others' conditions of worth leads to validation while failing to live up to others' conditions of worth leads to a perceived lack of personal worth, competence, and likeability.

During social interaction, people who seek external validation often use interpersonal situations to test or measure their personal worth, competence, or likeability. That is, other people—their peers, employers, teachers, and romantic partners—are seen as sources of external validation and as social yardsticks by which to measure one's personal worth (Dykman, 1998). Positive outcomes generally leave the validation-seeking individual feeling rather accepted and validated. The adjustment problems surface following negative outcomes because these problems imply a lack of personal worth, competence, or likeability.

In contrast to validation-seeking individuals, growth-seeking individuals center their personal strivings around learning, improving, and reaching personal potential. Seeking growth leads one to adopt a pattern of thinking in which situations and relationships are seen as opportunities for personal growth, learning, or self-improvement. As with validation-seeking individuals, positive outcomes from interpersonal interaction (e.g., social inclusion, interpersonal acceptance, athletic or academic successes) generally leave the growth-seeking individual feeling validated as well because the growth-seeking individual experiences a sense of progress. Unlike validation-seeking individuals, however, negative interpersonal outcomes (e.g., exclusion, rejection, failure) fail to usher in adjustment problems because negative outcomes simply identify and communicate information about life areas that are in need of improvement.

The Goal Orientation Inventory (GOI; Dykman, 1998) measures validation-seeking and growth-seeking strivings as relatively enduring personality characteristics. The respondent is asked to agree or disagree on whether the item describes how she thinks and acts in general:

> Instead of just enjoying activities and social interactions, most situations to me feel like a major test of my basic worth, competence, or likeability. (Validation-Seeking)

> Personal growth is more important to me than protecting myself from my fears. (Growth-Seeking)

The distinction between striving for validation versus growth is important because it predicts vulnerability to mental health difficulties. For instance, the more people strive for validation, the more likely they are to suffer anxiety during social interaction, fear of failure, low self-esteem, poor task persistence, and high depression (see the first column of numbers in Table 15.3). In contrast, the more people strive for growth, the more likely they are to experience low interaction anxiety, low fear of failure, high self-esteem, high task persistence, and low depression (see the second column of numbers in Table 15.3). In terms of self-actualization, growth-seeking individuals are more likely to view themselves as living in the present (highly time competent) and behaving in accordance with one's own principles (inner directed; see Table 15.3).

Table 15.3 Correlations with Indices of Psychological Well-Being for the Two Goal Orientations of Validation-Seeking and Growth-Seeking

Dependent Measure	Validation-Seeking Scale of the GOI	Growth-Seeking Scale of the GOI
Interaction anxiety	.46**	−.48**
Social anxiety	.42**	−.41**
Fear of failure	.50**	−.48**
Self-esteem	.59**	−.56**
Task persistence	−.40**	.55**
Depression	.38**	−.36**
Self-actualization:		
Time competence scale	−.51**	.20*
Inner directedness scale	−.56**	.31**

*p < .05; **p < .01. N ranged from 101 to 251 for each correlation reported above.

Note: The personality scale for each measure listed above was as follows: Interaction anxiety, Interaction Anxiousness Scale (Leary, 1983); social anxiety, Social Anxiety Subscale of the Self-Consciousness Scale (Fenigstein, Scheier, & Buss, 1975); fear of failure, Fear of Failure Scale (Dykman, 1998); self-esteem (reverse scored), Rosenberg's Self-Esteem Scale (Rosenberg, 1965); task persistence, Hope Scale (Snyder et al., 1991); depression, Beck Depression Inventory (Beck et al., 1979); and self-actualization, Personality Orientation Inventory (Shostrom, 1964, 1974).

Source: From "Integrating Cognitive and Motivational Factors in Depression: Initial Tests of a Goal-orientation Approach," by B. M. Dykman, 1998, *Journal of Personality and Social Psychology, 74,* pp. 139–158. Copyright 1998 by American Psychological Association. Adapted with permission.

This distinction between validation-seeking and growth-seeking is another way of expressing Maslow's distinction between deficiency and growth needs. Seeking validation is the pursuit to restore one's deficiency needs, at least at the interpersonal level, whereas seeking growth is the pursuit of looking for opportunities to realize one's potential. The distinction also expresses a climate of conditional positive regard versus a climate of unconditional positive regard. Seeking validation is a striving that grows out of parent-child interactions characterized by critical, conditional, and perfectionistic parenting (the lower half of Figure 15.2), whereas seeking growth is a striving that grows out of parent-child interactions characterized by supportive, nonjudgmental, and acceptance parenting (the upper half of Figure 15.2; Blatt, 1995; Dykman, 1998).

HOW RELATIONSHIPS SUPPORT THE ACTUALIZING TENDENCY

The extent to which individuals develop toward congruence and adjustment depends greatly on the quality of their interpersonal relationships. At one extreme, relationships take on a controlling tone as others force their agendas on other people, pushing them toward heteronomy and a commitment to conditions of worth. At the other extreme, relationships take on a supportive tone as they promote autonomy by affording people the opportunity and flexibility necessary to move from heteronomy toward autonomy. Such relationships nurture the actualizing tendency.

In humanistic therapy, for example, a client moves toward health and psychological congruence when his therapist brings the following characteristics into the relationship: warmth, genuineness, empathy, interpersonal acceptance, and confirmation of the other person's capacity for self-determination (Kramer, 1995; Rogers, 1973, 1980, 1995). *Warmth* essentially means caring for and enjoying spending time with the other person. *Genuineness* acknowledges that each person must be fully present in and open to the relationship's here and now, offering personal authenticity rather than a professional facade of being a therapist, or "the expert." *Empathy* relates to listening to and hearing all the messages the other is sending and also truly understanding and willingly adopting the other's perspective on experience. Empathy occurs as one person gains the capacity to enter into the private perceptual world of the other and becomes thoroughly at home in that world. *Interpersonal acceptance* means that each person in the relationship experiences a basic acceptance and trust from the other (unconditional positive regard). Finally, *confirmation of the other person's capacity for self-determination* acknowledges that the other person is capable and competent and possesses an inherently positive developmental direction. Within a humanistic framework, these five characteristics reflect the quality of an interpersonal relationship.

Helping Others

Interpersonal relationships become constructive, helpful relationships when a person becomes, by virtue of her contact with another, more mature, more open to experience, and better integrated (Rogers, 1995). Helping, in the humanistic tradition, does not involve an expert rushing in to solve the problem, to fix things, to advise people, or to mold and manipulate them in some way. Instead, helping involves letting the other person discover, and then be, herself. This last insight communicates the antithesis of conditions of worth.

Relatedness to Others

One index of healthy psychosocial development is the extent to which the individual accepts social conventions, accommodates the self to the society, internalizes cultural values, cooperates with others, shows respect for others, and so on. Rather than being independent, selfish, and socially detached, self-actualizers are actually good citizens. What motivates the willingness to accommodate the self to others is the need for relatedness (Goodenow, 1993; Ryan & Powelson, 1991). Interpersonally, relatedness (Chapter 5) refers to the quality of the relationship between socializer and socializee. When one person feels emotionally connected to, interpersonally involved with, liked by, respected by, and valued by another person, relatedness is high and internalization of external regulations occurs willingly (Ryan & Powelson, 1991).

But relatedness can come with a price—a hidden agenda in which one person asks for compliance from the other before granting love or approval (Gruen, 1976). Conditions of worth, for instance, essentially mean that the other person's (or society's) love, approval, care, and emotional connectedness are contingent on compliance with socialization standards and norms. But there is another type of relatedness between people besides a conformity-demanding conditional positive regard—namely, the unconditional acceptance and support between people (Hodgins, Koestner, & Duncan, 1996; Ryan, 1993). Consider relatedness in both childhood and adult development. The quality of relatedness in early attachments (infant and caretaker) depends on how sensitive and responsive caregivers are to the infant's needs and initiatives (Colin, 1996). The paradoxical conclusion that emerged from Mary Ainsworth's classic program of research on infant attachment was that infants who received warm, need-satisfying, responsive, sensitive care from mothers did not become dependent or needy; instead, nurturance enabled and even liberated the child's autonomy (Ainsworth, 1989). Relationships rich in relatedness paradoxically facilitate autonomy (Hodgins, Koestner, & Duncan, 1996). In contrast, when others provide contingent conditions of worth, people often forgo autonomy in order to preserve relatedness. In optimal development, neither autonomy nor relatedness is forgone (Ryan, 1993).

Freedom to Learn

Rogers continually lamented contemporary educational practices. He did not like the idea of a "teacher" because he felt that the only learning that really mattered was self-initiated learning (Rogers, 1969). As a teacher looking back at the results of his own efforts, Rogers felt that he was responsible for more damage than good. Little of consequence occurs when a teacher gives out heaps of information for students to digest. Instead of "teacher," Rogers preferred "facilitator," a term that describes the classroom leader as one who creates and supports an atmosphere conducive to students' learning. Learning does not follow teaching. Rather, learning follows having one's interests identified, facilitated, and supported. Self-discovery and self-evaluation are of prime importance, while criticisms and evaluation by teachers are inconsequential or harmful. Thus, education is not something a teacher can give to (or force on) a student. Rather, education must be acquired by the student through an investment of his energies and interests.[1]

In practice, humanistic education typically manifests itself in three themes (Allender & Silberman, 1979):

- The facilitator (i.e., teacher) functions as a structuring agent in an open classroom.
- Students take responsibility for initiating their own learning.
- Students learn cooperatively and in a context of the peer group.

A facilitator relies on setting up learning centers or stations in the classroom to encourage students' choices and initiatives, and the facilitator focuses most of her attention on identifying and supporting students' needs, desires, interests, and preferences (McCombs & Pope, 1994). Personal responsibility for learning moves students out of the role of passive receivers of knowledge and into the role of active learners who construct their own understandings. Peer-based cooperative learning facilitates individual learning by allowing students to communicate their ideas to others as well as to learn from the feedback, modeling, and insight of their peers (Johnson & Johnson, 1985). When classrooms support students' initiatives (rather than teach them what to learn), students gain academic confidence, show greater mastery motivation, and participate more actively during learning activities (deCharms, 1976; Ryan & Grolnick, 1986). To be fair, contemporary educational psychology research shows many benefits from traditional teaching (Ausubel,

---

[1]Golfer Ben Hogan, in a Rogerian spirit, gave the following reply to answer why he had not written another instructional book: "Golf is a game that cannot be taught; it must be learned."

1977). So Rogers's contribution to educational practice was more to add a student-centered approach to the educator's repertoire rather than to replace teacher-centered instruction in the schools.

Self-Definition and Social Definition

Self-definition and social definition are personality processes related to how individuals conceptualize who they are (Jenkins, 1996; Stewart, 1992; Stewart & Winter, 1974). Socially defined individuals accept external definitions of who they are. Self-defined individuals resist these external definitions and instead favor internal definitions of the self. Many people conceptualize themselves as using both sources of information, but some people rely rather fully either on self-definition or on social definition processes.

Self-definition and social definition processes are particularly instructive in the developing identities of women (Jenkins, 1996). Compared to their socially defined counterparts, self-defined women are more autonomous and independent in their interpersonal relationships (they depend less on others) and social roles (they may prefer nontraditional occupations). They take decisive and successful goal-directed actions, as in occupational decisions and strategies for career development. They organize their goals around self-determined aspirations, including their own personal decisions to get married or not and to have children or not. They are also less invested in so-called traditional roles, such as wife and mother. In contrast, socially defined women prefer to work with and depend on others. They prefer traditional female roles both at home and at work. They are typically willing to compromise in terms of their plans, college-degree aspirations, career persistence, and relationships in general. Decisions and experience flow not from the self but, instead, from the social support of others and the beliefs, abilities, and aspirations of those others. And by depending on others, socially defined married women hope for husbands who can provide them with a life that is stimulating and challenging.

THE PROBLEM OF EVIL

Much of the spirit of humanistic psychology follows the questionnable assumption that "human nature is inherently good." But do we as a society dare trust people who follow their inner guides? Freedom and self-determination are fine if human nature is benevolent, cooperative, and warmhearted. But what if human nature is malevolent, selfish, and aggressive? What if human nature is evil, or at least partly evil?

Humanistic thinkers wrestle with the nature of evil (Goldberg, 1995; Klose, 1995). The discussion typically takes one of two forms. On the one hand, the discussion asks *how much* of human nature is evil? This question asks, "If family, political, economic, and social systems were benevolent and growth-promoting, then would human evil be reduced to zero or would some residual ferociousness remain?" (Maslow, 1987). On the other hand, the discussion tries to understand evildoers (e.g., murderers, rapists) who confess to enjoying what they do and express a willingness to continue doing such acts (Goldberg, 1995).

Evil is the deliberate, voluntary, intentional infliction of painful suffering on another person without respect for his humanity or personhood. Rogers's conviction was that evil was not inherent in human nature. He argued that if caretakers provided enough nurturance and acceptance and if they established a genuine connectedness with those they cared for, then people would inevitably choose good over evil (Rogers, 1982). Hence, human beings behave malevolently only to the extent that they have been injured or damaged by their experience. Violence reflects a history of relationships steeped in power and control (Muehlenhard & Kimes, 1999), while altruism reflects a history of relationships steeped in empathy and care (Batson, 1991).

Other humanists see more ambiguity in human nature. They assume that benevolence *and* malevolence are part of everyone. In this view, under one set of social conditions, the actualizing tendency pairs itself with life-affirming values and adopts constructive ways for relating and behaving; but under another set of conditions, the actualizing tendency pairs itself with malicious values and leads to cruelty and destructive behavior (May, 1982). Thus, a person needs a value system (standards of right and wrong) to support and complement the organismic valuation process. If adults (parents) do not provide a child with a benevolent value system, then that child will grab a value system wherever it is available, be it among equally confused peers on the street, the college fraternity world, or Wall Street (Maslow, 1971). The recent study of suicide terrorists shows that these individuals were pretty much normal people who were intensely committed to a cause and to a set of values that they saw as greater than themselves (Atran, 2003). If a society cannot provide a benevolent value system for all its members, then it must build safeguards and structures into its social systems to renounce cruelty and to counter impulses to do evil (Bandura, 1999).

When people *desire* to act in ways that promote evil, they possess a malevolent personality (Goldberg, 1995). The descent into a malevolent personality is a slippery course of choices and developmental progressions (Baumeister & Campbell, 1999; Fromm, 1964; Goldberg, 1995). Evil develops (Stuab, 1999): (1) Adults shame and scorn the child such that the child comes to the conclusion that she is flawed and incompetent as a human being; (2) the child incubates a negative self-view and comes to prefer lies and self-deceit over critical self-examination; (3) a transition occurs from being a victim to becoming an insensitive perpetrator; (4) the person initiates experimental malevolence; and (5) the malevolent personality is forged through a rigid refusal to engage in critical self-examination. The self becomes unwilling to examine itself (e.g., scapegoating is used as a strategy for sacrificing others to preserve one's own self-image; Baumeister, Smart, & Boden, 1996), and success in intimidation fosters the self-aggrandizement that counteracts the need for self-examination (Goldberg, 1995).

This view argues that evil springs out of a person's grandiosity and damaged concept of self to explain heinous acts. The cause seems to have its origin in enculturation, not in human nature. It is difficult to determine whether or not evil is inherent in human nature. Within a supportive interpersonal climate, people's choices move them in the direction of greater socialization, improved relationships, and toward what is healthy and benevolent (Rogers, 1982). Therefore, as murder, war, and prejudice continue unabated throughout human history, the culprit might not be the evil in human nature but, alternatively, the sickness in culture. As long as society offers people choices, the possibility remains that its members will internalize a pathological value system that makes possible the descent into evil and the forging of a malevolent personality (May, 1982).[2]

POSITIVE PSYCHOLOGY AND MENTAL HEALTH

Positive psychology looks at people's mental health and the quality of their lives to ask, "What could be?" (Seligman & Csikszentmihalyi, 2000). It seeks to build people's strengths and competencies. It does not ask that people put on rose colored glasses or adopt Pollyanna as a role model. Instead, positive psychology makes the case that strengths are as important as are weaknesses, resilience is as important as is vulnerability, and the life long task to cultivate wellness is as important as is an intervention attempt to remedy pathology. A sampling of the human strengths that comprise the subject matter of positive psychology appears in Table 15.4 (from Snyder & Lopez, 2002).

The building of the strengths in Table 15.4 yield two interrelated outcomes: (1) fostering personal growth and well-being and (2) preventing human sickness (e.g., depression, suicide) from ever taking root within the personality. For insight how this might be so, consider the two illustrative strengths of optimism and meaning.

Optimism

Most people are neither realistic nor accurate in how they think. Most of us think we are better than average, and most of us think we are better than average in all sorts of domains (e.g,. driving, teaching, honesty, you name it). Many of us harbor within us a positivity

Table 15.4   Personal Strengths Investigated as the Subject Matter of Positive Psychology

* Happiness	* The Passion to Know
* Enjoyment	* Wisdom
* Resilience	* Authenticity
* Capacity for Flow	* Toughness
* Personal Control	* Self-Determination
* Optimism	* Forgiveness
* Optimistic Explanatory Style	* Compassion
* Hope	* Empathy
* Self-Efficacy	* Altruism
* Goal-Setting	* Humor
* Meaning	* Spirituality

---

[2]A final question asks whether human evil can be healed. One constant in humanistic thinking is that it never condemns without an affirmation of hope. But the malevolent personality is a tough one. Four reasons exist to explain the difficulty in healing evil: (1) the malevolent personality's closed nature (unwillingness to engage in critical self-examination), (2) the rarity of the malevolent personality's genuine motivation to change, (3) the odds against the malevolent personality finding those supportive conditions in which motivation for personal change can take root and fulfill itself, and (4) the strong influence of the individual's choice to change or not (Klose, 1995).

bias. This pervasive tendency to see ourselves in a positive light is associated with well-being and enhanced performance (Taylor, 1989; Taylor & Brown, 1988). Optimism grows out of this positivity, and can be understood as a positive attitude or a good mood that is associated with what one expects to unfold in his or her immediate and, especially, long-term future (Peterson, 2000).

Wishful thinking can do more harm than good (Oettingen, 1996), but empirical evidence supports the conclusion that people who are optimistic live more worthwhile lives than do people who are not optimistic. Optimists experience better psychological and physical health (Scheier & Carver, 1992), undertake more health-promoting behaviors (Peterson, Seligman, Yurko, Martin, & Friedman, 1998), show greater persistence and more effective problem solving, and are more socially popular (Peterson, 2000). The reason this is so is because optimism gives people a sense of hope and motivation that their future can indeed be improved, as in cases like increasing school achievement, improving personal health, and growing an interpersonal relationship (Seligman, 1991).

Optimism can be taught and learned (Seligman et al., 1995), but it also seems to be inherent in our nature. When equipped with optimism, optimism colors our expectations and emotions and we generally live up to our self-fulfilling (optimistic) prophecy by coping and performing better than when we are more sanguine.

Meaning

From a motivational point of view, meaning in life grows out of three needs (Baumeister & Vohs, 2002). The first need is purpose. To give today's activity and struggle a sense of purpose, it helps if the person generates future-oriented goals, such as trying to graduate high school, fall in love during a summer vacation, or go to heaven in the afterlife. Connecting the activity of the day with a future goal effectively endows day-to-day activity with a sense of purpose it otherwise would not have. The second need is for values. Values define what is good and what is right, and when we internalize or act on a value we affirm a sense of goodness in us. The third need is for efficacy. Having a sense of personal control or competence is important because it enables us to believe that what we do makes a difference. Collectively, a sense of purpose, internalized values, and high efficacy to affect changes in the environment cultivate meaning in life (Baumeister & Vohs, 2002).

Creating meaning is an active process in which people interpret the events in their lives (Taylor, 1983), find the benefit in these events (Davis, Nolen-Hoeksema, & Larson, 1998), and discover the significance of what happens to them (Park & Folkman, 1997). So meaning arises as much out of the specific events in our lives—what happens to us—as it does the needs for purpose, values, and efficacy. That is, people create meaning in response to a health crisis (e.g., cancer), the loss of a loved one, academic failure, unemployment, and career burnout (Baumeister & Vohs, 2002). People who successfully create meaning within a particular life experience typically do so by first framing the event as a burden or bad event. They then explain how that bad event set in progress a developmental trajectory in which the bad event is ultimately translated into a positive outcome. In doing so, they essentially use the burden as a springboard to create a self endowed with strengths like purpose, moral goodness, and strong efficacy (McAdams, Diamond, de St. Aubin, & Mansfield, 1997). In contrast, people who do not counter life's burdens with purpose, moral goodness, and efficacy (i.e., meaning) are significantly more likely to suffer mental pathology in the wake of the bad event (McAdams, 1993, 1996). From this point of view, the act of creating meaning helps prevent future sickness (e.g., depression).

CRITICISMS

After spending a few hours reading Maslow, Rogers, or an article on positive psychology, it is easy to feel good and optimistic about yourself and about human beings in general. For instance, if you read any one of the 15 chapters in Rogers's (1980) *A Way of Being*, you will likely experience a sense of personal enrichment. Still, one must square the optimism of humanism with daily reality and wonder if it is not overly naive to conceptualize human nature as intrinsically good. If human nature is something to be nurtured rather than constrained, then one wonders why hatred, prejudice, crime, exploitation, and war persist throughout human history without interruption (Geller, 1982). Perhaps people are not so intrinsically honorable and trustworthy. Perhaps people have within themselves not only positive human potentialities but also the potential to destroy themselves and others (Baumeister & Campbell, 1999; May, 1982; Staub, 1999). One can imagine the potentially adverse consequences of a parent or a government that presupposes benevolent inner guides and therefore gives a wide lattitude to misbehaving children or citizens (Bandura, 1999). It seems that the humanistic view emphasizes only one part of human nature.

A second criticism is that humanistic theorists use a number of vague and ill-defined constructs. It is difficult to pinpoint precisely what an "organismic valuation process" and a "fully functioning individual" are, for example. Any theoretical construct that evades a precise operational definition must remain scientifically dubious. For this reason, humanistic views on motivation have been harshly criticized (Daniels, 1988; Neher, 1991). The critics essentially recommend we drop these quasi-scientific concepts. But there is a middle ground that recognizes the relative infancy or newness of humanistic study (O'Hara, 1989). So far in humanistic psychology's balance between method and topic, topic gets more attention than does method. As humanistic psychology matures, its study is slowly leaving behind armchair speculation in favor of a more scientific understanding of the origins, dynamics, and consequences of human potentiality. Evidence for this movement toward rigorous scientific methodologies is clearly seen in the emerging field of positive psychology.

A third criticism questions how one is to know what is *really* wanted or what is *really* needed by the actualizing tendency (Geller, 1982). Like an inherent actualizing tendency, early learning, socialization, and internalizations can also yield the personal conviction that a way of thinking or behaving is right and natural. For example, if a person is 100% confident that abortion is bad, wrong, and something to be refused, then how is that person to know for sure that such a preference is a product of the organismic valuation process rather than an internalization of societal conditions of worth? Knowledge of right and wrong can be difficult to trace back to the origins of its true source. If standards of right and wrong are introjected from infancy, a person can be self-deceived into thinking that their preferences are their own rather than their parents'.

"Feelingism" is a fourth criticism (Rowan, 1987). Humanism sometimes presents feelings as "the royal road to the true self" (to twist a Freudian phrase), such that feelings provide markers for identifying the inner guides of the actualizing tendency and organismic valuation process. "Feelingism" becomes a problem, however, when humanists afford feelings a conceptual status above all other aspects of experience, such as thinking. Some humanistic clinicians who practice group therapy do rather exhault feelingism, such as those spoofed in popular movies such as *Couch trip* starring Dan Akroyd. Collectively, these four criticisms strongly suggest that one's enthusiasm toward humanistic and positive psychology be constrained to recognize that they address only one piece of the overall motivation puzzle—not the whole puzzle of motivation study.

SUMMARY

Humanistic psychology stresses the notions of inherent potentialities, holism, and strivings toward personal fulfillment. In practice, humanistic psychology is about identifying and developing human potential. Positive psychology looks at people's mental health and how they live their lives to ask, "What could be?" In practice, positive psychology seeks to build people's strengths and competencies so to cultivate psychological wellness.

For Maslow, self-actualization referred to the full realization and use of one's talents, capacities, and potentialities. In his need hierarchy, Maslow made the distinction between deficiency needs and growth needs. Despite its intuitive appeal and widespread popularity, empirical research actually finds little support for the need hierarchy. Maslow's contribution to contemporary motivation study is not in the hierarchy but, rather, in his insights about why people fail to self-actualize and what actions they can take to encourage their personal growth toward self-actualization.

For Rogers, one fundamental need—the actualizing tendency—subsumed and coordinated all other motives so to serve the collective purpose of enhancing and actualizing the self. With socialization, children learn societal conditions of worth on which their behavior and personal characteristics are judged. As a consequence, all of us live in two worlds—the inner world of the actualizing tendencies and organismic valuation and the outer world of social priorities and conditions of worth. When people move away from organismic valuing and toward external conditions of worth, they adopt facades and reject or deny personal characteristics, preferences, and beliefs. The terms "congruence" and "incongruence" described the extent to which an individual denies and rejects personal qualities (incongruence) or accepts the full range of his personal characteristics and desires (congruence). The congruent, fully functioning individual lives in close proximity to the actualizing tendency and therefore experiences a marked sense of autonomy, openness to experience, and personal growth.

Causality orientations reflect the extent of self-determination in the personality and concern differences in people's understanding of what causes and regulates their behavior. For the person with an autonomy-causality orientation, behavior arises in response to needs and interests with a full sense of personal choice. For the person with a control-causality orientation, inner guides are relatively ignored. Instead, behavior arises in response to feelings of pressure to comply with what is expected or with what should be done. Autonomy-oriented individuals experience relatively greater positive functioning than do control-oriented individuals, including the long-term maintenance of the behavior changes they attempt to accomplish in their lives, such as losing a lot of weight.

A strong commitment to societal conditions of worth leads people into a process of seeking validation from others. In social interaction, validation-seeking individuals strive to prove their self-worth, competence, and likeability. In contrast, growth-seeking individuals center their strivings on learning, improving, and reaching personal potential. The distinction between the two is important for two reasons. First, validation-seeking individuals are more vulnerable to losing their sense of self-worth and to experiencing anxiety and depression. Second, the distinction between validation-seeking and growth-seeking is a nice way to express (1) Maslow's distinction between deficiency and growth needs and (2) Rogers' distinction between conditional positive regard and unconditional positive regard.

Interpersonal relationships support the actualizing tendency in at least four ways: helping others (as in therapy), relating to others in authentic ways, promoting the freedom to learn (as in education), and defining the self. Interpersonal relationships characterized by warmth, genuineness, empathy, interpersonal acceptance, and confirmation of the other person's capacity for self-determination provide the social climate that optimally supports the actualization tendency in another person. Another problem with which humanistic thinkers wrestle is that of evil—namely, how much of human nature is inherently evil and why do some people enjoy inflicting suffering on others? Some humanistic thinkers argue that evil is not inherent in human nature—that human nature is inherently good and evil arises only when experience injures and damages the person. Other humanists assume that both benevolence and malevolence are inherent in everyone—that human nature needs to internalize a benevolent value system before it can avoid evil.

Positive psychology looks at people's mental health and the quality of their lives to ask, "What could be?" It seeks to build people's strengths and competencies, and it makes the study of these strengths and competencies its subject matter. To illustrate how positive psychology investigates human strengths, the chapter looked in depth into optimism and meaning.

The chapter concludes by offering a number of criticisms of a humanistic understanding of motivation, including Pollyanna optimism, unscientific concepts, unknown origins of inner guides, and "feelingism."

READINGS FOR FURTHER STUDY

Humanistic Theorists

HARDEMAN, M. (1979). A dialogue with Abraham Maslow. *Journal of Humanistic Psychology, 19*, 23–28.

ROGERS, C. R. (1959). A theory of therapy, personality, and interpersonal relationships, as developed in the client-centered framework. In S. Koch (Ed.), *Psychology: A study of science* (Vol. 3, pp. 184–256). New York: McGraw-Hill.

ROGERS, C. R. (1995). What understanding and acceptance mean to me. *Journal of Humanistic Psychology, 35*, 7–22.

Empirical Tests of Humanistic Hypotheses

BAUMEISTER, R. F., & Campbell, W. K. (1999). The intrinsic appeal of evil: Sadism, sensational thrills, and threatened egotism. *Personality and Social Psychology Review, 3*, 210–221.

DECI, E. L., & Ryan, R. M. (1985). The General Causality Orientations Scale: Self-determination in personality. *Journal of Research in Personality, 19*, 109–134.

DYKMAN, B. M. (1998). Integrating cognitive and motivational factors in depression: Initial tests of a goal-orientation approach. *Journal of Personality and Social Psychology, 74*, 139–158.

FORD, J. G. (1991). Inherent potentialities of actualization: An initial exploration. *Journal of Humanistic Psychology, 31*, 65–88.

JENKINS, S. R. (1996). Self-definition in thought, action, and life path choices. *Personality and Social Psychology Bulletin, 22*, 99–111.

Positive Psychology

SELIGMAN, M. E. P., & CSIKSZENTMIHALYI, M. (2000). Positive psychology: An introduction. *American Psychologist, 55*, 5–14.

Chapter 16

Conclusion

Your neighbor drops by looking distressed and like she is at the end of her rope. Her daughter is doing very poorly in school and is even considering dropping out. Your neighbor's face turns serious as she seeks your advice, "What can I do? How can I motivate my daughter?" After reading and reflecting on 15 chapters in a book entitled, *Understanding Motivation and Emotion*, it has come down to this—to a knock on the door and the distressed face of a concerned parent. What can you recommend?

Would offering her a monetary incentive for good grades or for continued attendance be a good strategy? This is a popular strategy, but is it a good enough strategy that you would recommend it? What about suggesting that your neighbor talk to her daughter about school and what it means to her? The conversation could explore the daughter's interests and goals, about her sense of competence in school, about her future and the possible selves she embraces for herself, or about whether school can or cannot help her become the person she wants to become. Or, the conversation might focus on the quality of the relationships she has with her teachers. Would this be a good strategy? Would you recommend it? Can you suggest something better? You see before you a real motivational problem that is affecting the lives of people you care about, and you see the pain on the mother's face that tells you rather clearly that she has not been able to solve the problem. Can you do any better with this particular motivational problem?

Understanding motivation and emotion is an important and worthwhile undertaking because it pays off. That is, motivation produces. If we can learn how to motivate students, then we can improve students' engagement during learning activities. If we can learn how to motivate employees, then their productivity and job satisfaction increase. If we can learn how to motivate athletes, then their skills develop and they are more likely to become lifelong participants in their sport. If physicians can learn how to motivate their patients, then their health improves.

UNDERSTANDING AND APPLYING MOTIVATION

By now, you have gained some level of confidence in your own understanding of motivation and emotion. Just how much confidence you now possess likely depends on the extent to which you can do the following:

1. Explain why people do what they do.
2. Predict in advance how conditions will affect motivation and emotion.
3. Apply motivational principles to solve practical problems.

In the spirit of answering these three questions, this final chapter pursues three goals. The opening section checks on your understanding of motivation, asking questions such, Can you explain motivation? Can you explain why we do what we do? Can you explain why we want what we want and fear what we fear? Can you predict changes in people's motivation before they occur? Can you forecast the conditions under which motivational and emotional states will rise and fall? Can you apply principles of motivation to help people solve the practical and everyday problems they face in their lives? Can you help empower others to improve their performances and to overcome their motivational deficits or vulnerabilities? The more you can answer these questions, the more you will be able to explain, predict, and apply motivational principles.

The middle section of the chapter adopts a very practical tone. Its pages ask you to apply your knowledge about motivation, first, to the task of motivating the self and, second, to the task of motivating others.

The final section concludes the book by offering a series of case studies to stir your imagination about trying to solve common motivational problems. The section also presents a series of success stories in which motivational psychologists have designed and implemented interventions programs to improve people's lives.

Explaining Motivation: Why We Do What We Do

Explaining the reasons for behavior—explaining why we do what we do—requires the ability to generate psychologically satisfying answers to questions such, Why did he do that? Why does she want that? Why is he so afraid of or resistant against a particular course of action? Answers to these questions lie in understanding the source of motivation and how motives, once aroused, intensify, change, and fade.

To explain why we do what we do, Chapter 1 listed two dozen theories of motivation (see Table 1.5, page 18). Each theory provides a piece of the uncompleted puzzle that is the grand effort to explain human wants, desires, fears, and strivings. Working down the list of theories in Table 1.2, for instance, achievement motivation theory explains why people sometimes react to a standard of excellence with positive emotion and approach behavior but other times show negative emotion and seek only to avoid it. Learned helplessness theory explains why people turn markedly passive and self-defeating when they are exposed to an environment in which they think offers them little or no personal control. Collectively, these theories address most of the circumstances in which the reader might be interested.

To explain motivational states, it helps to have an empirically validated and familiar motivation theory at your side. The theory will explain why a particular motivational phenomenon rises, persists, and declines, and which particular conditions in the person, in the social context, and in the culture, affect the phenomenon in these ways. With such a theory in mind, it becomes easier to answer questions such as the following: Why do people set high goals for themselves? Why do people procrastinate when it is so obvious that there is work to be done? Why do people engage in risky behaviors like parachute jumping or driving really, really fast? Why do separated friends go to so much trouble to keep in touch? Taken together, motivation theories provide a means of understanding and explaining why we do what we do and why we want what we want.

Predicting Motivation: Identifying Antecedents

Motivation study pays close attention to the conditions that give rise to motivational and emotional states, asking questions such as, Which antecedent conditions energize and direct behavior? An understanding of motivation and emotion includes the ability to predict what effect various environmental, interpersonal, intrapsychic, and physiological conditions will have on motivation and emotion.

Consider the motivational implications of the following events. What are some expected motivational implications of being exposed to a highly competent role model? What implications does such an observational experience have for an elementary grade student who watches a peer solve math problems on the chalkboard? What about for a company salesperson who watches her supervisor interact smoothly and flawlessly with clients? What about for an athlete who watches a video-recorded performance of a champion performer? For the 4th-grade math student, the corporate employee, and the aspiring athlete, what effect will an exposure to an expert model have on their self-efficacy? On their goal setting? On their sense of mastery versus helpless? On the possible selves they might embrace? On their capacity for autonomous self-regulation?

Test yourself on a few antecedents covered in the earlier chapters. For each antecedent, check whether or not a helpful theory comes to mind that allows you to offer a confident prediction as to what effect that condition might have on a person's motivation:

- 24 hours of deprivation (from food, people)
- presence of a warm, genuine, and empathic friend who listens carefully
- cultural pressures (e.g., toward thinness or high grades)

- a choice of what to do
- an expected, tangible reward (e.g., money)
- a standard of excellence
- unresponsive, uncontrollable environments
- autonomy-supportive teacher
- feedback about one's goal-directed performance
- an obstacle to one's plans that seems illegitimate or unjust

Applying Motivation: Solving Problems

The more you understand the principles of motivation and emotion, the greater will become your capacity to find workable solutions to real-world motivational problems. Solving motivational problems means empowering people toward optimal experiences, healthy development, and positive functioning and away from immature defenses, intentional avoidance, and overwhelming negative emotionality.

The two questions that define the effort to apply motivational principles are, "How do I motivate myself?" and "How do I motivate others?" Motivationally empowering self and others involves amplifying strengths and repairing weaknesses. Amplifying strengths involves nurturing, supporting, and building motivational resources so that people can develop and use these resources to improve their functioning. Repairing weaknesses involves reversing motivational deficits so that people can reduce vulnerabilities and overcome pathologies. The implication is that finding workable solutions to the motivational problems of the self and others will lead to proportional gains in their functioning and well being.

Consider first the effort to amplify strengths and improve functioning—to increase effort in school, performance in athletics, productivity at work, resiliency in therapy, personal growth in old age, and so on. Each chapter provided some insight into the practical task of amplifying strengths, but here are some reminders. Test yourself again, this time by asking what could I do to promote this motivational state in myself and in others?

- promote resilient self-efficacy beliefs
- cultivate personal autonomy
- set up conditions that promote the flow experience
- nurture growth needs and become a fully functioning individual
- develop a mastery motivational orientation
- adopt positive social identities
- set difficult, specific goals
- encourage learning goals over performance goals
- encourage incremental theories over entity theories
- encourage differentiation and integration of the self
- nurture mature ego development
- enhance autonomous and more capable self-regulation

Consider, second, the effort to repair weaknesses and overcome pathology—student apathy, achievement anxiety, helplessness, depression, immature coping strategies, challenge avoidance, worker absenteeism, breakdowns in relationships, and breakdowns in regulation such as ignoring physiological cues for hunger or personal preferences for what one wants to do. Again, each chapter provided some insight into the effort to repair weaknesses and reverse vulnerabilities, but here are some reminders. Test yourself one final time by asking what could I do to overcome the pathology in myself and in others?

- promote a constructive rather than destructive reaction to failure
- avoid the hidden costs of reward
- reverse the restraint release that leads to binge eating
- channel aggressive impulses into productive outlets
- reverse doubt-plagued and fear-dominated decision making
- prevent helplessness and its deficits
- challenge entity thinking so to find the value in effort
- redefine the meaning of failure
- reverse pessimistic expectancies and explanatory styles
- overcome addictions
- solve the paradox of thought suppression
- identify immature defense mechanisms and find the courage to give them up

MOTIVATING SELF AND OTHERS

Much of the appeal in studying motivation lies in its potential to speak to motivating ourselves and others. We want to promote effort, achievement, challenge seeking, and excellence in self, and we want to promote these same outcomes for those who are important to us. We also want to help self and others reverse and overcome pessimism, anxiety, doubt, worry, hesitancy, and helplessness.

Motivating Self

Imagine that you cannot generate within yourself the motivation to study, exercise, or practice. How do you motivate a sense of initiative within yourself? Or, imagine that you cannot stop yourself from smoking, eating, or coping in an angry-hostile way. How do you motivate a sense of restraint within yourself? As one illustration, consider suffering through the motivational problem of hesitancy, procrastination, or outright avoidance in not really wanting to practice a skill, like playing the piano. How does one nurture engagement-fostering needs, cognitions, and emotions? How does one surround oneself with engagement-fostering environments and supportive interpersonal relationships?

In terms of needs, energy and direction might arise from a perception of competence or a need for achievement but might fall from a perception of incompetence and the fear of failure. In terms of cognition, energy and direction might arise from self-efficacy beliefs, mastery goals, or an optimistic explanatory style but might fall from doubt, a performance-avoidance goal, and a pessimistic explanatory style. In terms of emotion, energy and direction might arise from interest, joy, and hope but fall from fear, anger, and embarrassment. In terms of environments and relationships, energy and direction might arise from the challenge of a competition or an upcoming test or from the listening and informational feedback from an autonomy-supportive teacher but might fall from a critical audience or the directives and commands from a controlling teacher.

The effort to motivating the self, therefore, is to undertake a critical examination to diagnose potentials and deficits in one's current needs, cognitions, emotions, environmental surroundings, and interpersonal relationships. For instance, does playing the piano adequately challenge and involve one's competence need, or does it generally induce an experience of apathy or anxiety? Is one's piano-playing associated with expectations of efficacy, flow, and personal control, or with expectations of being overwhelmed by the experience? While playing the piano or while thinking about playing the piano in the future, does one feel mostly interest and joy or anger and resentment? As one plays, how do the people around you respond—are they supportive or demanding and pushy? If one can diagnose why approach motivation is low or why avoidance motivation is high, then constructive steps can be made toward solving the motivational problems and deficits one currently faces.

The effort to motivate self and the effort to motivate others differ in some important ways. Figure 16.1 shows that all efforts to motivate involve the introduction and management of environmental conditions, including the offering of incentives, optimal challenges, environmental threats, and interesting things to do (line b). What is unique about motivating the self, however, is the lifelong task of developing inner motivational resources, as shown in the figure's line a. What is unique about motivating others is the offering of high quality interpersonal relationships, as shown in the figures line c.

Cultivating inner motivational resources involves the developmental effort to build effectance motivation, strong and resilient self-efficacy beliefs, a mastery motivational orientation, robust personal control beliefs, achievement strivings, a healthy sense of self and identity, sense of competence, an autonomy causality orientation, mature defense mecha-

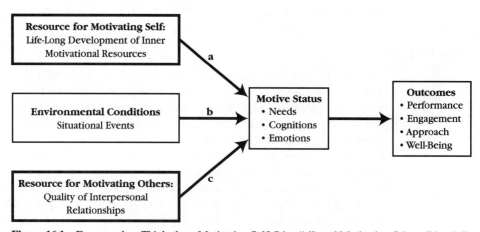

Figure 16.1 Framework to Think about Motivating Self (Line "a") and Motivating Others (Line "c")

nisms, the capacity for setting goals, self-regulation abilities, interests and preferences, an optimistic explanatory style, and so on. Developing inner motivational resource means growing one's approach-oriented needs, cognitions, and emotions. The more one cultivates and develops strong, resilient, and productive inner motivational resources over the life span, the more frequently he or she will experience strong, resilient, and productive motivational states in a given situation (see line a in Figure 16.1). For instance, when taking a foreign-language class in college, the student with a possible self of "traveler" or with an intention to one day become a "high school Spanish teacher" herself, then that student will engage in the college class with the motivational ally of an inner motivational resource (the possible self).

Given the motivational benefits of inner motivational resources, consider trying to solve the motivational problem of a fear of public speaking that motivates avoidance behavior. Part of the problem can be understood in the situation's environmental conditions (line b in Figure 16.1), as might be the case if one faces a hostile, critical, controlling, or competitive audience. So part of the problem can be found in the environment or in the person's perception of the environment. That not withstanding, the presence of inner motivational resources can support a speaker's motivation even in the face of a nonsupportive environment. People can build within themselves strong efficacy beliefs that can silence their doubt and anxiety. People can learn to leave behind their performance-avoidance goals ("during your speech, don't forget your lines") and adopt performance-approach goals ("during your speech, communicate three main points"). And people can learn to embrace incremental theories about their public speaking abilities to counter and replace their entity beliefs that leave them vulnerable to patterns of avoidance when things go wrong. So when people set goals, encounter failure feedback, or need to marshal great efforts to face the challenges in their lives, it helps if they have inner motivational resources to maintain a sense of purpose, buffer stress, silence doubt, and maintain positive emotionality.

The key to motivating self is the lifelong undertaking to cultivate a reservoire of productive inner motivational resources. From this point of view, much of the effort to motivate the self becomes the effort to figure out how to nurture inner motivational resources within oneself. Motivating the self is therefore not so much a situational event that one undertakes to solve today's problem as it is a developmental undertaking that one undertakes to empower the self throughout the lifetime.

Motivating Others

What is unique about motivating others is that the person facing a motivational problem does so within the context of an interpersonal relationship, as shown in line c in Figure 16.1. As one person attempts to motivate another, the person being motivated reacts in one of three prototypical ways—namely, passively, aggressively, or constructively (deCharms, 1987). Repeated interactions between the motivator and motivatee teaches the person who is trying to solve his or her motivational problem either (1) the passivity of amotivation and learned helplessness, (2) the aggressive negativity of stubborn reactance when others try to shape or control his or her thoughts and behaviors, or (3) the constructive cooperative effort of learning new ways of thinking, feeling, and behaving that change one's situation for the better.

BOX 16   *Four Case Studies*

Question: Why is this information important?

Answer: To build your capacity to explain, predict, and solve motivational problems.

Consider four case studies in which a different person faces a motivational issue. Use each case study to practice the three-fold task of (1) explaining, (2) predicting, and (3) applying motivation. The goal is to explain why the person's motivation is what it is, predict how his or her motivation would change in response to different events, and design an intervention attempt to intentionally affect the person's motivation for the better.

Child at Home

Child resists brushing her teeth at night before going to bed. She does not like it. She does not do it. And, when she does brush her teeth, she does it poorly and half-heartedly. But her parents see high value in her brushing and they encourage her to do so, though they dread having to deal with their daughter's resistance night after night.

Employee at Work

A sales representative for a large company receives a monthly sales quota from her supervisor and is told that everything is fine so long as she continues to meet or exceed her quota. She feels that she has the skills for the job, but job turnover among her follow employees is high because 90% of the calls she makes fail to produce a sell. The day-to-day experience on the job is one of rejection and frustration. She is thinking about quitting and looking for another job.

Athlete or Musician

An athlete (or musician) performs well, and she very much enjoys her sport (instrument). She loves to play and practice, but she would like to develop her talents further, much further in fact. For some reason, her rate of improvement recently has been slow. She wants to become an elite performer, but it does not seem to be happening.

Medical Patient

Physician tells the patient that he needs to lose 40 pounds or risk a heart attack. The patient understands the need to make a lifestyle change. Though he agrees with the idea, he is nevertheless pessimistic that he will ever take his physician's advice and make the lifestyle change. Exercise and a healthy diet are just not his thing. In his heart, he doubts that the lifestyle change is worth all the fuss.

The first two outcomes within the motivator-motivatee relationship are negative, as they pit motivatee against motivator. The third outcome of the relationship is positive and places the person into a learning-to-do-for-yourself, cooperative relationship between motivator and motivatee. With the third outcome, the person learns how to solve his own motivational problem, how to build his own skills, how to originate and initiate his own actions. In other words, he learns personal causation. Alternatively, manifestations of passivity or aggressive reactivity are tell-tale signs that the relationship is making the person's motivational problem worse, not better (deCharms, 1987).

Most attempts to motivate others take place within the context of a relationship that involves some interpersonal power differential between the motivator and the person being motivated (Deci & Ryan, 1987). For example, consider the following interpersonal relationships in which the first person has some responsibility for motivating the other: teachers motivating students, parents motivating children, employers motivating employees, doctors motivating patients, therapists motivating clients, coaches motivating athletes, clergy motivating parishioners, experts motivating novices, and therapists motivating clients.

In each relationship, the first person has some influence over the second, whether the basis of that influence manifests itself in expertise, rewards, force, status, or position. Consequently, the person who is one down in the relationship is vulnerable to being controlled or bossed around by the person who is one up in power. Controlling and bossing other people generally produces patterns of motivation that can be characterized as the passivity of helplessness or the aggressive negativity of reactance. This directive, take-charge approach to motivating others can be seen in military leaders, hard-line employers, extremely competitive athletic coaches, controlling teachers, take-charge politicians, authoritarian parents, and patronizing doctors.

Those who productively motivate others focus on the quality of the relationship they provide to those they seek to motivate. They seek to cultivate personal causation in others by using the relationship as a conduit to energize the constructive, cooperative, growth-promoting effort in less able, less powerful, or less motivated others to learn new and more adaptive ways of thinking, feeling, and behaving.

Given this introduction, it is helpful to ask two questions when trying to motivate others:

1. Who is motivating the person?
2. Is the social context supporting the person's personal causation and inner motivational resources, or is it robbing this person of these assets?

As to the first question, the motivator will be either the person himself, or it will be some outside force, such as a supervisor or coach. The second question presents any interpersonal relationship as a two-edged sword that can either support or undermine the person's motivation. These two questions point to the conclusion that, in the art and practice of motivating others, the primary goal is not to produce compliance or a predetermined pattern of desired behavior in the other but, instead, is to enhance the other's capacity for personal causation.

Feedback on How the Effort to Motivate Self and Others Is Going

Fostering initiative, agency, and personal causation in self and others is as much an art as it is a science. But, even artists need feedback. Ongoing changes in emotion, behavior, and well being make for excellent sources of feedback.

Emotions readout the status of a person's motivational status, as discussed in Chapter 12. When you engage in an activity and feel interest, enjoyment, and optimism, things are going well, motivationally speaking, and when you feel apathy, anger, and pessimism then things are not. And when you see interest, enjoyment, and optimism in those you try to motivate, things are likely going well; just as things are likely going poorly when those you try to motivate express apathy, anger, and pessimism.

Another feedback mechanism to use while motivating self and others is the expression of their overt behaviors, including effort, persistence, and latency to begin (as discussed in Chapter 1). Attempts to motivate self and others are going well in proportion to which behavior shows intense effort, short latency, long persistence, high probability of occurrence, facial and gestural expressiveness, and focus or goal-directedness.

Changes in vitality and well-being also signal motivational progress and growth versus motivational stagnation. Motives energize us, and improvements in our motivational states can been seen in the vitality and well-being we express.

When the reader relies on her knowledge of theories to generate motivational strategies, she can then attend closely to emotional, behavioral, and well-being feedback to signal how things are going in the art of motivating others. Once done, the reader will begin to realize the amazing capacity that an understanding of motivation and emotion has to improve people's lives.

DESIGNING MOTIVATIONAL INTERVENTIONS

After 15 chapters, I hope you will agree that those who study motivation and emotion know a lot. These researchers collectively devote an enormous amount of time and energy to developing, testing, and refining ever-more sophisticated theories of motivation. That is fine but, in some sense, the real payoff of motivation study is using that knowledge to improve people's lives. This section discusses several success stories of how those who study motivation have designed and implemented successful motivational interventions to improve people's lives in important ways.

Before looking at some of these success stories, however, it helps to take a step back and recognize just how difficult and precarious it can be to translate advances in scientific knowledge into practical improvements that change people's lives for the better. Consider the sorry success rate of medical research, for instance. Researchers have developed a successful vaccine for Alzheimer's in rats. They have enabled paralyzed rats with severe spinal cord injuries to walk again. And, they have cured an impressive range of different types of cancer in laboratory rats. Still, for humans, there is no cure for Alzheimer's, spinal cord injury, or cancer, not to mention multiple sclerosis, Parkinson's disease, osteoporosis, cystic fibrosis, etc. Many valid reasons exist to explain the gap between gains in theoretical understanding and success in practical applications of that knowledge, but the point is that practical application of theoretical knowledge is not something one can take for granted.

When you began reading this book, you likely did so with a sort of implicit agreement that if you labored through 450 pages of text, then, in the end, all this effort would pay off because you would gain some practical, real-world strategies to cope successfully with the motivational problems you cared about most. Fortunately, motivation researchers have been largely successful in their efforts to translate their theories into solutions, though this has been true only in the last decade or so.

Below are several case studies to spark your imagination of the motivational problems people face. These case studies are followed by four success stories in which those who study motivation have successfully applied their ideas to solve important motivational problems.

Four Case Studies

Consider the four case studies featured in Box 16. In each case, a person faces a different motivational issue. The child at home finds it difficult to generate the motivation she needs to engage in an uninteresting, devalued course of action. The salesperson faces the challenge of maintaining her confidence, interest, optimism and hope in the face of frequent failure and potential burnout. The athlete wants to develop talent and enhance performance, but is having a difficult time doing so. The patient faces the difficult, energy-demanding task of initiating and maintaining a lifestyle change.

In reading each case study, attempt to accomplish the three objectives listed in the beginning of this chapter—namely, explaining motivation, predicting motivation, and applying motivation. First, attempt to diagnose why the person is currently experiencing that particular motivational experience. You will not, of course, have access to the important details of his or her situation, but you can still generate a number of possible hypotheses to explain why the person is experiencing that level of motivation and that type of motivation. Second, once you have a couple of hypotheses to work with, identify the key sources of the person's motivation. What conditions could affect the person's motivation? Third, apply your knowledge of motivation to generate a productive course of action for each person to help them better generate the energy and direction they need in their day-to-day behavior to solve the motivation issue. As you read each case study and think about the person's needs, cognitions, emotions, environmental circumstances, and interpersonal relationships, recall the contents of the previous 15 chapters. Also, think about the larger developmental goals of building and amplifying strengths and also repairing weaknesses and reversing deficits.

Four Success Stories

If you look for them, you will see several attempts to design motivational interventions around you each day. At a health club, for instance, you might see a poster like the one in Figure 16.2 hanging on the wall next to the treadmill machines. The poster, in effect, is inviting the would-be runner to hop on the treadmill and start exercising by pursuing a series of short-term goals (daily 5 mile runs) that lead to a larger, long-term goal (26.2 miles). Running "My Marathon" is an explicit goal-setting program. Its motivational purpose is to create in the would-be runner an *intention to act,* that is, an intention to run. A health-club member with an intention to act will be more motivated than would a health-club member with no such intention to act. No data exist to evaluate whether this poster actually produces a motivational effect, and this is true for most of the motivational interventions you will encounter. But researchers make the effort to test the effectiveness of their motivational interventions, and some of their findings appear below.

One such goal-setting intervention occurred in a work setting. Researchers concerned with boosting working attendance worked with a group of employees to discuss ways to overcome the obstacles in their daily lives that were interfering with their ability to come to work (Frayne & Latham, 1987). During the intervention, the employees set specific, difficult goals for their attendance and attempts were made to improve their self-regulatory skills by monitoring ways in which their environment either helped or interfered with their attendance. Three months later, the employees' self-efficacy increased (as they become agents in exercising influence over their attendance behavior) as did their attendance, relative to a control group of workers who did not receive the intervention effort. A follow up study showed that the increases in self-efficacy and attendance both continued nine months later (Latham & Frayne, 1989).

My Marathon
Run 26.2 miles in 2 Weeks

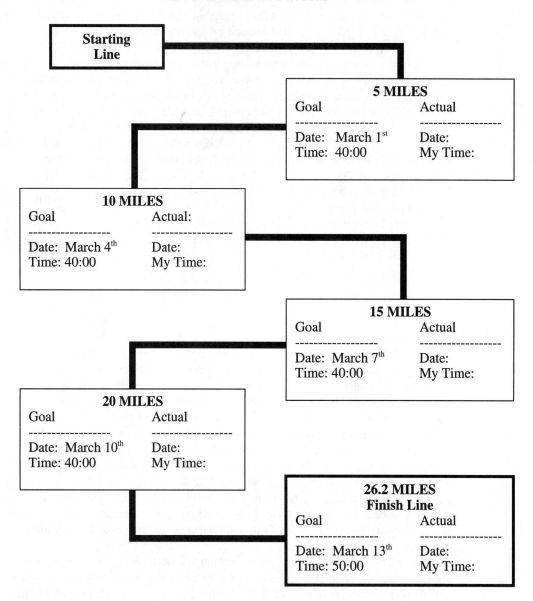

Figure 16.2 Motivational Poster to Encourage Goal Setting and the Expenditure of Effort

Attaining Personal Goals

In several studies, researchers worked with college students over the course of a semester to ask them to list several goals that they planned to strive for (Koestner, Lekes, Powers, & Chicoine, 2002). Some goals were academic (write a research paper), some goals were health-related (sleep at least 8 hours each night), while other goals were social, fun-related, or personal chores. The student also rated the extent to which each goal reflected their personal interests and values. Some students participated in an intervention program to set implementation intentions in which they learned to specify a time and a place for pursuing their goal. They also developed self-management plans by identifying possible sources of distraction and a counterbehavior for each distractor. One woman who set the goal of reading *Paradise Lost* specified a time and place in which the reading would occur and identified her boyfriend and phone interruptions as possible distractors. Her counter-behaviors included scheduling to see her boyfriend later in the day, turning off the phone, and reminding herself how important it was to finish the book.

On their own, students completed about 62% of the goals they set for themselves. Students completed a significantly higher percentage of the goals that were high in self-concordance (those that reflected their personal interests and values). Most importantly, participants in the experimental group were especially likely to accomplish their self-concordant goals for which they set implementation intentions. Participants also reported rather strong positive affect and well-being upon accomplishing their self-concordant goals. Thus, the unique combination of having both self-concordant goals and clear implementation intentions to overcome obstacles and distractions resulted in especially high levels of goal progress and accomplishment (and also a corresponding boost in positive affect). This success story shows that all the knowledge researchers have gained in understanding goal-setting, personal strivings, self-determination theory, and implementation intentions pays off by showing that people make maximal progress toward personal goals when they work deliberately through not only what they want to accomplish (goals) but also why they are pursuing these particular goals (self-concordance) and how they plan to reach them (implementation intentions).

Motivating Students

In one school, students were attending relatively infrequently and their academic achievement was poor. A team of motivation researchers volunteered to spend several years at the school working with teachers to bolster students' motivational development. Teachers received a workshop experience and on-going collaboration designed around the goal of promoting in their students a greater sense of "personal causation" (or perceived self-determination, an internal perceived locus of causality) in regard to their schoolwork (deCharms, 1976, 1984). The workshop involved a variety of activities, discussions, and self-assessments. For instance, one discussion focused on nurturing a desire to improve in students when that desire does not initially exist by introducing an ideal self that develops over time. One activity was to highlight what it motivationally felt like to be an "origin" (high self-determination, an internal locus of causality) versus a "pawn" (low self-determination, an external locus of causality). In this activity, the teacher passed out sheets of paper with numbers and dots. For students, the task was to connect the dots. The picture was of a simple house on the left with a tree on the right. Acting in an authoritarian way, the teacher treated the students like pawns by telling them to pick up their pencils, connect dot #1 to dot #2, put down their pencils, pick up their pencils, connect dot #2 to dot #3, put down their pencils, pick up their pencils, connect dot #3 to dot #4, et cetera. After the exercise, the teacher discussed the pawn concept with the students. The teacher asked them to think about other times in which they acted like Pawns or were treated like Pawns, and the discussions often lasted for the remainder of the class period. Two days later, the teacher introduced the "connect the dots" exercise a second time. This time, students were encouraged to be creative. They were to connect the dots in any way, add color and details. They were free to ask for help, but were encouraged to do it on their own. When done, the students discussed the origin concept with their teacher. This time the discussion centered on self-determination and being personally responsible for one's own work.

Some teachers in the school were randomly assigned into the experimental group (to receive the motivational training) while others were assigned into the control group. Researchers tracked all students' motivational development, attendance, and academic achievement through the 5th, 6th, and 7th grades. Fifth-grade scores served as a baseline measure, and researchers expected to see origin-like changes emerge in the 6th and 7th grades. The effort to support students' motivational development was a success, as shown in children's greater personal causation (or perceived self-determination; see left panel in Figure 16.3), achievement motivation (see middle panel in Figure 16.3), attendance, and academic achievement (see right panel in Figure 16.3). Follow-up studies showed a beneficial long-term effect for these middle school students as significantly more of the students with participating teachers graduated from high school than did students with teachers who did not participate in the motivational training (deCharms, 1984). This success story shows that motivation is often rooted in interpersonal relationships with others, and also that researchers can translate their knowledge of how to motivate others into classrooms capable on cultivating students' healthy motivational development.

Suppressing Hunger, Reversing Obesity

Most motivational interventions attempt to increase people's motivation. Some interventions, however, seek to decrease hyperactive motivational states that, because of their unusual intensity, are associated with unhealthy ways of behaving. Appetite and cravings can lead people to overeat and, hence, toward obesity, which is an unhealthy way of behaving because of its association with diabetes, heart disease, high blood pressure, and other health disorders. Researchers know that direct stimulation of certain brain sites can increase hunger while direct stimulation of other sites can increase satiety. A drug capable of targeting the excitation and inhibition of hunger-related brain structures can therefore affect the motivational experience of hunger. One such drug (Zonegran, or zonisamide) stimulates satiety via serotonin release, synthesis, and turnover (reuse) in the striatum, and it also alters taste by taking some of the pleasure out of high calorie foods via dopamine agonists (inhibitors) in the striatum.

Knowing this, researchers gave the drug to 30 obese adults for 12 weeks and tracked their week-by-week weight loss (Gadde, Franciscy, Wagner, & Krishnan, 2003). While

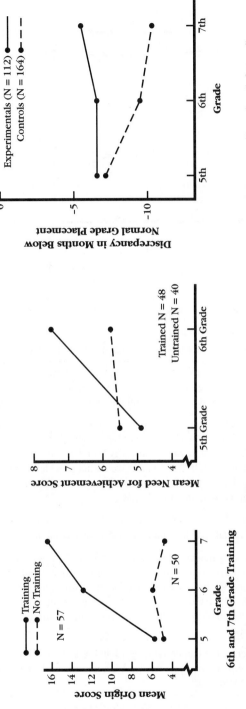

Figure 16.3 Benefits to Students When their Teachers Promote their Motivational Development: Greater Personal Causation (left panel), Achievement Motivation (middle panel), and Academic Achievement (right panel)

Source: From "Enhancing Motivation: Change in the Classroom," by R. deCharms, 1976, New York: Irvington Publishers.

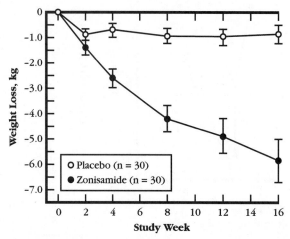

Figure 16.4 Pattern of Weight Change from Baseline to Week 16 in Obese Adults Who Took the Drug or a Placebo

Source: Gadde, K. M., Franciscy, D. M., Wagner II, H. R., & Krishnan, K. R. R. (2003). Zonisamide for weight loss in obese adults. *JAMA: Journal of the American Medical Association, 289*, 1820–1825.

Table 16.1 Parents' Attempt to Help Their Daughter Solve a Motivational Dilemma

Jennifer, 10 years old, has taken dance lessons since she was 4. In the fall, she announced to her parents that she was quitting dance in favor of team sports: basketball, softball, and soccer. "All my friends are playing on these teams," she told her father. "I'm tired of feeling left out."

Her parents anticipated a number of problems with this plan. First, Jennifer was not particularly good at team sports. On top of this, she was highly sensitive to the competitive aspects of sports. In other words, her feelings were often and easily hurt. Second, Jennifer had especially liked being in the limelight at dance recitals. Team sports would not provide such a loving showcase. Third, her parents had invested a great deal of time and money in dance lessons. Jennifer was finally getting good. It seemed an inopportune time to quit.

How could they handle this? Should they force Jennifer to continue dance because she had invested so much and could easily see how much Jennifer was giving up? What was best for their daughter?

Jennifer's mother, weighing all these complex issues, talked with her daughter about the possible consequences of quitting dance. She stressed, however, that the ultimate decision was Jennifer's. Jennifer stuck to her decision. She opted for sports. Although she was by no means a star, she made great progress in handling the competition and the inevitable disappointments. Her parents supported her at events and picked up the pieces when she was upset at the end of a losing game. Jennifer learned to persevere.

In late spring, much to her parent's surprise, Jennifer announced that she would like to dance again. She might continue in a team sport or two, but not as intensely. Her parents bit their tongues. There weren't any "I told you so's."

Source: Grolnick, W. S. (2003). *The psychology of parental control: How well-meant parenting backfires.* Mahwah, N.J.: Lawrence Erlbaum.

30 adults taking a placebo lost little weight, the adults taking the experimental drug consistently dropped pounds, as shown in Figure 16.4. The drug's motivational one-two punch (stimulate serotonin, stimulate dopamine agonists) stimulated satiety and made high-caloric foods taste blander. This success story shows that all the knowledge researchers have gained in understanding the motivated and emotional brain (Chapter 3) are beginning to pay off in important and literally life changing and health-promoting ways.

Autonomy-Supportive Parenting

The final success story is not a research investigation but, instead, a parent's story (Grolnick, 2003). Table 16.1 tells the story of how this parent negotiated the tricky task of supporting her daughter's motivational strivings during a difficult period. Common sense and popular books on parenting lead to advice like leading children down the path of optimal development with a take-charge controlling approach that uses tools like rewards and praise. Instead, what these parents did was acknowledge their daughter's feelings. They did not take control of their situation and impose their more experienced will on their daughter.

In brief, what these parents did right in motivating their daughter was that they supported her autonomy. In doing so, they successfully sidestepped the two pitfalls in motivating others by keeping at bay their daughter's amotivation/learned helplessness and aggressive reactance against the parents' intervention effort. They were able to motivate their daughter through a constructive do-it-for-yourself relationship.

On a larger level, the parent-researcher was able to do something more—something I hope the reader will also be able to do in the years to come. The parent used her deep understanding of motivation to help inform her understanding about what motivates her daughter. With this knowledge, she constructed an effective approach to motivating others.

References

Aarts, H., Dijksterhuis, A., & Midden, C. (1999). To plan or not to plan: Goal achievement of interrupting the performance of mundane behavior. *European Journal of Social Psychology, 29,* 971–979.

Abe, J. A. A., & Izard, C. E. (1999). The developmental functions of emotions: An analysis in terms of differential emotions theory. *Cognition and Emotion, 13,* 523–549.

Abramson, L. Y., & Alloy, L. B. (1980). Judgment of contingency: Errors and their implications. In A. Baum & J. Singer (Eds.), *Advances in environmental psychology: Applications of personal control* (Vol. 2, pp. 111-130). Hillsdale, NJ: Lawrence Erlbaum.

Adelmann, P. K., & Zajonc, R. B. (1989). Facial efference and the experience of emotion. *Annual Review of Psychology, 40,* 249–280.

Adkins, K. K., & Parker, W. (1996). Perfectionism and suicidal preoccupation. *Journal of Personality, 64,* 529–543.

Adolph, E. F. (1980). Intakes are limited: Satieties. *Appetite, 1,* 337–342.

Adolphs, R., Tranel, D., Damasio, H., & Damasio, A. (1994). Impaired recognition of emotion in facial expressions following bilateral damage to the human amygdala. *Nature, 372,* 669–672.

Aggleton, J. P. (1992). The functional effects of amygdala lesions in humans: A comparison with findings from monkeys. In J. P. Aggleton (Ed.), *The amygdala: Neurobiological aspects of emotion, memory, and mental dysfunction* (pp. 485–503). New York: Wiley.

Agnati, L. F., Bjelke, B., & Fuxe, K. (1992). Volume transmission in the brain. *American Scientist, 80,* 362–373.

Ainley, M., Hidi, S., & Berndorf, D. (2002). Interest, learning, and the psychological processes that mediate their relationship. *Journal of Educational Psychology, 94,* 545–561.

Ainsworth, M. D. S. (1989). Attachments beyond infancy. *American Psychologist, 44,* 709–716.

Ainsworth, M. D. S., Blehar, M. C., Waters, E., & Wall, S. (1978). *Patterns of attachment: A psychological study of the strange situation.* Hillsdale, NJ: Lawrence Erlbaum.

Alexander, P. A., Kulikowich, J. M., & Jetton, T. L. (1994). The role of subject-matter knowledge and interest in the processing of linear and nonlinear text. *Review of Educational Research, 64,* 201–252.

Algozzine, B., Browder, D., Karvonen, M., Test, D. W., & Wood, W. M. (2001). Effects of interventions to promote self-determination for individuals with disabilities. *Review of Educational Research, 71,* 219–277.

Allender, J. S., & Silberman, M. L. (1979). Three variations of student-directed learning: A research report. *Journal of Humanistic Psychology, 19,* 79–83.

Alloy, L. B., & Abramson, L. T. (1979). Judgment of contingency in depressed and nondepressed students: Sadder but wiser? *Journal of Experimental Psychology: General, 108,* 441–485.

Alloy, L. B., & Abramson, L. T. (1982). Learned helplessness, depression, and the illusion of control. *Journal of Personality and Social Psychology, 42,* 1114–1126.

Alloy, L. B., & Abramson, L. Y. (1988). Depressive realism: Four theoretical approaches. In L. B. Alloy (Ed.), *Cognitive processes in depression* (pp. 223–265). New York: Guilford.

Alloy, L. B., & Seligman, M. E. P. (1979). On the cognitive component of learned helplessness and depression. *The Psychology of Learning and Motivation, 13,* 219–276.

Amabile, T. M. (1979). Effects of external evaluations on artistic creativity. *Journal of Personality and Social Psychology, 37,* 221–233.

Amabile, T. M. (1983). *The social psychology of creativity.* New York: Springer-Verlag.

Amabile, T. M. (1985). Motivation and creativity: Effect of motivational orientation on creative writers. *Journal of Personality and Social Psychology, 48,* 393–399.

Amabile, T. M. (1998). How to kill creativity. *Harvard Business Review, 76,* 76–87.

Amabile, T. M., DeJong, W., & Lepper, M. R. (1976). Effects of externally-imposed deadlines on subsequent intrinsic motivation. *Journal of Personality and Social Psychology, 34*, 92–98.

Amabile, T. M., Hennessey, B. A., & Grossman, B. S. (1986). Social influences on creativity: The effects of contracted-for reward. *Journal of Personality and Social Psychology, 50*, 14–23.

American Psychiatric Association. (1994). *Diagnostic and statistical manual of mental disorders* (4th ed.), Washington, DC: American Psychiatric Association.

Ames, C. A. (1987). Enhancing student motivation. In M. Maehr & D. Kleiber (Eds.), *Recent advances in motivation and achievement: Enhancing motivation* (Vol. 5, pp. 123–148). Greenwich, CT: JAI Press.

Ames, C. A., & Archer, J. (1988). Achievement goals in the classroom: Student learning strategies and motivational processes. *Journal of Educational Psychology, 80*, 260–267.

Ames, R., & Ames, C. A. (1984). Introduction. In R. Ames & C. A. Ames (Eds.), *Research on motivation in education: Student motivation* (Vol. 1, pp. 1–11). Orlando, FL: Academic Press.

Anand, B. K., Chhina, G. S., & Singh, B. (1962). Effect of glucose on the activity of hypothalamic feeding centers. *Science, 138*, 597–598.

Anastasi, A. (1982). *Psychological testing* (5th ed.). New York: Macmillan.

Andersen, B. L., & Cyranowski, J. M. (1994). Women's sexual self-schema. *Journal of Personality and Social Psychology, 67*, 1079–1100.

Anderson, C. A. (1989). Temperature and aggression: Ubiquitous effects of heat on occurrence of human violence. *Psychological Bulletin, 106*, 74–106.

Anderson, G., & Brown, R. I. (1984). Real and laboratory gambling sensation seeking and arousal. *British Journal of Psychology, 5*, 401–411.

Anderson, K. J. (1990). Arousal and the inverted-U hypothesis: A critique of Neiss's Reconceptualizing arousal. *Psychological Bulletin, 107*, 96–100.

Anderson, R., Manoogian, S. T., & Reznick, J. S. (1976). The undermining and enhancing of intrinsic motivation in preschool children. *Journal of Personality and Social Psychology, 34*, 915–922.

Andreassi, J. L. (1986). *Psychophysiology: Human behavior and physiological response* (2nd ed.). Hillsdale, NJ: Lawrence Erlbaum.

Applerloo, M. J. A., van der Stege, J. G., Hoek, A., & Schultz, W. C. M. W. (2003). In the mood for sex: The value of androgens. *Journal of Sex and Marital Therapy, 29*, 87–102.

Appley, M. H. (1991). Motivation, equilibration, and stress. In R. A. Dienstbier (Ed.), *Nebraska symposium on motivation* (Vol. 38, pp. 1–67). Lincoln: University of Nebraska Press.

Arnett, J. (1991). Still crazy after all these years: Reckless behavior among young adults aged 23–27. *Personality and Individual Differences, 12*, 1305–1313.

Arnold, M. B. (1960). *Emotion and personality* (Vols. 1 & 2). New York: Columbia University Press.

Arnold, M. B. (1970). Perennial problems in the field of emotion. In M. B. Arnold (Ed.), *Feelings and emotions* (pp. 169–185). New York: Academic Press.

Aronson, E. (1969). The theory of cognitive dissonance: A current perspective. In L. Berkowitz (Ed.), *Advances in experimental social psychology* (Vol. 4, pp. 1–34). New York: Academic Press.

Aronson, E. (1988). *The social animal* (5th ed.). San Francisco: W. H. Freeman.

Aronson, E. (1992). The return of the repressed: Dissonance theory makes a comeback. *Psychological Inquiry, 3*, 303–311.

Aronson, E. (1999). Dissonance, hypocrisy, and the self-concept. In E. Harmon-Jones & J. Mills (Eds.), *Cognitive dissonance: Progress on a pivotal theory in social psychology* (pp. 103–126). Washington, DC: American Psychological Association.

Aronson, E., Fried, C. B., & Stone, J. (1991). Overcoming denial and increasing the intention to use condoms through the induction of hypocrisy. *American Journal of Public Health, 81*, 1636–1637.

Aronson, E., & Mills, J. (1959). The effect of severity of initiation on liking for a group. *Journal of Abnormal and Social Psychology, 59*, 177–181.

Ashby, F. G., Isen, A. M., & Turken, A. U. (1999). A neuropsychological theory of positive affect and its influence on cognition. *Psychological Review, 106*, 529–550.

Aspinwall, L. G. (1998). Rethinking the role of positive affect in self-regulation. *Motivation and Emotion, 22*, 1–32.

Atkinson, J. W. (1957). Motivational determinants of risk-taking behavior. *Psychological Review, 64*, 359–372.

Atkinson, J. W. (1964). A theory of achievement motivation. In *An introduction to motivation* (pp. 240–268). New York: Van Nostrand.

Atkinson, J. W. (1981). Studying personality in the context of an advanced motivational psychology. *American Psychologist, 36*, 117–128.

Atkinson, J. W. (1982). Motivational determinants of thematic apperception. In A. J. Stewart (Ed.), *Motivation and society* (pp. 3–40). San Francisco: Jossey-Bass.

Atkinson, J. W., & Birch, D. (Eds.). (1970). *The dynamics of action.* New York: Wiley.

Atkinson, J. W., & Birch, D. (1974). The dynamics of achievement-oriented activity. In J. W. Atkinson & J. O. Raynor (Eds.), *Motivation and achievement* (pp. 271–325). Washington, DC: Van Nostrand Reinhold.

Atkinson, J. W., & Birch, D. (1978). *Introduction to motivation* (2nd ed.). New York: Van Nostrand.

Atkinson, J. W., Bongort, K., & Price, L. H. (1977). Explorations using computer simulation to comprehend TAT measurement of motivation. *Motivation and Emotion, 1*, 1–27.

Atkinson, J. W., Heyns, R. W., & Veroff, J. (1954). The effect of experimental arousal of the affiliation motive on thematic apperception. *Journal of Abnormal and Social Psychology, 49*, 405–410.

Atran, S. (2003). Genesis of suicide terrorism. *Science, 299*, 1534–1539.

Austin, J., Alvero, A., & Olson, R. (1998). Prompting patron safety-belt use at a restaurant. *Journal of Applied Behavior Analysis, 31*, 655–657.

Austira, J., Hatfield, D. B., Grindle, A. C., & Bailey, J. S. (1993). Increasing recycling in office environments: The effects of specific, informative cues. *Journal of Applied Behavior Analysis, 26*, 247–253.

Ausubel, D. P. (1977). The facilitation of meaningful verbal learning in the classroom. *Educational Psychologist, 12*, 162–178.

Averill, J. R. (1968). Grief: Its nature and significance. *Psychological Bulletin, 70*, 721–748.

Averill, J. R. (1979). The functions of grief. In C. Izard (Ed.), *Emotions in personality and psychopathology* (pp. 339–368). New York: Plenum.

Averill, J. R. (1980). A constructivist view of emotion. In R. Plutchik & H. Kellerman (Eds.), *Theories of emotion* (pp. 305–340). New York: Academic Press.

Averill, J. R. (1982). *Anger and aggression: An essay on emotion.* New York: Springer-Verlag.

Averill, J. R. (1983). Studies on anger and aggression. *American Psychologist, 38*, 1145–1160.

Averill, J. R. (1985). The social construction of emotion: With special reference to love. In K. Gergen & K. Davis (Eds.), *The social construction of the person* (pp. 89–109). New York: Springer-Verlag.

Averill, J. R. (1990). Emotions as related to systems of behavior. In N. L. Stein, B. Leventhal, & T. Trabasso (Eds.), *Psychological and biological approaches to emotion* (pp. 385–404). Hillsdale, NJ: Lawrence Erlbaum.

Averill, J. R. (1994). In the eyes of the beholder. In P. Ekman & R. J. Davidson (Eds.), *The nature of emotion: Fundamental questions* (pp. 7–14). New York: Oxford University Press.

Azar, B. (1994, October). Seligman recommends a depression vaccine. *APA Monitor, 27*, 4.

Azar, B. (2000, January). Two computer programs 'face' off. *Monitor on Psychology*, 48–49.

Azrin, N. H., Rubin, H., O'Brien, F., Ayllon, T., & Roll, D. (1968). Behavioral engineering: Postural control by a portable operant apparatus. *Journal of Applied Behavior Analysis, 2*, 39–42.

Bailey, J. M., Gavlin, S., Agyei, Y., & Gladue, B. A. (1994). Effects of gender and sexual orientation on evolutionary relevant aspects of human mating psychology. *Journal of Personality and Social Psychology, 66*, 1081–1093.

Bailey, J. M., & Pillard, R. C. (1991). A genetic study of the male sexual orientation. *Archives of General Psychiatry, 48*, 1089–1096.

Bailey, J. M., Pillard, R. C., Neale, M. C., & Agyei, Y. (1993). Heritable factors influence sexual orientation in women. *Archives of General Psychiatry, 50*, 217–223.

Baize, H. R., & Schroeder, J. E. (1995). Personality and mate selection in personal ads: Evolutionary preferences in a public mate selection process. *Journal of Social Behavior and Personality, 10*, 517–536.

Baldwin, J. D., & Baldwin, J. I. (1986). *Behavior principles in everyday life* (2nd ed.). Englewood Cliffs, NJ: Prentice-Hall.

Banaji, M., & Hardin, C. (1996). Automatic stereotyping. *Psychological Science, 7*, 136–141.

Bandura, A. (1977). Self-efficacy: Toward a unifying theory of behavioral change. *Psychological Review, 84*, 191–215.

Bandura, A. (1982). Self-efficacy mechanism in human agency. *American Psychologist, 37*, 122–147.

Bandura, A. (1983). Self-efficacy mechanisms of anticipated fears and calamities. *Journal of Personality and Social Psychology, 45*, 464–469.

Bandura, A. (1986). Self-efficacy. In *Social foundations of thought and action: A social cognitive theory* (pp. 390–453). Englewood Cliffs, NJ: Prentice-Hall.

Bandura, A. (1988). Self-efficacy conception of anxiety. *Anxiety Research, 1*, 77–98.

Bandura, A. (1989). Human agency in social cognitive theory. *American Psychologist, 44*, 1175–1184.

Bandura, A. (1990). Conclusion: Reflections on nonability determinants of competence. In R. J. Sternberg & J. Kolligian Jr. (Eds.), *Competence considered* (pp. 315–362). New Haven, CT: Yale University Press.

Bandura, A. (1991). Self-regulation of motivation through anticipatory and self-regulatory mechanisms. In R. A. Dienstbier (Ed.), *Nebraska symposium on motivation: Perspectives on motivation* (Vol. 38, pp. 69–164). Lincoln: University of Nebraska Press.

Bandura, A. (1993). Perceived self-efficacy in cognitive development and functioning. *Educational Psychologist, 28*, 117–148.

Bandura, A. (1997). *Self-efficacy: The exercise of control.* New York: W. H. Freeman.

Bandura, A. (1998). Health promotion from the perspective of social cognitive theory. *Psychological Health, 13*, 623–649.

Bandura, A. (1999). Moral disengagement in the perpetration of inhumanities. *Personality and Social Psychology Review, 3*, 193–209.

Bandura, A., & Adams, N. E. (1977). Analysis of self-efficacy theory of behavioral change. *Cognitive Therapy and Research, 1*, 287–308.

Bandura, A., Adams, N. E., Hardy, A. B., & Howells, G. N. (1980). Tests of the generality of self-efficacy theory. *Cognitive Therapy and Research, 4*, 39–66.

Bandura, A., & Cervone, D. (1983). Self-evaluative and self-efficacy mechanisms governing the motivational effects of goal systems. *Journal of Personality and Social Psychology, 45*, 1017–1028.

Bandura, A., & Cervone, D. (1986). Differential engagement of self-reactive influences in cognitive motivation. *Organizational Behavior and Human Decision Processes, 38*, 92–113.

Bandura, A., Cioffi, D., Taylor, C. B., & Brouillard, M. E. (1988). Perceived self-efficacy in coping with cognitive stressors and opioid activation. *Journal of Personality and Social Psychology, 55*, 479–488.

Bandura, A., Reese, L., & Adams, N. E. (1982). Microanalysis of action and fear arousal as a function of differential levels of perceived self-efficacy. *Journal of Personality and Social Psychology, 43*, 5–21.

Bandura, A., & Schunk, D. H. (1981). Cultivating competence, self-efficacy, and intrinsic interest through proximal self-motivation. *Journal of Personality and Social Psychology, 41*, 586–598.

Bandura, A., Taylor, C. B., Williams, S. L., Mefford, I. N., & Barchas, J. D. (1985). Catecholamine secretion as a function of perceived coping self-efficacy. *Journal of Consulting and Clinical Psychology, 53*, 406–414.

Bandura, A., & Wood, R. E. (1989). Effect of perceived controllability and performance standards on self-regulation of complex decision making. *Journal of Personality and Social Psychology, 56*, 805–814.

Barrett, K. C. (1995). A functionalist approach to shame and guilt. In J. P. Tangney & K. W. Fischer (Eds.), *Self-conscious emotions: The psychology of shame, guilt, embarrassment, and pride* (pp. 25–63). New York: Guilford Press.

Bassett, G. A. (1979). A study of the effects of task goal and schedule choice on work performance. *Organizational Behavior and Human Performance, 24*, 202–227.

Basson, R. (2001). Human sex-response cycles. *Journal of Sex and Marital Therapy, 27*, 33–43.

Basson, R. (2002). Women's sexual desire—disordered or misunderstood? *Journal of Sex and Marital Therapy, 28*, 17–28.

Basson, R. (2003). Commentary on "In the mood for sex—The value of androgens." *Journal of Sex and Marital Therapy, 29*, 177–179.

Batson, C. D. (1991). *The altruism question: Toward a social-psychological answer*. Hillsdale, NJ: Lawrence Erlbaum.

Batson, C. D., Coke, J. S., Chard, F., Smith, D., & Taliaferro, A. (1979). Generality of the "glow of goodwill": Effects of mood on helping and information acquisition. *Social Psychology Quarterly, 42*, 176–179.

Baucom, D. H., & Aiken, P. A. (1981). Effect of depressed mood on eating among obese and nonobese dieting and nondieting persons. *Journal of Personality and Social Psychology, 41*, 577–585.

Baumeister, R. F. (1987). How the self became a problem: A psychological review of historical research. *Journal of Personality and Social Psychology, 52*, 163–176.

Baumeister, R. F., & Campbell, W. K. (1999). The intrinsic appeal of evil: Sadism, sensational thrills, and threatened egotism. *Personality and Social Psychology Review, 3*, 210–221.

Baumeister, R. F., Campbell, J. D., Krueger, J. I., & Vohs, K. D. (2003). Does high self-esteem cause better performance, interpersonal success, happiness, or healthier lifestyles? *Psychological Science in the Public Interest, 4*, 1–44.

Baumeister, R. F., Heatherton, T. F., & Tice, D. M. (1994). *Losing control: How and why people fail at self-regulation*. San Diego: Academic Press.

Baumeister, R. F., & Leary, M. R. (1995). The need to belong: Desire for interpersonal attachments as a fundamental human motivation. *Psychological Bulletin, 117*, 497–529.

Baumeister, R. F., Smart, L., & Boden, J. M. (1996). Relation of threatened egotism to violence and aggression: The dark side of self-esteem. *Psychological Review, 103*, 5–33.

Baumeister, R. F., Stillwell, A. M., & Heatherton, T. F. (1995). Interpersonal aspects of guilt: Evidence from narrative studies. In J. P. Tangney & K. W. Fischer (Eds.), *Self-conscious emotions: The psychology of shame, guilt, embarrassment, and pride* (pp. 255–273). New York: Guilford Press.

Baumeister, R. F., & Vohs, K. D. (2002). The pursuit of meaningfulness in life. In C. R. Snyder & S. J. Lopez (Eds.), *Handbook of positive psychology* (pp. 608–618). New York: Oxford University Press.

Beach, F. A. (1955). The descent of instinct. *Psychological Review, 62*, 401–410.

Beatty, W. W. (1982). Dietary variety stimulates appetite in females but not in males. *Bulletin of the Psychonomic Society, 19*, 212–214.

Beauvois, J. L., & Joule, R. V. (1996). *A radical dissonance theory*. London: Taylor & Francis.

Beck, A. T. (1976). *Cognitive therapy and the emotional disorders*. New York: International Universities Press.

Beck, A. T., Rush, A. J., Shaw, B. F., & Emery, G. (1979). *Cognitive therapy of depression*. New York: Guilford Press.

Beck, R. C. (1979). Roles of taste and learning in water regulation. *Behavioral and Brain Sciences, 1*, 102–103.

Beck, S. P., Ward-Hull, C. I., & McLear, P. M. (1976). Variable related to women's somatic preferences of the male and female body. *Journal of Personality and Social Psychology, 34*, 1200–1210.

Becker, L. J. (1978). Joint effect of feedback and goal setting on performance: A field study of residential energy conservation. *Journal of Applied Psychology, 63*, 428–433.

Belfoire, P. J., Browder, D. M., & Mace, C. (1994). Assessing choice making and preference in adults with profound mental retardation across community and center-based settings. *Journal of Behavioral Education, 4*, 217–225.

Bell, A. P., Weinberg, M. S., & Hammersmith, S. K. (1981). *Sexual preference: Its development in men and women*. Bloomington: Indiana University Press.

Bem, D. J. (1967). Self-perception: An alternative interpretation of cognitive dissonance phenomena. *Psychological Review, 74*, 183–200.

Bem, D. J. (1972). Self-perception theory. In L. Berkowitz (Ed.), *Advances in experimental social psychology* (Vol. 6, pp. 1–62). New York: Academic Press.

Bem, D. J., & McConnell, H. K. (1970). Testing the self-perception explanation of dissonance phenomena: On the salience of premanipulation attitudes. *Journal of Personality and Social Psychology, 14*, 23–31.

Beninger, R. J. (1982). The behavioral function of dopamine. *Behavioral and Brain Sciences, 5*, 55–56.

Beninger, R. J. (1983). The role of dopamine in locomotor activity and learning. *Brain Research, 287*, 173–196.

Benjamin, L. T., Jr., & Jones, M. R. (1978). From motivational theory to social cognitive development: Twenty-five years of the Nebraska Symposium. *Nebraska symposium on motivation* (Vol. 26, pp. ix–xix). Lincoln: University of Nebraska Press.

Bennett, W. I. (1995). Beyond overeating. *New England Journal of Medicine, 332*, 673–674.

Benware, C., & Deci, E. L. (1984). The quality of learning with an active versus passive motivational set. *American Educational Research Journal, 21*, 755–765.

Berenbaum, S. A., & Snyder, E. (1995). Early hormonal influences on childhood sex-typed activity and playmate preferences: Implications for the development of sexual orientation. *Developmental Psychology, 31*, 31–42.

Bergmann, G., & Spence, K. W. (1941). Operationalism and theory construction. *Psychological Review, 48*, 1–14.

Berkowitz, L. (1962). *Aggression: A social psychological analysis*. New York: McGraw-Hill.

Berlyne, D. E. (1966). Curiosity and exploration. *Science, 153*, 25–33.

Berlyne, D. E. (1967). Arousal and reinforcement. In D. Levine (Ed.), *Nebraska symposium on motivation* (Vol. 15, pp. 1–110). Lincoln: University of Nebraska Press.

Berlyne, D. E. (1975). Behaviourism? Cognitive theory? Humanistic psychology? To Hull with them all. *Canadian Psychological Review, 16*, 69–80.

Berman, L. A., & Berman, J. R. (2000). Viagra and beyond: Where sex educators and therapists fit in from a multidisciplinary perspective. *Journal of Sex Education and Therapy, 25*, 17–24.

Bernard, L. L. (1924). *Instinct: A study of social psychology*. New York: Holt.

Bernieri, F. J., & Rosenthal, R. (1991). Interpersonal coordination: Behavior matching and interactional synchrony. In R. S. Feldman & B. Rimeí (Eds.), *Fundamentals of nonverbal behavior* (pp. 401–432). New York: Cambridge University Press.

Berry, D. S., & McArthur, L. Z. (1985). Some components and consequences of a babyface. *Journal of Personality and Social Psychology, 48*, 312–323.

Berry, D. S., & McArthur, L. Z. (1986). Perceiving character in faces: The impact of age-related craniofacial changes on social perception. *Psychological Bulletin, 100*, 3–18.

Berry, J. M., & West, R. L. (1993). Cognitive self-efficacy in relation to personal mastery and goal setting across the life span. *International Journal of Behavioral Development, 16*, 351–379.

Berry, S. L., Beatty, W. W., & Klesges, R. C. (1985). Sensory and social influences on ice cream consumption by males and females in a laboratory setting. *Appetite, 6*, 41–45.

Betz, N. E., & Hackett, G. (1986). Applications of self-efficacy theory to understanding career choice behavior. *Journal of Social and Clinical Psychology, 4*, 279–289.

Bexton, W. H., Heron, W., & Scott, T. H. (1954). Effects of decreased variation in the sensory environment. *Canadian Journal of Psychology, 8*, 70–66.

Binder, L. M., Dixon, M. R., & Ghezzi, P. M. (2000). A procedure to teach self-control to children with attention deficit hyperactivity disorder. *Journal of Applied Behavior Analysis, 33*, 233–237.

Bindra, D. (1959). *Motivation: A systematic reinterpretation.* New York: Ronald Press.

Bindra, D. (1979). *Motivation, the brain, and psychological theory.* Unpublished manuscript, Psychology Department, McGill University, Montreal.

Birch, H. G. (1956). Sources of odor in maternal behavior in animals. *American Journal of Orthopsychiatry, 26*, 279–284.

Birch, L. L., & Fisher, J. A. (1996). The role of experience in the development of children's eating behavior. In E. D. Capaldi (Ed.), *Why we eat what we eat: The psychology of eating.* Washington, DC: American Psychological Association.

Birch, L. L., Johnson, S. L., Anderson, G., Peters, J. C., & Schulte, M. C. (1991). The variability of young children's energy-intake. *New England Journal of Medicine, 324*, 232–235.

Birch, L. L., Zimmerman, S. I., & Hind, H. (1980). The influence of social affective context on the formation of children's food preferences. *Child Development, 51*, 856–861.

Birney, R. C., Burdick, H., & Teevan, R. C. (1969). *Fear of failure.* New York: Van Nostrand.

Blackburn, G. (1995). Effect of degree of weight loss on health benefits. *Obesity Research, 3*, 211S.

Blai, B., Jr. (1964). An occupational study of job satisfaction and need satisfaction. *Journal of Experimental Education, 32*, 383–388.

Blais, M. R., Sabourin, S., Boucher, C., & Vallerand, R. J. (1990). Toward a motivational model of couple happiness. *Journal of Personality and Social Psychology, 59*, 1021–1031.

Blanchard, D. C., & Blanchard, R. J. (1972). Innate and conditioned reactions to threat in rats with amygdaloid lesions. *Journal of Comparative Psychological Psychology, 81*, 281–290.

Blandler, R. (1988). Brain mechanisms of aggression as revealed by electrical and chemical stimulation: Suggestions of a central role for the midbrain periaqueductal grey region. In A. N. Epstein & J. M. Sprague (Eds.), *Progresses in psychobiology and physiological psychology* (Vol. 13, pp. 67–154). San Diego, CA: Academic Press.

Blank, P. D., Reis, H. T., & Jackson, L. (1984). The effects of verbal reinforcements on intrinsic motivation for sex-linked tasks. *Sex Roles, 10*, 369–387.

Blankenship, V. (1987). A computer-based measure of resultant achievement motivation. *Journal of Personality and Social Psychology, 53*, 361–372.

Blascovich, J., Brennan, K., Tomaka, J., Kelsey, R. M., Hughes, P., Coad, M. L., & Adlin, R. (1992). Affect intensity and cardiac arousal. *Journal of Personality and Social Psychology, 63*, 164–174.

Blasi, A. (1976). Concept of development in personality theory. In J. Loevinger (Ed.), *Ego development* (pp. 29–53). San Francisco: Jossey-Bass.

Blass, E. M., & Hall, W. G. (1976). Drinking termination: Interactions among hydrational, Orogastric, and behavioral controls in rats. *Psychological Review, 83,* 356–374.

Blatt, S. J. (1994). *Therapeutic change: An objects relations approach.* New York: Plenum.

Blatt, S. J. (1995). The destructiveness of perfectionism: Implications for the treatment of depression. *American Psychologist, 50,* 1003–1020.

Boggiano, A. K., & Barrett, M. (1985). Performance and motivational deficits of helplessness: The role of motivational orientations. *Journal of Personality and Social Psychology, 49,* 1753–1761.

Boggiano, A. K., Barrett, M., Weiher, A. W., McClelland, G. H., & Lusk, C. M. (1987). Use of the maximal-operant principle to motivate children's intrinsic interest. *Journal of Personality and Social Psychology, 53,* 866–879.

Boggiano, A. K., Flink, C., Shields, A., Seelbach, A., & Barrett, M. (1993). Use of techniques promoting students' self-determination: Effects on students' analytic problem-solving skills. *Motivation and Emotion, 17,* 319–336.

Boggiano, A. K., Main, D. S., & Katz, P. A. (1988). Children's preference for challenge: The role of perceived competence and control. *Journal of Personality and Social Psychology, 54,* 134–141.

Boggiano, A. K., & Ruble, D. N. (1979). Competence and the overjustification effect: A developmental study. *Journal of Personality and Social Psychology, 37,* 1462–1468.

Bolger, N. (1990). Coping as a personality process: A prospective study. *Journal of Personality and Social Psychology, 59,* 525–537.

Bolger, N., & Zuckerman, A. (1995). A framework for studying personality in the stress process. *Journal of Personality and Social Psychology, 69,* 890–902.

Bolger, N., & Shilling, E. A. (1991). Personality and the problems of everyday life: The role of neuroticism in exposure and reactivity to daily stressors. *Journal of Personality, 59,* 355–386.

Bolles, R. C. (1972). A motivational view of learning, performance, and behavior modification. *Psychological Review, 81,* 199–213.

Bolles, R. C. (1975). *A theory of motivation* (2nd ed.). New York: Harper & Row.

Bolles, R. C., & Fanselow, M. S. (1980). A perceptual-defensive-recuperative model of fear and pain. *Behavioral and Brain Sciences, 3,* 291–323.

Bolm-Avdorff, J., Schwammle, J., Ehlenz, K., & Kaffarnik, H. (1989). Plasma level of catecholamines and lipids when speaking before an audience. *Work and Stress, 3,* 249–253.

Boneau, C. A. (1990). Psychological literacy: A first approximation. *American Psychologist, 45,* 891–900.

Booth, A., Shelley, G., Mazur, A., Tharp, G., & Kittok, R. (1989). Testosterone and winning and losing in human competition. *Hormones and Behavior, 23,* 556–571.

Borecki, I. B., Rice, T., Peírusse, L., Bouchard, C., & Rao, D. C. (1995). Major gene influence on the proximity to store fat in trunk versus extremity depots: Evidence from the Quebec family study. *Obesity Research, 3,* 1–8.

Bosenbaum, M., Leibel, R. L., & Hirsch, J. (1997). Obesity. *New England Journal of Medicine, 337,* 396–407.

Bowlby, J. (1969). *Attachment and loss: Vol. 1. Attachment.* New York: Basic Books.

Bowlby, J. (1973). *Attachment and loss: Vol. 2. Separation: Anxiety and anger.* New York: Basic Books.

Bowlby, J. (1980). *Attachment and loss, Vol. III. Loss, sadness, and depression.* New York: Basic Books.

Bowles, T. (1999). Focusing on time orientation to explain adolescent self concept and academic achievement: Part II. Testing a model. *Journal of Applied Health Behavior, 1,* 1–8.

Boyatzis, R. E. (1972). *A two factor theory of affiliation motivation.* Unpublished doctoral dissertation, Harvard University.

Boyatzis, R. E. (1973). Affiliation motivation. In D. C. McClelland & R. S. Steele (Eds.), *Human motivation: A book of readings.* Morristown, NJ: General Learning Press.

Bozarth, M. A. (1991). The mesolimbic dopamine system as a model reward system. In P. Willner & J. Scheol-Kroger (Eds.), *The mesolimbic dopamine system: From motivation to action* (pp. 301–330). New York: Wiley.

Branden, N. (1984). *The six pillars of self-esteem*. New York: Bantam Books.

Brandstatter, V., Lengfelder, A., & Gollwitzer, P. M. (2001). Implementation intentions and efficient action initiation. *Journal of Personality and Social Psychology, 81*, 946–960.

Brehm, J. W. (1956). Postdecision changes in the desirability of alternatives. *Journal of Abnormal and Social Psychology, 52*, 384–389.

Brehm, J. W. (1966). *A theory of psychological reactance*. New York: Academic Press.

Brehm, S. S., & Brehm, J. W. (1981). *Psychological reactance: A theory of freedom and control*. New York: Academic Press.

Brewer, M. B. (1979). Ingroup bias in the minimal intergroup situation: A cognitive-motivational analysis. *Psychological Bulletin, 86*, 307–324.

Brickman, P., Coates, D., & Janoff-Bulman, R. (1978). Lottery winners and accident victims: Is happiness relative? *Journal of Personality and Social Psychology, 36*, 917–927.

Brigham, T. A., Maier, S. M., & Goodner, V. (1995). Increased designated driving with a program of prompts and incentives. *Journal of Applied Behavior Analysis, 28*, 83–84.

Broadbent, D. E., Cooper, P. F., FitzGerald, P., & Parkes, K. R. (1982). The cognitive failures questionnaire (CFQ). *British Journal of Clinical Psychology, 21*, 1–16.

Brobeck, J. R. (1960). Food and temperature. *Recent Progress in Hormone Research, 16*, 439.

Brophy, J. (1981). Teacher praise: A functional analysis. *Review of Educational Research, 51*, 5–32.

Brophy, J. (1999). Toward a model of the value aspects of motivation in education: Developing appreciation for particular learning domains and activities. *Educational Psychologist, 34*, 75–85.

Brothers, K. J. (1994). Office paper recycling: A function of container proximity. *Journal of Applied Behavior Analysis, 27*, 153–160.

Brouwers, M., & Wiggum, C. D. (1993). Bulimia and perfectionism: Developing the courage to be imperfect. *Journal of Mental Health Counseling, 15*, 141–149.

Brown, A. S. (1991). A review of the tip-of-the-tongue experience. *Psychological Bulletin, 109*, 204–223.

Brown, I., Jr., & Inouye, D. K. (1978). Learned helplessness through modeling: The role of perceived similarity in competence. *Journal of Personality and Social Psychology, 36*, 900–908.

Brown, J. S. (1961). *The motivation of behavior*. New York: McGraw-Hill.

Brown, L. T., Ruder, V. G., Ruder, J. H., & Young, S. D. (1974). Stimulation seeking and the change seeker index. *Journal of Consulting and Clinical Psychology, 42*, 311.

Brownell, K. D. (1991). Dieting and the search for the perfect body: Where physiology and culture collide. *Behavior Therapy, 22*, 1–12.

Bryne, D. (1961). Anxiety and the experimental arousal of affiliation need. *Journal of Abnormal and Social Psychology, 63*, 660–662.

Buck, R. (1984). *The communication of emotion*. New York: Guilford Press.

Buck, R. (1986). The psychology of emotion. In J. LeDoux & W. Hirst (Eds.), *Mind and brain: Dialogues in cognitive neuroscience* (pp. 275–300). New York: Cambridge University Press.

Buck, R. (1988). *Human motivation and emotion*. New York: John Wiley & Sons.

Buckner, C. E., & Swann, W. B. Jr. (1996, August). *Physical abuse in close relationships: The dynamic interplay of couple characteristics*. Paper presented at the annual meeting of the American Psychological Association, Washington, DC.

Bugental, J. F. T. (1967). *Challenges and humanistic psychology*. New York: McGraw-Hill.

Burger, J. M. (1984). Desire for control, locus of control, and proneness to depression. *Journal of Personality, 52*, 71–89.

Burger, J. M. (1985). Desire for control and achievement-related behaviors. *Journal of Personality and Social Psychology, 48*, 1520–1533.

Burger, J. M. (1986). Desire for control and illusion of control: The effects of familiarity and sequence of outcomes. *Journal of Research in Personality, 20*, 66–76.

Burger, J. M. (1990). Desire for control and interpersonal interaction style. *Journal of Research in Personality, 24*, 32–44.

Burger, J. M. (1992). *Desire for control: Personality, social, and clinical perspectives*. New York: Plenum.

Burger, J. M., & Arkin, R. M. (1980). Prediction, control, and learned helplessness. *Journal of Personality and Social Psychology, 38*, 482–491.

Burger, J. M., & Cooper, H. M. (1979). The desirability of control. *Motivation and Emotion, 3*, 381–393.

Burger, J. M., Oakman, J. A., & Bullard, N. G. (1983). Desire for control and the perception of crowding. *Personality and Social Psychology Bulletin, 9*, 475–479.

Burger, J. M., & Schnerring, D. A. (1982). The effects of desire for control and extrinsic rewards on the illusion of control and gambling. *Motivation and Emotion, 6*, 329–335.

Buss, D. M., & Schmitt, D. P. (1993). Sexual strategies theory: An evolutionary perspective on human mating. *Psychological Review, 100*, 204–232.

Bussey, K., & Bandura, A. (1999). Social cognitive theory of gender development and differentiation. *Psychological Review, 106*, 676–713.

Buston, P. M., & Emlen. S. T. (2003). Cognitive processes underlying human mate choice: The relationship between self-perception and mate preference in Western society. *Proceedings of the National Academy of Sciences, 100*, 8805–8810.

Byrne, B. M. (1984). The general/academic self-concept nomological network: A review of construct validation research. *Review of Educational Research, 54*, 427–456.

Byrne, B. M. (1986). Self-concept/academic achievement relations: An investigation of dimensionality, stability, and causality. *Canadian Journal of Behavioral Science, 18*, 173–186.

Byrne, B. M. (1996). Academic self-concept: Its structure, measurement, and relation with academic achievement. In B. A. Bracken (Ed.), *Handbook of self-concept*. New York: Wiley.

Cabanac, M., & Duclaux, P. (1970). Obesity: Absence of satiety aversion to sucrose? *Science, 168*, 496–497.

Calhoon, L. L. (1988). Explorations in the biochemistry of sensation seeking. *Personality and Individual Differences, 9*, 941–949.

Cameron, J., & Pierce, W. D. (1994). Reinforcement, reward, and intrinsic motivation: A meta-analysis. *Review of Educational Research, 64*, 363–423.

Campfield, L. A., Smith, F. J., & Burn, P. (1997a). The OB protein (leptin) pathway: A link between adipose tissue mass and central neural networks. *Hormone and Metabolic Research, 28*, 619–632.

Campfield, L. A., Smith, F. J., & Burn, P. (1997b). OB protein: A hormonal controller of central neural networks mediating behavioral, metabolic and neuroendocrine responses. *Endocrinology and Metabolism, 4*, 81–102.

Campfield, L. A., Smith, F. J., & Burn, P. (1998). Strategies and potential molecular targets for obesity treatment. *Science, 280*, 1383–1387.

Campfield, L. A., Smith, F. J., Rosenbaum, M., & Hirsch, J. (1996). Human eating: Evidence for a physiological basis using a modified paradigm. *Neuroscience and Biobehavioral Reviews, 20*, 133–137.

Campion, M. A., & Lord, R. G. (1982). A control systems conceptualization of the goal-setting and changing process. *Organizational Behavior and Human Performance, 30*, 265–287.

Camras, L. (1977). Facial expressions used by children in a conflict situation. *Child Development, 48*, 1431–1435.

Camras, L. A. (1992). Expressive development and basic emotions. *Cognition and Emotion, 6*, 269–283.

Cannon, W. B. (1927). The James-Lange theory of emotion: A critical examination and an alternative theory. *American Journal of Psychology, 39*, 106–124.

Cannon, W. B. (1929). *Bodily changes in pain, hunger, fear, and rage*. New York: Appleton.

Cannon, W. B. (1932). *The wisdom of the body*. New York: W. W. Norton.

Cantor, N., Markus, H., Niedenthal, P., & Nurius, P. (1986). On motivation and the self-concept. In R. M. Sorrentino & E. T. Higgins (Eds.), *Handbook of motivation and cognition* (Vol. 1, pp. 96–121). New York: Guilford Press.

Carlsmith, J. M., Ellsworth, P. C., & Aronson, E. (1976). *Methods of research in social psychology*. New York: Random House.

Carlson, N. C. (1988). *Discovering psychology*. Boston: Allyn & Bacon.

Carnelley, K. B., Pietromonaco, P. R., & Jaffe, K. (1994). Depression, working models of others, and relationship functioning. *Journal of Personality and Social Psychology, 66*, 127–140.

Carnevale, P. J. D., & Isen, A. M. (1986). The influence of positive affect and visual access on the discovery of integrative solutions in bilateral negotiation. *Organizational Behavior and Human Decision Processes, 37*, 1–13.

Carstensen, L. L. (1993). Motivation for social contact across the life span. In J. Jacobs (Ed.), Nebraska Symposium on Motivation: Developmental perspectives on motivation (Vol. 40, pp. 209–254). Lincoln: University of Nebraska Press.

Carstensen, L. L. (1995). Evidence for a life-span theory of socioemotional selectivity. *Current Directions in Psychological Science, 4*, 151–156.

Carstensen, L. L., Gottman, J. M., & Levenson, R. W. (1995). Emotional behavior in long-term marriage. *Psychology and Aging, 10*, 140–149.

Carter, R. (1988). *Mapping the mind*. Berkeley: University of California Press.

Carver, C. S., & Scheier, M. F. (1998). *On the self-regulation of behavior*. Cambridge, United Kingdom: Cambridge University Press.

Carver, C. S., & Blaney, P. H. (1977). Avoidance behavior and perceived control. *Motivation and Emotion, 1*, 61–63.

Carver, C. S., & Scheier, M. F. (1981). *Attention and self-regulation: A control theory approach to human behavior*. New York: Springer-Verlag.

Carver, C. S., & Scheier, M. F. (1982). Control theory: A useful conceptual framework for personality: Social, clinical, and health psychology. *Psychological Bulletin, 92*, 111–135.

Carver, C. S., & Scheier, M. F. (1990). Origins and functions of positive and negative affect: A control-process view. *Psychological Review, 97*, 19–35.

Carver, C. L., & White, T. L. (1994). Behavioral inhibition, behavioral activation, and affective responses to impending reward and punishment: The BIS/BAS scales. *Journal of Personality and Social Psychology, 67*, 319–333.

Chen, M., & Isen, A. M. (1992). *The influence of positive affect and success on persistence on a failed task*. Unpublished manuscript, Cornell University.

Chen, R. (1993). Responding to compliments: A contrastive study of politeness strategies between American English and Chinese speakers. *Journal of Pragmatics, 20*, 49–75.

Cioffi, D. (1991). Beyond attentional strategies: A cognitive-perceptual model of somatic interpretation. *Psychological Bulletin, 109*, 25–41.

Clark, L. A., Watson, D., & Leeka, J. (1989). Diurnal variation in the positive affects. *Motivation and Emotion, 13*, 205–234.

Clark, L. A., Watson, D., & Mineka, S. (1994). Temperament, personality, and the mood and anxiety disorders. *Journal of Abnormal Psychology, 103*, 103–116.

Clark, M. S. (1984). Record keeping in two types of relationships. *Journal of Personality and Social Psychology, 47*, 549–557.

Clark, M. S., & Mills, J. (1979). Interpersonal attraction in exchange and communal relationships. *Journal of Personality and Social Psychology, 37*, 12–24.

Clark, M. S., Mills, J., & Powell, M. C. (1986). Keeping track of needs in communal and exchange relationships. *Journal of Personality and Social Psychology, 51*, 333–338.

Clark, M. S., Ouellette, R., Powell, M. C., & Milberg, S. (1987). Recipient's mood, relationship type, and helping. *Journal of Personality and Social Psychology, 53*, 94–103.

Clement, R., & Jonah, B. A. (1984). Field dependence, sensation seeking and driving behavior. *Personality and Individual Differences, 5*, 87–93.

Clifford, M. M. (1984). Thoughts on a theory of constructive failure. *Educational Psychologist, 19*, 108–120.

Clifford, M. M. (1988). Failure tolerance and academic risk-taking in ten- to twelve-year-old students. *British Journal of Educational Psychology, 58*, 15–27.

Clifford, M. M. (1990). Students need challenge, not easy success. *Educational Leadership, 48*, 22–26.

Cofer, C. N., & Appley, M. H. (1964). *Motivation: Theory and research*. New York: John Wiley.

Cohen, S., Sherrod, D. R., & Clark, M. S. (1986). Social skills and the stress-protective role of social support. *Journal of Personality and Social Psychology, 50*, 963–973.

Cohn, J. F., Zlochower, A. J., Lien, J., & Kanade, T. (1999). Automated face analysis by feature point tracking has high concurrent validity with manual FACS coding. *Psychophysiology, 36*, 35–43.

Coles, M. G. H., Ponchin, E., & Porges, S. W., (Eds.) (1986). *Psychophysiology: Systems, processes, and applications*. New York: Guilford Press.

Colin, V. L. (1996). *Human attachment*. New York: McGraw-Hill.

Condry, J. (1977). Enemies of exploration: Self-initiated versus other-initiated learning. *Journal of Personality and Social Psychology, 35*, 459–477.

Condry, J. (1987). Enhancing motivation: A social development perspective. *Advances in motivation and achievement: Enhancing motivation, 5*, 23–49.

Condry, J., & Chambers, J. (1978). Intrinsic motivation and the process of learning. In M. R. Lepper & D. Greene (Eds.). *The hidden costs of reward: New perspectives on the psychology of human motivation* (pp. 61–84). Hillsdale, NJ: Lawrence Erlbaum.

Condry, J., & Stokker, L. G. (1992). Overview of special issue on intrinsic motivation. *Motivation and Emotion, 16*, 157–164.

Connell, J. P. (1990). Context, self, and action: A motivational analysis of self-system processes across the life-span. In D. Cicchetti (Ed.), *The self in transition: From infancy to childhood* (pp. 61–97). Chicago: University of Chicago Press.

Connell, J. P., & Wellborn, J. G. (1991). Competence, autonomy, and relatedness: A motivational analysis of self-system processes. In M. R. Gunnar & L. A. Sroufe (Eds.), *Self processes in development: Minnesota symposium on child psychology* (Vol. 23, pp. 167–216). Chicago: University of Chicago Press.

Connolly, K., & Smith, P. K. (1972). Reactions of pre-school children to a strange observer. In N. G. Blurton-Jones (Ed.), *Ethological studies of child behavior*. Cambridge: Cambridge University Press.

Cooper, K. H. (1968). *Aerobics*. New York: Bantam Books.

Cooper, K. J., & Browder, D. M. (1998). Enhancing choice and participation for adults with severe disabilities in community-based instruction. *Journal of the Association for Persons with Severe Handicaps, 23*, 252–260.

Cooper, M. L., Frone, M. R., Russell, M., & Mudar, P. (1995). Drinking to regulate positive and negative emotions: A motivational model of alcohol use. *Journal of Personality and Social Psychology, 69*, 990–1005.

Cooper, W. H. (1983). An achievement motivation nomological network. *Journal of Personality and Social Psychology, 44*, 841–861.

Cordova, D. I., & Lepper, M. R. (1996). Intrinsic motivation and the process of learning: Beneficial effects of contextualization, personalization, and choice. *Journal of Educational Psychology, 88*, 715–730.

Costa, P. T., Jr., & McCrae, R. R. (1980). Influence of extraversion and neuroticism on subjective well-being: Happy and unhappy people. *Journal of Personality and Social Psychology, 38,* 668–678.

Costa, P. T., & McRae, R. R. (1992). *Revised NEO Personality Inventory (NEO PI-R) and NEO Five-Factor Inventory Professional manual.* Odessa, FL: Psychological Assessment Resources.

Costello, C. G. (1978). A critical review of Seligman's laboratory experiments on learned helplessness and depression in humans. *Journal of Abnormal Psychology, 87,* 21–31.

Covington, M. (1984a). The self-worth theory of achievement motivation: Findings and implications. *The Elementary School Journal, 85,* 5–20.

Covington, M. (1984b). Motivation for self-worth. In R. Ames & C. A. Ames (Eds.), *Research on motivation in education* (Vol. 1, pp. 77–113). New York: Academic Press.

Covington, M. W., & Omelich, C. L. (1984). Task-oriented versus competitive learning structures: Motivational and performance consequences. *Journal of Educational Psychology, 76,* 1038–1050.

Cox, B. S., Cox, A. B., & Cox, D. J. (2000). Motivating signage prompts safety-belt use among drivers exiting senior communities. *Journal of Applied Behavior Analysis, 33,* 635–638.

Cox, R. (1987). The rich harvest of Abraham Maslow. In A. Maslow's, *Motivation and personality* (3rd ed., pp. 245–271). New York: Harper & Row.

Coyne, J. C. (1976a). Towards an interactional description of depression. *Psychiatry, 39,* 28–40.

Coyne, J. C. (1976b). Depression and the response of others. *Journal of Abnormal Psychology, 85,* 186–193.

Coyne, J. C., & DeLongis, A. (1986). Going beyond social support: The role of social relationships in adaptation. *Journal of Consulting and Clinical Psychology, 54,* 454–460.

Crago, M., Yates, A., Beutler, L. E., & Arizmendi, T. G. (1985). Height-weight ratios among female athletes: Are collegiate athletics the precursors to an anorexic syndrome? *International Journal of Eating Disorders, 4,* 79–87.

Crandall, C. S. (1988). Social cognition of binge eating. *Journal of Personality and Social Psychology, 55,* 588–598.

Crary, W. G. (1966). Reactions to incongruent self-experiences. *Journal of Consulting Psychology, 30,* 246–252.

Crews, F. (1996). The verdict on Freud. *Psychological Science, 7,* 63–67.

Crick, F., & Mitchison, G. (1986). REM sleep and neural networks. *Journal of Mind and Behavior, 7,* 229–250.

Cross, S. E., & Markus, H. R. (1991). Possible selves across the life span. *Human Development, 34,* 230–255.

Cross, S. E., & Markus, H. R. (1994). Self-schemas, possible selves, and competent performance. *Journal of Educational Psychology, 86,* 423–438.

Crowne, D. P., & Marlowe, D. (1964). *The approval motive.* New York: Wiley.

Csikszentmihalyi, M. (1975). *Beyond boredom and anxiety: The experience of flow in work and play.* San Francisco: Jossey-Bass.

Csikszentmihalyi, M. (1982). Toward a psychology of optimal experience. *Review of Personality and Social Psychology, 3,* 13–36.

Csikszentmihalyi, M. (1990). *Flow: The psychology of optimal experience.* New York: Harper & Row.

Csikszentmihalyi, M. (1997). *Finding flow: The psychology of engagement with everyday life.* New York: Basic Books.

Csikszentmihalyi, M., & Csikszentmihalyi, I. (Eds.) (1988). *Optimal experiences: Psychological studies of flow in consciousness.* New York: Cambridge University Press.

Csikszentmihalyi, M., & Nakamura, J. (1989). The dynamics of intrinsic motivation: A study of adolescents. In C. A. Ames & R. Ames (Eds.), *Research on motivation in education* (Vol. 3, pp. 45–61). San Diego: Academic Press.

Csikszentmihalyi, M., Rathunde, K., & Whalen, S. (1993). *Talented teenagers: The roots of success and failure*. New York: Cambridge University Press.

Cui, X., & Vaillant, G. E. (1996). The antecedents and consequences of negative live events in adulthood: A longitudinal study. *American Journal of Psychiatry, 152*, 21–26.

Cummings, D. E., Weigle, D. S., Frayo, R. S., Breen, P. A., Ma, M. K., Dellinger, E. P., & Purnell, J. Q. (2002). Plasma ghrelin levels after diet-induced weight loss or gastric bypass surgery. *New England Journal of Medicine, 346*, 1623–1630.

Cummings, D. E., Purnell, J. Q., Frayo, S., Schmidova, K., Wisse, B. E., & Weigle, D. S. (2001). A prandial rise in plasma ghrelin levels suggests a role in meal initiation in humans. *Diabetes, 50*, 1714–1719.

Cunningham, M. R. (1986). Measuring the physical in physical attractiveness: Quasi-experiments on the sociobiology of female facial beauty. *Journal of Personality and Social Psychology, 50*, 925–935.

Cunningham, M. R., Barbee, A. P., & Pike, C. L. (1990). What do women want? Facialmetric assessment of multiple motives in the perception of male facial physical attractiveness. *Journal of Personality and Social Psychology, 59*, 61–62.

Cunningham, M. R., Roberts, A. R., Barbee, A. P., Druen, P. B., & Wu, C. (1995). Their ideas of beauty are, on the whole, the same as ours: Consistency and variability in the cross-cultural perception of female physical attractiveness. *Journal of Personality and Social Psychology, 68*, 261–279.

Curry, L. A., Snyder, C. R., Cook, D. L., Ruby, B. C., & Rehm, M. (1977). The role of hope in student-athlete academic and sport achievement. *Journal of Personality and Social Psychology, 73*, 1257–1267.

D'Amato, M. R. (1974). Derived motives. *Annual Review of Psychology, 25*, 83–106.

Daniels, M. (1988). The myth of self-actualization. *Journal of Humanistic Psychology, 28*, 7–38.

Darwin, C. A. (1859). *On the origin of species by means of natural selection*. London: John Murray; New York: Modern Library, 1936.

Darwin, C. A. (1872). *The expression of the emotions in man and animals*. London: John Murray.

Davidson, P., Turiel, E., & Black, A. (1983). The effects of stimulus familiarity in the use of criteria and justification in children's social reasoning. *British Journal of Developmental Psychology, 1*, 49–65.

Davidson, R. J. (1994). On emotion, mood, and related affective constructs. In P. Ekman & R. J. Davidson (Eds.), *The nature of emotion: Fundamental questions* (pp. 51–55). New York: Oxford University Press.

Davidson, R. J. (2003). Affective neuroscience and psychophysiology: Toward a synthesis. *Psychophysiology, 40*, 655–665.

Davidson, R. J., Ekman, P., Saron, C., Senulis, J., & Friesen, W. V. (1990). Approach/withdrawal and cerebral asymmetry. *Journal of Personality and Social Psychology, 58*, 330–341.

Davies, J., & Brember, I. (1999). Reading and mathematics attainments and self-esteem in years 2 and 6—an eight-year cross-sectional study. *Educational Studies, 25*, 145–157.

Davis, C. G., Nolen-Hoeksema, S., & Larsen, J. (1998). Making sense of loss and benefiting from the experience: Two construals of meaning. *Journal of Personality and Social Psychology, 75*, 561–574.

Davis, M. (1992). The role of the amygdala in conditioned fear. In J. P. Aggleton (Ed.), *The amygdala: Neurobiological aspects of emotion, memory, and mental dysfunction* (pp. 255–305). New York: Wiley.

Davis, M., Hitchcock, J. M., & Rosen, J. B. (1987). Anxiety and the amygdala: Pharmacological and anatomical analysis of the fear-potentiated startle paradigm. *The Psychology of Learning and Motivation, 21*, 263–305.

Davis, M., & Whalen, P. J. (2001). The amygdala: Vigilance and emotion. *Molecular Psychiatry, 6*, 13–34.

Davis, S. (2000). Testosterone and sexual desire in women. *Journal of Sex Education and Therapy, 25*, 25–32.

Day, J. D., Borkowski, J. G., Punzo, D., & Howsepian, B. (1994). Enhancing possible selves in Mexican American students. *Motivation and Emotion, 18*, 79–103.

Deaux, K., Reid, A., Mizrahi, K., & Ethier, K. A. (1995). Parameters of social identity. *Journal of Personality and Social Psychology, 53*, 281–295.

DeCastro, J. M., & Brewer, E. M. (1991). The amount eaten in meals by humans is a power function of the number of people present. *Physiology and Behavior, 51*, 121–125.

deCharms, R. (1968). *Personal causation.* New York: Academic Press.

deCharms, R. (1976). *Enhancing motivation: Change in the classroom.* New York: Irvington.

deCharms, R. (1984). Motivation enhancement in educational settings. In R. E. Ames & C. A. Ames (Eds.), *Research on motivation in education: Student motivation* (Vol. 1, pp. 275–310). New York: Academic Press.

deCharms, R. (1987). The burden of motivation. In M. L. Maehr & D. A. Kleiber (Eds.), *Advances in motivation and achievement: Enhancing motivation* (Vol. 5, pp. 1–21). Greenwhich, CT: JAI Press.

deCharms, R., & Moeller, G. H. (1962). Values expressed in American children's readers: 1800–1950. *Journal of Abnormal and Social Psychology, 64*, 136–142.

Deci, E. L. (1971). Effects of externally mediated rewards on intrinsic motivation. *Journal of Personality and Social Psychology, 18*, 105–115.

Deci, E. L. (1972). Intrinsic motivation, extrinsic reinforcement, and inequity. *Journal of Personality and Social Psychology, 22*, 113–120.

Deci, E. L. (1975). *Intrinsic motivation.* New York: Plenum.

Deci, E. L. (1980). *The psychology of self-determination.* Lexington, MA: Lexington Books.

Deci, E. L. (1992a). On the nature and function of motivation theories. *Psychological Science, 3*, 167–171.

Deci, E. L. (1992b). The relation of interest to the motivation of behavior: A self-determination theory perspective. In K. A. Renninger, S. Hidi, & A. Krapp (Eds.), *The role of interest in learning and development* (pp. 43–60). Hillsdale, NJ: Erlbaum.

Deci, E. L. (1995). *Why we do what we do: Understanding self-motivation.* New York: Penguin Books.

Deci, E. L., & Casio, W. F. (1972, April). *Changes in intrinsic motivation as a function of negative feedback and threats.* Paper presented at the meeting of the Eastern Psychological Association, Boston, MA.

Deci, E. L., Connell, J. P., & Ryan, R. M. (1989). Self-determination in a work organization. *Journal of Applied Psychology, 74*, 580–590.

Deci, E. L., Eghrari, H., Patrick, B. C., & Leone, D. R. (1994). Facilitating internalization: The self-determination theory perspective. *Journal of Personality, 62*, 119–142.

Deci, E. L., Koestner, R., & Ryan, R. M. (1999). A meta-analytic review of experiments examining the effects of extrinsic rewards on intrinsic motivation. *Psychological Bulletin, 125*, 627–668.

Deci, E. L., Nezlak, J., & Sheinman, L. (1981). Characteristics of the rewarder and intrinsic motivation of the rewardee. *Journal of Personality and Social Psychology, 40*, 1–10.

Deci, E. L., & Ryan, R. M. (1985a). *Intrinsic motivation and self-determination in human behavior.* New York: Plenum.

Deci, E. L., & Ryan, R. M. (1985b). The General Causality Orientations Scale: Self-determination in personality. *Journal of Research in Personality, 19*, 109–134.

Deci, E. L., & Ryan, R. M. (1987). The support of autonomy and the control of behavior. *Journal of Personality and Social Psychology, 53*, 1024–1037.

Deci, E. L., & Ryan, R. M. (1991). A motivational approach to self: Integration in personality. In R. Dienstbier (Ed.), *Nebraska symposium on motivation: Perspectives on motivation* (Vol. 38, pp. 237–288). Lincoln: University of Nebraska Press.

Deci, E. L., & Ryan, R. M. (1995). Human autonomy: The basis for true self-esteem. In M. Kernis (Ed.), *Efficacy, agency, and self-esteem* (pp. 31–49). New York: Plenum.

Deci, E. L., Ryan, R. M., & Williams, G. C. (1995). Need satisfaction and the self-regulation of learning. *Learning and Individual Differences, 8*, 165–183.

Deci, E. L., Schwartz, A., Scheinman, L., & Ryan, R. M. (1981). An instrument to assess adult's orientations toward control versus autonomy in children: Reflections on intrinsic motivation and perceived competence. *Journal of Educational Psychology, 73*, 642–650.

Deci, E. L., Spiegel, N. H., Ryan, R. M., Koestner, R., & Kauffman, M. (1982). Effects of performance standards on teaching styles: Behavior of controlling teachers. *Journal of Educational Psychology, 74*, 852–859.

De La Ronde, C., & Swann, W. B., Jr. (1998). Partner verification: Restoring shattered images of our intimates. *Journal of Personality and Social Psychology, 75*, 374–382.

Delisle, J. (1986). Death with honors: Suicide among gifted adolescents. *Journal of Counseling and Development, 64*, 558–560.

DeLongis, A., Coyne, J. C., Dakof, G., Folkman, S., & Lazarus, R. S. (1982). Relations of daily hassles, uplifts, and major life events to health status. *Health Psychology, 1*, 119–136.

DeLongis, A., Folkman, S., & Lazarus, R. S. (1988). The impact of daily stress and mood: Psychological and social resources as mediators. *Journal of Personality and Social Psychology, 54*, 486–495.

Dember, W. N. (1965). The new look in motivation. *American Scientist, 53*, 409–427.

Dember, W. N. (1974). Motivation and the cognitive revolution. *American Psychologist, 29*, 161–168.

Dembroski, T. M., MacDougall, J. M., & Musante, L. (1984). Desirability of control versus locus of control: Relationship to paralinguistics in the Type A interview. *Health Psychology, 3*, 15–26.

Dempsey, E. W. (1951). Homeostasis. In S. S. Stevens (Ed.), *Handbook of experimental psychology* (pp. 209–235). New York: John Wiley.

Denham, S. A., Mitchell-Copeland, J., Strandberg, K., Auerbach, S., & Blair, K. (1997). Parental contributions to preschooler's emotional competence: Direct and indirect effects. *Motivation and Emotion, 21*, 65–86.

DePaulo, B. (1992). Nonverbal behavior and self-presentation. *Psychological Bulletin, 111*, 203–243.

Depue, R. A., & Monroe, S. M. (1978). Learned helplessness in the perspective of the depressive disorders: Conceptual and definitional issues. *Journal of Abnormal Psychology, 87*, 3–20.

de Rivera, J. (1977). *A structural theory of the emotions.* New York: International Universities Press.

de Rivera, J. (1981). The structure of anger. In J. de Rivera (Ed.), *Conceptual encounter: A method for the exploration of human experience.* Washington, DC: University Press of America.

Deutsch, J. A., & Gonzalez, M. F. (1980). Gastric nutrient content signals satiety. *Behavior Neural Biology, 30*, 113–116.

Deutsch, J. A., Young, W. G., & Kalogeris, T. J. (1978). The stomach signals satiety. *Science, 201*, 165–167.

Di Chiara, G., Acquas, E., & Carboni, E. (1992). Drug motivation and abuse: A neurobiological perspective. *Annals of New York Academy of Sciences, 654*, 207–219.

Dickerson, C., Thibodeau, R., Aronson, E., & Miller, D. (1992). Using cognitive dissonance theory to encourage water conservation. *Journal of Applied Social Psychology, 22*, 841–854.

Diener, C. I., & Dweck, C. S. (1978). An analysis of learned helplessness: Continuous changes in performance, strategy, and achievement cognitions following failure. *Journal of Personality and Social Psychology, 36*, 451–462.

Diener, C. I., & Dweck, C. S. (1980). An analysis of learned helplessness: II. The processing of success. *Journal of Personality and Social Psychology, 39*, 940–952.

Diener, E., & Diener, M. (1995). Cross-cultural correlates of life satisfaction and self-esteem. *Journal of Personality and Social Psychology, 68*, 653–663.

Diener, E., & Diener, C. (1996). Most people are happy. *Psychological Science, 7*, 181–185.

Diener, E., & Emmons, R. A. (1984). The independence of positive and negative affect. *Journal of Personality and Social Psychology, 47*, 105–1117.

Diener, E., & Iran-Nejad, A. (1986). The relationship in experience between various types of affect. *Journal of Personality and Social Psychology, 50*, 1031–1038.

Diener, E., Sandvik, E., Pavot, W., & Fujita, F. (1998). Extraversion and subjective well-being in a U.S. national probability sample. *Journal of Research in Personality, 26*, 205–215.

Dienstbier, R. A. (1991). Introduction. In R. A. Dienstbier (Ed.), *Nebraska symposium on motivation* (Vol. 38, pp. ix–xiv). Lincoln: University of Nebraska Press.

Dimberg, U. (1982). Facial reactions to facial expressions. *Psychophysiology, 19*, 643–647.

Diserens, C. M. (1925). Psychological objectivism. *Psychological Review, 32*, 121–125.

Dollinger, S. J., & Thelen, M. H. (1978). Over-justification and children's intrinsic motivation: Comparative effects of four rewards. *Journal of Personality and Social Psychology, 36*, 1259–1269.

Donovan, J. M., Hill, E., & Jankowiak, W. R. (1989). Gender, sexual orientation, and truth-or-consequences in studies of physical attractiveness. *Journal of Sex Research, 26*, 264–271.

Driver-Linn, E. (2003). Where is psychology going? Structural fault lines revealed by psychologists' use of Kuhn. *American Psychologist, 58*, 269–278.

Druss, R. G., & Silverman, J. A. (1979). Body image and perfectionism of ballerinas. *General Hospital Psychiatry, 2*, 115–121.

Duffy, E. (1957). Psychological significance of the concept of arousal or activation. *Psychological Review, 64*, 265–275.

Dunker, K. (1945). On problem-solving. *Psychological Monographs, 58*, Whole No. 5.

Dunlap, K. (1919). Are there any instincts? *Journal of Abnormal Psychology, 14*, 35–50.

Dunn, J., & Munn, P. (1987). Development of justification in disputes with mother and sibling. *Developmental Psychology, 23*, 791–798.

Dupue, R. A., & Collins, P. F. (1999). Neurobiology of the structure of personality: Dopamine facilitation of incentive motivation and extraversion. *Behavioral and Brain Sciences, 22*, 491–569.

Dweck, C. S. (1975). The role of expectancies and attributions in the alleviation of learned helplessness. *Journal of Personality and Social Psychology, 31*, 674–685.

Dweck, C. S. (1986). Motivational processes affecting learning. *American Psychologist, 41*, 1040–1048.

Dweck, C. S. (1990). Motivation. In R. Glaser & A. Lesgold (Eds.), *Foundations for a cognitive psychology of education*. Hillsdale, NJ: Lawrence Erlbaum.

Dweck, C. S. (1999). *Self-theories: Their role in motivation, personality, and development*. Philadelphia: Psychology Press.

Dweck, C. S., & Elliot, E. S. (1983). Achievement motivation. In P. Mussen & E. M. Hetherington (Eds.), *Handbook of child psychology* (pp. 643–692). New York: Wiley.

Dweck, C. S., & Leggett, E. L. (1988). A social-cognitive approach to motivation and personality. *Psychological Review, 95*, 256–273.

Dweck, C. S., & Repucci, N. D. (1973). Learned helplessness and reinforcement responsibility in children. *Journal of Personality and Social Psychology, 25*, 109–116.

Dykman, B. M. (1998). Integrating cognitive and motivational factors in depression: Initial tests of a goal-orientation approach. *Journal of Personality and Social Psychology, 74*, 139–158.

Eagle, M. (1984). *Recent developments on psychoanalysis*. New York: McGraw-Hill.

Earley, P. C., Connolly, T., & Ekegren, G. (1989). Goals, strategy development and task performance: Some limits on the efficacy of goal setting. *Journal of Applied Psychology, 74*, 24–33.

Earley, P. C., & Perry, B. C. (1987). Work plan availability and performance: An assessment of task strategy priming on subsequent task completion. *Organizational Behavior and Human Decision Processes, 39*, 279–302.

Earley, P. C., Wojnaroski, P., & Prest, W. (1987). Task planning and energy expended: Exploration of how goals influence performance. *Journal of Applied Psychology, 72,* 107–113.

Eaves, L. J., Eysenck, H. J., & Martin, N. G. (1989). *Genes, culture, and personality: An empirical approach.* San Diego: Academic Press.

Eccles, J. S. (1984a). Sex differences in achievement patterns. In T. Sonderegger (Ed.), *Nebraska symposium on motivation: Psychology and gender* (Vol. 32, pp. 97–132). Lincoln: University of Nebraska Press.

Eccles, J. S. (1984b). Sex differences in mathematics participation. In M. Steinkamp & M. L. Maehr (Eds.), *Advances in motivation and achievement* (Vol. 2, pp. 93–137). Lincoln: University of Nebraska Press.

Eccles-Parsons, J. E., Adler, T. F., & Kaczala, C. M. (1982). Socialization of achievement attitudes and beliefs: Parental influences. *Child Development, 53,* 310–321.

Eccleston, C., & Crombez, G. (1999). Pain demands attention: A cognitive-affective model of the interruptive function of pain. *Psychological Bulletin, 125,* 356–366.

Eckenrode, J. (1984). Impact of chronic and acute stressors on daily reports of mood. *Journal of Personality and Social Psychology, 46,* 907–918.

Eckert, T. L., Ardoin, S. P., Daly III, E. J., & Martens, B. K. (2002). Improving oral reading fluency: A brief experimental analysis of combining an antecedent intervention with consequences. *Journal of Applied Behavior Analysis, 35,* 271–281.

Edwards, R., Manstead, A. S. R., & MacDonald, C. J. (1984). The relationship between children's sociometric status and ability to recognize facial expressions of emotion. *European Journal of Social Psychology, 14,* 235–238.

Eibl-Eibesfeldt, I. (1971). *Love and hate.* London: Methuen.

Eibl-Eibesfeldt, I. (1972). Similarities and differences between cultures in expressive movements. In R. A. Hinde (Ed.), *Nonverbal communication.* Cambridge: Cambridge University Press.

Eibl-Eibesfeldt, I. (1989). *Human ethology.* New York: Aldine De Gruyter.

Eidelson, R. J. (1980). Interpersonal satisfaction and level of achievement: A curvilinear relationship. *Journal of Personality and Social Psychology, 39,* 460–470.

Eisenberger, R., Pierce, W. D., & Cameron, J. (1999). Effects of reward on intrinsic motivation: Negative, neutral, and positive: Comment on Deci, Koestner, and Ryan (1999). *Psychological Bulletin, 125,* 677–691.

Ekman, P. (1972). Universal and cultural differences in facial expression of emotion. In J. R. Cole (Ed.), *Nebraska symposium on motivation* (Vol. 19, pp. 207–284). Lincoln: University of Nebraska Press.

Ekman, P. (1992). An argument for basic emotions. *Cognition and Emotion, 6,* 169–200.

Ekman, P. (1993). Facial expression and emotion. *American Psychologist, 48,* 384–392.

Ekman, P. (1994a). All emotions are basic. In P. Ekman & R. J. Davidson (Eds.), *The nature of emotion: Fundamental questions* (pp. 15–19). New York: Oxford University Press.

Ekman, P. (1994b). Strong evidence for universals in facial expressions: A reply to Russell's mistaken critique. *Psychological Bulletin, 115,* 268–287.

Ekman, P., & Davidson, R. J. (1993). Voluntary smiling changes regional brain activity. *Psychological Science, 4,* 342–345.

Ekman, P., & Davidson, R. J. (Eds.). (1994). *The nature of emotion: Fundamental questions* (pp. 20–24). New York: Oxford University Press.

Ekman, P., & Friesen, W. V. (1971). Constants across cultures in facial expressions of emotion. In J. K. Cole (Ed.), *Nebraska symposium on motivation* (pp. 207–283). Lincoln: University of Nebraska Press.

Ekman, P., & Friesen, W. V. (1975). *Unmasking the face.* Englewood Cliffs, NJ: Prentice-Hall.

Ekman, P., & Friesen, W. V. (1978). *Facial action coding system.* Palo Alto, CA: Consulting Psychologists Press.

Ekman, P., & Friesen, W. V. (1986). A new pan-cultural facial expression of emotion. *Motivation and Emotion, 10,* 159–168.

Ekman, P., Levenson, R. W., & Friesen, W. V. (1983). Autonomic nervous system activity distinguishes between emotions. *Science, 221,* 1208–1210.

Ekman, P., & Rosenberg, E. (1997). *What the face reveals.* New York: Oxford University Press.

Ekman, P., Sorenson, E. R., & Friesen, W. V. (1969). Pan-cultural elements in facial displays of emotion. *Science, 164,* 86–88.

El-Haschimi, K., Pierroz, D. D., Hileman, S. M., Bjorbake, C., & Flier, J. S. (2000). Two defects contribute to hypothalamic leptin resistance in mice with diet-induced obesity. *Journal of Clinical Investigation, 105,* 1827–1832.

Ellingson, S. A., Miltenberger, R. G., Stricker, J. M., Garlinghouse, M. A., Roberts, J., Galensky, T. L., & Rapp, J. T. (2000). Analysis and treatment of finger sucking. *Journal of Applied Behavior Analysis, 33,* 41–52.

Elliot, A. J. (1997). Integrating the "classic" and "contemporary" approaches to achievement motivation: A hierarchical model of approach and avoidance achievement motivation. In M. L. Maehr & P. R. Pintrich (Eds.), *Advances in motivation and achievement* (Vol. 10, pp. 143–179). Greenwich, CT: JAI Press.

Elliot, A. J. (1999). Approach and avoidance motivation and achievement goals. *Educational Psychologist, 34,* 169–189.

Elliot, A. J., & Church, M. (1997). A hierarchical model of approach and avoidance achievement motivation. *Journal of Personality and Social Psychology, 72,* 218–232.

Elliot, A. J., & Devine, P. G. (1994). On the motivational nature of cognitive dissonance: Dissonance as psychological discomfort. *Journal of Personality and Social Psychology, 66,* 382–394.

Elliot, A. J., & Harackiewicz, J. (1996). Approach and avoidance goals and intrinsic motivation: A mediational analysis. *Journal of Personality and Social Psychology, 70,* 461–475.

Elliot, A. J., & McGregor, H. (1999). Test anxiety and the hierarchical model of approach and avoidance achievement motivation. *Journal of Personality and Social Psychology, 76,* 628–644.

Elliot, A. J., & Sheldon, K. (1997). Avoidance achievement motivation: A personal goals analysis. *Journal of Personality and Social Psychology, 73,* 171–185.

Elliot, A. J., Sheldon, K., & Church, M. (1997). Avoidance personal goals and subjective well-being. *Personality and Social Psychology Bulletin, 23,* 915–927.

Elliot, A. J., & Thrash, T. M. (2002). Approach-avoidance motivation in personality: Approach and avoidance temperament and goals. *Journal of Personality and Social Psychology, 82,* 804–818.

Elliot, E., & Dweck, C. (1988). Goals: An approach to motivation and achievement. *Journal of Personality and Social Psychology, 54,* 5–12.

Elliot, T. R., Witty, T. E., Herrick, S., & Hoffman, J. T. (1991). Negotiating reality after physical loss: Hope, depression, and disability. *Journal of Personality and Social Psychology, 61,* 608–613.

Ellsworth, P. C. (1994). William James and emotion: Is a century of fame worth a century of misunderstanding? *Psychological Review, 101,* 222–229.

Ellsworth, P. C., & Smith, C. A. (1988a). From appraisal to emotion: Differences among unpleasant feelings. *Motivation and Emotion, 12,* 271–302.

Ellsworth, P. C., & Smith, C. A. (1988b). Shades of joy: Patterns of appraisal differentiating pleasant emotions. *Cognition and Emotion, 2,* 301–331.

Elman, D., & Killebrew, T. J. (1978). Incentives and seat belts: Changing a resistant behavior through extrinsic motivation. *Journal of Applied Social Psychology, 8,* 73–83.

Elmquist, J. K., Elias, C. F., & Saper, C. B. (1999). From lesions to leptin: hypothalamic control of food intake and body weight. *Neuron, 22,* 221–232.

Emmons, R. A. (1989). The personal striving approach to personality. In L. A. Pervin (Ed.), *Goal concepts in personality and social psychology* (pp. 87–126). Hillsdale, NJ: Lawrence Erlbaum.

Emmons, R. A. (1996). Striving and feeling: Personal goals and subjective well-being. In P. M. Gollwitzer & J. A. Bargh (Eds.), *The psychology of action: Linking cognition and motivation to behavior* (pp. 313–337). New York: Guilford Press.

Emmons, R. A., & Diener, E. (1986). Influence of impulsivity and sociability on subjective well-being. *Journal of Personality and Social Psychology, 50,* 1211–1215.

Engerman, J., Austin, J., & Bailey, J. (1997). Prompting patron safety-belt use at a supermarket. *Journal of Applied Behavior Analysis, 30,* 577–579.

Epstein, A. N. (1973). Epilogue: Retrospect and prognosis. In A. N. Epstein, H. R. Kissileff, & E. Stellar (Eds.), *The neuropsychology of thirst: New findings and advances in concepts* (pp. 315–332). New York: Wiley.

Epstein, J. A., & Harackiewicz, J. H. (1992). Winning is not enough: The effects of competition and achievement orientation on intrinsic interest. *Personality and Social Psychology Bulletin, 18,* 128–138.

Erdelyi, M. H. (1985). *Psychoanalysis: Freud's cognitive psychology.* New York: W. H. Freeman.

Erdelyi, M. H. (1990). Repression, reconstruction, and defense: History and integration of the psychoanalytic and experimental frameworks. In J. L. Singer (Ed.), *Repression and dissociation* (pp. 1–31). Chicago: University of Chicago Press.

Erdelyi, M. H., & Goldberg, B. (1979). Let's not sweep repression under the rug: Toward a cognitive psychology of repression. In J. F. Kilstrom & F. J. Evans (Eds.), *Fundamental disorders of memory.* Hillsdale, NJ: Lawrence Erlbaum.

Erez, M. (1977). Feedback: A necessary condition for the goal setting performance relationship. *Journal of Applied Psychology, 62,* 624–627.

Erez, M., Earley, P. C., & Hulin, C. L. (1985). The impact of participation on goal acceptance and performance: A two-step model. *Academy of Management Journal, 28,* 50–66.

Erez, M., & Kanfer, F. H. (1983). The role of goal acceptance in goal setting and task performance. *Academy of Management Review, 8,* 454–463.

Erez, M., & Zidon, I. (1984). Effects of goal acceptance on the relationship to goal difficulty and performance. *Journal of Applied Psychology, 60,* 69–78.

Ericsson, K. A., Krampe, R. T. C., & Tesch-Romer, C. (1993). The role of deliberate practice in the acquisition of expert performance. *Psychological Review, 100,* 363–406.

Ericsson, K. A., & Charness, N. (1994). Expert performance: Its structure and acquisition. *American Psychologist, 49,* 725–747.

Estrada, C. A., Isen, A. M., & Young, M. J. (1994). Positive affect improves creative problem-solving and influences reported source of practice satisfaction in physicians. *Motivation and Emotion, 18,* 285–299.

Estrada, C. A., Isen, A. M., & Young, M. J. (1997). Positive affect influences integration of information and decreases anchoring in reasoning among physicians. *Organizational Behavior and Human Decision Making Processes, 72,* 117–135.

Ethington, C. A. (1991). A test of a model of achievement behaviors. *American Educational Research Journal, 28,* 155–172.

Evans, G. E., Shapiro, D. H., & Lewis, M. (1993). Specifying dysfunctional mismatches between different control dimensions. *British Journal of Psychology, 84,* 255–273.

Exline, R. V. (1962). Need affiliation and initial communication behavior in problem solving groups characterized by low interpersonal visibility. *Psychological Reports, 10,* 79–89.

Exner, J. E., Jr. (1986). *The Rorschach: A comprehensive system* (Vol. 1, 2nd ed.). New York: Wiley-Interscience.

Eysenck, H. J. (1986). Can personality study ever be scientific? *Journal of Social Behavior and Personality, 1,* 3–19.

Eysenck, H. P. (1991). Biological dimensions of personality. In L. A. Pervin (Ed.), *Handbook of personality* (pp. 244–276). New York: Guilford Press.

Eysenck, S. B., Eysenck, H. J., & Barrett, P. (1985). A revised version of the psychoticism scale. *Personality and Individual Differences, 6*, 21–29.

Faust, I. M., Johnson, P. R., & Hirsch, J. (1977a). Adipose tissue regeneration following lipectomy. *Science, 197*, 391–393.

Faust, I. M., Johnson, P. R., & Hirsch, J. (1977b). Surgical removal of adipose tissue alters feeding behavior and the development of obesity in rats. *Science, 197*, 393–396.

Fazio, R. H., Jackson, J. R., Dunton, B., & Williams, C. J. (1995). Variability in automatic activation as an unobtrusive measure of racial attitudes: A bona fide pipeline? *Journal of Personality and Social Psychology, 69*, 1013–1027.

Fazio, R. H., Zanna, M., & Cooper, J. (1977). Dissonance and self-perception: An integrative view of each theory's proper domain of application. *Journal of Experimental Social Psychology, 13*, 464–479.

Fazio, R. H., Zanna, M., & Cooper, J. (1979). On the relationship of data to theory: A reply to Ronis and Greenwald. *Journal of Experimental Social Psychology, 15*, 70–66.

Feather, N. T. (1961). The relationship of persistence at a task to expectation of success and achievement related motives. *Journal of Abnormal and Social Psychology, 63*, 552–561.

Feather, N. T. (1963). Persistence at a difficult task with alternative tasks of intermediate difficulty. *Journal of Abnormal and Social Psychology, 66*, 604–609.

Feeney, J. A., & Noller, P. (1990). Attachment style as a predictor of adult romantic relationships. *Journal of Personality and Social Psychology, 58*, 281–291.

Fehr, B., Baldwin, M., Collins, L., Patterson, S., & Benditt, R. (1999). Anger in close relationships: An interpersonal script analysis. *Personality and Social Psychology Bulletin, 25*, 299–312.

Fehr, B., & Russell, J. A. (1984). Concept of emotion viewed from a prototype perspective. *Journal of Experimental Psychology: General, 113*, 464–486.

Felson, R. B. (1984). The effect of self-appraisals of ability on academic performance. *Journal of Personality and Social Psychology, 47*, 944–952.

Feltz, D. L. (1992). Understanding motivation in sport: A self-efficacy perspective. In G. C. Roberts (Ed.), *Motivation in sport and exercise* (pp. 93–105). Champaign, IL: Human Kinetics.

Fenigstein, A., Scheier, M. F., & Buss, A. H. (1975). Public and private self-consciousness: Assessment and theory. *Journal of Consulting and Clinical Psychology, 43*, 522–527.

Fernald, A. (1992). Human maternal vocalizations to infants as biologically relevant signals: An evolutionary perspective. In J. H. Barkow, L. Cosmides, & J. Tooby (Eds.), *The adapted mind* (pp. 391–428). New York: Oxford University Press.

Fernandez-Dols, J. M., & Ruiz-Belba, M. A. (1995). Are smiles a sign of happiness? Gold medal winners at the Olympic games. *Journal of Personality and Social Psychology, 69*, 1113–1119.

Feshbach, S. (1984). The personality of personality theory and research. *Personality and Social Psychology Bulletin, 10*, 446–456.

Festinger, L. (1957). *A theory of cognitive dissonance*. Stanford: Stanford University Press.

Festinger, L., & Carlsmith, J. M. (1959). Cognitive consequences of forced compliance. *Journal of Abnormal and Social Psychology, 58*, 203–210.

Festinger, L., Riecken, H. W., & Schachter, S. (1956). *When prophecy fails*. Minneapolis: Minnesota University Press.

Festinger, L., Riecken, H. W., & Schachter, S. (1958). When prophecy fails. In E. E. Maccoby, T. M. Newcomb, & E. L. Hartley (Eds.), *Readings in social psychology* (pp. 156–163). New York: Holt, Rinehart & Winston.

Findley, M. J., & Cooper, H. M. (1983). Locus of control and academic achievement: Literature review. *Journal of Personality and Social Psychology, 44*, 419–427.

Fischer, H., Andersson, J. L. R., Furmark, T., Wik, G., & Fredrikson, M. (2002). Right-sided human prefrontal brain activation during acquisition of conditioned fear. *Emotion, 2*, 233–241.

Fischer, K. W., Shaver, P. R., & Carnochan, P. (1990). How emotions develop and how they organise development. *Cognition and Emotion, 4*, 81–127.

Fisher, C. D. (1978). The effects of personal control, competence, and extrinsic reward systems on intrinsic motivation. *Organizational Behavior and Human Performance, 21*, 273–288.

Fisher, S., & Greenberg, R. P. (1977). *The scientific credibility of Freud's theories and therapy.* New York: Basic Books.

Fisher, S., & Greenberg, R. P. (1996). *Freud scientifically reappraised: Testing the theories and therapy.* New York: John Wiley & Sons.

Fisher, W., Piazza, C., Cataldo, M., Harrell, R., Jefferson, G., & Comer, R. (1993). Functional communication training with and without extinction and punishment. *Journal of Applied Behavior Analysis, 26*, 23–36.

Flegel, K. M., Carroll, M. D., Kucznarski, R. J., & Johnson, C. L. (1998). Overweight and obesity in the United States: Prevalence and trends, 1960–1994. *International Journal of Obesity Relat. Matabolism Disorder, 22*, 39–47.

Flink, C., Boggiano, A. K., & Barrett, M. (1990). Controlling teaching strategies: Undermining children's self-determination and performance. *Journal of Personality and Social Psychology, 59*, 916–924.

Flink, C., Boggiano, A. K., Main, D. S., Barrett, M., & Katz, P. A. (1992). Children's achievement-related behaviors: The role of extrinsic and intrinsic motivational orientations. In A. K. Boggiano & T. S. Pittman (Eds.), *Achievement and motivation: A social-developmental perspective* (pp. 189–214). New York: Cambridge University Press.

Foch, T. T., & McClearn, G. E. (1980). Genetics, body weight, and obesity. In A. E. Stunkard (Ed.), *Obesity* (pp. 48–61). Philadelphia: W. B. Saunders.

Foder, E. M., & Farrow, D. L. (1979). The power motive as an influence on the use of power. *Journal of Personality and Social Psychology, 37*, 2091–2097.

Foder, E. M., & Smith, T. (1982). The power motive as an influence on group decision making. *Journal of Personality and Social Psychology, 42*, 178–185.

Folkman, S., & Lazarus, R. S. (1985). If it changes it must be a process: Study of emotion and coping during three stages of a college examination. *Journal of Personality and Social Psychology, 48*, 150–170.

Folkman, S., & Lazarus, R. S. (1990). Coping and emotion. In N. Stein, B. Leventhal, & T. Trabasso (Eds.), *Psychological and biological approaches to emotion* (pp. 313–332). Hillsdale, NJ: Lawrence Erlbaum.

Folkman, S., Lazarus, R. S., Dunkel-Schetter, C., DeLongin, A., & Gruen, R. J. (1986). Dynamics of a stressful encounter: Cognitive appraisal, coping, and encounter outcomes. *Journal of Personality and Social Psychology, 50*, 992–1003.

Foote, N. N. (1951). Identification as the basis for a theory of motivation. *American Sociological Review, 16*, 14–21.

Ford, J. G. (1991a). Inherent potentialities of actualization: An initial exploration. *Journal of Humanistic Psychology, 31*, 65–88.

Ford, J. G. (1991b). Rogerian self-actualization: A clarification of meaning. *Journal of Humanistic Psychology, 31*, 101–111.

Ford, J. G. (1995). The temperament/actualization concept: A perspective on constitutional integrity and psychological health. *Journal of Humanistic Psychology, 35*, 57–67.

Forest, D., Clark, M. S., Mills, J., & Isen, A. M. (1979). Helping as a function of feeling state and nature of the helping behavior. *Motivation and Emotion, 3*, 161–169.

Fowles, D. C. (1988). Psychophysiology and psychopathology: A motivational approach. *Psychophysiology, 25*, 373–391.

Frankl, V. E. (1960). Paradoxical intention: A logotherapeutic technique. *American Journal of Psychotherapy, 14*, 520–525.

Frayne, C. A., & Latham, G. P. (1987). The application of social learning theory to employee self-management of attendance. *Journal of Applied Psychology, 72*, 387–392.

Freud, A. (1946). *The ego and mechanisms of defense*. New York: International Universities Press.

Freud, S. (1914). *Psychopathology of everyday life* (A. A. Brill, Trans.). New York: Macmillan. (Original work published 1901)

Freud, S. (1915). Instincts and their vicissitudes (translated by J. Riviere, 1949). In *Collected papers of Sigmund Freud* (Vol. 4, pp. 60–83). London: Hogarth.

Freud, S. (1917). *Wit and its relation to the unconscious* (A. A. Brill, Trans.). New York: Moffat, Yard. (Original work published 1905)

Freud, S. (1920). *A general introduction to psychoanalysis* (J. Rivieíre, Trans.). New York: Liverright. (Original work published 1917)

Freud, S. (1922). *Beyond the pleasure principle* (J. Strachey, Trans.). London: Hogarth. (Original work published 1920)

Freud, S. (1927). *The ego and the id* (J. Rivieíre, Trans.). London: Hogarth. (Original work published 1923)

Freud, S. (1932). *The interpretation of dreams* (A. A. Brill, Trans.). London: Allen & Irwin. (Original work published 1900)

Freud, S. (1949). Instincts and their vicissitudes. In J. Rivieíre (Trans.), *Collected papers of Sigmund Freud* (Vol. 4, pp. 60–83). London: Hogarth. (Original work published 1915)

Freud, S. (1958). *Civilization and its discontents* (J. Rivieíre, Trans.). London: Hogarth Press. (Original work published 1930)

Freud, S. (1959). Inhibitions, symptoms, and anxiety (A. Strachey & J. Strachey, Trans.). In J. Strachey (Ed.) *The standard edition of the complete psychological works of Sigmund Freud* (Vol. 20). London: Hogarth Press. (Original work published 1926)

Freud, S. (1961). Humour (J. Rivieíre & J. Strachey, Trans.). In J. Strachey (Ed.) *The standard edition of the complete psychological works of Sigmund Freud* (Vol. 21). London: Hogarth press. (Original work published 1927)

Freud, S. (1964). New introductory lectures on psychoanalysis. In J. Strachey (Ed. and Trans.), *The standard edition of the complete psychological works of Sigmund Freud*. London: Hogart Press.

Fridlund, A. J. (1992). *The behavioral ecology and sociality of human faces*. In M. S. Clark (Ed.), Emotion. Newbury Park, CA: Sage.

Fried, C. B., & Aronson, E. (1995). Hypocrisy, misattribution, and dissonance reduction. *Personality and Social Psychology Bulletin, 21*, 925–933.

Frijda, N. H. (1986). *The emotions*. New York: Cambridge University Press.

Frijda, N. H. (1988). The laws of emotion. *American Psychologist, 43*, 349–358.

Frijda, N. H. (1993). The place of appraisal in emotion. *Cognition and Emotion, 7*, 357–388.

Frijda, N. H. (1994). Universal antecedents exist, and are interesting. In P. Ekman & R. J. Davidson (Eds.), *The nature of emotion: Fundamental questions* (pp. 155–162). New York: Oxford University Press.

Fromm, E. (1941). *Escape from freedom*. New York: Rinehart.

Fromm, E. (1956). *The art of loving*. New York: Harper & Brothers.

Fromm, E. (1964). *The heart of man*. New York: Harper & Row.

Fromm, E. (1986). *For the love of life*. New York: The Free Press.

Frost, R. O., Marten, P., Lahart, C., & Rosenblate, R. (1990). The dimensions of perfectionism. *Cognitive Therapy and Research, 14*, 449–468.

Gable, S. L., Reis, H. T., & Elliot, A. J. (2000). Behavioral activation and inhibition in everyday life. *Journal of Personality and Social Psychology, 78*, 1135–1149.

Gadde, K. M., Franciscy, D. M., Wagner II, H. R., & Krishnan, K. R. R. (2003). Zonisamide for weight loss in obese adults. *JAMA: Journal of the American Medical Association, 289*, 1820–1825.

Gagnon, J. H. (1974). Scripts and the coordination of sexual conduct. In J. K. Cole & R. Diensteiber (Eds.), *Nebraska symposium on motivation* (Vol. 21, pp. 27–59). Lincoln: University of Nebraska Press.

Gagnon, J. H. (1977). *Human sexualities.* Glenview, IL: Scott Foresman.

Gallagher, M., & Chiba, A. A. (1996). The amygdala and emotion. *Current Opinion in Neurobiology, 6*, 221–227.

Gallagher, S. M., & Keenan, M. (2000). Independent use of activity materials by the elderly in a residential setting. *Journal of Applied Behavior Analysis, 33*, 325–328.

Garbarino, J. (1975). The impact of anticipated reward upon cross-aged tutoring. *Journal of Personality and Social Psychology, 32*, 421–428.

Gardner, H. (1985). *The mind's new science: A history of the cognitive revolution.* New York: Basic Books.

Gecas, V., & Burke, P. J. (1995). Self and identity. In K. S. Cook, G. A. Fine, & J. S. House (Eds.), *Sociological perspectives on social psychology* (pp. 41–67). Boston: Allyn & Bacon.

Geller, E. S. (1988). A behavioral science approach to transportation safety. *The New York Academy of Medicine, 64*, 632–661.

Geller, E. S., Altomari, M. G., & Russ, N. W. (1984). *Innovative approaches to drunk driving prevention.* Warren, MI: Societal Analysis Department, General Motors Research Laboratories.

Geller, E. S., Casali, J. G., & Johnson, R. P. (1980). Seat belt usage: A potential target for applied behavior analysis. *Journal of Applied Behavior Analysis, 13*, 669–675.

Geller, E. S., Rudd, J. R., Kalsher, M. J., Streff, F. M., & Lehman, G. R. (1987). Employer-based programs to motivate safety-belt use: A review of short-term and long-term effects. *Journal of Safety Research, 18*, 1–17.

Geller, L. (1982). The failure of self-actualization theory: A critique of Carl Rogers and Abraham Maslow. *Journal of Humanistic Psychology, 22*, 56–63.

Gerard, H. (1992). Dissonance theory: A cognitive psychology with an engine. *Psychological Inquiry, 3*, 323–327.

Gershoff, E. T. (2002). Corporal punishment by parents and associated child behaviors and experiences: A meta-analytic and theoretical review. *Psychological Bulletin, 128*, 539–579.

Gibson, E. J. (1988). Exploratory behavior in the development of perceiving, acting and the acquiring of knowledge. *Annual Review of Psychology, 39*, 1–41.

Gilovich, T., Medvec, V. H., & Chen, S. (1995). Commission, omission, and dissonance reduction: Coping with regret in the Monty Hall problem. *Personality and Social Psychology Bulletin, 21*, 182–190.

Gjesme, T. (1981). Is there any future in achievement motivation? *Motivation and Emotion, 5*, 115–138.

Goebel, B. L., & Brown, D. R. (1981). Age differences in motivation related to Maslow's need hierarchy. *Developmental Psychology, 17*, 809–815.

Goffman, E. (1959). *The presentation of self in everyday life.* Garden City, NY: Doubleday.

Gold, M. S., & Fox, C. F. (1982). Antianxiety and opiates. *Brain and Brain Sciences, 3*, 486–487.

Gold, M. S., Pottash, A. L. C., Extein, I., & Kleber, H. D. (1980). Chonidine in acute opiate withdrawal. *New England Journal of Medicine, 302*, 1421–1422.

Goldberg, C. (1995). The daimenic development of the malevolent personality. *Journal of Humanistic Psychology, 35*, 7–36.

Goldsmith, H. H. (1994). Parsing the emotional domain from a developmental perspective. In P. Ekman & R. J. Davidson (Eds.), *The nature of emotion: Fundamental questions* (pp. 68–73). New York: Oxford University Press.

Goldstein, K. (1939). *The organism.* New York: American Book Company.

Goleman, D. (2003). *Destructive emotions: How can we overcome them?* New York: Bantam Books.

Gollwitzer, P. M. (1993). Goal achievement: The role of intentions. In W. Stroebe & M. Hewstone (Eds.), *European review of social psychology* (Vol. 4, pp. 141–185). Chichester, England: Wiley.

Gollwitzer, P. M. (1996). The volitional benefits of planning. In P. M. Gollwitzer & J. A. Bargh (Eds.), *The psychology of action: Linking cognition and emotion to behavior* (pp. 287–312). New York: Guilford Press.

Gollwitzer, P. M. (1999). Implementation intentions: Strong effects of simple plans. *American Psychologist, 54,* 493–503.

Gollwitzer, P. M., & Bargh, J. A. (Eds.). (1996). *The psychology of action: Linking cognition and motivation to behavior.* New York: Guilford Press.

Gollwitzer, P. M., & Brandstatter, V. (1997). Implementation intentions and effective goal pursuit. *Journal of Personality and Social Psychology, 73,* 186–199.

Gollwitzer, P. M., & Moskowitz, G. B. (1996). Goal effects on action and cognition. In E. T. Higgins & A. W. Kruglanski (Eds.), *Social psychology: Handbook of basic principles* (pp. 361–399). New York: Guilford Press.

Gollwitzer, P. M., & Schaal, B. (1998). Metacognition in action: The importance of implementation intentions. *Personality and Social Psychology Review, 2,* 124–136.

Gonas, G. (1977). Situation versus frame: The interactionist and the structuralist analysis of everyday life. *American Sociological Review, 42,* 854–867.

Goodenough, F. L. (1932). Expressions of emotions in a blind-deaf child. *Journal of Abnormal and Social Psychology, 27,* 328–333.

Goodenow, C. (1993). The psychological sense of school membership among adolescents: Scale development and educational correlates. *Psychology in the Schools, 30,* 79–90.

Goodman, R. A. (1968). On the operationality of Maslow's need hierarchy. *British Journal of Industrial Relations, 6,* 51–57.

Gottfried, A. (1985). Academic intrinsic motivation in elementary and junior high school students. *Journal of Educational Psychology, 77,* 631–645.

Gras, M. E., Cunill, M., Planes, M., Sullman, M. J. M., & Oliveras, C. (2003). Increasing safety-belt use in Spanish drivers: A field test of personal prompts. *Journal of Applied Behavior Analysis, 36,* 249–251.

Gray, J. A. (1982). *The neuropsychology of anxiety: An inquiry into the functions of the septo-hippocampal systems.* Oxford, England: Oxford University Press.

Gray, J. A. (1987). Perspectives on anxiety and impulsivity: A commentary. *Journal of Research in Personality, 21,* 493–509.

Gray, J. A. (1987). *The psychology of fear and stress* (2nd ed.). Cambridge, United Kingdom: Cambridge University Press.

Gray, J. A. (1994). Three fundamental emotion systems. In P. Ekman & R. J. Davidson (Eds.), *The nature of emotion: Fundamental questions* (pp. 243–247). New York: Oxford University Press.

Gray, J. R., Braver, T. S., & Raichle, M. E. (2002). Integration of emotion and cognition in the lateral prefrontal cortex. *Proceedings of the National Academy of Science, 99,* 4115–4120.

Green, C. W., Reid, D. H., White, L. K., Halford, R. C., Brittain, D. P., & Gardner, S. M. (1988). Identifying reinforcers for persons with profound handicaps: Staff opinion versus systematic assessment of preferences. *Journal of Applied Behavior Analysis, 21,* 31–43.

Greenberg, J. R., & Mitchell, S. (1983). *Object relations in psychoanalytic theory.* Cambridge, MA: Harvard University Press.

Greenberg, J. R., & Pyszczynski, T. (1985). Compensatory self-inflation: A response to the threat to self-regard of public failure. *Journal of Personality and Social Psychology, 49,* 273–280.

Greenberg, J. R., Solomon, S., Pyszczynski, T., Rosenblatt, A., Burling, J., Lyon, D., Simon, L., & Pinel, E. (1992). Why do people need self-esteem? Converging evidence that self-esteem serves an anxiety-buffering function. *Journal of Personality and Social Psychology, 63,* 913–922.

Greenberg, R., & Pearlman, C. (1993). An integrated approach to dream theory: Contributions from sleep research and clinical practice. In A. Moffitt, M. Kramer, & R. Hoffman (Eds.), *The functions of dreaming* (pp. 363–380). Albany: State University of New York.

Greene, D., & Lepper, M. R. (1974). Effects of extrinsic rewards on children's subsequent intrinsic interest. *Child Development, 45,* 1141–1145.

Greeno, C. G., & Wing, R. R. (1994). Stress-induced eating. *Psychological Bulletin, 115,* 444–464.

Greenwald, A. G., (1992). New look 3: Unconscious cognition reclaimed. *American Psychologist, 47,* 766–779.

Greenwald, A. G., Spangenberg, E. R., Pratkanis, A. R., & Eskenazi, J. (1991). Double-blind tests of subliminal self-help audiotapes. *Psychological Science, 2,* 119–122.

Gregory, L. W., Cialdini, R. B., & Carpenter, K. M. (1982). Self-relevant scenarios as mediators of likelihood estimates and compliance: Does imagining make it so? *Journal of Personality and Social Psychology, 43,* 89–99.

Grilo, C. M., & Pogue-Geile, M. F. (1991). The nature of environmental influences on weight and obesity: A behavior genetics analysis. *Psychological Bulletin, 110,* 520–537.

Grilo, C. M., Shiffman, S., & Wing, R. R. (1989). Relapse crises and coping among dieters. *Journal of Consulting and Clinical Psychology, 57,* 488–495.

Grolnick, W. S. (2003). *The psychology of parental control: How well-meant parenting backfires.* Mahwah, NJ: Lawrence Erlbaum.

Grolnick, W. S., Deci, E. L., & Ryan, R. M. (1997). Internalization within the family: The self-determination perspective. In J. E. Grusec & L. Kuczynski (Eds.), *Parenting and children's internalization of values: A handbook of contemporary theory* (pp. 135–161). New York: Wiley.

Grolnick, W. S., Frodi, A., & Bridges, L. (1984). Maternal control styles and the mastery motivation of one-year-olds. *Infant Mental Health Journal, 5,* 72–82.

Grolnick, W. S., & Ryan, R. M. (1987). Autonomy in children's learning: An experimental and individual difference investigation. *Journal of Personality and Social Psychology, 52,* 890–898.

Gross, J. J. (1999). Emotion regulation: Past, present, future. *Cognitive and Emotion, 13,* 551–573.

Gross, J. J., Carstensen, L. L., Pasupathi, M., & Tsai, J. (1997). Emotion and aging: Experience, expression, and control. *Psychology and Aging, 12,* 590–599.

Gross, N., Mason, W. S., & McEachern, A. W. (1958). *Explorations in role analysis: Studies of the school superintendency role.* New York: Wiley.

Gruen, A. (1976). Autonomy and compliance: The fundamental antithesis. *Journal of Humanistic Psychology, 16,* 61–69.

Guay, A. T. (2001). Decreasing testosterone in regularly menstruating women with decreased libido: A clinical observation. *Journal of Sex and Marital Therapy, 27,* 513–519.

Guisinger, S., & Blatt, S. J. (1994). Individuality and relatedness: Evolution of a fundamental dialectic. *American Psychologist, 49,* 104–111.

Hackett, G. (1985). The role of mathematics self-efficacy in the choice of math-related majors of college women and men: A path analysis. *Journal of Counseling Psychology, 32,* 47–56.

Haggbloom, S. J., Warnick, R., Warnick, J. E., Jones, V. K., Yarbrough, G. L., Russell, T. M., Borecky, C. M., McGahhey, R., Powell, J. L., Beavers, J., & Monte, E. (2002). The 100 most eminent psychologists of the 20th century. *Review of General Psychology, 6,* 139–152.

Hall, H. K., & Byrne, A. T. J. (1988). Goal setting in sport: Clarifying recent anomalies. *Journal of Sport and Exercise Psychology, 10,* 184–198.

Hall, J. F. (1961). *Psychology of motivation.* Philadelphia: J. B. Lippincott.

Hall, R. V., Axelrod, S., Tyler, L., Grief, E., Jones, F. C., & Robertson, R. (1972). Modification of behavior problems in the home with a parent as observer and experimenter. *Journal of Applied Behavior Analysis, 5*, 53–64.

Hall, W. G. (1973). A remote stomach clamp to evaluate oral and gastric controls of drinking in the rat. *Physiology and Behavior, 173*, 897–901.

Hamachek, D. E. (1978). Psychodynamics of normal and neurotic perfectionism. *Psychology, 15*, 27–33.

Hamann, S. B., Ely, T. D., Hoffman, J. M., & Kilts, C. D. (2002). Ecstasy and agony: Activation of the human amygdala in positive and negative emotion. *Psychological Science, 13*, 135–141.

Hamer, D. H., Hu, S., Magnuson, V. L., Hu, N., & Pattatucci, A. M. L. (1993). A linkage between DNA markers on the X chromosome and male sexual orientation. *Science, 261*, 321–327.

Hansford, B. C., & Hattie, J. A. (1982). The relationship between self and achievement/performance measures. *Review of Educational Research, 52*, 123–142.

Harackiewicz, J. (1979). The effects of reward contingency and performance feedback on intrinsic motivation. *Journal of Personality and Social Psychology, 37*, 1352–1363.

Harackiewicz, J. M., Barron, K. E., Carter, S. M., Lehto, A. T., & Elliot, A. J. (1997). Predictors and consequences of achievement goals in the college classroom: Maintaining interest and making the grade. *Journal of Personality and Social Psychology, 73*, 1284–1295.

Harackiewicz, J. M., & Elliot, A. J. (1993). Achievement goals and intrinsic motivation. *Journal of Personality and Social Psychology, 65*, 904–915.

Harackiewicz, J. M., & Manderlink, G. (1984). A process analysis of the effects of performance-contingent rewards on intrinsic motivation. *Journal of Experimental Social Psychology, 20*, 531–551.

Harackiewicz, J. M., Sansone, C., & Manderlink, G. (1985). Competence, achievement orientation, and intrinsic motivation: A process analysis. *Journal of Personality and Social Psychology, 48*, 493–508.

Hardaway, R. A. (1990). Subliminally activated symbiotic fantasies: Facts and artifacts. *Psychological Bulletin, 107*, 177–195.

Hardeman, M. (1979). A dialogue with Abraham Maslow. *Journal of Humanistic Psychology, 19*, 23–28.

Hardre, P. L., & Reeve, J. (2003). A motivational model of rural students' intentions to persist in, versus drop out of, high school. *Journal of Educational Psychology, 95*, 347–356.

Harlow, H. F. (1953). Motivation as a factor in the acquisition of new responses. In M. R. Jones (Ed.), *Nebraska symposium on motivation* (Vol. 1, pp. 24–49). Lincoln: University of Nebraska Press.

Harmon-Jones, E., & Mills, J. (1999). An introduction to cognitive dissonance theory and an overview of current perspectives on the theory. In E. Harmon-Jones & J. Mills (Eds.), *Cognitive dissonance: Progress on a pivotal theory in social psychology* (pp. 3–21). Washington, DC: American Psychological Association.

Harper, R. M., Frysinger, R. C., Trelease, R. B., & Marks, J. D. (1984). State-dependent alteration of respiratory cycle timing by stimulation of the central nucleus of the amygdala. *Brain Research, 306*, 1–8.

Harris, R. N., & Snyder, C. R. (1986). The role of uncertain self-esteem in self-handicapping. *Journal of Personality and Social Psychology, 51*, 451–458.

Harrison, A. A., & Saeed, L. (1997). Let's make a deal: An analysis of revelations and stipulations in lonely hearts advertisements. *Journal of Personality and Social Psychology, 35*, 257–264.

Harter, S. (1974). Pleasure derived by children from cognitive challenge and mastery. *Child Development, 45*, 661–669.

Harter, S. (1978a). Effectance motivation reconsidered: Toward a developmental model. *Human Development, 21*, 34–64.

Harter, S. (1978b). Pleasure derived from optimal challenge and the effects of extrinsic rewards on children's difficulty level choices. *Child Development, 49*, 788–799.

Harter, S. (1981). A model of mastery motivation in children: Individual differences and developmental changes. In W. A. Collin (Ed.), *Aspects of the development of competence* (Vol. 14, pp. 215–255). Hillsdale, NJ: Erlbaum.

Harter, S. (1988). The construction and conservation of the self: James and Cooley revisited. In D. K. Lapsle & F. C. Power (Eds.), *Self, ego, and identity: Integrative approaches* (pp. 43–60). New York: Springer-Verlag.

Harter, S. (1990). Causes, correlates and the functional role of global self-worth: A life-span perspective. In R. J. Sternberg & J. Kolligian, Jr. (Eds.), *Competence considered* (pp. 67–97). New Haven, CT: Yale University Press.

Harter, S. (1993). Causes and consequences of low self-esteem in children and adolescents. In R. Baumeister (Ed.), *Self-esteem: The puzzle of low self-regard* (pp. 87–116). New York: Plenum Press.

Harter, S., & Park, R. (1984). The pictorial perceived competence scale for young children. *Child Development, 55*, 1969–1982.

Hartmann, H. (1958). *Ego psychology and the problem of adaptation* (D. Rapaport, Trans.). New York: International Universities Press.

Hartmann, H. (1964). *Essays on ego psychology: Selected problems in psychoanalytic theory*. New York: International Universities Press.

Harvey, J., & Ashford, M. L. J. (2003). Leptin in the CNS: Much more than a satiety signal. *Neuropharmacology, 44*, 845–854.

Hatfield, E., Cacioppo, J. T., & Rapson, R. L. (1993a). *Emotional contagion*. Cambridge: Cambridge University Press.

Hatfield, E., Cacioppo, J. T., & Rapson, R. L. (1993b). Emotional contagion. *Current Directions in Psychological Science, 2*, 96–99.

Hatfield, E., Hsee, C. K., Costello, J., Weisman, M. S., & Denney, C. (1995). The impact of vocal feedback on emotional experience and expression. *Journal of Social Behavior and Personality, 10*, 293–312.

Haviland, J. J., & Lelwica, M. (1987). The induced affect response: Ten-week old infants' responses to three emotion expressions. *Developmental Psychology, 23*, 997–1004.

Haviland, J. M., & Kramer, D. A. (1991). Affect-cognition relationships in adolescent diaries: The case of Anne Frank. *Human Development, 34*, 143–159.

Hazan, C., & Shaver, P. (1987). Romantic love conceptualized as an attachment process. *Journal of Personality and Social Psychology, 52*, 511–524.

Heath, R. G. (1964). Pleasure response of human subjects to direct stimulation of the brain. In R. G. Heath (Ed.), *The role of pleasure in behavior* (pp. 219–243). New York: Harper & Row.

Heatherton, T. F., Herman, C. P., & Polivy, J. (1991). Effects of physical threat and ego threat on eating behavior. *Journal of Personality and Social Psychology, 60*, 138–143.

Heatherton, T. F., Polivy, J., & Herman, C. P. (1989). Restraint and internal responsiveness: Effects of placebo manipulations of hunger state on eating. *Journal of Abnormal Psychology, 98*, 89–92.

Hebb, D. O. (1949). *The organization of behavior*. New York: Wiley.

Hebb, D. O. (1955). Drives and the C.N.S.: Conceptual nervous system. *Psychological Review, 62*, 245–254.

Heckhausen, H. (1967). *The anatomy of achievement motivation*. New York: Academic Press.

Heckhausen, H. (1977). Achievement motivation and its constructs: A cognitive model. *Motivation and Emotion, 1*, 283–329.

Heckhausen, H. (1980). *Motivation and Handeln*. New York: Springer-Verlag.

Heckhausen, H. (1982). The development of achievement motivation. In W. W. Harup (Ed.), *Review of child development research* (Vol. 6, pp. 600–668). Chicago: University of Chicago Press.

Heider, F. (1958). *The psychology of interpersonal relations*. New York: John Wiley.

Heimer, L. (1995). *The human brain and spinal cord* (2nd ed.). New York: Springer-Verlag.

Heise, D. R. (1979). *Understanding events: Affect and the construction of social action.* New York: Cambridge University Press.

Heise, D. R. (1985). Affect control theory: Respecification, estimation, and tests of the formal model. *Journal of Mathematical Sociology, 1,* 191–222.

Heise, D. R. (1989). Effects of emotion displays on social identification. *Social Psychology Quarterly, 52,* 10–21.

Heise, D. R. (1991). *INTERACT 2: A computer program for studying cultural meanings and social interaction.* Department of Sociology, University of Indiana: Bloomington, IN.

Helmke, A., & van Aken, M. A. G. (1995). The causal ordering of academic achievement and self-concept of ability during elementary school: A longitudinal study. *Journal of Educational Psychology, 87,* 624–637.

Henderlong, J., & Lepper, M. R. (2002). The effects of praise on children's intrinsic motivation: A review and synthesis. *Psychological Bulletin, 128,* 774–795.

Hendrick, S. S., & Hendrick, C. (1987). Love and sexual attitudes, self-disclosure, and sensation seeking. *Journal of Social and Personal Relationships, 4,* 281–297.

Hennessey, B. A., & Amabile, T. M. (1998). Reward, intrinsic motivation, and creativity. *American Psychologist, 53,* 674–675.

Henry, M. C., Hollander, J. E., Alicandro, J. M., Casara, G., O'Malley, S., & Thode, H. C. Jr. (1996). Prospective countrywide evaluation of the effects of motor vehicle safety device use on hospital resource use and injury severity. *Annals of Emergency Medicine, 28,* 627–634.

Herman, C. P., & Mack, D. (1975). Restrained and unrestrained eating. *Journal of Personality, 43,* 647–660.

Herman, C. P., Polivy, J., & Esses, J. M. (1987). The illusion of counter-regulation. *Appetite, 9,* 161–169.

Heron, W. (1957). The pathology of boredom. *Scientific American, 196,* 52–56.

Hewitt, P. L., & Dyck, D. G. (1986). Perfectionism, stress, and vulnerability to depression. *Cognitive Therapy and Research, 10,* 137–142.

Hewitt, P. L., & Flett, G. L. (1991a). Dimensions of perfectionism in unipolar depression. *Journal of Abnormal Psychology, 100,* 98–101.

Hewitt, P. L., & Flett, G. L. (1991b). Perfectionism in the self and social contexts: Conceptualization, assessment, and association with psychopathology. *Journal of Personality and Social Psychology, 60,* 456–470.

Heyman, G. D., & Dweck, C. S. (1992). Achievement goals and intrinsic motivation: Their relation and their role in adaptive motivation. *Motivation and Emotion, 16,* 231–247.

Hidi, S. (1990). Interest and its contribution as a mental resource for learning. *Review of Educational Research, 60,* 549–571.

Hill, J. O., Pagliassotti, M. J., & Peters, J. C. (1994). In C. Bouchard (Ed.), *Genetic determinants of obesity* (pp. 35–48). Boca Raton, FL: CRC Press.

Hill, J. O., & Peters, J. C. (1998). Environmental contributions to the obesity epidemic. *Science, 280,* 1371–1374.

Hiroto, D. S. (1974). Locus of control and learned helplessness. *Journal of Experimental Psychology, 102,* 187–193.

Hiroto, D. S., & Seligman, M. E. P. (1975). Generality of learned helplessness in man. *Journal of Personality and Social Psychology, 31,* 311–327.

Hochschild, A. R. (1983). *The managed heart.* Berkeley: University of California Press.

Hodgins, H. S., & Knee, C. R. (2002). The integrating self and conscious experience. In E. L. Deci & R. M. Ryan's (Eds.), *Handbook of self-determination* (pp. 65–86). Rochester, NY: University of Rochester Press.

Hodgins, H. S., Koestner, R., & Duncan, N. (1996). On the compatibility of autonomy and relatedness. *Personality and Social Psychology Bulletin, 22,* 227–237.

Hodgins, H. S., Liebeskind, E., & Schwartz, W. (1996). Getting out of hot water: Facework in social predicaments. *Journal of Personality and Social Psychology, 71*, 300–314.

Hodgson, R., & Rachman, S. (1974). Desynchrony in measures of fear. *Behaviour Research and Therapy, 12*, 319–326.

Hoebel, B. G. (1976). Brain stimulation reward and aversion in relation to behavior. In A. Wauquier & E. T. Rolls (Eds.), *Brain stimulation reward* (pp. 355–372). New York: Elsevier.

Hokoda, A., & Fincham, F. D. (1995). Origins of children's helpless and mastery achievement patterns in the family. *Journal of Educational Psychology, 87*, 375–385.

Holahan, C. K., & Holahan, C. J. (1987). Self-efficacy, social support, and depression in aging: A longitudinal analysis. *Journal of Gerontology, 42,* 65–68.

Holmes, D. S. (1974). Investigation of repression: Differential recall of material experimentally or naturally associated with ego threat. *Psychological Bulletin, 81*, 632–653.

Holmes, D. S. (1990). The evidence for repression: An examination of sixty years of research. In J. L. Singer (Ed.), *Repression and dissociation* (pp. 85–102). Chicago: University of Chicago Press.

Holmes, T. H., & Rahe, R. H. (1967). The social readjustment rating scale. *Journal of Psychosomatic Research, 11*, 213–218.

Holstedge, G., Kuypers, H. G. J. M., & Dekker, J. J. (1977). The organization of the bulbar fibre connections to the trigeminal, facial, and hypoglossal motor nuclei: II. An autoradiographic tracing study in cat. *Brain, 100*, 265–286.

Holt, E. B. (1931). *Animal drive and the learning process.* New York: Holt.

Holt, R. R. (1989). *Freud reappraised: A fresh look at psychoanalytic theory.* New York: Guilford Press.

Hom, H. L., Jr. (1994). Can you predict the overjustification effect? *Teaching of Psychology, 21*, 36–37.

Hong, Y., Chiu. C., Dweck, C. S., Lin, D. M.-S., & Wan, W. (1999). Implicit theories, attributions, and coping: A meaning system approach. *Journal of Personality and Social Psychology, 77*, 588–599.

Horney, K. (1939). *New ways in psychoanalysis.* New York: Norton.

Horney, K. (1937). *The neurotic personality of our time.* New York: W. W. Norton.

Horowitz, M. J., Wilner, N., Kaltreidr, N., & Alvarez, W. (1980). Signs and symptoms of posttraumatic stress disorder. *Archives of General Psychology, 37*, 85–92.

Horvath, P., & Zuckerman, M. (1993). Sensation seeking, risk appraisal, and risky behavior. *Personality and Individual Differences, 14*, 41–52.

Horvath, T. (1979). Correlates of physical beauty in men and women. *Social Behavior and Personality, 7*, 145–151.

Horvath, T. (1981). Physical attractiveness: The influence of selected torso parameters. *Archives of Sexual Behavior, 10*, 21–24.

Hosobuchi, Y., Adams, J. E., & Linchitz, R. (1977). Pain relief by electrical stimulation at the central gray matter in humans and its reversal by naloxone. *Science, 197*, 183–186.

Huber, V. L. (1985). Effects of task difficulty, goal setting, and strategy on performance of a heuristic task. *Journal of Applied Psychology, 70*, 492–504.

Huebner, R. R., & Izard, C. E. (1988). Mothers responses to infants facial expressions of sadness, anger, and physical distress. *Motivation and Emotion, 12*, 185–196.

Hull, C. L. (1943). *Principles of behavior.* New York: Appleton-Century-Crofts.

Hull, C. L. (1952). *A behavior system: An introduction to behavior theory concerning the individual organism.* New Haven, CT: Yale University Press.

Hull, J. G. (1981). A self-awareness model of the causes and effects of alcohol consumption. *Journal of Abnormal Psychology, 90*, 586–600.

Hupka, R. B. (1984). Jealousy: Compound emotion or label for a particular situation. *Motivation and Emotion, 8*, 141–155.

Hymbaugh, K., & Garrett, J. (1974). Sensation seeking among skydivers. *Perceptual and Motor Skills, 38*, 1–18.

Isaacson, R. L. (1982). *The limbic system* (2e.). New York: Plenum.

Isen, A. M. (1970). Success, failure, attention, and reactions to others: The warm glow of success. *Journal of Personality and Social Psychology, 15*, 294–301.

Isen, A. M. (1984). Toward understanding the role of affect in cognition. In R. Wyer & T. Srull (Eds.), *Handbook of social cognition* (pp. 179–236). Hillsdale, NJ: Erlbaum.

Isen, A. M. (1987). Positive affect, cognitive processes, and social behavior. In L. Berkowitz (Ed.), *Advances in experimental social psychology* (Vol. 20, pp. 203–253). New York: Academic Press.

Isen, A. M. (2002). A role for neuropsychology in understanding the facilitating influence of positive affect on social behavior and cognitive processes. In C. R. Snyder & S. J. Lopez (Eds.), *Handbook of positive psychology* (pp. 528–540). New York: Oxford University Press.

Isen, A. M., Clark, M. S., & Schwartz, M. F. (1976). Duration of the effects of good mood on helping: Footprints in the sands of time. *Journal of Personality and Social Psychology, 34*, 385–393.

Isen, A. M., Daubman, K. A., & Nowicki, G. P. (1987). Positive affect facilitates creative problem-solving. *Journal of Personality and Social Psychology, 51*, 1122–1131.

Isen, A. M., & Geva, N. (1987). The influence of positive affect on acceptable level of risk: The person with a large canoe has a large worry. *Organizational Behavior and Human Decision Processes, 39*, 145–154.

Isen, A. M., Johnson, M. M. S., Mertz, E., & Robinson, G. F. (1985). The influence of positive affect on the unusualness of word associations. *Journal of Personality and Social Psychology, 48*, 1413–1426.

Isen, A. M., & Levin, P. F. (1972). The effect of feeling good on helping: Cookies and kindness. *Journal of Personality and Social Psychology, 21*, 384–388.

Isen, A. M., & Means, B. (1983). The influence of positive affect on decision-making strategy. *Social Cognition, 2*, 18–31.

Isen, A. M., Niedenthal, P., & Cantor, N. (1992). An influence of positive affect on social categorization. *Motivation and Emotion, 16*, 65–68.

Isen, A. M., & Nowicki, G. P. (1981). *Positive affect and creative problem solving.* Paper presented at the annual meeting of the Cognitive Science Society, Berkeley, CA.

Isen, A. M., & Patrick, R. (1983). The effect of positive feelings on risk-taking: When the chips are down. *Organizational Behavior and Human Performance, 31*, 194–202.

Isen, A. M., & Reeve, J. (2003). *The influence of positive affect on intrinsic motivation.* Unpublished manuscript, Cornell University.

Isen, A. M., Rosenzweig, A. S., & Young, M. J. (1991). The influence of positive affect on clinical problem solving. *Medical Decision Making, 11*, 221–227.

Isen, A. M., Shalker, T., Clark, M., & Karp, L. (1978). Affect, accessibility of material in memory, and behavior: A cognitive loop? *Journal of Personality and Social Psychology, 36*, 1–12.

Iversen, L., & Sabroe, S. (1989). Psychological well-being among unemployed and employed people after a company closes down: A longitudinal study. *Journal of Social Issues, 44*, 141–152.

Iwata, B. A. (1987). Negative reinforcement in applied behavior analysis: An emerging technology. *Journal of Applied Behavior Analysis, 20*, 361–378.

Izard, C. E. (1971). *The face of emotion.* New York: Appleton-Century-Crofts.

Izard, C. E. (1980). Cross-cultural perspectives on emotion and emotion communication. In H. Triandis & W. J. Lonner (Eds.), *Handbook of cross-cultural psychology* (Vol. 3). Boston: Allyn & Bacon.

Izard, C. E. (1982). Comments on emotion and cognition: Can there be a working relationship? In M. S. Clark & S. T. Fiske (Eds.), *Affect and cognition.* Hillsdale, NJ: Lawrence Erlbaum.

Izard, C. E. (1984). Emotion-cognition relationships in human development. In C. E. Izard, J. Kagan, & R. B. Zajonc (Eds.), *Emotions, cognition and behavior* (pp. 17–37). Cambridge, United Kingdom: Cambridge University Press.

Izard, C. E. (1989). The structure and functions of emotions: Implications for cognition, motivation, and personality. In I. S. Cohen (Ed.), *The G. Stanley Hall lecture series* (Vol. 9, pp. 39–63). Washington, DC: American Psychological Association.

Izard, C. E. (1990). Facial expressions and the regulation of emotions. *Journal of Personality and Social Psychology, 58*, 487–498.

Izard, C. E. (1991). *The psychology of emotions*. New York: Plenum.

Izard, C. E. (1992). Basic emotions, relations among the emotions, and emotion-cognition relations. *Psychological Review, 99*, 561–565.

Izard, C. E. (1993). Four systems for emotion activation: Cognitive and noncognitive development. *Psychological Review, 100*, 68–90.

Izard, C. E. (1994). Innate and universal facial expressions: Evidence from developmental and cross-cultural research. *Psychological Bulletin, 115*, 288–299.

Izard, C. E., Fantauzzo, C. A., Castle, J. M., Haynes, O. M., Rayias, M. F., & Putnam, P. H. (1995). The ontogeny and significance of infants' facial expressions in the first nine months of life. *Developmental Psychology, 31*, 997–1013.

Izard, C. E., Hembree, E. A., Dougherty, L. M., & Spizzirri, C. C. (1983). Changes in facial expressions of 2- to 19-month-old infants following acute pain. *Developmental Psychology, 19*, 418–426.

Izard, C. E., Huebner, R. R., Risser, D., McGinnes, G., & Dougherty, L. (1980). The young infant's ability to reproduce discrete emotion expressions. *Developmental Psychology, 16*, 132–140.

Izard, C. E., & Malatesta, C. Z. (1987). Perspectives on emotional development: I. Differential emotions theory of early emotional development. In J. D. Osotsky (Ed.), *Handbook of infant development* (2nd ed., pp. 494–554). New York: Wiley-Interscience.

Jackson, W. T., Taylor, R. E., Palmatier, A. D., Elliott, T. R., & Elliot, J. L. (1998). Negotiating the reality of visual impairment: Hope, coping, and functional ability. *Journal of Clinical Psychology in Medical Settings, 5*, 173–185.

Jacobs, K. W., & Koeppel, J. C. (1974). Psychological correlates of the mobility decision. *Bulletin of the Psychodynamic Society, 3*, 330–332.

Jacobs, W. J., & Nadel, L. (1985). Stress-induced recovery of fears and phobias. *Psychological Review, 92*, 512–531.

Jacoby, L., & Kelly, C. M. (1992). A process-dissociation framework for investigating unconscious influences: Freudian slips, projective tests, subliminal perception, and signal detection theory. *Current Directions in Psychological Science, 1*, 174–179.

James, W. (1884). What is an emotion? *Mind, 9*, 188–205.

James, W. (1890). *The principles of psychology* (2 Vols.). New York: Henry Holt.

James, W. (1894). The physical basis of emotion. *Psychological Review, 1*, 516–529.

Janssen, E., Vorst, H., Finn, P., & Bancroft, J. (2002). The sexual inhibition (SIS) and Sexual excitation (SES) scales: I. Measuring sexual inhibition and excitation proneness in men. *The Journal of Sex Research, 39*, 114–126.

Jeffrey, D. B., & Knauss, M. R. (1981). The etiologies, treatments, and assessments of obesity. In S. N. Haynes & L. Gannon (Eds.), *Psychosomatic disorders: A psychophysiological approach to etiology and treatment* (pp. 269–319). New York: Praeger.

Jenkins, S. R. (1987). Need for achievement and women's careers over 14 years: Evidence for occupational structural effects. *Journal of Personality and Social Psychology, 53*, 922–932.

Jenkins, S. R. (1996). Self-definition in thought, action, and life path choices. *Personality and Social Psychology Bulletin, 22*, 99–111.

John, O. P., & Robins, R. W. (1994). Accuracy and bias in self-perception: Individual differences in self-enhancement and the role of narcissism. *Journal of Personality and Social Psychology, 66,* 206–219.

John, O. P., & Srivastava, S. (2000). The big five trait taxonomy: History, measurement, and theoretical perspectives. In L. A. Pervin & P. John (Eds.), *Handbook of personality: Theory and research* (2nd ed., pp. 102–138). New York: The Guilford Press.

Johnson, D. W., & Johnson, R. T. (1985). Motivational processes in cooperative, competitive, and individualistic learning situations. In C. A. Ames & R. Ames (Eds.), *Research on motivation in education: The classroom milieu* (Vol. 2, pp. 249–286). Orlando, FL: Academic Press.

Johnson-Laird, P. N., & Oatley, K. (1989). The language of emotions: An analysis of a semantic field. *Cognition and Emotion, 3,* 81–123.

Johnson-Laird, P. N., & Oatley, K. (1992). Basic emotions, rationality and folk theory. *Cognition and Emotion, 6,* 201–223.

Jones, E. E., & Davis, K. E. (1965). From acts to dispositions: The attribution process in person perception. In L. Berkowitz (Ed.), *Advances in experimental social psychology* (Vol. 2, pp. 214–266). New York: Academic Press.

Jones, E. E., & Gerard, H. B. (1967). *Foundations of social psychology.* New York: Wiley.

Josephs, R. A., Markus, H. R., & Tafarodi, R. W. (1992). Gender and self-esteem. *Journal of Personality and Social Psychology, 63,* 391–402.

Joussemet, M., Koestner, R., Lekes, N., & Houlfort, N. (2003). Introducing uninteresting tasks to children: A comparison of the effects of rewards and autonomy support. *Journal of Personality.*

Kahneman, D. (1973). *Attention and effort.* Englewood Cliffs, NJ: Prentice-Hall.

Kagan, J. (1972). Motives and development. *Journal of Personality and Social Psychology, 22,* 51–66.

Kanfer, R., & Ackerman, P. L. (1989). Motivation and cognitive abilities: An integrative aptitude treatment interaction approach to skill acquisition. *Journal of Applied Psychology, 74,* 657–690.

Kapp, B. S., Gallagher, M., Underwood, M. D., McNall, C. L., & Whitehorn, D. (1982). Cardiovascular responses elicited by electrical stimulation of the amygdala central nucleus in the rabbit. *Brain Research, 234,* 251–262.

Kapp, B. S., Pascoe, J. P., & Bixler, M. A. (1984). The amygdala: A neuroanatomical systems approach to its contributions to aversive conditioning. In N. Buttlers & L. R. Squire (Eds.), *Neuropsychology of memory* (pp. 473–488). New York: Guilford Press.

Karabenick, S. A., & Yousseff, Z. I. (1968). Performance as a function of achievement level and perceived difficulty. *Journal of Personality and Social Psychology, 10,* 414–419.

Karoly, P. (1993). Mechanisms of self-regulation: An overview. *Annual Review of Psychology, 44,* 23–52.

Kaschak, E., & Tiefer, L. (Eds.) (2002). *A new view of women's sexual problems.* Binghamton, NY: Haworth Press.

Kasser, T., & Ryan, R. M. (1993). A dark side of the American dream: Correlates of financial success as a central life aspiration. *Journal of Personality and Social Psychology, 65,* 410–422.

Kasser, T., & Ryan, R. M. (1996). Further examining the American dream: Differential correlates of intrinsic and extrinsic goals. *Personality and Social Psychology Bulletin, 22,* 280–287.

Kasser, T., & Ryan, R. M. (2001). Be careful what you wish for: Optimal functioning and the relative attainment of intrinsic and extrinsic goals. In P. Schmuck & K. M. Sheldon (Eds.), *Life goals and well-being: Toward a positive psychology of human striving.* Seattle, WA: Hogrefe & Huber.

Kasser, V. G., & Ryan, R. M. (1999). The relation of psychological needs for autonomy and relatedness to vitality, well-being, and mortality in a nursing home. *Journal of Applied Social Psychology, 29,* 935–954.

Kassirer, J. P., & Angell, A. (1998). Losing weight: An ill-fated New Year's resolution. *New England Journal of Medicine, 338*, 52–54.

Kast, A., & Connor, K. (1988). Sex and age differences in response to informational and controlling feedback. *Personality and Social Psychology Bulletin, 14*, 514–523.

Katz, J., Beach, S. R. H., & Anderson, P. (1996). Self-enhancement versus self-verification: Does spousal support always help? *Cognitive Therapy and Research, 20*, 345–360.

Katzman, M., & Wolchik, S. (1984). Bulimia and binge eating in college women: A comparison of personality and behavioral characteristics. *Journal of Consulting and Clinical Psychology, 52*, 423–428.

Kazdin, A. E. (1979). Imagery elaboration and self-efficacy in the covert modeling treatment of unassertive behavior. *Journal of Consulting and Clinical Psychology, 47*, 725–733.

Keating, C. F., Mazur, A., & Segall, M. H. (1981). A cross-cultural exploration of physiognomic traits of dominance and happiness. *Ethology and Sociobiology, 2*, 41–48.

Keesey, R. E. (1980). A set-point analysis of the regulation of body weight. In A. J. Stunkard (Ed.), *Obesity* (pp. 144–165). Philadelphia: Saunders.

Keesey, R. E. (1989). Physiological regulation of body-weight and the issue of obesity. *Medical Clinics of North America, 73*, 15–27.

Keesey, R. E., Boyle, P. C., Kemnitz, J. W., & Mitchell, J. S. (1976). The role of the lateral hypothalamus in determining the body weight set point. In D. Novin, W. Wyrwicka, & G. A. Bray (Eds.), *Hunger: Basic mechanisms and clinical implications* (pp. 243–255). New York: Raven Press.

Keesey, R. E., & Powley, T. L. (1975). Hypothalamic regulation of body weight. *American Scientist, 63*, 558–565.

Kelley, A. E., & Stinus, L. (1984). The distribution of the projection from the parataenial nucleus of the thalamus to the nucleus accumbens in the rat: An autoradiographic study. *Experimental Brain Research, 54*, 499–512.

Kelley, H. H. (1967). Attribution theory in social psychology. In D. Levine (Ed.), *Nebraska symposium on motivation* (Vol. 15, pp. 192–238). Lincoln: University of Nebraska Press.

Kelly, A. E., & Kahn, J. H. (1994). Effects of suppression of personal intrusive thought. *Journal of Personality and Social Psychology, 66*, 998–1006.

Kelly, D. D. (1991). Sexual differentiation of the nervous system. In E. R. Kandel, J. H. Schwartz, & T. M. Jessell (Eds.), *Principles of neural science* (3rd ed., pp. 959–973). Norwalk, CT: Appleton & Lange.

Keltner, D., & Buswell, B. N. (1997). Embarrassment: Its distinct form and appeasement functions. *Psychological Bulletin, 122*, 250–270.

Keltner, D., Ellsworth, P. C., & Edwards, K. (1993). Beyond simple pessimism: Effects of sadness and anger on social perception. *Journal of Personality and Social Psychology, 64*, 740–752.

Keltner, D., & Gross, J. J. (1999). Functional accounts of emotions. *Cognitive and Emotion, 13*, 467–480.

Keltner, D., & Haidt, J. (1999). Social functions of emotions at four levels of analysis. *Cognitive and Emotion, 13*, 505–521.

Kemper, T. D. (1987). How many emotions are there? Wedding the social and the autonomic components. *American Sociological Review, 93*, 263–289.

Kenrick, D. T., Groth, G. E., Trost, M. R., & Sadalla, E. K. (1993). Integrating evolutionary and social exchange perspectives on relationship: Effects of gender, self-appraisal, and involvement level on mate selection criteria. *Journal of Personality and Social Psychology, 64*, 951–969.

Kihlstrom, J. F. (1987). The cognitive unconscious. *Science, 237*, 1445–1452.

Kihlstrom, J. F., & Cantor, N. (1984). Mental representations of the self. In L. Berkowitz (Ed.), *Advances in experimental and social psychology* (Vol. 17, pp. 2–47). New York: Academic Press.

Kimble, G. A. (1990). Mother nature's bag of tricks is small. *Psychological Science, 1*, 36–41.

Kirkpatrick, L. A., & Shaver, P. (1988). Fear and affiliation reconsidered from a stress and coping perspective: The importance of cognitive clarity and fear reduction. *Journal of Social and Clinical Psychology, 7*, 214–233.

Kirschbaum, C., Wolf, O. T., May, M., Wippich, W., & Hellhammer, D. H. (1996). Stress and treatment-induced elevations of control levels associated with impaired declarative memory in healthy adults. *Life Sciences, 58*, 1475–1483.

Kirschenbaum, D. S. (1987). Self-regulatory failure: A review with clinical implications. *Clinical Psychology Review, 7*, 77–104.

Klein, C. S. (1967). Peremptory ideation: Structure and force in motivated ideas. In R. R. Holt (Ed.), Motives and thought: Psychoanalytic essays in honor of David Rapaport. *Psychological Issues, 5* (Monograph No. 18/19), 80–128.

Klein, H. J., Whitener, E. M., & Ilgen, D. R. (1990). The role of goal specificity in the goal-setting process. *Motivation and Emotion, 14*, 179–193.

Klesges, R. C., Coates, T. J., Brown, G., Sturgeon-Tillisch, J., Moldenhauer-Klesges, L. M., Holzer, B., Woolfrey, J., & Vollmer, J. (1983). Parental influences on children's eating behavior and relative weight. *Journal of Applied Behavioral Analysis, 16*, 371–378.

Klien, G. (1954). Need and regulation. In M. R. Jones (Ed.), *Nebraska symposium on motivation* (Vol. 2, pp. 224–274). Lincoln: University of Nebraska Press.

Kling, A. S., & Brothers, L. A. (1992). The amygdala and social behavior. In J. P. Aggleton (Ed.), *The amygdala: Neurobiological aspects of emotion, memory, and mental dysfunction* (pp. 353–377). New York: Wiley.

Klinnert, M. D., Campos, J. J., Sorce, J. F., Emde, R. N., & Suejda, M. (1983). Emotions as behavior regulators: Social referencing in infancy. In R. Plutchik & H. Kellerman (Eds.), *Emotion: Theory, research, and experience, emotions in early development* (Vol. 2, pp. 57–86). New York: Academic Press.

Klohnen, E. C., & Bera, S. (1998). Behavioral and experiential patterns of avoidantly and securely attached women across adulthood: A 31-year longitudinal perspective. *Journal of Personality and Social Psychology, 74*, 211–223.

Klose, D. A. (1995). M. Scott Peck's analysis of human evil: A critical review. *Journal of Personality and Social Psychology, 35*, 37–66.

Knee, C. R., & Zuckerman, M. (1996). Causality orientations and the disappearance of the self-serving bias. *Journal of Research in Personality, 30*, 76–87.

Knee, C. R., & Zuckerman, M. (1998). A nondefensive personality: Autonomy and control as moderators of defensive coping and self-handicapping. *Journal of Research in Personality, 32*, 115–130.

Knox, R. E., & Inkster, J. A. (1968). Postdecision dissonance at post time. *Journal of Personality and Social Psychology, 8*, 319–323.

Koestner, R., Bernieri, F., & Zuckerman, M. (1992). Self-regulation and consistency between attitudes, traits, and behaviors. *Personality and Social Psychology Bulletin, 18*, 52–59.

Koestner, R., Lekes, N., Powers, T. A., & Chicoine, E. (2002). Attaining personal goals: Self-concordance plus implementation intentions equals success. *Journal of Personality and Social Psychology, 83*, 231–244.

Koestner, R., Losier, G. F., Vallerand, R. J., & Carducci, D. (1996). Identified and introjected forms of political internalization: Extending self-determination theory. *Journal of Personality and Social Psychology, 70,* 1025–1036.

Koestner, R., Ryan, R. M., Bernieri, F., & Holt, K. (1984). Setting limits on children's behavior: The differential effects of controlling versus informational styles on intrinsic motivation and creativity. *Journal of Personality, 52*, 233–248.

Koestner, R., Zuckerman, M., & Koestner, J. (1987). Praise, involvement, and intrinsic motivation. *Journal of Personality and Social Psychology, 53*, 383–390.

Kohn, A. (1993). *Punished by rewards: The trouble with gold stars, incentive plans, A's, praise, and other bribes*. Boston: Houghton Mifflin.

Kohut, H. (1971). *The analysis of self*. New York: International Universities Press.

Kolb, J., Cooper, S, & Fishman, G. (1995). Recent developments in psychoanalytic technique: A review. *Harvard Review of Psychiatry, 3*, 65–74.

Koulack, D. (1993). Dreams and adaptation to contemporary stress. In A. Moffitt, M. Kramer, & R. Hoffman (Eds.), *The functions of dreaming* (pp. 321–340). Albany: State University of New York Press.

Kramer, P. D. (1993). *Listening to Prozac*. New York: Penguin books.

Kramer, R. (1995). The birth of client-centered therapy: Carl Rogers, Otto Rank, and "The Beyond." *Journal of Humanistic Psychology, 35*, 54–110.

Krantz, P. J., & McClannahan, L. E. (1993). Teaching children with autism to initiate to peers: Effects of a script-fading procedure. *Journal of Applied Behavior Analysis, 26*, 121–132.

Kraut, R. E., & Johnston, R. E. (1979). Social and emotional messages of smiling: An ethological approach. *Journal of Personality and Social Psychology, 37*, 1539–1553.

Krettek, J. E., & Price, J. L. (1978). Amygdaloid projections to subcortical structures within the basal forebrain and brainstem in the rat and cat. *Journal of Comparative Neurology, 178*, 225–254.

Kuhl, J. (1978). Standard setting and risk preference: An elaboration of the theory of achievement motivation and an empirical test. *Psychological Review, 85*, 239–248.

Kuhl, J., & Blankenship, V. (1979). The dynamic theory of achievement motivation. *Psychological Review, 86*, 141–151.

Kuhlman, D. M. (1975). Individual differences in casino gambling? In N. R. Eadington (Ed.), *Gambling and society*. Springfield, IL: Thomas.

Kuhn, T. S. (1962). *The structure of scientific revolutions*. Chicago: University of Chicago Press.

Kuhn, T. S. (1970). *The structure of scientific revolutions* (2nd ed.). Chicago: University Press.

Kulik, J. A., Mahler, H. I. M., & Earnest, A. (1994). Social comparison and affiliation under threat: Going beyond the affiliative-choice paradigm. *Journal of Personality and Social Psychology, 66*, 301–309.

Kuo, Z. Y. (1921). Giving up instincts in psychology. *Journal of Philosophy, 17*, 645–664.

Laird, J. D. (1974). Self-attribution of emotion: The effects of expressive behavior on the quality of emotional experience. *Journal of Personality and Social Psychology, 29*, 475–486.

Laird, J. D. (1984). Facial response and emotion. *Journal of Personality and Social Psychology, 47*, 909–917.

Laird, J. D., Wagener, J. J., Halal, M., & Szegda, M. (1982). Remembering what you feel: The effects of emotion on memory. *Journal of Personality and Social Psychology, 42*, 646–657.

Lane, J. D., & Wegner, D. M. (1995). The cognitive consequences of secrecy. *Journal of Personality and Social Psychology, 69*, 237–253.

Lang, P. J. (1994). The varieties of emotional experience: A mediation of James-Lange theory. *Psychological Review, 101*, 211–221.

Lange, C. (1922). The emotions. In K. Dunlap (Ed.), *The emotions* (Istar A. Haupt, Trans.; pp. 33–90). Baltimore: Williams & Wilkins. (Original work published 1885).

Lange, R. D., & James, W. (1922). *The emotions*. Baltimore: Williams & Wilkins.

Langer, E. (1975). The illusion of control. *Journal of Personality and Social Psychology, 32*, 311–328.

Langer, E., & Rodin, J. (1976). The effects of choice and enhanced personal responsibility for the aged: A field experiment in an institutionalized setting. *Journal of Personality and Social Psychology, 34*, 191–198.

Langsdorff, P., Izard, C. E., Rayias, M., & Hembree, E. (1983). Interest expression, visual fixation, and heart rate changes in 2- to 8-month old infants. *Developmental Psychology, 19*, 375–386.

Lann, E., & Everaerd, W. (1995). Determinants of female sexual arousal: Psychophysiological theory and data. *Annual Review of Sex Research, 6*, 32–76.

Lansing, J. B., & Heyns, R. W. (1959). Need affiliation and frequency of four types of communication. *Journal of Abnormal and Social Psychology, 58*, 365–372.

Lanzetta, J. T., Cartwright-Smith, J. E., & Kleck, R. E. (1976). Effects of nonverbal dissimulation of emotional experience and autonomic arousal. *Journal of Personality and Social Psychology, 33*, 354–370.

LaPointe, K. A., & Crandell, C. J. (1980). Relationship of irrational beliefs to self-reported depression. *Cognitive Therapy and Research, 4*, 247–250.

Lapore, S. J. (1992). Social conflict, social support, and psychological distress: Evidence of cross-domain buffering effects. *Journal of Personality and Social Psychology, 63*, 857–867.

LaPorte, R. E., & Nath, R. (1976). Role of performance goals in prose learning. *Journal of Educational Psychology, 68*, 260–264.

Larson, R., & Asmussen, L. (1991). Anger, worry, and hurt in early adolescence: An enlarging world of negative emotion. In M. Colton & S. Gore (Eds.), *Adolescent stress: Causes and consequences* (pp. 21–42). New York: Aldine de Gruyter.

Larsen, R. J. (1988, June). *Individual differences in affect intensity*. Paper presented at the Motivation and Emotion conference at Nags Head, NC.

Larson, R. J. (1989). A process approach to personality: Utilizing time as a facet of data. In D. Buss & N. Cantor (Eds.), *Personality psychology: Recent trends and emerging directions* (pp. 177–193). New York: Springer-Verlag.

Larsen, R. J., & Diener, E. (1987). Affect intensity as an individual difference characteristic: A review. *Journal of Research in Personality, 21*, 1–39.

Larsen, R. J., Diener, E., & Emmons, R. A. (1987). Affect intensity and reactions to daily life events. *Journal of Personality and Social Psychology, 51*, 803–814.

Larsen, R. J., Kasimatis, M., & Frey, K. (1992). Facilitating the furrowed brow: An unobtrusive test of the facial feedback hypothesis applied to unpleasant affect. *Cognition and Emotion, 6*, 321–338.

Larsen, R. J., & Ketelaar, T. (1991). Personality and susceptibility to positive and negative emotional states. *Journal of Personality and Social Psychology, 61*, 132–140.

Latham, G. P., & Baldes, J. J. (1975). The practical significance of Locke's theory of goal setting. *Journal of Applied Psychology, 60*, 122–124.

Latham, G. P., Erez, M., & Locke, E. A. (1988). Resolving scientific disputes by the joint design of crucial experiments by the antagonists: Application to the Erez-Latham dispute regarding participation in goal setting. *Journal of Applied Psychology, 73*, 753–772.

Latham, G. P., & Frayne, C. A. (1989). Self-management training for increasing job attendance: A follow-up and a replication. *Journal of Applied Psychology, 74*, 411–416.

Latham, G. P., & Kinne, S. B. (1974). Improving job performance through training in goal setting. *Journal of Applied Psychology, 59*, 187–191.

Latham, G. P., & Locke, E. A. (1975). Increasing productivity with decreasing time limits: A field replication of Parkinson's law. *Journal of Applied Psychology, 60*, 524–526.

Latham, G. P., Mitchell, T. R., & Dossett, D. L. (1978). Importance of participative goal setting and anticipated rewards on goal difficulty and job performance. *Journal of Applied Psychology, 63*, 163–171.

Latham, G. P., & Saari, L. M. (1979). Importance of supportive relationships in goal setting. *Journal of Applied Psychology, 64*, 151–156.

Latham, G. P., & Yukl, G. A. (1975). Assigned versus participative goal setting with educated and uneducated woods workers. *Journal of Applied Psychology, 60*, 299–302.

Latham, G. P., & Yukl, G. A. (1976). Effects of assigned and participative goal setting on performance and job satisfaction. *Journal of Applied Psychology, 61*, 166–171.

Laumann, E. O., Paik, A., & Rosen, R. C. (1999). Sexual dysfunction in the United States: Prevalence and predictors. *Journal of the American Medical Association, 281*, 537–544.

Lavrakas, P. J. (1975). Female preferences for male physiques. *Journal of Research in Personality, 9*, 324–334.

Law, A., Logan, H., & Baron, R. S. (1994). Desire for control, felt control, and stress inoculation training during dental treatment. *Journal of Personality and Social Psychology, 67*, 926–936.

Lazarus, R. S. (1966). *Psychological stress and the coping process.* New York: McGraw-Hill.

Lazarus, R. S. (1968). Emotions and adaptation: Conceptual and empirical relations. In W. J. Arnold (Ed.), *Nebraska symposium on motivation* (Vol. 16, pp. 175–266). Lincoln: University of Nebraska Press.

Lazarus, R. S. (1982). Thoughts on the relations between emotion and cognition. *American Psychologist, 37*, 1019–1024.

Lazarus, R. S. (1983). The costs and benefits of denial. In S. Bresnitz (Ed.), *The denial of stress* (pp. 1–32). New York: International Universities Press.

Lazarus, R. S. (1984). On the primacy of cognition. *American Psychologist, 39*, 124–129.

Lazarus, R. S. (1991a). *Emotion and adaptation.* New York: Oxford University Press.

Lazarus, R. S. (1991b). Progress on a cognitive-motivational-relational theory of emotion. *American Psychologist, 46*, 819–834.

Lazarus, R. S. (1994). Universal antecedents of the emotions. In P. Ekman & R. J. Davidson (Eds.), *The nature of emotion: Fundamental questions* (pp. 163–171). New York: Oxford University Press.

Lazarus, R. S., & DeLongis, A. (1983). Psychological stress and coping in aging. *American Psychologist, 38*, 245–254.

Lazarus, R. S., & Folkman, S. (1984). *Stress, appraisal, and coping.* New York: Springer-Verlag.

Leary, M. R. (1983). Social anxiousness: The construct and its measurement. *Journal of Personality Assessment, 47*, 66–75.

Leavitt, R. L., & Power, M. B. (1989). Emotional socialization in the postmodern era: Children and day care. *Social Psychology Quarterly, 52*, 35–43.

LeDoux, J. E. (1987). Emotion. In F. Plum (Ed.), *Handbook of psychology: I. The nervous system* (pp. 419–460). Bethesda, MD: American Physiological Society.

LeDoux, J. E. (1989). Cognitive-emotional interactions in the brain. *Cognition and Emotion, 3*, 267–289.

LeDoux, J. E. (1992a). Brain mechanisms of emotion and emotional learning. *Current Opinion in Neurobiology, 2*, 191–198.

LeDoux, J. E. (1992b). Emotion and the amygdala. In J. P. Aggleton (Ed.), *The amygdala: Neurobiological aspects of emotion, memory, and mental dysfunction* (pp. 339–351). New York: Wiley-Liss.

LeDoux, J. E. (2000). Emotion circuits in the brain. *Annual Review of Neuroscience, 23*, 155–184.

LeDoux, J. E., Iwata, J., Cicchetti, P., & Reis, D. J. (1988). Different projections of the central amygdaloid nucleus mediate autonomic and behavioral correlates of conditioned fear. *Journal of Neuroscience, 8*, 2517–2529.

LeDoux, J. E., Romanski, L. M., & Xagoraris, A. E. (1989). Indelibility of subcortical emotional memories. *Journal of Cognitive Neuroscience, 1*, 238–243.

Lee, K. A., Vaillant, G. E., Torrey, W. C., & Elder, G. H. (1995). A 50-year prospective study of the psychological sequelae of World War II combat. *American Journal of Psychiatry, 152*, 516–522.

Lefcourt, H. M., & Martin, R. A. (1986). *Humor and life stress: An antidote to adversity.* New York: Springer-Verlag.

Lehman, D. R., Ellard, D. R., & Wortman, C. B. (1986). Social support for the bereaved: Recipients and providers perspectives on what is helpful. *Journal of Consulting and Clinical Psychology, 54*, 438–446.

Leippe, M. R., & Eisenstadt, D. (1994). Generalization of dissonance reduction: Decreasing prejudice through induced compliance. *Journal of Personality and Social Psychology, 67,* 395–413.

Leon, I., & Hernandez, J. A. (1998). Testing the role of attribution and appraisal in predicting own and other's emotions. *Cognition and Emotion, 12,* 27–43.

Lepper, M. R. (1983). Social-control processes and the internalization of social values: An attributional perspective. In E. T. Higgins, D. N. Ruble, & W. W. Hartup (Eds.), *Social cognition and social development* (pp. 294–330). New York: Cambridge University Press.

Lepper, M. R., & Greene, D. (1975). Turning play into work: Effects of adult surveillance and extrinsic rewards on children's intrinsic motivation. *Journal of Personality and Social Psychology, 31,* 479–486.

Lepper, M. R., & Greene, D. (Eds.). (1978). *The hidden costs of reward.* Hillsdale, NJ: Erlbaum.

Lepper, M. R., Greene, D., & Nisbett, R. E. (1973). Undermining children's intrinsic interest with extrinsic rewards: A test of the overjustification hypothesis. *Journal of Personality and Social Psychology, 28,* 129–137.

Lepore, S. J. (1992). Social-conflict, social support, and psychological distress: Evidence of cross-domain buffering effects. *Journal of Personality and Social Psychology, 63,* 857–867.

Lerner, J. S., & Keltner, D. (2001). Fear, anger, and risk. *Journal of Personality and Social Psychology, 81,* 146–159.

Lerner, J. S., Goldberg, J. H., & Tetlock, P. E. (1998). Sober second thoughts: The effects of accountability, anger, and authoritarianism on attributions of responsibility. *Personality and Social Psychology Bulletin, 24,* 563–574.

Levenson, H. M. (1981). Differentiating among internality, powerful others, and chance. In H. M. Lefcourt (Ed.), *Research with the locus of control construct: Vol. 1. Assessment methods* (pp. 15–63). New York: Academic Press.

Levenson, R. W. (1992). Autonomic nervous system differences among emotions. *Psychological Science, 3,* 23–27.

Levenson, R. W. (1994a). Human emotion: A functional view. In P. Ekman & R. J. Davidson (Eds.), *The nature of emotion: Fundamental questions* (pp. 123–126). New York: Oxford University Press.

Levenson, R. W. (1994b). The search for autonomic specificity. In P. Ekman & R. J. Davidson (Eds.), *The nature of emotion: Fundamental questions* (pp. 252–257). New York: Oxford University Press.

Levenson, R. W. (1999). The intrapersonal functions of emotion. *Cognitive and Emotion, 13,* 481–504.

Levenson, R. W., Carstensen, L. L., Friesen, W. V., & Ekman, P. (1991). Emotion, physiology, and expression in old age. *Psychology and Aging, 6,* 28–35.

Levenson, R. W., Carstensen, L. L., & Gottman, J. M. (1994). Influence of age and gender on affect, physiology, and their interrelations: A study of long-term marriages. *Journal of Personality and Social Psychology, 67,* 56–68.

Levenson, R. W., Ekman, P., & Friesen, W. V. (1990). Voluntary facial action generates emotion-specific autonomic nervous system activity. *Psychophysiology, 27,* 363–384.

Levenson, R. W., & Gottman, J. M. (1983). Marital interaction: Physiological linkage and affective exchange. *Journal of Personality and Social Psychology, 45,* 587–597.

Levin, R. (1990). Psychoanalytic theories of the function of dreaming: A review of the empirical literature. In J. Masling (Ed.), *Empirical studies of psychoanalytic theories* (Vol. 3, pp. 1–53). Hillsdale, NJ: Analytic Press.

Levine, S. B. (2002). Reexploring the concept of sexual desire. *Journal of Sex & Marital Therapy, 28,* 39–51.

Lewinsohn, P. M., Mischel, W., Chaplin, W., & Barton, R. (1980). Social competence and depression: The role of illusory self-perceptions. *Journal of Abnormal Psychology, 89*, 203–212.

Li, N. P., Bailey, J. M., Kenrick, D. T., & Linsenmeier, J. A. W. (2002). The necessities and luxuries of mate preferences: Testing the tradeoffs. *Journal of Personality and Social Psychology, 82*, 947–955.

Lindsley, D. B. (1957). Psychophysiology and motivation. In M. R. Jones (Ed.), *Nebraska symposium on motivation* (Vol. 5, pp. 44–105). Lincoln: University of Nebraska Press.

Lindzey, G. (Ed.). (1958). *Assessment of human motives.* New York: Rinehart.

Linehan, M. M. (1997). Self-verification and drug abusers: Implications for treatment. *Psychological Science, 8*, 181–183.

Linville, P. W. (1982). Affective consequences of complexity regarding the self and others. In M. S. Clark & S. T. Fiske (Eds.), *Affect and cognition* (pp. 79–109). Hillsdale, NJ: Erlbaum.

Litle, P., & Zuckerman, M. (1986). Sensation seeking and music preferences. *Personality and Individual Differences, 4*, 575–578.

Locke, E. A. (1968). Toward a theory of task motivation and incentives. *Organizational Behavior and Human Performance, 3*, 157–189.

Locke, E. A. (1996). Motivation through conscious goal setting. *Applied and Preventive Psychology, 5*, 117–124.

Locke, E. A. (2002). Setting goals for life and happiness. In C. R. Snyder & S. J. Lopez (Eds.), *Handbook of positive psychology* (pp. 299–312). New York: Oxford University Press.

Locke, E. A., & Bryan, J. F. (1969). The directing function of goals in task performance. *Organizational Behavior and Human Performance, 4*, 35–42.

Locke, E. A., Chah, D. O., Harrison, S., & Lustgarten, N. (1989). Separating the effects of goal specificity from goal level. *Organizational Behavior and Human Decision Processes, 43*, 270–287.

Locke, E. A., & Kristof, A. L. (1996). Volitional choices in the goal achievement process. In P. M. Gollwitzer & J. A. Bargh (Eds.), *The psychology of action: Linking cognition and motivation to behavior.* New York: Guilford Press.

Locke, E. A., & Latham, G. P. (1984). *Goal-setting: A motivational technique that works!* Englewood Cliffs, NJ: Prentice Hall.

Locke, E. A., & Latham, G. P. (1990). *A theory of goal setting and task performance.* Englewood Cliffs, NJ: Prentice Hall.

Locke, E. A., & Latham, G. P. (2002). Building a practically useful theory of goal setting and task motivation. *American Psychologist, 57*, 705–717.

Locke, E. A., Shaw, K. N., Saari, L. M., & Latham, G. P. (1981). Goal setting and task performance: 1969–1980. *Psychological Bulletin, 90*, 125–152.

Loevinger, J. (1976). Stages of ego development. In J. Loevinger (Ed.), *Ego development* (pp. 13–28). San Francisco: Jossey-Bass.

Loewenstein, G. (1996). Out of control: Visceral influences on behavior. *Organizational Behavior and Human Decision Processes, 65*, 272–292.

Loftus, E. F., & Klinger, M. R. (1992). Is the unconscious smart or dumb? *American Psychologist, 47*, 761–765.

Longcope, C. (1986). Adrenal and gonadal androgen secretion in normal females. *Clinics in Endocrinology and Metabolism, 15*, 213–228.

Lorenz, K. (1965). *Evolution and modification of behavior: A critical examination of the concepts of the "learned" and the "innate" elements of behavior.* Chicago: The University of Chicago Press.

Lowe, M. R. (1993). The effects of dieting on eating behavior: A three-factor model. *Psychological Bulletin, 114*, 100–121.

Luborsky, L., & Crits-Christoph, P. (1990). *Understanding transference: The core conflictual relationship theme method.* New York: Basic Books.

Lucas, R. E., Diener, E., Grob, A., Suh, E. M., & Shao, L. (2000). Cross-cultural evidence for the fundamental features of extraversion. *Journal of Personality and Social Psychology, 79,* 452–468.

Lucas, R. E., & Fujita, F. (2000). Factors influencing the relation between extraversion and pleasant affect. *Journal of Personality and Social Psychology, 79,* 1039–1056.

Lykken, D., & Tellegen, A. (1996). Happiness is a stochastic phenomenon. *Psychological Science, 7,* 186–189.

MacKinnon, N. J. (1994). *Symbolic interactionism as affect control.* Albany, NY: SUNY Press.

MacLean, P. D. (1990). *The triune brain in evolution: Role in paleocerebral functions.* New York: Plenum Press.

MacLeod, A. K, Byrne, A., & Valentine, J. D. (1996). Affect, emotional disorder, and future-directed thinking. *Cognition and Emotion, 10,* 69–86.

Madsen, K. B. (1959). *Theories of motivation.* Copenhagen: Munksgaard.

Maehr, M. L., & Kleiber, D. A. (1980). The graying of achievement motivation. *American Psychologist, 36,* 787–793.

Mahoney, E. R. (1983). *Human sexuality.* New York: McGraw-Hill.

Main, M., Kaplan, N., & Cassidy, J. (1985). Security in infancy, childhood, and adulthood: A move to the level of representation. In I. Bretherton & E. Waters (Eds.), Growing points of attachment theory and research. *Monographs of the Society for Research in Child Development, 50,* 67–104.

Malmo, R. B. (1959). Activation: A neurological dimension. *Psychological Review, 66,* 367–386.

Manderlink, G., & Harackiewicz, J. M. (1984). Proximal versus distal goal setting and intrinsic motivation. *Journal of Personality and Social Psychology, 47,* 918–928.

Mandler, G. (1975). *Mind and emotion.* New York: John Wiley & Sons.

Mandler, G. (1984). *Mind and body: Psychology of emotion and stress.* New York: Norton.

Mandrup, S., & Lane, M. D. (1997). Regulating adipogenesis. *Journal of Biology and Chemistry, 272,* 5367–5370.

Manstead, A. S. R. (1991). Emotion in social life. *Cognition and Emotion, 5,* 353–362.

Markus, H. (1977). Self-schemata and processing information about the self. *Journal of Personality and Social Psychology, 35,* 63–68.

Markus, H. (1983). Self-knowledge: An expected view. *Journal of Personality, 51,* 543–565.

Markus, H., Cross, S., & Wurf, E. (1990). The role of self-esteem in competence. In R. J. Sternberg & J. Kolligian (Eds.), *Competence considered* (pp. 205–225). New Haven: Yale University Press.

Markus, H., & Nurius, P. (1986). Possible selves. *American Psychologist, 41,* 954–969.

Markus, H. R., & Ruvolo, A. P. (1989). Possible selves: Personalized representations of goals. In L. A. Pervin (Ed.), *Goal concepts in personality and social psychology* (pp. 211–241). Hillsdale, NJ: Lawrence Erlbaum.

Markus, H., & Sentisk, K. (1982). The self in social information processing. In J. Suls (Ed.), *Psychological perspectives on the self* (Vol. 1, pp. 41–60). Hillsdale, NJ: Erlbaum.

Markus, H., & Wurf, E. (1987). The dynamic self-concept: A social psychological perspective. *Annual Review of Psychology, 38,* 299–337.

Marlatt, G. P., & Parks, G. A. (1982). Self-management of addictive behaviors. In P. Karoly & F. H. Kanfer (Eds.), *Self-management and behavior change* (pp. 443–488). New York: Pergamon.

Marsh, H. W. (1990). Causal ordering of academic self-concept and academic achievement: A multivariate, longitudinal panel analysis. *Journal of Educational Psychology, 82,* 646–656.

Mascolo, M. F., Fischer, K. W., & Li, J. (2003). Dynamic development of component systems of emotions: Pride, shame, and guilt in China and the United States. In R. J. Davidson, K. R.

Scherer, & H. H. Goldsmith (Eds.), *Handbook of affective sciences* (pp. 375–408). New York: Oxford University Press.

Masling, J. (Ed.). (1983). *Empirical studies of psychoanalytic theories.* Hillsdale, NJ: Analytic Press.

Maslow, A. H. (1943). A theory of human motivation. *Psychological Review, 50,* 370–396.

Maslow, A. H. (1954). *Motivation and personality.* New York: Harper.

Maslow, A. H. (1968). *Toward a psychology of being.* New York: Van Nostrand.

Maslow, A. H. (1971). *The farther reaches of human nature.* New York: Viking Press.

Maslow, A. H. (1987). *Motivation and personality* (3rd ed.). New York: Harper & Row.

Mason, A., & Blankenship, V. (1987). Power and affiliation motivation, stress, and abuse in intimate relationships. *Journal of Personality and Social Psychology, 52,* 203–210.

Masters, W. H., & Johnson, V. E. (1966). *Human sexual response.* Boston: Little, Brown.

Mathes, E. W. (1981). Maslow's hierarchy of needs as a guide for living. *Journal of Humanistic Psychology, 21,* 69–72.

Matsui, T., Okada, A., & Inoshita, O. (1983). Mechanism of feedback affecting task performance. *Organizational Behavior and Human Performance, 31,* 114–122.

Matsumoto, D. (1987). The role of facial response in the experience of emotion: More methodological problems and a meta-analysis. *Journal of Personality and Social Psychology, 52,* 769–774.

May, R. (Ed.). (1961). *Existential psychology.* New York: Random House.

May, R. (1982). The problem of evil: An open letter to Carl Rogers. *Journal of Humanistic Psychology, 22,* 10–21.

Mayer, D. J. (1952). The glucostatic theory of regulation of food intake and the problem of obesity. *Bulletin of the New England Medical Center, 14,* 43.

Mayer, D. J. (1953). Glucostatic mechanism of regulation of food intake. *New England Journal of Medicine, 249,* 13–16.

McAdams, D. P. (1980). A thematic coding system for the intimacy motive. *Journal of Research in Personality, 14,* 413–432.

McAdams, D. P. (1982a). Intimacy motivation. In A. J. Stewart (Ed.), *Motivation and society.* San Francisco: Jossey-Bass.

McAdams, D. P. (1982b). Experiences of intimacy and power: Relationships between social motives and autobiographical memory. *Journal of Personality and Social Psychology, 42,* 292–302.

McAdams, D. P. (1993). *The stories we live by: Personal myths and the making of the self.* New York: Morrow.

McAdams, D. P. (1996). Personality, modernity, and the storied self: A contemporary framework for studying persons. *Psychological Inquiry, 7,* 295–321.

McAdams, D. P., Diamond, A., de St. Aubin, E., & Mansfield, E. (1997). Stories of commitment: The psychosocial construction of generative lives. *Journal of Personality and Social Psychology, 72,* 678–694.

McAdams, D. P., & Constantian, C. A. (1983). Intimacy and affiliation motives in daily living: An experience sampling analysis. *Journal of Personality and Social Psychology, 45,* 851–861.

McAdams, D. P., Healy, S., & Krause, S. (1984). Social motives and patterns of friendship. *Journal of Personality and Social Psychology, 47,* 828–838.

McAdams, D. P., Jackson, R. J., & Kirshnit, C. (1984). Looking, laughing, and smiling in dyads as a function of intimacy motivation and reciprocity. *Journal of Personality, 52,* 261–273.

McAdams, D. P., & Losoff, M. (1984). Friendship motivation in fourth and sixth graders: A thematic analysis. *Journal of Social and Personal Relationships, 1,* 11–27.

McAdams, D. P., & Powers, J. (1981). Themes of intimacy in behavior and thought. *Journal of Personality and Social Psychology, 40,* 573–587.

McAdams, D. P., & Vaillant, G. E. (1982). Intimacy motivation and psychosocial adaptation: A longitudinal study. *Journal of Personality Assessment, 46,* 586–593.

McAuley, E., & Tammen, V. V. (1989). The effect of subjective and objective competitive outcomes on intrinsic motivation. *Journal of Sport and Exercise Psychology, 11*, 84–93.

McCaul, K. D., Holmes, D. S., & Solomon, S. (1982). Facial expression and emotion. *Journal of Personality and Social Psychology, 42*, 145–152.

McClelland, D. C. (Ed.). (1955). *Studies in motivation.* New York: Appleton-Century-Crofts.

McClelland, D. C. (1961). *The achieving society.* Princeton, NJ: Van Nostrand.

McClelland, D. C. (1965). Achievement and entrepreneurship: A longitudinal study. *Journal of Personality and Social Psychology, 1*, 389–392.

McClelland, D. C. (1975). *Power: The inner experience.* New York: Irvington.

McClelland, D. C. (1978). Managing motivation to expand human freedom. *American Psychologist, 33*, 201–210.

McClelland, D. C. (1982). The need for power, sympathetic activation, and illness. *Motivation and Emotion, 6*, 31–41.

McClelland, D. C. (1985). *Human motivation.* San Francisco: Scott, Foresman.

McClelland, D. C. (1987). Characteristics of successful entrepreneurs. *The Journal of Creative Behavior, 21*, 219–233.

McClelland, D. C., Atkinson, J. W., Clark, R. A., & Lowell, E. L. (1953). *The achievement motive.* New York: Appleton-Century-Crofts.

McClelland, D. C., & Burnham, D. H. (1976, March–April). Power is the great motivator. *Harvard Business Review, 100–110*, 159–166.

McClelland, D. C., Colman, C., Finn, K., & Winter, D. G. (1978). Motivation and maturity patterns in marital success. *Social Behavior and Personality, 6*, 163–171.

McClelland, D. C., Constantian, C., Pilon, D., & Stone, C. (1982). Effects of child-rearing practices on adult maturity. In D. C. McClelland (Ed.), *The development of social maturity.* New York: Irvington.

McClelland, D. C., Davis, W. B., Kalin, R., & Wanner, E. (1972). *The drinking man: Alcohol and human motivation.* New York: Free Press.

McClelland, D. C., & Pilon, D. A. (1983). Sources of adult motives in patterns of parent behavior in early childhood. *Journal of Personality and Social Psychology, 44*, 564–574.

McClelland, D. C., & Teague, G. (1975). Predicting risk preferences among power-related tasks. *Journal of Personality, 43*, 266–285.

McClelland, D. C., & Watson, R. I., Jr. (1973). Power motivation and risk-taking behavior. *Journal of Personality, 41*, 121–139.

McCombs, B. L., & Pope, J. E. (1994). *Motivating hard to reach students.* Washington, DC: American Psychological Association.

McCoy, C. L., & Masters, J. C. (1985). The development of children's strategies for the social control of emotion. *Child Development, 56*, 1214–1222.

McCrae, R. R. (1990). Controlling neuroticism in the measurement of stress. *Stress Medicine, 6*, 237–241.

McCrae, R. R., & Costa, P. T. Jr. (1986). Personality, coping, and coping effectiveness in an adult sample. *Journal of Personality, 54*, 385–405.

McCrae, R. R., & Costa, P. T. (1987). Validation of the five-factor model of personality across instruments and observers. *Journal of Personality and Social Psychology, 52*, 81–90.

McCrae, R. R., & Costa, P. T. (1991). Adding Liebe und Arbeit: The full five-factor model and well-being. *Personality and Social Psychology Bulletin, 3*, 173–175.

McDougall, W. (1908). *Introduction to social psychology.* London: Methuen.

McDougall, W. (1926). *Introduction to social psychology.* Boston: Luce and Co.

McDougall, W. (1933). *The energies of men.* New York: Scribner.

McGinley, H., McGinley, P., & Nicholas, K. (1978). Smiling, body position and interpersonal attraction. *Bulletin of the Psychonomics Society, 12*, 21–24.

McGraw, K. O. (1978). The detrimental effects of reward on performance: A literature review and a prediction model. In M. R. Lepper & D. Greene (Eds.), *The hidden costs of reward* (pp. 33–60). New York: John Wiley.

McGraw, K. O., & McCullers, J. C. (1979). Evidence of detrimental effects of extrinsic incentives on breaking a mental set. *Journal of Experimental Social Psychology, 15*, 285–294.

McHugh, P. R., & Moran, T. H. (1985). The stomach: A conception of its dynamic role in satiety. In J. M. Sprague & A. N. Epstein (Eds.), *Progress in psychobiology and physiological psychology* (Vol. 11, pp. 197–232). Orlando, FL: Academic Press.

McIntosh, D. N. (1996). Facial feedback hypotheses: Evidence, implications, and directions. *Motivation and Emotion, 20*, 121–147.

McIntosh, D. N., Zajonc, R. B., Vig, P. S., & Emerick, S. W., (1997). Facial movement, breathing, temperature, and affect: Implications of the vascular theory of emotional efference. *Cognition and Emotion, 11*, 171–195.

McKeachie, W. J. (1976). Psychology in America's bicentennial year. *American Psychologist, 31*, 819–833.

McKeachie, W. J., Lin, Y., Milholland, J., & Issacson, R. (1966). Student affiliation motives, teacher warmth, and academic achievement. *Journal of Personality and Social Psychology, 4*, 457–461.

McNally, R. J. (1992). Disunity in psychology: Chaos or speciation? *American Psychologist, 47*, 1054.

McNulty, S. E., & Swann, W. B., Jr. (1994). Identity negotiation in roommate relationships: The self as architect and consequence of social reality. *Journal of Personality and Social Psychology, 67*, 1012–1023.

Mednick, M. T., Mednick, S. A., & Mednick, E. V. (1964). Incubation of creative performance and specific associative priming. *Journal of Abnormal and Social Psychology, 69*, 84–88.

Medvec, V. H., Madey, S. F., & Gilovich, T. (1995). When less is more: Counterfactual thinking and satisfaction among Olympic medalists. *Journal of Personality and Social Psychology, 69*, 603–610.

Meece, J., Blumenfeld, P., & Hoyle, R. (1988). Students' goal orientations and cognitive engagement in classroom activities. *Journal of Educational Psychology, 80*, 514–523.

Mellstrom, M., Jr., Cicala, G. A., & Zuckerman, M. (1976). General versus specific trait anxiety measures in the prediction of fear of snakes, heights, and darkness. *Journal of Consulting and Clinical Psychology, 44*, 83–91.

Mento, A. J., Steel, R. P., & Karren, R. J. (1987). A meta-analytic study of the effects of goal setting on task performance: 1966–1984. *Organizational Behavior and Human Decision Processes, 39*, 52–83.

Meston, C. M. (2000). The psychophysiological assessment of female sexual function. *Journal of Sex Education and Therapy, 25*, 6–16.

Meuhlenhard, C. L., & Kimes, L. A. (1999). The social construction of violence: The case of sexual and domestic violence. *Personality and Social Psychology Review, 3*, 234–245.

Mickelson, K. D., Kessler, R. C., & Shaver, P. R. (1997). Adult attachment in a nationally representative sample. *Journal of Personality and Social Psychology, 73*, 1092–1106.

Mikulincer, M. (1986). Motivational involvement and learned helplessness: The behavioral effects of the importance of uncontrollable events. *Journal of Social and Clinical Psychology, 4*, 402–422.

Mikulincer, M. (1988). The relationship of probability of success and performance following failure: Reactance and helplessness effects. *Motivation and Emotion, 12*, 139–152.

Mikulincer, M. (1994). *Human learned helplessness: A coping perspective.* New York: Plenum Press.

Miller, D. L., & Kelley, M. L. (1994). The use of goal setting and contingency contracting for improving children's homework performance. *Journal of Applied Behavior Analysis, 27*, 73–84.

Miller, E. K., & Cohen, J. D. (2001). An integrative theory of prefrontal cortex function. *Annual Review of Neuroscience, 24,* 167–202.

Miller, G. A., Galanter, E. H., & Pribram, K. H. (1960). *Plans and the structure of behavior.* New York: Holt, Rinehart & Winston.

Miller, N. E. (1948). Studies of fear as an acquirable drive: 1. Fear as motivation and fear-reduction as reinforcement in the learning on new responses. *Journal of Experimental Psychology, 38,* 89–101.

Miller, N. E. (1959). Liberalization of basic S-R concepts: Extensions to conflict behavior, motivation, and social learning. In S. Koch (Ed.), *Psychology: A study of a science* (Vol. 2, pp. 196–292). New York: McGraw-Hill.

Miller, N. E. (1960). Motivational effects of brain stimulation and drugs. *Federation Proceedings, Federation of American Societies for Experimental Biology, 19,* 846–853.

Millon, T. (1990). The disorders of personality. In L. A. Pervin (Ed.), *Handbook of personality: Theory and research* (pp. 339–370). New York: Guilford Press.

Mills, J., & Clark, M. S. (1982). Communal and exchange relationships. In L. Wheeler (Ed.), *Review of personality and social psychology* (Vol. 3, pp. 121–144). Beverly Hills, CA: Sage.

Mirenowicz, J., & Schultz, W. (1994). Importance of unpredictability for reward responses in primate dopamine neurons. *Journal of Neurophysiology, 72,* 1024–1027.

Mischel, H. N., & Mischel, W. (1983). The development of children's knowledge of self-control strategies. *Child Development, 54,* 603–619.

Mischel, W. (1996). From good intentions to willpower. In P. M. Gollwitzer & J. A. Bargh (Eds.), *The psychology of action: Linking cognition and motivation to behavior.* New York: Guilford Press.

Mischel, W., Coates, B., & Raskoff, A. (1968). Effects of success and failure on self-gratification. *Journal of Personality and Social Psychology, 10,* 381–390.

Mischel, W., Shoda, Y., & Rodriguez, M. L. (1989). Delay of gratification in children. *Science, 244,* 933–938.

Miserandino, M. (1996). Children who do well in school: Individual differences in perceived competence and autonomy in above-average children. *Journal of Educational Psychology, 88,* 203–214.

Mitchell, S. (1988). *Relational concepts in psychoanalysis.* Cambridge, MA: Harvard University Press.

Mittelman, W. (1991). Maslow's study of self-actualization: A reinterpretation. *Journal of Humanistic Psychology, 31,* 114–135.

Moffitt, A., Kramer, M., & Hoffman, R. (1993). *The functions of dreaming.* Albany: State University of New York.

Mogenson, G. J., Jones, D. L., & Yim, C. Y. (1980). From motivation to action: Functional interface between the limbic system and the motor system. *Progress in Neurobiology, 14,* 69–97.

Moltz, H. (1965). Contemporary instinct theory and the fixed action pattern. *Psychological Review, 72,* 27–47.

Money, J. (1988). *Gay, straight, and in-between: The sexology of erotic orientation.* New York: Oxford University Press.

Money, J., Wiedeking, C., Walker, P. A., & Gain, D. (1976). Combined antiandrogenic and counseling program for treatment of 46 XY and 47 XYY sex offenders. In E. J. Sachar (Ed.), *Hormones, behavior, and psychopathology, 66,* 105–109.

Mook, D. G. (1988). On the organization of satiety. *Appetite, 11,* 27–39.

Mook, D. G. (1996). *Motivation: The organization of action* (2nd ed.). New York: W. W. Norton.

Mook, D. G., & Kozub, F. J. (1968). Control of sodium chloride intake in the nondeprived rat. *Journal of Comparative and Physiological Psychology, 66,* 105–109.

Mook, D. G., & Wagner, S. (1989). Orosensory suppression of saccharin drinking in rat: The response, not the taste. *Appetite, 13,* 1–13.

Moran, T. H. (2000). Cholecystokinin and satiety: Current perspectives. *Nutrition, 16*, 858–865.

Morgenson, G. J., & Calaresu, F. R. (1973). Cardiovascular responses to electrical stimulation of the amygdala in the rat. *Experimental Neurology, 39*, 166–180.

Montague, P. R., Dayan, P., & Sejnowski, T. J. (1996). A framework for mesencephalic Dopamine systems based on predictive Hebbian learning. *Journal of Neuroscience, 16*, 1936–1947.

Morse, R. C., & Stoller, D. (1982, September). The hidden message that breaks habits. *Science Digest, 28*.

Moruzzi, G., & Magoun, H. W. (1949). Brain stem reticular formation and activation of the EEG. *EEG and Clinical Neurophysiology, 1*, 455–473.

Mossholder, K. W. (1980). Effects of externally mediated goal setting on intrinsic motivation: A laboratory experiment. *Journal of Applied Psychology, 65*, 202–210.

Muehlenhard, C. L., & Kimes, L. A. (1999). The social construction of violence: The case of sexual and domestic violence. *Personality and Social Psychology Review, 3*, 234–245.

Mueller, C. M., & Dweck, C. S. (1997). *Implicit theories of intelligence: Malleability beliefs, definitions, and judgments of intelligence*. Unpublished data.

Munarriz, R., Talakoub, L., Flaherty, E., Gioia, M., Hoag, L., Kim, N. N., Traish, A., Goldstein, I., Guay, A., & Spark, R. (2002). Androgen replacement therapy with dehydroepiandrosterone for androgen insufficiency and female sexual dysfunction: Androgen and questionnaire results. *Journal of Sex and Marital Therapy, 28*, 165–173.

Murray, H. A. (1937). Facts which support the concept of need or drive. *Journal of Personality, 3*, 115–143.

Murray, H. A. (1938). *Explorations in personality*. New York: Oxford University Press.

Murray, H. A. (1943). *Thematic apperception test*. Cambridge: Harvard University Press.

Nasby, W., & Yando, R. (1982). Selective encoding and retrieval of affectively information. *Journal of Personality and Social Psychology, 43*, 1244–1255.

Nauta, W. J. H. (1986). Circuitous connections linking cerebral cortex, limbic system, and corpus striatum. In B. K. Doane & K. E. Livingston (Eds.) *The limbic system: Functional organization and clinical disorder* (pp. 43–54). New York: Raven.

Neemann, J., & Harter, S. (1986). *The self-perception profile for college students*. [Manual]. Denver: University of Denver.

Neher, A. (1991). Maslow's theory of motivation: A critique. *Journal of Humanistic Psychology, 31*, 89–112.

Neiss, R. (1988). Reconceptualizing arousal: Psychobiological states in motor performance. *Psychological Bulletin, 103*, 345–366.

Neisser, U. (1967). *Cognitive psychology*. Englewood Cliffs, NJ: Prentice-Hall.

Newby, T. J. (1991). Classroom motivation: Strategies of first-year teachers. *Journal of Educational Psychology, 83*, 195–200.

Newcomb, M. D., & McGee, L. (1991). Influence of sensation seeking on general deviance and specific problem behaviors from adolescence to young adulthood. *Journal of Personality and Social Psychology, 61*, 614–628.

Newell, A., Shaw, J. C., & Simon, H. A. (1958). Elements of a theory of human problem solving. *Psychological Review, 65*, 151–166.

Newman, E. B., Perkins, F. T., & Wheeler, R. H. (1930). Cannon's theory of emotion: A critique. *Psychological Review, 37*, 305–326.

Newman, R. S. (1991). Goals and self-regulated learning: What motivates children to seek academic help? In M. L. Maehr & P. R. Pintrich (Eds.), *Advances in motivation and achievement* (Vol. 7, pp. 151–183). Greenwich, CT: JAI Press.

Nezu, A. M., Nezu, C. M., & Blissett, S. E. (1988). Sense of humor as a moderator of the relation between stressful events and psychological distress: A prospective analysis. *Journal of Personality and Social Psychology, 54*, 520–525.

Nicholls, J. G. (1978). The development of the concepts of effort and ability, perceptions of academic achievement, and the understanding that difficult tasks require more ability. *Child Development, 49*, 800–814.

Nicholls, J. G. (1979). Development of perception of own attainment and causal attributions for success and failure in reading. *Journal of Educational Psychology, 71*, 94–99.

Nicholls, J. G. (1984). Achievement motivation: Conceptions of ability, subjective experience, task choice, and performance. *Psychological Review, 91*, 328–346.

Niedenthal, P. M., Tangney, J. P., & Gavanski, I. (1994). "If only I weren't" versus "If only I hadn't": Distinguishing shame and guilt in counterfactual thinking. *Journal of Personality and Social Psychology, 67*, 585–595.

Nisbett, R. E., & Ross, L. (1980). *Human inference: Strategies and shortcomings of social judgment.* Englewood Cliffs, NJ: Prentice-Hall.

Nolen, S. B. (1988). Reasons for studying: Motivational orientations and study strategies. *Cognition and Instruction, 5*, 269–287.

Nolen-Hoeksema, S., Wolfson, A., Mumme, D., & Guskin, K. (1995). Helplessness in children of depressed and nondepressed mothers. *Developmental Psychology, 31*, 377–387.

Noller, P. (1984). *Nonverbal communication and marital interaction.* Oxford: Pergamon.

Nurius, P. (1991). Possible selves and social support: Social cognitive resources for coping and striving. In J. A. Howard & P. L. Callero (Eds.), *The self-society interface: Cognition, emotion, and action* (pp. 239–258). New York: Cambridge University Press.

Oatley, K., & Duncan, E. (1994). The experience of emotions in everyday life. *Cognition and Emotion, 8*, 369–381.

Oatley, K., & Jenkins, J. M. (1992). Human emotions: Function and dysfunction. *Annual Review of Psychology, 43*, 55–85.

Oatley, K., & Johnson-Laird, P. N. (1987). Toward a cognitive theory of emotions. *Cognition and Emotion, 1*, 29–50.

Oettingen, G. (1996). Positive fantasy and motivation. In P. M. Gollwitzer & J. A. Bargh (Eds.), *The psychology of action: Linking cognition and motivation to behavior* (pp. 236–259). New York: Guilford Press.

Oettingen, G., Honig, G., & Gollwitzer, P. M. (2000). Effective self regulation of goal attainment. *International Journal of Education Research, 33*, 705–732.

O'Hara, M. (1989). When I use the term humanistic psychology . . . *Journal of Humanistic Psychology, 29*, 263–273.

Oldham, G. R. (1975). The impact of supervisory characteristics on goal acceptance. *Academy of Management Journal, 18*, 461–475.

Olds, J. (1956). Pleasure centers in the brain. *Scientific American, 195,* 105–116.

Olds, J. (1969). The central nervous system and the reinforcement of behavior. *American Psychologist, 24*, 114–132.

Olds, J., & Milner, P. (1954). Positive reinforcement produced by electrical stimulation of septal area and other regions in the rat brain. *Journal of Comparative and Physiological Psychology, 47*, 419–427.

Olds, M. E., & Fobes, J. L. (1981). The central basis of motivation: Intracranial self-stimulation studies. *Annual Review of Psychology, 32*, 523–574.

Olds, M. E., & Olds, J. (1963). Approach-avoidance analysis of the rat diencephalon. *Journal of Comparative Neurology, 217*, 1253–1264.

Orbell, S., Hodgkins, S., & Sheeran, P. (1997). Implementation intentions and the theory of planned behavior. *Personality and Social Psychology Bulletin, 23*, 945–954.

Orbell, S., & Sheeran, P. (1998). "Inclined abstainers": A problem for predicting health-related behavior. *British Journal of Social Psychology, 37*, 151–165.

Orbell, S., & Sheeran, P. (2000). Motivation and volitional processes in action initiation: A field study of the role of implementation intentions. *Journal of Applied Social Psychology, 30,* 780–797.

Orlick, T. D., & Mosher, R. (1978). Extrinsic rewards and participant motivation in a sport related task. *International Journal of Sport Psychology, 9,* 27–39.

Ortony, A., & Clore, G. L. (1989). Emotion, mood, and conscious awareness. *Cognition and Emotion, 3,* 125–137.

Ortony, A., Clore, G. L., & Collins, A. (1988). *The cognitive structure of emotions.* Cambridge: Cambridge University Press.

Osgood, C. E., May, W. H., & Miron, M. S. (1975). *Cross-cultural universals of affective meaning.* Urbana: University of Illinois Press.

Osgood, C. E., Suci, G. C., & Tannenbaum, P. H. (1957). *The measurement of meaning.* Urbana: University of Illinois Press.

Overskeid, G., & Svartdal, F. (1996). Effects of reward on subjective autonomy and interest when initial interest is low. *The Psychological Record, 46,* 319–331.

Oyserman, D., & Markus, H. (1990). Possible selves and delinquency. *Journal of Personality and Social Psychology, 59,* 112–125.

Ozer, E. M., & Bandura, A. (1990). Mechanisms governing empowerment effects: A self-efficacy analysis. *Journal of Personality and Social Psychology, 58,* 472–486.

Pace, G. M., Ivancis, M. T., Edwards, G. L., Iwata, B. A., & Page, T. J. (1985). Assessment of stimulus preference and reinforcer value with profoundly retarded individuals. *Journal of Applied Behavior Analysis, 18,* 249–255.

Pallak, S. R., Costomiris, S., Sroka, S., & Pittman, T. S. (1982). School experience, reward characteristics, and intrinsic motivation. *Child Development, 53,* 1382–1391.

Panksepp, J. (1982). Toward a general psychobiological theory of emotions. *Behavioral and Brain Science, 5,* 407–467.

Panksepp, J. (1986). The anatomy of emotions. In R. Plutchik & H. Kellerman (Eds.), Emotion: Theory, research, and experience: Biological foundations of emotions (Vol. 5, pp. 91–124). New York: Academic Press.

Panksepp, J. (1994). The basics of basic emotion. In P. Ekman & R. J. Davidson (Eds.), *The nature of emotion: Fundamental questions* (pp. 20–24). New York: Oxford University Press.

Park, C. L., & Folkman, S. (1997). Meaning in the context of stress and coping. *Review of General Psychology, 1,* 115–144.

Parkes, A. S., & Bruce, H. M. (1961). Olfactory stimuli in mammalian reproduction. *Science, 134,* 1049–1054.

Parkinson, B. (1991). Emotional stylists: Strategies of expressive management among trainee hairdressers. *Social Psychology Quarterly, 5,* 419–434.

Parsons, J. E., & Ruble, D. N. (1977). The development of achievement-related expectancies. *Child Development, 48,* 1975–1979.

Patrick, B. C., Skinner, E. A., & Connell, J. P. (1993). What motivates children's behavior and emotion? Joint effects of perceived control and autonomy in the academic domain. *Journal of Personality and Social Psychology, 65,* 781–791.

Patterson, C. J., & Mischel, W. (1976). Effects of temptation-inhibiting and task-facilitating plans on self-control. *Journal of Personality and Social Psychology, 33,* 209–217.

Paul, J. P. (1993). Childhood cross-gender behavior and adult homosexuality: The resurgence of biological models of sexuality. *Journal of Homosexuality, 24,* 41–54.

Pederson, N. C., Plomin, R., McClearn, G. E., & Friberg, L. (1988). Neuroticism, extraversion, and related traits in adult twins reared apart and reared together. *Journal of Personality and Social Psychology, 55,* 950–957.

Penfield, W. (1958). *The excitable cortex in conscious man*. England: Liverpool University Press.

Pennebaker, J. W. (1990). *Opening up*. New York: Morrow.

Perls, F. S. (1969). *Gestalt therapy verbatim*. Lafayette, CA: Real People Press.

Pert, C. B. (1986, Summer). The wisdom of the receptors: Neuropeptides, the emotions, and body-mind. *Advances* (Intitute for the Advancement of Health), *3*, 8–16.

Peters, R. S. (1958). *The concept of motivation*. London: Routledge and Kegan Paul.

Peterson, C. (2000). The future of optimism. *American Psychologist, 55*, 44–55.

Peterson, C., & Barrett, L. C. (1987). Explanatory style and academic performance among university freshmen. *Journal of Personality and Social Psychology, 53*, 603–607.

Peterson, C., Maier, S. F., & Seligman, M. E. P. (1993). *Learned helplessness: A theory for the age of personal control*. New York: Oxford University Press.

Peterson, C., & Park, C. (1998). Learned helplessness and explanatory style. In D. F. Barone, V. B. Van Hasselt, & M. Hersen (Eds.), *Advanced personality* (pp. 287–310). New York: Plenum.

Peterson, C., & Seligman, M. E. P. (1984). Causal explanations as a risk factor for depression: Theory and evidence. *Psychological Review, 91*, 347–374.

Peterson, C., Seligman, M. E. P., & Vaillant, G. E. (1988). Pessimistic explanatory style is a risk factor for physical illness: A thirty-five year longitudinal study. *Journal of Personality and Social Psychology, 55*, 23–27.

Peterson, C., Seligman, M. E. P., Yurko, K. H., Martin, L. R., & Friedman, H. S. (1998). Catastophizing and untimely death. *Psychological Science, 9*, 49–52.

Pfaffmann, C. (1960). The pleasures of sensation. *Psychological Review, 67*, 253–268.

Pfaffmann, C. (1961). The sensory and motivating properties of the sense of taste. In M. R. Jones (Ed.), *Nebraska symposium on motivation* (Vol. 9, pp. 71–108). Lincoln: University of Nebraska Press.

Pfaffmann, C. (1982). Taste: A model of incentive motivation. In D. W. Pfaff (Ed.), *The physiological mechanisms of motivation* (pp. 61–97). New York: Springer-Verlag.

Pham, L. B., & Taylor, S. E. (1999). From thought to action: Effects of process- versus outcome-based mental simulations on performance. *Personality and Social Psychology Bulletin, 25*, 250–260.

Phillips, A. G., Pfaus, J. G., & Blaha, C. D. (1991). Dopamine and motivated behavior: Insights provided by in vivo analysis. In P. Willner & J. Scheel-Kruger (Eds.), *The mesolimbic dopamine system: From motivation to action* (pp. 199–224). New York: Wiley.

Phillips, D. (1984). The illusion of incompetence among academically competent children. *Child Development, 55*, 2000–2016.

Pierce, G. R., Sarason, B. R., & Sarason, I. G. (1991). General and specific support expectations and stress as predictors of perceived supportiveness: An experimental study. *Journal of Personality and Social Psychology, 63*, 297–307.

Pierce, K. L., & Schreibman, L. (1994). Teaching daily living skills to children with autism in unsupervised settings through pictorial self-management. *Journal of Applied Behavior Analysis, 27*, 471–481.

Pittman, T. S., Boggiano, A. K., & Ruble, D. N. (1983). Intrinsic and extrinsic motivational orientations: Limiting conditions on the undermining and enhancing effects of reward on intrinsic motivation. In J. Levine & M. Wang (Eds.), *Teacher and student perceptions: Implications for learning* (pp. 319–340). Hillsdale, NJ: Erlbaum.

Pittman, T. S., Davey, M. E., Alafat, K. A., Wetherill, K. V., & Kramer, N. A. (1980). Informational versus controlling verbal rewards. *Personality and Social Psychology Bulletin, 6*, 228–233.

Pittman, T. S., Emery, J., & Boggiano, A. K. (1982). Intrinsic and extrinsic motivational orientations: Reward induced changes in preference for complexity. *Journal of Personality and Social Psychology, 42*, 789–797.

Pittman, T. S., & Heller, J. F. (1988). Social motivation. *Annual Review of Psychology, 38*, 461–489.

Plutchik, R. (1970). Emotions, evolution, and adaptive processes. In M. B. Arnold (Ed.), *Feelings and emotions* (pp. 3–24). New York: Academic Press.

Plutchik, R. (1980). *Emotion: A psychoevolutionary analysis*. New York: Harper & Row.

Plutchik, R. (1985). On emotion: The chicken-and-egg problem revisited. *Motivation and Emotion, 9*, 197–200.

Polivy, J. (1976). Perception of calories and regulation of intake in restrained and unrestrained subjects. *Addictive Behaviors, 1*, 237–243.

Polivy, J., & Herman, C. P. (1976a). Clinical depression and weight change: A complex relation. *Journal of Abnormal Psychology, 85*, 338–340.

Polivy, J., & Herman, C. P. (1976b). Effect of alcohol on eating behavior: Influences of mood and perceived intoxication. *Journal of Abnormal Psychology, 85*, 601–606.

Polivy, J., & Herman, C. P. (1983). *Breaking the diet habit*. New York: Basic Books.

Polivy, J., & Herman, C. P. (1985). Dieting and binging. *American Psychologist, 40*, 193–201.

Pollak, L. H., & Thoits, P. A. (1989). Processes in emotional socialization. *Social Psychology Quarterly, 52*, 22–34.

Potter, S. H. (1988). The cultural construction of emotion in rural Chinese social life. *Ethos, 16*, 181–208.

Powley, T. L., & Keesey, R. E. (1970). Relationship of body weight to the lateral hypothalamus feeding syndrome. *Journal of Comparative and Clinical Psychology, 70*, 25–36.

Premack, D. (1959). Toward empirical behavior laws: I. Positive reinforcement. *Psychological Review, 66*, 219–233.

Price, R. A. (1987). Genetics of human obesity. *Annals of Behavioral Medicine, 9*, 9–14.

Quattrone, C. A. (1985). On the congruity between internal states and action. *Psychological Bulletin, 98*, 3–40.

Rachman, S. (1978). *Fear and courage*. San Francisco: Freeman.

Rachman, S., & Hodgson, R. I. (1974). Synchrony and desynchrony in fear and avoidance. *Behaviour Research and Therapy, 12*, 311–318.

Ramamurthi, B. (1988). Stereotactic operation in behaviour disorders. *Amygdalotomy and hypothalamotomy. Acta Neurochir* (Supplement), *44*, 152–157.

Rand, A. (1964). The objectivist ethics. In *The virtue of selfishness*. New York: Signet.

Rapaport, D. (1960). On the psychoanalytic theory of motivation. *Nebraska symposium on motivation* (Vol. 8, pp. 173–247). Lincoln: University of Nebraska Press.

Ravlin, S. B. (1987). A computer model of affective reactions to goal-relevant events. Unpublished master's thesis, University of Illinois, Urbana-Champaign. As cited in A. Ortony, G. L. Clore, & A. Collins (Eds.), *The cognitive structure of emotions*. Cambridge: Cambridge University Press.

Raynor, J. O. (1969). Future orientation and motivation of immediate activity: An elaboration of the theory of achievement motivation. *Psychological Review, 76*, 606–610.

Raynor, J. O. (1970). Relationship between achievement-related motives, future orientation, and academic performance. *Journal of Personality and Social Psychology, 15*, 28–33.

Raynor, J. O. (1974). Future orientation in the study of achievement motivation. In J. W. Atkinson & J. O. Raynor (Eds.), *Motivation and achievement*. Washington, DC: V. H. Winston.

Raynor, J. O., & Entin, E. E. (1982). *Motivation, career striving, and aging*. New York: Hemisphere.

Reber, A. (1992). The cognitive unconscious: An evolutionary perspective. *Consciousness and Cognition, 1*, 93–133.

Reeve, J. (1989). The interest-enjoyment distinction in intrinsic motivation. *Motivation and Emotion, 13*, 83–103.

Reeve, J. (1993). The face of interest. *Motivation and Emotion, 17*, 353–375.

Reeve, J. (1996). *Motivating others: Nurturing inner motivational resources*. Needham Heights, MA: Allyn and Bacon.

Reeve, J. (2002). Self-determination theory applied to educational settings. In E. L. Deci & R. M. Ryan's (Eds.), *Handbook of self-determination* (pp. 183–203). Rochester, NY: University of Rochester Press.

Reeve, J., Bolt, E., & Cai, Y. (1999). Autonomy-supportive teachers: How they teach and motivate students. *Journal of Educational Psychology, 91*, 537–548.

Reeve, J., & Deci, E. L. (1996). Elements of the competitive situation that affect intrinsic motivation. *Personality and Social Psychology Bulletin, 22*, 24–33.

Reeve, J., Deci, E. L., & Ryan, R. M. (2003). Self-determination theory: A dialectical framework for understanding the sociocultural influences on student motivation. In D. M. McInerney & S. Van Etten (Eds.), *Research on sociocultural influences on motivation and learning: Big theories revisited* (Vol. 4). Greenwhich, CT: Information Age Press.

Reeve, J., Jang, H., Hardre, P., & Omura, M. (2002). Providing a rationale in an autonomy-supportive way as a strategy to motivate others during an uninteresting activity. *Motivation and Emotion, 26*, 183–207.

Reeve, J., & Jang, H. (2003). *What teachers say and do to support students' autonomy during a learning activity.* Unpublished manuscript, University of Iowa.

Reeve, J., Nix, G., & Hamm, D. (2003). Testing models of the experience of self-determination in intrinsic motivation and the conundrum of choice. *Journal of Educational Psychology, 95*, 375–392.

Reeve, J., Olson, B. C., & Cole, S. G. (1985). Motivation and performance: Two consequences of winning and losing in competition. *Motivation and Emotion, 9*, 291–298.

Reifman, A. S., Larrick, R. P., & Fein, S. (1991). Temper and temperature on the diamond: The heat-aggression relationship in major league baseball. *Personality and Social Psychology Bulletin, 17*, 580–585.

Reis, H. T., Sheldon, K. M., Gable, S. L., Roscoe, R., & Ryan, R. M. (2000). Daily well-being: The role of autonomy, competence, and relatedness. *Personality and Social Psychology Bulletin, 26*, 419–435.

Reis, I. L. (1986). A sociological journey into sexuality. *Journal of Marriage and the Family, 48*, 233–242.

Reisenzein, R., & Hofman, T. (1993). Discriminating emotions from appraisal-relevant situational information: Baseline data for structural models of cognitive appraisals. *Cognition and Emotion, 7*, 271–293.

Renninger, K. A. (1996). Learning as the focus of the educational psychology course. *Educational Psychologist, 31*, 63–76.

Renninger, K. A., Hidi, S., & Krapp, A. (Eds.). (1992). *The role of interest in learning and development.* Hillsdale, NJ: Lawrence Erlbaum.

Renninger, K. A., & Wozniak, R. H. (1985). Effect of interest on attentional shift, recognition, and recall in young children. *Developmental Psychology, 21*, 624–632.

Revelle, W., Amaral, P., & Turriff, S. (1976). Introversion/extraversion, time stress, and caffeine: Effect on verbal performance. *Science, 192*, 149–150.

Reynolds, P. C. (1982). Affect and instrumentality: An alternative view on Eibl-Eibesfeldt's human ethology. *Behavioral and Brain Science, 5*, 267–268.

Rigby, C. S., Deci, E. L., Patrick, B. P., & Ryan, R. M. (1992). Beyond the intrinsic-extrinsic dichotomy: Self-determination in motivation and learning. *Motivation and Emotion, 16*, 165–185.

Rimé, B., Mesquita, B., Philippot, P., & Boca, S. (1991). Beyond the emotional event: Six studies on the social sharing of emotion. *Cognition and Emotion, 5*, 435–465.

Ritvo, L. B. (1990). *Darwin's influence on Freud: A Tale of Two Sciences.* New Haven, CT: Yale University Press.

Robbins, T. W., & Everitt, B. J. (1996). Neurobehavioural mechanisms of reward and motivation. *Current Opinion in Neurobiology, 6*, 228–236.

Roberts, D. C. S., Corcoran, M. E., & Fibiger, H. C. (1977). On the role of ascending catecholaminergic systems in intravenous self-administration of cocaine. *Pharmacology, Biochemistry, and Behavior, 6*, 615–620.

Roberts, G. C. (Ed.). (1992). *Motivation in sport and exercise.* Champaign, IL: Human Kinetics Books.

Robertson, L. S., Kelley, A. B., O'Neil, B., Wixom, C. W., Eiswirth, R. S., & Haddon, W. (1974). A controlled study of the effect of television messages on safety belt use. *American Journal of Public Health, 64*, 1071–1080.

Robinson, D. T., & Smith-Lovin, L. (1992). Selective interaction as a strategy for identity maintenance: An affect control model. *Social Psychology Quarterly, 55*, 12–28.

Robinson, D. T., Smith-Lovin, L., & Tsoudis, O. (1994). Heinous crime or unfortunate accident? The effects of remorse on responses to mock criminal confessions. *Social Forces, 73*, 175–190.

Rodin, J. (1981). Current status of the external-internal hypothesis for obesity. *American Psychologist, 36*, 361–372.

Rodin, J. (1982). Obesity: Why the losing battle? In B. B. Wolman (Ed.), *Psychological aspects of obesity: A handbook* (pp. 30–87). New York: Van Nostrand Reinhold.

Rodin, J., & Langer, E. J. (1977). Long-term effects of a control-relevant intervention with the institutionalized aged. *Journal of Personality and Social Psychology, 35*, 897–902.

Roediger, H. L. (1990). Implicit memory: Retention without remembering. *American Psychologist, 45*, 1043–1056.

Rofé, Y. (1984). Stress and affiliation: A utility theory. *Psychological Review, 91*, 251–268.

Rogers, C. R. (1951). *Client-centered therapy: Its current practice, implications, and theory.* Boston: Houghton Mifflin.

Rogers, C. R. (1959). A theory of therapy, personality, and interpersonal relationships, as developed in the client-centered framework. In S. Koch (Ed.), *Psychology: A study of a science* (Vol. 3, pp. 184–256). New York: McGraw-Hill.

Rogers, C. R. (1961). *On becoming a person.* Boston: Houghton Mifflin.

Rogers, C. R. (1963). Actualizing tendency in relation to motives and to consciousness. *Nebraska symposium on motivation* (Vol. 11, pp. 1–24). Lincoln: University of Nebraska Press.

Rogers, C. R. (1966). *A therapist's view of personal goals* [A Pendle Hill pamphlet, #108]. Wallingford, PA: Pendle Hill.

Rogers, C. R. (1969). *Freedom to learn: A view of what education might become.* Columbus, OH: Merrill.

Rogers, C. R. (1973). My philosophy of interpersonal relationships and how it grew. *Journal of Humanistic Psychology, 13*, 3–15.

Rogers, C. R. (1980). *A way of being.* Boston: Houghton Mifflin.

Rogers, C. R. (1982). Notes on Rollo May. *Journal of Humanistic Psychology, 22*, 8–9.

Rogers, C. R. (1995). What understanding and acceptance mean to me. *Journal of Humanistic Psychology, 35*, 7–22.

Rolls, B. J. (1979). How variety and palatability can stimulate appetite. *Nutrition Bulletin, 5*, 78–86.

Rolls, B. J., Bell, E. A., & Thorwart, M. L. (1999). Water incorporated into a food but not served with a food decreases energy intake in lean women. *American Journal of Clinical Nutrition, 70*, 448–455.

Rolls, B. J., Rowe, E. T., & Rolls, E. T. (1982). How sensory properties of food affect human feeding behavior. *Physiology and Behavior, 29*, 409–417.

Rolls, B. J., Wood, R. J., & Rolls, E. T. (1980). Thirst: The initiation, maintenance, and termination of drinking. In J. M. Sprague & A. N. Epstein (Eds.), *Progresses in psychobiology and physiological psychology* (Vol. 9, pp. 263–321). New York: Academic Press.

Rolls, E. T. (1992). Neurophysiology and the functions of the primate amygdala. In J. P. Aggleton (Ed.), *The amygdala: Neurobiological aspects of emotion, memory, and mental dysfunction* (pp. 143–165). New York: Wiley.

Rolls, E. T., Sanghera, M. K., & Roper-Hall, A. (1979). Latency of activation of neurons In the lateral hypothalamus and substantia innominata during feeding in the monkey. *Brain Research, 164*, 121–135.

Roney, C., Higgins, E. T., & Shah, J. (1995). Goals and framing: How outcome focus influences motivation and emotion. *Personality and Social Psychology Bulletin, 21*, 1151–1160.

Ronis, D., & Greenwald, A. (1979). Dissonance theory revised again: Comment on the paper by Fazio, Zanna, and Cooper. *Journal of Experimental Social Psychology, 15*, 62–69.

Rose, S., Frieze, I. H. (1989). Young singles scripts for a first date. *Gender and Society, 3*, 258–268.

Roseman, I. J. (1984). Cognitive determinants of emotion: A structural theory. In P. Shaver (Ed.), *Review of personality and social psychology: Emotions, relationships, and health* (Vol. 5, pp. 11–36). Beverly Hills, CA: Sage.

Roseman, I. J. (1991). Appraisal determinants of discrete emotions. *Cognition and Emotion, 5*, 161–200.

Roseman, I. J., Antoniou, A. A., & Jose, P. E. (1996). Appraisal determinants of emotions: Constructing a more accurate and comprehensive theory. *Cognition and Emotion, 10*, 241–277.

Rosen, B., & D'Andrade, R. C. (1959). The psychological origins of achievement motivation. *Sociometry, 22*, 185–218.

Rosenberg, E. L., & Ekman, P. (1994). Coherence between expressive and experiential systems in emotion. *Cognition and Emotion, 8*, 201–229.

Rosenberg, M. (1965). *Society and the adolescent self-image*. Princeton, NJ: Princeton University Press.

Rosenfeld, P., Giacalone, R. A., & Tedeschi, J. T. (1984). Cognitive dissonance and impression management explanations for effort justification. *Personality and Social Psychology Bulletin, 10*, 394–401.

Rosenhan, D. L., & Seligman, M. E. P. (1984). *Abnormal psychology*. New York: W. W. Norton.

Rosenholtz, S. J., & Rosenholtz, S. H. (1981). Classroom organization and the perception of ability. *Sociology of Education, 54*, 132–140.

Ross, M., & Shulman, R. (1973). Increasing the salience of initial attitudes: Dissonance versus self-perception theory. *Journal of Personality and Social Psychology, 28*, 138–144.

Rothkopf, E. Z., & Billington, M. J. (1979). Goal-guided learning from text: Inferring a descriptive processing model from inspection times and eye movements. *Journal of Educational Psychology, 71*, 310–327.

Rotter, J. B. (1966). Generalized expectancies for internal and external control of reinforcement. *Psychological Monographs*, Whole No. 80.

Rowan, J. (1987). Nine humanistic heresies. *Journal of Humanistic Psychology, 27*, 141–157.

Rozin, P., & Fallon, A. E. (1987). A perspective on disgust. *Psychological Review, 94*, 23–41.

Rozin, P., Haidt, J., & McCauley, C. R. (1993). Disgust. In M. Lewis & J. Haviland (Eds.), *Handbook of emotions* (pp. 575–594). New York: Guilford Press.

Rozin, P., Lowery, L., & Ebert, R. (1994). Varieties of disgust faces and the structure of disgust. *Journal of Personality and Social Psychology, 66*, 870–881.

Ruble, D. N., Crosovsky, E. H., Frey, K. S., & Cohen, R. (1992). Developmental changes in competence assessment. In A. Boggiano & T. S. Pittman (Eds.), *Motivation and achievement: A social-developmental perspective* (pp. 138–166). New York: Cambridge University Press.

Ruble, D. N., Parsons, J., & Ross, J. (1976). Self-evaluative responses of children in an achievement setting. *Child Development, 47*, 990–997.

Ruckmick, C. A. (1936). *The psychology of feeling and emotion*. New York: McGraw-Hill.

Rudd, J. R., & Geller, E. S. (1985). A university-based incentive program to increase safety belt use: Towards cost-effective institutionalization. *Journal of Applied Behavior Analysis, 18*, 215–226.

Ruderman, A. J., & Wilson, G. T. (1979). Weight, restraint, cognitions, and counter-regulation. *Behaviour Therapy and Research, 17*, 581–590.

Rummel, A., & Feinberg, R. (1988). Cognitive evaluation theory: A meta-analytic review of the literature. *Social Behavior and Personality, 16*, 147–164.

Russek, M. (1971). Hepatic receptors and the neurophysiological mechanisms controlling feeding behavior. In S. Ehrenpreis (Ed.), *Neuroscience research.* New York: Academic Press.

Russell, J. A. (1995). Facial expressions of emotion: What lies beyond minimal universality? *Psychological Bulletin, 118*, 379–391.

Russell, J. A., & Barrett, L. F. (1999). Core affect, prototypical emotional episodes, and other things call emotion: Dissecting the elephant. *Journal of Personality and Social Psychology, 76*, 805–819.

Russell, J. A., & Yik, M. S. M. (1996). Emotion among the Chinese. In M. H. Bond (Ed.), *The handbook of Chinese psychology* (pp. 166–188). Hong Kong: Oxford University Press.

Rutledge, L. L., & Hupka, R. B. (1985). The facial feedback hypothesis: Methodological concerns and new supporting evidence. *Motivation and Emotion, 9*, 219–240.

Ryan, E. D., & Lakie, W. L. (1965). Competitive and noncompetitive performance in relation to achievement motive and manifest anxiety. *Journal of Personality and Social Psychology, 1*, 342–345.

Ryan, R. M. (1982). Control and information in the intrapersonal sphere: An extension of cognitive evaluation theory. *Journal of Personality and Social Psychology, 43*, 450–461.

Ryan, R. M. (1991). The nature of the self in autonomy and relatedness. In J. Strauss & G. R. Goethals (Eds.), *The self: Interdisciplinary approaches* (pp. 208–238). New York: Springer-Verlag.

Ryan, R. M. (1993). Agency and organization: Intrinsic motivation, autonomy, and the self in psychological development. In J. E. Jacobs (Ed.), *Nebraska symposium on motivation: Developmental perspectives on motivation* (Vol. 40, pp. 1–56). Lincoln: University of Nebraska Press.

Ryan, R. M. (1995). Psychological needs and the facilitation of integrative processes. *Journal of Personality, 63*, 397–427.

Ryan, R. M., Avery, R. R., & Grolnick, W. S. (1985). A Rorschach assessment of children's mutuality of autonomy. *Journal of Personality Assessment, 49*, 6–12.

Ryan, R. M., & Connell, J. P. (1989). Perceived locus of causality and internalization: Examining reasons for acting in two domains. *Journal of Personality and Social Psychology, 57*, 749–761.

Ryan, R. M., & Deci, E. L. (2000a). Self-determination theory and the facilitation of intrinsic motivation, social development, and well-being. *American Psychologist, 55*, 68–78.

Ryan, R. M., & Deci, E. L. (2000b). Intrinsic and extrinsic motivations: Classic definitions and new directions. *Contemporary Educational Psychology, 25*, 54–67.

Ryan, R. M., & Deci, E. L. (2001). On happiness and human potentials: A review of research on hedonic and eudaimonic well-being. *Annual Review of Psychology, 52*, 141–166.

Ryan, R. M., & Frederick, C. M. (1997). On energy, personality, and health: Subjective vitality as a dynamic reflection of well-being. *Journal of Personality, 65*, 529–565.

Ryan, R. M., Frederick, C. M., Lepes, D., Rubio, N., & Sheldon, K. M. (1997). Intrinsic motivation and exercise adherence. *International Journal of Sport Psychology, 28*, 335–354.

Ryan, R. M., & Grolnick, W. S. (1986). Origins and pawns in the classroom: Self-report and projective assessments of individual differences in children's perceptions. *Journal of Personality and Social Psychology, 50*, 550–558.

Ryan, R. M., Koestner, R., & Deci, E. L. (1991). Ego-involved persistence: When free-choice behavior is not intrinsically motivated. *Motivation and Emotion, 15*, 185–205.

Ryan, R. M., & Lynch, J. (1989). Emotional autonomy versus detachment: Revisiting the vicissitudes of adolescent and young adulthood. *Child Development, 60*, 340–356.

Ryan, R. M., Mims, V., & Koestner, R. (1983). Relation of reward contingency and interpersonal context to intrinsic motivation: A review and test using cognitive evaluation theory. *Journal of Personality and Social Psychology, 45*, 736–750.

Ryan, R. M., Plant, R. W., & O'Malley, S. (1995). Initial motivations for alcohol treatment: Relations with patient characteristics, treatment involvement and dropout. *Addictive Behaviors, 20,* 586–596.

Ryan, R. M., & Powelson, C. L. (1991). Autonomy and relatedness as fundamental to motivation and education. *Journal of Experimental Education, 60,* 49–66.

Ryan, R. M., Rigby, S., & King, K. (1993). Two types of religious internalization and their relations to religious orientations and mental health. *Journal of Personality and Social Psychology, 65,* 586–596.

Ryan, R. M., Stiller, J., & Lynch, J. H. (1994). Representations of relationships to teachers, parents, and friends as predictors of academic motivation and self-esteem. *Journal of Early Adolescence, 14,* 226–249.

Ryff, C. D. (1989). Happiness is everything, or is it? Explorations on the meaning of psychological well-being. *Journal of Personality and Social Psychology, 57,* 1069–1081.

Ryff, C. D. (1991). Possible selves in adulthood and old age: A tale of shifting horizons. *Psychology and Aging, 6,* 286–295.

Ryff, C. D. (1995). Psychological well-being in adult life. *Current Directions in Psychological Science, 4,* 99–104.

Ryff, C. D., & Keyes, C. L. M. (1995). The structure of psychological well-being revisited. *Journal of Personality and Social Psychology, 69,* 719–727.

Ryff, C. D., & Singer, B. (2002). From social structure to biology: Integrative science in pursuit of human health and well-being. In C. R. Snyder & S. J. Lopez (Eds.), *Handbook of positive psychology* (pp. 541–555). New York: Oxford University Press.

Saarni, C. (1979). Children's understanding of display rules for expressive behavior. *Developmental Psychology, 15,* 424–429.

Saarni, C. (1997). Coping with aversive feelings. *Motivation and Emotion, 21,* 45–63.

Sackeim, H. A. (1983). Self-deception, self-esteem, and depression: The adaptive value of lying to oneself. In J. Masling (Ed.), *Empirical studies of psychoanalytic theories* (Vol. 1, pp. 101–157). Hillsdale, NJ: Analytic Press.

Sackeim, H. A., Greenberg, M. S., Weiman, A. L., Gur, R. C., Hungerbuhler, J. P., & Geschwind, N. (1982). Hemispheric-asymmetry in the expression of positive and negative emotion: Neurological evidence. *Archives of Neurology, 39,* 210–218.

Sacks, C. H., & Bugental, D. B. (1987). Attributions as moderators of affective and behavioral responses to social failure. *Journal of Personality and Social Psychology, 53,* 939–947.

Sakurai, T., Amemiya, A., Ishii, M., Matsuzaki, I., Chemelli, R. M., Tanaka, H., Williams, S. C., Richardson, J. A., Kozlowski, G. P., Wilson, S., Arch, J. R. S., Buckingham, R. E., Haynes, A. C., Carr, S. A., Annan, R. S., McNulty, D. E., Liu, W. S., Terrett, J. A., Elshourbagy, N. A., Bergsma, D. J., & Yanagisawa, M. (1998). Orexins and orexin receptors: A family of hypothalamic neuropeptides and G protein-coupled receptors that regulate feeding behavior. *Cell, 92,* 573–585.

Salomon, G. (1984). Television is easy and print is tough: The differential investment of mental effort in learning as a function of perceptions and attributions. *Journal of Educational Psychology, 76,* 647–658.

Sansone, C. (1989). Competence feedback, task feedback, and intrinsic interest: The importance of context. *Journal of Experimental Social Psychology, 25,* 343–361.

Sansone, C., & Harackiewicz, J. M. (2000). *Intrinsic and extrinsic motivation: The search for optimal motivation and performance.* San Diego, CA: Academic Press.

Sansone, C., & Smith, J. L. (2000). Self-regulating interest: When, why, and how. In C. Sansone & J. M. Harackiewicz (Eds.), *Intrinsic motivation: Controversies and new directions* (pp. 343–373). New York: Academic Press.

Sansone, C., Weir, C., Harpster, L., & Morgan, C. (1992). Once a boring task always a boring task?: Interest as a self-regulatory mechanism. *Journal of Personality and Social Psychology, 63,* 379–390.

Sanz, J. (1996). Memory biases in social anxiety and depression. *Cognition and Emotion, 10*, 87–105.

Sarason, B. R., Pierce, G. R., Shearin, E. N., Sarason, I. G., Waltz, J. A., & Poppe, L. (1991). Perceived social support and working models of self and actual others. *Journal of Personality and Social Psychology, 60*, 273–287.

Schaal, B., & Gollwitzer, P. M. (1999). *Implementation intentions and resistance to temptation.* Unpublished manuscript, New York University.

Schacter, D. L. (1992). Understanding implicit memory: A cognitive neuroscience approach. *American Psychologist, 47*, 559–569.

Schachter, S. (1959). *The psychology of affiliation.* Stanford, CA: Stanford University Press.

Schachter, S. (1964). The interaction of cognitive and physiological determinants of emotion. In L. Berkowitz (Ed.), *Advances in experimental social psychology* (Vol. 1, pp. 49–80). New York: Academic Press.

Schachter, S., & Singer, J. E. (1962). Cognitive, social, and physiological determinants of emotional states. *Psychological Review, 69*, 379–399.

Scharff, J. S., & Scharff, D. E. (1995). *The primer of object relations therapy.* Northvale, NJ: Jason Aronson.

Schafer, R. B., Wickram, K. A. S., & Keith, P. M. (1996). Self-concept disconfirmation, psychological distress, and marital happiness. *Journal of Marriage and the Family, 58*, 167–177.

Scheier, M. F., & Carver, C. S. (1992). Effects of optimism on psychological and physical well-being: Theoretical overview and empirical update. *Cognitive Therapy and Research, 16*, 201–228.

Scheier, M. A., & Kraut, R. E. (1979). Increasing educational achievement via self-concept change. *Review of Educational Research, 49*, 131–150.

Scheier, M. F., & Carver, C. S. (1988). A model of behavioral self-regulation: Translating intention into action. In L. Berkowitz (Ed.), *Advances in experimental social psychology* (Vol. 21, pp. 303–346). New York: Academic Press.

Scherer, K. R. (1984a). Emotion as a multicomponent process: A model and some cross-cultural data. In P. Shaver (Ed.), *Review of personality and social psychology* (Vol. 5, pp. 37–63). Beverly Hills, CA: Sage.

Scherer, K. R. (1984b). On the nature and function of emotion: A component process approach. In K. Scherer & P. Ekman (Eds.), *Approaches to emotion* (pp. 293–318). Hillsdale, NJ: Erlbaum.

Scherer, K. R. (1986). Vocal affect expression: A review and a model for future research. *Psychological Bulletin, 99*, 143–165.

Scherer, K. R. (1993). Studying the emotion-antecedent appraisal process: An expert systems approach. *Cognition and Emotion, 7*, 325–355.

Scherer, K. R. (1994a). An emotion's occurrence depends on the relevance of an event to the organism's goal/need hierarchy. In P. Ekman & R. J. Davidson (Eds.), *The nature of emotion: Fundamental questions* (pp. 227–231). New York: Oxford University Press.

Scherer, K. R. (1994b). Toward a concept of modal emotions. In P. Ekman & R. J. Davidson (Eds.), *The nature of emotion: Fundamental questions* (pp. 25–31). New York: Oxford University Press.

Scherer, K. R. (1997). Profiles of emotion-antecedent appraisal: Testing theoretical predictions across cultures. *Cognition and Emotion, 11*, 113–150.

Scherer, K. R., Schorr, A., & Johnstone, T. (Ed.) (2001). *Appraisal processes in emotion: Theory, methods, research.* New York: Oxford University Press.

Scherer, K. R., & Ekman, P. (1984). *Approaches to emotion.* Hillsdale, NJ: Lawrence Erlbaum.

Scherer, K. R., & Tannenbaum, P. H. (1986). Emotional experience in everyday life. *Motivation and Emotion, 10*, 295–314.

Scherhorn, G., & Grunert, S. C. (1988). Using the causality orientations concept in consumer behavior research. *Journal of Consumer Psychology, 13*, 33–39.

Schiefele, U. (1991). Interest, learning, and motivation. *Educational Psychologist, 26,* 299–323.

Schierman, M. J., & Rowland, G. L. (1985). Sensation seeking and selection of entertainment. *Personality and Individual Differences, 6,* 599–603.

Schildkraut, J. J. (1965). The catecholamine hypothesis of affective disorders: A review of supporting evidence. *American Journal of Psychiatry, 12,* 509–522.

Schmalt, H. D. (1982). Two concepts of fear of failure motivation. *Advances in Test Anxiety Research, 1,* 45–52.

Schmalt, H. D. (1999). Assessing the achievement motive using the grid technique. *Journal of Research in Personality, 33,* 109–130.

Schmitt, M. (1973). Influences of hepatic portal receptors on hypothalamic feeding and satiety centers. *American Journal of Physiology, 225,* 1089–1095.

Schmitz, B., & Skinner, E. A. (1993). Perceived control, effort, and academic performance: Interindividual, intraindividual, and multivariate time-series analyses. *Journal of Personality and Social Psychology, 64,* 1010–1028.

Schooler, C., Zahn, T. P., Murphy, D. L., & Buchsbaum, M. S. (1978). Psychological correlates of monoamine oxidase in normals. *Journal of Nervous and Mental Disease, 166,* 177–186.

Schraw, G., Flowerday, T., & Reisetter, M. F. (1996). The role of choice in reader engagement. *Journal of Educational Psychology, 90,* 705–714.

Schultz, D. P. (1987). *A history of modern psychology* (4th ed.). San Diego, CA: Harcourt Brace Jovanovich.

Schunk, D. H. (1989a). Self-efficacy and achievement behaviors. *Educational Psychology Review, 1,* 173–208.

Schunk, D. H. (1989b). Self-efficacy and cognitive skill learning. In C. A. Ames & R. Ames (Eds.), *Research on motivation in education: Goals and cognition* (Vol. 3, pp. 13–44). San Diego: Academic Press.

Schunk, D. H. (1991). Self-efficacy and academic motivation. *Educational Psychologist, 26,* 207–231.

Schunk, D. H., & Cox, P. D. (1986). Strategy training and attributional feedback with learning disabled students. *Journal of Educational Psychology, 78,* 201–209.

Schunk, D. H., & Hanson, A. R. (1989). Self-modeling and children's cognitive skill learning. *Journal of Educational Psychology, 83,* 155–163.

Schunk, D. H., & Zimmerman, B. J. (1997). Social origins of self-regulatory competence. *Educational Psychologist, 32,* 195–208.

Schwartz, M. W., Woods, S. C., Porte, D., Jr., Seeley, R. J., & Baskin, D. G. (2000). Central nervous system control of food intake. *Nature, 404,* 661–671.

Schwartz, G. E. (1986). Emotion and psychophysiological organization: A systems approach. In M. G. H. Coles, E. Ponchin, & S. W. Proges (Eds.), *Psychophysiology: Systems, processes, and applications* (pp. 354–377). New York: Guilford Press.

Schwartz, M. W., & Seeley, R. J. (1997). Neuroendocrine responses to starvation and weight loss. *New England Journal of Medicine, 336,* 1802–1811.

Schwartz, N., & Clore, G. L. (1983). Mood, misattribution, and judgments of well-being: Informative and directive functions of affective states. *Journal of Personality and Social Psychology, 45,* 513–523.

Sclafani, A. (1980). Dietary obesity. In A. J. Stunkard (Ed.), *Obesity* (pp. 166–181). Philadelphia: W. B. Saunders.

Sclafini, A., & Springer, D. (1976). Dietary obesity in adult rats: Similarities to hypothalamic and human obesity syndromes. *Physiology and Behavior, 17,* 461–471.

Segal, E. M., & Lachman, R. (1972). Complex behavior or higher mental process: Is there a paradigm shift? *American Psychologist, 27,* 46–55.

Segraves, R. T. (Ed.) (2001). Historical and international context of nosology of female sexual disorders [Special issue.]. *Journal of Sex and Martial Therapy, 27* (2).

Seligman, M. E. P., Reivich, K., Jaycox, L., & Gillham, J. (1995). *The optimistic child*. New York: Houghton Mifflin.

Seligman, M. E. P. (1975). *Helplessness: On depression, development, and death*. San Francisco: W. H. Freeman.

Seligman, M. E. P. (1991). *Learned optimism*. New York: Alfred A. Knopf.

Seligman, M. E. P., & Csikszentmihalyi, M. (2000). Positive psychology: An introduction. *American Psychologist, 55*, 5–14.

Seligman, M. E. P., & Maier, S. F. (1967). Failure to escape traumatic shock. *Journal of Experimental Psychology, 94*, 1–9.

Seligman, M. E. P., & Schulman, P. (1986). Explanatory style as a predictor of productivity and quitting among life insurance agents. *Journal of Personality and Social Psychology, 50*, 832–838.

Sepple, C. P., & Read, N. W. (1989). Gastrointestinal correlates of the development of hunger in man. *Appetite, 13*, 183–191.

Seyle, H. (1956). *The stress of life*. New York: McGraw-Hill.

Seyle, H. (1976). *Stress in health and disease*. Reading, MA: Butterworth.

Shaalvik, E. M., & Hagtvet, K. A. (1990). Academic achievement and self-concept. *Journal of Personality and Social Psychology, 58*, 292–307.

Shaffer, D. (1977). Suicide in childhood and early adolescence. *Journal of Child Psychology and Psychiatry, 45*, 406–451.

Shapira, Z. (1976). Expectancy determinants of intrinsically motivated behavior. *Journal of Personality and Social Psychology, 34*, 1235–1244.

Shapiro, D. H., Schwartz, C. E., & Astin, J. A. (1996). Controlling ourselves, controlling our world: Psychology's role in understanding positive and negative consequences of seeking and gaining control. *American Psychologist, 51*, 1213–1230.

Shaver, P., & Hazan, C. (1987). Being lonely, falling in love: Perspectives from attachment theory. *Journal of Social Behavior and Personality, 2*, 105–124.

Shaver, P., Schwartz, J., Kirson, D., & O'Connor, C. (1987). Emotion knowledge: Further exploration of a prototype approach. *Journal of Personality and Social Psychology, 52*, 1061–1086.

Shaver, P. R., Wu, S., & Schwartz, J. C. (1992). Cross-cultural similarities and differences In emotion and its representation: A prototype approach. In M. S. Clark (Eds.), *Review of personality and social psychology* (Vol. 13). Thousand Oaks, CA: Sage.

Sheeran, P., & Orbell, S. (1999). Implementation intentions and repeated behaviors: Augmenting the predictive validity of the theory of planned behavior. *European Journal of Social Psychology, 29*, 349–370.

Sheffield, F. D., & Roby, T. B. (1950). Reward value of a non-nutritive sweet taste. *Journal of Comparative and Physiological Psychology, 43*, 471–481.

Sheldon, K. M. (2001). The self-concordance model of healthy goal striving: When personal goals correctly represent the person. In P. Schmuck & K. M. Sheldon (Eds.), *Life goals and well-being: Towards a positive psychology of human striving* (pp. 18–36). Seattle: Hogrefe & Huber Publishers.

Sheldon, K. M. (2002). The self-concordance model of healthy goal striving: When personal goals correctly represent the person. In E. L. Deci & R. M. Ryan's (Eds.), *Handbook of self-determination* (pp. 65–86). Rochester, NY: University of Rochester Press.

Sheldon, K., M., & Elliot, A. J. (1998). Not all personal goals are personal: Comparing autonomous and controlled reasons as predictors of effort and attainment. *Personality and Social Psychological Bulletin, 24*, 546–557.

Sheldon, K., M., & Elliot, A. J. (1999). Goal striving, need-satisfaction, and longitudinal well-being: The self-concordance model. *Journal of Personality and Social Psychology, 76*, 482–497.

Sheldon, K., M., Elliot, A. J., Kim, Y., & Kasser, T. (2001). What is satisfying about satisfying events? Testing 10 candidate psychological needs. *Journal of Personality and Social Psychology, 80*, 325–339.

Sheldon, K. M., & Houser-Marko, L. (2001). Self-concordance, goal attainment, and the pursuit of happiness: Can there be an upward spiral? *Journal of Personality and Social Psychology, 80,* 152–165.

Sheldon, K. M., & Kasser, T. (1998). Pursuing personal goals: Skills enable progress but not all progress is beneficial. *Personality and Social Psychology Bulletin, 24,* 1319–1331.

Sheldon, K. M., & Kasser, T. (1995). Coherence and congruence: Two aspects of personality integration. *Journal of Personality and Social Psychology, 68,* 531–543.

Sheldon, K. M., Ryan, R. M., & Reis, H. T. (1996). What makes for a good day? Competence and autonomy in the day and in the person. *Personality and Social Psychology Bulletin, 22,* 1270–1279.

Sheldon, K. M., Ryan, R. M., & Reis, H. T. (1998). What makes for a good day? Competence and autonomy in the day and in the person. *Personality and Social Psychology Bulletin, 22,* 1270–1279.

Shields, J. (1976). Heredity and environment. In H. J. Eysenck & G. D. Wilson (Eds.), *A textbook of human psychology.* Baltimore: University Park Press.

Shipley, T. E., Jr., & Veroff, J. (1952). A projective measure of need for affiliation. *Journal of Experimental Psychology, 43,* 349–356.

Shirey, L. L., & Reynolds, R. E. (1988). Effect of interest on attention and learning. *Journal of Educational Psychology, 80,* 159–166.

Shostrom, E. L. (1964). An inventory for the measurement of self-actualization. *Educational and Psychological Measurement, 24,* 207–218.

Shostrom, E. L. (1974). *Manual for the personal orientation inventory.* San Diego, CA: EDITS.

Sid, A. K. W., & Lindgren, H. C. (1981). Sex differences in achievement and affiliation motivation among undergraduates majoring in different academic fields. *Psychological Reports, 48,* 539–542.

Silver, R. L. (1982). *Coping with an undesirable life event: A study of early reactions to physical disability.* Unpublished doctoral dissertation, Northwestern University.

Silverman, L. H. (1976). Psychoanalytic theory: The reports of my death are greatly exaggerated. *American Psychologist, 31,* 621–637.

Silverman, L. H., & Weinberger, J. (1985). Mommy and I are one: Implications for psychotherapy. *American Psychologist, 40,* 1296–1308.

Simon, L., Greenberg, J., & Brehm, J. (1995). Trivialization: The forgotten mode of dissonance reduction. *Journal of Personality and Social Psychology, 68,* 247–260.

Simon, W., & Gagnon, J. H. (1986). Sexual scripts: Permanence and change. *Archives of Sexual Behavior, 15,* 97–120.

Singh, D. (1993a). Adaptive significance of female physical attractiveness: Role of waist-to-hip ratio. *Journal of Personality and Social Psychology, 65,* 293–307.

Singh, D. (1993b). Body shape and women's attractiveness: The critical role of waist-to-hip ratio. *Human Nature, 4,* 297–321.

Singh D. (1995). Female judgment of male attractiveness and desirability for relationships: Role of waist-to-hip ratio and financial status. *Journal of Personality and Social Psychology, 69,* 1089–1101.

Sinha, R., & Parsons, O. A. (1996). Multivariate response patterning of fear and anger. *Cognition and Emotion, 10,* 173–198.

Skinner, B. F. (1938). *The behavior of organisms.* New York: Appleton-Century-Crofts.

Skinner, B. F. (1953). *Science and human behavior.* New York: Macmillan.

Skinner, B. F. (1986). What is wrong with daily life in the Western world? *American Psychologist, 41,* 568–574.

Skinner, E. A. (1985). Action, control judgments, and the structure of control experience. *Psychological Review, 92,* 39–58.

Skinner, E. A. (1986). The origins of young children's perceived control: Caregivers contingent and sensitive behavior. *International Journal of Behavioral Development, 9,* 359–382.

Skinner, E. A. (1991). Development and perceived control: A dynamic model of action in context. In M. Gunnar & L. A. Sroufe (Eds.), *Minnesota Symposium on Child Psychology* (Vol. 23). Hillsdale, NJ: Erlbaum.

Skinner, E. A. (1995). *Perceived control, motivation, and coping.* Newbury Park, CA: Sage.

Skinner, E. A., & Belmont, M. J. (1993). Motivation in the classroom: Reciprocal effects of teacher behavior and student engagement across the school year. *Journal of Educational Psychology, 85,* 571–581.

Skinner, E. A., Chapman, M., & Baltes, P. B. (1988). Control, means-ends, and agency beliefs: A new conceptualization and its measurement during childhood. *Journal of Personality and Social Psychology, 54,* 117–133.

Skinner, E. A., Zimmer-Gembeck, M. J., & Connell, J. P. (1998). Individual differences and the development of perceived control. *Monographs of the Society for Research in Child Development, 63,* Serial number 254.

Slade, L. A., & Rush, M. C. (1991). Achievement motivation and the dynamics of task difficulty choices. *Journal of Personality and Social Psychology, 60,* 165–172.

Smith, A. C., III, & Kleinman, S. (1989). Managing emotions in medical school: Students' contacts with the living and the dead. *Social Psychology Quarterly, 52,* 56–69.

Smith, C. A., & Ellsworth, P. C. (1985). Patterns of cognitive appraisal in emotion. *Journal of Personality and Social Psychology, 48,* 813–838.

Smith, C. A., & Ellsworth, P. C. (1987). Patterns of appraisal and emotion related to taking an exam. *Journal of Personality and Social Psychology, 52,* 475–488.

Smith, C. A., Haynes, K. N., Lazarus, R. S., & Pope, L. K. (1993). In search of the "hot" cognitions: Attributions, appraisals, and their relation to emotion. *Journal of Personality and Social Psychology, 65,* 916–929.

Smith, K., Locke, E., & Barry, D. (1990). Goal setting, planning and organizational performance: An experimental simulation. *Organizational Behavior and Human Decision Processes, 46,* 118–134.

Smith, P. K. (1982). Does play matter? Functional and evolutionary aspects of animal and human play. *Behavioral and Brain Sciences, 5,* 139–184.

Smith, R. A., Wallston, B. S., Wallston, K. A., Forsberg, P. R., & King, J. E. (1984). Measuring desire for control of health care processes. *Journal of Personality and Social Psychology, 47,* 415–426.

Smith, R. G., Iwata, B. A., & Shore, B. A. (1995). Effects of subject- versus experimenter-selected reinforcers on the behavior of individuals with profound developmental disabilities. *Journal of Applied Behavior Analysis, 28,* 61–71.

Smith-Lovin, L. (1990). Emotion as confirmation and disconfirmation of identity: An affect control model. In T. D. Kemper (Ed.), *Research agendas in the sociology of emotions.* New York: SUNY Press.

Smith-Lovin, L., & Heise, D. R. (Eds.). (1988). *Analyzing social interaction: Advances in affect control theory.* New York: Gordon & Breach.

Snyder, C. R. (1994). *The psychology of hope: You can get there from here.* New York: Free Press.

Snyder, M., & Ebbesen, E. B. (1972). Dissonance awareness: A test of dissonance theory versus self-perception theory. *Journal of Experimental Social Psychology, 8,* 502–517.

Snyder, C. R., Harris, C., Anderson, J. R., Holleran, S. A., Irving, L. M., Sigmond, S. T. Yoshinobu, L., Gibb, J., Langelle, C., & Harney, P. (1991). The will and the ways: Development and validation of an individual-differences measure of hope. *Journal of Personality and Social Psychology, 60,* 570–585.

Snyder, C. R., Lapointe, A. B., Crowson, J. J., Jr., & Early, S. (1998). Preferences of high-and low-hope people for self-referential input. *Cognition and Emotion, 12,* 807–823.

Snyder, C. R., & Lopez, S. J. (Eds.) (2002). *Handbook of positive psychology*. New York: Oxford University Press.

Snyder, C. R., Rand, K. L., & Sigmon, D. R. (2002). Hope theory: A member of the positive psychology family. In C. R. Snyder & S. J. Lopez (Eds.), *Handbook of positive psychology* (pp. 257–276). New York: Oxford University Press.

Snyder, C. R., Shorey, H. S., Cheavens, J., Pulvers, K. M., Adams, V. H. III, & Wiklund, C. (2002). Hope and academic success in college. *Journal of Educational Psychology, 94,* 820–826.

Sobal, J., & Stunkard, A. J. (1989). Socioeconomic status and obesity: A review of the literature. *Psychological Bulletin, 105,* 260–275.

Solomon, R. L. (1980). The opponent-process theory of motivation: The costs of pleasure and the benefits of pain. *American Psychologist, 35,* 691–712.

Solomon, S., Greenberg, J., & Pyszczynski, T. (1991). A terror management theory of social behavior: The psychological functions of self-esteem and cultural worldviews. In M. P. Zanna (Ed.), *Advances in experimental social psychology* (Vol. 24, pp. 93–159). San Diego: Academic Press.

Sorrentino, R. M., & Higgins, E. T. (1986). Motivation and cognition. In R. M. Sorrentino & E. T. Higgins (Eds.), Handbook of motivation and cognition: *Foundations of social behavior* (pp. 3–19). New York: Guilford Press.

Spangler, W. D., & House, R. J. (1991). Presidential effectiveness and the leadership motive profile. *Journal of Personality and Social Psychology, 60,* 439–455.

Spence, J. T., & Helmreich, R. L. (1983). Achievement-related motives and behavior. In J. T. Spence (Ed.), *Achievement and achievement motives: Psychological and sociological approaches* (pp. 10–74). San Francisco: W. H. Freeman.

Spencer, J. A., & Fremouw, W. J. (1979). Binge eating as a function of restrained and weight classification. *Journal of Abnormal Psychology, 88,* 262–267.

Spiegelman, B. M., & Flier, J. F. (2001). Obesity and the regulation of energy balance. *Cell, 104,* 531–543.

Spitzer, L., & Rodin, J. (1981). Human eating behavior: A critical review of studies in normal weight and overweight individuals. *Appetite, 2,* 293–329.

Sprecher, S., Sullivan, Q., & Hatfield, E. (1994). Mate selection preferences: Gender differences examined in a national sample. *Journal of Personality and Social Psychology, 66,* 1074–1080.

Squire, S. (1983). *The slender balance*. New York: Pinnacle.

Staats, H., van Leeuwen, E., & Wit, A. (2000). A longitudinal study of informational interventions to save energy in an office building. *Journal of Applied Behavior Analysis, 33,* 101–104.

Stacey, C. L., & DeMartino, M. F. (Eds.). (1958). *Understanding human motivation*. Cleveland, OH: Howard Allen.

Staub, E. (1999). The roots of evil: Social conditions, culture, personality, and basic human needs. *Personality and Social Psychology Review, 3,* 179–192.

Stevens, J., Cai, J., Pamuk, E. R., Williamson, D. F., Thun, M. J., & Wood, J. L. (1998). The effect of age on the association between body-mass index and mortality. *New England Journal of Medicine, 338,* 1–7.

Steele, C. M. (1988). The psychology of self-affirmation: Sustaining the integrity of the self. In L. Berkowitz (Ed.), *Advances in experimental social psychology* (Vol. 20, pp. 261–302). New York: Academic Press.

Steele, C. M., & Josephs, R. A. (1990). Alcohol myopia: Its prized and dangerous effects. *American Psychologist, 45,* 921–933.

Steele, R. S. (1977). Power motivation, activation, and inspirational speeches. *Journal of Personality, 45,* 53–64.

Stein, G. L., Kimiecik, J. C., Daniels, J., & Jackson, S. A. (1995). Psychological antecedents of flow in recreational sport. *Personality and Social Psychology Bulletin, 21,* 125–135.

Stein, N. L., & Trabasso, T. (1992). The organisation of emotional experience: Creating links among emotion, thinking, language and intentional action. *Cognition and Emotion, 6,* 225–244.

Stellar, J. R., & Stellar, E. (1985). *The neurobiology of motivation and reward.* New York: Springer-Verlag.

Stemmler, G. (1989). The autonomic differentiation of emotions revisited: Convergent and discriminant validity. *Psychophysiology, 26,* 617–632.

Stern, J. S., & Lowney, P. (1986). Obesity: The role of physical activity. In K. D. Brownell & J. P. Foreyt (Eds.), *Handbook of eating disorders: Physiology, psychology, and treatment of obesity, anorexia, and bulimia* (pp. 145–158). New York: Basic Books.

Stevens, J., Cai, J. W., Pamuk, E. R., Williamson, D. F., Thun, Ml J., & Wood, J. L. (1998). The effect of age on the association between body-mass index and mortality. *New England Journal of Medicine, 338,* 1–7.

Stevenson, J. A. F. (1969). Neural control of food and water intake. In W. Haymaker, E. Anderson, & W. J. H. Nauta (Eds.), *The hypothalamus.* Springfield, IL: Thomas.

Stewart, A. J. (1992). Self-definition and social definition: Personal styles reflected in narrative style. In C. P. Smith (Ed.), *Motivation and personality: Handbook of thematic content analysis.* New York: Cambridge University Press.

Stewart, A. J., & Rubin, Z. (1976). Power motivation in the dating couple. *Journal of Personality and Social Psychology, 34,* 305–309.

Stewart, A. J., & Winter, D. G. (1974). Self-definition and social definition in women. *Journal of Personality, 42,* 238–259.

Stipek, D. (1999). Differences between Americans and Chinese in the circumstances evoking pride, shame, and guilt. *Journal of Cross-Cultural Psychology, 29,* 616–629.

Stipek, D. J. (1983). A developmental analysis of pride and shame. *Human Development, 26,* 42–56.

Stipek, D. J. (1984). Young children's performance expectations: Logical analysis or wishful thinking? In J. G. Nicholls (Ed.), *The development of achievement motivation* (pp. 33–56). Greenwich, CT: JAI.

Stipek, D. J., & Gralinski, H. (1996). Children's beliefs about intelligence and school performance. *Journal of Educational Psychology, 88,* 397–407.

Stipek, D. J., & Kowalski, P. S. (1989). Learned helplessness in task-orienting versus performance-orienting testing conditions. *Journal of Educational Psychology, 81,* 384–391.

Stokols, D. (1972). On the distinction between density and crowding: Some implications for future research. *Psychological Review, 79,* 275–277.

Storm, C., & Storm, T. (1987). A taxonomic study of the vocabulary of emotions. *Journal of Personality and Social Psychology, 53,* 805–816.

Strack, F., Martin, L. L., & Stepper, S. (1988). Inhibiting and facilitating conditions of the human smile: Unobtrusive test of the facial feedback hypothesis. *Journal of Personality and Social Psychology, 54,* 768–777.

Strang, H. R., Lawrence, E. C., & Fowler, P. C. (1978). Effects of assigned goal level and knowledge of results on arithmetic computation: A laboratory study. *Journal of Applied Psychology, 63,* 446–450.

Straub, R. R., & Roberts, D. M. (1983). Effects of nonverbal oriented social awareness training program on social interaction ability of learning disabled children. *Journal of Nonverbal Behavior, 7,* 195–201.

Straub, W. F., & Williams, J. M. (Eds.). (1984). *Cognitive sport psychology.* Lansing, NY: Sport Science Associates.

Strauman, T. (1992). Self-guides, autobiographical memory, and anxiety and dysphoria: Toward a cognitive model of vulnerability to emotional distress. *Journal of Abnormal Psychology, 101,* 87–95.

Strayer, J. (1993). Children's concordant emotions and cognitions in response to observed emotions. *Child Development, 64,* 188–201.

Strube, M. J., Boland, S. M., Manfredo, P. A., & Al-Falaij, A. (1987). Type A behavior pattern and the self-evaluation of abilities: Empirical tests of the self-appraisal model. *Journal of Personality and Social Psychology, 52*, 956–974.

Stunkard, A. J. (1988). Some perspectives on human obesity: Its causes. *Bulletin of New York Academy of Medicine, 64*, 902–923.

Sullivan, H. S. (1953). *The interpersonal theory of psychiatry*. New York: Norton.

Suls, J., Green, P., & Hillis, S. (1998). Emotional reactivity to everyday problems, affective inertia, and neuroticism. *Personality and Social Psychology Bulletin, 24*, 127–136.

Sutherland, S. (1993). Impoverished minds. *Nature, 364*, 767.

Sutton, S. K., & Davidson, R. J. (1997). Prefrontal brain asymmetry: A biological substrate of the behavioral approach and inhibition systems. *Psychological Science, 8*, 204–210.

Swann, W. B., Jr. (1983). Self-verification: Bringing social reality into harmony with self. In J. Suls & A. Greenwald (Eds.), *Psychological perspectives on the self* (Vol. 2, pp. 33–66). Hillsdale, NJ: Lawrence Erlbaum.

Swann, W. B., Jr. (1985). The self as architect of social reality. In B. Schlenker (Ed.), *The self and social life* (pp. 100–125). New York: McGraw-Hill.

Swann, W. B., Jr. (1987). Identity negotiation: Where two roads meet. *Journal of Personality and Social Psychology, 53*, 1038–1051.

Swann, W. B., Jr. (1992a). Why people self-verify. *Journal of Personality and Social Psychology, 62*, 392–401.

Swann, W. B., Jr. (1992b). Seeking truth, finding despair: Some unhappy consequences of a negative self-concept. *Current Directions in Psychological Science, 1*, 15–18.

Swann, W. B., Jr. (1997). The trouble with change: Self-verification and allegiance to the self. *Psychological Science, 8*, 177–180.

Swann, W. B., Jr. (1999). *Resilient identities: Self, relationships, and the construction of social reality*. New York: Basic Books.

Swann, W. B., Jr., & Ely, R. J. (1984). A battle of wills: Self-verification versus behavioral confirmation. *Journal of Personality and Social Psychology, 46*, 1287–1302.

Swann, W. B., Jr., & Hill, C. A. (1982). When our identities are mistaken: Reaffirming self-conceptions through social interactions. *Journal of Personality and Social Psychology, 43*, 59–66.

Swann, W. B., Jr., Hixon, J. G., Stein-Seroussi, A., & Gilbert, D. T. (1990). The fleeting gleam of praise: Behavioral reactions to self-relevant feedback. *Journal of Personality and Social Psychology, 59*, 17–26.

Swann, W. B., Jr., & Pelham, B. W. (2002). The truth about illusions: Authenticity and positivity in social relationships. In C. R. Snyder & S. J. Lopez (Eds.), *Handbook of positive psychology* (pp. 366–381). New York: Oxford University Press.

Swann, W. B., Jr., Pelham, B. W., & Krull, D. S. (1989). Agreeable fancy or disagreeable truth: Reconciling self-enhancement and self-verification. *Journal of Personality and Social Psychology, 57*, 782–791.

Swann, W. B., Jr., & Pittman, T. S. (1977). Initiating play activity in children: The moderating influence of verbal cues on intrinsic motivation. *Child Development, 48*, 1125–1132.

Swann, W. B., Jr., & Predmore, S. C. (1985). Intimates as agents of social support: Sources of consolation or despair? *Journal of Personality and Social Psychology, 49*, 1609–1617.

Swann, W. B., Jr., & Schroeder, D. G. (1995). The search for beauty and truth: A framework for understanding reactions to evaluations. *Personality and Social Psychology Bulletin, 21*, 1307–1318.

Swann, W. B., Jr., Stein-Seroussi, A., & Giesler, B. (1992). Why people self-verify. *Journal of Personality and Social Psychology, 62*, 392–401.

Swann, W. B., Jr., Wenzlaff, R. M., & Tafarodi, R. W. (1992). Depression and the search for negative evaluations: More evidence of the role of self-verification strivings. *Journal of Abnormal Psychology, 101*, 314–317.

Sweeney, D. R., Gold, M. S., Ryan, N., & Pottash, A. L. C. (1980). Opiate withdrawal and panic anxiety. *APA Abstract, 123.*

Symons, D. (1992). What do men want? *Behavioral and Brain Sciences, 15,* 113.

Szagun, G., & Schauble, M. (1997). Children's and adults' understanding of the feeling experience of courage. *Cognition and Emotion, 11,* 291–306.

Tafrate, R. C., Kassinove, H., & Dundin, L. (2002). Anger episodes in high- and low-trait anger community adults. Journal of Clinical Psychology, 58, 1573–1590.

Talwar, S. K., Xu, S. H., Hawley, E. S., Weiss, S. A., Moxon, K. A., & Chapin, J. K. (2002). Behavioral neuroscience: Rat navigation guided by remote control—free animals can be 'virtually' trained by microstimulating key areas of their brain. *Nature, 417* (6884), 37–38.

Taubes, G. (1998). Obesity rates rise, experts struggle to explain why. *Science, 280,* 1367–1368.

Tauer, J. M., & Harackiewicz, J. M. (1999). Winning isn't everything: Competition, achievement orientation, and intrinsic motivation. *Journal of Experimental Social Psychology, 35,* 209–238.

Tavris, C. (1989). *Anger: The misunderstood emotion.* New York: Simon & Schuster.

Taylor, C. B., Bandura, A., Ewart, C. K., Miller, N. H., & DeBusk, B. F. (1985). Exercise testing to enhance wives' confidence in their husbands' cardiac capabilities soon after clinically uncomplicated acute myocardial infarction. *American Journal of Cardiology, 55,* 635–638.

Taylor, S. E. (1983). Adjustment to threatening events: A theory of cognitive adptation. *American Psychologist, 38,* 1161–1173.

Taylor, S. E. (1989). *Positive illusions: Creative self-deception and the healthy mind.* New York: Basic Books.

Taylor, S. E., & Brown, J. D. (1988). Illusion and well-being: A social psychological perspective on mental health. *Psychological Bulletin, 103,* 193–210.

Taylor, S. E., & Brown, J. D. (1994). Positive illusions and well-being revisited: Separating fact from fiction. *Psychological Bulletin, 116,* 21–27.

Taylor, S. E., Pham, L. B., Rivkin, I. D., & Armor, D. A. (1998). Harnessing the imagination: Mental simulation, self-regulation, and coping. *American Psychologist, 53,* 429–439.

Teasdale, J. D., & Fogarty, S. J. (1979). Differential effects of induced mood on retrieval of pleasant and unpleasant events from episodic memory. *Journal of Abnormal Psychology, 88,* 248–257.

Tellegen, A. (1985). Structures of mood and personality and their relevance to assessing anxiety, with an emphasis on self-report. In A. H. Tuma & J. D. Maser (Eds.), *Anxiety and the anxiety disorders* (pp. 681–706). Hillsdale, NJ: Erlbaum.

Tennen, H., & Affleck, G. (1987). The costs and benefits of optimistic explanations and dispositional optimism. *Journal of Personality, 55,* 377–393.

Terasaki, M., & Imada, S. (1988). Sensation seeking and food preferences. *Personality and Individual Differences, 9,* 87–93.

Terborg, J. R. (1976). The motivational components of goal setting. *Journal of Applied Psychology, 61,* 613–621.

Terhune, K. W. (1968). Studies of motives, cooperation, and conflict within laboratory microcosms. In G. H. Snyder (Ed.), *Studies in international conflict* (Vol. 4, pp. 29–58). Buffalo, NY: University of Buffalo.

Tesser, A. (1988). Toward a self-evaluation maintenance model of social behavior. In L. Berkowitz (Ed.), *Advances in experimental social psychology* (Vol. 21, pp. 181–227). New York: Academic Press.

Thibodeau, R., & Aronson, E. (1992). Taking a closer look: Reasserting the role of the self-concept in dissonance theory. *Personality and Social Psychology Bulletin, 18,* 591–602.

Thoits, P. A. (1984). Coping, social support, and psychological outcomes. In P. Shaver (Ed.), *Review of personality and social psychology* (Vol. 5, pp. 219–238). Beverly Hills, CA: Sage.

Thomas, D., & Diener, E. (1990). Memory accuracy in the recall of emotions. *Journal of Personality and Social Psychology, 59,* 291–297.

Thompson, S. (1981). Will it hurt less if I can control it? A complex answer to a simple question. *Psychological Bulletin, 90,* 89–101.

Thorton, J. W., & Jacobs, P. D. (1971). Learned helplessness in human subjects. *Journal of Experimental Psychology, 87,* 369–372.

Thorton, J. W., & Powell, G. D. (1974). Immunization to and alleviation of learned helplessness in man. *American Journal of Psychology, 87,* 351–367.

Tiedens, L. Z., & Linton, S. (2001). Judgment under emotional certainty and uncertainty: The effects of specific emotions on information processing. *Journal of Personality and Social Psychology, 81,* 973–988.

Tiggenmann, M., & Winefield, A. H. (1987). Predictability and timing of self-report in learned helplessness experiments. *Personality and Social Psychology Bulletin, 13,* 253–264.

Timberlake, W., & Farmer-Dougan, V. A. (1991). Reinforcement in applied settings: Figuring out ahead of time what will work. *Psychological Bulletin, 110,* 379–391.

Timpe, R. L. (1989). Perfectionism: Positive possibility or personal pathology. *Journal of Psychology and Christianity, 8,* 23–24.

Toates, F. M. (1979). Homeostasis and drinking. *Behavior and Brain Science, 2,* 95–139.

Tolman, E. C. (1923). The nature of instinct. *Psychological Bulletin, 20,* 200–218.

Tomaka, J., Blascovich, J., Kelsey, R. M., & Leitten, C. L. (1993). Subjective, physiological, and behavioral effects of threat and challenge appraisals. *Journal of Personality and Social Psychology, 65,* 248–260.

Toman, W. (1960). *An introduction to the psychoanalytic theory of motivation.* New York: Pergamon Press.

Tomkins, S. S. (1962). *Affect, imagery, and consciousness: The positive affects (Vol. 1).* New York: Springer.

Tomkins, S. S. (1963). *Affect, imagery, and consciousness: The negative affects (Vol. 2).* New York: Springer.

Tomkins, S. S. (1970). Affect as the primary motivational system. In M. B. Arnold (Ed.), *Feelings and emotions* (pp. 101–110). New York: Academic Press.

Tomkins, S. S. (1984). Affect theory. In K. R. Scherer & P. Ekman (Eds.), *Approaches to emotion* (pp. 163–196). Hillsdale, NJ: Lawrence Erlbaum.

Tooby, J., & Cosmides, L. (1990). The past explains the present: Emotional adaptations and the structure of ancestral environment. *Ethology and Sociobiology, 11,* 375–424.

Tourangeau, R., & Ellsworth, P. C. (1979). The role of facial response in the experience of emotion. *Journal of Personality and Social Psychology, 37,* 1519–1531.

Tronick, E. Z. (1989). Emotions and emotional communication in infants. *American Psychologist, 44,* 112–119.

Trope, Y. (1975). Seeking information about one's own ability as a determinant of choice among tasks. *Journal of Personality and Social Psychology, 32,* 1004–1013.

Trope, Y. (1983). Self-assessment in achievement behavior. In J. Suls & A. G. Greenwald (Eds.), *Psychological perspectives on the self* (Vol. 2, pp. 93–121). Hillsdale, NJ: Lawrence Erlbaum.

Trope, Y., & Brickman, P. (1975). Difficulty and diagnosticity as determinants of choice among tasks. *Journal of Personality and Social Psychology, 31,* 918–925.

Trudewind, C. (1982). The development of achievement motivation and individual differences: Ecological determinants. In W. Hartrup (Ed.), *Review of Child Development Research* (Vol. 6, pp. 669–703). Chicago: University of Chicago Press.

Tubbs, M. E. (1986). Goal-setting: A meta-analytic examination of the empirical evidence. *Journal of Applied Psychology, 71,* 474–483.

Tuiten, A., van Honk, J., Koppeschaar, H., Bernaards, C., Thijssen, J., & Verbaten, R. (2000). Time course of effects of testosterone administration on sexual arousal in women. *Archives of General Psychiatry, 57,* 149–153.

Turner, N., Barling, J., & Zacharatos, A. (2002). Positive psychology at work. In C. R. Snyder & S. J. Lopez (Eds.), *Handbook of positive psychology* (pp. 715–728). New York: Oxford University Press.

Turner, J. H. (1987). Toward a sociological theory of motivation. *American Sociological Review, 52*, 15–27.

Urist, J. (1977). The Rorschach test and the assessment of object relations. *Journal of Personality Assessment, 41*, 3–9.

Urist, J. (1980). Object relations. In R. W. Woody (Ed.), *Encyclopedia of clinical assessment* (Vol. 2, pp. 821–833). San Francisco: Jossey-Bass.

Vaillant, G. E. (1977). *Adaptation to life*. Boston: Little, Brown, & Company.

Vaillant, G. E. (1992). *Ego mechanisms of defense: A guide for clinicians and researchers*. Washington, DC: American Psychiatric Association.

Vaillant, G. E. (1993). *The wisdom of the ego*. Cambridge, MA: Harvard University Press.

Vaillant, G. E. (2000). Adaptive mental mechanisms: Their role in a positive psychology. *American Psychologist, 55*, 89–98.

Vallerand, R. J. (1997). Toward a hierarchical model of intrinsic and extrinsic motivation. In M. P. Zanna (Ed.), *Advances in experimental social psychology* (Vol. 29, pp. 271–360). San Diego, CA: Academic Press.

Vallerand, R. J., Deci, E. L., & Ryan, R. M. (1985). Intrinsic motivation in sport. In K. B. Pandolf (Ed.), *Exercise and sport sciences reviews* (Vol. 15, pp. 389–425). New York: Macmillan.

Vallerand, R. J., Gauvin, L. I., & Halliwell, W. R. (1986). Negative effects of competition on children's intrinsic motivation. *Journal of Social Psychology, 126*, 649–656.

Vallerand, R. J., Fortier, M. S., & Guay, F. (1997). Self-determination and persistence in a real-life setting: Toward a motivational model of high school dropout. *Journal of Personality and Social Psychology, 72*, 1161–1176.

Vallerand, R. J., Pelletier, L. G., Blais, M. R., Briere, N. M., Senecal, C., & Vallieres, E. F. (1992). The Academic Motivation Scale: A measure of intrinsic, extrinsic, and amotivation in education. *Educational and Psychological Measurement, 52*, 1003–1017.

Vallerand, R. J., & Reid, G. (1984). On the causal effects of perceived competence on intrinsic motivation: A test of cognitive evaluation theory. *Journal of Sport Psychology, 6*, 94–102.

Valtin, H. (2002). "Drink at least eight glasses of water a day." Really? Is there scientific evidence for "8 x 8"? *American Journal of Physiology: Regulatory, Integrative, and Comparative Physiology, 283*, R993-R1004.

van Dijk, W. W., Zeelenberg, M., & van Der Plight, J. (1999). Not having what you want versus having what you do not want: The impact of type of negative outcome on the experience of disappointment and related emotions. *Cognition and Emotion, 13*, 129–148.

van Hooff, J. A. R. A. M. (1962). Facial expressions in higher primates. *Symposium of the Zoological Society of London, 8*, 97–125.

van Hooff, J. A. R. A. M. (1972). A comparative approach to the phylogeny of laughter and smiling. In R. A. Hinde (Ed.), *Non-verbal communication*. Cambridge: Cambridge University Press.

Van Houten, R., & Retting, R. A. (2001). Increasing motorist compliance and caution at stop signs. *Journal of Applied Behavior Analysis, 34*, 185–193.

van IJzendoorn, M. H. (1995). Adult attachment representations, parental responsiveness, and infant attachment: A meta-analysis on the predictive validity of the adult attachment interview. *Psychological Bulletin, 117*, 387–403.

Veitch, R., & Griffitt, W. (1976). Good news bad news: Affective and interpersonal effects. *Journal of Applied Social Psychology, 6*, 69–75.

Veroff, J. (1957). Development and validation of a projective measure of power motivation. *Journal of Abnormal and Social Psychology, 54*, 1–8.

Veroff, J., Depner, C., Kulka, R., & Douvan, E. (1980). Comparison of American motives: 1957 versus 1976. *Journal of Personality and Social Psychology, 39,* 1249–1262.

Verplanken, B., & Faes, S. (1999). Good intentions, bad habits, and effects of forming implementation intentions on healthy eating. *European Journal of Social Psychology, 29,* 591–604

Viken, R. J., Rose, R. J., Kaprio, J., & Kosken, V. U. O. (1994). A developmental genetic analysis of adult personality: Extraversion and neuroticism from 18 to 59 years of age. *Journal of Personality and Social Psychology, 66,* 722–730.

Vinogradova, O. S. (1975). Functional organization of the limbic system in the process of registration of information: Facts and hypotheses. In R. L. Isaacson & K. H. Pribram (Eds.), *The hippocampus: 2. Neurophysiology and behavior* (pp. 1–70). New York: Plenum.

Volmer, F. (1986). Why do men have higher expectancy than women? *Sex Roles, 14,* 351–362.

Vroom, V. H. (1964). *Work and motivation.* New York: Wiley.

Wachtel, P. (1993). *Therapeutic communication.* New York: Guilford Press.

Wahba, M. A., & Bridwell, L. G. (1976). Maslow reconsidered: A review of research on the need hierarchy theory. *Organizational Behavior and Human Performance, 15,* 212–240.

Waterman, A. S. (1988). Identity status theory and Erikson's theory: Commonalities and differences. *Developmental Review, 8,* 185–208.

Watson, D., & Clark, L. A. (1984). Negative affectivity: The disposition to experience aversive emotional states. *Psychological Bulletin, 96,* 465–490.

Watson, D., & Clark, L. A. (1997). Extraversion and its positive emotional core. In R. Hogan, J. Johnson, & S. Briggs (Eds.), *Handbook of personality psychology* (pp. 767–793). San Diego, Ca: Academic Press.

Watson, D., & Clark, L. A. (1994). The vicissitudes of mood: A schematic model. In P. Ekman & R. J. Davidson (Eds.), *The nature of emotion: Fundamental questions* (pp. 400–405). New York: Oxford University Press.

Watson, D., Clark, L. A., McIntyre, C. W., & Hamaker, S. (1992). Affect, personality, and social activity. *Journal of Personality and Social Psychology, 63,* 1011–1025.

Watson, D., Clark, L. A., & Tellegen, A. (1988). Development and validation of brief measures of positive and negative affect: The PANAS scales. *Journal of Personality and Social Psychology, 54,* 1063–1070.

Watson, D., & Tellegen, A. (1985). Toward a consensual structure of mood. *Psychological Bulletin, 98,* 219–235.

Watson, D., Wiese, D., Vaidya, J., & Tellegen, A. (1999). The two general activation systems of affect: Structural findings, evolutionary considerations, and psychobiological evidence. *Journal of Personality and Social Psychology, 76,* 820–838.

Watson, J. B. (1919). *Psychology from the standpoint of a behaviorist.* Philadelphia: Lippincott.

Watson, J. B. (1924). *Behaviorism.* New York: W. W. Norton.

Wegner, D. M. (1989). *White bears and other unwanted thoughts.* New York: Guilford Press.

Wegner, D. M. (1992). You can't always think what you want: Problems in the suppression of unwanted thoughts. In M. P. Zanna (Ed.), *Advances in experimental social psychology* (Vol. 25, pp. 193–225). San Diego: Academic Press.

Wegner, D. M. (1994). Ironic processes of mental control. *Psychological Review, 101,* 34–52.

Wegner, D. M., & Erber, R. (1993). Hyperaccessibility of suppressed thoughts. *Journal of Personality and Social Psychology, 63,* 903–912.

Wegner, D. M., Schneider, D. J., Carter, S., III, & White, T. (1987). Paradoxical effects of thought suppression. *Journal of Personality and Social Psychology, 53,* 5–13.

Weinberg, A., & Minaker, K. (1995). Council of Scientific Affairs, American Medical Association: Dehydration evaluation and management in older adults. *Journal of the American Medical Association, 274,* 1552–1556, 1995.

Weinberg, R. S., Bruya, L., & Jackson, A. (1985). The effects of goal proximity and goal specificity on endurance performance. *Journal of Sport Psychology, 7,* 296–305.

Weinberg, R. S., Bruya, L., Longino, J., & Jackson, A. (1988). Effect of goal proximity and specificity on endurance performance of primary-grade children. *Journal of Sport and Exercise Psychology, 10,* 81–91.

Weinberg, R. S., Gould, D., & Jackson, A. (1979). Expectations and performance: An empirical test of Bandura's self-efficacy theory. *Journal of Sport Psychology, 1,* 320–331.

Weiner, B. (1972). *Theories of motivation: From mechanism to cognition.* Chicago: Rand McNally.

Weiner, B. (1979). A theory of motivation for some classroom experiences. *Journal of Educational Psychology, 71,* 3–25.

Weiner, B. (1980). *Human motivation.* New York: Holt, Rinehart & Winston.

Weiner, B. (1982). The emotional consequences of causal attributions. In M. S. Clark & S. T. Fiske (Eds.), *Affect and cognition* (pp. 185-209). Hillsdale, NJ: Lawrence Erlbaum.

Weiner, B. (1985). An attributional theory of achievement motivation and emotion. *Psychological Review, 92,* 548–573.

Weiner, B. (1986). *An attributional theory of motivation and emotion.* New York: Springer-Verlag.

Weiner, B. (1990). History of motivational research in education. *Journal of Educational Psychology, 82,* 616–622.

Weiner, B., & Graham, S. (1989). Understanding the motivational role of affect: Life-span research from an attributional perspective. *Cognition and Emotion, 3,* 401–409.

Weiner, B., Russell, D., & Learman, D. (1978). Affective consequences of causal ascriptions. In J. Harvey, W. J. Ickes, & R. F. Kidd (Eds.), *New directions in attribution research* (Vol. 2, pp. 59–88). Hillsdale, NJ: Erlbaum.

Weiner, B., Russell, D., & Learman, D. (1979). The cognition-emotion process in achievement-related context. *Journal of Personality and Social Psychology, 37,* 1211–1220.

Weingarten, H. P. (1985). Stimulus control of eating: Implications for a two-factor theory of hunger. *Appetite, 6,* 387–401.

Weinstein, N. D. (1984). Why it won't happen to me: Perceptions of risk factors and susceptibility. *Health Psychology, 3,* 431–457.

Weinstein, N. D. (1993). Optimistic biases about personal risks. *Science, 155,* 1232–1233.

Weiss, J. M. (1972). Psychological factors in stress and disease. *Scientific American, 226,* 104–113.

Weiss, J. M., Glazer, H. I., & Pohorecky, L. A. (1976). Coping behavior and neurochemical changes in rats: An alternative explanation for the original learned helplessness experiments. In G. Serban & A. King (Eds.), *Animal models in human psychobiology.* New York: Plenum.

Weiss, J. M., & Simson, P. G. (1985). Neurochemical basis of stress-induced depression.

Weiss, J. M., Stone, E. A., & Harrell, N. (1970). Coping behavior and brain norepinephrine level in rats. *Journal of Comparative and Physiological Psychology, 72,* 153–160.

Wellborn, J. G. (1991). *Engaged and disaffected action: The conceptualization and measurement of motivation in the academic domain.* Unpublished doctoral dissertation, University of Rochester.

Wertheimer, M. (1978). Humanistic psychology and the humane but tough-minded psychologist. *American Psychologist, 33,* 739–745.

Westen, D. (1990). Psychoanalytic approaches to personality. In L. Pervin (Ed.), *Handbook of personality: Theory and research* (pp. 21–65). New York: Guilford Press.

Westen, D. (1991). Social cognition and object relations. *Psychological Bulletin, 109,* 429–455.

Westen, D. (1998). The scientific legacy of Sigmund Freud: Toward a psychodynamically informed psychological science. *Psychological Bulletin, 124,* 333–371.

Westen, D., Klepser, J., Ruffins, S. A., Silverman, M., Lifton, N., & Boekamp, J. (1991). Object relations in childhood and adolescence: The development of working representations. *Journal of Consulting and Clinical Psychology, 59,* 400–409.

Whalen, P. J. (1998). Fear, vigilance, and ambiguity: Initial neuroimaging studies of the human amygdala. *Current Directions in Psychological Science, 7,* 177–187.

Wheeler, L., Reis, H. T., & Nezlek, J. (1983). Loneliness, social interaction, and sex roles. *Journal of Personality and Social Psychology, 45,* 943–953.

White, G. L. (1981). A model of romantic jealousy. *Motivation and Emotion, 5*, 295–310.

White, H. R., Labourvie, E. N., & Bates, M. E. (1985). The relationship between sensation seeking and delinquency: A longitudinal analysis. *Journal of Research in Crime and Delinquency, 22*, 197–211.

White, R. W. (1959). Motivation reconsidered: The concept of competence. *Psychological Review, 66*, 297–333.

White, R. W. (1960). Competence and the psychosexual stages of development. In M. R. Jones (Ed.), *Nebraska symposium on motivation* (Vol. 8, pp. 97–141). Lincoln: University of Nebraska Press.

Wicker, A. W. (1969). Attitudes versus action: The relationship of verbal and overt behavioral responses to attitude objects. *Journal of Social Issues, 25*, 41–68.

Wiederman, M. W. (1993). Evolved gender differences in mate preferences: Evidence from personal advertisements. *Ethology and Sociobiology, 13*, 331–352.

Wiersma, U. J. (1992). The effects of extrinsic rewards in intrinsic motivation: A meta-analysis. *Journal of Occupational and Organizational Psychology, 65*, 101–114.

Wilder, D. A., & Thompson, J. E. (1980). Intergroup contact with independent manipulations of in-group and out-group interaction. *Journal of Personality and Social Psychology, 38*, 589–603.

Williams, D. E., & Thompson, J. K. (1993). Biology and behavior: A set-point hypothesis of psychological functioning. *Behavior Modification, 17*, 43–57.

Williams, D. G. (1990). Effects of psychoticism, extraversion, and neuroticism in current mood: A statistical review of six studies. *Personality and Individual Differences, 11*, 615–630.

Williams, D. R., & Teitelbaum, P. (1956). Control of drinking by means of an operant conditioning technique. *Science, 124*, 1294–1296.

Williams, G. C., & Deci, E. L. (1996). Internalization of biopsychological values by medical students: A test of self-determination theory. *Journal of Personality and Social Psychology, 70*, 767–779.

Williams, G. C., Grow, V. M., Freedman, Z. R., Ryan, R. M., & Deci, E. L. (1996). Motivational predictors of weight loss and weight-loss maintenance. *Journal of Personality and Social Psychology, 70*, 115–126.

Williams, J. G., & Solano, C. H. (1983). The social reality of feeling lonely: Friendship and reciprocation. *Personality and Social Psychology Bulletin, 9*, 237–242.

Williams, K. J., Suls, J., Alliger, G. M., Learner, S. M., & Choi, K. W. (1991). Multiple role juggling and daily mood states in working mothers: An experience sampling study. *Journal of Applied Psychology, 76*, 664–674.

Willner, P., Ahlenius, S., Muscat, R., & Scheel-Kruger, J. (Eds.) (1991). The mesolimbic dopamine system. In P. Willner & J. Scheel-Kruger (Eds.), *The mesolimbic dopamine system: From motivation to action* (pp. 3–15). New York: Wiley.

Winchie, D. B., & Carment, D. W. (1988). Intention to migrate: A psychological analysis. *Journal of Applied Psychology, 18*, 727–736.

Windle, M. (1992). Temperament and social support in adolescence: Interrelations with depression and delinquent behavior. *Journal of Youth and Adolescence, 21*, 1–21.

Winefield, A. H. (1982). Methodological differences in demonstrating learned helplessness in humans. *Journal of General Psychology, 107*, 255–266.

Winefield, A. H., Barnett, A., & Tiggemann, M. (1985). Learned helplessness deficits: Uncontrollable outcomes or perceived failure? *Motivation and Emotion, 9*, 185–195.

Winne, P. H. (1997). Experimenting to bootstrap self-regulated learning. *Journal of Educational Psychology, 88*, 397–410.

Winson, J. (1992). The function of REM sleep and the meaning of dreams. In J. W. Barron, M. N. Eagle, & D. L. Wolitzky (Eds.), *Interface of psychoanalysis and psychology* (pp. 347–356). Washington, DC: American Psychological Association.

Winter, D. G. (1973). *The power motive*. New York: Free Press.

Winter, D. G. (1993). Power, affiliation, and war: Three tests of a motivational model. *Journal of Personality and Social Psychology, 65,* 532–545.

Winter, D. G. (1987). Leader appeal, leader performance, and the motive profiles of leaders and followers: A study of American presidents and elections. *Journal of Personality and Social Psychology, 52,* 196–202.

Winter, D. G. (1988). The power motive in women and men. *Journal of Personality and Social Psychology, 54,* 510–519.

Winter, D. G., & Stewart, A. J. (1978). Power motivation. In H. London & J. Exner (Eds.), *Dimensions of personality.* New York: Wiley.

Winterbottom, M. (1958). The relation of need for achievement to learning experience in independence and mastery. In J. Atkinson (Ed.), *Motives in fantasy, action, and society* (pp. 453–478). Princeton, NJ: Van Nostrand.

Wise, R. A. (1989). Opiate reward: Sites and substrates. *Neuroscience and Biobehavioral Reviews, 13,* 129–133.

Wise, R. A. (1996). Addictive drugs and brain stimulation reward. *Annual Review of Neuroscience, 19,* 319–340.

Wise, R. A., & Bozarth, M. A. (1984). Brain reward circuitry: Four circuit elements wired in apparent series. *Brain Research Bulletin, 12,* 203–208.

Wittrock, M. C. (1992). An empowering conception of educational psychology. *Educational Psychologist, 27,* 129–142.

Wolff, P. H. (1969). The natural history of crying and other vocalizations in early infancy. In B. M. Foss (Ed.), *Determinants of infant behavior* (pp. 81–109). London: Methuen.

Wood, R. E., & Bandura, A. (1989). Impact of conceptions of ability on self-regulatory mechanisms and complex decision making. *Journal of Personality and Social Psychology, 56,* 407–415.

Wood, R. E., Bandura, A., & Bailey, T. (1990). Mechanisms governing organizational performance in complex decision-making environments. *Organizational Behavior and Human Decision Processes, 46,* 181–201.

Wood, R. E., Mento, A. J., & Locke, E. A. (1987). Task complexity as a moderator of goal effects: A meta-analysis. *Journal of Applied Psychology, 72,* 416–425.

Woods, S. C., Seeley, R. J., Porte, D., Jr., & Schwartz, M. W. (1998). Signals that regulate food intake and energy homeostasis. *Science, 280,* 1378–1383.

Woodworth, R. S. (1918). *Dynamic psychology.* New York: Columbia University Press.

Woody, E. Z., Costanzo, P. R., Leifer, H., & Conger, J. (1981). The effects of taste and caloric perceptions on the eating behavior of restrained and unrestrained subjects. *Cognitive Research and Therapy, 5,* 381–390.

World Health Organization (1998). *Obesity: Preventing and managing the global epidemic.* World Health Organization, Geneva.

Wortman, C. B., & Brehm, J. W. (1975). Responses to uncontrollable outcomes: An integration of reactance theory and the learned helplessness model. In L. Berkowitz (Ed.), *Advances in experimental social psychology* (Vol. 8, pp. 277–336). New York: Academic Press.

Wren, A. M., Seal, L. J., Cohen, M. A., Brynes, A. E., Frost, G. S., Murphy, K. G., Dhillo, W. S., Ghatei, M. A., & Bloom, S. R. (2001). Ghrelin enhances appetite and increases food intake in humans. *The Journal of Clinical Endocrinology and Metabolism, 86,* 5992.

Wyrwicka, W. (1988). *Brain and feeding behavior.* Springfield, IL: Charles C. Thomas.

Yanovsky, S. Z., & Yanovsky, J. A. (2002). Drug therapy: Obesity. *New England Journal of Medicine, 346,* 591–602.

Yerkes, R. M., & Dodson, J. D. (1908). The relation of strength of stimulus to repidity of habit formation. *Journal of Comparative Neurology and Psychology, 18,* 459–482.

Young, P. T. (1961). *Motivation and emotion: A survey of the determinants of human and animal activity.* New York: Wiley.

Younger, J. C., Walker, L., & Arrowood, A. J. (1977). Postdecision dissonance at the fair. *Personality and Social Psychology Bulletin, 3*, 284–287.

Zajonc, R. B. (1980). Feeling and thinking: Preferences need no inferences. *American Psychologist, 35*, 151–175.

Zajonc, R. B. (1981). A one-factor mind about mind and emotion. *American Psychologist, 36*, 102–103.

Zajonc, R. B. (1984). On the primacy of affect. *American Psychologist, 39*, 117–123.

Zanna, M. P., & Cooper, J. (1976). Dissonance and the attribution process. In J. H. Harvey, W. J. Ickes, & R. F. Kidd (Eds.), *New directions in attribution research* (Vol. 1, pp. 199–217). Hillsdale, NJ: Lawrence Erlbaum.

Zajonc, R. B., Murphy, S. T., & Inglehart, M. (1989). Feeling and facial efference: Implications of the vascular theory of emotions. *Psychological Review, 96*, 395–416.

Zimmerman, B. J. (2000). Attaining self-regulation: A social cognitive perspective. In M. Boekaerts, P. R. Pintrich, & M. Zeidner's (Eds.), *Handbook of self-regulation* (pp. 13–39). San Diego, CA: Academic Press.

Zimmerman, B. J. (2002). Becoming a self-regulated learner: An overview. *Theory into Practice, 41*, 64–70.

Zimmerman, B. J., & Risemberg, R. (1997). Become a proficient writer: A social cognitive perspective. *Contemporary Educational Psychology, 22*, 73–101.

Zubek, J. P. (Ed.). (1969). *Sensory deprivation*. New York: Appleton-Century-Crofts.

Zuckerman, M(arvin). (1978). Sensation seeking. In H. London & J. E. Exner (Eds.), *Dimensions of personality* (pp. 487–559). New York: John Wiley.

Zuckerman, M. (1979). *Sensation-seeking: Beyond the optimal level of arousal*. Hillsdale, NJ: Erlbaum.

Zuckerman, M. (1994). *Behavioral expressions and biosocial bases of sensation seeking*. New York: Cambridge University Press.

Zuckerman, M., Ball, S., & Black, J. (1990). Influences of sensation seeking, gender, risk appraisal, and situational motivation on smoking. *Addictive Behaviors, 15*, 209–220.

Zuckerman, M., Bone, R. N., Neary, R., Mangelsdorff, D., & Brustman, B. (1972). What is the sensation seeker? Personality trait and experience correlates of the Sensation Seeking Scale. *Journal of Clinical Counseling Psychology, 39*, 308–321.

Zuckerman, M., & Neeb, M. (1980). Demographic influences in sensation seeking and expressions of sensation seeking in religion, smoking, and driving habits. *Personality and Individual Differences, 1*, 197–206.

Zuckerman, M., Tushup, R., & Finner, S. (1976). Sexual attitudes and experience: Attitude and personality correlates and changes produced by a course in sexuality. *Journal of Consulting and Clinical Psychology, 44*, 7–19.

Zuckerman, M(iron)., Klorman, R., Larrance, D. T., & Spiegel, N. H. (1981). Facial, autonomic, and subjective components of emotion: The facial feedback hypothesis versus the externalizer-internalizer distinction. *Journal of Personality and Social Psychology, 41*, 929–944.

Zuckerman, M., Kieffer, S. C., & Knee, C. R. (1998). Consequences of self-handicapping effects on coping, academic performance, and adjustment. *Journal of Personality and Social Psychology, 74*, 1619–1628.

Zullow, H. M., Oettingen, G., Peterson, C., & Seligman, M. E. P. (1988). Pessimistic explanatory style in the historical record: CAVing LBJ, presidential candidates, and East versus West Berlin. *American Psychologist, 43*, 673–682.

Zumoff, B., Strain, G. W., Miller, L. K., & Rosner, W. (1995). Twenty-four-hour mean plasma testosterone concentration declines with age in normal premenopausal women. *Journal of Clinical Endocrinology and Metabolism, 80*, 1429–1430.

AUTHOR INDEX

SUBJECT INDEX

CREDITS LIST

Figure 1.2   Adapted from "Cognitive Control of Action," by D. Birch, J. W. Atkinson, and K. Bongort in *Cognitive View of Human Motivation* (pp. 71–84), B. Weiner's (Ed.), 1974, New York: Academic Press.

Figure 3.2   From "The Excitable Cortex in Conscious Man," by W. Penfield, 1958. England: Liverpool University Press.

Table 3.3   From "Behavioral Inhibition, Behavioral Activation, and Affective Responses to Impending Reward and Punishment: The BAS/BIS Scales" by C. S. Carver and T. L. White, 1994, *Journal of Personality and Social Psychology,* 67, 319–333.

Figure 3.7   From "Mapping the Mind," by R. Carter, 1998. Berkeley, CA: University of California Press. Published by arrangement by Weidenfeld & Nicolson

Figure 4.4   From "The Pleasures of Sensation," by C. Pfaffmann, 1960, *Psychological Review,* 67, pp. 253–268. Copyright 1960 by the American Psychological Association. Reprinted with permission.

Table 4.1   From "Sensory and Social Influences on Ice Cream Consumption by Males and Females in a Laboratory Setting," by S. L. Berry, W. W. Beatty, and R. C. Klesges, 1985, Appetite, 6, pp. 41–45.

Figure 4.7   "Measuring the Physical in Physical Attractiveness: Quasi-Experiments on the Sociobiology of Female Facial Beauty," by M. R. Cunningham, 1986, *Journal of Personality,* 50, pp. 925–935. Copyright 1986 by the American Psychological Associated. Reprinted with permission.

Table 4.2   From "Mate Selection Preferences: Gender Differences Examined in a National Sample," by S. Sprecher, Q. Sullivan, and E. Hatfield, 1994, *Journal of Personality and Social Psychology,* 66, pp. 1074–1080. Copyright 1994 by the American Psychological Association. Adapted with permission.

Figure 5.4   Adapted from "Self-Determination and Persistence in a Real-Life Setting: Toward a Motivational Model of High School Dropout," by R. J. Vallerand, M. S., Fortier, and G. Guay, 1997, *Journal of Personality and Social Psychology,* 72, pp. 1161–1172. Copyright 1997 by American Psychological Association. Adapted by permission.

Table 5.2   Adapted from "Setting Limits on Children's Behavior: The Differential Effects of Controlling versus Informational Styles on Intrinsic Motivation and Creativity," by R. Kestner, R. M. Ryan, F. Bernier and K. Holt, 1984, *Journal of Personality,* 52, 233–248.

Figure 6.1   From "University–Based Incentive Program to Increase Safety Belt Use: Towards Cost-Effective Institutionalization," by J. R. Rudd and G. S. Geller, 1985, *Journal of Applied Behavior Analysis,* 18, pp. 215–226.

Figure 6.2   From "Modification of Behavior Problems in the Home with a Parent as Observer and Experimenter," R.V. Hall, S. Axelrod, L. Tyler, E. Grief, F. C. Jones, & R. Robertson, 1972, *Journal of Applied Behavior Analysis,* 5, pp. 53–64. Copyright 1972 by the Journal of Applied Behavior Analysis. Reprinted by permission.

Figure 6.3   From "Behavioral Engineering: Postural Control by Portable Operant Apparatus," N. H. Azrin, H. Rubin, F. O'Brien, T. Ayollon, and D. Roll, 1968, *Journal of Applied Behavior Analysis,* 2, pp. 39–42. Copyright 1968 by the Journal of Applied Behavior Analysis. Reprinted by permission.

Figure 6.4   From " Corporal Punishment by Parents and Associated Child Behaviors and Experiences: A Meta-Analytical and Theoretical Review," by E. T. Gershoff, 2002, *Psychological Bulletin,* 128, 539–579. Copyright 2002 by American Psychological Association. Adapted by permission.

Figure 6.5   From "Self-Determination Theory and Facilitation of Intrinsic Motivation, Social Development, and Well Being," by R. M. Ryan and E. L. Deci, 2000, *American Psychologists,* 55, pp. 68–78. Copyright 200o by American Psychological Association. Reprinted by permission.

Figure 6.6   From "Providing a Rationale in an Autonomy-Supportive Way as a Strategy to Motivate Others During an Uninteresting Activity," J. Reeve, H. Jang, P. Hardre, & M. Omura, 2002, *Motivation and Emotion,* 26, pp. 183–207. Copyright 2002, Plenum Press.

Figure 7.1   Adapted from "A Computer-Based Measure of Resultant Achievement Motivation," by V. Blankenship, 1987, *Journal of Personality and Social Psychology,* 53, pp. 361–372. Copyright 1987 by American Psychological Association. Adapted by permission.

Table 7.3   From "Achievement Goals in the Classroom: Students' Learning Strategies and Motivational Processes," by C. A., Ames and J. Archer, 1988, *Journal of Educational Psychology,* 80, pp. 260–267. Copyright 1988 by American Psychological Association. Adapted by permission.

Figure 7.2   From "A hierarchical model of approach and avoidance achievement motivation," by A. J. Elliot and M. Church, 1997, Journal of Personality and Social Psychology, 72, pp. 218–232. Copyright 1997 by American Psychological Association. Reprinted by permission.

Table 7.4   From "Approach and Avoidance Motivation and Achievement Goals," by A. J. Elliot, 1999, *Educational Psychologist,* 34, pp. 160–189.

Table 7.5   From "A Social Cognitive Approach to Motivation and Personality," by C. S. Dweck and E. L. Leggett, 1988, *Psychological Review,* 95, pp. 256–273. Copyright 1988 by American Psychological Association. Reprinted by permission.

Figure 8.3   Adapted from "A Computer Model of Affective Reactions to Goal-Relevant Events" by S. B. Ravlin, unpublished Master's thesis, University of

Illinois-Urbana-Champaign. Cited in A. Ortony, G. L. Clore, and A. Collins (Eds.), *The Cognitive Structure of Emotions,* 1987, New York: Cambridge University Press.

Figure 9.5   From "An Analysis of Learned Helplessness: Continuous Changes in Performance, Strategy, and Achievement Cognitions Following Failure," C. I. Diener and C. S. Dweck, 1978, *Journal of Personality and Social Psychology,* 36, pp. 451–462. Copyright 1978 by American Psychological Association. Adapted by permission.

Figure 9.6   Adapted from "Judgments on Contingency in Depressed and Nondepressed Students: Sadder but Wiser?" by L. B. Alloy and L. T. Abramson, *Journal of Experimental Psychology: General,* 108, pp. 441–485. Copyright 1979 by American Psychological Association. Adapted by permission.

Box 9   Adapted from "Controlling Ourselves, Controlling Our World: Psychology's Role in Understanding Positive and Negative Consequences of Seeking and Gaining Control," by D. H. Shapiro, Jr., C. E. Schwartz, and J. A. Astin, 1996, *American Psychologist,* 51, pp. 1213–1230. Copyright 1996 by American Psychological Association. Adapted by permission.

Figure 9.8   From "Responses to Uncontrollable Outcomes: an Integration of Reactance Theory and the Learned Helplessness Model," by C. B. Wortman and J. W. Brehm, 1975, in L. Berkowitz' (Ed.), *Advances in Experimental Psychology* (Vol. 8, pp. 277–336). New York: Academic Press. Copyright 1975 by Academic Press.

Table 10.1   From "Possible Selves in Adulthood and Old Age: A Tale of Shifting Horizons," by C. D. Ryff, 199, *Psychology and Aging,* 6, pp. 286–295. Adapted by permission from the Psychological Association.

Figure 10.1   From "Self-Verification: Bringing Social Reality into Harmony with Self," by W. B. Swann, Jr., 1983, in J. Suls and A. Greenwald (Eds.), *Psychological Perspectives on the Self* (Vol. 2, pp. 33–66). Hillsdale, NJ: Lawrence Erlbaum.

Figure 10.2   From "Possible Selves in Adulthood and Old Age: A Tale of Shifting Horizons," by C. D. Ryff, 1991, *Psychology and Aging,* 6, pp. 286–296. Adapted by permission from the American Psychological Association.

Figure 10.4   From "Goal Striving, Need Satisfaction, and Longitudinal Well-Being: The Self-Concordance Model," by K. M. Sheldon and A. J. Elliot, 1999, *Journal of Personality and Social Psychology,* 76, pp. 482–497. Copyright 1999 by American Psychological Association.

Figure 10.5   From "Goal Striving, Need Satisfaction, and Longitudinal Well-Being: The Self-Concordance Model," by K. M. Sheldon and A. J. Elliot, 1999, *Journal of Personality and Social Psychology,* 76, pp. 482–497. Copyright 1999 by American Psychological Association.

Figure 10.6   Adapted from "Self-Concordance, Goal Attainment, and the Pursuit of Happiness: Can There be an Upward Spiral?," by K. M. Sheldon and L. Houser-Marko, 2001, *Journal of Personality and Social Psychology,* 80,